THE TANGLED WEB

THE TANGLED WEB

A True Story of Lies

Richard Lee

Tegmen Publishing

Copyright © 2012 by Richard Lee

All rights reserved.
No part of this book may be reproduced, scanned, or distributed in any printed or electronic form without permission. Please do not participate in or encourage piracy of copyrighted materials in violation of the author's rights. Purchase only authorized copies.
For information, contact the author directly at
richle2012@hotmail.com

ISBN-10: 0615609627
ISBN-13: 978-0-615-60962-1

Printed in the United States

*This book is dedicated
to anyone whose life has been damaged
by the power of a lie.*

CONTENTS

Acknowledgements ix
Preface xi
Prologue xv

I	THE FLY IN THE WEB 1
1	Gayman 3
2	Jonathan 25
3	Week Ends 34
4	Opportunistic Infection 45
5	Business Drag 55
6	Glad to be Gay 61
7	Heart Conditions 70
8	Pride and Prejudice 82
9	Much Ado About Nothing 89
10	Chase 103
11	Destination Nowhere 116
12	Turn of Events 129
13	Exeunt 140

II	VERY STICKY WEBS 157
14	Evil Dan 159
15	Will & Grace 199
16	GayMan 216
17	In the Middle of the Wickedness 243
18	Moving to Mariah 259
19	Thanksgiving 265
20	Reversal of Fortune 270
21	X-mas 288
22	Unusual Jonathan 300

III THE OTHER FLIES 313

23	Gayboi 315
24	Desperate Measures 334
25	The One True Honest Person 350
26	Strange Days 358
27	Cliff@Jonathan.con 376
28	The Mother of Vice 392
29	Foundation of Sand 397
30	Easter 407
31	The Breaking Point 417
32	All's Well That Ends 431
33	Loose Threads 437
34	The Pretender 440

IV UNTANGLING 457

35	A Woman With Insight 459
36	Stalking Jonathan 485
37	A Very Dangerous Man 497
38	Johnny 505
39	Confrontation 516
40	Entr'acte 526
41	Undue Influence 538
42	Meeting Chase 568
43	Good Dan 586
44	Obstruction of Justice 606
45	Like a Thief in the Night 612
46	Getting Unstuck 623
47	Loose Threads, II 626
48	Déjà Vu All Over Again 632
49	Tied Threads 652

V UNMASKING THE MIMIC 669

A.	Unmasking the Insanity 671
B.	The Threads in the Web 676
C.	Escaping the Spider's Web 694
D.	Avoiding the Spider's Web 706

References 721
Index 725

ACKNOWLEDGEMENTS

First and foremost, I would like to thank those of "Johnny's" victims (or "survivors," to use the currently fashionable phrase) who shared their stories and insights with me. These include (in order of appearance) "Miranda," "Mike," "Terry," "Laura," "Andy," "Dan," and "Crystal."

I would like to thank my dear friend, D.M., who patiently, patiently, *patiently* waited for *nine years* for me to complete *her* book. In late 2002, I promised you the first copy of this book and I never forgot that promise. It *is your* book in more ways than one because I met you during the time that the drama of my relationship with "Jonathan" was playing itself out—in fact, the day that I confronted "Jonathan" with what I had learned about his "relationship" with "Andy" and when, in some sense, the *real* drama began—and you have been a part of my life ever since. I never could have imagined it at the time, but you have proven to be one of the *truest* friends I have ever had. This book is the *least* of what I owe to you.

I would also like to thank E.H. and A.H. for reading early drafts of this manuscript and offering invaluable critiques that ultimately strengthened the quality of the final draft. In addition, I would like to thank A.E. for helping me decode the legalese—a language I cannot master—that I encountered in my research and writing. Any errors of commission or omission are in the end my own.

And last—but really first—I would like to thank P.V.S., without whose encouragement at a critical time in my life this book—and undoubtedly the majority of my writing—would not exist.

"Richard Lee"
February 1, 2012

PREFACE

The term *psychopath* provokes a variety of associations in people's minds. For many people, the term conjures up visions of the remorseless serial killer who murders one hapless victim after another in order to fulfill some perverse and powerful compulsion that implacably reasserts itself again and again. Although serial killers have probably always existed, American society has, in recent decades, become increasingly captivated by this type of murderer, who is endlessly featured in both "true crime" and fictional accounts as the epitome of evil, the focus of fascination, and the embodiment of entertainment. What this fixation says about our society is open to debate, but there can be no doubt that in the popular imagination, *psychopath* = *serial killer*.

This, however, is a distortion of the truth. The psychopath, the person who functions with little or no conscience, takes many forms. Although they can take the form of the serial killer, they are far more likely to appear to us in the form of the con artist, the pathological liar, the swindler, the bully, the manipulator, the sadist and many other "subspecies" who suffer from (or, in *their* minds, revel in) the same dysfunction. Fundamentally, all psychopaths believe and behave as if the rest of us are not beings with rights and feelings and selves that *matter*, but *tools* to be used for their own perverse purposes, then discarded once our usefulness to them has been exhausted. They have *no* concern for how their behavior affects us because they have no understanding of the concept of "concern for others." In addition, the danger these individuals pose derives not simply from their behavior, but also from the fact that, on the surface, they often appear as normal as the rest of us. They wear what psychiatrist Hervey Cleckley called a "mask of sanity," luring us in with their intelligence, their charm, their seeming concern for our welfare, then snaring us in their web of deceit, manipulation, and damage from which it is often difficult to escape. Some never do, literally die trying. They prey not only on our ignorance and innocence, but also on our wants and weaknesses, often recognizing them when we don't, which makes them even more effective in their efforts to exploit us. The damage they cause to society and to the individuals who compose it is multifaceted and incalculable.

Thankfully, the vast majority of us will never encounter, directly, the psychopath in the guise of the serial killer. Unfortunately, we are far more likely to encounter one of their "lesser" forms, which can, however, do just as much to damage us—physically, emotionally, mentally, vocationally, socially, financially, spiritually—as their murderous counterparts. Estimated to comprise 3% of the adult male and 1% of the adult female population, the United States currently harbors at least five million psychopaths. And, this is only those who meet the *full* criteria for the disorder, not those who meet enough of the criteria to still pose a threat. Although some of these individuals are safely locked away in prison, most are not. Therefore, we are in far more danger from them than we are from the more flagrant type that figures so prominently in the popular imagination. Unfortunately, most of us are unaware of the less captivating menace that lurks all around us, that is far more likely to ensnare, damage, and possibly destroy us. The stories, the lessons, that come from them are no less dramatic and far more important.

In this book, I recount the details of my ten-month relationship with "Johnny," a psychopath whom I first encountered in the late spring of 2001 and with whom I was directly entangled for the next year. Apart from being a master manipulator, a vindictive bully, and a white-collar criminal, he was first and foremost a pathological liar who wove intricate, convincing stories about himself and his life—and others—that were designed either to reinforce his sense of self or to manipulate those who ran afoul of him into serving his psychopathic needs. The level of pathological lying that I saw in Johnny was beyond description, far worse than anything I had ever encountered outside a psychiatric textbook, and something that, for me, has intellectually always been the most intriguing aspect of his behavior. Unfortunately, it also caused the most damage. In this book, I also recount my attempts to untangle the intricate web of lies about himself and others—and me—that he wove not only throughout that time, but also in the months that followed. Further, I attempt to analyze his seemingly incomprehensible behavior and place it into some kind of comprehensible psychological framework. Finally, and perhaps most importantly, I try to detail the way in which these "characters" (an appropriate term, I believe, since they interact with us not as people, but as personas) operate, so that hopefully the reader can recognize and avoid becoming snared in their web of psychopathology.

The factual information in this book derives from multiple sources. The most important of these sources are direct interaction with "Johnny," some 1,800 hours' worth, that took place during the one-year period between June 16, 2001 and July 6, 2002 as well as approximately 450 e-mails that he sent to me between May 31, 2001, when we met, and July 7, 2002, when he viciously informed me that my attempts to expose him had failed, that it was now *his* turn to harm *me*. Two additional, if minor, direct sources are a small number of instant-message sessions that took place between mid-June and August 29, 2001 and telephone conversations that took place between June 6, 2001 and January 15, 2002.

Another no less important source of information about "Johnny" was some of his other victims, whose stories of the lies he had told to them and the damage those lies had done to them began to emerge within weeks of our breakup around the beginning of April 2002. These victims include, in order of appearance, "Miranda West," "Mike Harmon," "Terry Frazier," "Laura," "Andy Black," "Dan," and "Crystal." I spoke to all of these individuals directly, either in person or by phone, at least once and, in some cases, multiple times. I audio-recorded two of my conversations with "Miranda," which took place on May 16, 2002 and August 3, 2002, respectively, and these recordings total at least two and a half hours' worth of material. In addition, I have numerous e-mails from "Laura," "Andy," "Dan," and "Crystal" detailing what "Johnny" did to them and documenting our attempts to deal with the resulting damage. Finally, I have copies of several instant-message sessions with "Dan" and "Andy."

Another significant source of information about the workings of "Johnny's" mind are numerous sex ads using at least sixty different personas that he placed on various gay-oriented Internet message boards during the three-year period between April 15, 2000 and March 26, 2003. It was these ads that first raised my suspicions that "Johnny" might not be the person he had led me to believe he was.

Apart from the sources noted above, relevant information is taken, if not from memory, then from diary entries, credit card statements, bank statements, telephone records, a storage unit rental agreement, miscellaneous receipts, documents found in a briefcase that "Johnny" left behind at "Dan's," records from an online criminal background search that I performed in February 2011, information from "Crystal's" web site that dealt with "Johnny's" criminal activities, information from two web sites detailing two separate crimes that "Johnny" committed, police reports obtained from the police in "Paladin," photographs of "Johnny" and "Glenn," and photographs of the interior and exterior of the house on "Millstone Drive" in "Paladin."

I have dispensed with the cumbersome use of the word *sic* when quoting, having made minor changes in person and tense as well as occasional corrections when letters were transposed or omitted and inclusions when clarifying words were omitted. I have, however, left important misspellings or stylistic peculiarities intact whenever possible. In addition, at the risk of seeming sexist, I have dispensed with the cumbersome use of the phrase "he and she" and its derivatives and have used the generic pronoun "he" and its derivatives in most places. Apart from allowing the writing to flow more smoothly, the use of the masculine pronoun seems more fitting, since I am often referring to psychopaths when I use it and most psychopaths are male.

I have changed the names of all the people, places, and other entities involved. Any connection between the pseudonyms used and the actual names of persons, places, or other entities, past, present, or future, is purely coincidental. It is my hope that the reader will make no effort to uncover the true identities of the persons mentioned herein and interfere in their lives in any way. We have all suffered enough because of "Johnny's" behavior and should not have to suffer further because of some misguided, or perverse, desire to unmask identities. We all want, and expect, to be left in peace. What is important here is *what* happened, not *who* it happened to.

Although this book is written in a popular style and, therefore, some may view it simply as a "good read," I sincerely hope that the reader will come away from this book not only with a greater insight into the workings of at least one version of the psychopathic mind and an understanding of how to recognize and avoid psychopaths in general, but also with a greater insight into oneself. Psychopaths prey, first and foremost, on our personal weaknesses, especially the ones we have not yet recognized within ourselves. Perhaps this book will inspire the reader to embark on the path to self-understanding and self-improvement without having to encounter a psychopath to do it, permit the reader to grow stronger without gaining that strength through the struggle to escape the psychopath's snare. Ultimately, the greatest lesson, among many, that we can learn from an encounter with the psychopath is that *we* have the ability to tear down their webs of lies with the power of the truth about ourselves, even to prevent them from being able to weave the webs through which they ensnare and destroy us in the first place. Ultimately, we feed them with our inner weakness, but we can defeat them with our inner strength.

PROLOGUE

In 1998, I received my master's degree in psychology from the university in Hawthorn, my home town. Once I completed my degree, I began searching for a suitable position in which I could use it. For a number of reasons, I had been contemplating moving to the nearby larger city of Paladin and focused my job searching there. Apart from having more job opportunities than Hawthorn did, Paladin had one of the most active gay communities in the state, which I thought would give me the opportunities for having the kind of life as a gay man that Hawthorn had always been unable to provide.

Throughout the fall of 1998 and the first half of 1999, I worked at a variety of temporary jobs while I continued my search for a full-time one. One of them, an academic job that I held in the spring, was headquartered in the northwest corner of Paladin. In spite of the good economy, however, I didn't seem to be having much luck finding something more substantial. So, around the beginning of July, I decided to place my résumé on the Internet, a relatively new concept, in the hope that it would reach a broader audience.

For six more weeks, I received no responses. Then, around the middle of August, I received a phone call late one morning from the head of human resources for a company in Paladin. He explained that he had found my online résumé and told me that his boss, a doctor and businessman, was interested in doing research to determine if various substances were effective in treating psychological disorders. Because his boss couldn't do the job himself, he was looking for an assistant to help him and he thought I seemed like a perfect fit. The job, as described to me, seemed well defined and I felt I knew exactly what I was going to be doing and confident that I could do it. It sounded like a wonderful opportunity not only because it would give me a chance to use my master's degree in psychology, which was research oriented, but also because it would bring to an end an exhausting job search that had lasted for months. In addition, the job would finally allow me to live in Paladin. Perhaps once I was there, I could even have something of a love life, something that had been subordinated to the demands of school and job hunting for a very long time.

After a series of interviews that stretched throughout the rest of August, I was hired. Over the next month, I prepared, practically and psychologically, to move to Paladin. Eventually, I found an apartment in the northwest corner of the city, not too far from my new job and not too far from my old one. I had liked that job, liked the area, liked my new job, at least in principle. It seemed like a dream come true.

Once I arrived, however, the dream rapidly turned into a nightmare. The job, for one, proved to be one of the worst experiences I had ever had. Because my boss had just created my position—I was the first person to fill it—he was still in the process of deciding what he wanted the person in the position to do. That spelled trouble for me. Although I had been hired for what seemed to be a well-defined purpose, my boss quickly scrapped his original idea and began taking things in a variety of unrelated and constantly shifting directions. Consequently, I was left in a continuous state of uncertainty about what I was supposed to be doing. Compounding the problem, I perceived that I couldn't talk to my boss about my concerns without appearing inadequate to do the job and feeling that I was risking losing it. Soon I began functioning in a state of constant anxiety.

In addition, I had unwittingly moved into a ground floor apartment above which lived a family who seemed to have no understanding of the word *quiet*. The first night I was there, their children spent three hours, from 9:00 in the evening until midnight, playing what sounded like basketball. The ceiling shook continuously throughout that time, to the point that it almost dislodged the reflectors from an overhead light positioned directly beneath them. Sometime later, they decided to have a church meeting in their apartment. There must have been at least fifteen people there that night and the noise they were making was incredible. They were talking and laughing as loudly as they could, stomping their feet, playing tambourines and rhythm sticks, and singing hymns at the top of their lungs. This went on all evening, and since I was right below them, I was bearing the brunt of it. Although I complained on them and they were warned to be quieter, they never changed their behavior. There was only a narrow window of opportunity between midnight and 6:00 in the morning when I got any peace. Consequently, I was living beneath almost constant noise, which meant that I was living in a continuous state of tension.

Finally, although I did have a few friends in Paladin, I rarely saw them, and because I did most of my work at home, I had little contact with the people at work. In addition, I was living alone, which made me feel even more disconnected. I do like my solitude from time to time, but the constant isolation proved detrimental. Gradually, my emotional health started to decline.

Then, after only a month, my boss decided not only to "end our association," as he put it, but also to eliminate the position altogether simply because he had become tired of the whole venture. I could not have been more shocked because he had never indicated to me that he was unhappy about anything until the day he fired me. Consequently, I was left not only jobless, but also feeling that I had been fired for completely capricious reasons, which only added insult to injury. I didn't know what I was going to do.

By the time what I came to call the "Paladin Incident" was all over, I was mentally, emotionally, and physically exhausted. It wasn't just because of what had happened in the month that I had been in Paladin, however, but also because of all the stress I had experienced in the previous year or so from having my life in such a state of turmoil. I decided to move back to Hawthorn because, without the job, there was no material reason to stay there and, with an unbearable living situation, there was every psychological reason to leave. In addition, I needed to retreat to someplace familiar and comfortable and recoup.

Aware of my condition, my mother offered to let me move home for a while. Although I was reluctant to do it, I was so depleted that I needed help and there didn't seem to be anyone else willing or able to provide it. I was grateful, but also humiliated. Our society has always placed a very strong stigma on adult children who live with their parents, especially adult sons who live with their mothers, and being gay, I felt stigmatized enough. This prejudice is in some ways just as irrational and powerful as the one toward homosexuality and equally damaging. I felt like a pariah, becoming withdrawn and ashamed to reveal what had happened to me.

When I first came back in November, I felt relieved, but after I had been home for a few weeks, I began suffering from one illness after another, since my immune system had become weakened from the stress. I rang in the new millennium with one of the worst sore throats that I have ever suffered from. Worse, I began to sink into a depression. Fortunately, I was offered a part-time job teaching psychology at the college in Hawthorn in January, which helped to alleviate my financial worries somewhat, but it wasn't enough to curb my depression, which only grew worse. By February, my condition had grown so serious that my mother, afraid that I might try to kill myself, forced me to go to the doctor.

In the end, I went to a new doctor, a wonderful man who, knowing that I didn't have medical insurance, was reluctant to have me pay him even though his clinic required it. He had a soft spot for teachers, telling me that he was what he was because of them, and knowing how little many teachers got paid. To treat my depression, he put me on Prozac, supplying me with enough free samples to last me for months. Fortunately, it worked wonders and soon I began to feel better.

My teaching job, although rather routine, proved to be relatively stress free, and for the next year or so, I settled into a lifestyle in which my primary goal was to maintain the sense of equilibrium that I had finally regained. I wasn't happy about living at home again at my age, but if living at home allowed me to keep my life stable and sane, then that was what I was going to do for myself.

By the spring of 2001, I began to feel increasingly discontent with my situation. That was an encouraging sign, I believed, because it meant that I had regained a firm enough foundation of physical and mental health that I now felt motivated to build a bigger life on top of it. I began thinking about what I wanted to do professionally, if I wanted to return to school to obtain a doctorate in psychology and become a full-fledged psychologist or do something different. I was developing the drive to try again.

By April, I had been taking Prozac daily for fourteen months. My mental and emotional well-being had remained stable for quite some time and I wanted to see how well it would stay that way without the chemical crutch. Within two weeks, I noticed an extraordinary change. My emotions came alive in a way that they had not for well over a year. My feelings were roused much more easily and affected me much more intensely and the world began touching me with an undeniable vibrancy. I realized that although the Prozac had helped, it had also blunted my emotional responses.

That had also included my sexual feelings. It wasn't until I stopped taking the Prozac that I realized the rebuilding of my well-being had come at a price. While I was taking the drug, I had described myself as being "me, but better," but after I stopped taking it, I realized that it had been suppressing not only my depression, but also my sexuality. In looking back over the previous year, I could think of only three times when I had felt noticeably sexual. That was clearly abnormal for an otherwise healthy man in his early 30s. Later, I learned that Prozac caused decreased libido in a certain proportion of men who took it. I was one of them. Since I seemed to be doing well—in fact, in some ways, better—without it, I decided not to continue taking it.

Throughout the second half of the spring, I started noticing and reacting to men again in a way that I hadn't for a long time. By that point, it had been some time since I had been involved with someone and once again the prospect was becoming appealing.

My relationship history, though, was somewhat checkered, if that was the word, because I tended to attract men who kept secrets that eventually destroyed those relationships. One man named Cole managed to hide the fact that he was an alcoholic for two months before he could finally hide it no longer. Another man named Henri managed to hide the fact that he was involved in damaging sexual practices, again for two months, before he, too, could hide that no longer. Discovering the truth, the deception, was deeply damaging to my ability to trust and later hindered my ability to form other relationships. I wasn't stupid or naïve, but I *had* ignored my intuition, which, in both cases, had told me that something was seriously wrong even though I didn't have tangible facts to back up my feelings.

But those, and other, experiences were now in the past. I had either healed from them or built up defenses against them to the point that they no longer interfered with my ability to move forward. By May 2001, I had the confidence, the courage, to try again.

Only when it was too late would I realize that in doing so, I had become a fly that was headed directly into a spider's very sticky web.

I just want to be open with you. The more info that you take in the better you can understand who and what I am. There are really no, or very very few secrets(and they must be unconscious ones as I don't know what they would be at this point) here. What you see is what there is.

—Jonathan

*La vérité existe. On n'invente que le mensonge.
(Truth exists. Falsehood is only invented.)*

—Georges Braque

—I—
—The Fly in the Web—

I loved The Fly *(help me help me). It was so so tacky. I'm sure that Helene was fucking the brother. They were just too friendly at the end and nobody seemed too shattered that the husband was eaten by the spider. Now there's a lesson for life.*

—Jonathan

—1—
GAYMAN

Now it's your turn.

On the evening of Wednesday, May 30, 2001, I was staying up late—as I preferred to do. From the time that I was a teenager, I have been a night person, preferring the starlit hours to the sunlit ones, and my summer schedule, which didn't require me to rise early, allowed me to indulge my nocturnal inclinations. That summer, I was teaching a psychology class two afternoons a week in Viridian, a small town located between Hawthorn and Paladin. An astrologically minded person might say that my preference for the "night life" arose from the fact that the "planet" associated with my sun sign, Cancer, was the Moon. I have always maintained an ambivalent attitude toward astrology, saying, "I don't believe in astrology—but that's because I'm a Cancer and Cancers don't believe in astrology," but I *did* believe that the proposed Cancerian personality fit my true personality perfectly—or almost.

Cancers were supposed to be emotionally sensitive and I knew that some things affected me more deeply than they seemed to affect most. On the positive side, it made me empathetic, compassionate, and concerned about the suffering of others, but on the negative side, it made me more anxious, depressive, and easily hurt than the average person. That sensitivity, because of both its positive and its negative qualities, had promoted an interest in humanitarian issues, artistic expression, and psychology. In addition, Cancers were supposed to be homebodies who valued creating a comfortable sanctuary to which they could retreat when the world became too overwhelming. I was readily overstimulated and depleted by my interaction with others and preferred solitude to socializing. Further, Cancers were supposed to prefer stability and security to unpredictability and risk and I had a long history of clinging to what I had rather than risk losing it for something better or different. I did take risks, but not often, and found uncertain situation difficult to tolerate.

And, finally, Cancers were supposed to be intuitive, easily apprehending truths that bypassed the rational faculties. Here, though, I deviated the most from the presumed Cancerian pattern. I had been told that I had good intuition, but I didn't listen to it. I didn't trust it. At an early age, I had developed a strong interest in the sciences and a preference for rational, factual thinking, which I felt was superior. I thought of intuition as a kind of emotional "thinking"…and I had seen what happened when people "thought"—and behaved—emotionally. I came to attribute most of the problems in human society, in human nature, to the irrationality of emotion. Paradoxically, I was a very emotional person myself, and my "instincts" about situations, about people, generally proved to be true, but I still felt that concrete proofs, coupled with reason, proved the better way to understand the world, to live one's life, to keep from harm. Consequently, the brilliant light of the Sun, which symbolized Reason, not the pale light of the Moon, which symbolized Intuition, was my guiding light, was the *true* "planet" that symbolized me.

The evening of the 30th was warm and the sky was clear, not yet veiled by the haze that would come later in the summer and sometimes hide the dimmer stars from view. Taking advantage of the ideal conditions, I went outside around midnight to gaze at the stars. As I stepped out the back door, which faced toward the south, my eyes fixed on the assemblage of stars directly before me: a J-shaped string of suns that some ancient peoples had thought resembled a scorpion. The predominately blue-white stars that made up the string served not only to define the body of the creature, but also to highlight the bright reddish star at the center of the cephalothorax. The Arabs had called the star *kalb al-akrab* and the Romans *cor scorpionis*, both of which meant "heart of the scorpion," but I knew the star by its Greek name, Antares. The 30th of May was a special night for the brightest star in the assemblage because it was on this night that, at midnight, it reached its highest point in the sky. Drifting among the nearby stars were Mars and Pluto, the planets associated with the astrological sign Scorpio. The arachnid, it seemed, was exerting an especially powerful influence on that particular night.

Perhaps appropriately, I had, throughout the evening, been using the Internet, the worldwide system of interwoven computers that was also known as the Web. In part, I had been visiting different gay personals sites. For at least a month, I had been casually perusing the ads, and had occasionally thought about replying to one or even posting my own, but so far I had done neither. The situation wasn't right, the timing wasn't right, perhaps in some way *I* wasn't right, wasn't ready to take the next step. But I continued to look, working up my courage to make the leap back into a romantic life.

I had first begun "surfing the Net" in May 1997, four years before. I have always been interested in astronomy, and my initial impetus for going "online" was to find copies of the spectacular photographs that had been taken by the Hubble Space Telescope as well as other astronomical information and art. For the next three months, my Internet activities were confined almost exclusively to the scientific and the artistic. The thought that the Internet had other uses never entered my mind. Then one day in August, that all changed.

That day, I had gone to use the computer at the local university library and had found that someone who had used the computer before me had visited a gay-oriented site. Until I made this discovery, I hadn't thought about the potential for using the Internet to meet other gay men, since at that point the Internet was still something of a novelty and its possibilities, as well as its pitfalls, had not yet become established in the public's mind, or at least in *my* mind. Now, I *did* begin to think about the possibilities and find this method for connecting with other gay people in general, and other gay men in particular, to be especially appealing.

Meeting people through the Internet seemed both convenient and comfortable for me, given that I lived in a city in which the only clear methods for meeting other gay people were either to attend the meetings of the gay support group at the local university or to go to the city's one gay bar. The former I had found limiting, while the latter I had found uncomfortable. In addition, I found that looking through personals ads, in which people defined who they were and what they wanted in a few succinct phrases, seemed to be an efficient way of eliminating people who didn't have the qualities you wanted and finding those who did. Although the process was somewhat clinical and was based solely on how accurately and eloquently people presented themselves, it was at least a place to start.

Throughout the previous three and a half years, I had met various gay men and had met with varying degrees of success in my encounters, whether virtual or actual, with them. Although I had met at least two people who had "issues," as psychologists now euphemistically label *problems*, I had never encountered anyone who posed a genuine threat. I was always cautious, but I also figured that using the Web was no worse than any other way of meeting people.

At one point, I happened to be visiting a gay web site called *Gayteway*. It was, in fact, the site that I had discovered the day I had gone to use the computer at the library and was, therefore, the site that had opened the gay community to me. The site appeared to be quite thorough in its inclusion of material that would be of interest to gay people, including personals. It had become one of my favorite gay sites and I visited it often. Indeed, most of the gay men I had met through the Internet I had met through *Gayteway*.

Sometime around 1:00 in the morning of the last day of May, I went to the message board where gay men from my state posted their ads. Shortly thereafter, my attention fastened on a particular ad that had been placed there the evening before.

The ad was posted by someone who called himself "Gayman." He described himself as a "daddy"—gay parlance for an older man—who was looking for a "son"—a younger man—to date or possibly to form a long-term relationship with. Physically, "Gayman" described himself as being in his mid-40s—the ad implied 44—standing 5'8" and weighing 180 pounds. He was quick to add, however, that he was "not fat." In addition, he said that he had short salt-and-pepper hair and a goatee. Psychologically, he described himself as having a laid-back, "easy" personality, being emotionally secure, and not being a "control freak." Otherwise, he said he had "varied interests," but didn't elaborate. He said that he had just ended a ten-year relationship, but added that it had ended "friendly." He implied that he and his former partner had simply grown apart and that it had been time for the both of them to move on. He stated that he was planning to retire the next year at the age of 45, so "new possibilities" would be opening up. "Gayman" seemed to be someone who had reached a turning point in his life.

As far as the ideal partner was concerned, he said that he was looking for someone 40 or younger who was intelligent, attractive, and easy to get along with. He said that he would be willing to relocate the right person, if that was required. He said that the ideal man should like to travel both in the United States and overseas. Finally, he said that whether or not his boyfriend worked was up to him. I fully intended to work, but his statement reinforced the notion that he was financially secure. In general "Gayman" seemed more interested in having someone with whom to enjoy his retired life than anything else. As if to emphasize that fact, he ended the ad by saying that his last boyfriend and he had had a "great time" and encouragingly stated, "Now it's your turn."

As I read the ad, I was filled with what I can only describe as a *now!* feeling—a feeling that the time had finally come and the situation was finally right. The person who called himself "Gayman" seemed far more interesting, far more similar to me in some way than any of the other gay men I had encountered.

Over the next hour, I composed my reply to "Gayman's" ad. Around 2:00, I completed it and, with a mixture of excitement and hope, I sent it. I didn't know if or when the mysterious "Gayman" would respond, but I had at least made my interest known.

I took a bath and went to bed sometime around 2:30. I fell into a light sleep, too stimulated to drift any deeper.

The next morning, I checked my e-mail sometime around 10:00. I was pleased, and more than a little excited, to find that I had received a message, titled "Interested," from someone who called himself "Jonathan."

In the message, he began by telling me that I had written a "very interesting and attention getting note." He said that personality and intelligence were more important to him than looks, but that I appeared to have all three. In describing himself further, he said that he was originally from England and had been in the United States for just over five years. He said that he had lived in a Southern state[1] before being transferred to his current position in Paladin. He said that he also had a master's degree, although his was in "strategic planning." Since he didn't define his job and since I didn't know what "strategic planning" was, I wondered if he was in the military. He said that in addition to his home in Paladin, he had retained his former home in the South as well as his permanent home in London. He said that he was looking forward to retiring early the next year and doing some of the things the demands of his job had prevented him from doing.

Otherwise, he described himself as being "a masculine man who happen[ed] to be gay" as well as being "100% gay," as I had told him I was. He said that he was "healthy in every way," being STD- and HIV-negative, and that he enjoyed an active sex life. He said that he tried to be a sensitive lover but was looking for more than sex. Disparagingly, he said that "[g]etting laid was easy" and that sex, though important, was only one part of the equation.

He said that he had a good sense of humor and had the ability to recognized when he "fuck[ed] up" and could laugh at himself. He said his friends described him as thoughtful and considerate, something he hoped was true. He told me he was a dog lover and

---

[1] From here, I will refer to this state as the "Southern" state

currently lived with three poodles that were well behaved and didn't take over his home or life.

He ended by saying that it would be terrific to speak to me and, if there was mutual interest, to meet. He said that he looked forward to hearing from me soon.

Jonathan. The mystery man, "Gayman," was no longer so mysterious. I wasn't expecting "Gayman" to be anything but American, and the fact that he was British added an extra level of intrigue. I had never considered myself an Anglophile, but the fact of being from a different culture stimulated my curiosity about other peoples, other ways of thinking, perceiving, behaving, being. Yet, despite potential differences, we did seem to share similar values about sexuality, which I considered to be important, and neither of us seemed to take himself too seriously. I wasn't a dog person, having always shared my life with cats, but perhaps I would be willing to adapt. If things continued between us, things could become interesting indeed.

I spent a good part of the day composing a reply that comprehensively but concisely described my history and personality. After telling him my real name, I told him where I had been born, had been raised, and was currently living. I told him some of what had happened to me in the previous couple of years, including living in Paladin then returning to Hawthorn, although I spared him the details of the "Paladin Incident." I told him about some of my interests, including astronomy, metaphysics, and ancient cultures as well as writing, which was my main passion. I told him that at this point in my life, I was less interested in having casual sex than in forming a relationship with someone in which sex was only one part. I concluded by telling him that I was planning to come to Paladin in the near future to visit friends and suggested that while I was there, we could meet in some comfortable location. I suggested Tolliver's, a small restaurant and bar the co-owner of which was the boyfriend of a friend of mine. It not only was gay-oriented and would, therefore, permit us to talk openly about that aspect of our lives without feeling discomfort, but also had a comfortable, quiet atmosphere that was conducive to letting two people get to know each other better.

Later that evening, Jonathan sent me a second message, titled "Common Ground," which emphasized our similarities. After thanking me for my quick reply, he said that he also had a strong interest in ancient cultures and had actually wanted to be an archaeologist when he was younger. He said that he had started his career as an assistant curator at the British Museum in London, where he had worked with Chinese porcelain objects, before he had eventually switched to a career in business 18 years before. Mysteriously, he said that the circumstances that had led to the change were "too arcane to mention here"—which made me think that was a story I was going to have to encourage him to tell. He said that he had been fortunate enough to visit or actually work on digs in such far-flung locales as Peru, Bolivia, Israel, and Zimbabwe. He said that he still maintained an interest in archaeology and planned to reimmerse himself in the subject after retiring the next year.

As far as his "day job," as he called it, was concerned, he said that he was currently the chief officer of operations (COO) of an information technology company in Paladin. Later, I learned that he had moved to Paladin to assume the position in October 1999—ironically, the same month that I had moved there. He said that his company had been relatively unaffected by the recent downturn in the IT market because of the cutting-edge nature of their products. He said that during the previous eleven months he had been slowly cashing out and diversifying his financial base and would still retain a 5% equity position in his company after retiring, but he would not take an active role in managing the company after January, his intended retirement date.

As far as sex was concerned, Jonathan said that he had been "fairly wild early on," but that as he had "sort of" matured, he had discovered the "enhanced pleasure" of sleeping with someone "that you actually had a conversation with and could remember his name in the morning." He said that he "like[d] (!)" what he called "male sex," but was now only interested if it involved someone he wanted to know or someone he already knew but wanted to know better. In general, his attitude toward sex seemed to mirror my own.

Jonathan ended his message by saying that he would be happy to meet me the next time I visited Paladin. He said that he had never been to Tolliver's but that it sounded like a great place to go on a date. He gave me his phone number and said that although he traveled for business, he would be happy to give me days when he would be available so we could chat before I came. He said that I had piqued his interest and curiosity and that he looked forward to learning more.

I wasn't able to respond to Jonathan's second message until the next evening. Despite being exhausted from my busy day, I found enough energy to write a lengthy reply. I told him that I was envious of him to hear that he had once worked at the British Museum because I had often thought I would find it fulfilling to work in a museum that focused on collecting the artifacts of ancient cultures. Expanding on my interests in anthropology, I told him that I was especially intrigued by the Minoan culture, a highly sophisticated culture that had flourished on Crete between 3000 and 1450 BCE. I was also intrigued to hear about his work in Zimbabwe because, as it happened, I had actually been reading about the extensive ruins there within the previous couple of weeks. I looked forward to exploring our interest in anthropology in more detail.

Although I expressed my knowledge of archaeology, I had to confess my ignorance about business, in which I had little background. I mentioned that when he had told me that he had a degree in "strategic planning," I had thought that he might be involved in the *military*. I stood corrected. Ignorance aside, I told him I was glad to know that his company hadn't suffered the problems that had befallen the IT field in recent times and actually seemed to be flourishing, to the point that he could retire at such a young age and pursue the things he truly loved.

In the same message, I mentioned, reluctantly, that I was living with my family. That gave Jonathan, who said his full name was "Jonathan Iain Joshua Frazier," an opening to begin telling me about *his* family. Jonathan's father, Edward, was a prominent physician who lived in London. Jonathan described his father—whom he also called Papa or Da—as an imposing, intimidating figure to whom his children, and most people in general, felt compelled to defer. At 80, he was in perfect health and had been "in hospital" only once in his life, during World War II. Although he was retired from active practice, he had retired only the year before and remained active teaching and writing.

Jonathan compared his mother, Helena, who was 77, to Lovey Howell, Natalie Schafer's character on *Gilligan's Island*. "Mummy," as he called her, seemed to spend most of her time being chauffeured about England buying up every trinket and bauble she could lay her hands on. She appeared to be waited on hand and foot, with her personal staff going so far as to change her sheets every time she arose from taking a nap. Yet, despite being pampered, she was far from weak. She was the only member of the Frazier family who did not defer to her husband and seemed to be as formidable in her own way as he was.

At 54, Sarah was the oldest of the Frazier children. She lived in London with Reginald, her husband of 30 years who was also 30 years her senior. Sarah had met Reginald while she was studying law "at university," where he was one of her professors. They had become romantically involved, and because of the difference in their ages—and, more importantly, their backgrounds—the relationship had caused something of a scandal. Although her parents had forbidden her to marry him, Sarah had resisted their wishes and the two had married. Jonathan didn't indicate if Sarah's relationship with their parents was still strained, although I got the impression that, over time, their parents' feelings had mellowed. Reginald, now in his 80s, had recently been diagnosed with prostate cancer and the family was now dealing with that fact.

Jonathan's oldest brother, who was also named Reginald, was the only Frazier child who lived in Eiseley, the small town in England where Jonathan and his siblings had been born and raised. In his early 50s, Reginald had married well and had never worked, being instead a man of leisure. In that regard, he reminded me somewhat of Charles Darwin, who had married into the wealthy Wedgwood family of Wedgwood china fame and whose means had relieved him of the pressures of working, thereby allowing him to pursue his interest in natural science. Reginald served on the Eiseley town council and performed other community services, but even so, Jonathan still referred to him as a "slug." I received the distinct impression that this judgment was based not on some deeply-held belief in the value of industry, but on simple envy of his brother's ability to do as he pleased.

Temperamentally, Bettina seemed to be the most atypical of the Frazier children, being introverted and unassuming while the rest of her siblings seemed more extroverted and assertive. Indeed, her subdued character had earned her the nickname "Strange Bettina." Around 50, Bettina lived with her husband and four children in London but otherwise didn't appear to associate with her family or socialize in general to any significant degree.

In his late 40s, Michael was a don of economics at Cambridge. According to Jonathan, he had published in *The Economist*, an important British periodical, and otherwise lived the subdued life of the stereotypical academician. Jonathan felt that both Bettina and Michael had dealt with the stresses of life, the pressures to achieve and succeed that their parents had instilled in them, by retreating from them: Bettina into home life, Michael into academic life. In my opinion, life in academia was anything but pressure-free, but Jonathan seemed to think of the walls of Cambridge as some kind of ivory tower that protected Michael from the fray in the "real" world.

In her late 40s, Leandra was the Frazier child who was the most like her father. Indeed, Jonathan described Leandra as "my father in a dress," assertive to the point of aggression. Leandra also seemed to have a cruel streak, the type of person who had literally pulled the legs off insects when she was a child. Leandra lived in London with her second husband, having divorced her first husband, in part, because he was "boring." Leandra had several children and, in her late 40s, was expecting again. Although Jonathan once listed the names of all of Leandra's children, he gave details about only two.

The first was a younger son, Hamish, who was notable because of a dramatic incident that would happen later that summer in which he was involved. The second was Alcuin, the oldest son, who was attending university at Cambridge. In addition, Alcuin was Jonathan's favorite nephew and later, Alcuin would become important in Jonathan's life in ways that at the time I could not have imagined.

At 46, Charmaine was Jonathan's youngest sister and the sibling to whom he felt the closest. They corresponded frequently and Jonathan would often tell her things before he would tell other members of his family. Charmaine lived in London with her four children, her husband Marcus having died three and a half years before in an especially horrific accident that had taken place at Christmas. While attempting to hang an ornament at the top of the family Christmas tree, Marcus had lost his balance on the ladder on which he was standing and had fallen, hitting his head on the corner of a coffee table. The impact had killed him instantly. Adding to the horror, Charmaine and one of her children had witnessed the accident. Charmaine apparently had not adequately dealt with her husband's death and had still not dated after three and a half years.

At 38, Terrence was the baby of the family. He, like Jonathan, lived in the United States, having moved to the Northeast some 15 years before. An artist, Terrence had worked and socialized with various luminaries in his and related fields, people whose names I knew quite well. According to Jonathan, Terrence had been married and divorced three times, first to a Chinese woman, then to a Japanese woman, and finally to a Korean woman. I once quipped to Jonathan that it seemed as if Terrence were trying to work his way around the Pacific Rim. Jonathan said that he liked Terrence, but he also said that he wasn't close to him. Overall, I detected more than a hint of jealousy toward his younger brother. Jonathan seemed to feel that Terrence was his father's favorite and that he permitted him a degree of latitude to be and do whatever he wished that he did not permit to his other children—for instance, to be an artist instead of something more befitting his background.

Jonathan mentioned several relatives, but perhaps the most intriguing was his Aunt Elfriede. Her name didn't sound especially British and, as it turned out, Elfriede was not from England. An aunt through marriage to Jonathan's oldest maternal uncle, Elfriede had been born and had lived much of her early life in Germany. That included Nazi Germany. Apparently, Elfriede had fully assimilated Hitler's racist views and had actually worked as a secretary for one of Hitler's higher-ups. When the Nazi regime had fallen, however, Elfriede had fled to England, where she had not only met her husband-to-be, but also reversed her racist opinions. She was no longer married to Jonathan's uncle, but she was still considered a part of the Frazier family. Indeed, Jonathan said of Aunt Elfriede that she "fits right into our goofy family like she was born to it." Elfriede was Jonathan's favorite aunt, whom he described as "very dotty but also very funny." Perhaps because of her own experience in fleeing Germany, Aunt Elfriede had advised Jonathan, upon hearing that he was moving to the United States, to keep £5,000 (roughly $8,000 US) in cash and his passport on hand in case he needed to flee the country.

Jonathan's best friend in England was Colin, whom Jonathan described as like a ninth child in the Frazier family. Jonathan had met Colin when he had gone away to "public" (boarding) school, "per English traditions," at the age of eight and the two of them had been best friends ever since. Colin, as it happened, was also gay, which gave him and Jonathan an additional level of connection beyond that forged by shared interests and experiences. Another close friend included Harald, an antiques dealer from northern Europe, who had the distinction, as Jonathan put it, of being "the most sexually active person I know." Harald, too, was gay, and Jonathan recounted an incident when, one day, he had gone to Harald's to return a book and found him in the middle of an orgy. Jonathan mentioned other friends, but Colin and Harald were the two he mentioned the most frequently and who seemed to figure into his life the most prominently. Like Jonathan's nephew Alcuin, Colin would later assume a significance in Jonathan's life that I could not have anticipated.

Jonathan said that everyone in his family knew Glenn, his former boyfriend to whom he had alluded in his ad, and knew that Jonathan was gay. He said, though, that no one in his family made an issue of it and that it was merely considered "part of life." I had always perceived that British society was more accepting of homosexuality than American society was and Jonathan's comment seemed to reflect a level of acceptance that, unfortunately, still hadn't developed in the United States.

Overall, Jonathan described his upbringing as stereotypically "British" in nature, in which one is fundamentally taught to suppress one's emotions, especially when experiencing or expressing them would give an appearance of weakness or interfere with the efficient performance one's duties. In general, the Frazier children had been raised "to run the British Empire," as Jonathan once described it, which essentially meant that they were expected to achieve and maintain a high standard in every aspect of life and to let nothing—

emotion, sickness, excuses, weakness—deter them in the pursuit not simply of excellence, but seemingly of perfection.

I felt that Jonathan's upbringing was double-edged. On the one hand, Jonathan had been raised to believe that, by virtue of his upper-crust background, he was superior to others, but on the other hand, the drive to maintain this sense of superiority in tangible terms could often prove more burdensome than bolstering to one's sense of self. As someone who understood the psychological, and even physical, damage that could result from the excessive suppression of one's feelings, Jonathan and I had numerous debates on the relative merits of emotional suppression versus emotional expression. Jonathan's mentality was something that I could not fully appreciate from experience, but it was something that I strove to understand rather than criticize.

On the morning of Sunday, June 3, however, Jonathan allowed his stiff upper lip to quiver, if a little. After thanking me for my previous message, he lamented that life could be "so hectic and difficult sometimes" before telling me that one of his closest friends had unexpectedly died that morning. He said that his friend, whose name was Alexander, was 44, "same as [him]," and that he had known him for 14 years. He said that the two of them had spoken nearly every day and that he would miss him every day for the rest of his life. Jonathan described Alexander as a "dear, warm loving person who just wanted to be loved and happy" and hoped that he was "happy and loved now." He said that the funeral was that Tuesday in England, which meant that he couldn't go. He apologized for being so morose but said that he didn't know how to react. He said he felt like crying, but didn't seem to be able to.

I carefully composed what I hoped would be a compassionate and supportive response. Given the subject, I inevitably expressed my own beliefs about death and life after death and referred him to a metaphysical site that I had created about a year before on which I discussed various phenomena that seemed to suggest the existence of the soul. I hoped my message would comfort him.

In response, Jonathan thanked me for my e-mail and told me that he believed in many of the things that I had said in my message. Consequently, he wasn't too upset about missing the funeral because he believed that Alexander's spirit was gone and they were only putting his remains into the ground.

Then, he asked me if I knew or had heard of a woman named Miranda West. He described her as a "pretty well known seer, intuitive and...psychic" who lived in Paladin. He said they had met through the friend of a friend and had become acquaintances. He said that Miranda was very comforting about matters like Alexander's death and that "by coincidence" they were having dinner the next evening. He said that in the past Miranda had been "accurate to the point of scariness" and hoped I would be able to meet her sometime. He said that he wasn't one of those "New Age junkies" but did believe that some people had "insights or a gift of sensitivity" that others didn't; Miranda, he believed, had that gift.

I had never heard of Miranda, but I had been to several people in the previous several years who purportedly had "insights or a gift of sensitivity" that others didn't and I was certainly open to and intrigued by the possibility of meeting someone who was "accurate to the point of scariness." As with Jonathan's favorite nephew Alcuin and his best friend Colin, Miranda would eventually come to assume a level of importance that at the time I could not have foreseen, even if I myself had been psychic.

■

After we had corresponded by e-mail for about a week, I worked up my courage to call him. On the evening of Wednesday, June 6, I found some time when I could speak to him in private, so I decided that would be as good a time as any for our first conversation. With a mixture of nervousness and excitement, I called. After a few rings, a man answered, saying hello in a refined British accent. I asked if this was Jonathan, and when he said yes, I told him it was Richard. "Richard!" he exclaimed, the second R-sound missing from my name. "You've rescued me from these reports!" He went on to explain that he had been in the middle of reading through some reports for work but that he desperately needed to take a break.

I don't remember everything we discussed, but I do remember that our conversation was very broad ranging. Having an interest in linguistics and languages, I was curious to know how the Midwestern accent—my accent—sounded to him. He said that it sounded "flat," which I thought was an interesting perception. Although I didn't ask him this explicitly, I had received the impression that the British didn't have the same kind of fawning reaction to American accents that many Americans seemed to have toward British ones. I myself thought that although British accents were distinctive and interesting, they were no more distinctive and interesting than my own when viewed from a broader perspective. I believed that people who thought that British accents were cultured or romantic or quaint were a little ridiculous, since I had seen no evidence that the British were any more cultured or romantic or quaint than the Americans. To me, *what* Jonathan said was far more interesting than *how* he said it.

I asked him how he liked the Midwest and he said that he found the people friendly, adding that he thought the Midwest was a good place to find a boyfriend. I thought that was an encouraging sign.

At one point, Jonathan commented that, in reading my response to his ad, he had seen that I was 6'3". I told him that was right and he told me, uncertainly, that he was "kind of short." Although at 5'8" he was half a foot shorter than I was, height was not an issue for me. At 6'3", almost everyone was shorter than me, so I attached little importance to differences in height. In addition, I had once calculated that the average height of the men with whom I had been involved to that point was somewhere around 5'9", which was only an inch taller than Jonathan's stated height. Therefore, I was used to being involved with "short" men. I told him that if height wasn't an issue for him, then it wasn't an issue for me, but even though he didn't mention it again, I gathered that it *was* an issue for him, a source of perceived inferiority.

By the time we were through, we had talked for an hour and a half. Jonathan seemed very pleased with how our conversation had gone and enthusiastically asked me for a "second date." I accepted. After we hung up, I was left feeling excited and satisfied that things had gone so well, that things were going so well. Later that night, he sent me an e-mail, titled "Super," in which he thanked me for ringing and told me that he'd had a "super" time talking to me. Now, he was looking forward "even more" to meeting me and told me that, in his opinion, "the more contact there is, the better it seems to get." I agreed.

■

By the Saturday following our first conversation, I had worked up enough courage to send Jonathan a picture of myself—myself as an adult. Because I had suggested that we go to the zoo in Paladin for something to do on a date, I had sent him a picture of myself that had been taken there when I was six. In response to receiving the picture of my six-year-old self, he had said that I was "too cute for words" and that if I was "half as handsome as an adult as [I was as] a child then we [would] get along, on one level anyway, famously." Although his reaction was encouraging, he had not yet seen me at 34.

I had never been confident about my appearance, given that, with a slender ectomorphic build, I had always had less than the idealized male physique. By the time I was 15, I had reached my adult height of 6'3", but for the next ten years, my weight had remained stalled in the low 130s. After that point, I had begun to gain weight, but slowly, and it wasn't until I had reached my early 30s that I had managed to reach even 160. I had always thought of myself as being built more like an insect—possibly a walking stick—than like a person. Because my weight had always fallen below normal for my height, sometimes considerably so, some people thought I was malnourished, sick, or simply too thin to suit them, which made me feel extremely self-conscious. Although at 34 my weight, which averaged around 162, was now within the low normal range for my height, years of negative reactions had left me feeling deeply insecure about my body.

In addition, I had protruding ears that, although adorable as a child were not quite so lovable as an adult, and strabismus, which gave me a "lazy" left eye that became more apparent the farther away I focused. In pictures, I always tried to assume a three-quarter view that masked the ungainly angle of my ears and focus my eyes as if I were looking only a foot or so away to make them converge. Even so, I *did* think I had *some* redeeming features, which gave me enough courage to send a recent picture of myself to Jonathan.

His reaction seemed to be positive. In an e-mail he sent to me later that day, he told me that I was "handsomer then [he] had a right to expect" and that he saw "the child in the man and vise versa." He also commented that my hairstyle was "quite flattering to [my] face," and although to him appearance was not "Number 1," he said that he did like the way I looked. After receiving validation on an aspect of myself about which I felt insecure, I felt more confident.

Jonathan didn't send me a picture of himself, however, and sometime that next week, my curiosity about what *he* looked like finally overcame me. Instead of asking him for a photo of himself, I thought I might be able to find one of him online. Given that he was the COO of an information technology company, it seemed likely that the company would have a web site where his picture would be featured. He hadn't given me the name of the company for which he worked, so I decided to enter his name into a search engine and see what came up. I was rewarded with a most unexpected result.

I was offered a link that, when clicked, took me to a page containing biographies, and photographs, of several employees…all of whom were dressed like detectives. In reading the page, I ascertained that the people on the page were recruiters, hence the detective attire. I scrolled down the page and, at last, got my first glimpse of Jonathan.

Although the picture gave no indication of height or weight, it did seem to confirm what Jonathan had told me otherwise about his appearance. He was very much the "daddy" type, and the round glasses and pipe that he sported as part of the detective persona only heightened the "daddy" look. The biography described him as being classy and cultured and added that he even had "classy dogs!"—referring, of course, to Jonathan's poodles. Although he had told me that he was the COO of his company, I assumed that he also did a certain amount of recruiting, hence his inclusion on the recruiters' page. All in all, I did find him reasonably attractive and the biography also seemed to confirm what he had told me about himself, although his e-mails and our conversation had assured me that he was, in fact, classy, intelligent, cultured, and definitely interesting.

Around the same time, I became curious about Jonathan's family. Because his family seemed impressive, I thought I might also be able to find out more about them online. I searched for information about his family in England, but found nothing. I also searched for information about his brother Terrence, who lived in the United States. When I entered his name into a search engine, I was presented with a number of links that seemed to relate to Jonathan's brother. I clicked on one of the links and found a story that contained biographical information about Terrence. Perplexing information.

The story, strangely, said that "Terry," as he was called, was not from England, but from a state in the Midwest.[2] The *Midwest*? That made no sense. Did I have the right Terrence Frazier? I might have thought I was mistaken, but the story contained a picture of "Terry," who looked strikingly like Jonathan. In addition, the information the story provided about "Terry's" art matched what Jonathan had told me about him. Something, somewhere, was wrong. I assumed it was the information. Eventually, I put the issue into the back of my mind.

■

On the Saturday that I sent Jonathan the picture of myself, he e-mailed to say that he would call me sometime Monday evening. He did, and we ended up having another hour-and-a-half conversation. Later that evening, he sent me an e-mail in which he once again described our conversation as "super" and expressed his amazement at having spoken for 90 minutes; despite its length, he thought he could have continued for another 90. He said that it was great to find someone he enjoyed talking and listening to. He also said that he enjoyed me "more with each passing encounter" and expressed his hope that we could at least be good friends—though preferably more.

I enjoyed *him* more with each passing encounter. It was difficult for me not to. Every message, every conversation, did something for me that nothing else, that no *one* else, had done for me for a very

---

[2] From here, I will refer to this state as the "Midwestern" state

long time—if ever. At the time, I wasn't conscious of all the reasons why I found Jonathan so alluring, but in retrospect, I realized that in the beginning, a number of forces worked together to draw me irresistibly to him.

First of all, Jonathan was an excellent storyteller. Whether he was discussing his "goofy" family, his trials at work, his boyhood in England, his life in Paladin, his sexual interests, his personal losses, his challenges in the States, our developing relationship, he had an unparalleled ability to convey his experiences with a degree of realism that I found captivating. In reading his e-mails, I often felt as if I were with him, within him, experiencing his thoughts, perceptions, feelings, sensations as he experienced them. Jonathan's command of language may have been enhanced by his intelligence and honed by his education, but he had a natural talent. As someone who appreciated good writing, I felt that Jonathan's eloquent, evocative style allowed me to get to know him faster and better than I might have gotten to know someone less skilled at expressing himself.

Second, I enjoyed the fact that the sexual part of my life had opened up again. By the time I met Jonathan, I hadn't been sexually involved with anyone for two years, and even though the Prozac had left me largely uninterested in sex for one of them, I was still delighted to be sexually engaged with someone after an extended period of relative asexuality.

But, something that made our sexual interaction more appealing than it would have been with many was the way Jonathan approached it. Although we spoke frankly about our sexual interests, Jonathan infused his suggestiveness with a considerable amount of wit. For example, many of our sexual exchanges revolved around a medical condition that had stricken Jonathan at the same time he had met me, one that he said his doctor had diagnosed as "stiffyitis." He seemed to believe there was a causal link between the two events and, according to him, his doctor agreed. In a message he sent to me a week after we met, he told me that he had discussed the matter with his doctor, who had told him the condition was "common in Europeans dating Midwestern American college teachers." He said that to treat the condition, his doctor had advised him to "take a professor and go to bed."

A week later, he sent me a message in which he told me that his "condition" was getting worse and that he was starting to have attacks at random times throughout the day and was actually having an attack as he wrote to me. After asking, "What's a semi-young gentleman to do?" he signed the message "Woodenly yours." He expressed his concern that stiffyitis was "a chronic condition that may never have a complete cure," but suggested that since there were so many other maladies that ranked higher on the list of disorders in need of research, we should start our own "private" research program to investigate treatments for the condition. Jonathan's banter appealed to my intelligence and sense of humor as well as to my need to be eased back into a sexual life, something that despite my interest, I was finding a little awkward and anxiety-provoking after a lengthy period of celibacy.

Third, like the British Jonathan in the United States, I had always felt like a "stranger in a strange land," at odds with my social environment. Being gay was part of it, but far from all of it. I was an intellectual person who lived among people who seemed to have little interest in intellectual pursuits and sometimes disparaged those who did as "educated fools." When I did have the opportunity to interact with intellectual people, however, I found that many of them knew very little outside a limited area of specialization. My interests were more broad ranging, so it was a rarity to find someone who was not only intelligent, but also knowledgeable about a variety of topics. In addition to sharing certain interests, Jonathan often knew arcane facts about obscure subjects, which astonished and delighted me. But, at the same time, he knew a great deal about areas that in some ways I didn't—business, art, British culture—which made me feel that I had something, many things, to learn from him, that we weren't simply throwing back and forth the same information. Until I met Jonathan, I had met few people who were as intellectually stimulating.

Fourth, Jonathan appeared to be a cultured person and live a cultured life—a life that I needed. In addition to having spent the majority of my life surrounded by people who weren't intellectual and often denigrated those who were, I had spent my life surrounded by people who weren't cultured and often disparaged those who were. I didn't think that I was better than they were, but I did know that I was different from them and needed different things to be fulfilled. Jonathan seemed to be able to fulfill that need in a way that most others could not.

Fifth, Jonathan intrigued me for a specific and idiosyncratic reason. When I was a child, I became interested in entomology and fascinated by the accounts of the lives and adventures of the important naturalists of the 19th century, many of whom were British. Being intellectual and peaceful, I was attracted to refined, "gentlemanly" pursuits, such as studying insects, and as a child, I imagined having a Victorian-style study that would contain my collections of insects from all over the world, just as the pioneers in the natural sciences (at least as I imagined) had had. Although

Jonathan didn't have an interest in biology, I still found him intriguing, mainly on an unconscious level, because he was the first person I had met who seemed to be part of the same "gentlemanly" milieu as my childhood inspirations.

Far more important, however, Jonathan took an interest in me and my life that few people did and had for a long time. I felt that most people were interested more in telling me about themselves than in hearing about me, that they simply waited for me to stop talking so they could resume talking about themselves. Many people simply drowned me out, not even hearing me in the first place. Although we had a good relationship, my mother had an chronic habit of not letting me finish a sentence before speaking, which made me feel that what I had to say wasn't important. My sister had an even worse habit of keeping me on the phone, sometimes for two or three hours at a time, while she did nothing but talk about herself in a single unpunctuated sentence. Either because of my background in psychology or because I was perceived as a good listener, other people viewed me as a "dumping ground," as I was once described, and constantly unloaded their personal problems onto me without permitting me to do the same, something that left me feeling used. Experiences like these reinforced my natural tendency to be unsocial and introverted, since I got little gratification out of my interactions with most people.

Jonathan, however, was the opposite. He wanted to hear everything about me. In one e-mail in which he expressed his dismay over learning that in our telephone conversation the night before, I had allowed him to "rabbit on about all of [his] bullshit nonsense" when I had a real problem, he told me not to keep things to myself because he was "interested in everything about [me], the good as well as the not so good." In others, he told me that he "miss[ed me] and ha[dn't] even met [me] yet," that he "[thought] of [me] more then occasionally and always with a smile on [his] face," and that he "[was] already dreaming of [me] and [his] head ha[dn't] yet hit the pillow." It was flattering and thrilling to feel that I had made such an impression on someone who seemed so impressive.

Most important of all, perhaps, I felt that Jonathan could provide me with the material security that I needed. I wasn't looking for a sugar daddy who would pay for everything for me, but I *was* looking for someone who could provide the material stability that I feared I couldn't provide for myself. I had suffered from years of limiting, sometimes debilitating, social anxiety, agoraphobia, and depression and had come to have serious doubts about my ability to provide for myself because of how those impairments had interfered with my ability to meet the demands of everyday living. By the age of 34, I had overcome my agoraphobia and had a reasonable grasp on my social anxiety and depression, but I was still haunted by the ghosts of the past. My experience in Paladin only a year and a half before had reactivated my fears. Jonathan, who was the COO of a company and came from a wealthy family, was someone, it seemed, who would never want for anything, for whom mere survival, it seemed, had never been and never would be even a thought. At the time, I wasn't conscious of how powerful my need for material certainty was, but when I encountered Jonathan, someone who seemed both able and willing to provide for his boyfriend's material welfare in such an unfailing way, an unrecognized part of me found the possibility of finally having this fundamental need satisfied, this underlying fear pacified, irresistible.

Although Jonathan maintained an attitude of cautious optimism about what was happening between us, he also expressed his feeling that our meeting was more than an accident. In the message in which he told me about Alexander, he made the comment that it was strange how both of us had reached a crossroads in our lives at roughly the same time. The day after our first conversation, he had described things as getting "almost too eerie" between us as more of our similarities became evident. That included the fact that we had moved to Paladin not only at the same time, but also to the same area. When I had lived there, I had probably driven within a few blocks of his house, having no idea that our paths would eventually cross when we were living much farther apart. In a message he sent to me two days before I met him in person, he commented again on how odd it was that we had so many things in common. He mentioned that the Arabs called it *kismet*—fate. I didn't know if it was, but I did know that the similarities between us were striking and I did find it odd myself how I had once again been pulled back to that particular spot in Paladin.

■

Once, in discussing some difficulties I was having in understanding the way he related to things, he told me, "You've never met anyone like me before." I hadn't. Jonathan was unique. Everything I thought I wanted, needed, came together in Jonathan.

■

In the end, I agreed to meet Jonathan at his home in Paladin on Saturday, June 16, and if it proved desirable, to stay through Sunday, the 17th. The day before I met Jonathan in person, I had to work in the afternoon, but I made it back home by 4:00. Because my own car was 16 years old and was breaking down on a regular basis, I didn't trust it to make the trip to Paladin, despite the fact that I had been driving it half that distance to work for at least a year. I didn't want anything to go wrong, so I decided to rent one that seemed more roadworthy. After picking up the car, I went shopping and finished buying the toiletries and other items I would need for the weekend.

Later that evening, Jonathan wrote to tell me that he planned to rise early the next morning to make his house "inhabitable" so he wouldn't be embarrassed when I arrived. He added that I should know that he didn't go to such effort to clean the house for everybody, "actually anybody," but told me that he was doing so for me because he had a feeling that I was "worth it." I was beginning to feel he was worth it too.

That evening, I finished packing and that night, I slept peacefully. Surprisingly peacefully, given how nervous the upcoming situation might normally have made me. I was excited, but also relaxed. Things could not have been going better between Jonathan and me, and although I hoped things would continue to do so, I didn't feel emotionally committed to a particular outcome. Whatever would happen would happen, and even if things went badly, at least I would have tried. It would be a little adventure that I both wanted and needed, something that would not only break up the monotony, but also shake up my complacency and, regardless of outcome, mark the beginning of an expanded life.

The next morning, I checked my e-mail and found a message from Jonathan. Written the night before, he said that in anticipation of my visit, he had "cleaned and cleaned" his house and although it was "still not perfect" it was hopefully "good enough." His maid, the third one he'd had since he'd lived in Paladin, had been sick and unable to clean the house herself that week. Even so, he felt that she did only a fair job and he had been thinking about replacing her. He complained that since he'd been in Paladin he had been unable to find good help, saying that he had been able to find excellent help for half the price when he had lived in the South and help that would stay with you "til the last dog [came] home" in England. Housework didn't appear to be his forte, but I suspected that having come from a background in which others performed such menial work, Jonathan hadn't had much of an opportunity to develop those talents. Consequently, I appreciated the effort he seemed to be making on my behalf.

Concluding his message, he told me he was off to the "Land of Nod," a phrase that inspired him to reminisce about his childhood. He asked me if I knew the nursery rhyme, "Wynken, Blynken, and

Nod," who "one night / Sailed off in a wooden shoe." He said that when he was a child, the poem had been read to him so often that he had memorized it and he could recite it in its entirety. He said he still loved it as well as *The Wind in the Willows*, *Le Morte d'Arthur*, and a "whole host of other wonderful stories and poems that we heard every day." He had fond memories of being read to when he was a child while "eating pudding in [his] jammies." "Ah, childhood," he wrote wistfully, saying that he wasn't sure if he wanted to be a child again but that it had been great the first time. Ending his reverie, he told me that he would be "waiting happily at this end" for my arrival.

Less like Wynken, Blynken, and Nod than like Odysseus I "sailed off," expecting one kind of adventure, but ultimately receiving one that proved very different.

—2—
JONATHAN
You've never met anyone like me before.

Saturday, June 16 proved to be warm and bright, a typical June day in the Midwest and a perfect day for long-distance travel. I left for Paladin around 10:30 with the intention of arriving at Jonathan's around noon. As I made the hour-and-a-half trip from Hawthorn to Paladin, I was filled with a mixture of anticipation and excitement tempered by cooler feelings of cautious optimism and simple curiosity about this Englishman who had found his way to the American Midwest, this person from whom I was in some ways so different but to whom I seemed in some ways so similar. Over the Internet and over the phone, we seemed to have established something more than a casual connection and I was hopeful that direct contact and interaction would only strengthen it—which, unfortunately, can sometimes have the opposite effect. I have always been an anxious person, especially when meeting people for the first time, but that day I was not anxious at all.

As planned, I arrived in Jonathan's neighborhood sometime around noon. I knew the area well, so I had little trouble finding the general spot. I did, however, have somewhat more trouble finding the specific house, since I had never actually driven on Millstone Drive, the main street on which Jonathan lived. After about fifteen minutes of moderate frustration, I finally found it. I was already a little late and I didn't want anything to go wrong.

Jonathan's house was a one-story ranch that stood about a hundred feet back from the road. Intervening between house and street was a spacious front yard that was shaded by several large trees. The driveway lay to the right as one faced the house and ended in a parking area to the right of an attached garage. A brick sidewalk ran along the front of the house from the driveway to the front door. A small bench sat in the front yard to the left of the door. The house wasn't as ostentatious as I might have imagined, although I didn't have preconceived ideas about what it should look like, but it seemed spacious and attractive and consistent with the kind of home that someone in Jonathan's high position might have.

I pulled into the driveway and, after composing myself a little, I got out of the car. As I walked along the sidewalk that ran along the front of the house, I could hear dogs barking from within, having already been alerted to my presence. I stepped up on the porch and rang the doorbell. The dogs continued barking, and after a few seconds, I saw the pulled curtains of the large window that lay to the right of the door briefly part before once again falling closed. A few seconds later, the door opened, and, after my eyes adjusted to the relative darkness within the house, I saw Jonathan, in the flesh, for the first time.

In person, Jonathan looked rather different than he had in the picture on the web site. In place of the detective costume he had sported in the photo, he was now dressed in a short-sleeved, crew-neck shirt with navy blue and white horizontal stripes and a pair of light-colored short pants. He was also not wearing his glasses, thereby revealing the deep, dark circles beneath his brown eyes. In his ad he had said that he was "not fat," and although he was, overall, more stocky than fat, much of his weight seemed to have settled into a noticeable paunch. Except for his dark hair, dark eyes, and goatee, Jonathan bore a certain resemblance to actor Ian Holm, although Jonathan wasn't as handsome. Interestingly, I thought of Holm in his role as Ash, the android in the 1979 science-fiction/horror film *Alien*. Although I didn't think Jonathan was ugly, I didn't find him as attractive in person as I had in his photo. If I had gone there purely for sex, I might have politely excused myself and left, as shallow as that would have been. But, because I was there for something more, and because there did in fact seem to be *much* more to him than simply his looks, I ignored my initial reaction to his physical appearance and decided to see where things would otherwise lead.

"Richard?" he asked, the second R-sound missing from my name.

After affirming that I was in fact he, Jonathan opened the door more fully and allowed me into his home. When I stepped inside, I felt as if I had stepped into a museum. Although my view from the foyer was limited primarily to the living and dining rooms to my right, what I saw there said it all. The rooms were richly decorated in European-style art and antiques and, to a lesser extent, Asian ones as well. To my right, the living room furniture, which mainly consisted of a matching white sofa and loveseat decorated with roses, surrounded an oval-shaped, marble-faced coffee table that was covered with an assortment of items that Jonathan referred to as "tchotchkes." Defining the area was a rug that was also adorned with roses and edged with a green silken border. The border was torn along one edge, but that didn't detract from its appearance. Beyond sat a white chaise lounge, which Jonathan later referred to as the "psychiatrist's couch." The sofas were all buried in elaborately decorated embroidered pillows and the spaces that were not occupied by end tables holding expensive-looking lamps were occupied by equally expensive-looking vases as well as plant stands overflowing with artificial flowers.

On the wall across from the foyer hung several large paintings in various European styles. One was a painting in a golden frame of two neoclassical figures that appeared to be fleeing from some unseen menace. Another was a more modern, abstract piece in a thick, off-white frame that appeared to be a still life consisting of various objects reduced to their basic geometric forms. Beneath them stood a round table with a glass cover onto which had been painted a large image of a bare-breasted woman that reminded me somewhat of Gauguin's paintings of Tahitian women. The overall style could be described as Victorian with a modern edge.

Jonathan had told me that he owned three poodles, a breed of dog that I had always associated, whether rightly or wrongly, with refinement. The biographical blurb on the company web site had referred to them as "classy" dogs and they seemed to fit with Jonathan's personality and background. Two of the dogs, whose names were Sweetie and Frizzie, were young and energetic, sporting the curly white locks of their breed. Their hair had been left natural and had not been clipped into the stereotypical poodle style. The third, whose name was Prissy, was much older and showed her age. I later learned that she was 16, decidedly old for a dog. She was smaller than the others and some of her hair was missing. She was also less vigorous and seemed somewhat senile, occasionally behaving as if she didn't know where she was or what she was supposed to be doing. In addition, she hadn't been bathed in a very long time. She gave off a rank canine odor and I couldn't stand to let her get too close to me. Privately I started calling her Pig-Pen, after the *Peanuts* character who never bathed and went around in a cloud of his own stink. I thought she would have felt much better if Jonathan had bathed her and I wondered how much of her hair loss was due not to age, but to lack of hygiene. The dogs, which Jonathan called "the girls," trailed after him wherever he went, like courtiers obediently following their king.

In addition to his own dogs, Jonathan was taking care of a friend's dog, whose name was Sadie. Sadie was a Great Dane that belonged to a man named Horatio. Horatio had worked with Jonathan as an assistant and had come with him to his current place of business in Paladin. Horatio was on business in Japan—or "The Orient," as Jonathan called it—for an extended time and it was easier to leave Sadie at home than to take her with him. Sadie was friendly, but much larger than Jonathan's dogs and, on the whole, somewhat overwhelming. Jonathan treated her well, but I got the impression that he wasn't entirely happy to have the responsibility of caring for her while her owner was overseas.

He led me to the guest bedroom, which lay across the hall from his own. The bed was missing, and Jonathan explained why. He told me that he had donated one of his beds to a local hospice for people with AIDS, but that when the movers had come that morning to take the bed away, they had inadvertently taken the wrong bed. Therefore, it wouldn't be possible for me to sleep in the guest bedroom. In retrospect, I had to wonder if his story about the bed, which conveniently happened to have been carted away that very morning, wasn't some type of ruse to encourage me to sleep in the same bed with him.

He asked me if I wanted something to drink, to which I said yes. We headed toward the kitchen, and I saw that hanging on the dining room wall to the left of the kitchen door was a large charcoal portrait of a woman and four children. The woman, who was seated and depicted from the waist up in three-quarter view, was holding a baby. In the background to her left stood two girls who appeared to be somewhere between ten and early teens. In the lower right-hand corner stood a boy of perhaps seven with long, thick, curly hair and mischievous dark eyes. I knew at once who it was, since those eyes hadn't changed in 40 years. They were all dressed in refined, almost Victorian clothes and, on the whole, the subject and style were stereotypically upper-crust British. Jonathan explained that the woman was his mother and the baby in her arms was his younger brother Terrence, while the two girls were his two youngest sisters, Charmaine and Leandra.

All in all, the trappings that I saw about me were consistent with his story about having come from a cultured, upper-crust background in England as well as presently holding an important, well-paid position. If he were some kind of Internet fraud who was trying to make me believe he was something more than he was, then he had gone to a great deal of trouble to do it.

In the kitchen, Jonathan asked me what I wanted, then gave me the glass of water I had requested. After continuing to make small talk for several more minutes, he finally asked me if he could have a kiss. In spite of not finding him attractive at first, he had perhaps grown on me a little in the brief time I'd spent with him. I told him I thought he would never ask, then we kissed. It had been some time since I'd been kissed by a man and the kissing, and holding, felt good on more than just the sensual level. He remarked that I had beautiful eyes, and for the first time, I noticed the beauty of his own eyes. I told him that I thought he had beautiful eyes too, that they were the color of tea and that I liked tea. It was a silly remark, but it was the kind of remark that you make when you are happy and such remarks are, in their own way, not so silly.

He suggested that we continue our conversation in the sunroom, which lay around the corner from the kitchen. The room, which doubled as the den, proved to be an especially intimate and comfortable place to continue the process of getting to know each other. As I entered, I took stock of the room. Because every wall, except for the west one that faced the interior of the house, was dominated by tall awning windows, the breezy, light-filled room seemed much more spacious than it actually was. In the southwest corner to my right stood a tubular, stainless steel shelf approximately six feet high that held the television, the stereo, and an assortment of smaller items. Along the south wall, a door opened onto a small patio, and through the door, I could see patio furniture, a grill, and large metal dragonfly ornaments staked into the ground. On the east wall near the southeast corner stood an Art Deco display case filled with more tchotchkes, while a brown tweed sectional sofa occupied the left half of the east wall and most of the north. In the northwest corner stood a round, 1950s-style Formica table on which sat a lamp with a round, white, Asian-style paper shade. Between the table and the door stood a chair decorated in a white, striped fabric that contrasted starkly with the reddish square pillow covered with writhing Chinese dragons that lay in the seat. In front of the chair sat a round footstool that was also covered in a white fabric. Between the display case and the eastern section of the sofa stood a round chair upholstered in a purple fabric. Jonathan seated himself in the purple chair, while I seated myself on the north end of the sofa.

I don't remember everything we discussed, but I do remember one topic in particular that did arise: my previous relationships. Jonathan raised the issue, not I. To me, talking about your previous relationships on a first date was the last thing you did. His questions were very detailed and very pointed. He wanted to know how many relationships I had had, how long we had been together, and—most important of all, it seemed—whether or not we had lived together. I told him that I had had several relationships that had lasted for varying amounts of time, usually on the order of several months, but that I had never actually lived with any of the men with whom I had been involved. "So," he concluded, "you've never really had a long-term relationship." Although I didn't ask him this, I had to wonder how long he thought a relationship was supposed to last before it could be considered "long term." He also seemed to imply that because I had never actually lived with any of the men with whom I had been involved, I had never had a "real" relationship. At that point, I felt that I was less on a date than on a job interview and was having to justify my qualifications to be his next boyfriend. The exchange left me feeling somewhat uncomfortable, but eventually he changed the subject and we moved on to other matters.

Altogether we talked for about an hour. Around 1:30, Jonathan suggested that we head for the zoo. By that point, I hadn't visited the Paladin zoo for at least ten years and was looking forward to going, especially since the exhibits had been extensively upgraded since my last visit. After he changed into different clothing, replacing his striped shirt and short pants with a yellow Hawaiian shirt and jeans, we got into my car and headed to the zoo.

Although it was a clement Saturday afternoon in June, the zoo wasn't as crowded as I'd feared it might be, making our outing that much more pleasant. After Jonathan bought our tickets, we began our tour of the exhibits. One of the first exhibits we came to featured an animal that was depicted in Minoan frescoes. Jonathan had already mentioned that he had visited Crete, which made me even more jealous of him. When I mentioned the depictions of the animal, Jonathan responded that it was interesting because the animal wasn't native to Crete. I was impressed that he knew such an arcane fact, and although I already understood that Jonathan was well educated, I would continue to be astonished by the breadth of his knowledge.

I have always been particularly drawn to the desert life, the giraffes, and especially the big cats, while Jonathan seemed particularly drawn to the elephants. I had already noticed several instances of elephants in the décor of his home and, when asked, he confirmed that the elephant was his favorite animal. Because of our interest in African wildlife, we ended up spending a considerable amount of time in the African section of the zoo.

While we were there, something strange happened. At one point, I was looking at Jonathan when suddenly I was overcome by a feeling that I can only describe as *wrongness*. The feeling went far deeper than whatever misgivings I might have had about his appearance or his probing questions about my previous relationships.

It was an instinctive feeling that something about Jonathan wasn't quite right. The feeling lasted for only a few seconds before it relented, but it remained with me, in diminished form, for at least several minutes before it finally faded.

Because I could find no rational reason for having such a feeling, I explained it away. I told myself that I was just nervous, more nervous than I had thought, and that I was projecting my unpleasant feelings onto him. After a while, I had forgotten about it.

After viewing the exhibits for about an hour, we went to the concession area and bought something to drink. Taking our refreshments outside, we sat in the shade of the surrounding trees where we could watch the wildlife around us and continue to learn about each other.

We talked for another hour about various topics, and although I don't remember everything we discussed, I do remember that at one point our conversation turned to music. Since Jonathan was British and not much older than I was, I mentioned my interest in the British New Wave music of the 1980s. I told Jonathan that one of my favorite groups was Eurythmics and that I wanted copies of their videos, including one of a performance at Heaven, a nightclub in London, in 1983. I had first seen the performance on television in 1984 and it had resonated with and reinforced my emerging sexuality at a time in my life when little else had, making it special to me. Jonathan told me that he had actually spent a lot of time at Heaven, which, unbeknownst to me, was not only a gay-oriented nightclub, but also one of the most famous gay oriented nightclubs in the world. I was astounded that, by fate, I was actually talking to someone who was directly connected to something that had played a meaningful role in my development as a gay man. It gave me a strange sense of completion, of life having come full circle.

After we finished our drinks and, for the time, our discussions, we moved on to the monkeys and then to the lions, which were, unfortunately, thwarting my desire to take some clear, close-up pictures of them by staying well back from the fence.

By the time we completed our tour, it was approaching 5:00. We had been enjoying the exhibits for nearly three hours and decided it was time to call it an afternoon. After working our way to the parking lot and allowing the interior of the car, which had grown stiflingly hot in the midday sun, to cool down, we drove back to Jonathan's home, where we spent the next hour and a half chatting and resting after our active day.

Around 7:00, we drove to Tolliver's, the gay-oriented restaurant where I had suggested we have dinner. I had been there several times in the previous two years, but I had never been there on a date. I had described Tolliver's to Jonathan as having an intimate atmosphere and the fact that only a handful of other patrons were present that night made it seem even more intimate. I don't remember what Jonathan had to eat, although I do remember that I had veal parmigiana and spaghetti with iced tea, my favorite drink. I also don't remember what we discussed, although the content was probably not as important as the connection the conversation helped to forge. We stayed for about an hour and a half before making the half-hour drive back to Jonathan's home.

We arrived sometime between 9:30 and 10:00. For the next couple of hours we watched television and continued to connect. Then, around midnight, Jonathan suggested we go to bed. Although he had assured me that I could sleep elsewhere if I wanted, I had, in spite of some misgivings about him, come to feel comfortable enough with him to sleep with him in his bed. He lit some scented candles, and after watching TV together in bed for another half an hour while the flowery aroma filled the air, he banished the dogs from the room and turned out the lights. Once he did, the room was illuminated only by the flickering candlelight. After we discussed what we liked, we spent the next couple of hours by ourselves while the dogs, unaccustomed to being separated from their master, clawed and barked at the closed door. Despite their protests, we managed not to let them distract us. Afterwards, we allowed them in and fell asleep watching television. I slept surprisingly well, despite the fact that I usually didn't sleep well the first night I stayed in a strange place. The fact that I did said something about how comfortable I felt.

The next morning around 10:00, I arose to find Jonathan already awake and sitting in the sunroom reading the Sunday paper. He had already taken "the girls" outside to "make," as he called it, and had spoken to his parents, who regularly called their children on Sunday. I made some hot tea and rejoined him in the sunroom. As I tried to wake up, we talked about various topics for the next hour or so. As noontime approached, the conversation turned to the issue of lunch. Jonathan suggested having lunch at—appropriately enough—an English-style pub in one of the trendier sections of Paladin. Because the day was warm and sunny, we sat outside to enjoy the weather and watch the people. I don't remember what we discussed, although as had been true the night before at Tolliver's, the content of the conversation wasn't as important as the connection it promoted. We spent perhaps an hour there before we returned to Jonathan's home.

By the time we arrived, it was well after 1:00. We spent some time lounging together on the sectional in the sunroom, mainly watching television, but also "fooling around." We didn't have sex, although Jonathan tried to persuade me in that direction. By that time, I was feeling an increasing pressure to leave and didn't want to start something I couldn't finish. I needed to get the car back to the rental agency by 5:00, which meant that I would have to leave by 3:00, but I was also starting to feel somewhat overloaded by everything that had happened in the previous twenty-four hours and I needed some time alone to process it. Although I didn't admit the latter, I did mention the former, and Jonathan seemed to understand.

Around 3:00 I left. As I drove back to Hawthorn, I was suffused with a feeling of satisfaction and contentment. I felt that things couldn't have gone better, that things couldn't be going better. The time I'd spent with Jonathan, though brief, had, I felt, strengthened whatever bond was forming between us. At that point, I had no expectations, but I did have hopes that things would continue to go well, wherever they would lead. On that warm, sunny June afternoon, I felt very good.

I made it back home in time to turn in the car on time. After I returned home and unpacked, I relaxed a little and began to absorb what had happened, what had been happening. I wondered how Jonathan was feeling, wondered what would happen next.

That afternoon, I sent him a brief e-mail in which I told him I had arrived home safely and had enjoyed our weekend together. Later that evening, he sent me a longer e-mail in which he expressed his own feelings about our "week-end," as he wrote it. He said that although he felt the beginning had been "a bit nervey," he thought that we had become comfortable with each other fairly quickly. He said that he thought the fact that we'd had the opportunity to e-mail and talk beforehand had helped, which I thought it had as well. He reemphasized his position that although he didn't have trouble getting sex most of the time—"it's the accent," he explained—he wouldn't abandon the chance for a mature relationship if one presented itself. He concluded by apologizing if he had seemed "pushy" before I had left, but explained that I was "awfully cute." He assured me, though, that he could survive and that somehow he would muddle through until the next time.

Although I didn't have expectations, I was glad that he was looking forward to the "next" time. So was I. I didn't know when the next time would be, but I did know that it would undoubtedly be as memorable as the first. My life seemed to be taking a new, entirely unexpected path and I was intrigued to see where that path would lead.

I would not be disappointed.

—3—
WEEK ENDS

When do you want to come back...?

The next time that I saw Jonathan was the next weekend. The first two times that I saw him, I didn't spend the entire weekend—or *week end*, as he would usually write it—with him. The first time I saw him, the weekend of June 16, I spent only Saturday afternoon through Sunday afternoon with him, while the second time I saw him, the weekend of June 23, I spent only Friday night through Saturday afternoon with him.

The second weekend was different from the rest in at least two respects. First, this was the weekend that Jonathan met my sister, Kathryn. A few years older than me, she was a healthcare worker with three teenage children who also lived in Hawthorn. She was divorced from her children's father to whom she had been married for ten years because his drinking had made it impossible to remain together. In addition, she had just separated from her second husband of 12 years because of his problematic behavior and was now trying to pursue her life unfettered from an equally difficult relationship. She had planned to meet a friend in Paladin that Friday evening and the two of them had planned to spend the night together at a hotel that was by chance only a short drive from Jonathan's. I thought that if Kathryn were driving to Paladin, I could hitch a ride with her and avoid more wear and tear on my aged car. We went late in the afternoon on Friday after we had both gotten off work. After dropping me off at Jonathan's, she went to the hotel, planning to return around noon the next day.

That evening, Jonathan and I went to a Chinese restaurant for dinner. I don't remember what Jonathan ordered, but I ordered Kung

Pao chicken, which was covered with peanuts. Jonathan told me that he was severely allergic to peanuts and that if he were to eat them, he would go into anaphylactic shock. I found it ironic that someone who loved elephants so much couldn't eat peanuts himself.

We spent the night in bed watching science-fiction movies from the 1950s, including *The Fly* with Vincent Price.

The next day around noon, Kathryn came back to Jonathan's to pick me up and, after the two of them had chatted for about an hour, the three of us went to the English pub for lunch. I say the *two* of them chatted because the other notable feature of the second weekend was that I had developed laryngitis and spent much of the weekend unable to speak. I began losing my voice on Friday afternoon, and by the time I arrived at Jonathan's, it had almost disappeared, failing to return until Wednesday of the following week.

Kathryn and I left Paladin sometime around 2:00. Later that afternoon, Jonathan sent me an e-mail in which he gave me his thoughts about the weekend. He told me he was glad I had visited and described it as a "lovely though short visit." He said he thought we seemed to be very relaxed together, something that had happened quickly. He said he couldn't believe we had fallen asleep watching television, as we had the Saturday before, and mentioned *The Fly*. He said he was sure that Hélène, whose husband André had undergone the horrific fusion of man and fly, was "fucking the brother," François. He observed that Hélène and François were "just too friendly at the end and nobody seemed too shattered that the husband was eaten by the spider." He described the tale as a "lesson for life." Perhaps.

Turning to Kathryn, he said that he'd liked her but didn't know how she felt about him. I assumed that she had liked him as well, although she had a tendency to have subdued or unclear reactions to many things. He told me to feel better and stay in touch. He told me to "[e]mail, smoke signal [use] tom-tom drums," whatever worked best for me, and told me he looked forward to my next message. In an attempt to "persuade" me to stay in touch, he said he didn't want me to force him to e-mail Kathryn and tell her to go harass me. He concluded by asking me when I wanted to come back.

I went back just a few days later. The first full weekend that I spent with Jonathan was the weekend of June 30, the weekend of my 35th birthday. I was on summer break from school by that point, having both the last week of June and the first week of July free, and Jonathan invited me to spend as much of my break with him as I wanted. Altogether, I ended up staying with him for five days, from the afternoon of Friday, June 29 to the afternoon of Wednesday, July

4. I was flattered that someone who had known me for only a month and had spent only two days with me would want me to spend as much of my vacation with him as I wanted.

About a week after we met, Jonathan had told me that he was thinking about making a quick trip home around the beginning of July. One of the reasons he wanted to go then, it appeared, was to avoid being in the United States on the Fourth—a "sore point with us" [British], as he described it. After I corrected him when he attributed the "pursuit of happiness" statement from the Declaration of Independence to the Constitution, he said that he was still proud of himself for knowing the quote at all, considering how much time the British spent on American history in school, especially "THAT period." In spite of his aversion to "that period," however, he reported that he had several friends who worked at the American Embassy in London and that he had typically managed to get himself invited to various functions there, including the Fourth of July party he said they held. He described the party as always being a "great blow out" and said that he figured there was "some element of revenge in going and eating and drinking as much of the American's food and booze as [they] could hold." His attitude toward the United States in general and Americans in particular seemed ambivalent at best, although his feelings appeared to be based less on historical than on cultural differences. In the end he didn't go home, which made it, according to him, the first time he had remained in the States during the Fourth.

Friday night, Jonathan made dinner for me for my birthday, which I thought was a sweet gesture. Later, he asked me if I wanted my present then or the next day and I chose the next day.

The next morning, I joined Jonathan in the sunroom, where he was wrapped in a terrycloth robe and seated in the purple chair. He asked me if I wanted my present now and I said yes. He came over to the sectional where I was seated and sat down beside me. First, he gave me a card with a picture of a dog on the front that looked like Sadie and was sitting next to a toilet holding up a cup of toilet water. I don't remember what the card said, but I do remember it was funny and sweet.

Then, he presented me with a small, rectangular box wrapped in paisley paper. I unwrapped and opened it. Inside, nestled on a bedding of white gauze, rested a small, shiny, turquoise object, somewhere between oval and rectangular in shape, that measured about three-quarters of an inch long and about half an inch wide. The object bore several wedge-shaped cuts at one end, a T-shaped cut running across and down the lower half of the curved top, and several linear cuts running widthwise along the flattened bottom. The object was pierced lengthwise by a hole. At first, I didn't realize what it was. When he asked me if I knew and I told him I didn't, he told me the object was an Egyptian faience scarab. Suddenly, I recognized the wedge-shaped cuts as stylized eyes and mouthparts and the T-shaped cut as the lines that defined the elytra. Jonathan said that, knowing about my interest in ancient cultures in general and the Minoan culture in particular, he had tried to find something Minoan, but had been unable to do so. Instead, he had managed to find the scarab, which he had obtained from his friend Harald.

He told me that the scarab had come from the funeral wrappings of a mummy that had recently been acquired by the Egyptian Museum in Berlin. The body was that of a scribe who had lived during the Middle Kingdom period (c. 2040-1640 BCE), making the scarab more than 3,500 years old. Temporally, this corresponded to the high point of Minoan culture (c. 2000-1450 BCE), which made me feel that, even if it wasn't Minoan, it was still something connected to that time. In addition, given that Crete lay less than 250 miles to the north of Egypt at their closest points and the Minoans had carried on extensive trade relations with the Egyptians of the time, it also seemed to correspond to that place. Jonathan explained that the mummy had been draped with a kind of webbing onto which scarabs had been threaded, explaining the hole that ran lengthwise through the middle. The markings on the bottom was the scribe's name in what might be considered the "cursive" form of Egyptian. Although I wasn't certain how I felt about the casual sale of antiquities, which I believed rightly belonged not in private hands but to the world, the fact remained that I had never received a gift like that from someone with whom I was involved and I was a little overwhelmed.

Later that day, we went to an art museum in Paladin. Jonathan had a strong interest in art and had said that he had worked at the British Museum restoring art. We spent at least an hour and a half wandering among the exhibits. I remember running across an old painting that depicted the Charing Cross section of London. Jonathan assured me that the Charing Cross region, which was where the Heaven nightclub was now located, looked very different nowadays than it had when the painting had been produced. I could only imagine. I hoped to be able to see the change with my own eyes someday.

The first weekend that I had spent with him, he had mentioned that he wanted to sell one of the paintings that hung on the "museum" wall, as I had come to think of it. It was the still life in which the featured objects had been reduced to abstract forms. According to Jonathan, the work, titled *Still Life*, had been painted by an influential Cubist in the 1930s. I had become interested in art history when I was in college, but I knew more about some artists and movements than others and hadn't recognized the painting for what it was. Jonathan told me that his grandfather had acquired the painting in the mid-1950s and had eventually bequeathed it to him. Since the painting had been taken out of circulation, it had become a "lost" work, increasing its importance. Jonathan didn't like the painting, however, and believed it should be in a museum or at least in the collection of someone who appreciated it more than he did, so he began to make plans to sell it.

According to Jonathan, the painting had once been appraised at $750,000, but if he were going to sell it, he needed to have it reappraised to determine its current value. That summer, he made tentative plans to have someone from a major auction house come and look at the painting, but for different reasons, those plans always fell through. Among other reasons that he didn't like the painting was that it contained an object he thought was an insect. Although insects were my favorite group of animals, I myself wasn't inspired by the work.

Someone whose work I appreciated more than that of the Cubist was that of an important European Surrealist. Intriguingly, Jonathan owned some of his works, including two small paintings that he said Glenn had bought that hung in the bedroom and a decorated glass vase. Jonathan also owned a couple of limited-edition lithographs by an influential American artist whose artwork had caught my attention when I was young. Our artistic interests were strikingly similar, so art was something we could discuss.

Literature, however, was not. I have always been a literary person, read widely both fiction and non-fiction, and have written since I was a child. Although he was one of the most intelligent people I had ever met, and such people usually read as a matter of course, Jonathan seemed to have only limited interest in literature. The only books I ever saw in his home were ones on the care of poodles and some of the novels in the *Mapp and Lucia* series by E. F. Benson. The latter revolve around the exploits of Emmeline "Lucia" Lucas, a member of the British upper class during the 1920s and 1930s. Jonathan loaned me *Make Way for Lucia*, a compilation of the series, which I tried to read. I say *tried* to read because apart from the fact that the dense prose made reading it more of a challenge than a pleasure, I was not especially interested in the empty games of the bored upper crust. It did, however, give me some insight into the world from which Jonathan came or at least a world that appealed to him.

Throughout the remainder of my vacation stay, our activities were fairly unremarkable, consisting largely of what might be described as "domestic" activities. For the most part, we spent our time talking, watching television, shopping for food, eating in or eating out, and generally doing things that slowly strengthened the connection that was growing between us.

Something else that strengthened my feelings toward Jonathan was his sympathetic reaction to my telling him about the abuse I had suffered at the hands of my father. My mother had divorced my father when I was 11 after my father's drinking and general inability to deal with the demands of being a husband and a father had made staying married impossible. As time passed, both his drinking and his abusiveness had grown worse, the latter taking both verbal and physical form. My father wasn't physically abusive toward my mother or my sister, but he was toward me. He had occasionally tried to "discipline" me by beating me with his belt, although my mother had always stopped him, and as I got older, I had become better at fighting him off. Once, when I was ten, I had even punched him in the face for calling my mother names. Because I had generally been successful in defending myself, I had never suffered from the sense of powerlessness that most children would feel in that situation. Even so, when I raised the issue of my father's abuse during dinner Sunday night, Jonathan expressed a level of sympathy that deeply affected me. In a fairly short period of time, he seemed to have become concerned for me in a way that went beyond normal compassion.

When I returned to Hawthorn on the Fourth of July, I felt as if I had returned from the moon. I had been gone for only five days, but it was five days that had changed everything. I didn't realize until I returned and experienced the emotional aftermath just how things had changed. Returning to my "old" life left me feeling depressed and somehow diminished. I felt a distinct sense of loss. I couldn't believe that I had found someone who evinced such caring, such concern for me. I couldn't believe, either, that the person who seemed to care so much about me was someone of Jonathan's caliber, someone so intelligent, cultured, intriguing, strong. I had never met anyone like him, and to have him take such an interest in me, want to be with me, was a fantasy come true. Being away from him, then, left me feeling that something vital had been taken away from me.

I realized I was starting to become emotionally invested in the situation. What happened between us now *mattered*. I wasn't in love with Jonathan, but I now cared about him and what happened to him more than I did most.

■

By the end of June, I had fallen into a pattern of spending my "week ends" with Jonathan, a pattern that, with only one exception, would continue throughout the rest of the summer. The class I was teaching that summer in Viridian met on Monday and Friday afternoons from 1:00 until almost 3:00. I would go to Viridian on Friday afternoon, teach class, then go to Paladin, where I would stay with Jonathan until Monday morning. Then, I would drive back to Viridian and teach the Monday afternoon class before heading home to Hawthorn. By the first week of July, Jonathan had already given me a key to his house so I could let myself in if he was still at work when I arrived on Friday afternoon and lock the door when I left on Monday morning.

Our weekends together tended to follow a predictable pattern. After arriving at Jonathan's home sometime around 4:30 in the afternoon on Friday, he would escort me into the kitchen where we would get something to drink and chat for a few minutes before moving into the sunroom for a lengthier discussion of the events of the week. I would usually sit in the white chair, while Jonathan would invariably sit in the purple one. After talking for about an hour, I would go back out to my car to retrieve my clothes so I could change out of my "business drag," as Jonathan called work clothes, and into something more comfortable. Around this time, Jonathan would feed the girls in the kitchen while I would feed Sadie in the sunroom so she wouldn't eat the girls' food, which she often tried to do.

When they finished, Jonathan and I would take the dogs out into the front yard and let them "make" while we would sit together on the bench that stood near the front of the house. While the dogs enjoyed the warmth and freedom, we would discuss where we wanted to go for dinner. After running through the list of cuisines, we would eventually settle on one, more often than not Chinese or, less frequently, Mexican. After bringing the dogs back inside, we would usually go back into the sunroom and watch some television until it reached what Jonathan considered to be an appropriate dinner time, usually around 8:00. We would then go out to eat and return home, generally around 9:30 or 10:00. We would usually retire to the sunroom, where we would watch television and eat dessert—usually something involving ice cream or pie or, often, both—and remain until about midnight. Then, after clicking off the TV, the sound of which had become a conditioned stimulus that sent "the girls" into a frenzy of barking, we would go to bed.

Saturday morning, I would usually wake up to find that Jonathan had already arisen and, after having taken the dogs outside to "make," had seated himself in the purple chair to read the morning paper. I would invariably make a cup of steeped tea and, although I generally prefer my tea sweetened but otherwise "raw," as I describe tea without anything added, I eventually got into the habit of making it *à l'anglaise*, as I came to describe hot tea with cream. This happened after Jonathan was horrified to learn that, for the most part, I subsisted on Lipton's instant tea made with Hawthorn tap water. I would always boil the water in a teakettle, painted in primary colors, that Jonathan said he had picked up during a trip to South America. After the tea was fixed, I would join him in the sunroom where I would read the paper and watch some television.

We usually ate lunch somewhere different from where we ate dinner. One place we frequented throughout the summer was a restaurant with both indoor and outdoor seating that was located in the trendy neighborhood where the English pub was. Throughout the summer, we spent several sunny afternoons chatting and enjoying the weather at this and a couple of other restaurants in the area.

After eating lunch, we would often spend the afternoon visiting various antiques shops where Jonathan would spend a considerable amount of time searching for more tchotchkes to add to his collection. He would often search for examples of Venetian glass, which he loved, or pieces of Blue Willow china, which he favored as well. I got the impression that upon his arrival in Paladin, Jonathan had made ferreting out all the antiques shops a top priority, then frequenting them a central activity. That summer, we must have visited at least ten and I found that Jonathan was on a first-name basis with the owners of several.

Jonathan knew his antiques, if anyone did, and I was astonished at how accurately he was able to identify the styles and time periods as well as estimate the current values of a wide variety of pieces. Having been raised in a culture that stressed the importance of the past, and in a subculture that stressed the appreciation of things older and finer, it seemed inevitable that Jonathan would have developed a keen interest in the value of antiques. How much he might have assimilated the importance that many gay men place on antiques was difficult to say. Some gay men seemed as obsessed with antiques as they did with sex, although I myself had never shared the former obsession. Despite my lack of interest in the activity, it did at least give us the chance to be together.

During our outings, we would occasionally encounter people who would fawn over Jonathan because he was British. Once he opened his mouth, they would usually make some remark about how much they *loved* the way he spoke and otherwise be more solicitous to him than they might have been had he pronounced the Rs at the ends of his syllables as distinctly as I did. Jonathan would sometimes roll his eyes at me or otherwise express his dismay at the absurdity of their reactions. I had to agree. The way Americans reacted to British accents was ridiculous, but most of them seemed to be oblivious to how they embarrassed themselves.

In addition to antiques hunting, we would usually spend some of Saturday afternoon driving around Paladin looking at houses. Jonathan said that when he and Glenn had moved to Paladin, the house on Millstone Drive had been the only suitable one available near his workplace and that he had, therefore, felt forced into accepting it. He said that he felt somewhat isolated in his present home in a somewhat sparsely populated section of the city and that he preferred to be "in the middle of the wickedness," as he phrased it—an area where there was always something going on.

During the house hunting, we would often find ourselves downtown, in the area of Paladin that Jonathan referred to as "Boystown." This was an area of the city where, according to Jonathan, the well-to-do gay men seemed to cluster. In an effort to improve the appearance and appeal of the city, interested parties had embarked on a regentrification project that involved upgrading many of the older homes in downtown Paladin, some of which dated from the foundation of the city. Because a certain segment of the gay community seemed to love older, often Victorian, homes, it was only natural that those with the money to afford them would want to live in them. It was only natural, too, that Jonathan would as well, although *his* interest seemed based less on subcultural influences than on childhood experiences.

Although Jonathan would often do the driving, he was always concerned about being pulled over by the police for some driving violation. The reason, he said, was that he didn't have an American driver's license. He was supposed to have gotten one when he had arrived in the States but had failed to do so. Somehow, he had managed to drive for five years without one. I didn't understand why it was so difficult to get one when doing so would have relieved him of the emotional, and possibly legal, burden that came with not having one. I always felt, though, that he derived an almost adolescent satisfaction from feeling that he was getting away with something.

After returning home, we would usually relax and watch TV before deciding where we wanted to eat dinner. We would then repeat the pattern from the night before of going out to eat, returning home to watch more TV and eat dessert in the sunroom, and going to bed sometime around midnight.

Sundays were generally similar to Saturdays with the main exception that we would dine in, not out. In the afternoon, we would go to the grocery store, usually to Jonathan's favorite supermarket just north of his home, to buy the raw materials for the evening meal. Before we would go, though, Jonathan would usually spend a considerable amount of time poring over the paper in search of coupons. Even though he could well afford not to bother with something more typically reserved for someone on a budget, Jonathan told me that he *loved* coupons. He explained that they didn't use coupons in England and that his discovery of their widespread use in the States had been a revelation. Finding the best buys had become something of a game for him, so hunting for coupons appeared to count as part of his weekend fun.

Jonathan was a good cook—better than I, at least—and sometimes he would fix dishes from his homeland. British cooking has never had a reputation for refinement, but the meals he fixed were always filling. One dish in particular was called Windsor Castle Casserole, apparently a favorite of Queen Elizabeth's. According to Jonathan, the Queen's former cook had written a cookbook in which she gave the recipe for the dish, which the Queen would have for dinner every Monday night while she watched television. The dish consisted of strips of chicken, rice, cheese, and various greens and spices. We ate the casserole several times that summer. We would eat dinner in the breakfast nook that adjoined the kitchen while the dogs would beg us for food, their begging growing more plaintive as we ate.

As we ate, we would watch Jonathan's favorite shows on the small TV there. These included *Malcolm in the Middle*, *Sex and The City*, and *Queer As Folk*. Before spending Sunday nights at Jonathan's, I had never seen *Sex and The City*, which I derisively started calling *Sluts and The City* and, produced by a gay man and two straight women who described themselves as "gay men," I thought was more a gay man's fantasy than a straight woman's reality. I had also never seen *Queer As Folk*, the American version of a British series that, in the American version, revolved around the lives of a group of gay friends from Philadelphia. Much of the series focused on the relationship between Brian, a 30-year-old advertising executive who was pathologically narcissistic and ruthlessly promiscuous, and Justin, an 18-year-old artist who was in love with Brian and who suffered from Brian's self-centered behavior.

I despised *Queer As Folk*, which I stared calling *Queer Ass Folk*, because the main characters were unlikable and because it perpetuated stereotypes about gay men that I found detrimental, especially the one that maintains that gay men are inherently incapable of remaining sexually faithful. *I* certainly could, and even though Jonathan and I were not committed to each other, I didn't plan on seeing or having sex with anyone else while I was involved with him. I was interested in pursuing a *relationship* with someone and understood the importance of subordinating my sexual impulses for the sake of the integrity and the stability of a relationship. Jonathan had indicated to me that he felt the same way. I couldn't fathom why Jonathan found such a despicable show so appealing, but I tried to tolerate it.

After we had finished dinner, we would spend some time cleaning up before retiring to the sunroom to eat dessert and watch television until sometime around midnight, when we would go to bed.

Monday morning, Jonathan would leave for work sometime between 9:00 and 10:00 and I would get ready to head back to Viridian to teach my Monday afternoon class. After he would leave, I would usually have a cup of hot tea *à l'anglaise* and spend some time outside in the morning warmth, wandering around the yard or sitting at the metal garden table with a tile mosaic top where Jonathan and I occasionally sat, and collected my thoughts. Finally, I would pack my clothes, take them to the car and, after making the bed and making certain that everything was shut off and locked up, leave for Viridian. Each time I left, I felt that I was leaving a piece of myself behind.

I wanted Jonathan to visit me in Hawthorn, but having him come to me seemed fraught with complications. First, I didn't have my own space and the space I shared was small and unaccommodating. Second, coming to Hawthorn would require Jonathan to have someone look after his dogs, which proved difficult to arrange. Third, there was little to do in Hawthorn, so finding diversions was challenging. For these and other reasons, then, it seemed more feasible for me to go to Paladin, so I went. Even so, I did invite him several times, hoping we could work something out.

For the most part, my weekends with Jonathan were quite pleasant, and I began to feel that the new life that I had wanted was slowly forming for me, a life with an interesting, intelligent, well-educated, cultured English gentleman who, on top of it all, actually seemed to like me. Each weekend, I found going to Jonathan's on Friday that much easier and coming back home on Monday that much harder.

—4—
Opportunistic Infection

You should be nice to me because I have a heart condition.

Almost from the day I met him, Jonathan complained about not feeling well. His primary symptom was recurring nausea, which he sometimes tried to treat with a home remedy of ginger ale or some other soft drink. He attributed his nausea to stress, which made sense, given his highly stressful position. The first time he mentioned the symptom was on the afternoon of Saturday, June 9, when he wrote to tell me that he doubted he would go to a dinner party to which he had been invited that evening because his stomach felt "a bit dodgey." Later that night he wrote to tell me that he hadn't gone and had spent the night relaxing on the sectional in the sunroom, watching television, talking on the phone, and alternately sipping Coke and mango juice. He added that his stomach was still "a little queasy" but otherwise he felt "terrific."

The next evening, however, he wrote to tell me that he had a headache and that the "unease of [his] tummy" which had gotten better, had returned. Jokingly, he attributed it to a conversation he'd had with his parents in which his mother, who wanted to go "on holiday" in the States before going on a cruise in the Caribbean, had suggested that she and his father spend a couple of weeks with him. Jonathan was horrified. He said that although he loved his parents dearly, two weeks with them in Paladin would turn him into a candidate for "involuntary commitment." A couple of days later, he was still complaining of a "queasy stomach" but attributed it to nerves and said that he was drinking ginger ale in an attempt to treat it.

At the time, I could not have guessed that the trouble with his stomach might be a symptom of a larger problem.

Around 6:00 in the evening of Wednesday, June 20, Jonathan sent me an e-mail titled "A Day in the ER." Beginning the message by stating that day had been "the most frustrating and unusual since [he had] arrived in the States," he went on to tell me that at a meeting that morning, he had "sort of fainted." After a "very cute new young guy" at work had gotten him up, he had been taken to the emergency room "over [his] strenuous protest." After commenting on the "very very cute staff" at the hospital, which he thought was "mostly gay," he went on to say that after having undergone various tests, including an EKG, the doctors had discovered that he had "inverted T waves," which he said indicated that his heart wasn't receiving enough oxygen, and that his heart was now pointing to the right instead of straight down, which might be associated with the T-wave anomaly. He said the cause was "open for debate," but stress could be a factor. Although the doctors had urged him to stay overnight for observation and additional tests, he had refused to do so. After having encouraged him to return the next morning at 8:00 for more tests and having told him to return immediately if he had chest pain or felt faint, the doctors had released him and Jonathan had returned home, alone.

We instant-messaged for a while later that night, but our exchange added little new information. There was little new information to add. The situation was, of course, worrying. I didn't know what to think. I was, however, not surprised to hear that Jonathan had developed a *heart* condition because high-pressure, Type-A personalities and heart problems seemed to go hand in hand.

The next day he returned to the hospital's heart institute, where he endured a "rather full day of tests and assorted horseshit." After commenting on his cardiotherapist, whom he described as being "as cute as that staff in the ER," he went on to tell me the tests had revealed that he had abnormalities in his EKG at both rest and during exercise, that his T-waves were still "goofy," that his heart was pitched to the right at a 50-degree angle, and that the right side of his heart wasn't getting enough oxygen. The only thing that appeared normal was his blood pressure. He said he was supposed to see the cardiologist on Monday, the 25th to decide on a course of treatment. He said the cardiologist didn't want to hospitalize him unless he developed recurring attacks of angina, which he currently didn't have. His message implied that he'd been having chest pain, which he hadn't mentioned.

He said that different people from work had spent different parts of the day at the heart institute with him, which he thought was "awfully nice as they arranged it themselves unbeknownst to [him]." Their gesture seemed to indicate just how much Jonathan meant to them. He ended the message by concluding that "life [went] on at the moment."

Although he was not hospitalized, Jonathan was given nitroglycerin in case he experienced additional attacks of angina. Over the next several days, his condition remained relatively stable, if punctuated by occasional mild chest pain. On the morning of Friday, the 22nd, he wrote to tell me that he had made it through the night without having had an attack of angina or having had to take nitroglycerin and that it was "always a good sign to wake up alive."

When I spent the evening of Friday, the 22nd through the afternoon of Saturday, the 23rd with him, we discussed the unsettling events of the previous week. Jonathan told me that his cardiologist had raised the possibility of performing an angioplasty if he proved to have blocked arteries. Understandably, he was not thrilled, remarking that although he had been told the procedure wasn't serious, "those saying it [were] not the ones getting it." In his typical Type-A way, Jonathan seemed inconvenienced by having angioplasty and said that he "would rather do it as soon as possible and be finished with it and get on with [his] life." I encouraged, even insisted, that instead of feeling inconvenienced, he proceed with the treatment as planned, for all the good it did me.

On the morning of Sunday, the 24th, Jonathan wrote to tell me that he had once again woken up alive, which was "always a positive sign," and although he had suffered "a bit of chest pain," he hadn't had to take nitroglycerin and the pain had gone away on its own.

On the morning of Monday, the 25th, the day he was supposed to see the cardiologist, he wrote to tell me that he felt "so tired" and that he wished he could "escape for a day or two" but that it wasn't possible. Then, later that evening, he wrote to tell me that he had rescheduled his appointment, which had been scheduled for 3:30, because he was "tied up in meetings" all day and was "too involved just to leave" at the appointed time. Knowing I wouldn't be happy with his decision, he said that he wasn't "in critical condition or anything approaching real distress" and reminded me that even Kathryn, who knew about his condition, had said that it didn't require immediate attention, so another day or two wouldn't "shatter the Earth." Even though I understood, I *wasn't* happy.

I was even less happy the next day when Jonathan sent me an e-mail in which he told me, unbelievably, that the heart institute had lost his test results. He said that his primary care physician, who had been waiting to see the results since the previous Friday, had finally contacted the institute that morning to obtain them, only to discover that the institute couldn't find *any* of Jonathan's records. All they had been able to find was an empty file with his correct Social Security number and address listed, but with his name misspelled. The institute had claimed they had sent the records to the hospital where Jonathan had been taken the day he had fainted, but the hospital had claimed they didn't have them. He said that unless they found the records, there was no point in going in the next day, which was the day to which he had rescheduled his appointment. Frustrated by what had happened, he quipped that since "[his] records [were] gone, [he] must be cured" and that it was a "miracle."

On Friday, the 27th, Jonathan sent me an e-mail, titled "Deja Vu All Over Again," in which he said that because the heart institute couldn't find his test results, he'd had to repeat the tests. He said the institute had rationalized their repetition of the tests by claiming that it gave them a clearer picture of his condition when in fact the *real* reason was that the "incompetent fools," as Jonathan called them, couldn't locate his records and if anything happened to him, the institute would be held accountable. He said that he'd spent three hours repeating the tests and that they were supposed to call him the next day with the results and decide where to go from there. I could only hope their medical care was better than their record keeping.

By the end of June, the doctors had decided that Jonathan's condition most likely resulted from stress. Jonathan's highly responsible position was also highly stressful and Jonathan's emotional suppression only heightened the possibility of physiological damage. He appeared to deal with stress by not dealing with it, which left him poorly prepared to cope with his stress-related illness in a more constructive way. Therefore, the doctors thought he would benefit from stress-reduction training and referred him to the hospital's Stress Center, where he could learn to deal with the stress that seemed to be damaging his heart. He started going the first week of July.

Jonathan's condition remained stable throughout most of the next week. Then, on Friday, the 6th, he received some upsetting news, which aggravated his condition. Around 7:30 that evening, he sent me an alarming e-mail in which he told me that he was having chest pain. He said that although the nitroglycerin helped, the pain returned in fifteen minutes and radiated to his shoulder, arm, and upper back. He said that if he didn't feel better that night, he might have to go to the emergency room.

I was alarmed, thinking he might be having a heart attack. I called him so I could speak to him directly and implore him to go to the hospital. When he refused, I informed him that if he didn't go, I was going to drive to Paladin that night and force him to go myself. I was serious and frustrated that he wasn't taking things more seriously. In the end, the pain seemed to subside and he convinced me that he would be all right. Even so, this sudden worsening of his condition worried me greatly and I felt thwarted and somewhat helpless to do anything direct, since I was an hour and a half away.

The next morning, he wrote to tell me that he still had "a little discomfort" but that the nitroglycerin seemed to be keeping it in check. He said that if he "seriously" didn't feel well he would go to the ER, but that he couldn't run there "for every twinge." Twinge or not, I still wasn't happy with the way Jonathan seemed to be in denial, or at least downplaying, the magnitude of his condition, but there was little I seemed to be able to do to make him take his situation more seriously.

Because I had just left Jonathan's on Wednesday, July 4, after having spent five days with him, I didn't return the following weekend. That was the first, and only, weekend that I didn't spend with Jonathan that summer. I did, however, decide to return on Monday, the 9th and stay at least until the next afternoon. I was very worried about him and felt that someone needed to be there to take care of him.

On Tuesday afternoon, we went out for lunch and while we ate, we discussed some of the more philosophical aspects of his illness. Jonathan explained that he felt that his illness was not only a weakness, but also a failure, and that he felt "ashamed" of his condition. When I tried to convince him there was no need to feel ashamed for having human weaknesses, he replied that he was supposed to be superhuman. I was beginning to realize that his attitude toward his illness was in some ways as much of a problem as the illness itself. I tried to be positive and encouraging, but I didn't know what I could do to counteract 44 years of conditioning.

After we returned to Jonathan's, he checked his e-mail and, in the process, he told me that he kept my e-mails in a special folder, which I found touching. I left later that afternoon, still concerned about his condition, both physical and emotional, but also hopeful that my presence had helped.

Later that night, Jonathan sent me an e-mail that was even more touching. In it, he told me that he was "very glad and touched to know [me] and to be with [me]" and that I had "made [his] life better." He said that whatever happened, he only knew how to be who and what he was. He said it was extremely frustrating to be sick the way he was and to be "limited by [himself]." He said that he had always been able to overcome every obstacle that life had thrown at him but now he didn't know how to deal with what was happening to him. Disturbingly, he told me that he may be "sicker then [I knew]," stating that his condition wasn't an "acquired illness but just [his] body wearing out in places." Trying to find something positive in the situation, he said that he felt he still had some "mileage" left in him and "intend[ed] to get the best ride that [he could]." He concluded by thanking me for being "so close and good." I felt honored that he viewed me as a positive part of his life at what was proving to be more of a turning point than he'd realized when he'd written his personals ad only six weeks before.

On Wednesday, the 11th, Jonathan returned to the hospital for more tests. For various reasons, I wasn't happy with the way his doctors seemed to be handling his case and had told Jonathan how I felt. Jonathan had also starting having trouble holding down his food and frequently threw up after eating. I never saw him throw up, but I certainly heard plenty of retching noises coming from behind closed bathroom doors. Hoping to help, I gave him some advice about his diet, which largely involved switching to blander foods that he could keep down. Finally, around the middle of June, his father had been diagnosed with colon cancer and his family was expecting Jonathan to fly to England to be there for the surgery, which was scheduled for the week of July 16. That created yet another level of unhealthy stress.

In response to my reactions, Jonathan said that his doctors had told him he couldn't travel at the moment, since they had found additional abnormalities in his EKG and had put him on medication and wanted him nearby so they could monitor his condition. He said he didn't know how he was going to tell his parents that he wouldn't be able to come, saying that he feared his mother would "go ballistic," since it was so important to her that everyone be there. One of his doctors had suggested that it might be better to wait and go after his father was home, while another one seconded the opinion, stating that he'd had surgery for colon cancer five years before and had wanted to be left alone for the next two weeks because he felt so bad. Encouragingly, Jonathan said his stomach was better, but stated he refused to eat "shit," reminding me that he preferred to eat "fresh decent stuff," rarely drank, and didn't smoke. He said he did need to do a better job of keeping hydrated and said that his assistant at work was now keeping him supplied with bottled water with lemon all day regardless of where he was in the office. He ended by saying his doctors were wanting him to wear some telemetry the following week so they could have a more complete record of his heart activity, something he agreed to do.

During the week of the 16th, Jonathan suffered through the inconvenience of the telemetry. On Thursday of that week, he saw his primary doctor with the hope of having "some definition about what to do for [himself]." When he did, he learned that the doctors had finally discovered what was really wrong with him...and nothing, including our relationship, was ever the same.

That Friday, I went to Jonathan's. After we had discussed other matters, Jonathan told me there was something he thought I should know. He explained that the doctors had finally diagnosed him with endocarditis, an inflammation of the innermost layer of tissue in the heart. The disease is typically caused by a bacterium, which meant that Jonathan was suffering from an infection. I asked him where he thought he could have contracted something like that and he told me that when he had vacationed in Venice, one of his favorite cities, two years before, he had come down with a mysterious flu-like illness and had been deathly sick for ten days. He thought that he might have become infected then and that after the initial illness, the bacteria had gone dormant until something had triggered them to begin multiplying again. I felt somewhat relieved because after a month of uncertainty, his doctors finally seemed to know what was wrong with him, and if it *was* a bacterial infection, then it could be treated with antibiotics and further damage could be averted.

Jonathan informed me, however, that it wasn't that simple. His doctors were concerned that he might be suffering from a drug-resistant strain, which were becoming more common. He said they had taken blood samples and were going to culture the bacterium to see if they could find an antibiotic capable of killing it. He said that one of the people at the hospital had commented that endocarditis was the disease that Barbara Hershey's character in *Beaches* had died from. This appeared to be a little more serious than the "stiffyitis" that had afflicted him a few weeks before.

I didn't know how to react to this disturbing news. Hopefully, the particular strain that was affecting Jonathan was susceptible. We would just have to wait and see.

Over the next several days, Jonathan, and I, waited for the results of the tests. They seemed to be taking longer than Jonathan had anticipated, which concerned him. I tried to console him by telling him that just because things were taking a little longer than he'd expected, that didn't mean there was a problem. He replied that he wasn't "stupid" and was convinced there was. I wasn't, but I didn't seem to be able to think of anything else to make him feel better.

By early the next week, it was clear there *was* a problem. Jonathan never actually came out and told me, at least at first, that the doctors had discovered the bacteria were, in fact, drug-resistant and his condition was, therefore, incurable. Instead, he conveyed this information indirectly by telling me about ways of treating, if not curing, the disease. He told me about one procedure in particular that was informally known as a "cut down." Although the disease could not be cured, its progression could be slowed by replacing some of his own blood with uninfected blood, thereby "cutting down" on the total proportion of bacteria in his system. Apparently that was the only thing the doctors could do.

Over the next few days, Jonathan continued to complain of nausea. I suspected that now it wasn't just physical but psychological. He said that one of his doctors had prescribed Phenergan, an anti-nausea drug, which he said wasn't helping. He was also supposed to see the doctors that week to arrange the "cut down," but kept claiming he was too busy to go. Among other things, the doctors were wanting to install stents so they wouldn't have to keep reinserting IV lines. I felt that his "inability" to go was actually just an inability to accept what was happening to him.

Finally, on the morning of Tuesday, the 31st, Jonathan confessed that he didn't feel well and hadn't for several days. I knew he hadn't, but for him to make such a bald admission was unusual. He said that it wasn't just his stomach, although he didn't specify further, and stated that he was seeing the doctor at 9:00 that morning. I was disturbed to hear that he was doing worse, but was glad that something had finally prodded him strongly enough to go back to the doctor.

That day, I talked to Kathryn about Jonathan's condition and she suggested that his nausea might be caused by his infection, something I hadn't considered. I mentioned this possibility with the hope that it would serve as an added encouragement for him to begin his treatments. In addition, the doctors were experimenting with different combinations of antibiotics in the hope that one of these combinations would prove effective where a single antibiotic would not and I asked him if he'd heard anything about the tests they'd been doing on his cultures.

In response he told me that the doctors had ordered him not to travel until he felt better, which forced him to send another executive from work to California, where he said he was originally supposed to go on business. He told me the doctors had told him the same thing that Kathryn had suggested about his nausea, that it was partly caused by the infection. He stated that he'd had the infection for over two years, if he was right about the illness he'd suffered in Venice, and that it was "very opportunistic." He reported that his doctors had concocted various IV mixtures that were designed to treat both his infection and his dehydration and that he was scheduled to take his first treatment the next day. He wasn't looking forward to it because the doctors had told him that at first the treatments would make him sicker, so he had prepared himself for "days of vomiting."

When he reported on the treatment he took the next day, he told me that it was the first in a series of nine. He told me that he felt more alert but had been very sick to his stomach. He restated that the latter had been expected and that he had been "somewhat" prepared. The next morning he wrote to tell me that he'd had an "OK" night but wasn't having a treatment that day, just some lab work.

A few days later, he felt the need to know exactly where he stood, medically, and pressed his doctor for answers. Unfortunately, he didn't receive as much clarification as he would have liked. On Monday, August 6, he e-mailed me to tell me that his doctor expected his treatment to last at least six weeks, but had also stated that he wasn't certain that Jonathan actually had endocarditis. Frustrated, Jonathan remarked that he was once again in the same position in which he'd found himself for the past several weeks and complained that he didn't feel well and was very tired. I felt just as frustrated as he did as well as very concerned.

The doctors, however, proceeded on the assumption that Jonathan did in fact have bacterial endocarditis. Interestingly, Kathryn learned that week that the daughter of a friend of one of her coworkers had developed bacterial endocarditis in the spring after having visited Italy the previous winter. In addition, she said that another patient who was bedfast and who was, therefore, exposed only to people who came into her house, had developed drug-resistant bacterial endocarditis after being exposed to family members who had visited Greece. Kathryn wanted me to ask Jonathan if he knew the specific strain of bacterium that was causing *his* endocarditis. She wanted to find out if there was a connection because, if so, the cases might be part of a larger problem that needed to be recognized and reported, if it hadn't already. In response, he told me that from what he understood, drug-resistant strains of bacterial endocarditis were fairly new and becoming more prevalent and that although he didn't know the name of his particular strain, he did know that the National Institutes of Health was monitoring the situation. Since this was an emerging phenomenon, there seemed to be little else they could do.

■

Jonathan's condition rapidly became a dominant feature in our relationship—often, *the* dominant feature. Because I was now dealing with a sick—possibly dying—man, I gave him much more latitude than I would have had he been well. I overlooked many of the things he did to me or didn't do for me because of the physical limitations his illness imposed or because of a feeling that he was acting out of an inability to accept the fact that his health was deteriorating, perhaps irreversibly. In addition, I didn't want to cause him unnecessary stress because I was afraid it would exacerbate not only his physical problems, but also his emotional ones—*especially* his emotional ones.

Unfortunately, he sometimes seemed to use his illness to avoid dealing with anything unpleasant or inconvenient, especially when it came to our relationship. If I tried to get him to take responsibility for something unacceptable he had done, he would sometimes respond by saying, "You should be nice to me because I have a heart condition." He would always say it somewhat jokingly, in the tone of a seven-year-old who felt he was being picked on, but it was obvious that he was trying to shut me down. I knew that he was trying to manipulate me, disown responsibility, but sometimes I didn't press certain issues because I genuinely didn't want to cause him needless stress. That didn't mean that I let him get away with *anything*, but it did mean that I was much more tolerant of his behavior than I otherwise might have been. Under normal circumstances, I wouldn't have tolerated many of the things that he did or would do, but circumstances were hardly normal, and I tried to do the best that I could under those circumstances.

—5—
BUSINESS DRAG

Currently I am the COO of a technology company…

In his second e-mail to me, Jonathan told me that he was employed as the COO of an information technology company based in Paladin. Later, he told me that the name of the company was OutSource. Jonathan said that he had been recruited to his current position while he was still working for a company called TekNetium, located in the Southern state, and had accepted the position because it would allow him to exert more influence over the direction of a business or, as he described it, to be "a bigger fish in a smaller sea." In his position as COO, Jonathan's primary responsibility was to oversee the daily operation of the company, a multimillion-dollar concern that employed some 350 people. Apparently, Jonathan had been quite successful professionally in the two years he had worked there, increasing the company's profits almost 40% above expected each year. Jonathan's current job was certainly an indication of how far he had come since his days of "dusting the relics" at the British Museum, as he had once described his duties there.

Although I was unclear about Jonathan's résumé during the 13 years between working for the British Museum and working for TekNetium, he did once mention working for a bank in a country in northern Europe, although he didn't elaborate on what he had done there. In any event, Jonathan had, by any standard, done exceedingly well for himself in a very short time.

Yet, despite his success, Jonathan had grown tired of the burdensome demands and frenetic pace of his high-prestige, but high-pressure, career where he worked "24 by 7," as he described it, and was never free of an onerous sense of responsibility for the management of a multimillion-dollar company. That summer, he looked into other jobs that were less demanding, but his real desire throughout was to leave the world of work behind.

During the previous several years, with the acquisition of higher and better paid positions, he had finally begun to draw the kinds of salaries that, through the help of wise investing, would allow him to retire at the age of 45. At one point, Jonathan told me that as COO of OutSource, he not only drew a base salary of $20,000 a month—almost $250,000 a year—but also received monthly profit distributions that, allowing for fluctuations in the economy, typically amounted to approximately $50,000 a month—$600,000 a year. Altogether, then, Jonathan's income at OutSource worked out to almost $850,000 a year. That was a *little* more than I was earning as a part-time college teacher.

What he seemed to consider "pocket change" was very different from what I did. I remember one Saturday night in particular, not because of where we went or what we did, but because of what Jonathan did before we went out to eat. Before we got into his car, a champagne-colored Cadillac, he opened the trunk and removed a backpack that he kept there. Reaching into the backpack, he pulled out a huge wad of cash and, after counting it, announced that he had $2,000, which he said he had gotten out for the weekend. I was both startled and concerned that he was carrying around so much cash, but I supposed that to someone of Jonathan's financial background, $2,000 to him was like $20 to me. At the time, it mainly had the effect on me of emphasizing the financial disparity between us.

The inequality in our incomes was not only extreme, but also uncomfortable because money was power and I didn't have much power. Even so, I didn't want Jonathan's money and always paid my fair share in whatever we did to minimize the imbalance. I wasn't looking for a sugar daddy who paid for everything then expected *me* to pay an even higher price in other ways. For many reasons, I strove to keep our relationship as equal as possible.

Throughout the two and a half weeks between our Internet meeting and our physical meeting, Jonathan gave me some insight into his work life, insight that made it clear to me why he wanted to retire. In an e-mail from Wednesday, June 6, he told me that because of the day he'd had at work, he had been so tired the night before that he had fallen asleep "as soon as [he had] hit the pillow" and had gone into a "near coma" until 5:30 in the morning, when the phone had begun ringing and his day had started "with a bang." Apparently, there had been a technical problem at his company's site in Sweden, which had required him to "be nice and get on the phone to Malmo and speak Swedish to a distraught female techie who ha[d] no business sense whatsoever" and calm her down.

On Thursday, June 7, he e-mailed me to tell me that he'd had a "long meeting [that] morning from 8 to 12, [a] break for lunch but it really wasn't as [he] had lunch with people from the meeting, then another session from 1 to 3." Although there had been another meeting scheduled at 4:00, he had told someone else to go in his place and his assistant that he'd had enough for one day and had come home. He remarked that "[k]nowing that [he was] retiring in 6 months [was] beginning to give [him] a bit [of] an attitude," then hastened to add that he was "only kidding."

On Sunday, June 10, he e-mailed me to tell me that his plans to engage in cultural activities that day had been derailed when another technical problem had arisen at his company's site in Israel, forcing him to go into the office on his day off to take care of it. He explained that the latest software his company was producing was in beta testing and that the problems that had arisen at the site in Israel were similar to the ones that had arisen in Sweden just a few days before. Since similar problems had now materialized in two places, it was even more crucial to find out what was happening, especially given that his company was due to release the software in October. He said that although they had switched the technical support from the site in Israel to their server farm in France, which had solved the problem in the short term, they now had two teams working on both the short-term problems and the longer-term issues, respectively. He said that he would probably be going back into work later that night to see where things stood. He remarked, "[n]o wonder that I have a queasy stomach and headaches" and complained, "I am not being paid enough!"

The next morning, I checked my e-mail and found that Jonathan had sent me a message at 2:30 that morning. In it, he said that he had just gotten home from work and told me they were still in the process of comparing the incidents in Sweden and Israel, hoping for a third so they could find the commonality that connected them. He said that one of the groups was working on test scripts to try to reproduce the problem, but so far they hadn't found the bug. He said he had to be back in the office at 7:30 in the morning to talk to people in Israel again before he attended a staff meeting at 8:30. That meant he would get at most four hours of sleep. He said they had added a meeting about the beta test problems on a Monday that was already "filled up with meetings." He concluded by saying, "Yuck."

After midnight on Wednesday, June 13, he wrote to tell me about his upcoming day. He said that his Wednesday would consist of a meeting with the finance committee—which he described as "the most boring 2 hours ever conceived by mere mortals"—a meeting with his boss over lunch, a meeting with human resources about benefits, and another meeting with the quality assurance people working on the beta test problem. He also said that the search committee that was looking for his successor was meeting that week as well. He said that although he was on the committee, he tried to remain unobtrusive because even though no one would be selected without his approval, he didn't want to be seen as dictating who his replacement would be; his successor needed to be seen as a power center in his or her own right. He said that since he would be retaining equity in the company, he didn't want any hints of failure after he left. The meeting, which had originally been scheduled for Wednesday, had been moved to Friday. He concluded by thanking God because he "couldn't take one more meeting tomorrow."

Through the summer, I continued to receive almost daily updates about his extensive, and sometimes intensive, business activities. On Monday, June 25, Jonathan e-mailed me at 1:30 in the morning to tell me that his boss had called him around 9:00 the evening before to come to his house to meet with representatives of a company in California that wanted to buy a small piece of equity in OutSource. Jonathan said that even though his boss's house was just down the street from his, he hadn't been in the mood to go. He said that he had asked his boss if, in return for the favor he had done for him, he could have the following weekend off. He said that by the time he had gotten back at 1:00 in the morning, he was "pooped."

Later that day, he wrote to tell me that he was having dinner with the representatives from the company in California again that night. He said that although they were wanting only a 3.5% stake in OutSource, the marque value they could provide was even more important, so he felt compelled to meet with them. He said that in light of the recent beta test problem, the representatives from the company were "crawling all over everything," which made him nervous. There hadn't been any further trouble since the incident in Israel two weeks before, and after talking to members of one of the teams working on the failures, the representatives seemed satisfied that the problem had been solved, which permitted Jonathan to take his anxiety level down "a notch or two."

The next day, Jonathan wrote to tell me that he'd had a "usual" day in spite of the negotiations with the company in California thrown on top of everything else. He said the representatives would finally be leaving the next day. He said that second-quarter figures and projections were coming in and that they "[didn't] seem to have any nasty surprises, thank God." Although the numbers were only a little above expected, given the state of the information technology market, Jonathan thought they were "OK."

Jonathan told me that his boss, Mike Harmon, and he had a good, if sometimes intense, working relationship. Mike's wife Alicia and he had three daughters, whose names all began with the letter A. The oldest was Andrea, who was going to be going off to college in the fall, something her parents viewed with ambivalent feelings. Jonathan said that Mike and Alicia were somewhat controlling and wanted to keep Andrea under their thumb. In August, when Andrea finally left for college, Mike and Alicia went with her, less, it seemed, out of helpfulness than out of a need to control. On Tuesday, August 7, Jonathan e-mailed me to tell me that Mike hadn't returned yet and that apparently neither Mike nor his wife could bear to leave their eldest daughter at school until she was "PERFECTLY" settled in. In the same e-mail, Jonathan quipped that "[i]f I were Andrea, I would run out and fuck ever[y]one in sight just to celebrate being liberated from that shit."

Jonathan said that Mike was extensively remodeling his mansion and told me that, among other things, he was including an indoor pool and tennis court. Jonathan pointed the house out to me one time when we happened to drive past and I found the house impressive, but excessive, especially if what Jonathan had told me about the remodel was true. I supposed, though, that if Mike were the CEO of a successful company, he had earned it.

One Saturday night around the middle of July, Jonathan came into the sunroom after checking e mails and informed me that he'd gotten an e-mail from Mike telling him that he wanted him to come right over. It was 11:00 at night, and although I couldn't understand what couldn't wait until morning, I also understood that the business world operated with a sense of urgency that sometimes seemed obsessive. Jonathan left at 11:00 and didn't return until midnight. When he returned, he told me about the meeting, which to me seemed like more of the same. What didn't seem like more of the same was that Jonathan had told Mike that he was seeing me. Jonathan had told me that Mike knew he was gay and had no problem with it and had met Glenn before Jonathan and he had separated. Mike seemed interested, asking him what Jonathan thought of me. Jonathan said that he'd told Mike that he liked me and said that he thought I liked him. I did and it somehow gave me a feeling of recognition, of validation, that I found reinforcing.

When I would stay with him during the week, Jonathan would usually leave for work around 9:00 or 10:00 in the morning and return home around 3:00 or 4:00 in the afternoon. He didn't go to the office every weekday, but he did most of them. I assumed he could do, and did, some of his work from home, given his white-collar position in information technology. When he would go to the office, though, he always wore casual clothes, usually a pullover shirt and short pants, which seemed unprofessional to me. I never saw him don a business suit, although I did see a picture of him in which he was wearing a suit, minus the jacket, and was standing in an office setting. Perhaps OutSource had a casual dress code or perhaps Jonathan changed into his "business drag" at work. Why he would do that, though, escaped me, but Jonathan clearly did some things differently than I did.

■

Around the beginning of August, Jonathan told me about an employee named Ben. Apparently, money had come up missing and, because of his access to the funds in question, Ben had become the prime suspect. Because small amounts of money had disappeared over a long period of time, the theft hadn't been detected as quickly as it would have if a large sum had disappeared at once. Jonathan said that he had spoken to Ben privately, who had said that he was having "problems," but that didn't appear to be enough. On Monday, the 6th, Jonathan sent me an e-mail in which he said that he'd suspended Ben and was having the human resources department initiate a fuller investigation not just of Ben, but of everyone. Jonathan seemed dismayed that someone he liked and had apparently trusted had descended into stealing from his company. I was dismayed, too, for Jonathan, and was glad that I was not in his position.

The "Ben situation" would arise again many months later—though in a form that at the time I couldn't have imagined.

—6—
GLAD TO BE GAY

Getting laid is easy.

The day we began corresponding with each other and finding out the basic facts about each other, Jonathan had told me that sexually, he had been "fairly wild early on" and still enjoyed an "active" sex life. I didn't have a clear idea of what he meant by that until he quantified it for me. In the end, he calculated that, in his lifetime, he had probably had sex with *three thousand* men. I wasn't entirely certain that I believed that estimate, thinking that either he had miscalculated or he was exaggerating, but I also knew that some gay men did, in fact, have thousands of partners in their lifetimes. The latter fact had, unfortunately, been a major cause of the spread of HIV in the United States in the early 1980s. He also explained that in England in the 1970s and 1980s, when most of his "wildness" had taken place, gay liberation was at its height and everyone was "glad to be gay"—or "gladdy," for short, as the attitude was described. This "gladness" took the form of unrestrained sexual expression, as it had in the United States during the same period. He said it wasn't unusual to have sex with five different people in one day and he knew people who had had far more partners than him. Therefore, I thought it was at least plausible that he had in fact had as many partners as he claimed he had.

He also mentioned that much of the sex he'd had was unprotected or "bareback," to use the currently fashionable phrase. I asked him if he had ever thought at the time about how dangerous that was, but he said that AIDS hadn't yet become the issue in England that it had in the United States. He said that if he had been in the States at the same time doing the same thing he probably would be dead. I probably had to agree.

Jonathan claimed that he had had liaisons with at least two famous people during his "fairly wild early on" period. The first was the conductor of the London Philharmonic Orchestra. The experience, as he described it, was fairly harrowing. He said that they had spent the night together and that at one point, he discovered that he had been locked in his apartment. When he got the impression that the conductor intended to do something to him, he managed to escape out the window. He didn't say whether or not he had encountered the conductor later, but I supposed that if you were as promiscuous as Jonathan claimed to be, it only increased the likelihood of encountering someone who was disturbed.

The second person with whom he claimed to have been involved was the renowned Russian ballet dancer Rudolph Nureyev. He said that he had become involved with Nureyev while the dancer was staying in London, when Jonathan would have been around 20. According to Jonathan, they had been involved for approximately four months. Among other remembrances of his relationship that Jonathan recounted were ones of going bike riding with Nureyev and, of course, watching him perform. He also said that at one point during their relationship, he had become ill and had had to be hospitalized. Knowing that Jonathan's favorite color was blue, Nureyev had had a bouquet of blue flowers delivered to Jonathan's room every hour. Yet, despite such displays of sensitivity, Jonathan also said that Nureyev had displayed his more infamous issues with intimacy, insisting that Jonathan call him *Nureyev*, not *Rudolph*. Jonathan claimed that he still had a shirt that Nureyev had given to him, although I never saw it. I remember one afternoon that summer Jonathan was flipping channels and happened upon a program that featured Nureyev. Jonathan reacted to the sight of the dancer with a wistful longing. It was a strange experience to see him react that way to someone who was as far removed from me and my life as anyone could be.

I didn't know what to think about Jonathan's claims of having been involved with Nureyev. I had no way to verify whether or not the story was true but didn't feel driven to do so, since whether or not it was true had little impact on my life. Even so, I thought it might be possible. First, I reasoned that if Jonathan did come from an upper-class background, then it seemed more likely that his social circle would eventually intersect with that of a well-known individual than if he had come from a class lower down. In addition, it seemed more likely that he would have encountered a well-known person in a place like London than in other locales, since London was, of course, one of the world's most important cities.

Second, while visiting the library a few months later, I finally decided to learn more about Nureyev. I found a couple of biographies on the dancer, and although neither mentioned Jonathan—but why would they when Nureyev was notoriously promiscuous—they *did* mention an intriguing, if indirect, piece of support for Jonathan's claim. According to the biographers, Nureyev had been in London from 1976 to 1978, where he had performed in *Romeo and Juliet* as well as *Swan Lake*. Jonathan had told me that he had been born in mid-November 1956, which meant that he would have ranged from 19 to 21 while Nureyev was there. This, of course, was merely suggestive, but at least the time frame was correct.

Finally, Nureyev was the only celebrity, apart from the conductor, with whom Jonathan claimed to have been involved, which made the story sound more plausible than if he had simultaneously claimed that he had been involved with numerous well-knowns. Indeed, he even downplayed the significance of the relationship, saying that to Nureyev, he had just been "the flavor of the month."

Jonathan mentioned several other men with whom he had been involved. One was a man named Lucas. Lucas was middle-aged and married, but according to Jonathan, his wife turned a blind eye to his interest in other men. Jonathan described his relationship with Lucas as meaningful, but abusive. He said that Lucas had written him many inspiring letters about life, which Jonathan said he still had. In addition, Lucas was Jewish and this had led Jonathan to develop a deep respect for the Jewish people and an almost Zionistic sympathy for Israel. Unfortunately, Lucas was also controlling and had expected Jonathan to behave in certain ways, especially when they were with Lucas's friends. Apparently, Lucas wasn't above using physical "persuasion" to keep Jonathan in line. Jonathan said that once, when he was playing bridge with Lucas and his friends, he had done something minor of which Lucas disapproved and Lucas had slapped him across the face. Because of his abusiveness and the tension created by the conflict of trying to maintain two different types of incompatible sexual lives, their relationship had ended after a few months.

Another man was James. Like his friend Harald, James was an antiques dealer. Jonathan said that James collected Impressionist art and had original pieces by several famous Impressionists in his home. Jonathan said that it was incredible to wake up in his bedroom with "Monet on one wall, Cézanne on another, and Degas on another."

Yet another man was David Garrett. Though not as renowned as Nureyev, David was also a dancer and Jonathan recounted his memories of watching him rehearse and perform. Beyond that he didn't offer much detail about his relationship with David, but he always spoke fondly of him.

The most unusual—and to me disturbing—story Jonathan told me about his sexual past, however, involved not famous figures, but the priests who taught at the Catholic boarding school he said he had attended from the ages of eight to sixteen. He told me that some of the priests who were gay regularly had sex with the male students—including *him*. He said that he had started sleeping with his teachers when he was around 11 or 12 and had done so until he had left school. He said the first adult he ever saw ejaculate was one of the priests. He added that his reaction had been to think, "Cool!" He said that "everyone did it" and that no one had thought there was anything odd about it. Of course not, I thought, since it's easy to indoctrinate naïve and unknowing children into believing that almost anything is normal and acceptable, no matter how abnormal and unacceptable it is. I wondered if his parents had known and, if so, what their reaction had been, although I was certain they hadn't.

He did seem to understand, though, that not everyone thought such behavior was normal. I remember one evening in July when we were eating at a Chinese restaurant we frequented that summer and he raised the issue. He asked me if I had ever slept with any of my teachers when I was growing up and I told him *no*. I further told him that in *this* country, it wasn't considered normal for children to have sex with their teachers any more than it was considered normal for children to have sex with adults in general. I doubted it was considered normal in England, either. In response, he seemed rebuffed, as if he were in fact sensitive about the issue. I had to wonder how his experiences had affected his sexual development. He certainly seemed to find a broader range of sexual attitudes and behaviors acceptable than I did. Although much of the difference came from having been raised in different cultures at different times, I couldn't help thinking that his experiences, no matter how much they might have been "normalized" for him, had left a lasting impression.

■

Jonathan said that he had been faithful to Glenn, but after their relationship had ended, he had resumed a promiscuous, or at least "active," pattern. By the time I met him a little more than a year later, he had been involved with a number of men from Paladin.

Almost every time we went out together, Jonathan would see someone he claimed he had either had a relationship with or had slept with. After a while, I began to lose count.

The first time I encountered one of his former flings was shortly after I had started spending my weekends with him. One Saturday afternoon around the end of June, Jonathan wanted to visit a particular antiques shop in downtown Paladin to purchase scented candles. He used them instead of air freshener, saying that Europeans preferred scented candles to scented sprays for freshening the air. He also told me that he had once been involved with the owner of the shop, a young man named Kyle. He didn't tell me this, however, until we were about to step into the shop. Before we entered, he mentioned that he had dated Kyle "a couple of times" and left it at that. Being unprepared to encounter one of Jonathan's former paramours, my first visit to Kyle's shop proved rather uncomfortable.

Kyle, who was tall and athletic and appeared to be in his late 20s, was standing at the register. Jonathan spoke to him and asked him about his mother. Kyle noticed me, giving me a look that seemed to bore right through me. I don't know if he really was or if I was simply viewing his behavior through the lens of my discomfort, but I felt as if I had suddenly been thrust beneath a microscope turned to the highest setting. Throughout the rest of the time we remained in the shop, I found myself mainly trying to avoid Kyle and his gaze, which seemed to follow me wherever I went. I told Jonathan how I'd felt and he agreed, but added that it was only to be expected. I was a little dismayed by Jonathan's behavior as well because he had failed to appreciate my feelings about deliberately encountering one of his old flames both before and after the fact, but I didn't make an issue of it.

Later, Jonathan confessed that, instead of dating each other "a couple of times," he and Kyle had actually been involved with each other for *four months*. I didn't ask him why he hadn't told me that in the first place, although I wondered if he had thought it might bother me even more, in encountering Kyle, to know that he and Kyle had actually been much more deeply involved. I *liked* to think that, although I really didn't know why he hadn't initially been more forthcoming.

Whatever Jonathan's motives, I learned much more about Kyle and his relationship with him. Jonathan said that Kyle had given him the lamp with the Asian-style shade that sat on the Formica table in the sunroom, the one next to the chair in which I usually sat. Subsequently, I came to view that particular piece of the décor differently than I had before. He described Kyle as uninhibited, saying that he could be "really silly" and would sometimes do "the funniest things," although he didn't offer specific examples. He said that he and Kyle had actually taken a trip to Prague at some point during their relationship. He said, however, that Kyle had been "bitchy" during the trip and his bitchiness in general was part of what had ultimately undone their relationship. They had obviously remained friends, however, in spite of their differences, and Jonathan described Kyle as "all right."

Kyle was not, however, the only person from the shop whom Jonathan had dated. He had also dated another worker at the shop named Javier. Javier was from Argentina and, according to Jonathan, they had dated for about a month. Javier had a college degree and spoke five languages, but in spite of his credentials, he preferred to work in Kyle's antiques shop instead of doing something more significant. Overall, Jonathan didn't think he was very ambitious, although Jonathan was judging him by his own standards of ambition, which were rather high. Jonathan said they had stopped dating when they had run out of things to say to each other. We eventually visited Kyle's shop at least a couple of more times, and on one of these occasions, Javier was working. Like Kyle, he was tall, athletic, and handsome, but unlike Kyle, he seemed much friendlier.

One Saturday afternoon in June, Jonathan and I went to investigate a house downtown where he thought he might like to live. The young man who showed us the house, who was gay, was someone who surprisingly knew not only Jonathan, but also me. Although I didn't recognize him, he said that he had seen me in Hawthorn, apparently as I had gone to and from the university I had attended. I was surprised that there were gay men who not only noticed me, but also remembered me so well after so long when we'd never actually met. I didn't realize I was that memorable.

In any event, when the young man left, Jonathan looked at me with a slightly startled expression and said, "I think I made out with his boyfriend."

He recounted the story, which involved an encounter with the young man and his boyfriend on a previous occasion in which the boyfriend, who apparently wasn't quite as committed, had come on to Jonathan and the two of them had somehow ended up in a closet, where they had briefly made out. When I criticized Jonathan for doing that, he claimed that he hadn't known the two of them were together and added that at that point, it had been a long time since he'd had any kind of physical contact with another man and he hadn't had the restraint he might otherwise have had. I didn't know what to think about the situation, but I hoped that a similar incident didn't happen again.

Then there was Frank, the butcher. Frank worked at the supermarket that Jonathan frequented. He told me that he and Frank had dated for a while, although nothing serious had developed between them. Jonathan hoped to point him out to me when we went to the supermarket, although it wasn't until the third attempt that I finally saw him. Frank, in some ways, reminded me of Kyle and Javier, at least in that he was tall, dark-haired, and handsome. Unlike Kyle, but like Javier, Frank was equally friendly to the both of us. Jonathan later told me that Frank was the one who had taught him the difference between "tenderloin and prime cut." I could only imagine.

Then there was Lester. Lester was apparently a one-night stand. One Saturday morning sometime in July, Jonathan and I ate breakfast at a seedy coffee shop on the east side of town. As it turned out, there was a story behind how Jonathan had discovered such an unlikely place. Apparently, it was one of Lester's favorite hangouts and Jonathan and he had gone there to have breakfast the morning after their one-night stand. After a while, I began to wonder if there was *any* place in Paladin that wasn't somehow associated with Jonathan's sex life. He had obviously been quite busy in the year between breaking up with Glenn and meeting me.

Jonathan also seemed to attract his share of attention from people. For example, one Sunday afternoon in July, we went to Starbuck's for something chocolatey. After ordering, we took our desserts and drinks outside and sat down at one of the tables. I was facing away from most of the tables, while Jonathan was facing most of them, where he had a clear view of the handful of other patrons sitting around us. Directly behind me sat a young man whom I couldn't see, but who Jonathan claimed was flirting with him. Several times after that, Jonathan claimed that various people, both men and women, were flirting with him, although sometimes I wondered if he were mistaking fascination for flirtation. Sometimes it was difficult to tell, but I *did* know how people reacted to him when he *spoke*.

Jonathan had a metaphysical explanation for his "magnetism." He explained that Miranda had told him that because he was a Scorpio, he had a strong personality that commanded attention. I knew that Scorpios were also supposed to be especially sexual, so perhaps that meant he was supposed to command *sexual* attention. Less metaphysical was Jonathan's other explanation, which was that he conveyed what he called a "fuck me" look. Apparently this was an intensified version of the more demure "come-hither" look, although he never demonstrated it to me.

I suspected that if people weren't reacting to his British accent, then they were reacting to something behavioral that he did either consciously or unconsciously. I doubted they were reacting to his appearance, since he wasn't that good-looking. Sometimes, though, I thought it was all in his head and told him that he reminded me of Blanche Devereaux, the man-hungry southern belle played by Rue McClanahan on *The Golden Girls* who believed that every man wanted her whether he did or not. Jonathan felt insulted by the comparison, but he claimed there were so many people who wanted him that it seemed difficult to know what to believe. It was clear, however, that for whatever reason, Jonathan did have an uncanny ability to draw people to him and into his life.

■

On the evening of Friday, July 20, Jonathan and I went to see *A.I.* starring Haley Joel Osment in his Pinnochio-esque role as David, the android who wanted to be a boy. Afterwards, we had dinner at Half-Time, a gay-oriented restaurant and bar in Paladin. It had a quiet, intimate quality that reminded me of Tolliver's and we ate there two or three times throughout the summer.

While we were there, Jonathan seemed to recognize our waiter and asked him if he knew someone named Andy Black. I don't recall what the waiter said, but I do recall what *I* said. I asked him who Andy was and Jonathan explained to me that Andy was someone he had dated for a couple of months before the two of us had met. Although he didn't tell me how old Andy was, I got the impression he was young, perhaps in his early 20s. He did tell me that Andy worked in transportation. He also told me, with feigned reluctance, that Andy, the waiter, and he had ended up in bed together at one point and had smoked some marijuana in the process. I could only shake my head at yet *another* of Jonathan's sexual exploits. Jonathan said that although things had not worked out between him and Andy, they had remained friends and that he "liked" Andy. The way he said "liked" had an odd quality to it, but I couldn't quite place what was odd about it.

Throughout the next several months, Andy's name would arise from time to time, but six months later, on a cold afternoon in January, I would learn something about Jonathan's relationship with Andy that, on that warm evening in July, I could never have imagined.

■

Despite the carefree attitude that his behavior seemed to suggest, Jonathan's feelings about his sexuality in general were somewhat negative. He once described homosexuality as being a form of narcissism, of "loving one's own image," as he described it, which derived from an outdated psychoanalytic notion originally proposed by Sigmund Freud. I found it ironic that Jonathan, someone who seemed to be so "glad" about his sexuality, could simultaneously have such a questionable view of it. Then, again, I realized, from painful personal experience, how the conscious mind could hold one set of thoughts, feelings, and perceptions, while the unconscious mind could hold quite another. If I believed anything that Freud had proposed, it was that we are often driven by potent unseen forces that we do not recognize, let alone control. And, for some of us, that blindness can lead to our undoing.

■

I didn't know how Jonathan had behaved sexually with other partners, but with me, his behavior tended to be self-centered. He seemed to feel that his sexual satisfaction came first and that mine came second—if at all. Indeed, there were many times when he would be satisfied, then seem to be done. Sometimes, it didn't seem to occur to him that *I* wanted to be satisfied. I would have to ask him to do so and sometimes he would seem aggravated, as if I were asking him to perform some burdensome chore. When I would be "demanding," I would never hear about it overtly at the time, but I would usually hear about it subtly the next day. He would usually make some seemingly joking comment about how I was "very aggressive in bed last night" but that it was "okay"—something that told me he thought it was *not*. He refused, usually passively, to engage in certain acts that I liked and I received little satisfaction in our sexual relationship.

I tolerated his sexually selfish behavior because I knew he was sick, stressed, and not sixteen. I wasn't involved with Jonathan primarily for the sex, but if he had been healthier and younger, his lack of interest in sex in general and my pleasure in particular might have worked more forcefully to undermine our relationship. I was young and healthy with a normal sex drive and couldn't pretend that sex was unimportant. Understanding the circumstances, however, I tried to accept the fact that the quality of our sex life wasn't Jonathan's highest priority. Although sexually the relationship wasn't satisfying, I tried to focus on those aspects of it that were.

—7—
Heart Conditions

It was one of the most intense relationships I've ever had.

Over time, Jonathan expanded on the details about his relationship with Glenn. According to Jonathan, he and Glenn had met in England about 15 years earlier. One evening, a close friend of Jonathan's had brought Glenn to dinner at Jonathan's home in London. They seemed to click, and over time, their relationship had evolved until finally they had decided to live together. Jonathan and Glenn had lived together in London for several years until Jonathan had gotten his job working for the American arm of TekNetium in the South sometime in the spring of 1996. Glenn and he had lived there for a total of three and a half years before Jonathan was offered a position as COO of OutSource in the fall of 1999. That fall, Jonathan and Glenn had moved to Paladin. Although moving to Paladin had seemed like a good thing, it was there that their relationship had begun to unravel.

Jonathan explained that, over time, he and Glenn had grown apart. Jonathan said that Glenn was my age, 35, which meant that Glenn would have been only 20 when he and Jonathan, then 30, would have met. It didn't surprise me that they had grown apart, since someone who is 30 has already begun to figure out who he is and what he wants in life, while someone who is only 20 is still in the process of "finding himself." Jonathan summarized the quality of his nine-year relationship with Glenn by saying that "the first five years were excellent, the next two years were okay, and the last two years were shitty." Finally, after an extended period of deterioration, they had decided to go their separate ways. Sometime in the spring of 2000, Glenn had gone back to England, while Jonathan had remained in Paladin.

In spite of how things had ended, Jonathan said that he and Glenn had continued to remain friends and that he had made certain that Glenn would be provided for. Jonathan said that he had bought Glenn a car and a flat in London and had given him £45,000 (roughly $72,000 US). Jonathan told me that, as of that summer, Glenn was living and working in England and was involved with someone new. Jonathan said he got the impression that Glenn wasn't happy with his new life, but he also said that it wasn't his problem. I agreed because I believed it was no one's responsibility to make another person happy; indeed, I believed that it was an impossibility, since happiness comes from within, not from without.

From the beginning, I had known about Glenn, but it wasn't until later that I learned about Marcus. Jonathan had first met Marcus when the two of them were still in school. Marcus was somewhat older than Jonathan and appeared to be a kind of "golden boy," not only because of his fair complexion, but also because of his intelligence and ambition. Jonathan said that while they were still in school, he and Marcus were just acquaintances and otherwise did not operate in the same circles. They went their separate ways, but eventually, they met up again in London. Although Jonathan generally didn't give dates, I concluded that this had happened sometime around 1983, when Jonathan was 26. He said that he and Marcus became interested in each other and eventually fell in love. Jonathan said that emotionally, his relationship with Marcus was the most intense relationship he had ever had. He stated that "you don't love someone like that except when you're young."

Jonathan said that he and Marcus had lived together for the next three years. Jonathan said that Marcus, who was driven by ambition, encouraged him to be more ambitious in his own aspirations. Indeed, Jonathan credited Marcus for redirecting him from a career in archaeology to a career in business. In one of his first e-mails to me, Jonathan had said that because of circumstances "too arcane" to mention then, he had switched to a business career some 18 years before; as it turned out, those "circumstances" were Marcus. Marcus had apparently felt that Jonathan was wasting his time "dusting the relics" at the museum and had encouraged him to do something more significant and lucrative. Jonathan had agreed. At that point, Jonathan had enrolled in the London School of Economics, where he had eventually earned his master's degree in strategic planning, and had begun working in "The City," the historical core of London where the city's business and financial seat was located.

For three years, Jonathan and Marcus enjoyed their intense, youthful romance and seemed destined to spend the rest of their lives together.

Then, on the day after Christmas, the day that in England is known as Boxing Day, everything changed.

That year, Jonathan had bought Marcus a motorcycle for Christmas. On Boxing Day, Marcus had driven the motorcycle to a pub, where he had spent the afternoon drinking. Although he hadn't become drunk, he had drunk enough to impair his coordination and increase his reaction time. The roads on which he was driving were winding and icy. Before Marcus had left home, Jonathan, who had wanted him to stay home with him, had expressed his displeasure with him and had informed him that he expected him to be home by a specific time. Marcus, whom Jonathan described as having a "need for speed," and who was possibly rushing to arrive home in time to keep Jonathan from being mad, had lost control of the motorcycle and was thrown over the handlebars, landing on the pavement headfirst. Jonathan commented that the only outward wound that Marcus had received was a gash across his forehead. Inward, however, the damage was much greater: Marcus was left brain dead.

According to Jonathan, Marcus had lingered on life support for the next week. Finally, his stepmother had intervened and had had the doctors pull the plug. Jonathan had always hated Marcus's stepmother, but her decision to remove her stepson from life support, even though it was the *only* decision, had served to increase his animosity toward her even further. As 1986 ended, so did Marcus's life.

Jonathan said that he had been so grief-stricken over Marcus's death that he didn't date or have sex for months. Then, about a year after Marcus died, Jonathan's friend introduced him to Glenn. Given that Jonathan had told me he and Glenn had dated for about a year before deciding to live together, I inferred they had started living together sometime around the end of 1988, remaining together until they had separated in the spring of 2000. Although that meant that he and Glenn had been together for at least eleven years, not the nine years Jonathan had initially stated, I assumed I had made some mistake in estimating the time frames, although I couldn't determine where I had miscalculated. I didn't question it further, however, since the basic facts seemed more important.

After he and Glenn separated, Jonathan, in spite of having become involved with several men in the ensuing months, never found anyone with whom he fell in love. Then, he had met Cliff.

I didn't learn about Cliff until after Jonathan and I had known each other for about a month. The first Sunday of July was the first full Sunday that I spent with Jonathan, and that afternoon, we were lying in bed when Jonathan seemed to become preoccupied.

"Did I tell you about Cliff?" he asked.

By that point, Jonathan had told me about so many former lovers that I was beginning to lose count. Thinking at the time that he had, I said yes, but if I had really known the full story about Cliff, I would have been left with no doubt.

Jonathan told me that he and Cliff had met sometime in the summer of 2000. He was never specific about how they had met, although certain things he said seemed to suggest they had met in some fashion through what Jonathan described as the "gay elite here [in Paladin] that is very involved in business and politics." However they met, he said that when they had, they had experienced an instant, intense attraction to each other. He said they had spent the entire first night they had known each other talking and had been "together after that." Jonathan said that he and Cliff had been so intensely bonded that they would "not go buy a pair of socks without the other going with him" and would even rearrange their business schedules so they could always be together when the other had to travel. He said that he had loved Cliff "physically, mentally, and spiritually" and described the relationship as "one of the most intense relationships [he had] ever had." He said there was nothing wrong in the relationship and that, in a word, the relationship was "perfect."

Unfortunately, they could not remain together. Around the end of 2000, Cliff had gotten an opportunity to advance his career by obtaining a position at a company in California. Jonathan said that he had actually helped Cliff prepare for the interviews even though he knew what it would mean if Cliff got the job. Jonathan knew that he wouldn't follow him to California because he didn't want to be what he described as an "appendage" of Cliff's. Cliff did get the job, and in late 2000, he left.

The break was so traumatic that, according to Jonathan, the only way they had felt they could both survive emotionally was to cut off all further contact with each other. He also explained that was why he hadn't told me about him before then, since the subject was too painful. I thought their agreement not to have contact with each other was questionable, involving as it did the suppression and avoidance of their feelings, but I had also come to understand that, for Jonathan, this was a deeply ingrained, lifelong pattern that would probably never change. Apparently Jonathan and Cliff had had no contact with each other in the six months since their relationship had been torn asunder.

The subject of Cliff arose on that day because Jonathan told me that he had received an e-mail from Cliff. He told me this was the first time that Cliff had contacted him since they had separated and that he was questioning his current situation. He told me that Cliff had said that since they had broken up, he had become involved with another man named Loren. Cliff said that he loved Loren but that he wasn't *in* love with him, that he was, in fact, still in love with Jonathan. Mirroring Jonathan's words, he stated that his relationship with Jonathan was "the most intense relationship [he had] ever had" and that he hadn't been happy since he and Jonathan had broken up. Apparently Loren was wanting himself and Cliff to become a committed couple, but Cliff felt ambivalent about doing so because of his lingering, and more passionate, feelings for Jonathan. To resolve the issue for himself, Cliff had decided to contact Jonathan to apprise him of the situation and to see if there was any possibility of their rekindling their relationship. Cliff had also informed him that he was planning to return to the Midwest in the near future, which made a renewed relationship between Jonathan and him feasible. Cliff had told Jonathan that if he agreed to rekindle their relationship, he would leave Loren for Jonathan, but if not, he would commit to Loren.

I thought that Cliff's attitude was self-centered and manipulative, a maneuver more suited to an adolescent than to a 35-year-old man, but since I understood that people often do self-centered things out of unhappiness, and since I felt awkward about voicing my opinion, I kept my feelings to myself. I also didn't know how to take this unexpected news, not only the revelation of an apparently passionate and "perfect" relationship that had ended only a few months before—something I thought Jonathan should have told me about earlier—but also the question it posed about what it meant for *us*.

When I left on the Fourth of July, Jonathan seemed preoccupied. The morning after I got back to Hawthorn, he sent me an e-mail in which he explained that he'd been upset about Cliff. He claimed that he was over him but that sometimes it was best to "let the dead bury the dead." He said that he had waited for six months before he had tried dating again to make sure he wouldn't be on the rebound, something he saw as unfair to himself as well as the person with whom he was involved. He said that in those six months he had done his share of what he called "sport fucking" to "reestablish [his] ego," but now felt it was time to move on.

I spent a considerable amount of time composing what I hoped would be a thoughtful and comforting message regarding his doomed relationship with Cliff. In response, Jonathan said he felt that what had happened between him and Cliff was like "the pay back for [him] of who and what [he'd] been for the last 18 years," meaning that he felt he had let business come before personal happiness. He said that he had loved Cliff "more then [he could] tell [me]," but that it wasn't possible for them to remain together. Fatalistic, he told me that "[y]ou can't have everything so be careful what you ask for," saying that both he and Cliff had gotten what they'd wanted professionally but that it had destroyed what they'd had romantically. He concluded that "[l]ittle did either of us know that what we wanted wasn't what we needed" and that in the end their choice had proven to be bad.

Trying to be optimistic, though, he said that fortunately life was "organic and growing" and that things, and people, changed. He said that six months before, he couldn't be involved with anyone, but in that time "the earth [had] rotated and so [had he]." He said it was still upsetting to think about Cliff, what they'd had and what they'd lost, so it was important for the both of them to keep their agreement to stay out of each other's lives or "both of [them] would go mad."

In the message, he explained that he had revealed so much about his relationship with Cliff to me, that he wanted to reveal as much about himself as he could to me because "[t]he more info[rmation] that [I took] in, the better [I could] understand who and what [he was]." He told me that he harbored "really no, or very very few secrets," or that if he did, "they must be unconscious ones as [he didn't] know what they would be at this point." He assured me, "What you see is what there is." Otherwise, he told me that if I ever wanted to know anything about him just to ask him and he would tell me the truth, saying, "I always tell the truth" because "the truth [was] easier." He had already told me some unflattering things about himself, which suggested that he was willing to present himself in a negative light. He told me that he expected me to tell him the truth in return, saying that "[o]therwise any relationship is built on sand and can't stand for long." I liked to believe he was telling me the truth now because previous relationships had been destroyed by concealed lies, had definitely been built on sand, and I hoped I wouldn't have to go through that pain again.

On Thursday, Jonathan seemed merely wistful, but on Friday, that drastically changed.

Friday afternoon around 4:00, Jonathan sent me an e-mail titled "Please email soon" in which he told me that he had just received a "really upsetting" message from Cliff and was not handling it well. He said he was feeling "very weak and vulnerable" and said he could "hardly breathe."

Immediately I called Jonathan. Jonathan told me that he had just received an e-mail from Cliff titled "Little White Lie" in which Cliff had told him that, instead of planning to move back to the Midwest in the near future, he had actually returned in April and had been there, only 100 miles from Paladin—and Jonathan—for over two months. Jonathan was distraught, unable to comprehend how Cliff could have been so dishonest. Eventually, he calmed down, but he was still deeply troubled.

Around 7:30 that evening, he sent me an even more distressing e-mail in which he said that what Cliff had admitted had put him into a "bad tailspin" and that he was now having pain in his chest that radiated to his shoulder, arm, and upper back. He said that he'd been taking nitroglycerin but that the pain returned in fifteen minutes and that if it got worse he might go to the emergency room. He couldn't comprehend how someone he had loved so intensely could have done something so cruel and said that what Cliff had done had put him "in the deepest recess in hell." He told me he was depressed, which wasn't his normal mood, and the zest was gone from life. He said he tried to treat people the way he wanted to be treated but it didn't seem to work, mentioning again his inability to understand how someone he loved so much could have hurt him so much. He said that if Cliff had told him in April that he'd returned he would have joined him, but now, in July, he would never speak to him again, which was difficult to accept. He concluded that perhaps he didn't understand America, although I thought what had happened was a more universal problem. He ended the e-mail by saying that he was too upset to continue and would write more later.

Fearing that he might be having a heart attack, I called him and implored him to go to the hospital. He resisted, and eventually, the pain seemed to subside. Talking about what Cliff had done to him seemed to help. He told me that he "wouldn't treat a dog like this," referring to the callous way in which Cliff had delivered his revelation. He restated that if he had known that Cliff had been living only 100 miles away, he would have tried to reunite with him, since the 2,000 miles that separated my state from California had been the only thing that had separated *them*. He said, however, that because of the way that Cliff had hidden his secret from him, he could no longer trust him and that reuniting with him was now out of the question. He said he would never be able to trust him again. Once he got his feelings off his chest figuratively, that seemed to help the pressure in his chest literally. Even so, I was still greatly concerned about the turn of events, the downturn of Jonathan's health that they seemed to have precipitated.

Around 11:30, he e-mailed me to tell me that he was feeling better but that he couldn't sleep. He said that Colin had called, stating that although it was 4:00 in the morning in England, Colin hadn't been able to sleep either. They had talked about Cliff, who Colin had thought loved Jonathan as much as Jonathan loved him.

He said that he felt like an "open wound." He also expressed a desire to move, saying that he was unhappy in his house because too many bad things had happened there and that he wanted to be somewhere "safe and friendly."

In the same e-mail, Jonathan told me that a man named Dan, who was one of his best friends, was planning to come to Paladin on Saturday to see him. I had never met Dan, but Jonathan had told me that he lived in a small town called Credence, about an hour's drive from Paladin, and was gay. Apparently he had told Dan what had happened and Dan, concerned for him, had decided to come to Paladin to be with him. I was glad that someone would be with him when I couldn't.

On Saturday it was raining. The weather seemed to be a fitting reflection of Jonathan's mood. He wrote to me that morning, hoping that Dan would come as planned but wasn't sure that he would because Dan was "a bit of an old lady driver" who hated to drive in bad weather or traffic. He also told me that even though he'd had a fitful night, he felt better and had begun to put what had happened into some kind of perspective. He said that in spite of now knowing that Cliff was only 100 miles away, nothing had really changed. He said that even though he had once loved him and would have done anything for him "without qualification," he had moved beyond those feelings and just had to get back into that mindset again. Again, he commented on Cliff's callousness, stating that it was a quality that he had "never observed up close before in anyone," which seemed like a naïve perception from the otherwise worldly Jonathan. I assumed, though, that his feelings were simply magnifying what Cliff had done. In what seemed like a case of sour grapes, Jonathan said that he thought that in the end, Cliff might be the bigger loser and hoped that Loren was as devoted as he would have been. Even though he said he was feeling better, I still hoped that Dan would come and give Jonathan the distraction and support that would counteract his ruminations.

Later that day, Jonathan wrote to tell me that Dan had decided to come. Throughout the day, he updated me on their activities and, more importantly, on his condition. Around 6:00, he e-mailed me to tell me that he and Dan had eaten lunch at the English pub where we'd previously eaten while they had "watched all of the cuties parade past." He said that later, they had gone shopping and he described in detail what they had bought. Dan had bought "a lovely old Austrian chocolate set all hand painted with roses" as a wedding present for his niece and Jonathan had bought "a Ven[e]tian glass paperweight shaped and coloured like [a] peach," which he intended to give as a gift to the host of a party to which he'd been invited on

Sunday. Jonathan said that because Dan didn't think he was in fit condition to be left alone he was going to spend the night. Jonathan was quick to add that they were "just friends," as if to allay any jealousy or concern on my part. Although he'd also been invited to a cocktail party that evening, he had decided not to go because he had felt faint earlier in the day and wasn't in the mood to see anyone with "red, glassy eyes."

Later that evening, he and Dan went to Tolliver's, where Jonathan and I had gone on our first date. Jonathan told me, however, that he would "rather have the company from [his] first visit there," which made me feel honored but sad that I wasn't there. He said that while he was there, a man had hit on him, which had made him feel desirable. He said that he and Dan had also gone to another gay-oriented restaurant where a man had hit on Dan. Even so, Dan had foregone pursuing the matter in part because he was planning to spend the night. Jonathan said that he was "terribly depressed," so he was glad that Dan had decided to stay. Jonathan told me that "an e-mail would be appreciated" and that he needed to "feel the connection." Again, I was flattered that he had turned to me, but I regretted that physically I couldn't be there.

Unfortunately, the diversion that Dan's visit had provided didn't have the desired effect. Around 4:00 the next morning, Jonathan sent me an e-mail in which he told me that he was having a rough night and wasn't able to sleep. He said that he couldn't stop thinking about not only Cliff, but also Glenn, Marcus, and everyone he had ever cared about, wondering what he had done wrong to deserve the misfortune that had befallen him. He said he felt he was experiencing some kind of karmic retribution for his sins. He said that Dan, who was sleeping in the same bed, had finally had to go sleep in the sunroom because Jonathan was tossing and turning so much. He said that "[e]ven the dogs complained." Around noon, he wrote again, repeating some of what he'd offered in his previous message because he hadn't yet heard from me and didn't know if I'd received his previous e-mail. In addition to what I already knew, he added that Dan, exhausted, had left around 11:00 and that he himself, also depleted, had decided not to go to the party. He told me he appreciated what Dan had done for him and so did I. Although I had just been there, I wished I could have been there myself.

Jonathan hadn't heard from me because I had spent most of the morning composing what I hoped would be a thoughtful message in which I tried to counteract his depressive thinking. My message was partly successful, but only partly. Although he thanked me for taking the time to "go through [his] neuroses," he went on to give his reasons for why he thought each of his previous relationships had ended in disaster. In the case of Glenn, he thought it was simply a matter of having grown apart. In the case of Cliff, why Cliff had done what he had was still a mystery to him. He told me that Dan had called him a "piece of shit" and to forget him, although Jonathan said it wasn't that simple. In the case of Marcus, he said that having been raised Catholic, he still carried a great deal of guilt because he had bought the motorcycle that Marcus was riding when he was injured. He said he believed that his current suffering was divine retribution and that he had been "waiting for the thunderbolt for the past 20 years." I thought that was ridiculous, was just a product of Jonathan's unhappiness and need to make sense out of something that seemed senseless, but nothing that I, or anyone else, did at that point, it appeared, was going to reach him.

I felt incredibly sorry for Jonathan. Although my perception of the situation was that Cliff had behaved as he had because he was trying to move on with his life but emotionally was still trapped between the old one and the new, I also believed that Cliff's behavior had been self-centered and thoughtless. I hated the thought of Jonathan being alone and distraught, so I decided to go to Paladin after class on Monday to keep him company for a day or two and do what I could to help him.

Because the Cliff situation had made his misgivings about remaining in the house, where they had lived, especially keen, Jonathan decided to take a look at other places he thought he might like to live. One of these options was a penthouse apartment downtown, and on Tuesday afternoon, we went to see it. I thought that was a good diversion and hoped it would make Jonathan feel that he was doing something constructive in furthering his goal of leaving the house on Millstone Drive.

After we arrived, we spoke with a young woman about the apartment. In the process of gathering basic information about him, she asked Jonathan what he did for a living. Since the rent on the apartment was $2,000 a month, having an adequate source of income was paramount. When she asked Jonathan where he worked, he told her that he worked at "Intellex." That was the first time that I had heard of "Intellex." Jonathan had told me that he worked at *OutSource*, but I wondered if OutSource might be a division of "Intellex." I didn't ask for clarification on the point, however, because I didn't consider it important.

After chatting for a while, we went to see the apartment. The view from the penthouse was spectacular. At thirty stories up, you could see most of Paladin stretching away for miles in every direction until it faded into the hazy, discernibly curved horizon. From that vantage, the city looked like an architect's model instead of the real thing. The view in broad daylight was breathtaking enough; I couldn't imagine what it looked like at night, the city ablaze and alive with a million lights, like some kind of bioluminescent creature that inhabited the ocean's unlighted depths. I could imagine even less what it would be like to be greeted with that view *every* night and, possibly, even come to take it for granted.

I left later that day, hoping that between Dan and me we had made some kind of difference, had done something useful to help Jonathan through the unexpected shock and the resurgence of painful feelings that he had believed, falsely, were permanently buried. I didn't want to leave him alone, but I had to attend to my life at home. Even so, I planned to return on Friday.

Around 12:30 Friday morning, Jonathan sent me an e-mail that ended on a mysterious note. After telling me about his day, he told me that a lot of things were going on and that we needed to talk. He assured me, though, that it wasn't a bad "let's go on *Jerry Springer*" talk, but just a "catch up" talk. I wondered what had happened, but his message gave no clue.

After I had arrived on Friday and had changed out of my "business drag," Jonathan and I went out into the front yard, where we talked.

"I got another e-mail from Cliff," he told me.

This was the news? I was underwhelmed. "Oh—I thought you were going to tell me that you'd slept with someone." At that point our relationship, it would not have been a major issue for me, since I was recently arrived on the scene and we were far from making a commitment.

"No," he said, shaking his head and sounding as if what I'd thought was absurd. "As long as I'm seeing you, I would never do that." Perplexed, he said, "I didn't think he'd write again."

"Really? *I* did."

"Did you?"

"Of course." *Of course* he was going to write again. He wasn't going to raise such an important issue then just let it drop. Although I had deeply ambivalent feelings about the reemergence of Cliff into Jonathan's life, I did feel that Cliff's approach of trying to deal directly with his unresolved feelings, regardless of Jonathan's reactions, was healthier than Jonathan's approach of emotional denial.

Jonathan told me he had pictures of Cliff that were sealed in an envelope. Apparently, he couldn't bring himself to look at them because of the emotion he feared they would provoke. Later that summer, however, he finally showed me the pictures. They depicted a man who resembled actor James Spader in his role as archaeologist Daniel Jackson in the 1994 science-fiction film *Stargate*.

Jonathan drew an analogy between the situation that existed among himself, Cliff, and me and that among the characters of Carrie, Aidan, and Big on *Sex and The City*. In the series, Carrie felt torn between Aidan, who was stable, responsible, and caring, and Big, who was dashing, debonair, and exciting. I was placed in the role of Aidan, while Cliff was placed in the role of Big. Despite Jonathan's decision not to rekindle his relationship with Cliff, I still felt second best and insecure about what ultimately would happen.

After Cliff's reappearance in Jonathan's life around the beginning of July, he never left. He remained part of Jonathan's life, at least indirectly, from then on. As far as I knew, Jonathan and Cliff had no physical contact, but they did stay in touch by e-mail and by phone. I thought this was healthier in some ways for the both of them, regardless of the divergent directions in which their lives had otherwise gone, but I retained my ambivalence about Cliff's continued presence. I thought it was distracting at best, destabilizing at worst. I tried to be supportive, but it was difficult. I thought that in some ways it would have been easier for me if Cliff had simply been gone, had simply abided by the deal that he and Jonathan had made not to have any further contact with each other. I knew, though, that was selfish of me, thought that their psychological well-being was more important and that if renewed contact helped them heal, then I shouldn't thwart it. At first, Jonathan seemed to suffer tremendously because of Cliff's presence, felt that he had reopened a very deep wound that had started to close, and seemed to keep on suffering because of Cliff for months to come. I assumed Cliff, in his own way, was doing the same.

In time, it would become clear who was suffering the greater harm.

—8—
PRIDE AND PREJUDICE

I love my black brothers and sisters. I think everyone should own one.

For all of his appealing qualities, I was not blind to the fact that Jonathan was not Prince Charming, at least if that character is used to symbolize the perfect partner. For each of his positive qualities, Jonathan possessed a negative one that counterbalanced it. While Jonathan was intelligent, well educated, cultured, and seemingly capable of genuine caring, he was also arrogant, bigoted, and critical of others while incapable of accepting criticism himself.

One of Jonathan's most offensive traits was his bigotry. He was prejudiced, not surprisingly, against Americans, whom he found aggressive, uncouth, and uncultured. He routinely made unfavorable comparisons between the British and the Americans, although he delivered most of these comments in an offhanded rather than aggressive manner. Having been raised as a member of the British upper crust, it seemed inevitable that he would be instilled with this standard-issue prejudice. Although I was irritated by some of his remarks, I also tried to keep in mind that he was a stranger in a strange land who had limited experience with American culture and that his comments probably reflected not only his ignorance, but also his anxieties about being in a foreign place.

His more flagrant bigotry was reserved for the members of specific groups, especially black people. One of the first things that I had noticed when I had visited his home for the first time was his collection of "black mammy" objects, including an Aunt Jemima cookie jar, a pair of salt and pepper shakers in the form of an Old South-style black maid and butler, and a measuring spoon holder in the form of a black butler. When I commented on them, he said that lots of people in England had them, that they were very collectible, and that no one thought anything about them. He also referred to black people as "Negroes," a word that made me wince. I informed him that we no longer used the word *Negro* in the United States because it was now considered offensive and that he should refrain from using it. He didn't.

Jonathan's most disturbing behavior toward black people manifested itself during our afternoon drives around Paladin. More often than not, our drives would take us through what Jonathan referred to as the "Hood," the areas of Paladin that contained a preponderance of black residents. He clearly relished these opportunities to see the people he referred to as "the babies." Because we would be driving through these areas on summer afternoons, when the weather would encourage people to be outdoors, we would always find plenty of black people sitting on their porches, working in their yards, walking along the streets, or engaging in some other public activity. To Jonathan, their presence was an irresistible invitation to engage in public activities of his own, invariably of an insulting nature. Jonathan might see a black woman with blond hair and yell, "Hey, baby, dat sho' is a nice 'do! You a *natural* blond?" He might see a heavyset black woman and yell, "Hey, honey, you sho' do gots some junk in da trunk!" He might see a black woman standing in a yard or, worse still, on a street corner, and yell, "Hey, baby, how much you chargin'?" Every time he would do this I would cringe, but there seemed to be little I could do to stop him.

Unfortunately, if he was the one doing the driving, there was little I could do get him to avoid these areas—indeed, he would actively seek them out—and if *I* was the one doing the driving, I would often find myself in the "Hood" inadvertently after Jonathan and I had been meandering through the residential areas in search of potential houses. If I was driving, I would always try to leave as fast as I could, although Jonathan always tried to make at least one scene.

His antipathy toward blacks, which normally expressed itself in more subdued forms, exploded one day in August into outright hostility. Around 5:00 in the afternoon of Wednesday, August 1, Jonathan sent me an e-mail in which he told me that he'd gone to the water company earlier that day to pay his bill. He said that after having been gone for only ten or fifteen minutes, he had returned to his car to find that someone had stolen his expensive wire hubcaps. He said that he had been parked in plain view of the security guard who was on duty, but that when he had gone to talk to him about what had happened, he had found him playing solitaire, oblivious to what was going on around him. He said the guard had called down "some fancy black person" who had told him that it wasn't their responsibility and had instructed him to contact his insurance agency regarding the matter. Jonathan described the man as "[v]ery dismissive and condescending." By that point, I knew Jonathan well enough to know that he was angrier than he was admitting.

Then, about 9:30 that evening, he wrote again, and this time, his true feelings toward the "fancy black person" had boiled to the surface. He stated that he was angrier than he had originally thought not only about the theft, but also about the attitude of "that fucking nigger," as he now blatantly called him. He claimed that even though he was angry, he would "let it go." He never mentioned the incident again, but I knew that he hadn't "let it go."

Whenever I would tell him that he was racist, he would dismiss my charges that he was a "racialist," as he called it, by saying, "I love my black brothers and sisters—I think everyone should own one." I was not amused. Eventually, whenever the issue of his racial attitudes would arise and I would remind him of his statement that everyone should own a black person, Jonathan would say, "Actually, I think they should own *two*."

Yet, despite his prejudice toward blacks, Jonathan became obsessed with soul food throughout that summer. Although he never fixed any himself, he spent the entire summer talking about how he wanted to sample various selections, especially chitterlings. The second weekend I spent with him, we bought barbecue from a local black-owned restaurant, which seemed to trigger his obsession. After leaving prematurely the next day because of the laryngitis I was suffering at the time, he wrote on Sunday to tell me that a friend of his had called him that morning and that he, along with a few others, had gone on a picnic for which they had gotten soul food from the same restaurant. According to Jonathan, the menu had consisted of "ribs, pigs feet, chicken and all the fixins" but no chitterlings. Although he didn't have the opportunity to try chitterlings throughout most of that summer, he was always trying to get me to try them, which I never had and which, given what they were—fried pig intestine—I didn't think I wanted to.

Finally, Jonathan's dream of eating chitterlings came true in August when he traveled to the Midwestern state. He had mentioned having friends who lived there, but this time, it was business that took him there. On Friday, the 17th, he wrote to tell me that while he was there, one of the representatives from the company he was doing business with, who was black, had taken everyone to a "real in the hood soul food place" for lunch. The restaurant was owned by his aunt, whose name was Luella. Jonathan said that when she saw her nephew come in, she "started bringing out food and didn't stop." The menu consisted of "neck bones, feet(pig and chicken), fried chicken, lamb shanks, greens , corn hash, beans, potatos fixed 3 ways, sweet potato pie, pecan pie and homemade carmel ice creme." He said that there was more but that it was "beyond [his] stomach or mind to figure some of it out." He said that Friday was traditionally chitterlings day in black families, so they were also on the menu. He said they tasted like "fried air" and had "[m]ore texture then taste but with an underflavor." I was amused that his dream of trying chitterlings had finally come true.

He said that Aunt Luella had adopted him and told him that he would have to come back and stay with her, which I thought was a rather generous gesture toward a complete stranger. Jonathan said that she wouldn't let them pay, so he had some flowers and a music box sent to her, which reminded me somehow of the gifts that he and even Dan had bought during their shopping trip the weekend Dan had stayed with him in the aftermath of Cliff's revelation. He stated that he'd sent her those tokens of appreciation instead of a bottle of liquor as he'd originally intended because Aunt Luella had informed him that she was a "church goin' woman" and didn't touch "the devil's brew."

Obviously one could love the cuisine of a particular group and still hate the members of that group unless, of course, they were performing a function that reinforced the stereotypes that the prejudiced had of them, such as Luella's performing her approved role as Jonathan's servant. I wondered what Luella would think of Jonathan's idea that everyone should own one—or two—black people.

Jonathan's bigotry was not, however, confined to blacks. He was also prejudiced toward Hispanics, once asking me, "I know you call a little Negro a pickaninny, but what do you call a little spic?" He also ridiculed my use of the term "Hispanic" instead of "Mexican," thinking it was too politically correct. Although certain areas of Paladin had concentrations of Hispanic people and we occasionally drove through or ate at Hispanic-owned Mexican restaurants in these neighborhoods, fortunately he didn't behave toward them the way he did toward blacks.

He also seemed to have a particular problem with Indians, Pakistanis—or "Pakis," as he called them—and, most of all, Arabs, who to him were synonymous with Muslims. He believed that the Indians and the "Pakis," especially the doctors he had encountered, were nothing but money-grubbers and would later comment that they were only interested in "MONEYMONEYMONEY." I had told him about my bad experience working for the businessman in Paladin, who happened to be Indian, and how he seemed obsessed with money. Although his being Indian was incidental, Jonathan took my experience with him as just another example of how Indians cared about money to the exclusion of everything else. To try to sway his opinion in a less prejudiced direction, I told Jonathan about my doctor, who was also Indian and who didn't want me to pay him for his services. Jonathan acted, however, as if this were an exception that proved the rule.

Because of his affinity for the Jews, Jonathan had come to hate the Arabs, especially the Palestinians, who had been trying for decades to reclaim what they believed to be their rightful land from the Jews of Israel. In an e-mail he sent to me on September 11, he described Arabs in particular and Muslims in general as "scum and baby killers" and expressed his hope that people now understood how the Israelis suffered because of them. He concluded the message by stating that the United States should "nuke the Arab bastards and wipe every one...[of] those fuckers out."

Ironically, Jonathan seemed to be blind to the potency of his own bigotry. In an e-mail he sent to me on September 12, the day after he had sent me the e-mail referring to Arabs as "scum and baby killers," he said that as Dan had watched footage of Arabs in Baghdad dancing in the streets at the news of what had happened in New York the day before, he had been screaming "kill the fuckers." Of that Jonathan said that while he "agree[d] with the sentiment," he thought Dan's reaction was "a little over the edge." In my opinion, there was little difference between Dan's reaction and Jonathan's, but Jonathan never saw it.

Indeed, Jonathan seemed to harbor some level of prejudice against everyone whose skin was not as lily-white as his own and referred to everyone whose skin was darker than his as "mud people."

One group of people who I soon noticed were conspicuously absent from Jonathan's life was women. Aside from his sister Charmaine, he appeared to have no meaningful relationships of any kind with women. The women who played any role in Jonathan's life were either female relatives or ones whose roles were purely functional, such as his secretary or his maid.

Indeed, the only people with whom he seemed to want to be friends or even to socialize were other gay men. Even here, however, he sometimes evinced the same disdain for them that he revealed toward others. In several e-mails he sent to me throughout June, Jonathan described, in disparaging terms, the "gay yuppie scum" he had encountered in Paladin. He derided them for their superficiality and conformity to various gay stereotypes as well as their lack of self-awareness and awareness of the wider cultural world. He accused most of them of being pretentious, having bad taste, being "pseudo-sophisticated," and being "provincial trying to be worldly." He described their world as a "piss elegant pseudo social scene" and believed that they accepted him only because he was British and possessed the presumed sophistication that went along with it. He said that his accent, background, position, and experiences impressed them "but for the wrong reasons" and said that he thought he could "pee in the wine glasses as long as [he] said something with [his] English accent whilst [he] was doing it." He said that perhaps *he* was the real snob, but that he couldn't help looking down on them for their pretensions.

To me, there was no "perhaps" about his being a snob. Several months later, during an argument in which I accused him—rightly—of thinking that he was better than everyone else because of the way he was raised, he replied, with all the condescension he could muster, "We *are* better!" Having been raised in an upper-crust British family, in which a belief in his innate superiority had been explicitly instilled and consistently reinforced, I suppose I couldn't have expected anything different.

In addition, I couldn't understand how he could be prejudiced. Apparently he had learned nothing about how it felt to be the victim of prejudice from being gay. So much for the "sensitization" hypothesis that stated that people who were the members of groups that suffered prejudice would be less prejudiced themselves because they knew what it was like and would be unwilling to mistreat others the way they themselves had been mistreated. Jonathan wasn't the only bigoted gay person I had ever met, but he was certainly the worst. I realized that prejudice was not determined by a single variable, that it usually had multiple sources, but it still perplexed me how suffering prejudice oneself frequently seemed to do nothing to soften a victim's attitude toward other targeted groups.

I thought I understood why Jonathan was the way he was, but I didn't like it. Coming from a value system in which people were judged on their "backgrounds" instead of their characters, I felt that he was missing a few things. For the most part, though, his arrogance, his belief in his own superiority, didn't manifest itself too often, but it was always there, beneath the surface, waiting to rear its ugly head with its eyes that looked down at most of the rest of us with disdain.

Under different circumstances, I would not have tolerated such flagrant bigotry and probably would have separated myself from someone who espoused such repugnant attitudes. I believed, however, that Jonathan, who had been raised "to run the British

Empire"—an empire that was infamous for its racism and prejudice in general—might benefit from exposure to someone who had been raised in a country that, in its better moments, upheld the ideals of equality and tolerance. In spite of having an IQ in the upper two percent of the population and 35 years of life experience, I was actually stupid enough to believe that I could somehow change him.

Jonathan was far more inclined to point out the failings of others, real or imagined, than he was to recognize his own. Indeed, almost from the beginning, I realized that one of Jonathan's favorite defense mechanism was *projection*, a Freudian term for a process in which people disown responsibility for their negative traits by accusing others of having the same traits. He was exquisitely sensitive to criticism, although he usually tried to maintain a façade of imperturbability. Failing that, he would react with condescension or derision, but rarely did he react with outright hostility. His hostility, I later came to learn, was saved for very specific threats to his sense of self.

His arrogance, his condescension, his blindness to his own faults and his inability to accept, or even acknowledge, the effects they had on the people around him eventually led to our first fight.

—9—
Much Ado About Nothing

I think that you are way too sensitive and over the edge.

There comes a point in every relationship when the "initial niceness," as a friend of mine once described it, wears off and whatever nastiness has been lying dormant finally erupts to the surface. Around the middle of July, six weeks into our relationship, Jonathan and I finally had our first major fight.

Initially, Jonathan didn't seem to have any problem with any aspect of my appearance. Despite my insecurity about sending him a picture of me, I had received a positive response. After he saw me in the flesh, however, his feelings seemed to change. From the day we met, he began to point out things about my appearance that he felt I needed to modify. Although his comments were always delivered in a seemingly benign, joking, well-meaning way, it soon became clear that he was serious.

The first thing that had to go was my underwear. The first time he made a comment about them was the first night we spent together. I usually wore basic white briefs and saw no reason to wear anything else. Jonathan, however, did. He described my briefs, which he called "knickers," as "grandpa pants" and said they looked "poor." He said that I should wear bikini briefs—as he did—because they were not only better looking, but also more functional, since you only had to pull down the waistband to urinate instead of having to use the fly. He said that European men usually wore bikini briefs and implied they were somehow more sophisticated than the ones I wore. In order to "persuade" me to do as he wished, he even told me that

Kyle had started wearing them after he had suggested he do so. I responded by telling him that was *Kyle's* problem.

Jonathan even made a special point to mention my underwear in several e-mails that he sent to me between the middle of June, after our first meeting, and the middle of July. During the five days that I spent with him around the beginning of July, the issue seemed to attain special significance. In the two days that followed my return home, he sent me at least two e-mails in which he commented on the "problem." In the first, he expressed his hope that someone had given me new underwear for my birthday. In the second, he told me that Dan was coming to Paladin and the two were going shopping, so he asked me for my waist size "in case we see some decent panties." He even claimed he had discussed the matter with Horatio, almost making it seem as if it were the *only* matter relating to me that he had discussed with him.

At first, I didn't take his remarks too seriously—it was such an odd thing to focus on that surely he had to be joking—and I responded by joking back. But, as time passed, I realized that, for him, it was no joke. Every time we were together, he would make some comment about my underwear, sometimes saying something about them several times in one day. Eventually, it became clear to me that he really *didn't* like my underwear and really *did* want me to wear a different kind. And, eventually, his comments went from being ridiculous and harmless to being irritating, even insulting.

Then there was my hair. When I met Jonathan, my hair was almost shoulder length and permed. In addition, I had changed the color from a flat medium brown suffused with a little gray to an even golden brown. Although he had initially described my hairstyle as "flattering," he began to feel that I would look better with a different one. In particular, he thought I should get a buzz cut, a style that many young men were wearing that summer. I felt that because of a flat spot on the back of my head, combined with my protruding ears, I would look terrible with a buzz cut and didn't plan to get one. Even so, Jonathan expended considerable effort trying to convince me that I would look good with one. He told me that my hair was "overprocessed" and expressed his opinion that people looked better with their natural hair color. As for the latter, he told me that my hair looked "peach" colored and often referred to my "peachy" hair. He pointed out men on television who had buzz cuts then raved about how good they looked and how good *I* would look with one. Every time we went out and saw some young man with a buzz cut, Jonathan would point him out and point out how good it looked on him. He told me that getting a new haircut would give me a new attitude, although I wasn't sure what was wrong with the attitude I had. Over time, I became tired of hearing the constant refrain about how unflattering my hair apparently looked.

Then there was my driving. Apparently I didn't drive as fast or as forcefully as Jonathan thought I should and he began referring to me, as he did to Dan, as an "old lady" driver. I was cautious about my driving, but apart from simply understanding the importance of being careful, I was also driving in a city with one of the highest automobile accident rates in the country and had been in several near-collisions because of the recklessness of some Paladin drivers. In addition, I was driving a car that was becoming increasingly dilapidated and not knowing how I was going to afford a new one in the near future, I had further incentive to be careful. None of this mattered to Jonathan. As time went on, I heard more and more about the inadequacies of my driving habits.

Jonathan's behavior continued for a month before I decided to make some comments of my own.

The weekend of July 14, I was once again staying with Jonathan. It was our fifth time together, and for the fifth time in a row, Jonathan took aim at my underwear, my hair, and my driving. Mainly to appease him, I agreed to go shopping for new underwear. We went to a shopping mall where I ended up buying a three-pack of bikini briefs. I did the driving, which didn't please him, and I did the buying, which did. In retrospect, *he* should have done the driving and *he* should have done the buying, since *he* was the one who had the problem. To strike some kind of acceptable compromise between what he wanted and what I wanted, I bought the blandest colors possible: black, white, and gray.

By the time the weekend was over, my level of discomfort had finally reached the point that I could no longer conceal it. Although I didn't say anything to Jonathan about its source, I became increasingly withdrawn, increasingly preoccupied not with *whether* I would tell him about the comments and the effect they were having on me, but with *how* I would tell him. This was the first semi-serious issue that had arisen between us and I was reluctant to be the one to spoil what had, so far, remained relatively unspoiled.

Sunday night, I dressed in pajamas instead of simply stripping down to my underwear, not only because I wanted it to be a sign to Jonathan that I was not feeling sexual, but also because I did not want to be hassled once again about my underwear. (He had also had comments to make about my "jammies," saying that Glenn had worn them and implying there was something juvenile about them.) He commented that I seemed "brittle," which was one criticism with which I fully agreed. Unlike many men, I have never been able to separate my feelings from sex well enough to be able to have sex with someone at whom I am pissed off.

Monday morning, after Jonathan had left for work, I wandered around the house for a while, contemplating whether or not to write him a note in which I addressed his constant comments about my underwear, my hair, my driving, me. On the shallowest level, I had simply grown tired of the comments, which I felt had gotten out of hand.

On a deeper level, I didn't like the fact that his criticisms largely concentrated on my appearance. I had always been sensitive about my appearance, a feeling that had been fostered not only by the values of a society in which women died from eating disorders trying to become thin and men destroyed their bodies with steroids trying to become "buff," but also by the values of the gay subculture in which looks seemed to mean everything, seemed to make the difference between having love and being alone.

My deepest concern, however, was that his "suggestions" that I change my underwear, my hair, reflected an underlying desire to change *me*, to *control* me. In his ad, Jonathan had said that he wasn't a "control freak," but I began to wonder if the reason he had mentioned that particular fact was that the issue had arisen before.

I knew how control freaks operated. They always started out small, suggesting that you do something minor, like change the kind of underwear you wore. In addition, they wouldn't try to effect the change they wanted through coercion or force, but through subtlety and manipulation. They would tell you that you would somehow be better off if you did what they wanted, making you feel that they only had your best interest at heart, or they might tell you that if you *really* cared about them, you would do it to make them happy, making you feel uncaring or unreasonable for not doing something so trivial. By taking the subtle, manipulative approach, it made it much more difficult for you to see what they were really doing, what was really happening and, therefore, much more difficult to resist. Once they had succeeded in getting you to comply with smaller "requests," they could then more easily persuade you to comply with larger ones as you gradually became conditioned to feel that what you were doing was natural. Eventually, you had not only started wearing different underwear, but also cut yourself off from your family and friends and become the prisoner of a person who had, through your own unwitting complicity, deprived you of your self-determination and personal power. If Jonathan were in fact a control freak, then I needed to know and it needed to stop.

By that point, we had already had some smaller disagreements, based largely on cultural differences. When I had told him, for example, that I had tried to find additional information about his family on the Internet and had found information about him and Terrence, he had disapproved of what I had done, calling it "ill-bred." He said that in the social world from which he came, a person's privacy was paramount and that violating it was a serious breach of social etiquette. This was, after all, a subculture in which everyone was supposed to keep everything to themselves. I countered by telling him that the information I had found was on the *Internet*, where it couldn't be any more *public*. It wasn't as if I'd gone snooping through his personal things or even that deeply into his personal life. He may have felt that he had a right to privacy, but I also had a right to know whom I was involved with. Even so, Jonathan seemed to place a high value on his privacy and didn't want anyone prying too deeply into his life. As some kind of measure of his feeling on this point, when I had mentioned finding the web page on which he was dressed as a detective, the page had mysteriously disappeared just a few days later. Jonathan was obviously behind the deletion, although I never asked him about it. He clearly behaved as if he didn't want anyone to find out anything about him.

By that point, I was bothered by other things as well. In the beginning, he had seemed as interested in me and my life as I had his, but rather swiftly, the focus shifted from us to him. Our conversations became dominated by stories of *his* family, *his* friends, *his* past, *his* plans, *his* thoughts, *his* feelings, *his* wants, *his* needs, *his* drama, his *everything*. Whenever I would tell him about *my* life, it would seem to go in one ear and out the other unless it related to him in some way. Otherwise, much of what I had to say about myself and my life seemed irrelevant. After several weeks, I felt that he still had a limited understanding of me and didn't seem as interested in me on *my* terms, for *my* sake as he should have been for someone who otherwise seemed so enthusiastic about knowing me. I was beginning to wonder if he was interested in me for me or if he merely wanted a warm body around to satisfy his needs. I was starting to feel devalued, especially in light of his incessant comments about how I should "improve" myself.

In the end, I decided not to write a note but to call him when I returned home from work. Later that afternoon, I called. I told him I had something I wanted to discuss with him, but was initially hesitant to be more forthcoming. Finally, Jonathan told me that if I had something to say, then I should just say it. Somewhat falteringly, I told him that I didn't understand why he was making such an issue out of such superficial features as my underwear and hair and that it was almost as if he were trying to change me.

His reaction was one of irritation and dismissal. He told me I was blowing things out of proportion precisely because his suggestions were so minor. He told me that I was overly sensitive and that I reacted to what people said as if I were viewing it in a shaving mirror that made things seem much bigger than they actually were. He said that because I had never been in a long-term relationship, I didn't understand how things worked in relationships, that what he had been saying and doing was simply a normal part of the interchange that went on between two people. He even told me I was acting like a "sod," a British term of contempt.

By the time he was finished, I felt as if I had been slapped in the face. I was surprised, and stunned, by the vehemence of his reaction. I was also frustrated and dismayed because I felt that he hadn't understood me at all, didn't seem to want to understand. Perhaps because I was taken aback, and because I didn't want to prolong the fight, I backed down.

After our conversation, I started to compose an e-mail in which I tried to explain, in more coherent form, why I was disturbed by his constant nitpicking. I tried to make the point that his specific behaviors were, for me, indicators of a bigger, more troubling issue: a seeming attempt to change me into something that *he* wanted me to be that was becoming more intensive as time passed. I wasn't trying to provoke another fight, only to clarify what I had previously said.

By 11:00 that night, I still hadn't completed it. Around that time, Jonathan sent me a brief e-mail that was light in tone. It began by expressing mock surprise over the fact that I hadn't sent him my usual evening e-mail, then warned me—jokingly, it seemed—not to take him for granted because other men had expressed interested in him. He then went on to tell me that he was exhausted and was going to bed because he had a full if typical day at work the next day and was planning to look at a loft at 6:00 the next evening. He ended by telling me that he looked forward to hearing from me "eventually." The message, though vaguely manipulative, revealed no animosity, but gave the impression that he felt he had won, had succeeded in squelching my concerns.

For me, however, the issues had not been resolved, only dismissed. Although I softened my message somewhat in response to his lightened tone, I remained firm in my position. Later that night, I finally completed and sent it, hoping it would have a constructive effect.

It didn't.

Instead, I received another, even harder slap in the face. The next morning around 8:00, I received his reaction. Largely restating his remarks from the previous day, he began by voicing his opinion that

I was "way too sensitive and over the edge," indicating that he thought there were bigger problems than my underwear or my hairstyle. According to him, I always expected to be insulted and he "really, truly" felt that because I lived "where and how" I did—that is, lived in a smaller Midwestern city and was relatively unsocial—it had "limited [my] vistas and narrowed [my] outlook." In his opinion, I hadn't become fully socialized, not just into the gay community in particular, but also into mainstream society in general. He said that since I had never had, in his estimation, a "serious, long term gay relationship"—something that he found unusual at my age—I didn't understand how relationships worked, didn't understand in general how people related to each other. He also commented on how I didn't seem to have any close men friends, gay or otherwise, and consequently didn't seem to understand that close friends discussed everything—such as his discussing his dislike for my underwear with Horatio. He said that he had other close friends, including some Americans, and that they discussed everything as well, no matter how personal. He stated that although he wasn't perfect, *he* understood how personal relationships worked and the compromises that people needed to make. He congratulated himself on having been successful on a personal level and having been able to maintain "all types" of relationships for "long periods" of time. Although he had expressed the opinion that my lack of understanding about relationships came in part from living in Hawthorn, he finally suggested that my social isolation stemmed not from where I lived, but from something deeper. He made it clear that he was not going to censor what he said or worry if the next thing that came out of his mouth upset me.

Not content to stop at me, he dragged my family into the fray by stating that it "greatly concerned" him that I came from a family in which *no* one seemed to be able to maintain long-term intimate relationships. He observed that my parents lived solitary lives and that my sister had her "own pattern with men"—that is, had left two marriages. He suggested that because I had never seen a long-term relationship, I didn't understand how they worked. By that point, he had come to view Kathryn as self-absorbed and told me that in my own way I was just as self-absorbed as she was, but with "more awareness of other people"—though, apparently, not *much* more.

He reminded me that my two "semi relationships" with Cole and Henri had been of "extremely short" duration and that instead of fighting for those relationships when problems had arisen, I had fled. He expressed the opinion that in spite of leaving for reasons that "seemed real to [me]," I should have done more to help Cole overcome his drinking if I had really loved him. In addition, he questioned my claim that Henri had kept his sexual behavior secret as long as he had, stating that people weren't that devious or at least the ones that *he* had known had not been able to maintain façades long term and in time the truth about them had always emerged. Unwilling or unable to deal with relationship problems, I took the easy way out and ran off at the first sign of trouble.

Then, generalizing from his interpretation of my behavior in those situations, he expressed his opinion that *nothing* seemed important enough to me to fight for it. He reminded me that when things had gotten tough for me in Paladin, I had "[run] back to Mummy" in Hawthorn instead of staying and fighting to rebuild my life there. He congratulated himself on how, despite the fact that things were difficult for him now, *he* wasn't running back to England where he could have an easy life. His comment suggested that he believed the disparity between the life he was living in Paladin and the one he could be living in England was far greater than the disparity between the life I was living in Hawthorn and the one I had lived in Paladin, which made his fortitude appear even grander.

He ended his assault by telling me that if these "minor" things had assumed such importance, then perhaps our relationship wasn't progressing the way he wanted either. He told me we should carefully think about what we wanted to happen next and ask ourselves what he called the "Dear Abby" question: Was I better with him or without him? The next move, he said, was mine.

I found his diatribe insulting and infuriating. I was shocked at the way he had taken pieces of what I had told him about myself and had rearranged them to produce a picture of someone who, at 35, had no understanding of even the most basic elements of human interaction. If he had bothered to absorb more information about me, he might have had a clearer picture of who I was. In spite of having always been unsocial, I had been social enough that in my 35 years, I had participated in all of the different types of relationships that people had and knew very well how they functioned. Worse, he had painted me as someone who was fundamentally unable to form and maintain close relationships of *any* kind because of some deep-seated flaw in my psychological makeup. Did he really think of me in those terms? If he really felt that I was so horribly flawed, why had he continued to date me? Or, was he simply using whatever ammunition he had—or *thought* he had—to avoid taking any kind of personal responsibility?

Despite his claim that he was able to maintain "all types" of relationships, that did not appear to be true. Although he found it peculiar that I didn't have men, including gay ones, as friends, I found it equally peculiar that *he* didn't have anything *but gay men* as friends. This appeared to be a lifelong preference. Even here, though, he often seemed to look down on them. Other types of people were conspicuously absent from his life, including *heterosexual* men and—especially—*women*. Apart from his sister Charmaine—who was, after all, his *sister*—Jonathan had *no* female friends and didn't appear to have ever had. Indeed, he demonstrated an aversion to women, especially to women's sexuality. Whenever we would see a naked woman on TV—and especially if we would see two women being sexual—Jonathan would invariably make some comment about how he couldn't watch, how it was making him ill. He would always say it jokingly, but beneath the façade of humor, he evinced a palpable dislike for women. My lack of male friends, gay or otherwise, was largely situational, but Jonathan's overabundance of gay male friends appeared to be primarily psychological. If he found the absence of close men friends, gay or otherwise, from my life a cause for concern, I found the absence of non-gay men, and especially women, from his equally troubling, if not more so.

In addition to what he had said about me, I was shocked at the way he had dragged my family into the fight, accusing my mother and sister of having the same inability to maintain "long term intimate relationships" that I allegedly had. Once again I wondered how long a relationship had to last before he considered it "long term." My mother had been married for 21 years, while my sister had been married for 10 and 12 years, respectively. The shortest of those three marriages had lasted longer than *his* relationship with *Glenn* had, which was apparently his longest-lasting relationship. By his own standards, he himself didn't seem to be able to maintain "long term intimate relationships." He did not, however, seem to consider how his *own* standards applied to *himself*.

I did not allow his attack go unchallenged.

In response, I told him that I found his tirade not only presumptuous and ill-informed, considering that he had known me for only a few weeks, but also self-flattering at my expense. I told him that for someone who was supposed to be so well-bred, dragging my mother and sister into the argument was gratuitous and low and reminded him that my mother and sister had, in my opinion, had no choice but to end relationships that ultimately had lasted longer than his longest one. I told him that if he had bothered to find out more about me instead of always talking about himself, he might by now have a better and more accurate understanding of who I really was.

Making certain he understood more fully how his self-important behavior had affected me, I pointed out how the focus had, in short order, shifted from *us* to *him*. First, he had gone from wanting to hear everything about me to wanting to talk only about himself. Second, he had never offered to come to Hawthorn to visit me, having always expected me to come to him, and had never offered to help me buy gas when I had a limited income and he could well afford it. And, finally, I reminded him that in spite of having known him for only six weeks, I had done my best to be supportive of him as the problems in his life had accumulated. This was especially true in regard to the situation between him and Cliff, which had placed me in the uncomfortable position of helping him deal with his feelings toward an ex-boyfriend whose presence in his life, it seemed, was emotionally more powerful than mine. However he decided to respond, I had at least told him how I felt about the more important issues that had been troubling me.

In response, he essentially repeated and rationalized what he had said the first time, although now, he seemed to have cooled down. He began by telling me that in his previous message, he was simply trying to be as frank as possible with me. He maintained his belief that most of his observations were valid and claimed that he had mentioned my mother and sister only because they served as role models for my own relationship behavior. He claimed that he was "not criticizing, only observing," making an objective assessment of my situation. He expressed his belief that he wasn't congratulating himself regarding his own relationships, restating that he knew how to form and maintain friendships over a long period of time and that his ability to assess people's strengths and weaknesses, a skill that he had developed in his work, was transferable to his personal life.

In addition, he claimed that he had talked about himself and his relationships as much as he had not to be self-centered, but to give me a clearer picture of who he was. A couple of weeks before, he had told me that, in his opinion, the more information I had about him, the better I could understand who he was and he had just been acting in accordance with that belief.

Further, he pointed out that I had led him to believe that it wasn't a strain, either financially or practically, to come to Paladin, which was why he didn't feel compelled to come to Hawthorn. He said that even though he hadn't given me money for gas, he understood that I was on a budget and had tried to minimize my expenses by paying for meals and other items. Although I had paid what I believed to be my fair share, he referred to the "occasional" times I had done this as a "nice gesture."

Moreover, he claimed that he had never come to Hawthorn because I had never invited him. That was untrue, but I had mentioned the qualification that because of my living situation, having him stay the night would be impossible. As if I didn't know how to invite someone to do something and needed to be told, he explained to me, "Why don't you come over on Saturday?" telling me that was how it was done.

He ended the message by telling me that although he appreciated my support over the past several weeks, finding my concern for him both kind and loving, and had tried to reciprocate it, he was a strong person and would persevere. He was dismayed that things between us were turning ugly and, although he liked me a great deal, perhaps it was better to separate than to allow things to continue in such a confrontational mode. He told me we needed to think about what we wanted for ourselves, both as individuals and as a couple.

By the time the exchange was over, I was exhausted. I felt that he hadn't really heard me, that he didn't *want* to hear me, that he hadn't really taken responsibility for his thoughtless behavior. I was dismayed that things had gotten so out of hand, that he had reacted the way he had. I would never have anticipated unleashing such a torrent of recrimination, especially in someone whom I had thought was more civilized and self-aware.

Around 7:30 that evening, he sent me an e-mail in which he told me about the telemetry the doctors were requiring him wear to monitor his heart condition. In addition, he mentioned that his father was feeling "a bit nervey," but didn't mention why. The message ended on an uncertain note, stating that he would see me on Friday, "if that [was] still [my] plan." He expressed his opinion that the situation between us had gotten out of control and he expressed his hope that things had settled down because enough was happening.

Later that evening, I sent a placative e-mail in which I expressed my desire not to fight. I also mentioned some other, less incendiary issues. Strangely, I didn't hear from him the next day and by that evening, I wondered why I hadn't. Was he still angry? I sent him a message late that evening in which I commented that I hadn't heard from him all day. It wasn't until Thursday morning around 8:00 that I finally received a response.

After commenting, accusingly, that he hadn't heard from *me* the day before, he went on to inform me that Wednesday had been a "full and tough day." For one, that was the day that his father had undergone his cancer surgery. He reported that although the procedure itself had gone well, his father had suffered an episode of cardiac/respiratory distress, which was unexpected and upsetting. Fortunately, he had recovered, but the surgeon had stated that his father might need chemotherapy to make certain the cancer was fully eliminated. His doctors had not previously recommended it, so the unexpected change in treatment was concerning.

Then, he proceeded to inform me that because he hadn't gone to England to be present for the surgery, which his family had expected, he had been given "total hell" from almost every member of his family, especially Leandra, and had officially been branded "the worst child and sibling." But, even though his family had been condemning, others had been supportive. Colin had visited Jonathan's mother at home and had sent Jonathan at least three e-mails with updates about his father's condition. One of his nephews had sent flowers to his father and had e-mailed Jonathan to see how both he and his father were doing. After hearing about the confrontation with Leandra, Dan had offered to come to Paladin to stay with Jonathan, as he had when Jonathan had received the devastating news from Cliff two weeks before. Even Glenn had written to him not once but twice inquiring about his father. "It's nice to have good friends," he commented.

This was in contrast to *me*, who had, in Jonathan's eyes, been thoughtless not to have remembered that Wednesday had been the day of his father's surgery. In several places throughout the message, he expressed his dismay over my seeming lack of interest. In telling me that he had heard from many of his friends, he casually suggested that perhaps I had been too busy to inquire. In another place, he outright told me that he was disappointed that he hadn't heard from me. In yet another place, his sarcasm was especially unrestrained, commenting that he didn't know if I had been too busy, had been preoccupied with our fight, or believed that each e-mail had to be answered before another one could be sent. His "It's nice to have good friends" remark was meant not to praise his friends, but to condemn me.

Then, dropping the inflammatory issue of my perceived lack of interest in his father, he moved on to more neutral ones. First, he told me that Wednesday had been the day that his doctor had required him to wear the heart telemetry, which had been removed around 5:00. Otherwise, he said little about it, stating only that he was supposed to see his primary doctor that afternoon at 4:00. In addition, he had attended a management committee meeting regarding the company in California that wanted to buy into OutSource. The meeting, which had lasted for more than two hours, had ended in a non-binding, preliminary vote with six members in favor, two opposed, and one abstaining. Although the meeting had clarified the situation for him, it had also now put him in the position of trying to figure out the best way to handle it.

In the message, he told me I was welcome to come over that weekend, but his invitation seemed formal and I didn't feel welcome. He ended the message with an equally bland request to let him know if I was coming.

After reading the message, I felt terrible. I hadn't meant to forget that Jonathan's father's surgery had been scheduled for Wednesday, something that Jonathan hadn't mentioned for more than three weeks, or Jonathan's heart telemetry. I felt that through my sin of omission, I had worsened, or certainly hadn't bettered, a raw situation. I didn't feel that the Internet was the most productive method for resolving the issue, so I wrote to Jonathan and told him that I wanted to talk to him directly. Having cooled down, he agreed to call me.

That afternoon around 3:30, the phone rang. It was Jonathan. He began by asking me not to be "cross." Apparently he didn't want to fight any further. We had what proved to be a civilized conversation in which we discussed, calmly, not only the issues that had provoked the fight, but also some other goings-on in his life, including the aftermath of his father's surgery and his impending doctor's visit. We spoke for only about twenty minutes, and although the conversation was civilized, it was somewhat strained by lingering tension. Even so, I affirmed that I was planning to come on Friday and thought that after everything that had happened, we needed to see each other, directly, regardless of what ultimately happened between us.

When I went to Jonathan's that Friday afternoon, I felt apprehensive about what might happen. I was prepared for the worst and was prepared to leave that night, if the situation warranted it. That, however, did not happen. Although our conversation about what had happened between us earlier in the week was rather tense, and ultimately he didn't take as much responsibility for the fight as I would have liked, we did manage to come to a certain understanding about each other. Later that evening, we went to see *A.I.* By that point, we were feeling civil enough to hold hands throughout the movie. The rest of the weekend went well, and on Sunday afternoon, Jonathan said that he was feeling a lot better about things than he had been two days before. So was I, to say the least. By the time I left, things had gotten back to the way they had been before the problems had arisen and were perhaps even better, in fact, because we had largely cleared the air about certain things that had been bothering us and had put them behind us.

When I arrived home Monday afternoon, I wrote to tell him not only that I'd arrived safely, but also that I came away feeling that things between us were once again headed in the right direction.

Later that evening around 10:30 he replied. His tone was much lighter, more conciliatory, than it had been the week before. After making some small talk by commenting on how he'd just gotten home after a long day and how hot the day had been, he assured me that everything between us was fine. He reemphasized a point that he had made while I was there, which was that he wanted "no grudges, no repercussions, no pay backs" to operate in our relationship. He said that although he knew we would disagree and probably argue in the future, he expressed his wish to avoid the same kind of blowup again by not stockpiling petty grievances until our feelings got out of control. Although I felt that some of my grievances weren't "petty," I also felt that his attitude was mature and reasonable and I couldn't have agreed more.

After that, I didn't hear any more about the issues that had provoked the fight. Other, larger issues would, however, arise to take their place.

—10—
CHASE

I am not a good liar or cheater or cover up[p]er.

The five days that I spent with Jonathan during the first week of July marked a turning point in our relationship in more ways than one. In addition to the reemergence of Cliff into Jonathan's life, the first week of July witnessed the introduction of a new character into the *dramatis personae*: Chase. According to Jonathan, Chase was a 22-year-old pianist from Paladin who was studying music at the university in Hawthorn where I had studied. Unfortunately, Chase had developed stage fright, which was interfering not only with his ability to complete his music program in particular, but also with his ability to function in his career in general. To help him overcome his anxieties, he had been referred to the Stress Center, where he was participating in the same stress-reduction classes as Jonathan. Chase, as it turned out, was also gay and, the instant he had laid eyes upon him, he had taken an interest in Jonathan. Chase, who appeared to be extroverted and assertive, did not hesitate in letting Jonathan know how he felt.

Jonathan first told me about Chase while I was visiting him during the first week of July. Jonathan seemed flattered that someone that young was interested in him, but he questioned the foundation on which Chase's feelings were built. Because Chase seemed to be intrigued with Jonathan mainly because he was British, Jonathan felt that Chase saw him not as an individual, but as a symbol—a symbol of the refinement, sophistication, and upper-crust life of which he wished to be a part. Chase made this clear when he explicitly told Jonathan that he had "always dreamed of having an English boyfriend and someday living in London," as Jonathan reported.

Jonathan had found that many Americans reacted to him as a symbol, not as a person, and found it dismaying. In addition, Chase was much younger than Jonathan was, fully half his age. Jonathan was middle aged, while Chase was barely past adolescence. Jonathan seemed more amused than anything by Chase's youthfulness and persistence and didn't seem to take it too seriously.

The Thursday after I returned home from my five-day stay, Jonathan sent me an e-mail in which he told me the latest about the situation between him and Chase. He said that while he had been at the Stress Center that afternoon, he had seen Chase. He described Chase as being "cute and a little unsophisticated" and said that his attempts to get his attention were "obvious" but "sweet." He said that Chase had learned about him through a friend of a friend, though Jonathan didn't elaborate on the connection. As far as their activities at the Center that day were concerned, he said that they had done relaxation exercises and had drunk a lemonade together before he had gone back to the office and Chase had disappeared. He said that although he was flattered that someone Chase's age was interested in him, he was "way too young" for him. "Besides," he said, "I am sort of interested in someone else." At the time, I found the situation amusing as well and didn't expect anything to come of it. The fact that Jonathan didn't mention Chase in any of his e-mails to me the following week only seemed to confirm that he wasn't taking the situation too seriously.

The week after that, however, the "relationship" between Jonathan and Chase took a different turn. On Monday, the 16th, Jonathan and I had our first fight, and on Tuesday, the fight that had started on the phone erupted online and raged throughout that day. On Wednesday, Jonathan's father underwent his surgery and Jonathan suffered the reproach of his family, who had attacked him for not having come to England to be with his father. Those incidents, combined with Jonathan's continuing stresses at work and problems with health, drove Jonathan to feel that he needed to get away from things for a while.

As it happened, he chose to do so with Chase. On the evening of Wednesday, the 18th, he and Chase went out to have dinner and "hit a bar or two," as Jonathan described it. He said that it was "fun to get away and not have all kinds of problems or issues to deal with." He added that he had come home "alone."

In spite of having come home "alone," this was the first time that Jonathan and Chase had engaged in any "extracurricular" activities—done anything outside of the Stress Center. I understood Jonathan's need to relieve his stress, but his barhopping with Chase didn't relieve *mine*. In addition, I felt that Jonathan was making an unfavorable comparison between Chase and me, suggesting, it seemed, that while Chase was problem free, I was problem full. I wished *I* had had someone "fun" to get away with—Jonathan wasn't the *only* one with stress—but I didn't. I was starting to become dismayed by the situation.

The following week, after Jonathan and I had made up, Jonathan told me that Chase's feelings, and the forcefulness of his pursuit, were only growing stronger. On Monday, the 23rd, Jonathan wrote to tell me that he had seen Chase that day and, realizing that the situation was getting out of hand, he had had a long talk with him about his feelings toward him in an attempt to quell them. Unfortunately, Chase wasn't listening. He had told Jonathan that he was in love with him and, having watched *Queer As Folk* the night before, he had compared Jonathan with Brian and himself with Justin. Jonathan said that he had told Chase he was seeing someone, but Chase had told him that it didn't matter because *he* was right for Jonathan, not me. Jonathan said that he had told Chase he was twice his age, but Chase had told him that it didn't matter because he liked older men who had some sophistication. Jonathan said that he had told Chase he was a foreigner and didn't understand Chase's life or lifestyle, but Chase had told him that it didn't matter because he had always dreamed of having an English boyfriend and living in London. Jonathan said that he had told Chase he wouldn't go out with him again, but Chase had told him that he would, that it was only a matter of time before Jonathan realized he loved him and they belonged together. Jokingly, Jonathan told me that he guessed he was going to have to break up with me since his "other" boyfriend wouldn't let him date other men. Then, seriously, he told me that Chase wasn't going to give up and that although the situation was "somewhat funny," it was also "not funny at all." He asked me for advice about what to do.

In response, I pointed out the obvious, which was that Chase's interest in and pursuit of him appeared to be based entirely on what *Chase* wanted, not on what *Jonathan* wanted, that it was, all in all, a predictable outgrowth of Chase's immaturity and resulting inability to distinguish fantasy from reality. I told Jonathan that perhaps the best way to fend him off was to continue to assert why a relationship between the two of them wouldn't work, to reinforce that he was, in fact, a *real* person, not a fantasy creation. I realized that although Chase didn't appear to be listening to reason, I hoped that if Jonathan repeated his points long enough, Chase would eventually come to his senses.

The next afternoon, Jonathan wrote to tell me that he had been too busy at work to go to the Stress Center, so he hadn't seen Chase.

He had come to the conclusion that in some ways he was going to distance himself from him, but not entirely avoid him, since he did like him as a person and didn't want to hurt him. Given that it had been only a few days since our first fight, Jonathan quipped that perhaps I could tell Chase how awful he was, which might help to drive him away. He said that he certainly wouldn't sleep with him or allow himself to be alone with him if possible. He said that Chase was scheduled to go back to school in Hawthorn in three weeks, which would take care of the immediate problem. He agreed with me that Chase viewed him as "an emblem not a real person" and that it was all about *his* needs. Even so, Jonathan seemed slighted that I had suggested Chase saw nothing genuine in him, especially when it came to his looks. He "reminded" me that he wasn't considered a "complete dog" and that it was possible for someone to find him "vaguely" attractive. That hadn't been my intention, but the comment seemed to reveal his insecurities about his appearance.

For the next few days, Jonathan tried to walk a fine line between being friendly toward Chase but not being *too* friendly. He didn't want to give Chase any encouragement when Chase seemed to need little. Even so, Chase was persistent. On Thursday, the 26th, Jonathan reported that Chase and he had gone on their first "date"—as Chase defined it. Jonathan said that Chase had asked him to have lunch with him and that he'd done it because he didn't want to give Chase the impression he was avoiding him. He said that he had "[k]ept it light" but also said that on Chase's part, there had been "[l]ots of smiling and being cute." He said that Chase had tried to play footsie with him under the table but that he had "gently but firmly pulled [his] foot back." He said that they had hugged goodbye but hadn't set a "next date." All in all, Jonathan thought that things had gone well and that in spite of describing Chase as "very cute…[a]lmost too cute," indicating a certain amount of sexual attraction on Jonathan's part, he had managed to stay on the friendly side of the line that separated simple friendliness from sexual encouragement.

On Saturday, the 28th, Jonathan and I drove downtown to visit the shops. Later, I learned that while we were out, someone had seen the two of us together: Chase. Apparently, Chase had been either entering or leaving a music store downtown when we had driven past. For the first time, Chase had gotten a good look at me and—perhaps predictably—had not been pleased with what he saw. The next time he saw Jonathan, he had described me as "withered" and "red-haired"—the latter apparently an insult—and looking "much older" than 35. I understood that his reaction was a predictable expression of his rivalrous feelings toward me, but since no one likes to be insulted, and since I had always been sensitive about being thin, I was irritated by the comments. In addition, I felt it was unfair that *I* hadn't gotten a look at *Chase* and, therefore, couldn't offer *my* opinion.

That same weekend, I went with Jonathan to have his hair buzz-cut. By that point, he had been "encouraging" me for weeks to have my own hair buzz-cut, which I refused to do, so he decided to get a buzz cut himself. The cut turned out very well and flattered Jonathan's features about as well as any haircut could.

Jonathan's new look did not escape Chase's notice. The following Tuesday, Jonathan sent me an e-mail in which he told me about Chase's reaction to *both* our looks. Jonathan told me that Chase, whom he'd seen that day at the Stress Center, loved his new haircut and had commented that Jonathan looked "too hot for Paladin," innocently adding "whatever than means," and that Chase had said that he wanted to take him "around the world," exclaiming that he *did* know what *that* meant. Jonathan went on to say that Chase was "very straight forward" and had suggested that the two of them should have sex before he went back to school, saying that Jonathan couldn't really know how he felt about him until they did. Although Jonathan said there was a "certain logic" to Chase's proposal, he didn't tell him that. I found Chase's attitude typically adolescent and, if Chase wasn't kidding, I was dismayed that Jonathan seemed to think it was "logical."

As far as my "withered old red haired skinny white self," as Jonathan said Chase had described me, was concerned, Jonathan said that Chase had commented that I looked "way way too old" for Jonathan and had told him he thought that I had lied to Jonathan about my age. Jonathan had assured him I was 35, but Jonathan refused to tell me what Chase had said in response, not wanting to antagonize me. He ended the message by saying that he found the whole situation "really amusing on a level," but that he didn't have the time to deal with it then.

I didn't find it amusing. I was aggravated by Chase's adolescent insults and felt that Jonathan wasn't adequately defending me. I was also tired of his sexual advances, which Jonathan seemed to be taking too lightly. I felt that Jonathan was actually more than "amused" with the situation and actually enjoyed the seeming competition between Chase and me.

By the end of July, I was getting sick of hearing about Chase and wished that Jonathan would take a firmer stand with him. On Wednesday, August 1, I wasn't feeling well, either physically or emotionally, and sent Jonathan a message in which I told him that if Chase had insulted me "as usual," I would prefer not to know about it, since I was not in the mood for his adolescent nastiness. Jonathan wrote back and told me that, although he had in fact seen the "Chasester," as he called him, that day and that apparently he *had* made further comments about me, he would "skip the detail as per my request." Otherwise, he didn't seem to be taking Chase's behavior or my reactions to it very seriously.

According to Jonathan, Chase had been working on music inspired by and dedicated to him. I thought that was ridiculous and juvenile and not simply because I was feeling rivalrous. Chase didn't view Jonathan as a real person and his 22-year-old infatuation seemed to be growing exponentially with each passing day. On Wednesday, August 1, Jonathan also wrote to tell me about Chase's latest attempt to woo him. Apparently, Chase had finally asked Jonathan to come to dinner at his parents' that Friday night to hear the music he'd been composing. Jonathan said that he'd declined, however, stating that he refused to be put into "any type of dating or romantic situation" with Chase.

He said that Chase had asked to visit, but Jonathan had told him to call first, since he didn't like unannounced visitors. He claimed that Chase had been understanding, even subdued, seeming to have felt rebuffed. Jonathan said that if Chase would "calm down a bit," he would like to be friends with him, since he found him bright, creative, and "really quite nice" and hoped that he would get over his infatuation with him, which was based on the fact that he was "from London and older." The message, which revealed the maturity and sense of responsibility that a 44-year-old should have, helped to restore my faith in Jonathan, which had been somewhat shaken by the adolescent attitude the situation had occasionally brought out in him.

By the next week, however, Jonathan's feelings about maintaining boundaries between him and Chase had changed. On the afternoon of Wednesday, the 8th, Jonathan wrote to tell me that Chase had offered him another invitation to his parents' house, but this time, Jonathan had decided to accept. Jonathan claimed that as part of the therapy for his stage fright, Chase was going to perform in front of a group of his friends. He said that his parents were having a cookout and that about ten people would be in attendance. Jonathan thought it should be "pretty safe." Even so, I felt he was crossing some kind of line.

Later that evening, Jonathan sent me another e-mail in which he emphasized that it was "very important" to Chase that he go, so he had promised him that he would. Jonathan also said that there was "safety in numbers so this [was] the best way to support him and still be OK." I had mixed feelings about what Jonathan was planning, but the situation did seem to be "safe." I didn't know what to think, though, about Jonathan's implication that if he and Chase were alone, things might *not* be "OK." Later that evening, I spoke to Jonathan by phone, but he largely just repeated his intention to go, the importance of going. I was not entirely reassured. I went to bed Wednesday night wondering what was happening, what *would* happen.

■

For several weeks, I had been receiving e-mails from Jonathan at regular intervals throughout the day and could always rely on his sending me one early in the morning. In addition, I could usually catch him online.

Then, on the morning of Thursday, August 9, that changed.

When I checked my e-mail sometime between 8:00 and 8:30, I was surprised to find that I still hadn't received an e-mail from Jonathan. That was strange, since I had gotten one from him by that time every morning that I hadn't spent with him since early June, the day of his father's surgery notwithstanding. In addition, he wasn't even online, which again was peculiar. I waited online myself to see if he would log on, but as time passed, he did not.

Something was different. Something was wrong.

I started becoming concerned.

My first thought was his health. I began to wonder if he'd had some kind of episode. I became so worried, in fact, that I actually called the hospital to see if he had been admitted, but they had no record of his having been brought in. I began to fear that he'd collapsed at home and, incapacitated, was unable to get to help. Because I didn't know what had happened, because I could only imagine, I gradually became more anxious. I didn't know what to do.

Finally, around 9:30, Jonathan appeared online. I cannot describe how relieved I was to know that he was alive and apparently well enough to use the computer. We instant-messaged and he told me he had gotten up late. I sensed, though, that he was holding something back, that something specific had caused him to get up late, but he didn't elaborate. He told me he would write more later. I was satisfied with the explanation he gave to me and waited for further information.

My feeling of relief lasted for about four hours. Around 2:00 that afternoon, Jonathan dropped a bomb on me.

He began by telling me that he needed to talk to me soon. Assuring me that I had done nothing wrong and that things between us were still good, he went on to inform me that he had done something that I "may or may not need to be aware of." My anxiety now provoked by that foreboding preface, I read on.

He said that although we were still dating, our relationship hadn't reached the point of "exclusivity or live in or deep commit[t]ment" and that since we had known each other for only a couple of months, our relationship couldn't be at that point yet and still be "sane and rational." He said that although we saw each other on a regular basis, we didn't see each other every day, and our feelings were still developing. Then, getting more to the point, he assured me that he was not a "good liar or cheater or cover up[p]er" and that in the nine years that he had been involved with Glenn he had never cheated on him. He said that he hadn't been sure if he would tell me about what he had done before I was scheduled to come the next day or tell me in person, but he had decided to tell me before and then let me decide if I still wanted to come.

Waiting until the end to admit what he had done, he began by telling me that after the performance the night before, he and Chase had gone out for drinks. He said that Chase's best friend had also gone with them but that eventually he had left, leaving the two of them alone. Finally, he admitted to doing what I knew, what I feared, he had done: He had slept with Chase. That, he explained, was why it had taken him longer than normal to get online that morning. I had gotten online myself that afternoon as he was writing the message and, seeing that I was on, he told me he would send the message, give me time to absorb it, then instant-message with me later.

My heart began pounding furiously, painfully. How could Jonathan have *done* something like this? How could he have allowed something like this to happen? Although Chase had somehow manipulated Jonathan into sleeping with him, had been manipulating him from the beginning, Jonathan was fully aware of what Chase was doing, what he wanted, and had resolved not to cross certain lines because of the problems that doing so would create. Jonathan had claimed that the only reason he'd accepted the invitation to Chase's parents' the night before was that there would be "safety in numbers" and that the chances of being angled into a compromising situation would be lessened. But left alone with Chase or not, why couldn't Jonathan have exerted more self-control? Although both people were adults and, therefore, responsible for their actions, I felt that Jonathan, at 44, should have been the mature one, the responsible one, the one who should have had the sense and self-control to stop a problem like this before it even started. Especially when he knew what kind of effect *not* doing so would have on *me*. Hadn't he been thinking about *me* at *all*? What *had* he been thinking? I hated the manipulative little bastard that was Chase more than ever and was dismayed at how easily Jonathan had apparently given in to him. I was distraught. Everything had changed. What I had feared might happen *had* happened and the upper hand I felt I'd maintained had been destroyed in a night of thoughtless passion.

I don't recall the instant-message session that followed, but I do recall having to wait three hours until Jonathan returned home and I could speak to him by phone. During that time, with nothing else to do, I paced around the house in a maddening state of agitation from which I could find no relief.

When I finally did speak to him sometime around 5:00, I tried to be as calm, as rational, as possible, which was far from easy in my state. I wanted to understand what had happened, why he had done what he had, instead of arguing and accusing. It was only by understanding why it had happened, I believed, that the problem that had led to it could be resolved.

I don't remember the conversation in detail, but Jonathan began by reiterating what he had told me in his e-mail. In addition, he told me he thought that Chase's friend's "dropping out" had been prearranged by Chase and him so that Chase could be alone with Jonathan. I didn't see how it mattered, although learning about yet another instance of Chase's manipulativeness made me hate Chase even further. He then repeated, in expanded form, what he had told me in brief in his message. Although outwardly I seemed calm, inwardly, I remained in very deep turmoil. Nothing that Jonathan had added, had tried to explain, had helped.

I could barely sleep that night. I was still so agitated that every time I began to drift off to sleep, I jerked back awake. The most uncomfortable and upsetting part of the experience was that my heart wouldn't stop pounding. It pounded in my chest, in my neck, sending shock waves into my head. I had experienced few things physically so awful, so uncontrollable in my life. I thought about calling my doctor and having him give me some tranquilizers, something I had taken only once before—for shingles. I also thought about taking a less medical approach and buying a bottle of strong liquor. I knew, though, that neither of those options would ultimately give me the relief I wanted, which would come only from some kind of resolution to the situation that had caused it.

The next day, I was physically and emotionally exhausted. I had gotten perhaps a couple of hours of sleep and my heart was still beating disconcertingly hard. Worse, I had to teach that day, which meant that I had to make a one-hour trip to work, try to focus, for two hours, on psychology instead of my upturned life, then make another one-hour trip home. Somehow, I got through class, but on the drive home, I almost fell asleep at the wheel.

After I returned home around 4:00, I e-mailed Jonathan to tell him that I didn't think I was feeling well enough to make the trip to Paladin. I wasn't. I knew he was online when I sent the message and, therefore, he would be alerted to its arrival at once. I stayed online while I gave him time to read it and, hopefully, to respond.

Around 5:00, he finally sent me an instant message that started an exchange that lasted for the next two hours.

Jonathan began by asking me if he should "fire the bullet" or I should. Confused, I asked him what he meant. He responded by saying that things between us seemed to be "all out of kilter with some resentment or bitterness on both sides." That was certainly true. He commented that my "illness" was "opportune" and that if we both felt that dealing with what had happened was still important to the both of us we would be trying harder than we were. I told him my illness wasn't "opportune," but resulted from the agitation and sleeplessness I had been suffering over what had happened and told him about having almost fallen asleep at the wheel of my car. Once he seemed convinced I wasn't faking, we continued to discuss what had happened between him and Chase and, perhaps more importantly, what we wanted to happen between us.

He said that our relationship, he felt, was starting to enter "deeper waters," which provoked a certain amount of anxiety. He said that his life had become a "constant barrage" and that he needed a "safe, quiet place" to relax. He expressed his opinion that relationships should be that place, and if they weren't, then it was time to move on, as it had finally become with him and Glenn.

He described Chase as a "safe harbour" who "never hassle[d] [him] about anything and trie[d] to distract [him] with fluff," something that he found appealing. He also said that Chase had the advantage of being there all the time, while I did not, and that his constant onslaughts were like "water on a rock" that had gradually worn him down. He said that wasn't an excuse but a partial explanation for what had happened.

He said that as far as we were concerned, he felt he did better in a relationship but didn't want to make a "huge mistake" by going too fast. I wondered if he was referring to Cliff, which is exactly what had happened with them. He said, though, that he liked coming home to someone with whom he got along and could share his life and missed being in a relationship more than he'd realized. He said of Chase that in spite of all his appealing qualities, he was very self-absorbed, as many creative people were, and related to Jonathan through that self-absorption. In other words, it was all about him. In addition, the immature way he dealt with life, with people, was irritating. Jonathan said it was nice to be able to escape into

"Chaseland," as he called it, from time to time but he couldn't live there and would be bored with him "within the year." He said that as someone in his 40s, he wanted more than Chase could offer.

Throughout it all, I tried to be understanding. In the end, I felt that I had gained even greater insight into what had motivated him to sleep with Chase and hoped that, if Jonathan understood too, a similar incident wouldn't happen in the future.

We discussed plans to get together to talk, in person, about what had happened. I told Jonathan that I would be willing to come to Paladin the next day, if I felt able. Dan had invited Jonathan to come to his house for dinner, but Jonathan said he would cancel those plans if I decided to visit. I told him I would let him know first thing in the morning. I hoped that whatever happened, I would sleep better that night than I had the night before, although I was starting to feel calm enough—and was already exhausted enough—to feel confident that I would.

Before we got off, Jonathan told me that he'd received an e-mail from Chase twenty minutes before, telling him that he had driven past his house on his way home from the Stress Center and hadn't seen my car there "as usual." I wondered how often Chase had driven by when I was there. Jonathan quipped that he needed to move someplace that wasn't so visible from the street.

Jonathan said he was at work but since it was now going on 7:00, he told me he needed to get off and go home and feed the dogs. Even though I didn't have dogs to feed, I myself felt that the two hours we had chatted either had been enough or never would be.

Afterwards, I felt much better. What had happened still remained, but I felt that we had at least addressed some of the underlying issues that had led to what had happened. I didn't know where things were going, but I felt encouraged by his attempts at self-analysis and reconciliation. I felt calmer, saner. I lay down and fell asleep around 9:00. The next thing I knew, it was around 3:00.

When I got up, I was feeling better than I had in two and a half days. I decided to e-mail Jonathan to tell him I would be coming to Paladin after all. I felt now that I was up to the trip and needed to make it if I possibly could. When I got online, I discovered that Jonathan was too. He wanted to know what I was doing online so late and, after explaining, I asked him the same thing. He said that he had just gotten back from spending the evening with Chester and Devon, an on-again, off-again gay couple who were part of the "gay elite" in Paladin. Because they were concerned about him, they had invited him to spend the night. They had watched monster movies until it had gotten late, but instead of staying the night, as originally planned, Jonathan had decided to return home.

Saturday morning, I went to Jonathan's. In spite of our attempts to begin dealing with the issue of his having slept with Chase and everything that implied, the weekend began with a fair amount of uncertainty. We began with Jonathan's reiterating what had happened and why it had happened. Later, we tried to recapture some sense of normality by doing mundane things, such as going to a local home improvement store to purchase a part for Jonathan's washer and grabbing a sandwich at a nearby fast-food restaurant. After returning to Jonathan's, I found that at first I had an aversion to the bedroom, the "scene of the crime," but after Jonathan had made some comment about having changed the sheets and coaxing me to enter, I finally did. I sat down on the bed, trying not to think, or at least be neurotic, about what had happened there a few days before. Eventually, I grew more comfortable sitting there and Jonathan and I stayed there for a while watching television.

As the weekend wore on and we followed our familiar routine, I slowly began to feel that our relationship was returning to normal. By the time I left Monday morning, I was feeling infinitely better about our relationship than I had just a few days before.

Monday, the 13th was my last class of the summer semester. It had been an easy, pleasant class and I was going to miss it. In addition, my summer-long pattern of going to work in Viridian on Friday afternoons, going to Jonathan's later that day, spending the "week end" with him in Paladin, returning to work in Viridian on Monday afternoons, and finally returning home to Hawthorn later that day ended as well. The fall semester was going to start in two weeks and although I wouldn't know until the last minute how many classes I would be teaching or where I would be teaching them, I knew that everything would be different.

I also hoped that things would be different between not only Jonathan and me, but also Jonathan and Chase. That day, Jonathan sent me an e-mail in which he told me about a pinning ceremony for graduates from the Stress Center. At the ceremony, he had encountered Chase. That was the first time they had seen each other since the previous Wednesday night. All that Jonathan said about him, though, in an otherwise detailed message, was that he and Chase had talked for a while and that their conversation had been "light and OK." He said that he had hugged him, but described it as an "OK hug." That, I hoped, was as far as their physical behavior ever went. I did not want to go through what I had gone through again. I hoped, too, that once Chase returned to school, he would forget about Jonathan and I could forget about Chase.

Regardless of how things turned out, I know that when he admitted to sleeping with Chase, I should have ended my relationship with Jonathan. Although we didn't have a commitment, he had told me that while we were involved he wouldn't see other people and his behavior, two months into the relationship, betrayed problems with self-centeredness and self-control that I found disturbing. I wondered if they would continue, what forms they would take, and how much they ultimately would hurt me. Even so, I stayed.

Before Jonathan had "picked" me over Chase, I had held onto the relationship in part because I wasn't going to let an overgrown child whom I despised have Jonathan. *I* was going to have Jonathan if Jonathan would have me. I was *not* going to allow someone to destroy what I felt I had tried to build. Unfortunately, I wasn't immune to jealousy and the feelings of rivalry that stem from it. Whatever feelings of competitiveness I had were enflamed by the challenge and *I* was the one who was going to win.

After Jonathan had "picked" me over Chase, I also felt that Jonathan owed me something for what he had put me through. At first I didn't know what, but he owed me *something*, even if it was simply the continued presence, and preference, of someone who, in spite of his obvious flaws, had a set of qualities that I had never found unified in one person. I wasn't going to lose what I had waited so long to gain and if he could give me something to replace what he had taken, then I was going to accept it.

Although neither of these motivations was particularly noble, I was left feeling that the incident had left Jonathan with a greater awareness of why he had behaved the way he had and that he would be less inclined to fall into the same kind of trap again. Learning experiences could be painful, for everyone involved, but if a lesson was learned and a mistake was not repeated, then perhaps it was worth it. In addition, it had proven to be a difficult, disorienting summer for him and I realized that from the beginning he had been functioning in a weakened state. Therefore, I was willing to give him the benefit of the doubt. I hoped that he had changed for the better and that we could move forward in our relationship.

—11—
DESTINATION NOWHERE

Fancy a trip to London…?

Only a couple of weeks after we met, Jonathan raised the possibility of our going "on holiday" together. He said that because of his executive privilege, he usually had no difficulty getting away when he wanted and said that normally he made it back to England every couple of months or so to visit. Since I hadn't gone anywhere on vacation in ages, I relished the opportunity to get out of my rut and do something exciting.

The first time Jonathan raised the possibility was on Friday, June 15, the day before we met, which was something that helped to heighten my feelings of confidence about the continued progression of what was proving to be a fascinating relationship. By that point, Jonathan had told me that his father was having health problems, although it wasn't yet understood that he had cancer, and he thought he might go home to visit him around the end of June. In addition, it had been a couple of months since he had visited and it seemed time. Since my birthday was around the end of June, he asked me if I "fancied" a trip to London and "boring old Eiseley," telling me it would be a great way to ring in the next year of my life.

On the 19th, he told me that he was still planning to go to England the following week and that I was welcome to come, but added that going under the current circumstances wouldn't be the best introduction to "London, [t]he UK in general, and [his] bizarre family in particular." Having also learned that I didn't have a passport, he informed me that in the United States, passports weren't issues immediately, requiring a wait of at least two to three weeks.

Consequently, it appeared that I wouldn't be able to go to England around the end of June.

The Friday night of the second weekend I spent with him, Jonathan suggested another possible destination. He asked me if I had ever heard of the island of Margarita, which I hadn't. He said that it lay off the northern coast of Venezuela and was the ideal tropical retreat. He described it as the kind of place you went when you wanted to be as cut off from civilization as possible, but not so cut off that you didn't retain *some* amenities. The rooms were devoid of televisions and telephones, but you could still lie on the beach and relax. He said that he and Glenn had vacationed there several times and had enjoyed it. I forced myself to accept the possibility of spending a week or so in a tropical paradise.

If I was going to do that, however, I still needed a passport. I assumed that Jonathan was accurate about the time frame in which they were processed, but as it turned out, he wasn't. When I contacted the passport office about obtaining one, I was informed that the process would take not two or three weeks, but *six*. When I told Jonathan what I had learned, he was taken aback. Given that it was nearing the end of June, it would be at least the middle of August before we could go on vacation. He also doubted that, given our schedules, I would be able to go with him to England that summer.

Because of the passport issue, Jonathan suggested that maybe we could go to the Southern state, where he still had a house and where I wouldn't need a passport. He made this suggestion, however, around the time he fainted at work and became embroiled in medical tests to determine why. On Saturday, June 23, he wrote to tell me that he had rethought the issue and with everything that was going on—his father's illness, his own illness, his probable trip to England to see his father around the end of June—he had decided it would be better to stay in the Paladin area.

Although I felt presumptuous for feeling this way, I couldn't help feeling disappointed. Birthdays had ceased to be a major affair in my family, since Kathryn's children had grown, and with everyone's disparate schedules, we usually celebrated birthdays not on the appropriate day but whenever it proved convenient, if at all. Consequently, there was nothing holding me in Hawthorn, in the United States, and the prospect of receiving a trip to England as a birthday present was enticing.

Because I developed laryngitis on the Friday of the second weekend that I spent with Jonathan, my condition made it impossible for me to take care of business not just over the phone, but also in person for several days. Therefore, in spite of the urgency in getting the passport process underway, that would, unfortunately, have to wait until I could talk. Jonathan was not happy. He became somewhat pushy, and although I understood his desire to go on vacation when we both could and have nothing get in the way, I still became irritated by his insistence and seeming inability to understand my situation. I finally e-mailed him and told him that until my voice returned, the passport issue would have to wait.

In response, he apologized, explaining that the attitude he took in business, which was one of "just getting things done," inadvertently spilled over into his personal life. He said that in business, taking that attitude was the only way to be successful because otherwise someone else would do what you were planning before you did and you would be out of luck. He said that he didn't realize how forceful he could be with his expectations and needed to learn that although things weren't always done the way he wanted them to be done, they still got done. He told me that in the same way he expected people to accept him the way he was, he needed to do the same to others. He assured me that he had no desire to change me and told me to continue doing things the way I wanted to do them. Because his attempts to change me had not yet grown to the point that they obviously belied that statement, I appreciated his seeming self-awareness and accepted his apology.

By Wednesday, my voice had returned enough for me to be able to complete the process of getting the passport. I wrote to tell him about my progress and he seemed pleased that things were finally underway.

Part of the pressure Jonathan was putting on me to get the passport seemed to be driven in part by his need to get away. On Thursday, July 5, he sent me an e-mail titled "Destination Anywhere" that described at length the difficult day he'd endured and his desperate desire to leave his life behind, if just for a while.

On the morning of Thursday, the 12th, I went to the mailbox and was stunned to find that I had received my passport four full weeks before it had been scheduled to arrive. That Friday, when I went to Jonathan's, I told him that I had a surprise for him. We were sitting outside at the time, so I went inside to retrieve the passport from my suitcase, then returned to where Jonathan was seated. I told him to close his eyes, and when he did, I slipped the passport into his hands. When he opened his eyes and saw what he was holding, his eyes grew wide and he became elated. He kept exclaiming, "This is *great!*" and I was happy that he was happy. *We* could now go anywhere in the world.

Throughout July, we refined our travel plans. Although Jonathan said he could go essentially anytime he wanted, I was more restricted. The earliest I would be able to go would be the middle of August, during my between-semester break. The summer term would end on Friday, August 17, while the fall term would begin on Monday, August 27. If we left on the evening of the 17th, we could arrive in England on Saturday, the 18th, and if we left England on the following Saturday, allowing me to arrive home in time to return to work on the 27th, we could spend at least a week in Jonathan's homeland. Later, it occurred to me that the only reason I didn't feel I could leave until the 17th was that I had planned to give my class their final exam that afternoon, and that if I rescheduled their exam for the previous Monday, we could then have four additional days. I discussed the matter with my class and, not surprisingly, no one objected, since they were glad to be done with the course a little earlier than expected. Consequently, Jonathan and I would, in theory, be able to spend almost the entire second half of August in England.

Despite the excitement, I was somewhat intimidated about meeting Jonathan's family and friends. In an e-mail that I sent to a friend on Monday, July 30, only two weeks before we were scheduled to go, I discussed my anxieties about meeting "Zeus and Lovey Howell," considering that I would be Jonathan's first American boyfriend they had ever met and that their feelings about Americans were lukewarm at best. I told my friend that I felt like an ambassador for my country and couldn't screw up. I also expressed my anxieties about meeting Glenn, which I told my friend would be "interesting"—my all-purpose word for something I felt unsure about. I ended my e-mail by telling my friend that Jonathan and I were planning to visit Stonehenge while we were there, which I felt was a good thing because I was sure I would feel an especially strong need to pray. I hoped the experience of meeting his family and Glenn wouldn't be as nerve-wracking as I feared, but I felt uncertain about the situation.

As the time approached, I became more preoccupied with the final preparations. I bought some new clothes especially for the trip and my mother generously pitched in and bought me a new pair of shoes. Although clothing wasn't an issue, I was somewhat concerned about having enough money. I didn't make much the way it was, and since I was teaching only one class that summer, my income was reduced from what it normally was. In addition, I had been spending more than normal for the previous two months, since I was traveling and eating out much more than I had been when I had been unattached. By the beginning of August, my savings had dwindled to about $650, but since much of that needed to go for other expenses, I could take only a fraction of it. I also didn't know yet how many classes I would be teaching in the fall, so I felt the need to be conservative. Although Jonathan had told me that he would buy me whatever I wanted and otherwise pay for all of my expenses, I did not view Jonathan as a sugar daddy and planned to pay for my fair share, despite the tremendous disparity in our incomes.

On Friday, August 3, Jonathan sent me an e-mail in which he updated me on conditions in London. If things continued as he reported them, the trip we were about to take might be a "trip" in more ways than one. He informed me that a car bomb had exploded around midnight in Ealing Broadway, a trendy part of West London. Apparently, Leandra's son, Hamish, who was in the area at the time, had been mildly injured when he was hit by flying glass as he and his friends were walking to dinner after a late showing of the film *The Mummy Returns*. Jonathan said that four of his nephew's friends had been injured seriously enough to be taken to the hospital, but none of their injuries had been life-threatening. Jonathan speculated that the incident was part of an IRA summer bomb campaign, which he said they'd once waged for several consecutive summers. He informed me that he had lived through three previous IRA bomb campaigns and was "almost blown up" in the Harrods car bombing on December 17, 1983, which had claimed the lives of six people. He ended his e-mail by asking, "What is this world coming to?"

I had to agree. I could hardly wait to get killed on my first trip abroad.

On Wednesday, August 8, Jonathan sent me an extensive list of departure options. Option 1 was to leave on Saturday, the 18th, as scheduled. Option 2 was to leave on Wednesday, the 15th through New York. Although this option would give us three more days than Option 1, we would have to fly coach, which would be "hell," as Jonathan described it, since the plane would be almost full. Option 3 was to leave on Thursday, the 16th through Washington, D.C. He said we could upgrade, but only to business class, not to first. Even so, he thought it might be acceptable. Option 4 was to leave on the 16th through New York. We could upgrade to first class, but because of flight schedules that would require at least one layover, it would be the longest of the flights. Finally, Option 5 was to leave on Friday, the 17th, but this was Jonathan's least favorite option, since it would give us only one extra day. Leaving the decision to me, he encouraged me, "Vote on your choice of flights to Europe!! Vote now. Vote often."

Wednesday, August 8 was also the day that Jonathan slept with Chase.

After Jonathan had admitted to sleeping with Chase, I was more determined than ever to let Jonathan treat me to a trip to England. I felt that after the emotional turmoil I had endured because of his thoughtless behavior, he owed it to me. In addition, although I am ashamed to admit it, I also felt that by letting Jonathan take me to England rather than Chase—who wanted to go to England with Jonathan in my place—I would be getting back at Chase for everything he had done to hurt me and, perhaps more importantly, reasserting my claim on Jonathan. For me, then, the England trip would make right a lot of things that had gone wrong in the previous two months and nothing would stop me from going. I did not, however, admit any of this to Jonathan.

Eventually, we decided to depart the weekend of August 18. That would give us only a little more than a week before I had to be back in Hawthorn to go to work on the 27th, but that was better than nothing. Much better.

On the morning of Tuesday, August 14, however, I checked my e-mail and found a lengthy message from Jonathan with the urgent title, "Read Now. I'll write more when I know more." The message brought some unwelcome news. He informed me that he and Mike had met earlier that morning and Mike had informed him that, in his opinion, now was not the time for Jonathan to be taking a trip to England. Mike had cited a number of reasons why he thought Jonathan needed to stay in the States. First, he believed that OutSource had reached a crucial point in their negotiations with the company in California and he expected Jonathan to go to California in the following days to meet with their representatives in person. Second, OutSource was pushing to release their new software by October 1, only a few weeks away, and Mike felt that if Jonathan went on vacation at such a critical point, it would send the message that getting the software released on schedule wasn't that serious of an issue. And, third, Mike was concerned about the Ben situation, which had arisen only days before, and expected Jonathan to continue to oversee it, directly, especially if it could affect their dealings with the company in California.

Mike had also questioned why Jonathan felt the need to go home now if part of the reason was to visit his father. He reminded Jonathan that he hadn't visited him when he'd had his surgery in July, when he was much sicker, and knowing he was better, he didn't understand why Jonathan felt the urgency to visit him now. In addition, Mike reminded him that with his health problems, it was better for Jonathan to stay in Paladin, near his doctors.

Jonathan said, though, that in spite of the seemingly valid reasons Mike had given to him, they were really just "window dressing" that decorated Mike's true feelings. Apparently, Mike had been aggravated with Jonathan for the past week because he had been expecting him to come to him and tell him he was delaying his trip home; because he hadn't, Mike had come to feel that Jonathan wasn't committed to him, his job, and his responsibilities. Not helping matters was the fact that Mike had heard through the grapevine that Jonathan had been speaking to other companies, which seemed to underscore Jonathan's lack of dedication.

Jonathan said he knew that Mike was "a little hysterical" because of the pressures that meeting the release deadline had placed on him, which was why Jonathan had asked for a 30-minute break to give Mike time to cool down and himself time to write to me. He said he hoped he could still reason with him, but he seemed doubtful. He apologized profusely for having to cancel our plans but said that sometimes business intervened and that he'd scheduled the trip when he had primarily because of when I would be available. He said he was "sorry beyond words" and would write more when he knew more.

Naturally, I was disappointed. Even so, I felt worse for Jonathan. In fact, I was worried about him, about the effect this would have on him. He said he got home, on average, every couple of months, but by the middle of August, it had been several. There also seemed to be no clear idea of when he would be able to go. Going home on a regular basis seems to be crucial to his sense of well-being. Apart from having family and friends and history there, he simply needed to be with other British people, it seemed, in order to maintain a feeling of sanity and stability. Since Jonathan had been in Paladin, he had encountered only a handful of other British people, but was otherwise surrounded almost entirely by Americans and American culture, something to which he had only partially adjusted. Therefore, he often felt like a stranger in a strange land—something I thought I understood.

His experience was similar, I believed, to my experience of being gay in Hawthorn. Throughout my 35 years there, I had encountered only a limited number of gay people and knew how isolating and detrimental the experience of not being able to interact with others of your own kind could be. Like many gay people, who must operate within a heterosexual culture that they cannot fully understand, that is largely alien to who and what they are, the experience could be disorienting and destabilizing. Under normal circumstances, that would have been bad enough, but with all of the misfortune that had befallen him that summer, going home now seemed more crucial than ever. I was very concerned about the effect this latest blow would have on him.

I wrote him a long message in which I assured him that I wasn't angry or upset with him for what had happened, since he had no control over the situation. I told him I thought I understood how he felt, how important the trip was for him. I told him I didn't know when he would be able to do it, but I wanted to see him take the first flight to England that he could get whether I could go or not. I told him this wasn't about me; it was about him, and I was far more concerned about the implications for him than I was about those for me, which were minimal. I told him I didn't see how I could possibly focus on how this was affecting me when it was affecting him so much worse. I concluded by telling him if he needed to talk, I was there for him.

In response, he wrote the next morning to tell me that he'd had coffee with Mike but that he was adamant about Jonathan's remaining in Paladin. Jonathan said that he was angry with Mike over what he had done and that it would take a long time for him to get over it. I knew how Jonathan could carry a grudge, so I knew he meant it. He said his feelings toward Mike were making other job offers seem more appealing but he knew that was just because he was angry and would do nothing out of emotion. Jonathan concluded by saying that he needed to go to a meeting but told me before he went that I had shown him a lot about myself through the way I'd reacted to the cancellation of the trip, implying that I had shown that I was interested less in what he could do for me than in *him*, and told me that he liked what he'd seen.

I was flattered that he had responded so positively to my understanding why we couldn't go to England. In spite of how I had been left feeling in the wake of the Chase situation, ultimately I wasn't interested in Jonathan for the fascinating places he could take me; I was interested in Jonathan for *him*. I couldn't have cared less if I was with him in England or in my state or Nowhere. Because Jonathan was upset, I suggested that I come to Paladin on Thursday, but he told me that he had to go to the Midwestern state on business on Thursday and thought that waiting until Friday as usual would be better. He told me that "maybe [I] could stay longer then usual," which made me feel that he not only needed me around, but also wanted me around.

Because Jonathan ended up having to stay out of state an additional day, I ended up not going to Paladin until Saturday. I arrived around noon to find him aggravated, but not openly depressed. I knew, however, that he didn't normally show his emotions, so it was difficult to know how he might actually be feeling. I hoped, though, that if what he was feeling wasn't good, my presence would help.

That Saturday, I finally met Jonathan's friend, Dan. From the time I had met him, Jonathan had mentioned a variety of friends and had tentatively planned at certain points for us to get together with some of them, but for whatever reason that had never happened. Therefore, Dan had the distinction of being the first of Jonathan's friends whom I met in person.

There were several people whom Jonathan considered best friends. Colin was his best friend in general. Another man named Greg Carroll, who, like Jonathan, worked for an information technology company and lived near Terrence, was his best friend "in the United States." Dan was his best friend "in [my state]." Jonathan had told me that when he and Glenn had been planning to come to my state, they had posted messages on the Internet inquiring about what gay life there was like. Dan was one of the people who had responded. Apparently he had replied with several long, thoughtful messages and eventually he and Jonathan had become friends.

Dan had been a nurse in the army, but was now retired and spent much of his time painting. Dan had also been married, but had eventually divorced when he could no longer lead a heterosexual life. He had one son who was around 30 and with whom he had a strained relationship, in part because of his inability to accept his father's sexuality. Like many gay men who lived in small towns, Dan led a closeted, furtive life, fearful of being exposed and destroyed. In fact, Jonathan later told me that Dan had said he would "commit suicide" if the people in Credence found out that he was gay.

Yet, despite his fears, Dan apparently led an active sex life and Jonathan described him as "the most sexually active person [he knew]." That was saying a lot, coming from someone who had been as sexually active as he had and had friends like Harald. It seemed, too, that Dan didn't exercise the greatest caution or selectivity in procuring partners, most of whom he culled from the Internet or met through cruising at local parks. More troublesome perhaps, Dan apparently had a drinking problem to an unknown degree. One of these compulsive behaviors by itself was bad enough, but having both together, to my mind, was like having gasoline next to fire and the combination worried me. Jonathan told me that Cliff hadn't liked Dan because of his drinking, and under Cliff's considerable sway, Jonathan had avoided him for two months. Jonathan seemed to regret that decision, but it didn't appear to have caused irreparable damage in Jonathan and Dan's friendship.

Dan was in town that weekend to attend a nursing reunion. He had driven to Jonathan's and Jonathan had driven him to the reunion. Jonathan was supposed to pick him up sometime around noon. We drove to where the reunion was being held and Dan was waiting on the building's steps. As we drove up, Jonathan waved out the window and flirtatiously yelled, "Hey, honey!" I wondered how Dan, who was fearful of exposure, reacted inwardly to that. Outwardly, he didn't appear to react, although we were largely alone and we were not in Credence.

At the time, I wasn't clear on how old Dan was. Dan seemed evasive about his age, sometimes lying to make himself seem younger. Based on his appearance and his son's age, I estimated that Dan was somewhere in his mid- to late 50s. (Much later, I learned he was actually in his early 60s.) He was tall and muscular, but also somewhat heavy. His blond hair appeared to be graying and his face, along with his body, belied the ages that he liked others to believe he was. I wondered how much his drinking and the stresses in his life had aged him. Otherwise, my initial impression was of someone who seemed likeable and to whom I could in some ways relate.

On our way back to Jonathan's, Dan told us a little about the reunion. In addition, we talked a little about not only Dan's sex life, but also finding sex partners in general. When Dan gave Jonathan suggestions, Jonathan made a comment about how he wasn't "married"—indicating that he wasn't committed. I was put off by the remark because, although we hadn't made a formal commitment, I still thought it said something about his attitude toward me. I wondered if Dan knew that Jonathan and I were an "item." Perhaps because I had similar feelings about our commitment at that point, given what had just happened between him and Chase, I tried to overlook the comment.

When we arrived at Jonathan's, the three of us sat at the kitchen table and talked for about half an hour. That conversation revolved around Dan's sex life as well. Apparently, he had arranged an encounter with someone who, to both Jonathan and me, sounded questionable. We were both concerned about him and dissuaded Dan from meeting him. Dan also discussed his other sexual activities, which seemed to be numerous. Jonathan restated to Dan his opinion that Dan was the most sexually active person he knew, but Dan complained that his encounters were sporadic, that although he did have a lot of partners, he usually had only one encounter with each. In my opinion, his behavior was risky, even reckless, but not knowing Dan, I didn't feel that it was my place to voice my thoughts.

Sometime around 1:00, Dan left in his green SUV. After he was gone, Jonathan asked me what I thought of him. I thought he seemed nice enough and he had certainly been a good friend to Jonathan, but I was concerned about his compulsive behaviors. He seemed troubled in some ways and I was worried about what might happen to him.

Later, I learned that Dan didn't have an entirely favorable impression of *me*. According to Jonathan, Dan had told him that he didn't like the fact that I wasn't as "forceful" as Cliff had been. That seemed like an odd quality to focus on and I wondered how his military background might have affected his perceptions of what mattered. Since I was largely comfortable with my level of "forcefulness," however, I wasn't bothered by his judgment and felt that his perception was his problem. Overall, though, it didn't do much to affect my impression of Dan.

I ended up staying at Jonathan's until the following "week end." My stay in Paladin was a poor substitute for a trip to England, but I was far more concerned about the effect the canceled plans might have on Jonathan than on me.

During my stay, Jonathan finally revealed something about his life that until then he had never mentioned: his brother Malcolm. According to Jonathan, Malcolm was the ninth child in the Frazier family and, although he wasn't clear on the point, I got the impression that Malcolm was somewhere around Michael's age. Or, would have been, had he lived. According to Jonathan, Malcolm had died as a child when he had fallen out of an upper-story window. Although he wasn't clear about Malcolm's age when he was killed, I got the impression that while he was old enough to walk, he wasn't older than about five. Jonathan said the loss had been so traumatic for his family that his parents never spoke about it and forbade his siblings to discuss it as well, although obviously they had disobeyed their parents on the matter because the incident had happened before Jonathan had been born and he had heard the story from them. Jonathan was troubled by the incident, although strangely, he seemed more troubled than might be expected over something that he had not directly experienced, that had happened before he was born.

Then, a few days later, I found out why Jonathan was more troubled about Malcolm's death than seemed explicable. Jonathan hadn't told me the exact truth. Finally, Jonathan revealed that Malcolm had died not as a child, but as an adult. The fact of his death was not the problem as much as the manner of his death was: Malcolm, according to Jonathan, had committed suicide.

He told me a horrific story about Malcolm coming home from college and hanging himself in a closet in the family home in Eiseley. Although he didn't leave a suicide note or apparently discuss the reasons why he wanted to take his life, his family had gotten the impression that the pressure to live up to the Frazier standard of perfection had become too much for him to bear. Unfortunately, instead of taking something as shattering as their child's suicide as a wake-up call that they needed to change their approach to life, the Frazier family remained as unrelenting as ever and had simply decided to put the incident behind them, pretend that it had never happened, and continue to live life as they always had.

I was shocked by what had happened and appalled that his parents had dealt with their child's death in such a seemingly callous fashion. I realized that denial was usually the first defense mechanism that came into play after a loss, especially one of such magnitude, and could persist for years, but the "business as usual" attitude Jonathan's family took seemed to be the result less of psychological defenses than of cultural expectations that said that "running the British Empire" was more important than the single human life. For a group of people who thought they were superior, I felt they did much to knock themselves off their self-created pedestal.

The issue arose because of Jonathan's own doubts about his ability to live up to the Frazier standard of perfection that his family, his upbringing, had set for him. His failing health was undermining his life on many levels and he no longer felt he could achieve as he once had. That had been a recurring theme since the beginning of July, but as time had passed, the theme of defeat had grown increasingly dominant. He never talked about committing suicide, but the fact that he was now discussing his brother, who had and whom he had never before mentioned, was worrying. In spite of the problems we had had, did have, I felt more of a need to take care of Jonathan than ever.

Possibly because of his preoccupations, Jonathan was fairly unaffectionate during the time I was there. In the eight days that I spent with him, he hugged me twice—once when I came and once when I left—and we had sex twice, although it was fairly passionless sex. I tried not to make too much out of it, tried to understand his lack of interest, but it was still frustrating.

In addition, Jonathan said something to me while I was there that left me feeling odd. One day while we were out, he made a comment to the effect that although he had been honest with me about sleeping with Chase and always told the truth, maybe he was really just giving me enough truth to make me think that he was being truthful about everything when he really wasn't. Then, as soon as he said it, he smiled and assured me that he was just "having [me] on"—that is, joking with me. I liked to believe that he *was* joking, but I wasn't sure what would make him say something like that. Even so, I had never seen any solid evidence that he had been anything but truthful, so I continued to assume he was. Although his remark left me with a strange feeling, I attributed it to the reactivation of my feelings about my past betrayals, my realizations that I couldn't trust the person with whom I was involved, something to which I was exquisitely sensitive and possibly too sensitive.

Yet, despite the unpleasant asides, the week that I spent with Jonathan was generally fun. While I was there, we mainly engaged in the same kinds of nondescript, "domestic" activities that we generally did during our weekends. Although we still weren't living together, we might as well have been.

I left Jonathan's on the afternoon of Sunday, the 26th, the day before the fall semester began. It was the longest stretch of time that we had spent together. I was reluctant to leave, but I had to return to Hawthorn, to my "other" life. In addition, Jonathan had to leave for California that afternoon on business. He was still angry with Mike for keeping him from going to England, but he tried not to let his feelings interfere with business and focused on trying to get the best deal possible. Jonathan seemed to find it difficult for me to leave as well, saying that leaving was like "pulling a bandage off," something best done quickly rather than slowly and prolong the agony.

I arrived home sometime after 3:00. I went online to let Jonathan know I had gotten home safely only to find that he was online as well. Catching him on instant messenger, I told him I was home and asked him where he was. He told me he was at the airport with another coworker, having arrived only five minutes before. He asked me if I was okay, since he thought I seemed down when I had left. I told him that I had hated to leave and that he had seemed down himself. He said that he hadn't liked to see me go, either, and that the previous week had been "almost like living together." He lamented that "we [were] in different places yet again."

We didn't have much time to talk. Mike was instant-messaging him as well and Mike had to take precedence over me. He concluded the session by telling me that he had a layover in Minneapolis before he headed to California.

I tried to relax for the rest of the day. My between-semester break was coming to an end and I was facing the beginning of a new semester, so I wanted to be well rested. Although my time with Jonathan was supposed to be a vacation, it had left me exhausted. I was also readjusting to being home after the longest period that I had been gone for almost two years. I hoped the semester would go well, but I never knew what I was going to find, what kind of students I would have, and the fall semester, which was always more complex than the summer one was, would make work, life, more challenging than it had been during the previous three months. Even so, I hoped the fall would be as simple as possible.

I had no idea how complicated the next three months would actually be.

—12—
TURN OF EVENTS

Strange days are upon us.

The first day of the new semester proceeded uneventfully. This time, instead of teaching only one class, as I had done throughout the summer, I was teaching three: one in Hawthorn on Monday and Friday mornings, one in Viridian on Tuesday evenings, and one in a small town near Hawthorn called Clarian on Monday evenings. On Monday morning, I met with my Hawthorn class, and that evening, I met with my Clarian one. I was pleasantly surprised to find that a friend of mine with whom I had once worked had enrolled in my class in Clarian. I wouldn't be meeting with my Viridian group until the following night. It was going to be at least three times bigger than my summer one, which had only had about ten students. Yet, aside from new classes and mostly new faces, I expected everything else in my life to remain the same.

Unfortunately, it did not.

By the end of August, Jonathan had been wanting to leave the house on Millstone Drive for at least two months. The most superficial reason was that he preferred to be "in the middle of the wickedness," something that his current home, far from downtown, didn't allow. A more serious reason was that, as he had described it, "[t]oo many bad things ha[d] happened [t]here"—losing Glenn, losing Cliff, getting sick—and he wanted to be somewhere "safe and friendly." In the end, the most significant reason was that Jonathan's doctors had finally told him that his medical condition had grown serious enough that he should no longer live by himself.

Although Jonathan could have gotten some type of home healthcare to solve the latter problem, the house itself was gradually becoming unlivable. Beginning in mid-June, the house had become plagued by extensive electrical problems that had left the house without any hot water throughout most of the summer. Although the water heater had been repaired around the end of June, it had malfunctioned again almost at once. I had taken more than one ice-cold bath at the house that summer and was thankful that it wasn't winter. In an e-mail from Thursday, July 5, Jonathan told me that, on further inspection, an electrician had determined that there were "electrical problems, probably of long standing, with the whole wiring leads to the water heater and the furnace." The electrician wanted to "rewire the whole box and upgrade the service," which would cost somewhere between $12,000 and $15,700. Jonathan commented that he was "curious as to why this [hadn't] show[n] up in the structural and engineering inspection before closing" and that he "intend[ed] to get answers as this [couldn't] be a new or undiscovered problem that [had] just materialized 3 weeks ago."

Jonathan was never clear if his landlord, Ted Kanner, was unable or unwilling to pay for the repairs or if Ted was expecting Jonathan to pay for them himself, but it appeared that they weren't going to get done anytime soon. I wondered about the legality of what Ted was allowing to happen, but I knew that even if Jonathan pressed the matter legally, it would still take some time before the electrical problems, which reduced the quality of life in the house, were resolved.

Beyond the electrical issues, the carpeting throughout most of the house had been destroyed because Jonathan often allowed the dogs to "make" on it. Not deliberately, but neglectfully. Prissy, who was senile, was the worst offender, but Sweetie and Frizzie contributed as well. I was always finding fresh piles of feces and sometimes dried piles that had apparently not been discovered or removed for some time. In addition, the carpets were saturated with urine and I had quickly gotten into the habit of wearing my shoes at all times when I was in the house so I wouldn't step in some pile or puddle. Judging from their condition, Jonathan had apparently allowed the dogs to "make" in the house for some time before I had arrived, so the carpeting, which seemed damaged beyond repair, would have to be replaced. Jonathan was not the best housekeeper and seemed to have little luck with maids. I tried to do what I could to keep things clean while I was there, but the damage was so extensive and the problem so persistent that it remained largely outside my control. I never mentioned the situation to Jonathan because it wasn't my house or my place to do so, but it made being in the house somewhat uncomfortable.

Throughout the summer, he—and often we—had investigated different possibilities for a new place to live, but none of them had proven suitable or viable for one reason or another. In the end, Jonathan had decided not to rent the penthouse we had seen in July or any of the other places that he or we had investigated. At first, it seemed a matter of simply finding the right place and the right situation, but once he did, we assumed he would be free of the mess that the house, that his life, on Millstone Drive had become.

Then, in August, Jonathan told me that he had spoken with Ted, who had informed him of a stipulation in his contract that he had failed to fully appreciate. According to the terms of the lease, Jonathan had to continue to pay the rent for the house for a period of four months after informing Ted that he was planning to move out, whether he was living in the house or not. Therefore, if Jonathan moved out of the house before the four months was up, he would have to pay not only the rent on his new place, but also the rent on his old one until the four months' rent was paid in full. I didn't understand all the details of the agreement, which sounded odd, but I did understand that Jonathan was left feeling trapped in a place he had come to despise, a place he could no longer manage, a place where he was alone at a time when he could not be alone.

Then, on Tuesday, August 28, Jonathan sent me an e-mail, titled "Too Soon???" in which he informed me of an unexpected resolution to the situation. Still in California, he said that he had just spoken with "asshole" Ted Kanner and they had worked out a deal regarding the house. He said that according to the deal, he would move out, the house would be appraised, and he would get the difference between the appraisal price and the mortgage price. If the appraisal price was lower than the mortgage price, which he suspected it would be because of its condition, then Ted would take the loss. Although it sounded like a good deal, there was, unfortunately, one catch: Ted wanted Jonathan out by Labor Day, which was the following Monday. He said, though, that he was willing to accept the deal because then he wouldn't have to be responsible for the house any longer and wouldn't have to deal with the hassle of a showing. Jonathan didn't seem to want to deal with people any more than he had to, especially when it involved a situation that I perceived he found embarrassing.

He told me that Dan had offered to let him come and stay with him for a while until he figured out what to do in the long term. Another friend of his named Art, who lived in downtown Paladin and rented out sections of his large house, had also offered to let

Jonathan stay with him, but Jonathan had refused, thinking Dan the better choice. Although this wasn't exactly the way that either Jonathan or I had envisioned his departure from the house on Millstone Drive, at least he *was* departing.

Overwhelmed by everything he was going to have to do in the next few days, he naturally turned to me for help. He asked me if I would rent a moving van for him, since he didn't have an American driver's license, and help him pack. He said he hoped to get a few additional friends to help him with the packing. He planned to pack on Thursday and Friday, then move on Saturday and Sunday. Ending the message on an urgent note, he told me that he needed to know as soon as possible if I could help because Ted wanted his answer, which he had not yet given, by the next morning.

In spite of the complications, I was excited by the news. I told him that although it was short notice, I was thrilled to hear that he was leaving the house he had come to despise and that I didn't think his departure was "too soon." I was not only willing, but eager, to help him move and told him he could count on me to do whatever I could to help him.

Later that day, I happened to catch him online and we continued through instant messaging where e-mailing had left off. During our exchange, Jonathan opened up and confessed his fears, saying that he was "scared about the move, [his] health, [his] job, nearly everything." He repeated his plan to go to Dan's, where he now thought he might spend the entire winter, and try to regroup. He said he was so exhausted both physically and mentally that once he arrived he thought he would "sleep for a week." Living with Dan seemed ideal, since Dan had been a nurse and was qualified to take care of his physical health. Jonathan also repeated something that had become somewhat of a refrain, which was that he didn't feel "safe" in the house on Millstone Drive anymore but thought he would feel safe at Dan's.

He also voiced his feeling, which had been growing for some time, that he wanted to quit his job not in January, as originally planned, but much sooner. He said the trip to California had proven to be "enough" and although he felt he would be abandoning ship if he quit before October, when the software was scheduled for release, he wondered what difference it would make if he was dead.

His experience seemed to give him some insight into why I had left Paladin and had returned to Hawthorn when I had lost my job instead of toughing it out, something about which he had always seemed judgmental. Although he wasn't moving back home, he *was* attempting to alleviate as much stress as possible and allowing someone else to help take care of him and things until he recuperated, as I had. It seemed that he finally understood how things could get to the point that there was no alternative.

Through it all, I tried to reassure him that I would do what I could to help him, that I was there for him. He was especially concerned about losing his things that gave him, as he described it, "some security in a foreign place." I assured him that I wouldn't allow that to happen.

Throughout the exchange, he berated himself for being a "burden" and a "failure," something I vehemently tried to counteract. He didn't mention Malcolm by name, but I knew that he was placing himself in the same category as his dead brother and, for many reasons, I wanted to dissuade him from that line of thinking.

Around 5:00, I left for Viridian, but because I was so focused on the unfolding crisis with Jonathan, I dismissed class early and was home by 8:30. Around 11:30, when Jonathan had told me he would next be available, I got online to find him online as well. After asking me how class had gone, he told me that he had told his parents what he was planning to do. He said that, to his amazement, his father had been supportive, telling him that he should make his physical and mental health his priority. Jonathan attributed his father's attitude to his memory of what had happened to Malcolm and not wanting to see Jonathan go down that path. His mother, however, wasn't as understanding. She had apparently told Jonathan to "get over it" and keep his mind on fulfilling his duties. He described his mother as more of an "elitist" than his father was and reminded me that she never discussed what had happened to Malcolm, in part because Malcolm represented a failure. I though her attitude was disgusting but didn't interject my thoughts. I was glad to know, however, that Jonathan was receiving at least partial support from his parents when it could have been none.

We didn't instant-message for long because it was earlier in California than it was in the Midwest and Jonathan was still involved in meetings. He told me he would be home the next afternoon and I told him I would try to make firmer arrangements regarding the move the next day.

He concluded by telling me, "I would be totally out of it if it weren't for you" and added, "You always come through for me. Always." I was flattered and didn't want to let him down, especially when he seemed to need me so much.

I tried to get some sleep that night. I worried about Jonathan being alone in California in his condition, in his situation. I also knew that tomorrow would be a big day for me, since I now had the responsibility of finding not only a moving van, but also a suitable place to store Jonathan's precious things for however long it took him to find another place of his own to live.

The next morning, I woke up to find an e-mail from Jonathan. Describing himself as a "wreck," he said it was the middle of the night but he couldn't sleep. He told me that he had gone to bed and had "literally" passed out but had woken up only an hour later and was too anxious to go back to sleep. He said that he was worried about getting everything moved, especially a triple dresser from his bedroom and an armoire from the guest bedroom, both of which were large and heavy. Even the movers who had brought his things to the house had run into trouble moving them and he didn't want to leave them behind.

Then, he repeated his thought that he didn't want to work anymore and confessed that he felt as if he were having a "meltdown" from everything that was happening to him. He apologized for unloading on me, but told me that I was the only person he could admit his true feelings to. He further stated that if I didn't or couldn't help him, he would just give up. He thanked me for helping him and, after telling me he would call me as soon as he got home, he thanked me again.

Before I could respond, he sent me another message. Addressing me as "My Dear Richard," he informed me not only that he had spoken to Ted and had accepted Ted's deal, based on the help that both Dan and I had said we would give to him, but also that Ted had agreed to give him a few more days to vacate the house. Instead of having to be out by Monday, Jonathan now didn't have to be out until 5:00 in the afternoon on Wednesday. With everything there would be to do, the two extra days was a merciful extension. Jonathan knew that I had to work on Tuesday evening and apologized for taking so much of my time over the next week but told me that he relied on me. He reminded me that he would be home from California later that day and would call me as soon as he walked in the door so we could talk about everything that was happening directly, something we had not yet been able to do. Ending his message on a hopeful note, he told me that he missed me and that perhaps we could both be together in Paladin after the beginning of the year.

After reading his messages, I got busy trying to find storage facilities near Jonathan's soon-to-be-vacant home. In the end, I found three. In calling to make arrangements, I learned that the closest was booked up, but the second-closest had space available. I found that we could rent a $10' \times 15'$ room for $104 a month, and if that wasn't enough, we could rent two. That was perfect. Jonathan had wanted to rent a moving van for Saturday and Sunday, but when I inquired about them, I learned that none of the three facilities had one available, at least on Saturday. That wasn't perfect.

Later that morning, I caught Jonathan online. I told him what I had learned about the rooms and he seemed pleased. He had been concerned about getting a van on the weekend, but with the extra time we now had, it wasn't crucial to get one on Saturday, as would have originally been required. He suggested trying to get one for Sunday and Monday, which would then leave Tuesday and Wednesday free for taking care of smaller things. That seemed easier to arrange and I assured him I would look into it.

He told me that he was planning to take his clothes as well as some pictures and mementos to Dan's, the latter in order to "give [him] some sense of who [he was]." It seemed crucial to him to maintain his identity in a space that was not his own. He also said that Dan had refused to accept rent, welcoming him as his guest. Jonathan was amazed, but I told him Dan's attitude just emphasized what a good friend he was.

Even so, Jonathan was concerned because even though he agreed and described Dan as a "doll," he also pointed out that Dan drank and could be "very touchy." He was also concerned about how Dan would react to the dogs. According to Jonathan, Dan was almost obsessively clean and the dogs were dirty to varying degrees and didn't always act housebroken. He said, though, that he was now planning to spent maybe a couple of months at Dan's and that he and the dogs would try to stay out of Dan's way.

He also mentioned his ongoing negotiations with the company that wanted to buy shares of OutSource. Saying first that it was nearly 8:00 his time but later correcting that to 9:00, he stated that he had another meeting in a few minutes. He said that he'd met with the executive vice president at 6:30 that morning and had obtained a "handshake" deal. He said he had gotten a little more money and a shorter pay-in than expected, so he thought Mike should be happy. As part of the deal, Jonathan explained, OutSource could veto the second 10% if they were unhappy with how things were going and the other company had to resell their shares to them or OutSource would have the power to veto the company's decisions about whom they could sell their shares to. The only exception was if the other company was sold as a whole entity. He concluded by telling me that the other company had been given only one seat on OutSource's board of directors instead of two, which is what they had originally wanted. He seemed to feel it was a good deal and I agreed, insofar as I understood business.

Knowing that he needed to get to his meeting, I told him not to worry about the arrangements that needed to be made for the move, that I would take care of everything. In response, Jonathan told me, "You are the best" and added, "The only thing that I got lucky with recently was meeting you." After our exchange, I was even more motivated to help.

After I got offline, I called the second-closest facility and placed a hold on one of the rooms. In addition, I asked about the van. Although we needed the largest size available, I was informed that they didn't have the size we needed on all the days we needed it. In the end, however, I found a fourth facility some distance from where Jonathan lived that did. I didn't put a hold on the van, however, because I wanted to get Jonathan's approval. Although the issues of the room and the van were now settled, that was in some ways only the beginning.

Later that afternoon, Jonathan, who had finally gotten home, called. His voice was so different, so odd, that if I couldn't have told from the caller ID that it was him, I might not have known at first who it was. Apart from sounding extremely fatigued, his accent, strangely, had "flattened" to the point that he no longer sounded British, but American. As we spoke, his accent returned to normal, but it worried me because I didn't know what it said about his condition.

Before we got down to discussing the arrangements I had managed to make, Jonathan told me about a disturbing incident that had taken place before he had left California. He informed me that he had fainted in the lobby of the hotel at which he was staying. He seemed to brush it off, however, attributing it not to his illness or stress or lack of rest but to hypoglycemia from not eating properly. I was unsettled by the news because I suspected there was something more behind it than low blood sugar, that it was in fact an effect of his faltering health. I was relieved, however, to know that he had made it home alive if not entirely well.

Hoping it would help him feel that at least some of the burden had been taken off him, I told him that I had made all the necessary arrangements and just needed him to okay them. He did, so once we got off the phone, I reserved the van and otherwise made certain that the plans were in place.

Later that evening, I called him and told him that everything was set. Although he was still exhausted, at least this time he sounded British. During both conversations, Jonathan mentioned that instead of outright quitting, he was seriously thinking about telling Mike that he needed to take a leave of absence. If he could arrange it, that sounded like the best solution, at least in the short term, to the dilemma of allowing him to keep his job, but also giving him some time to stabilize his health and life.

Later that night, Jonathan sent me an e-mail that was both concerning and touching. He began by telling me that after we'd gotten off the phone, he'd begun to get undressed and had passed out again. He said that after he'd come to, he had just lain on the floor for a while before getting up. He assured me, though, that he was all right and once again attributed his fainting to hypoglycemia, which I didn't accept. He then went on to tell me that I was "so good" to him and that he wished I had been there when he had gotten home. He said that he was "lonely and a little scared" that night and that he missed me "more then usual." For more reasons than one, I wanted to be with him more than usual.

He told me that he had decided to meet with Mike the next morning and insist that he grant him a one-month medical leave. He said he wanted to use September to collect himself and try to feel normal again. Anguished, he confessed that it was "gutwrenching" to put all of his belongings in storage and go live in someone else's house, but added that he didn't have much choice. Referencing Jim Morrison, he said that "strange days" were upon us, something with which I wholeheartedly agreed. He said he was planning to go to Dan's the next afternoon to take some more of his "precious things" and would be back later that night only to have to go to the doctor at 8:30 Friday morning. He ended his message by saying that he was like "that Elvis song—lonely tonight."

The next morning, Jonathan sent me another message in which he expressed his feelings about what he was facing. He said he was still "completely freaked out" but was trying to cope. He said that he was running late but had a full day that consisted of going to the doctor, then to the office, then to Dan's. I was somewhat confused because Jonathan had originally said his doctor's appointment was Friday, not Thursday, but I assumed that either he'd miswritten or I'd misread his previous message. He told me that the next week would be "the most stressful of [his] life" and stated again that he was "totally freaked out." He said, though, that he "could not do this or make it without [me] and [my] help." He admitted that it was hard for him to ask for help and that he appreciated what I was doing to help him. Thus ended the last e-mail that he sent to me from the house on Millstone Drive.

I planned to give him as much help as possible. My plan was to go to Paladin on Friday after teaching my morning class and remain there, at least until the following Wednesday, when the move would be complete. I couldn't wait to get Jonathan out of that house, out of that life.

■

Sometime that week, I happened to visit the *Gayteway* board for my state. While I was there, I found that on the evening of Friday, August 10, someone calling himself "GayDaddy" had posted an ad on the board. In this ad, "GayDaddy" began by saying that at 10:00 he had just gotten home after a "shit" day at work and was "horny as hell." He described himself as being in his mid-40s, weighing 170 pounds, and standing 5'8". In addition, he described himself as a "top Daddy" and as "cut 7", thick." He said that he wanted oral sex—or "head," as he described it. After stating that he just wanted "no strings fun," he said that he would check the board again around 11:00 or midnight then "jerk off" if no one was interested.

Then, less than twenty minutes later, "GayDaddy" had posted another message that, perhaps, revealed his level of sexual desperation. After repackaging his previous posting, he told respondents to leave him a way to contact him, then said, "let's do it." He ended the message by informing respondents that he was "for real" and asked them if they were too.

Finally, a little over an hour later, "GayDaddy," who had apparently gotten no "takers," posted a final message in which, almost condemningly, he announced to the users of the board that he had been forced to "jerk off."

GayDaddy. Something about that name caught my attention. Its structure was similar to that of "Gayman," in which the first component, "Gay," and the second component were written as one word. "Gayman" was, of course, the alias that Jonathan had given in his personals ad that I had answered. The way that "GayDaddy" described himself, however, was even more striking. His statistics were essentially identical to Jonathan's. First, "GayDaddy" described himself as "cut 7", thick," while in his ad that I had answered, Jonathan had described himself as "7+ cut thick." Second, Jonathan sometimes described oral sex as "getting head." Third, just days before—around the time that "GayDaddy" would have posted his ad, in fact—Jonathan had used the term "top daddy" in a conversation we'd had in reference to himself.

And, finally, there was the date: August 10. That was the day I had received an e-mail from Jonathan around 10:00 that evening in which he had described the bad day he'd had with repeated uses of the word "shit." In it, he told me he had come home from work to find that the dogs had "shit" in the back hall. He told me that work had been difficult and that Mike had given him lots of "shit." He commented that "shit" flowed downhill and everyone was below him. Finally, he told me that the dogs had gotten into the popcorn he'd fixed himself for dinner, which he figured would give them the "shits." All in all, there were four uses of the word "shit" in a message that was roughly 130 words long. It seemed to be his word of the day.

I didn't know what to think. Was the person who had posted the ad Jonathan? Or was it simply someone who had found Jonathan's ad that I had answered—which was still posted—and incorporated fitting phrases from it into his own? People, lacking imagination or writing skills, sometimes resorted to that. The poster had, however, described himself as having had a "shit" day at work, something that Jonathan had not included in his public personals ad, but *had* included in his *private* e-mail to me. In addition, both Jonathan and "GayDaddy" had been using the computer at the same time: 10:00 P.M. If it *was* Jonathan, then what did that mean? Was he soliciting sex behind my back? But why would he be so devious when he had freely admitted to sleeping with Chase just the day before "GayDaddy"—he?—had posted his ad? Perhaps because I had no way of deciding the issue one way or another, I didn't think about it further—at least consciously.

Unconsciously, however, the lack of resolution continued to exert an influence. In spite of Jonathan's assurance that there were "really no, or very, very few secrets" that he held, that if I wanted to know anything about him all I needed to do was to ask him and he would tell me the truth, he had also made the comment—jokingly—that perhaps he was giving me just enough truth to make me think he was being truthful with me about everything when he wasn't. Which was true? I couldn't shake the growing feeling that Jonathan had not revealed to me everything there was to know about him, that perhaps he wasn't as truthful as he had led me to believe, as I liked to believe.

—13—
EXEUNT

*I am sad at leaving my home and it is gutwrenching to put all of
my things away and go live in someone else's house but I have
not much choice.*

On the last day of August, I arrived at Jonathan's sometime around noon to find Jonathan in the initial stages of sorting. We settled on an agenda for the remainder of the day, part of which involved going to the doctor at 1:00.

The doctor's office was, ironically, located in the same complex in which I had worked during my ill-fated tenure in Paladin some two years before. The buildings that comprised the complex were arranged around a courtyard and the building in which Jonathan's doctor had his office was located directly across from the one in which my former employer had his. That was about as close as I wanted to get to that office, that part of my life, again.

As we walked to the door, Jonathan said that he had decided not to have anything further to do with Chase. He shook his head and threw up his hand, indicating that he couldn't deal with him, with the situation, anymore. He said that he realized now what was important, *who* was important. He said that since Chase would be returning to college in Hawthorn and would no longer be going to the Stress Center, that would make the detachment simpler.

While I waited the forty-five minutes it took Jonathan to finish his visit, I spent some time wandering around the premises. This was the first time I had been to the building since I had lost my job and the emotional reaction that I had to being there again surprised me. Although I wanted to avoid my former office, the avoidance was based less on a need to stay away from something unpleasant than on a simple lack of interest in something that no longer mattered. In the two years that had passed since the "Paladin Incident," I had built a life that, although financially not as satisfying as the one I'd had in Paladin, was, nonetheless, *emotionally* satisfying, a feeling that no amount of money could buy. Although I had become discontent with my job in recent times for different reasons, teaching psychology was, as jobs went, more gratifying than many other things I could have been doing, which was part of why I continued to do it. In addition, in spite of the emotional roller coaster I had been riding for the past two months, my relationship with Jonathan did fulfill certain needs, which was part of why I tried to overlook some of the difficulties that had arisen. Because my life seemed better now than it had two years before, I felt that after experiencing the failure of two years before, I had somehow returned in triumph.

We returned to Jonathan's sometime around 2:00. Shortly thereafter, Laura, a friend of Jonathan's from the Stress Center, arrived to help. By that point, Jonathan had provided me with some information about Laura. Laura, who lived in the nearby town of St. Alban, had started going to the Stress Center around the beginning of August. She had lost her job in the spring and had been having difficulty dealing with the stress of being unemployed. In addition, she was divorced with two teenage sons, named Chuck, who was around 20, and Jack, who was around 18, whom she was trying to raise alone, something that had only added to her stress. While at the Center, she had met Jonathan and they had become friends. Apparently, their friendship had evolved rapidly enough in the few short weeks they had known each other that Jonathan felt comfortable involving her in the move. Perhaps he also felt desperate for help in the daunting task before him, but the intimate atmosphere of the support group—informally known as "Group"—to which they belonged had undoubtedly helped to foster an immediate closeness that had accelerated the development of their friendship.

Laura was slightly older than Jonathan but seemed younger, not only because she had an athletic build that made her look younger than she actually was, but also because she possessed a vitality that gave her a youthful quality. She was very friendly and seemed eager to pitch in and do whatever she could to help someone in need. I liked her immediately. I also liked the fact that she got my Americanized sense of humor, something that sometimes seemed lost on Jonathan.

We started in the kitchen and spent the better part of the afternoon sorting, wrapping, and packing the items there. In the process, Jonathan found a package of 4" × 6" prints, some of which were of Glenn. The pictures appeared to have been taken on

Christmas Day, 1999, the first and only Christmas that Jonathan and Glenn had spent together in Paladin. The only picture of Glenn that I had previously seen had been one of him and Jonathan standing on a boat that Jonathan kept on the dresser in his bedroom. Because that picture had been taken at something of a distance, their images were relatively small, and because they were both wearing sunglasses, their faces were obscured. Therefore, I had never gotten a good look at Glenn. One picture in particular showed Glenn dressed in long underwear, standing somewhere between the living room and dining room, grinning broadly for the camera. Glenn appeared to be taller than Jonathan, somewhere between his height and mine, and have a stocky build, similar to Jonathan's. Actually, the most striking aspect of Glenn's appearance was how much he looked like Jonathan, at least in a general way. He had a rounded, flattened, somewhat full face, like Jonathan's, and short, thick, black hair, also like Jonathan's. They didn't look like twins, but they definitely looked as if they could be related, which I found interesting.

Later that afternoon, we decided to quit for the day. Before Laura left, she and Jonathan spent some time chatting at the door. Her manner toward Jonathan seemed overly friendly, almost flirty. When he closed the door, he looked at me and, rolling his eyes, said, "I feel like an hors d'oeuvre." I wasn't sure how to interpret her behavior.

Because we had been so helpful, Jonathan decided to treat Laura and me to dinner. That evening, she drove back to Jonathan's and Jonathan drove the three of us to one of the Chinese restaurants where Jonathan and I had eaten before, the one where Jonathan had raised the issue of whether or not I, as a child, had ever slept with any of my teachers.

During the trip home, Laura reminded Jonathan to tell Glenn to take his medication. When I asked Jonathan what kind of medication it was, he told me that Glenn had trouble with his stomach and that it was stomach medicine. I felt no need to inquire further about Glenn's medicine or condition.

■

Later that night, I was lying on the sofa in the sunroom, watching TV, while Jonathan checked his e-mail. After my busy day, I was half-dozing by the time Jonathan finally reappeared. He sat down on the sofa and took me by the arms. I sat up, coming fully awake. Pensive, Jonathan said, "When two people have been together for a while, there comes a point when they should start thinking about living together."

Living together. This was often as close to a marriage proposal as a gay man got. He had hinted at the idea of living together, but until then, he had never been explicit about it. Because of the way I had come to feel, I was open to the idea, in spite of the problems that we had recently experienced. He restated his plan to spend the next couple of months at Dan's, while he got himself together, and voiced his hope that doing so would be a good thing. Then, he said that although he couldn't make promises, we should afterwards find a place in Paladin and move in together.

I felt flattered and touched that he wanted us to live together. I felt special because, in spite of having other options, he had chosen *me*. In addition, I felt that through adversity and uncertainty, I had somehow persevered and was now reaping the reward. That day marked an ending and a beginning, a turning point for us in more ways than one.

■

On the morning of Saturday, September 1, we were up by 8:30. Our plan was to investigate the storage unit that I had tentatively reserved, then return to Jonathan's and resume packing.

I got dressed in the bedroom while Jonathan got ready in the adjoining bathroom. At one point, I looked into the bathroom to see him standing before the mirror crossing himself. Then, he broke down and began crying.

I hurried into the bathroom and asked him what was wrong. He looked up at me with tortured, tear-filled eyes and said, "I'm losing my home!"

I reached out and pulled him close, his head pressed against my chest. I told him it was all right, to let it out, but then he said that he was sorry, that he needed to be strong, but couldn't. I looked down at him, into his pain-filled eyes and told him that I would be strong for the both of us. "All right," he said, in a tone and with a look of resignation that reminded me, eerily, of the expressions of a child more than those of an adult. *I* would have to be the strong one now.

After he had recovered and dressed, I drove us to the storage facility. While we were sitting in the car before we went in, he broke down once again. He told me that he didn't know if he could do this, and I told him that with my help he could. Perhaps with that encouragement, he stiffened his upper lip and we went in.

After getting the key to the unit, we walked to the warehouse-like building behind the main office to inspect the room. The 10′ × 15′ space proved smaller than either of us had envisioned, and the walls of the room were unfinished, having neither insulation nor drywall. Jonathan expressed his discomfort at leaving his things in such a cramped space where they would be subject to the vagaries of weather and temperature far more than was ideal. I had to agree.

We went back to the main office to see about getting a better room and, as it turned out, the largest room they had, a 29' × 15', climate-controlled space, was available. We went back to the units to inspect the larger room, which proved to be vastly superior to the smaller one we had seen. The room, which actually consisted of three smaller rooms that had been joined together, was constructed of painted, well-mortared concrete blocks, was equipped with cooling and heating vents, and sported an abundance of fluorescent lighting. Although the cost for this space was considerably higher than the cost for the other—$229 a month as opposed to $104—we had already anticipated renting two of the smaller rooms, for a combined cost of $208 a month. Consequently, the additional $21 a month, especially in light of the superior quality of the larger room, seemed entirely acceptable.

When the time came to complete the rental agreement, Jonathan said that he was too upset about leaving his home and too confused from the effects of his illness to do it. He also said that he was too upset and confused even to fill out the check for the first month's rent. Then, he asked me if I would fill out the agreement and make the payment myself. He told me to give him the bills as they came in and he would pay them. Because he seemed so dysfunctional and desperate, and because we now seemed committed in a way that we had not before, I agreed. I filled out the contract myself and, because it seemed easier, I placed the charge on my credit card and authorized the facility to automatically charge my credit card each month that his things remained in storage.

■

After returning to Jonathan's, we resumed the chores of moving. By 10:00, no one had shown up and Jonathan expressed his concerns that no one would. The thought that the two of us might be the only ones to perform the daunting task ahead of us prompted him to express something that, in one way, he already had, but that he wanted to reaffirm. At one point, he stopped me in the foyer and said, "It's just the two of us—not just today, but from now on." Then, for the first time, he uttered the "L" word. He told me that he loved me and I told him, in return, that I loved him. He commented that I hadn't said that before and kissed me. With that, our relationship moved to yet another level.

I hadn't told him that I loved him before then, not only because I wasn't emotionally prepared to take the risk of stating that, but also because I didn't know what I would have meant by it. I loved Jonathan, but I wasn't *in* love with him—an important distinction. I did have a strong affection for him, in spite of some of the things he had done to hurt me, and I felt an equally strong sympathy toward him. He was going through a difficult time and, over the past couple of months, I had seen how his life had slowly unraveled. He seemed to be good to me in some important ways and lately had become so dependent on me, beyond everyone else, which not only flattered me, but also provoked in me a powerful reciprocal response. By that point, I had certainly developed strong feelings toward him, but it was still difficult for me to define precisely what those feelings were. "Love" seemed to be the closest I could get.

As it turned out, Jonathan's concerns that we alone would be left to move him proved unfounded. Later that morning, Laura returned and more of Jonathan's friends from the Stress Center also showed. Until the middle of August, I hadn't met any of Jonathan's friends, but now, it seemed, I was being inundated with them. One person who came the second day was Greg—not his best friend Greg, but "fat" Greg, as Jonathan made the distinction. Jonathan claimed that Greg weighed 500 pounds, but whether he did or didn't, Greg was, indisputably, one of the most heavyset people I had ever met. Although he was decidedly obese, his fat was layered over a powerfully muscular build and the fat itself seemed dense instead of loose, giving him a solid, surprisingly defined look. For someone who weighed so much, he was also surprisingly energetic and agile and had no difficulty helping us with the moving. In fact, Greg was able to do things that the rest of us couldn't and I was astonished to watch him on several occasions lift heavy items over his head as easily as I might have lifted a piece of paper. Greg seemed friendly and I was happy to have someone that strong on hand to help us. In addition, Greg was gay, so I didn't have to deal with the homophobia that I often found in heterosexual men.

Greg also brought his friend Cheryl, who proved highly focused and organized. Although I wasn't sure of the relationship between the two, I got the impression that Cheryl fell into the "fag hag" category, a heterosexual woman who wanted male companionship, but didn't want the sexual pressure that frequently accompanied it. Sometime that afternoon, a lesbian couple from the Stress Center dropped past briefly to visit for a while and generally wish Jonathan well. I was surprised to see that Jonathan actually had friends who were lesbian, given the disdain he seemed to have for them.

It was on the same day that Jonathan gave Sadie away. Horatio seemed to have abandoned her and Jonathan was no longer able to care for her. Someone from the Stress Center, who loved dogs and seemed to be able to provide her with a good home, took Sadie. I had always liked her, even if she could be overwhelming, and was sad to see her go. So was Jonathan. Her loss from the life on Millstone Drive only added more sadness to an already sad situation.

At one point, Jonathan and I found ourselves sitting in the living room alone. He was holding the Surrealist vase and told me that he was going to leave it to me—meaning, in his will. When I told him that I didn't want it, he asked me if I didn't want something to remember him by. I told him that wasn't what I meant and tried to steer him away from such morbid thoughts. At that moment, his despair over having to leave his home on Millstone Drive seemed deeper than ever.

■

Later that afternoon, Laura and I found ourselves in Jonathan's office, sorting through the innumerable pieces of clothing that Jonathan owned, some of which he had stuffed into the sliding closet the room contained. Jonathan said that Cliff had once remarked that he owned more clothes than anyone he knew—altogether, we counted *four hundred* shirts and that was *only* the shirts—and sorting and packing all that clothing proved to be a major preoccupation during the move. We developed a system in which we would simply pull a plastic trash bag over a bundle of fifteen or twenty shirts, poke the hanger hooks through the bottom, then secure the bag by wrapping tape around the hangers' necks. Most of the rest of Jonathan's clothes went into trash bags and in the end we had dozens of bags in addition to everything else we had to store.

As Laura and I worked, we had what proved to be an enlightening—but disturbing—conversation about Jonathan.

"So, how do you know Jonathan?" she asked.

How did I know Jonathan? "We've been seeing each other for the past two and a half months."

"Oh, really?" she said, surprised.

"Yes. Didn't he tell you?"

"No. When I asked him about you, all he said was, 'I think he likes me'."

"Really." I didn't know what to think about that statement, which seemed like a very casual way to describe our relationship. Eventually, I learned that in spite of the fact that we had been involved with each other for close to three months and the fact that he had been going to the Stress Center for at least two, he had never mentioned me to anyone there. I felt more than a little dismayed.

Eventually the conversation drifted to what Jonathan had been discussing in Group. He hadn't been discussing *me*, but apparently, he *had* been discussing Glenn. That was understandable, though, given that Jonathan almost certainly had residual issues from his nine-year relationship with Glenn, but Jonathan had never actually mentioned anything in particular to me. He had, however, been more specific, more revealing, with the people in Group. Laura told me that Jonathan had said that he was still having problems coping with the fact that during their relationship, Glenn was beating him up.

Beating him up? I was stunned. The most Jonathan had told me was that he and Glenn had grown apart, which naturally would cause dissatisfaction and friction, but he had *never* indicated to me, in any way, that things had become *violent* between them.

"So, Jonathan was in an abusive relationship?" I said, wanting to make no mistake.

"Yes."

I asked her how long the abuse had gone on and she indicated it had done so for some time.

Then she added, "Glenn was schizophrenic."

Schizophrenic? Jonathan had *definitely* never told *me* that Glenn was *schizophrenic.* He had, in fact, never indicated that he was mentally ill in any way, only perhaps somewhat unhappy with his current life. Were we talking about the same person? I was beginning to feel uncomfortable about what I was learning, about what not learning it sooner, from Jonathan, implied.

At some point, the conversation came around to Jonathan's sexual behavior. Laura already knew that he had slept with Chase and I told her about the "GayDaddy" ad, which I suspected Jonathan had authored. I wasn't *certain* it was him, but I couldn't shake the feeling that perhaps it was. In any event, I told her I thought that based on what I knew about his past and his present, he was sexually compulsive, something to which she seemed to agree.

I mentioned to Laura that I was the one who was paying for the move and had already placed the charge for the first month's rent for the storage unit on my credit card. The charge for first month's rent was $229.95, and although I didn't yet know how much the moving van would ultimately cost, I had been quoted a price of $40 a day, so for four days, the charge would be at least $160; together, then, that amounted to almost $400. On my salary, I didn't have $400 to throw away and began to wonder if I could trust Jonathan to repay me. I began to wonder if I could trust Jonathan, period. Laura, too, seemed concerned.

When the conversation turned serious, Laura and I slipped outside to the driveway to continue our discussion, out of earshot of Jonathan.

Resuming the theme of his sexual behavior, Laura told me how she and Jonathan had come to meet. She said that one day shortly after she had started going to the Stress Center, she had said something somewhat derogatory about gay people in front of Jonathan. She said that someone had then informed her that Jonathan was gay. Feeling bad for what she had said, she apologized to Jonathan, telling him she didn't realize he was gay.

In response, Jonathan had said—seductively—"I'm not *completely* gay."

Laura then went on to say that Jonathan had propositioned her, saying, "He wanted me to join him in a threesome."

I knew how flirty Jonathan could be, so perhaps she had gotten the wrong impression. Even so, I was beginning to feel as if we were talking about two different people. I didn't know how to process, to put together, everything I was learning.

A few minutes later, Jonathan appeared. He seemed nervous and asked us if everything was all right. It wasn't, but we pretended it was. I was going to have to have a talk with Jonathan and I wasn't looking forward to it.

Later that afternoon, I had the opportunity to talk to Greg. He, too, asked me how I knew Jonathan and he, too, was surprised when I told him we were seeing each other, since he had never mentioned me to anyone in Group. He *did* say, though, that in Group, Jonathan *did* mention Cliff, saying that was almost all Jonathan talked about. It was always "Cliff, Cliff, Cliff," he said. I realized Jonathan had unresolved issues with Cliff, but I also felt that I could have been mentioned sometime to someone, since I liked to think I was important too. I was very dismayed.

After my enlightening conversation with Greg, I went back to working in the house. Later that afternoon, first Greg then Laura left. When Laura left, Jonathan went out to her car with her, while I stayed inside. About fifteen or twenty minutes later, I was standing in the living room when Jonathan came into the room through the kitchen door. He came up to me and, wide-eyed with what seemed to be surprise, he said, "Why didn't you tell me that Laura was in love with me!"

"What?"

"Laura just told me she was in love with me!"

"She didn't tell *me* she was in love with you." I probably would have had a different, more stunned, reaction to Laura's declaration, but I was too focused on, too consumed by, our earlier conversation—and the one I would have to have with Jonathan.

Ignoring for the time what had just happened, I said, "Jonathan, we need to have a talk."

"I knew there was something wrong," he said in an aggravated tone.

"Why don't we sit down."

We went into the sunroom and seated ourselves, I in the white chair and he in the purple one. "So what's wrong?" he asked.

I got right to the point. "Laura told me that you told the people in Group that Glenn was schizophrenic."

Jonathan paused for a moment, again thinking before answering. "I did *not* say that Glenn was *schizophrenic*. I said that his behavior was schizophrenic-*like*. He would go into these states where he would suddenly become the opposite of the way he normally was."

"She also told me that Glenn abused you."

After a moment of hesitation, Jonathan finally admitted that while he had led me to believe that he and Glenn had simply grown apart, the *real* reason he and Glenn had broken up was that during the last few months of their relationship, Glenn had turned violent and had started beating him up. Until that point, Glenn had never been physical with him, but during one argument, Glenn suddenly punched him in the face. Afterwards, Glenn had apologized, and Jonathan had tried to brush the incident off, viewing it as an "aberration" where Glenn's emotions had "boiled over" and assuming it would never happen again.

Unfortunately, it did. Some time later, Jonathan and Glenn had gotten into another fight that had started off verbal, but had ended up physical. This time, the beating Jonathan had suffered was far more severe. According to Jonathan, Glenn had broken out a tooth, bloodied his nose, and blacked an eye. I had noticed before that one of Jonathan's teeth was missing and its absence now seemed to have an explanation. Jonathan said that because of the condition of his eye, he had been forced to go to a business meeting the next day wearing sunglasses to cover the evidence of what had happened. He also said that the fight had taken place in the guest bedroom and had been so violent that it had actually left bloodstains on the wall from where Glenn had bloodied his nose and the blood had splattered onto the wall.

At that point, Jonathan decided that if Glenn's behavior was going to become a pattern, they could no longer remain together. Jonathan never made it clear whether or not he ever attempted to obtain some kind of help for Glenn, to find out why he had suddenly turned violent and what could be done to stop his behavior. He did say, however, that since Glenn no longer had any reason to remain in the United States, he had decided to return to England.

Jonathan claimed that even when they had gone to the airport the day that Glenn had returned to England, Glenn had threatened to kill him and had pushed him down an escalator, injuring him. Jonathan had several long scratches that ran along his left arm, which I had previously noted and asked him about. He had explained that he had gotten them when he had lost his balance and had fallen down the escalator as he had attempted to help Horatio carry unwieldy baggage. Now, however, he admitted that he had incurred the scratches not by *falling* down the escalator trying to help *Horatio*, but by being *shoved* down the escalator by *Glenn*.

"Why didn't you tell me any of this?" I asked

"It's difficult for me to talk about it," he said.

I could appreciate his feelings, but I still felt that I should have been told about it. "I feel I deserved to know this," I told him. "I feel I had a right to know that you'd been in an abusive relationship because that has an effect on me, on our relationship."

By this point, Jonathan was becoming flustered. "I don't like the fact that Laura was discussing things with you that I discussed in Group. That information is supposed to be confidential."

I found that statement ironic, given that Jonathan *constantly* discussed the problems of the people in the Group with *me*, including more lately Laura's, and had once stated that the main reason he continued to go when he didn't feel it was doing him much good was that the drama in the lives of the people who came was "better than a soap opera."

I asked him why no one in Group seemed to have heard of me. I told him that when Laura had asked him who I was, he had replied, "I think he likes me."

Jonathan explained that she had misreported what he had said. He told me that when Laura had asked him who I was, he had said, "I think he *likes* me" in an exaggerated, suggestive tone that was supposed to indicate to her that we were romantically involved. Perhaps, then, she had just misunderstood, but Jonathan seemed to believe there was more to it than that. He had told me that Laura had just acknowledged that she was in love with him, and he believed that she had actually twisted the information she had given to me to drive a wedge between us, in effect, to eliminate the competition. He believed that, despite having told her that he *was* "completely" gay, she couldn't accept that and was now determined to do whatever she could to keep him to herself.

I didn't know what to believe, but I considered the possibility that Jonathan might be right. Laura had come across as too enthusiastic, too eager to help, too sweet. She had known Jonathan for only four weeks, which made me wonder where the intensity of her desire originated. She had been unemployed since spring, by that point several months, and she didn't seem to be able to hold a job for an extended period of time. She also knew that Jonathan had money—lots of it—as the most cursory glance at his belongings attested. Perhaps she saw Jonathan as her ticket to Easy Street and was now determined to do whatever she could to insinuate herself into his life as fully as possible, regardless of what she had to do to accomplish it. The love of money was indeed the root of many evils and people had certainly done far more to have far less than what Jonathan had.

At that point, I began to dislike, and distrust, Laura.

■

On the morning of Sunday, the 2nd, we went to the facility from which I had intended to rent the moving van. In spite of what had happened the day before, I placed the charge for the van on my credit card, which, I was assured, was $40 a day.

I thought I would have no difficulty driving the van myself, but as it turned out, the van was a stick shift, not an automatic, and I had almost no experience driving the former. Jonathan, who told me that virtually all automobiles in England were stick shifts, said that he would drive the van himself. In spite of everything that I was already doing and had already done, I still felt guilty that I couldn't drive the van myself and thereby spare Jonathan the burden of trying to maneuver such an unwieldy vehicle.

Despite the fact that he didn't have an American driver's license, Jonathan drove the van to his home. Somehow, he managed to maneuver the van into the front yard and park it in front of the front door. Although I had felt bad about not being able to drive the van myself, I did feel better when Jonathan later told Laura and Greg that driving the big van made him feel "very butch."

The next three days were a blur of packing, loading, moving, unloading, storing, returning and repeating the process all over again. The process was occasionally punctuated by secondary considerations called "eating" and "sleeping." Thankfully, the early September weather remained sunny, if somewhat warm. The temperatures rose into the 80s during the day, and although the humidity remained comparatively low, the effects of our exertion made it seem much hotter than it actually was. Although we had an ample supply of cold drinks and ice on hand, I felt constantly thirsty and was functioning in a state of dehydration. In addition, I was so stimulated that I had lost much of my appetite and my ability to sleep, which meant that I wasn't replenishing my energy at the same rate I was expending it. Although Jonathan was helping with the move, I was worried about him overexerting himself in his depleted condition, so I felt compelled to do as much as possible. In addition, I was always mindful of the Wednesday deadline that loomed ever closer and was driven by a desire to make sure that Jonathan didn't have to leave any of his things behind.

At one point, we were cleaning out the Art Deco display case when Jonathan pulled out a small white box. I had seen that kind of box before. After removing the lid, he showed us two Egyptian scarabs like the one he had given to me for my birthday. He told us that he had gotten three because he had thought they were "neat." I remember hoping at the time that in the disorder of the move he didn't lose them. Many months later, I would learn about the fate of one of them.

■

At some point during the move, Jonathan went into the office to use the computer. After a while, he called to me. He wanted to know the location of Mariah, a city in my state. Although I had heard of Mariah, I had never thought about it and didn't know precisely where it was. I did know about certain famous people who had come from there, but beyond that, Mariah to me was as *terra incognita* as Timbuktu.

He wanted to know because while he was online, he had found out about an executive position at a hospital in Mariah that he thought he might be able to do. Although Jonathan had been granted medical leave from OutSource, he had begun to feel that his increasingly poor health no longer allowed him to do his former job, forcing him to either get a job that was more manageable or go on long-term disability. By this point, Jonathan was no longer thinking about retiring in January, and although I didn't understand why he couldn't retire four months early, I half-assumed that taking his retirement before a certain time would adversely affect his retirement income or that taking a leave and the resulting cut in pay would now require him to work longer. From what I understood, the job in Mariah involved restructuring the hospital to make its operation more cost-effective. The job seemed much less demanding than his position at OutSource did and would allow him to do something productive rather than simply sit around and stagnate, a prospect that he didn't find desirable. Once we figured out where Mariah was, Jonathan decided to look into the position.

On that day, I knew next to nothing about Mariah, but in the months to come, I would learn more about it than I had ever thought I would.

■

On the evening of Tuesday, the 4th, I had to teach in Viridian. That meant making a one-hour trip instead of a two-hour trip to the campus in Hawthorn, something for which I was thankful. Somehow, I managed to summon the energy to spend the day moving in weather that turned out to be hotter than they had predicted before heading to my "second," and somehow secondary, job teaching. After leaving the storage unit around 4:30, I hurried back to Jonathan's house to clean off the sweat and grime of the day's labor and change into my "business drag" before making the trip to Viridian. That was the first time I had been alone since the move had begun. Although the solitude was delightful, getting ready was frustrating not only because there was no hot water, as there hadn't been for the past two months, but also because the toilet in the guest bathroom, which had become "my" bathroom, had decided to back up. It didn't overflow, but it came perilously close. The house seemed to be falling apart piece by piece, strangely mirroring the way that Jonathan's life had done the same. I was glad that by the same time tomorrow, Jonathan would no longer be burdened with the house, with the mess that it had become in more ways than one.

Class that evening proceeded uneventfully and proved a welcome respite from the preoccupation with the move. I dismissed class somewhat early, however, since I faced a long drive, at night, back to Paladin and was tired enough as it was.

I arrived back at Jonathan's sometime around 10:00. The driveway was empty and the house was deserted. After returning the moving van, which we no longer needed, Jonathan and Laura had planned to drop off some of Jonathan's belongings at Dan's before returning to Paladin. I assumed they had simply taken longer than expected to complete their task, but I half-wondered if something more significant had happened to delay them. All I could do, however, was wait.

I went into the house, which had been left lighted. The girls greeted me at the door, as they had done for nearly three months now, then went about their business once they saw I was friend and not foe. I was starved, so I went into the kitchen to see what might be left to eat. In the end, I dined on potato chips and cheese dip washed down with a soft drink.

Although I had been alone in the house earlier that afternoon, this was the first time since the move had begun that I had been alone in the house with my thoughts—about the house, about everything. By now, the house had been almost totally emptied with only a few stray belongings, boxes, and bits of packing material left to furnish the rooms. Apart from the emptiness, I noticed that the acoustical quality inside the house had changed—without the presence of so many objects to absorb and dampen the sound, the sound waves reflected sharply, almost cavernously, off the walls. Somehow, that only emphasized the emptiness.

I felt that in some way I, too, was being emptied. For almost three months, the house had been the stage for the drama, the comedy, the tragedy that had been my relationship with Jonathan, an unlikely combination of people from different countries, different cultures, different classes, different consciousnesses. That act of the play had now come to an end and the set on which it had been performed was now being dismantled. After tomorrow, that part of the play would become part of the past, transferred from physical reality to phantasmal memory.

Despite the heat of the day, the night had turned off somewhat cool. At one point, I went out to my car to retrieve my jacket. As I did, an SUV appeared on Millstone Drive, heading my way. As it approached, it slowed then turned into the driveway. I saw that it was Dan's SUV. When it parked, I was surprised to see Jonathan and Laura get out. While I had been gone, I learned, I had missed some excitement.

They told me that on their way to return the moving van, it had run out of gas. They hadn't been able to make it to a gas station before it had run out, but eventually they had managed to find someone who had been willing to sell them a gallon of gas for five dollars—some three times the current price. Then, after they had decided to stop by the storage facility on their way to the facility from which we'd rented the van, it had broken down as they were parking it. I wasn't surprised to hear about the breakdown because, according to the odometer, the van had already accrued over 134,000 miles. Therefore, they had been forced to leave the van at the storage facility, not the one from which we'd rented it.

Then, when they had gotten to Dan's, Jonathan's *own* car had broken down. Jonathan said that he had called the school from Dan's to tell me what had happened, but I had already left. In the end, Dan had loaned Jonathan his SUV so that he and Laura could get back to Paladin.

I couldn't believe the turn of events. It seemed like some kind of bizarre comedy of errors. Somehow, though, it seemed appropriate, a fitting end to a summer of drama.

After Laura left and Jonathan and I made certain the girls, which he had planned to leave there for the night, would be all right, we left. Jonathan took Dan's SUV and I took my car. Along the way, we stopped off at a fast-food restaurant for something more substantial to eat, then around 11:30, we headed off for Credence. I had never been to Credence before, so I let Jonathan lead the way. The way was straightforward, even monotonous, and the monotony, combined with the effects of my exhausting day, began to have an effect on me. Several times along the way I almost fell asleep at the wheel, but somehow managed in the end to stay awake enough to get to Credence without incident.

By the time we arrived, Dan was already in bed. We slipped in quietly and prepared to bed down. Dan's house was quiet, cool, and clean, a striking counterpoint to the chaos, disorder, and general discomfort of Jonathan's. I managed to get a little sleep, despite the fact that I have always had trouble sleeping in a strange place the first night. Although tomorrow would mainly involve taking care of some odds and ends instead of the hard labor of the previous days, I was thankful for the rest I received.

On the morning of Wednesday, the 5th, Dan fixed us a filling breakfast, then Jonathan and I headed back to Paladin. We took my car, and by the time we reached the outer limits of the city, I was running low on gas. We stopped at a convenience store and after I had finished filling up, Jonathan went inside to pay.

After being gone for what seemed like an unusually long time, he finally returned with unexpected news. He had apparently tried to pay with a company credit card, but the card had been deactivated. Mike, it seemed, had wasted no time in suspending Jonathan's executive privileges. Although Mike was well within his rights to deny Jonathan his work-related privileges if Jonathan was on leave, the rapidity with which Mike had acted seemed to be a reflection of Mike's aggravation over Jonathan's decision to take some time for himself. I though Mike could have shown Jonathan a little more understanding, but I understood myself that, in business, the only thing that ultimately mattered was the bottom line. Money came first, people came second, it seemed, which was a primary reason I had never pursued a career in business. I told Jonathan that I could, and would, pay for the gas myself.

We got back to the house sometime between 10:00 and 11:00. The girls seemed happy to see us and seemed no worse for having spent the night alone. After five days of packing and moving, there was little left to do. There were still some odds and ends that needed to be removed, but there were so few they would easily fit into my car. Jonathan would, however, be leaving some things behind. He would be leaving the furniture that had been stored in the basement, since it had proven too difficult to remove, given the constraints of time and resources. In addition, he would be leaving the table in the garden where we had occasionally sat and where I, alone, had occasionally sat on Monday mornings while I drank my tea and collected my thoughts. And, he would be leaving the bench in the front yard where we had often sat while the dogs ran free, while we made our plans, while we talked about life. Those props, those pieces of stage dressing, would not be used in the next act of the drama that was Jonathan's life.

■

Ted Kanner was scheduled to take possession of the house at 5:00 that afternoon. Jonathan said he didn't want to be there to see him when he came, and, under the circumstances, I couldn't blame him. We planned, then, to be long gone before he arrived. By 3:00, we had finished packing everything Jonathan would be taking and searching the property to make certain that nothing that was going would be left behind.

At the end, we found ourselves in the kitchen, where, in our last act of clearing the house, we had gone to pack up the groceries that remained in the refrigerator. Jonathan looked around for a moment, then said, "This was a good house. It wasn't the best, but it was okay. The next one will be better."

On that hopeful, if poignant, note, we gathered the girls and placed them in the car. Then, after Jonathan locked the front door for the last time, we got into the car and, with a feeling of finality, drove away. An invisible curtain that had parted for Jonathan some two years before and for me some three months before finally drew closed. This act of the play was completed, and now, the players who had been left on the stage at the end had taken their final cue: *exeunt*—they exit.

—II—
—Very Sticky Webs—

Remember, despite your motives, you have lied and concocted a whole person to someone else. You can rationalize it any way you want to but this is awful and out of control...

—Jonathan

—14—
EVIL DAN

This is like being committed to a looney bin.

We arrived at Dan's sometime around 4:00. Jonathan had been awake during the first half of the trip, talking about how the green of the foliage in that part of the state looked different from the green of the foliage in England, but eventually he dozed off and slept for most of the second half of the trip. The girls were well behaved and dozed along with him. With the driving pressure of the move now relieved, I felt like dozing myself, but managed to resist.

Credence was as rural as Paladin was urban, as far removed from the hustle and bustle of city life as you could get and still remain within the confines of civilization. The peaceful, pastoral setting was relieving and relaxing and, I hoped, restorative. I hoped that here, Jonathan would find the respite from the stresses that had torn down his life.

In thanks for letting him stay with him, Jonathan gave Dan his painting *The Tempest*, which Dan had admired. This was the painting of the two neoclassical figures running from an unseen menace, which apparently was an approaching storm. Although we had stored almost all of his belongings at the storage unit, Jonathan did bring a few things with him, beyond the necessities, to "give [him] a sense of who [he was]," as he had described it. That included, among other things, the Surrealist vase that I had refused to take and would not take if he were giving it away because he believed he was dying. Although his condition didn't appear to be good, I thought his bequeathing of his belongings reflected his hopelessness more than his healthiness and I wasn't going to encourage the morbidity of his thinking. I did, however, hold on to a few of his things, looking forward to the day when they could reside in a home of Jonathan's own, hopefully a home of *our* own.

Dan was friendly and gracious, but he was also fanatical about cleanliness. The house was immaculate and he expected it to stay that way. All food had to be eaten in the kitchen and crumbly food, like potato chips, had to be eaten outside. The shower had to be cleaned and disinfected and the sink had to be wiped out and the stopper polished after each use. Although I prefer things to be clean myself, I found Dan's standards to be both obsessive and oppressive. Perhaps the habits of the army died hard. And now, Jonathan had brought three dogs, none of which had been groomed, one of which he never bathed, and all of which made messes on the floor, into Dan's house. I wondered how long that would last.

Despite the potential for problems, the first evening that Jonathan was officially there was peaceful. Dan fixed dinner, which we ate in the breezy kitchen, and we watched TV while we talked about nothing of importance. That evening was a far cry from the constant motion, the constant stress, of the previous week.

That night, however, was a different story. Sleeping was challenging, especially for Jonathan. This was the first night the girls had spent at Dan's house and, consistent with Dan's fastidiousness, Dan expected them to remain downstairs in the den, where their uncleanness could be confined. They were decidedly unhappy to be separated from Jonathan, especially Sweetie. Whenever he would leave her to go upstairs, she would start barking and continue, without stopping, until he returned. That, combined with the fact that poodles, like many small dogs, have a penetrating, high-pitched bark, made it difficult to sleep. The only thing that stopped her from barking was having Jonathan stay downstairs with her, which forced him to remain with her throughout much of the night. When he was able to return, he found it difficult to sleep, not only because of his agitation over Sweetie in particular and his situation in general, but also because the bedroom window was sealed shut, making it impossible to let fresh air into what proved to be a stuffy room. I hoped the dogs settled down once they adjusted to their new circumstances, not only for their sake, but also for Jonathan's.

I returned home on Thursday. By that point, I had been gone for almost a week and had to teach class on Friday. Anymore, it seemed as if I spent more time away than at home and that wasn't always good. I still had a life in Hawthorn and in the area that surrounded it, and now that the fall semester had started, it demanded far more of my time and attention than it had during the summer.

The day I left, Jonathan created a new e-mail account, since the one through which we had been corresponding since I'd met him had been eliminated with the Internet service he'd lost in the move. The username of the new account was based on one of Dan's, which began with the first two letters of my state followed by three of his initials: *xxjif*, in which *xx-* stood for the initials of my state.

I left Credence sometime around 5:00. As I was leaving, I went to hug Jonathan. He seemed reluctant to hug me and I didn't understand why. After some hesitation, he finally embraced me, but his embrace was brief and his reaction to me was odd. Then again, Jonathan could be odd and his oddity seemed to be enhanced by his odd circumstances.

The trip home from Credence took nearly three hours. Although I stopped for gas in one of the small towns close to Credence and got lost for about fifteen minutes near another small town where one of the main roads I was taking turned into another in a confusing way, the main reason for the delay was that I had to drive through so many small towns and along so many twisting roads. Credence was *very* out of the way. If Jonathan had wanted to get away from the craziness of the city in order to rest and recuperate, he had certainly selected the ideal spot. I planned to take a more direct route the next time I visited him, which, I hoped, would be the following weekend.

By the time I reached home, I was exhausted. The previous week had been one of the most demanding weeks of my life and I hadn't eaten or slept as well as I could have throughout that week. When I weighed myself a couple of days later, I found that I had lost at least five pounds, which for me was a notable amount of weight. I needed some time to rest and recuperate myself, but since I would have to be up the next morning by 7:30 to teach at 8:30, I wouldn't have the luxury of sleeping in.

The next morning, I checked my e-mail after class. I found that I had received an e-mail from Jonathan in which he reported on his situation as it stood that morning. Despite the fact that he was referring to both himself and me with Indian names, the humor failed to soften the fact that after only one day, problems had arisen.

He informed me that Dan, who Jonathan said was viewing him as his "pal/companion/audience," had asked him not to make any "toll calls." Dan's stated reason was that he was afraid not that Jonathan wouldn't pay for them, which Jonathan had said he would, but that the increased long-distance activity would raise his phone rates. In addition, Dan had told him that his room was too messy, so Jonathan, who was supposed to rest, was planning to spend the day cleaning it. Further, Jonathan said that he still hadn't heard anything about his car, which had now been in the shop for almost three days.

Finally, in addressing the state of our relationship, an issue that had arisen during the move, Jonathan told me that in spite of the "current turmoil," he felt that things were going well between us. He added, though, that we would have to talk about the issue in person because it involved "very personal things" and his "privacy even to write" was limited, since Dan seemed to be monitoring the computer. He added a postscript telling me that Sweetie seemed calmer and although she had defecated on the floor, Dan "didn't bat an eye," which was *one* bit of good news.

Although I found the message reassuring, I also found it unsettling. I knew that living with Dan would not be carefree; I had already anticipated problems because of the dogs—and, possibly, Dan's drinking—but I *hadn't* anticipated Dan's attempting to curtail Jonathan's ability to connect with the outside world. He was restricting his phone use as well as his computer use, and with his car still in the shop, Jonathan had become confined to Dan's home. I felt uncomfortable with the turn the situation was taking.

Although I was exhausted, I replied as quickly as I could. I told him that I wanted to talk to him that evening, if he would be around, and asked him if there were good and bad times to call. I knew that Dan went to bed early, usually by 9:00, and didn't want to wake him. The last thing I wanted to do was to cause Jonathan further problems.

When he finally wrote back around 1:30 that afternoon, things had apparently calmed down. Inspired by the fact that Dan was painting an "oriental"-style watercolor, he was now referring to me with a Japanese version of my name. He reported that they'd gone into town to get food for both themselves and the dogs but had otherwise been relaxing at home. He told me it was all right to call whenever I wanted, which I found encouraging.

He also told me, though, that Dan was already making plans for him, which included going to an arts festival in Rowen, a city near Credence, on Sunday, and washing the floors at the art center in Rowen, where the art club to which Dan belonged met, on Wednesday. My impression was that Jonathan had gone to Dan's to rest and recuperate, not to engage in strenuous labor and generally be dragged around. He said that he had skipped doctors' appointments both the previous day and that day, not because Dan was hindering him, but because he was sick of seeing doctors, was "sick of being sick," and wanted a break from it all. Although I wasn't happy about some of the things that were happening, I was glad that things had settled down.

The calm didn't last the afternoon, however. Around 4:00, Jonathan sent me an e-mail with the urgent title "SOS—I have to move again." In it, he informed me that one of the dogs had defecated on the floor by the washer and that Dan had unknowingly set something down onto the mess then picked it back up, getting feces on his hands and pants. Dan, who was fanatically hygienic, was extremely upset, informing Jonathan that he couldn't tolerate the dogs' dirtiness and smelled urine throughout the house. Therefore, Jonathan needed to figure out someplace else that he and the dogs could go. Jonathan said that he realized it wasn't right to go into another person's home and upset his life, but he was stumped about what to do and needed my help.

I was stumped as well. I called him early that evening and we discussed his options in addition to the pros and cons associated with each. None of his options, it seemed, was without complications.

Later that night, he sent me an e-mail around 11:00 in which he reviewed, in writing, the options we had discussed. After telling me about the rest of his evening, which had consisted of visiting Dan's sister, who also lived in Credence, being forced to watch an old movie that Dan liked, and waiting until Dan finished answering his e-mails to answer his own, Jonathan restated his need to live with someone or in some type of group setting. Laura wanted him to move in with her, "but at what price," he wondered. I wondered, too, because in spite of her profession of "love" for him, I suspected that she loved his money more and having him live with her would better allow her to use him. Cliff wanted him to move in with him, but doing so would send various messages, including the one that Jonathan wanted to reignite his relationship with him. Art had wanted him to move in with him but was now "super pissed off" that he hadn't, so he didn't know if that was still an option. Finally, Glenn had offered to come back and take care of him, but that, too, was filled with "undercurrents" that he found problematic. Jonathan made the valid point that he had become homeless based on Dan's assurance that he could keep his dogs with him. He said he had realized that Dan would get fed up with them eventually, but not as quickly as he had. Jonathan had thought he would have at least a month to figure something out, but now, it appeared, he had only days.

In addition, Dan had made the comment that he hoped Jonathan wasn't planning to have "too much company." He said that Dan was interested in meeting Terrence, who was tentatively planning to visit Jonathan the following Thursday, but "the implications about visitors [were] there."

After apologizing for being a "burden," Jonathan said that he was seriously considering returning home, thinking it might be the only viable solution. It was an extreme decision, but he was in an extreme situation.

As far as his activities in Credence were concerned, Dan was taking Jonathan to a funeral the next day. In addition, Dan's sister and niece were coming for dinner and Dan had volunteered Jonathan to prepare the meal, a "typical English dinner," without having asked him. He also told me that on Sunday, Dan was planning to take him to church, where he was going to be "the guest of honor at the post-service coffee"—again, without having asked him. Afterwards, Dan was planning to take him to the arts festival in Rowen—again, without having asked him. Although Jonathan was supposed to be taking it easy, his life, he commented, had suddenly become "very busy."

I liked very little of what Jonathan had said in his e-mail. I was unsettled to learn that Dan was inventing additional ways to cut Jonathan off from the world around him, in an attempt, it seemed, either to keep Jonathan's life from intruding on his any more than it already had or, more disturbingly, to keep Jonathan all to himself. In addition, none of Jonathan's options for getting away from Dan sounded like options to me and all of them would have some kind of adverse effect on me, either damaging or destroying my relationship with him. I wished that he could have come to live with me, but under the circumstances, that was out of the question. Things were getting tricky and quicker than expected.

On Saturday morning, I checked my e-mail and found a message that Jonathan had sent around 3:00. The message, titled "Can't sleep," sounded more desperate than ever. He told me he was "too upset about the dogs, being homeless and having to move again so fast" to be able to sleep. He now felt that giving up his home and taking a leave of absence had been a huge mistake because at least before he'd had a roof over his head and control over his life. He said he had talked to his father, but his father had informed him that he'd gotten himself into his mess and now he was going to have to get himself out of it—without his help. That was an unfortunate reversal of the supportive stance he'd taken only a few days before. Jonathan had no idea what to do. He apologized for venting, but explained that, on top of everything else, it was the middle of the night, he was feeling sick, and since the air conditioning wasn't on and he couldn't raise his window, he felt uncomfortably hot.

I hadn't been able to sleep either. I had gone to sleep around midnight but had woken up around 5:00 and had stayed awake. I was in almost as much turmoil about Jonathan's situation as he was and felt that I needed to come up with some kind of desirable, and viable, solution. When I wrote, I suggested the possibility of finding a place in or near Hawthorn so that he could be living not only in a place that was quieter and calmer than, say, Paladin, but also in the same city that I was, which would allow me take care of him. I told him I thought that moving back to England was a drastic decision and one that, to be selfish, I didn't want to see happen. Surely there had to be a better solution.

On Saturday morning, I had to attend a teachers' meeting. When I got home, I checked my e-mail and found a message from Jonathan in which he tried to put everything into perspective. He said that although moving to Hawthorn was a possibility, he had the dogs to consider. He said that if he would be willing to give them up or kennel them, he would just stay with Dan, who, in spite of his flaws and his difficulty adjusting to guests, was basically a kind, concerned person who had been trying to make him feel at home and help him recover his health. He mentioned that since he'd been at Dan's, he'd thrown up only twice, which was "a huge step forward." He said, though, that he didn't want to give up his dogs because he needed to have some "mental balance and security" and they provided him with that when everything else he owned was either in a storage unit or otherwise gone. He didn't know what to do and was afraid of making another bad decision that might make things even worse.

Again, he apologized to me for putting me in the middle of his mess and told me that if I decided to "bail" he wouldn't blame me, since all he seemed to do was to bounce from crisis to crisis. He told me not to become too consumed by his problems because "[o]ne of us fixated on [him] was enough." Unfortunately, it wasn't that easy. He concluded by telling me that he'd just gotten back from the "Holy Roller" funeral, which he said was not the way they did them in England, but then added that like Dorothy in *The Wizard of Oz*, he wasn't home anymore. Unfortunately, he wasn't.

To provide him with yet another level of "mental balance and security," I assured him that I had *no* intentions of bailing out on him just because things had gotten tough. I reminded him that I hadn't bailed out at earlier points, when I was less emotionally invested in our relationship than I was now and when worse things than his present situation had occurred, because—in spite of his past accusations to the contrary—I felt that our relationship was worth fighting for.

I concluded by telling him that it was strange being home on a Saturday, since it was the first time I'd been home on Saturday in two months. I told him I was still planning to resume the tradition of not being home on Saturday the following Saturday if Dan wouldn't feel too overburdened with guests. In addition, Jonathan suggested that Terrence might still be there on Saturday, and since his family hadn't had the opportunity to meet me in August as planned, I also didn't want to miss the chance for Jonathan's youngest sibling to scrutinize me and report back to the folks at home. I told Jonathan I thought it should be an "interesting" weekend…and I would be sure to pack an extra bottle of Prozac. I did think it would be genuinely interesting, though, to meet another member of Jonathan's family and I half-thought about taking the opportunity to ask him about the article that I had found in June that had made the strange claim that he was actually from the Midwest.

The messages Jonathan sent to me on Sunday revealed more of what was becoming his new routine, but were mainly rehashes of the ongoing and growing complications in his new life. In the first one, which he sent around 8:30 that morning, he told me that Sunday was the "one" day they ate breakfast and that he'd had to be up by 8:30 to eat and get ready for church. Dan was an elder, so he had to be there early. He reminded me that today he would be the "chief attraction," and that since the people there had never met an English person, he supposed he was expected to be "a cross between Mary Poppins, the Queen, and Paul McCartney."

He went on to say that "fat" Greg, who had helped us with the move, had been asking Dan a number of personal questions about him, and when Jonathan had questioned Greg about it, Greg had become "all sulky and pouty." Jonathan said, though, that he couldn't care less about Greg's reaction, and although Greg had been a great help during the move, there was, in his judgment, an "obvious disconnect" in someone who weighed 500 pounds.

Although the dogs were adjusting to their new surroundings and settling down, Dan was still pushing Jonathan to get rid of them and had been asking him if he'd made arrangements to do it. Jonathan had hoped that he would be able to wait until Terrence arrived on Thursday to leave, but thought that if not, going to Laura's—temporarily—might be an option. I wasn't thrilled about the idea, but if it *was* just temporary, then perhaps it would be tolerable.

Around 3:00 that afternoon, Jonathan wrote again to inform me that Dan's feelings of imposition had finally reached a critical point. He said that Dan had finally told him, outright, that the dogs had to go. Jonathan was feeling desperate enough to think that now, he would just go back to Paladin, rent a house, get his things out of storage, and move on with his life, in spite of his health. Again, he thought that staying with Laura might be a solution in the short term, though he knew it wasn't in the long term, since that situation might ultimately create even more problems than he was suffering at Dan's. He said that Greg had told him that Dan had "blurted out" that the only reason he'd asked Jonathan to stay with him was that Jonathan had had nowhere else to go and Dan was a Christian. It seemed to me, however, that his Christian charity came with a lot of conditions.

Jonathan concluded, forlornly, that Dan's would not be the "safe place" he'd hoped to find and, after living on his own in some form since he was eight, he was deeply discouraged about what he had been reduced to.

Jonathan also told me that Cliff had called again, which apparently he had done every day since he'd been at Dan's, to check on him. He said that Cliff meant well, but that dealing with him, in addition to everything else, was too difficult for him. He said that he cried every time he called. Although Cliff's calls were supposed to be helping, they were in fact having the opposite effect.

Then, Jonathan told me something that I found outrageous. He told me that the pastor at Dan's church had made a pass at him. He said that he was married, which Jonathan thought was an arrangement. He said the pastor had asked Jonathan to lunch on Tuesday and had actually let his hand brush along Jonathan's butt. He said his wife belonged to the same art club that Dan did, but he didn't tell Dan what had happened. Jonathan stated firmly that he wasn't going to lunch with him and was dismayed by what had happened.

The pastor's behavior also seemed to be another instance of Jonathan's strange ability to attract sexual attention. Otherwise, I wasn't as shocked as I could have been, since I realized the situation with the conflicted pastor was an all-too-common one.

The next morning, I woke up around 5:30, which was much earlier than I wanted to wake up. I had to teach in both the morning and the evening and wasn't looking forward to it. With everything going on, I wasn't up to it either physically or mentally, but like a performer, I felt that "the show must go on." One aspect of teaching that I had always hated was the feeling that I was on stage with a spotlight shooting down on me, my students scrutinizing, reacting to, and criticizing everything I said and did, sometimes for as long as three hours at a time. Sometimes I felt trapped or, as I described it to Jonathan in the e-mail that I sent to him before I went to work that morning, "like a cornered animal." Yet, despite my own difficulties, I tried to focus on Jonathan's, whose problems seemed more dire than mine, and asked him what I could do to make his life better.

When he responded around 1:00 that afternoon, he told me that he was "a bit of a nervous wreck" as well, but that Dan had gone to a pastel class at the art center and the dogs had settled down. In addition, he had called about a couple of houses, apparently in Paladin, that sounded promising. He said that Laura had told him she would try to visit him that afternoon and that Greg had called him the previous night to make up. Apparently, Greg had become so upset that Jonathan was angry with him that he had spent the entire day in bed eating Oreo cookies to make himself feel better. Greg had told Jonathan that he might stop by on his way back home from the Stress Center, where he had an appointment, but Jonathan said that he "[might] or [might] not answer the door."

Around 8:30 that evening, Jonathan wrote to tell me that he'd spoken with someone about a "great" house in Paladin. Located near the art museum we had visited in June, it had four bedrooms, three bathrooms, and an indoor pool. In addition, the rent was $200 less a month than the rent on his old house had been. He also said that his car, which had now been in the shop for nearly a week, would be ready on Wednesday. That would allow him to regain some of the freedom that Dan had been trying to curtail. Jonathan said that he wanted to view the house on Thursday and, since I was off work that day, I suggested that we meet there so I could offer feedback and, more importantly, so we could be together. Although it had been only a few days since we'd last seen each other, it felt like a few days too many.

On the night of Monday, September 10, I went to bed in a world that, despite the personal drama into which I'd been drawn, was fundamentally the same as it had always been. The next morning, however, I woke up into a world that had fundamentally changed.

On the fateful morning of September 11, Jonathan sent me an e-mail in which he related the events of the morning—*his* morning, not *the* morning, since he sent his message at 8:48, roughly the same time that the first of the World Trade Center towers was attacked. Referring to Credence as "Hooterville," he began by telling me that Dan had gone to a "poobah conference" at Patty's, a friend of Dan's who ran a convenience store in Credence. Jonathan said that he had met Patty at church on Sunday but had gotten the impression that she didn't like him. Consequently, he hadn't been invited to the "confab," as he called it. He said that Dan was in a sour mood because the "trick" he'd invited over that morning had failed to show and that after going into a "snit" about several things, he had left without telling Jonathan "bye or eat shit or anything." Dan's rudeness, however, appeared to be the least of Jonathan's problems.

He went on to tell me that although he wanted to see me and have me give him my opinion about the house, he didn't know if he would be able to go. He said that Dan was going to make our seeing each other as difficult as possible, since he didn't want Jonathan to have visitors—by which he seemed to mean *overnight* visitors—and since Jonathan was now afraid to leave the dogs alone with Dan for an extended time, concerned that he might do something to them. He informed me that both Laura and Greg had been at Dan's at different times on Monday and neither of them could smell the urine that Dan claimed permeated the air. Dan, it seemed, was just looking for—or inventing—excuses.

Jonathan told me that if two things could change, his situation would improve immeasurably. He said that first, he needed to find some way to keep his dogs with him, and second, he needed to be able to see his friends when he needed to see them. He had already stated that having his dogs with him was crucial to his emotional equilibrium and now added that not being able to socialize without being under surveillance was reinforcing his feelings of isolation, which was one of the reasons he had decided to leave his house in Paladin.

Although Jonathan needed to get away from Dan in both the near term and the long term, two things were preventing either from happening. First, Jonathan had learned that his car might not be ready by Wednesday, in which case he would be stranded even longer than he had anticipated. Second, Jonathan had managed to get an interview for the job at the hospital in Mariah, which had originally been scheduled for Wednesday, but because he wasn't sure that he would have his car by then, he had rescheduled his meeting to Friday to give himself some leeway. After stating that his situation was making him nervous and that he needed a solution, he ended by telling me to have a restful day.

My day, along with that of every other American, was far from restful. Like most Americans, I focused mainly on the immediate implications of what had happened, such as getting a full tank of gas before gas prices, it was feared, skyrocketed, as well as the larger implication of whether or not what had happened that day was only a harbinger of worse things to come.

When Jonathan wrote next, around 1:00 that afternoon, he began by mentioning the events not in New York, which by then had captivated everyone else's attention, but in Credence. Stating that he could now "operate the lawn mower," he said that he had tried to mow some of Dan's yard but that Dan had made him stop, since his rows weren't straight enough to suit him. "As if he would know what straight anything is," Jonathan quipped. He said that he had also swept the driveway and walkways, which amazingly *did* suit Dan. I wasn't certain how this was supposed to be helping Jonathan's health.

Finally turning to the events in New York, he mentioned that the IRA bomb campaigns in London had "never never" been anything like this. He said the IRA had always given a five-minute warning to minimize casualties, but the agency behind the World Trade Center attack had obviously had a different aim. As the day wore on, it became increasingly clear that the attacks were the work of Muslim extremists, apparently associated with Al-Qaeda. Assuming this to be true, Jonathan described the Arabs in general and the Muslims in particular as "scum and baby killers" and hoped that people now understood what Israel suffered at their hands every day. He ended the message by offering his solution to the problem, which was to "nuke the Arab bastards and wipe every one...[of] those fuckers out." Having struck a nerve, Jonathan's infamous prejudice needed little encouragement to rear its head.

Perhaps because his own personal drama seemed more pressing, Jonathan's messages throughout the remainder of the day focused primarily on the problems he was experiencing living with Dan, especially the extent of Dan's drinking. In an e-mail he sent to me around 2:45, he told me that Dan drank anywhere from half a gallon to a full gallon of wine every night, a description that finally quantified the extent of his drinking problem for me. Jonathan said that he usually had half a glass to keep him company and to be able to tolerate hearing Dan tell the same stories again and again. Fortunately, Dan's pastor had wanted all the elders in the church to attend a community service that evening in a nearby town for the victims of the attack. (Jonathan quipped, "Maybe he wants to sneak out during the service to come suck my dick.") He also said that Dan had an administrative meeting at the church the next morning, so he hoped that meant he would have a quiet night without being forced to admire Dan's "hideous" paintings or listen to his "drunken ramblings." He ended the e-mail by saying that, apart from everything that was wrong, "everything...was perfect."

As it turned out, my school decided to hold classes that night. Life, in some form, tried to go on. Even so, my students and I were in a strange mood, preoccupied to varying degrees with what had happened in New York, so no one could focus on psychology. Consequently, I decided to let class out after an hour and was home by 8:00. Unfortunately, I came home to even more drama, though of a more personal kind.

Around 9:00 that evening, Jonathan sent me another message, his most urgent yet. Titled "I have to get out of here now," it almost made the events in New York pale by comparison. Calling Dan's house a "looney bin," Jonathan said that Dan was drunk and slurring his words. He wasn't clear if Dan had gone to the meeting, but it appeared that he hadn't. Dan was still insisting that the smell of the dogs permeated the house and had been screaming at them so loudly that they were running under the furniture until Jonathan had gotten out of bed and had coaxed Dan upstairs. Worse, Dan was now telling Jonathan that he could use the phone for only five minutes at a time and could use the computer only at certain times because he was expecting e-mails from his "boyfriends," as he referred to them.

Although Jonathan was sick and had spent the afternoon and evening in bed, Dan was still expecting him to scrub floors at the art center the next morning. Because Jonathan still didn't have his car, he couldn't leave. Although he was supposed to get his car back the next day, Dan had claimed that he couldn't drive him to the garage in Rowen, where his car was being fixed, because he was afraid that gas prices would skyrocket because of hoarding and he didn't want to waste gas. Unfortunately for Dan, however, he had forgotten that he had to go to the art center and, therefore, he didn't have a valid excuse for not taking him. Obviously, Jonathan's having his car back would give him a level of freedom that Dan didn't seem to want him to have.

In addition, Jonathan informed me that Dan had tightened, or clarified, his position on overnight guests. Dan had gone from saying that he *preferred* that Jonathan not have overnight visitors to saying that he did *not want* Jonathan to have overnight visitors. That meant, of course, that I was no longer welcome to spend the night, although my name in particular had not been mentioned. I wondered, though, if I was welcome at all. Since the round trip between Hawthorn and Credence using the most direct route would take five hours, going to Credence just to spend a few hours with Jonathan before having to leave made my visiting him at Dan's impractical, if not impossible.

Jonathan didn't know what he was going to do. He had been at Dan's for less than a week and now he was going to have to leave. He said he was feeling very sick and couldn't deal with it. He didn't understand how Dan, who was a nurse and allegedly a good friend, could treat him not like a patient but like a servant. He ended the e-mail by insisting that he needed to get *out* as soon as possible.

With everything that had happened that day, I wondered if my own life could get any crazier. I had no idea how to get Jonathan "out," and now that Dan had made it clear that he didn't want overnight guests, making it virtually impossible for me to visit, there seemed to be no way for me to get "in" to be with and help him.

By Wednesday, Americans were beginning to orient themselves to the insane situation that had befallen them. In a similar fashion, Jonathan was beginning to orient himself, at least somewhat, to the insane situation that had befallen *him*. Around 9:00 that morning, he wrote to say that Dan had sobered up and was now being nice. He said, however, that it was the "up and down aspects" of Dan's behavior, with Dan being reasonable one moment and impossible the next, that were making him "looney." Jonathan hoped that his car would be ready that day, which would finally give him the ability to escape from the "looney bin" whenever he wanted and needed. Terrence, who lived in the Northeast, had informed him that he would have to postpone his visit because the disaster in New York had disrupted his plans. Now, it appeared, he wouldn't be able to come until sometime the following week. I had hoped that Terrence might be able to provide some direct familial support as well as a much-needed buffer between Jonathan and Dan, but now, Jonathan would be deprived of both.

Around 4:45 that afternoon, Jonathan reported that he had just gotten back from a "full day" at the art center, where he had "washed and buffed floors in the main studio, kitchen and halls." In addition, Dan had actually taken Jonathan to see about his car, but unfortunately, it still wasn't ready as of 4:00 that afternoon, which he found discouraging. The people at the garage had told him to check back the next day, although they didn't seem to be making any promises.

Far more concerning, however, was that Glenn had called but Dan hadn't told Jonathan. Apparently, Glenn had actually called eight times in the previous two days but Dan hadn't told him anything about it. Dan claimed that the repeated calls were "harassment" and was placing a block on the phone. Jonathan found what Dan had done, was planning to do, particularly frightening because now he wouldn't even know when someone was calling. Jonathan said that for some reason he didn't understand, Dan became furious when Glenn called. In addition, he said that while they had been at the art center, Greg, who had happened to be in Rowen, had driven by and seen Dan's SUV and had stopped in. Jonathan said that Dan had gotten angry even about that. He said that he was beginning to feel very isolated. He said he would write more, but Dan was "sort of looking over [his] shoulder."

I was very disturbed by this turn of events. Jonathan had been living at Dan's for only a week, and in that time, Dan had managed to gain a dismaying amount of control over Jonathan's life, over Jonathan himself. The situation was starting to remind me somewhat of Stephen King's novel *Misery* in which a mentally ill fan gains total control over an invalid author whose fictional worlds she retreats into because of her inability to deal with reality. I didn't know what to do.

About an hour later, Jonathan wrote to tell me the latest, to explain why he thought Dan was behaving as he was. The message was unsettling. Dan, who had by that time drunk at least four glasses of wine, had told Jonathan that he enjoyed having *him* there but the dogs had to go. Jonathan theorized that Dan was trying to isolate him because he was lonely and wanted him all to himself. Even so, Dan seemed to be continuing to ignore Jonathan's needs and already had their Thursday planned out without any input from Jonathan. Although Dan was wanting to go to Rowen—to go shopping—he told Jonathan that they would go to the garage to see about his car "if they're still open." Jonathan said that he hadn't felt well for a couple of days and needed to see his doctor and refill some of his prescriptions, which would run out in a few days. He ended his e-mail by saying that he was starting to feel "a bit like a prisoner."

I was disturbed by Jonathan's description of himself as a "prisoner." To try to counteract his feelings of isolation, I suggested that if he didn't get his car back in time to see the house in Paladin on Thursday, perhaps we could meet there that weekend and not only look at the house, but also get his prescriptions filled and do whatever else needed to be done.

In response, Jonathan reiterated that he didn't know if he would be able to do that since he was afraid to leave the dogs alone with Dan for more than a couple of hours. He said that Dan knew about his fears and played on them in order to keep him at the house. Even so, he generously described Dan not as "bad," but as "misguided and odd." He said that when he was sober, Dan was a good person, but when he was drunk, he changed for the worse.

By the time that Jonathan sent his message, it was 9:00, and by then, Dan was drunk enough that he couldn't negotiate the stairs, which kept him from coming down to the den, where Jonathan and the dogs were hiding out, and bothering him. Jonathan said that Dan had been screaming "Kill the fuckers!" at the TV during dinner when they had shown footage of Arabs dancing in the streets in Baghdad over the news of the destruction in New York. Jonathan said he agreed with the sentiment—one that he himself had expressed the day before—but thought that Dan's reaction had been "a little over the edge." I wasn't sure how Dan's comment about "killing" the "fuckers" was any more extreme than Jonathan's comment about "wiping out" the "fuckers," unless Dan had proposed doing it by some method more extreme than using a nuclear weapon, which Jonathan had proposed. His blindness to his own prejudice was evident, but given there were more important issues to deal with, it wasn't the time to mention it.

Once again, Jonathan repeated his familiar refrain about not knowing what to do but being afraid to make another decision that proved to be a mistake. He said that he wasn't going to make any plans beyond getting his car back. I could only hope that Dan, when he was sober the next day, would decide to take Jonathan to get it. He ended his e-mail by saying, "This is hell." He also mentioned the unfortunate fact that the previous six days was the longest we'd gone without seeing each other since mid-June.

It had been less than a week, but it seemed like a month.

The next afternoon, Jonathan sent me an e-mail in which he told me that he had finally gotten his car back. Although this should have been good news, the reclaiming of his car hadn't gone as planned. Describing himself as a "nervous wreck," Jonathan said that the repairs had cost around $645, which was $100 over the estimate. He said the car still wasn't running properly and wondered what they'd done to it for $645. To make matters worse, the garage wouldn't accept his check because his account wasn't with a local bank and the check number was too low. Consequently, he had gotten Dan to write the garage a check off his own account and Jonathan had written Dan one off his. Dan wasn't happy about it, Jonathan said, but neither was he. He said that he had returned to Dan's after he'd dropped him off at the garage but that Dan hadn't returned himself. He said that otherwise, they had spent the morning in a nearby town walking around several stores that Dan frequented "looking for men [for Dan] to ogle"—something that Jonathan described as a "major activity" of Dan's.

I didn't understand why Dan should have a problem with Jonathan's check. Although it would take longer for Dan to get his money, he would still get it. It just seemed to be yet another in a growing list of grievances that Dan was drawing up against Jonathan.

∎

Over the next several days, Jonathan's e-mails described, in agonizing detail, Dan's attempts to isolate him from the rest of the world, the magnitude of Dan's drinking, and the compulsivity of Dan's pursuit of casual sex. Throughout it all, Jonathan's health continued to deteriorate, both from his doctors' uncertainty about how to treat it and from the stress he had fled into instead of away from. But, throughout it all, Jonathan also held out hope that somehow he would be able to escape before Dan's list of real or invented complaints reached their limit and Dan threw him and the girls out on the street.

As far as his isolation was concerned, Dan finally decided that he didn't want Greg visiting. Jonathan reported that when Greg had come to the house to visit Jonathan on Thursday afternoon, Dan had been "visibly agitated" and his behavior had been "bordering on rude." When Jonathan had pressed Dan to explain why he'd behaved that way, Dan had told him that he didn't want people seeing Greg coming in and out of the house because he was so fat that Dan was afraid people would think he was "weird." As an elder in his church, Dan explained, he couldn't be involved with "weird" people—a truly Christian attitude. In addition, everyone in Rowen apparently knew Greg was gay, which was even more reason not to be seen associating with him.

The only saving grace, it seemed, was the possibility of getting the job at the hospital in Mariah and leaving. Jonathan now thought that if he did, he would move near there for a few months while he figured out what to do. Having that as an option, however, was contingent on his getting the job.

On Friday, Jonathan went to Mariah for his first interview. Fortunately, things went extremely well. He said that the meeting, which had originally been scheduled for an hour to an hour and a half, had ended up lasting three hours. He said he was now scheduled to go back the following Wednesday to spend the afternoon with the CEO.

Unfortunately, Jonathan had come back to a "bad problem" that had ruined the good feeling the meeting had left him with. While he had been gone, one of the dogs had defecated on the cheap carpet that Dan had laid in the basement bathroom. Jonathan said that, in response, Dan had gone "berserk." Dan said that he was going to rip up the carpet, that he would always smell it, that the dogs were a mess... When Jonathan wrote, it was around 7:00, by which point Dan was drunk and had gone to one of the parks in Rowen to "cruise." He had given Jonathan orders to stay downstairs and not come up when he came home unless he gave him the okay because he might have a "trick" with him. Jonathan voiced his hope that Dan got arrested.

Again, he mentioned that Laura wanted him to move in with her but he was reluctant to do so because of the problems he feared he would encounter there. He told me that she had actually told him that if he came, she wanted him to share her bed—a comment that only highlighted those problems. He didn't know, though, where else he could go in the short term. Again, he said that he didn't feel well and couldn't cope with what was happening, saying that the stress he was enduring was the worst that he had ever suffered. He said that he had felt desperate enough to e-mail his father, asking for his advice. He ended his message by telling me that he didn't know where his next e-mail would be coming from.

Alarmed by his final statement, I hurriedly replied, asking him if it was all right for me to call. A few minutes later he answered, telling me that Dan was gone and to call him then. When I did, he largely repeated what he had already told me. After talking for a while, Jonathan seemed calmer, but since I knew it was only a matter of time until the next crisis erupted, *I* didn't.

I didn't hear from Jonathan again until after 11:00 the next morning. Around that time, he e-mailed me to tell me what had happened after we'd gotten off the phone the night before. He said that Dan had staggered in about 10:00, alone. He had told Jonathan that he'd met someone at the park but had lost him while the man was following him back to Credence. Dan thought the man might actually have been an undercover cop because another car had pulled out from somewhere along the way and was following them. Jonathan said that Dan had been "really loaded" when he'd come home, which meant that he'd driven a good 30 miles drunk.

Jonathan said that earlier that morning they had gone to Rowen again to do some shopping but the trip had turned into an "expedition." He said that Dan had stopped at the park again not once but twice, cruised the restrooms at Wal-Mart, and driven by a lumberyard to ogle the workers. Jonathan said that he had just gone to get dog food and was planning to go alone until Dan invited himself to go along. Obviously, Dan wasn't satisfied, or scared, after what had happened the night before.

Jonathan also said that he had gotten an "interesting" e-mail from a friend of his named Logan, a "casualty" (emergency room) doctor back home and a "very nice guy." Jonathan had never mentioned Logan, but then again, Jonathan seemed to have so many friends that it wasn't surprising that I hadn't heard of them all and new names were always emerging. In the e-mail, Logan had theorized that Dan behaved the way he did toward Jonathan to keep Jonathan "depressed and stressed and therefore…dependent" on him. Logan had also suggested that Dan didn't want Jonathan to take the job at the hospital because he thought Dan might be in love with him and taking the job would take Jonathan away from him. Jonathan was skeptical about the latter, but he did think that what Logan had said otherwise had some validity. He thought that if Dan did want to keep Jonathan around, it was because he was British and Dan received some kind of reinforcement by showing off his English friend to everyone. Jonathan ended his e-mail by informing me that Dan was planning to go back to the park again but that he himself thought he would "have a headache."

I didn't know if Dan was in love with Jonathan, either, but I did agree with Logan's assessment that Dan was playing some kind of mind game with Jonathan to maintain the control over him that Dan seemed to have lost in the rest of his life.

Around 5:00 that afternoon, Jonathan wrote to tell me that he and Dan had eaten lunch at 11:30 so Dan could go back to the park to do more cruising—his third visit that day and his fifth in twenty-four hours. Consequently, he'd had a quiet afternoon, having slept most of the time. He said, though, that when Dan returned, he was in a foul mood because when they had been at the park earlier that day, Jonathan had commented that a couple of the men there were attractive but no one would speak to Dan when he had returned. After giving it further thought, Jonathan agreed with Logan that Dan was behaving the way he was in part to keep him off balance. He said that while the dogs had caused problems from the beginning, Dan only made an issue of it when it seemed to suit some unrelated purpose. Bolstering his opinion, Jonathan said that Greg had witnessed some of Dan's behavior and had called it "nuts."

One bright spot in an otherwise dreary message was Jonathan's mention that Dan was planning to be out of town all day the following Saturday. If Dan was gone, then the dogs would be safe, and Jonathan and I could finally have an opportunity to see each other. By that point, it would have been over two weeks, which seemed like two months. He suggested that we could meet in Paladin and possibly go to the gay bathhouse there. Jonathan said he knew the latter suggestion was "gross," to which I had to agree, but he said it would be "cheap and gay," which made it somehow more appealing than other options. *Any* opportunity to get away from Dan and be together, however, was appealing.

Jonathan ended the message by telling me that he was looking forward to "a scintillating night of Dan drinking wine, yelling at the TV and crying." He remarked, as he had before, that the experience was like "being committed to a looney bin" and added that maybe he had been. There was no "maybe" about it.

Around 8:00 that evening, Jonathan sent me an e-mail in which he kept me informed about Dan's drinking. He said that instead of staying home and inflicting himself on him, Dan had drunk not one but *five* glasses of wine and had gone back to the park for the *fourth* time that day, the *sixth* time in twenty-four hours. Seemingly oblivious to what had happened the night before, Dan had told Jonathan that he hoped he would meet "that cute guy from last night," whom Dan himself suspected of being an undercover cop.

He said that before Dan had left, he and Dan had gone to Dan's sister's, where Dan had seen a man fishing. Jonathan said that Dan had been ogling him so hard that the man had become uncomfortable and left. Although Dan seemed to believe that no one in Credence knew he was gay, Jonathan pointed out that in a small town, you couldn't go around behaving the way Dan did and expect to keep it a secret. Apparently, everyone already knew that Jonathan had gone to Mariah the day before and had been asking him how things had gone. He described the situation as "[s]weet but also a little frightening." Unfortunately, the feeling of intimacy that a small town could offer could easily turn into one of invasion. Jonathan, who was an especially private person, felt especially uncomfortable.

Jonathan once again voiced his hope that Dan got arrested at the park. Sarcastically, he said that since he didn't have enough money on him, he wouldn't be able to bail him out until Monday, which would give him a quiet Sunday. More seriously, he said that being arrested would destroy the façade of heterosexuality, of "normality," that Dan liked to believe he projected. He said the hypocrisy of being a church elder and "anti this and anti that" while constantly cruising public parks for gay sex was too much to take. Jonathan said he hoped the public exposure, which Dan had said would make him "commit suicide," would finally stop him. He said he couldn't believe that Dan had gone back to the park yet again and called it a "sickness." I had to agree. Jonathan ended his message by asking me how I liked being single again, telling me he was "angry and pissed off and a little bitter" about the enforced separation. He wasn't the only one.

The next morning around 7:30, Jonathan e-mailed to tell me that Dan had finally returned around 11:00 the night before and was angry because he had been at the park for three hours and no one had even spoken to him. He had drunk more wine then had gone to bed, but today, which was Sunday, he was getting ready for church. Jonathan once again remarked on how the hypocrisy in Dan's behavior was too much, which it was.

Jonathan also updated me on the situation between him and Laura. Apparently Laura had called the night before while Dan was gone and they had talked for nearly an hour. He said she was getting "too serious" about him, stating that even though she knew he was gay, it didn't matter to her. Jonathan quipped that to him, that was a "big obstacle." Laura was planning to visit for the day, probably on Thursday. Dan didn't seem to have the same kind of problem with Laura that he did with Greg, primarily, it seemed, because Laura's presence furthered the illusion of heterosexuality that Dan liked to believe he was projecting.

The situation with Laura was ludicrous, but the situation with his health was worrisome. Jonathan reported that in addition to having had a headache since Thursday, which he attributed to tension, he had developed pain and weakness in his left arm, shoulder, and leg—actually down his whole left side. He said that at first, he'd written it off as having slept on his left side wrong, but the problem was persisting. He said that he planned to call the doctor on Monday. I was concerned, having always associated weakness on one side of the body with stroke, but it could have been any number of things ranging from trivial to serious, so I hoped he did in fact talk to the doctor the next day.

As if what he was enduring wasn't enough, Dan was dragging him to church for the second Sunday in a row, the church where the closeted pastor who had come on to him the Sunday before was waiting. Jonathan was still angry about what had happened, but this time was prepared. He told me "that fucking minister" had better keep his "damn hands" to himself or he was going to say, very loudly, "What are you doing?" I wondered, though, if that would extinguish the situation or enflame it.

Throughout it all, the only thing I could do was listen and comfort, but because of the constraints in my own life, I could do little else.

Around noon, Jonathan sent me an e-mail that sorely tested the limits of my ability to sympathize and console. The title of the message, "Cliff Has Done it To Me Again," said it all.

Jonathan explained that Cliff had been calling him on a regular basis to see how he was doing. He said, though, that in spite of Cliff's invitations to have him come and live with him, he had persistently refused, stating that he didn't have the same level of trust in Cliff now that he'd had before and, therefore, couldn't be committed to him in the way they had been before. After two months of refusals, however, Cliff's attitude had finally changed. When he had contacted Jonathan in July, he had told him that he wasn't sure if he wanted to commit to Loren if he could recommit to Jonathan. Now, Cliff had decided that he had been rebuffed long enough. He had called that morning to tell Jonathan that he and Loren were now officially a couple. Cliff explained to Jonathan that although he was still in love with him, he'd waited long enough for him to change his mind and had reluctantly decided to move on with his life.

Jonathan said that although he knew he couldn't be with Cliff, he had loved him "madly and deeply," which made it feel as if someone had died. He said that he hadn't felt so depressed since his relationship with Glenn had disintegrated or Marcus had died. He apologized for being so self-absorbed, but even though he'd been half-expecting to hear what Cliff had called "the dreaded news" for some time, it had still hit him hard. "Another day in America," he concluded morosely.

My first thought was, *What the hell did you expect?* Since the beginning of July, Cliff had been angling to resume his relationship with Jonathan but Jonathan had steadfastly refused. It was only a matter of time before Cliff grew tired of the constant rejection and decided to move on with his life. Although I thought that Cliff had generally behaved in a selfish and insensitive way toward Jonathan, I didn't blame Cliff one bit for doing what he did. By this point, I'd heard enough and had enough of the emotional mess between Jonathan and Cliff and I wondered how far the new boyfriend was expected to go in consoling, in caring.

I was agitated myself and needed to get out of the house and think. Having nothing better to do, I went to the local university and wandered around the campus. At one point, I wandered into the building where the music classes were held. That made me think of Chase. Knowing that Chase had returned to school that fall, I found myself trying to find out more about him. I had already tried to find him through the campus directory, but had come up empty-handed. While I was in the music building, I did find a list of music students, including one named "Chase," but that Chase had a different last name from the one that Jonathan had given to me. Chase, in spite of the major impact he had indirectly had on my life, remained elusive.

When I returned home, I was still dismayed, but kept those feelings to myself. Having acquired a clearer head, I wrote Jonathan one of my long, supportive—and, given the topic, longsuffering—messages. Hoping that he would now begin to put the Cliff situation truly behind him—for *everyone's* sake—I told him that I didn't believe he had ever truly dealt with the feelings associated with losing Cliff, given his habit of walling himself off from his emotions, and that perhaps now that his emotions were closer to the surface than they normally were, it might be easier for him to deal with and release them. I told him that I knew he was upset and depressed about what had happened and his natural reaction would probably be to avoid those feelings however he could, but if he ever wanted to start feeling better, he couldn't do that. I concluded by saying that I hated not being able to be there with him, which, in spite of my aggravation, I did.

After all my effort, the message did not have the desired effect. Around 5:45 that evening, he sent me an e-mail that he started by saying that his day had gone from one bad thing to another. He said that he had told Laura what had happened, but instead of being sympathetic, she was upset with him for being upset about Cliff. Apparently, Laura was expecting him to rely on her alone for emotional support. Jonathan also stated that she "[wasn't] too thrilled" about our relationship, either, which didn't surprise me. Laura seemed to think that Jonathan shouldn't have a relationship with anyone but her. He said that no one seemed to understand how much he had been relying on Cliff for emotional support—including, he implied, me. He stated his belief that once you love someone, you always love them in some form, so Cliff's decision had done nothing to lessen those feelings. Jonathan compared himself to Job and said that his need to escape was stronger than ever. At the end, he summed up his feelings in two words: "Life stinks."

In response, my longsuffering stopped and some of my frustration surfaced. I felt that he was almost treating me as if *I* weren't important and I asked him where *I* stood in the scheme of things. Around 10:00 that night, he replied, assuring me that, apart from certain members of his family, I was possibly the most important person in his life. As far as Cliff was concerned, Jonathan explained that Cliff had been calling him every day, sometimes several times a day, to check on him and reminded me that Cliff had offered to deliver him from his "hell hole." He said that Cliff knew how to encourage him and make him feel better, which he needed more than ever. Since they had cared about each other so intensely and since their relationship had ended not because of problems but because of circumstances, losing Cliff had been—and again was—extremely difficult. Jonathan said that he would always love him, but he also realized that their chance at having a relationship was gone, especially now that he could no longer fully trust him. I understood that, but I was still tired of hearing about Cliff and the adverse effect that his "caring" was having on Jonathan.

As far as *we* were concerned, he said that we needed to be able to spend time together to regain the momentum we'd had before he'd gone to Dan's. He said that he feared our relationship was "loosing steam" because we didn't see each other and could rarely talk freely and because of the constant negativity surrounding us. He said that had to change, but given the circumstances and the complications, neither of us knew how it could.

Feeling the way I'd felt earlier that day, Jonathan said that when he "just couldn't bare it any longer" he had gotten into his car and had driven around for at least four hours. He said that he had gone to Mariah, then had gone to a city located between Mariah and Credence, then had gotten lost on his way back to Credence. I felt the fact that he'd left the girls alone with Dan for that long was a measure of his desperation.

Unfortunately, the stress of everything that had happened that day had undone some of the progress he'd made in regaining his health. He ended his e-mail by telling me that he'd thrown up at least three times that night. He begged me to write.

By that point, it was after 10:30 and I was exhausted. In addition, I had to get up early the next day and teach. Even so, I tried to put aside the feelings that Jonathan's e-mails from earlier in the day had provoked and sent him an e-mail in which I assured him that I didn't feel our separation was weakening our relationship as much as it was simply putting it on hold. I told him that I believed things would eventually change for the better, return to normal, and that in the meantime, I wasn't going anywhere. I didn't tell him this, but I felt that he was overreacting about our "separation," which had so far lasted for only a week and a half. I realized that he had been through a lot in that week and a half, on top of everything he had been through in the previous several, but I still thought that he was making too much out of our inability to be physically together.

Jonathan didn't respond until 8:30 the next morning. When he did, his e-mail, titled "Bad Night Worse Morning," focused primarily not on us, but on Dan. Jonathan said that he had gone to bed around 11:00 the night before and had fallen into a deep sleep for about forty-five minutes before waking up; after that, he had been up and down for the rest of the night. He said that he'd thrown up again around 3:00, waking up Dan. Apparently irritated, Dan hadn't spoken to him that morning even when he'd asked him a direct question. Finally, after considerable prodding, Dan had launched into a diatribe about how Jonathan needed to do laundry and, as always, how he needed to do something about the dogs. Jonathan described Dan as someone who had "severe intimacy and relationship issues," having cut off his own son after receiving one critical e-mail from him. Apparently, Dan had hosted "guests" before, but none of them had lasted for more than nine days. Having been there a few days longer than that, Jonathan now held the record—or had simply overstayed his welcome. The reasons his other guests had been asked to leave ranged from leaving a mess in the bathroom to allegedly stealing his loose change. All of Dan's reasons were petty, indicating that he was either unwilling or unable to make even minor adjustments to other people.

Then, Jonathan confessed the *real* reason why Dan didn't want him to have visitors—especially me. Although Jonathan said that he had intended to wait until he could speak to me in person, Dan had mentioned the reason again that morning and he had "fucking had it." Apparently, Dan didn't want Jonathan to have any visitors, except for Laura, because, in Dan's opinion, all of Jonathan's male friends were "too obviously gay" and he didn't want the neighbors to talk. Dan thought Jonathan was acceptable because he didn't "look or act gay," in Dan's judgment. Dan hadn't mentioned anyone in particular, but since I was Jonathan's only "sleep-in friend," the finger seemed to be pointing mainly at me.

Too obviously gay? How was I appearing or acting that might make people think I was gay, at least in *Dan's* mind? I knew that I wasn't usually perceived as macho or hypermasculine, but I also knew that I wasn't usually perceived as "faggy" or feminine, although some people who held well-defined gender stereotypes did sometimes perceive me as gay because I wasn't as stereotypically masculine as the average man in the conservative Midwest in which I lived. If anything, I was usually perceived as somewhat nerdy. I was infuriated, not because I felt insulted, but because Dan's self-hatred, projected onto me and others, had now become "too obvious" in the way it was interfering not only with Jonathan's ability to have social interaction, but also with my ability to maintain my relationship with Jonathan.

Beyond that, I found Dan's attitude self-deluding and sick. He had been in the army, but he had also been a nurse. He tried to maintain a façade of heterosexuality by having a "girlfriend," whom, I had learned, the people in Credence believed his friend Patty was, as well as being an elder in the church, but he was also a "bottom" who compulsively cruised the Internet and local parks for "tops," something that could not have remained secret in the time he had lived in the small town of Credence. Who did he think he was fooling? I hated Dan more than ever, not for what he had said about me, but for what he was doing to Jonathan and me.

That Monday, Jonathan barraged me with e-mails that focused on Dan. His behavior was becoming increasingly disturbing, even dangerous, and Jonathan was becoming even more desperate. In the first, titled "Got to get out of here ASAP," Jonathan said he was "on the verge of just killing Dan or walking out or something inbetween." He said that in spite of having spent the day doing laundry and cleaning, which should have appeased him, Dan had continued to harass him about the dogs. He said that Dan knew he was feeling sick, stressed, and vulnerable about the dogs and he seemed to be using that vulnerability against him.

Although that was bad enough, there was now a new twist: Jonathan could eat only at dinner. Dan was on a diet and was eating only one meal a day; even though Jonathan wasn't, Dan didn't want him fixing anything for himself because, he claimed, Jonathan always left the kitchen a mess and always left crumbs. I knew how fanatical Dan was about neatness, remembering how I had been required to eat crumbly foods, like potato chips, outside, but his fastidiousness had reached a new extreme. Jonathan quipped that he could stand to lose weight, but "forced starvation" wasn't the method he preferred to use. The stress of being deprived of regular meals, along with everything else, was driving him to tears.

In response to his request for his father's advice, his father had counseled him to look around and make a smart, not a hasty, decision so he didn't end up in an even worse situation. He said that his father had been condemning, calling him an "idiot" for getting himself into the situation he had. Jonathan, discouraged, said that his father was probably right.

Around 2:00 that afternoon, Jonathan sent me a lengthy e-mail that began by informing me that Dan had once again gone to the park. Sarcastically, he said he guessed that wasn't "too obviously gay." Dan's parting comment, and now constant refrain, was that the dogs had to go, since he could smell them in the kitchen. Jonathan quipped that he could still smell the spray paint from the twelve picture frames Dan had painted, so smelling the dogs over that must require "quite a feat of sniffing." He said he didn't miss eating during the day, since he wasn't hungry anyway, but realized it was just another way for Dan to exert his control over him. He said that he was finishing up the last load of laundry and had been forced to refold the laundry he'd previously done because Dan had told him he wasn't folding it right. He stated that Dan's nastiness was making him sicker.

After repeating his previous thoughts about Cliff, and me in relation to Cliff, Jonathan said that Logan had suggested that Dan was trying to keep him off balance so he wouldn't do well at his meeting at the hospital on Wednesday. He said Logan viewed Dan as a "very dark personality" and had suggested that Dan could become dangerous, since Dan didn't respect or seem to need other people and was filled with self-hatred, which was revealed in his attitude toward other gay men.

In addition to hearing from Laura, who had e-mailed him twice primarily to tell him she was spending the day in bed and baking brownies, assuring him that she would save him some, he had heard from Horatio. He had called to tell Jonathan that he was going to California, in Jonathan's place, to meet with the company that was buying into OutSource. He said that Horatio had commented that the office was "weird" without him, since he was "not gone but [he wasn't] there either." Horatio had also said that Mike kept asking him if Jonathan had ever discussed certain issues with him. In response, Horatio had told Mike to call Jonathan himself, but he understood that Mike was still angry with Jonathan for having taken a leave of absence and probably wouldn't. Even so, Horatio had asked the vice president of sales, who was sitting in for Jonathan during his leave, to arrange a conference call. I liked to think that Jonathan and Mike could take that opportunity to begin to heal the hard feelings that Jonathan's leave had obviously caused.

Yet, in the midst of the adversity and uncertainty, some positive things had happened. Jonathan told me that his father, in spite of his criticisms, had finally softened up and sent him £10,000—roughly $16,000 US—for emergencies. Although it wouldn't arrive for a week, it would arrive. At least his father was now standing behind him to this limited degree. He also told me that Terrence was once again planning to visit now that the situation in New York had begun to improve, but unfortunately he wouldn't be able to get there until the end of the following week. I wondered if Jonathan would even be there by then.

Around 6:45 that evening, Jonathan sent me an e-mail titled "Twilight Zone." After beginning by telling me he felt as if he was going to "break," Jonathan informed me that Dan had spent the entire afternoon at the park. When he finally returned around 5:00, he had ignored Jonathan, refused to talk to him, made himself not one but three waterglass-size vodkas on the rocks, and left again, presumably to go back to the park. Jonathan was certain that Dan was working up his courage to tell him to leave. If he did, Jonathan said, he would then be homeless and living out of his car. He said he had hoped to be able to remain at Dan's until he went to his meeting in Mariah on Wednesday then leave in an "orderly, sensible manner," but he doubted now that Dan would allow that to happen.

Jonathan complained that he had given up his house in part because of Dan's invitation to stay with him, which he now seemed on the verge of retracting. He was worried that he wouldn't be able to get all of the things that he'd taken to Dan's, which were some of his most precious possessions, into his car and no longer trusted Dan enough to leave them there. He said he was frightened, was in tears, and didn't know what to do. He ended the message by begging me to come and help him if he had to leave quickly.

Since he had been living at Dan's, Jonathan had never evinced quite this level of desperation. In response, I told him that I would do anything in my power to help him, that he could count on me. I told him that if he needed to get out fast, I would come to Credence as quickly as I could and get him, the girls, and his belongings—all of them—out. Jonathan had told me that Horatio had a townhouse in Paladin and that it might be a possible place to which he could flee, but I told him that whatever he decided, I would help him get out if he needed to get out, that all he needed to do was to give me the word. I told him that I was there for him. In trying to comfort him, I was also trying to comfort myself.

When he finally replied around 10:30, he seemed relieved that I was home from work, since he said it made him feel more secure knowing that he could reach me at once if he needed. He told me that Dan had come home around 9:00 and was so drunk that he had run over the reflector at the end of the driveway in addition to the solar lights that lined one side. After managing to get into the house, Dan had called a man from a nearby town whom he had met online but not in person and had made arrangements for him to come over so they could have sex. Dan had then ordered Jonathan to stay downstairs, even if it was for the rest of the night. Resigning himself to the situation, Jonathan said that would at least give him a chance to spend the night with the girls.

Jonathan found Dan's behavior increasingly bizarre and frightening and said that he made each day a little worse than the day before. Reviewing his possibilities for escape, he answered my question about possibly staying at Horatio's. He said that although Horatio was in California on business, he would ask him about it when he got back. Again, he confessed how frightened he felt at the prospect of becoming homeless and having nowhere to turn.

He ended the message by informing me that the "trick de jour" had just shown up, sending the dogs into a fit of barking and causing Dan to yell at him to shut them up. "Why is he so mean?" he asked. I knew, or at least I thought I knew, why Dan was mean, but I didn't launch into a lengthy psychological explanation in response because I knew that on a practical level, it would do no good. Jonathan just needed to get out and leave Dan and his dysfunction to himself.

Around 8:30 the next morning, Jonathan sent me an e-mail in which he reported on the events of the previous night. He said that after Dan's partner had arrived, the two of them had finished off the remaining vodka before having sex. Jonathan had remained downstairs until things had grown quiet, at which point he had fled upstairs and into his room. He said that he never saw the man but described his voice as "loud and coarse." Dan's lack of selectivity was quite evident.

That morning, Dan not only was hung over but also had added "the new shitty thing of the day" to his growing list of irrational rules. In addition to not being allowed to fix breakfast, Jonathan was now not allowed to fix coffee. Dan's reason was that although he made enough for the both of them, he ended up throwing most of it out. Jonathan was, however, still allowed to fix tea, since it was his, but he had to be finished and have the kitchen cleaned by 8:30. In addition, Dan had also reinforced his rule about having no food outside the kitchen, so Jonathan couldn't take even a drink into the den or into his room. "He must enjoy the power," Jonathan remarked, which seemed obvious. He reminded me that his meeting in Mariah was the next day and that after that he would plan "the great escape." He ended the message by hoping I was doing better than he was.

I wasn't sure that I was.

That afternoon, however, Jonathan wrote to tell me that things had calmed down. Calling me by my "Indian" name, he told me that

Dan was now being nice, presumably to make up for being a "shit" earlier in the day. Dan had made lunch, which Jonathan interpreted as a peace offering, and had explained that sometimes he had trouble adjusting to people and keeping friends. Apparently, his friendship with Jonathan, which had lasted for two years, was the longest one Dan had maintained. Perhaps because Dan's attitude toward Jonathan had softened, Jonathan's toward Dan had softened as well; now, Jonathan had returned to his earlier opinion that Dan was basically a good person but also deeply conflicted. He said he felt calmer now that the hostility Dan had displayed that morning had passed. Jonathan ended the message by expressing his wish that we could have spent the day together.

Throughout the remainder of the day, Dan continued to be good. Around 4:30, Jonathan wrote to tell me that he'd had a quiet afternoon, with Dan having stayed in the kitchen painting and himself having remained in the den watching TV and playing with the dogs. Mentioning our tentative plans to meet that Saturday in Paladin, Jonathan said that he saw no problem doing so if Dan was going to be gone, although he would have to return later that day to take care of the dogs. He told me he was looking forward to getting together after a couple of difficult weeks and so was I. Given everything that had happened in those two weeks, it had been two weeks too long.

Around 11:00 that evening, Jonathan e-mailed me for the fourth time that day. In this e-mail, he began referring to the two disparate personalities that Dan manifested as Good Dan and Evil Dan. He informed me that Good Dan was continuing to visit, although wondering when Evil Dan would return was nerve-wracking. That evening, Jonathan had needed to go to Rowen to buy dog food and Dan had invited himself along. They had gone to Wal-Mart, where Dan had cruised, then to a "hole in the wall" restaurant, where they'd eaten tenderloin sandwiches. All in all, the evening had gone uneventfully, though no one knew when that might change.

Jonathan did have one piece of unfortunate news. Because of the events in New York, Dan's trip had been postponed to Saturday, the 29th. Since Jonathan was afraid to leave the dogs alone with Dan, that meant that we wouldn't be able to meet in Paladin that Saturday as planned. I understood Jonathan's plight, but I wondered how long it would be now before I was able to see him. He asked for suggestions, but since I couldn't visit and he couldn't leave, I could think of no alternatives.

I was unhappy that we wouldn't be able to meet in Paladin that Saturday, but Jonathan felt optimistic, if nervous, about his interview at the hospital the next day, which partly made up for it. If everything went well, he said, he would then begin looking at houses in and around Mariah, which would "get [him] back into [his] own space"—something he desperately needed to do.

He ended his message to me by saying that he missed me and that our situation was "like being divorced." The next morning, though, when our e-mails crossed, indicating to Jonathan that we "really still [were] on the same wave length," he amended what he had said about our "marital status" by saying not to think of us as divorced but to think of him as a "Reservist called up for active duty in the Twilight Zone." That seemed like the best description of himself, his life, that I had heard yet.

When he returned from Mariah later that day, he wrote to tell me that things had gone "as well as anyone could hope." He told me that he would be going back later to meet the three vice presidents and a member of the board of directors whom he hadn't met. I was heartened that things had gone so well and hoped that it represented another step along the path to getting away from Dan and getting on with his life.

Yet, in spite of the encouraging news, the lift the meeting had given to him was once again deflated by what he had returned to. While he was gone, Dan had locked the dogs in a small room at the back of the basement to keep them confined. That, however, was only the beginning. Jonathan's messages throughout the rest of the evening indicated quite clearly that Evil Dan was back.

Around 8:00, he wrote to tell me that Dan was "almost falling down drunk." Once again, he had launched into a tirade about how intolerable the dogs were and how they would not be allowed out of the basement room. Jonathan commented, as he had before, that Dan always seemed to behave this way when he was at a business meeting or generally doing something that might weaken Dan's feeling of control over him. Jonathan said that Dan's behavior was "planned and purposeful and mean" and stated that he was now beginning to hate him.

Provoked once again into reviewing his options for escape, he still believed that going to Laura's might ultimately be the best solution. Going to Horatio's was an option only for a night or two since his townhouse had only one bedroom and wasn't very accommodating. Therefore, at least for the time, he was stuck at Dan's.

After mentioning again that we couldn't meet in Paladin on Saturday, he lamented the fact that we seemed to have resumed "very separate lives." Our relationship was drifting off course, he felt, through no fault of our own, and although Jonathan was upset, he didn't know what to do about it. Neither did I. Again, he mentioned how Dan's behavior destroyed the positive feeling he obtained from interacting with normal people and was convinced that Logan was right in his assessment of the motivation behind Dan's actions. Disgusted with the situation and tired of repeating himself, Jonathan abruptly dropped the subject.

He ended his message by informing me that he was planning to go to Rowen to keep from having to be around Dan and to keep from punching him, something he seemed half-serious about doing. Jonathan had never displayed and didn't seem capable of serious physical aggression, but his comment raised the disturbing possibility that given the right—or wrong—stimulus, the situation between Jonathan and Dan could turn violent.

When Jonathan returned a few hours later, the situation had reached the breaking point. In an e-mail titled "Urgent—leaving Dan's By Sunday," he began by telling me that he had just tried to call but the line had been busy. He told me that he had gone to an all-night restaurant in Rowen, where he had sat and drunk coffee until 11:30—some three hours—before he had returned to Dan's. When he'd gotten back, he had found that Dan had left a nasty note on his pillow, informing him that if he didn't do something with the dogs by the end of the week, he would take them to the pound.

Dan's ultimatum, it appeared, had been provoked by Jonathan's attempts to put him off regarding the dogs, which had been exposed as subterfuge. Apparently, Jonathan had told Dan that Laura had agreed to take the dogs when her older son moved out—something that was a half-truth, since Laura was willing to take them only if Jonathan came with them. Wanting to see Jonathan, Laura had invited herself to Dan's the next day, but far from being annoyed, Dan was eagerly awaiting her arrival, since her presence helped to perpetuate the façade of heterosexuality he was trying to maintain for the neighbors. Because Jonathan didn't feel prepared to deal with her, he had told her that he wouldn't be available, then had told Dan that she had a job interview and wouldn't be able to come. While Jonathan was out, however, Laura had called and talked to Dan, exposing the lie that Jonathan had told him.

Angered by the thoughts that the dogs wouldn't be leaving anytime soon and that Jonathan had lied to him, Dan had given him the ultimatum. Consequently, Jonathan had decided that he was going to go to Laura's on Sunday. He wasn't thrilled about the idea, but didn't feel he had a choice. He was expecting to have a confrontation with Dan the next morning over the dogs and feared that Dan might throw him out then. Venting his feelings in various directions, Jonathan said that before he left, he planned to expose Dan to Patty as well as to the pastor of his church, revealing to them both who and what Dan really was. He ended his message by expressing his opinion that Dan cared for nothing, not even his own child. His final words were a plea for help.

Sometime after midnight, Jonathan called again and finally got through. The desperation that was clear in his message was equally clear in his voice. I spent the next forty-five minutes listening to him vent and assuring him that I would do whatever I could to help him. Even if he couldn't come to live with me, I could at least rescue him from Dan by taking him, the girls, and his things to Laura's. He thanked me profusely for being there for him and after deciding that he'd burdened me long enough, we hung up. That did not, however, break the mental and emotional connection that I had to him or his problems and, in fact, only made it stronger.

The next morning around 9:00, Jonathan sent me an e-mail, titled "Stop The Insanity," in which he told me that the feared confrontation hadn't happened. Instead, Good Dan had reappeared and was now "all sweetness" toward him. Once again, Dan explained that the dogs were the issue, not Jonathan, and that he enjoyed having *him*. Jonathan said that, as a show of goodwill, he had hugged Dan "at his request," biting his tongue, though, as he did it. He wondered what went through Dan's brain and wasn't sure how to react to "this rollercoaster." Neither was I.

He then went on to compliment me for being "so wonderful and sweet" the night before and apologize for "those desperate middle of the night save me calls" but said that I was the one to whom he turned for comfort and advice. Now that things had calmed down, he asked me if he should go to Laura's, which would involve "an entirely different set of problems," or stay at Dan's. Jonathan knew that Laura thought the two of them living together would be a *Will & Grace* type of situation, but he observed, "Have you noticed that Will never has a boyfriend?" He also realized that sleeping in the same bed, which he said Laura wanted them to do, posed its own set of problems. He thought that Laura wanted him to live with her in part because she wanted her family and friends to think they were a couple. "A couple of whats?" he asked. As if the combination of Dan's attempts to isolate him and Laura's attempts to exploit him had intensified his feelings, he ended his message by telling me that he missed me.

I was relieved to know that Dan had settled down for the time being, but I knew it wouldn't last. In twenty-four hours, he had gone from being Good Dan to being Evil Dan to being Good Dan again. Dan's mood, destabilized by his drinking, was unpredictable and I was certain that before the day was out Evil Dan would once again assume control of the body.

I told him I thought that, all things considered, staying with Laura instead of Dan might be the better choice, at least in the short term. Or, more accurately, the *less bad* choice, given that neither arrangement was optimal and came equipped with its own set of problems. I reassured him, though, that whatever he decided to do, he could count on me to help him. It had heartened me that I was the one he'd chosen to call the night before when he'd felt desperate, which was how it was supposed to work if things were moving in the right direction. For whatever it was worth, I also told him that my mother knew about his situation and was concerned about him as well. My mother had no tolerance for hypocrites and alcoholics anyway, but the way Dan had been treating him, especially when he was sick, had pushed *all* the wrong buttons for her. Consequently, she was on his side as much as anyone else was.

In response, Jonathan began by thanking me for what he described as my "lovely" message, saying that it had brought tears to his eyes. He said that he didn't realize that my mother knew about his situation and supposed that she thought he was "10 varieties of idiot, like [his] father" did for getting himself into it. That wasn't true, but it seemed to say something about his feelings toward himself.

He went on to say that he was still trying to decide whether he should remain at Dan's or move to Laura's. He didn't like either option. He was now thinking that he would try to stall both of them until he found out whether or not he had gotten the job at the hospital. He said the hospital had called and had wanted references from places where he'd completed projects. There were numerous people at TekNetium as well as at another company, an American one, that he had not previously mentioned who could vouch for him. He said that at the latter, his former boss was now COO and *loved* him still. Now that he had actually been there, he liked the idea of living in Mariah, saying that it was a beautiful town with great houses and was an easy commute from Paladin. If he did get the job, he now planned to rent an apartment there for six months and try to establish the peace and quiet that he needed to recoup but that he knew now he would never find at Dan's.

Yet, in spite of the turmoil he caused, Good Dan was still controlling the body and was being his "jolly self," as Jonathan described him. Jonathan said that Dan had spent the day painting "more potential museum pieces" but had otherwise left him alone. Dan was in such a good mood that apparently he had brought Jonathan's lunch down to him so he wouldn't have to climb the stairs. Jonathan was disoriented by Dan's erratic behavior and commented that Dan needed a "resident therapist."

He ended the e-mail by telling me how much he appreciated me and everything I did for him and how I cared for him. He said he looked forward to getting his life back on track and moving forward with our lives. He restated his opinion from two weeks before that taking a leave of absence had been a disaster and thought that perhaps Mike knew more than he had given him credit for. He told me to be well and safe and added, "At least one of us then will be." Uncharacteristically he signed the e-mail, "With Love."

When I heard from Jonathan again sometime around 5:30 that afternoon, he informed me that Good Dan was still visiting. He said that Dan had spent the afternoon cruising the Internet and that after five hours he had finally convinced a graduate student at a nearby university to come over by telling him that he was in his 40s and in good shape. Jonathan said that the student was supposed to come over around 5:30 and that he thought he might go into town "to avoid that whole scene." Even if he didn't show, he still thought he would leave if Dan started drinking and wouldn't return until he thought it was "safe."

Otherwise, he said that he had spent all afternoon in his bedroom because he didn't feel well "at all" and wanted the maximum amount of privacy, peace, and quiet he could get. He told me that his heart doctor had called that day and had expressed his unhappiness at Jonathan's situation, asking him why he wasn't living in an assisted-care setting. He said that when he had told the doctor where he was, about his situation, he had burst into tears. His doctor had informed him that he needed to live in a peaceful, stress-free environment where he received supplemental care if he expected to recover. Concerned about his condition, his doctor had decided to see him the next Monday when he went for one of his "cut down" treatments, which he was supposed to have started receiving in early August, even though Jonathan hadn't been scheduled to see him. He ended his message by asking, "Some life, huh?" That didn't begin to describe it.

Later that night, Evil Dan returned. Around 9:00, Jonathan reported that Dan had drunk three tumblers of vodka and was close to passing out. In addition, he had been drinking wine and was cursing and stumbling around. Dan was also furious because the student hadn't shown up. Jonathan said that earlier he had been planning to escape to Rowen if the student had shown up and, knowing he might be going out, Dan had asked him to buy another double bottle of vodka, since the one Dan had bought on Monday, only three days before, was now gone. In the end, however, he didn't go, so Dan was limited to only the three tumblers.

Otherwise, Jonathan reported that he had spent almost all of the day in bed. He said that he wasn't feeling well and that the stress of living with Dan wasn't helping. He also stated that he hadn't been able to eat that day, Dan's restrictions notwithstanding, but didn't care because he was so tired and had no appetite. He said he had to leave for Mariah the next morning before 9:00 so he planned to crawl back into bed as soon as he could.

He said that Greg was planning to come over the next evening to keep Dan from being able to "pull his shit." He said that after seeing how Dan behaved, Greg wanted to protect him. Dan didn't like having Greg at the house, but from what I inferred, Dan hadn't reached the point that he had actually forbidden Greg to come. Jonathan then told me that he felt better knowing that I was home and he could reach me at once if he needed to, a fact that he told me helped him get through what he was suffering. Poignantly, he ended his message by saying, "I will go into my own space and the hospital can arrange some help for me and I will be quiet with my girls and you can come when convenient and I'll be OK... That is all that I want now." That, it appeared, was all he felt he could hope for.

In response, I tried to be encouraging, but it was difficult to know what to say. I wished him the best of luck with his meeting the next morning, telling him that if it went well, it could be the beginning of a better life in which he would once again have his own space and we could work, unfettered, on regaining the momentum he felt the development of our relationship had lost. I hoped it helped.

The next morning around 7:30, Jonathan wrote me a brief message in which he lamented how moving to Dan's had undermined his health, his life, and his relationship. He said that even if he didn't get the job in Mariah, his doctor was still unhappy about his current situation and would have social services find a better place for him. I didn't know what that meant for us. He concluded by telling me that he needed to leave but would e-mail me when he got back to let me know how things had gone.

Later that afternoon, Jonathan wrote to tell me about his meeting in Mariah as well as how Dan had, once again, tried to undermine the uplift it had given to him and reassert his sick control over him. He told me that after five hours of meetings and having met with "every fucking person alive who ever worked at that place, or so it seemed," he thought that things had gone well and said that they would be informing him of their decision by the end of the following week. In the course of the interview, he had learned more about the precise nature of his job. Apparently, he would be put in the position of the "designated bad guy" whose function would be to "shake up the environment" by instituting changes that the old guard, who wanted to maintain the status quo, wouldn't necessarily like. Although he would be the lightning rod in the potential storm, he also said that by reporting to the CEO, who fully supported the need to make the hospital's operation more cost-efficient, he would be protected. He wasn't sure what to think, saying that on the drive back, he had gone back and forth on the issue and was now in the middle.

Yet, in spite of his misgivings, Jonathan felt hopeful about the position and his chances of getting it. Unfortunately, as soon as he had returned to Dan's, Dan had tried, as he had before, to destroy the positive feeling the meeting had given to Jonathan. The moment Jonathan had walked in the door, Dan had complained that the dogs had barked so much while he was gone that they had given him a headache. Jonathan wisecracked—to me—that it was probably the gallon of vodka that Dan had drunk the night before that had given him the headache.

He also reported that Dan had been "rotten" that morning as well. When Jonathan had finished dressing in a pinstriped suit adorned with a silkscreened tie designed by a well-known artist, Dan had remarked that it was the ugliest tie he had ever seen. Jonathan said that Dan was so ignorant about art that his hatred of the tie only served to reinforce his liking of it. He remarked that all you had to do was to look around at Dan's house to see what kind of taste he had, since much of the décor appeared to come from low-end craft stores. That, apparently, was the only comment Dan had made to him to send him on his way. Jonathan was more convinced than ever that Logan was right about the reason for Dan's behavior. He ended the message by saying that he was going to change out of his ugly tie.

Around 6:15 that evening, he e-mailed me to tell me that although Dan was already drunk for the evening and was slurring his words, he was having to drive him to Rowen to buy more vodka. Unfortunately, Greg had never shown nor called, but Jonathan hoped that Dan would pass out, giving him some peace.

Around 10:00, Jonathan sent me an e-mail with the provocative title, "Ride of Death." Apparently, Dan had insisted on driving home from Rowen even though he was drunk. Jonathan had tried to get his keys away from him, but Dan had refused to give them up. In the end, Jonathan was able to get Dan to stay in Rowen long enough to sober up to the point that he was somewhat more in control, although when they had left, he was still impaired. Jonathan quipped that the incident was exactly what he needed to be stress free and regain his health. He wondered what would happen next.

Alarmed, I e-mailed him immediately to ask him if he was alone and we could speak. He wrote back almost at once to say that he was, so I called. As we had two nights before, we talked for about forty-five minutes during which he expanded on the upsetting events that had taken place that night. In response, I offered my opinions about what I thought he should do, since he always seemed to want my advice. Unfortunately, we had trouble seeing things from the other's point of view and ended up talking past each other. Perhaps because he had been so barraged with so many possibilities in so short a time while under so much stress, he was feeling overwhelmed, so I backed off. I only hoped he could get away from Dan as soon as he could and not in a way that would end our relationship.

The next day, I didn't hear from Jonathan in the morning, as I normally did. After writing early that afternoon to find out how he was doing, he finally replied around 3:00. He told me that he'd spent much of the day on the phone. He didn't clarify if Dan had been gone or had relented on his restrictions on using the phone, but I assumed the former. He said that his friend Greg Carroll had called and said that he'd spoken to Terrence, who had told him what was happening in Jonathan's life. He said that later, Terrence himself had called and that they had spoken for more than two hours. Jonathan said that even though he and Terrence had never been close, Terrence was being "incredibly nice." Terrence was horrified at how far Jonathan had fallen in so short a time and had told him that he didn't want the same thing that had happened to Malcolm to happen to him. Jonathan said he wasn't contemplating suicide at all but understood how the circumstances of his life could suggest to anyone that he might be.

He said that, in spite of not being close, Terrence wanted him to come and live with him. Terrence wanted to come within the next week or two and they would leave Jonathan's belongings in the storage unit but pack up the car with everything that he had taken to Dan's, which wasn't much. Jonathan wasn't sure that he wanted to do that, in part because he didn't know how he felt about living with Terrence. Jonathan was also suspicious that their father had put Terrence up to making the offer, which meant that it wasn't Terrence's idea. In spite of his reservations, however, Jonathan thought he would add it to his growing list of imperfect options for escaping from Dan's.

As far as Dan was concerned, Jonathan said simply that Dan was being Dan. He said that he had gone from being good to bad to good to bad since 9:00 that morning. Jonathan said that he was meeting "Big" Greg in Rowen for dinner and would try to stay out until at least 11:00 by which point Dan would be either asleep or passed out. After thanking me for having called the night before, he ended his e-mail by telling me that he missed me. I missed him too and wished we could be together for many reasons.

■

Around the middle of August, I had started having subtle problems with the engine of my car. By the middle of September, the problems had grown to the point that the engine didn't want to turn over half the time. I thought—I *hoped*—that my car just needed a new battery, but when I had it checked, I was told that the engine was wearing out and nothing could be done to fix it. Although it was unwelcome news, since that meant I would now have to buy another car on my limited income, it wasn't surprising news, given how old my car was. I had my suspicions that all of the driving I had done the week of the move had finished it off, since I estimated that I had driven at least 500 miles that week, but it was really just a matter of time.

On the afternoon of Sunday, September 23, Kathryn and I spent the afternoon looking at cars when there were no salespeople to pester us. We went to a dealership in Clarian and I ended up finding a car there that became a strong possibility.

When I returned home, I found that Jonathan had sent me three pictures of himself that Dan had taken. They were large, clear, color "portraits" of him and the first photos that I'd had of him in the four months that we'd been seeing each other. This was also the first time that my mother saw what Jonathan looked like. Her comment about his appearance was that he looked "mischievous," as if he were always trying to figure out what kind of trouble to get into next. I thought that was an interesting perception because it mirrored my own when I had first seen the portrait of his mother and some of his siblings that depicted him around the age of seven.

Then, around 11:00 that evening, Jonathan sent me his most depressed, discouraged message yet since living at Dan's. He began by telling me that Dan had gotten so drunk that he had dropped his glass, which had shattered all over the floor. As if calculated to increase his concern for the girls, Dan had told Jonathan that he'd had his son's dog put to sleep when his son was 12 because she kept urinating on the floor. He said that Frizzie had reached the point that she cowered at the sound of Dan's voice and he was certain that Dan had hit her.

He said that, in addition, Cliff had called again that day. Having reduced him to tears, Jonathan had cried for more than half an hour. He wanted Cliff to leave him alone or at least stop being so hurtful, saying that he still loved Cliff but needed to be separate from him. He then addressed the situation between us, saying it had been so long since he had seen me—by that point, more than two weeks—that the situation caused him almost as much pain as the situation with Cliff did, though for different reasons. As he had before, he compared the situation to a divorce or a sudden death. He stated that although our relationship had drifted off course from the lack of contact, he felt that it could be put back on track "with work."

He ended his e-mail by telling me that the next day would be a long day of doctors and that although Dan was going with him, it was undoubtedly to ogle the men at the hospital. He told me he was tired and was going to bed. Quoting from the lyrics of Carole King, he lamented that I was "so far away." The physical distance was the least of it.

∎

On Monday, September 24, I decided to drive to the hospital in Paladin to see if I could, by chance, catch Jonathan there. I hadn't seen him since I'd left Credence more than two weeks before, although it seemed like more than two months, and I hoped to be able to see him, if only briefly, before he returned to the seeming prison of Dan's. After teaching my Monday morning class, I came home, ate breakfast, and wrapped a gift that I had purchased for him, a videotape of *Victor/Victoria*, which Jonathan said he enjoyed but hadn't seen for some time. Around 11:00, I got into my car, uncertain that it would make the three-hour round trip, and headed for Paladin.

Amazingly, my car, with its half-dead engine, made it all the way to the hospital. Although I had driven past the hospital numerous times while Jonathan was still living in Paladin, I had never actually driven into the complex, since until that point I had had no incentive to do so. Now, however, I saw, up close, the hospital where Jonathan had been taken on that fateful day in June when he had fainted at work and where the drama of his illness had, for the past three months, partly played out. I also drove past the infamous Stress Center where Jonathan had met the fag hag Laura, the 500-pound Greg—Chase—and others who, in ways both major and minor, had played their own parts in the drama of the previous months. To say that I had mixed emotions about the place would be an understatement and I spent little time in its presence.

I drove around the parking lot several times to see if I could spot Jonathan's car. I never saw it. I even stopped and checked at the main desk to see if he was there, but they had no record of him. He should have been there and I couldn't understand why he wasn't. Discouraged, feeling that I had wasted my gas and time and had brought my car that much closer to collapse for no good reason, I headed back to Hawthorn.

By the time I got home, sometime around 3:00, I was exhausted. I tried to rest before I had to make the trip to Clarian to teach for three hours. Somehow, I made it through the evening and back home without falling asleep at the wheel.

When I got home, I checked my e-mail, only to find that I hadn't received a message from Jonathan. That was unusual. Either Dan wasn't letting him use the computer or…something had happened.

—15—
WILL & GRACE

Things here are distinctly odd and very Will & Grace-*like in a Stephen King way.*

After not having heard from Jonathan all day Monday, I started checking my e-mail around 9:00 in the evening to see if I'd gotten any messages from him and kept checking until almost 1:00 the next morning when I saw I wasn't getting anything. In between, I spent a lot of time online seeing if I'd hear from him. I knew something was wrong when I wasn't hearing from him but I wasn't sure what to do. I might have called, but I didn't know if I should call so late, thinking that if Dan were asleep I might wake him and he would be angry. It didn't seem to take much and I didn't want to provoke him, for Jonathan's sake.

When I checked my e-mail again the next morning, I saw that I still hadn't received anything from him. To try to get his attention, I sent him a message titled "Are You OK?" in which I told him that I hadn't heard from him since Sunday night, was concerned, and wanted him to e-mail or call me as soon as he could.

Finally, around 10:15 that morning, Jonathan sent me a cryptic—and disturbing—response. Saying that he was *not* okay, he explained that Monday had been "nuts" and that he was now at Laura's. He said that he had tried to call the night before but my line was busy until after midnight. I had a dial-up connection that blocked the phone line while I was online, so ironically, *my* attempts to contact *him* had thwarted *his* attempts to contact *me*.

I wrote him back, telling him that I would stay off the phone if he wanted to call. Since I didn't have Laura's number, I couldn't call him. Finally, around 4:00 that afternoon he called and explained why the previous day had been "nuts" and why he was now living with Laura.

According to Jonathan, he and Dan had gone to the hospital the day before, despite my inability to find them. Everything had gone fine—until they had gotten home. There, Dan had given Jonathan an ultimatum about the issue that had been an issue from before the beginning: the dogs. He said that Dan had finally become so disgusted by the dogs that he had told him that if he didn't get rid of them at once, they would have to go live in his car. Apparently, he meant that literally. Feeling that he had reached his own breaking point, Jonathan had, in desperation, called Laura and asked her if he could come and live with her. That afternoon, Laura and her sons had driven to Dan's and had rescued Jonathan from him, taking his dogs and belongings back with them to St. Alban.

That, however, was not the only thing that had happened—or even the most important. Jonathan told me that something had happened to Glenn. Glenn had been visiting his mother and stepfather, who were living on one of the Caribbean Islands, and had started to leave a couple of days before. According to friends, he had gone to the airport with the intention of returning home, but had failed to board the plane. He then disappeared and no one had heard from him since. Although he was an adult and had been missing for only a couple of days, the fact that he hadn't gotten in touch with anyone to inform them of his whereabouts seemed worrisome.

Jonathan had previously mentioned that Glenn had a habit of disappearing for several days at a time when he felt overly stressed, and knowing that his relationship with his stepfather was fraught with problems, I wondered if something had happened between them to shove Glenn to his limit. He seemed to be having difficulties anyway, if Jonathan's information about how much Glenn had been calling—or trying to call—him while he was living at Dan's was correct. He had said only two weeks before that Glenn had tried to call him eight times in two days, which suggested a considerable measure of desperation. Unfortunately, Dan had blocked Glenn's calls, so Jonathan had been unable to determine what was happening to Glenn, let alone try to help him.

Although things had ended badly between them, they still cared about each other and Jonathan still felt responsible for him. Consequently, Jonathan was taking the news very hard, which had been dropped on top of the untoward events that had happened to *him* the same day.

I didn't know what to say. Jonathan's life seemed to be going from bad to worse with no end in sight. Laura had reminded him that although Glenn had a habit of disappearing when he became overwhelmed he always returned and I reminded him of the same. I told him I thought it would be only a matter of time before Glenn reappeared and everything was all right, which I genuinely believed.

I wasn't able to talk as long as I would have liked because I had to teach that evening and had to leave by 5:00. When I got to work, I checked my e-mail and found a message from Jonathan. In it, he thanked me for the moral support I had tried to give to him but told me he was unhappy about "so many things," especially Glenn. In spite of Laura's and my assurances about his past disappearances, Jonathan insisted that he wouldn't be at peace until Glenn reappeared, safe and sound, stating that if anything happened to him, he wouldn't be able to live with himself. He said that he had made an appointment with Miranda West to see if she could "feel something." Although I was skeptical, I hoped she could offer him comfort.

Beyond that, he said that although he'd gotten everything from Dan's, he wasn't unpacking at Laura's, which he described as a "total shit house." He added, however, that her sons were "great" and Laura "tried." He said he was planning to look at houses in Mariah on Thursday in case he got the job there. He ended the message by reporting that he'd had to sleep in the same bed with Laura the night before but that he'd fallen asleep "immediately."

When I got home that evening, I replied, trying to be encouraging and assuring him that I was there for him if he needed me. I slept somewhat more soundly that night knowing that even if the situation at Laura's was fraught with its own complications, Jonathan had at least escaped from Dan's clutches. I was also hopeful that if Jonathan's attempts to establish a new life in Mariah continued to progress as well as they already had, he would shortly escape from *Laura's* clutches.

The next day, I resumed my car search. Eventually I settled on the car that I had seen in Clarian, a slightly used one-year-old car with less than 14,000 miles on it. It was saddening to part with my old car, which had been with me through a lot, but it was time for it to go and for me to enter a new phase of my life.

I didn't contact Jonathan that day because I was waiting for him to contact me, if he would. I didn't call him because I didn't know how Laura felt about my calling or what kind of repercussions it might have for Jonathan. In addition, I didn't e-mail him because I didn't want to tie up the phone line in case he wanted to call. I thought it would be better to wait for him to make the next move in an uncertain situation.

I didn't hear from Jonathan again until Thursday. It had gotten to the point that when I didn't hear from him, even for one day, I began to fear the worst. When I did finally hear from him, he told me that e-mail had been down the previous day, so he hadn't been able to write. He didn't say anything about Glenn, but did comment on other aspects of his life. He said that the situation at Laura's was "almost as goofy as Dan's but the dogs [were]n't being harassed." He also implied that he had gotten the job at the hospital, which was incredible news. The hospital had negotiated his employment package the previous day and they were now waiting for the steering committee of their board of directors to approve it. He expected that to happen either that day or the next. He concluded by saying that he was going to go look at four houses in Mariah and added that Laura was going with him. Sarcastically, he appended the word "wow" capitalized and followed by an exclamation mark. I could only imagine what *that* experience would be like, as if he didn't already have enough to deal with.

Since he hadn't raised the issue, I asked him if he had heard anything more about Glenn, and I commented on some of the other things he'd mentioned. I also told him I felt that the "separation thing," as it had come to be called, had gotten out of hand and had to be reversed. I felt that since we would probably be able to work around Laura more easily than we had been able to work around Dan, since Jonathan didn't have to worry about leaving his dogs alone with her and St. Alban was closer to Paladin than Credence was, we should start seeing each other again as much as possible. To that end, I suggested that we get together in Paladin on Sunday if it was feasible. I likened the past month to "an excursion through some kind of disorienting parallel universe" and expressed my hope that we could get to the wormhole out as quickly as possible. Trying to find some comedy within the tragedy, I concluded by telling him that when he and Laura found a house the two of them liked to let me know what they would like as a wedding present.

Jonathan's reply was short, but not sweet. On Friday, he informed me that he'd had a "horrible couple of days." He hadn't heard from Glenn, whom he now feared was dead. In addition, he had told off Dan, who was now claiming that Jonathan had stolen from him, although Jonathan didn't specify what Dan was accusing him of having stolen. He said that things at Laura's were "ok…but a bit ackward," which, to my mind, was an improvement over what they had been at Dan's. He didn't mention the "separation thing," but did end his message by asking me why he wasn't hearing from me, what had happened with my car, and if he didn't "count" anymore.

I was put off by his implication that I wasn't staying in touch with him as much as he liked, given that I felt I had been doing that as much as I could in spite of the obstacles involved, but I also understood that he was having a hard time and was reacting to things emotionally, not rationally. I wrote back, telling him that he *did* count, and asked him if I could call him, allowing me to communicate with him directly. He said yes, so I called him around 7:00 that evening and we talked further. In the process, I learned more about some of the things to which he had alluded in his last e-mail, although not much more. After we hung up, I hoped he was satisfied, however, that I thought he *did* "count" and that my perceived lack of interest in his life had been just a misperception.

Saturday morning around 10:00, he sent me an e-mail in which he described the situation at Laura's as "distinctly odd and very *Will&Grace*-like in a Stephen King way." He said there was a "below surface tension" between Laura and him, although he didn't specify if it was sexual or something else, but said he wasn't concerned because he didn't think he would have to stay with her very long. He said he had placed an offer on a house in Mariah as well as on a backup in case the offer on the first house wasn't accepted. I hoped that one or the other panned out because as soon as it did, he could flee from Laura's.

He went on to specify that Dan was accusing him of having stolen *money* from him—something he insisted wasn't true—and of being ungrateful. He partly blamed Dan for Glenn's disappearance, believing that if Dan hadn't limited his communication with Glenn, he might not have disappeared. Jonathan said he would never forgive Dan for that and for the unhealthy ways in which he had tried to control his life. He said that Dan still retained possession of *The Tempest*—which Jonathan had presumably given to Dan as a gift but which he now wanted back—and had turned threatening toward him, although he didn't specify how. Jonathan said that he intended to "tear down his facade of lies and show what a true sexual predator he [was] in that small community" of Credence. He didn't say what he was planning, if anything, but his statement was indicative of the magnitude of his antipathy toward Dan.

Jonathan said that although he wanted to see me the next day, he would have to ask Laura if he could leave. His rationale was that because he wasn't living in his own home, he wasn't in control. I thought that was an odd attitude. Even if he wasn't living in his own home, why did he have to ask for permission to leave? He was an adult, after all. Was Laura really that possessive? If *I* was the reason for his reservations, then he didn't have to tell her whom he was meeting. He had said that he hadn't lived at home since he was eight, and in some ways, he seemed to relate to the person who owned the house in which he lived the way an eight-year-old related to his parents. I realized that Jonathan had been conditioned to react and relate to things very differently than I had, though, so I tried to be understanding.

That Saturday morning, I went to pick up my new car, and later that day, I e-mailed Jonathan to tell him about it. A little past 7:30 that evening, he replied, wishing me *mazel tov* on the car. Then, he reported that his offer on the first house in Mariah had been rejected. He said that he and the owner had settled on a price but that the owner had wanted a month-to-month contract, refusing to give him a lease with specific terms. The situation seemed unstable and unacceptable. His agent was now trying to make a deal on the backup house.

Raising the subject of Dan, he said he now thought that Dan *did* have a crush on him and was now behaving like a "high school girl who got dumped." He wondered how he could tell the people in Credence the truth about Dan. He said that Dan had already told everyone in Credence that Jonathan had stolen from him, so if Jonathan said anything about Dan, it would simply be viewed as an attempt to get back at Dan and wouldn't be believed.

Moving to the subject of Glenn, he said that he was haunted by Glenn and tried to talk to him but couldn't feel his presence. He said that he was afraid of what might have happened to him and that if something had, he wouldn't be able to live with himself. Again, he accused Dan of having a hand in Glenn's disappearance by keeping them from being able to communicate and for that Jonathan would destroy him. He said that he rarely hated but he hated Dan. He ended the e-mail abruptly by saying that he wanted to change the subject.

By that point, I was starting to get pulled into Jonathan's attempts to expose and injure Dan. Dan had made his life a living hell, had kept him from communicating with Glenn, had kept us from being together because of his internalized homophobia and pathological desire to have Jonathan to himself. Whether directly or indirectly, he had done a considerable amount of damage to a considerable number of people. In addition, he lived a life that was nothing but a lie, filled to overflowing with hypocrisy and deceit. I am not normally a vengeful person, but I feel that sometimes people's behavior becomes so egregious that not forcing them to suffer the consequences of their actions is almost a kind of passive approval. I found myself suggesting to Jonathan that he send letters to some of the more relevant people in Credence detailing his activities. I told him not only that he had my blessing to do whatever he needed to do to damage Dan, but also that I would do whatever I could to help.

Jonathan and I finally arranged to meet that Sunday at the bathhouse he had mentioned, which was located in a semi-seedy area of Paladin. It purported to be a fitness club for men, but the fact that it contained rooms with beds and closed-circuit TVs playing gay porn belied its stated nature. Unfortunately, there seemed to be no other place where we could meet and be intimate, if we wanted to be, something we had not been able to be for at least a month. When I arrived sometime around 2:00, I found that Jonathan had already arrived and had gotten us a room. We spent the rest of the afternoon there.

While we were there, Jonathan told me that he had posted a message on the *Gayteway* board for my state in which he had outed Dan, revealing his real name, address, and other vital information. I knew, however, that the only people who would see the message were people who didn't matter. I wondered, though, how Dan, who frequented the board, would react. Given his almost pathological fear of exposure, I assumed he would be mortified.

In addition, we discussed Glenn, who had by then been missing for at least a week. There was still no word as to what had happened to him. Jonathan didn't know what to do to find him and I didn't know what to tell him.

Finally, we discussed the state of our relationship. Until that day, we hadn't seen each other for almost a month, the longest we'd gone without seeing each other since we'd met. Perhaps because of everything Jonathan had been through, he seemed to feel that the separation had caused more damage to our relationship than I did. Jonathan had always seemed to place a greater emphasis on being physically together than I did in maintaining the health of a relationship. I told him that I wanted to try to get back to the place we were before he went to Credence, but I wasn't sure how. Beyond occasional meetings, I felt there was little we could do to overcome the "separation thing" until we could get into a situation in which we no longer had to be separated.

Jonathan said that he would have to leave in time to be home for dinner because Laura was fixing dinner and she wanted him to be home to eat. Before we left, he called her to tell her that he'd be home soon, as if he were eight or they were married.

When we went to the parking lot, Jonathan got his first look at my new car. Before we parted ways, I retrieved the gift-wrapped copy of *Victor/Victoria* that I'd intended to give to him the day he'd left Dan's and gave it to him. When he unwrapped it, he seemed overwhelmed and expressed guilt over accepting it. I told him that he shouldn't feel that way, but when he finally left, he was still in an emotional state. In my own way so was I, since I didn't know when I would be seeing him again.

After making the trip back to Hawthorn, I wrote to Jonathan to let him know that I had gotten home. In my e-mail, I repeated some of the issues that we had discussed that afternoon, including his plans to get revenge on Dan, the situation with Glenn, and the state of our relationship.

Around 10:30 that night, Jonathan replied. He reported that he had posted additional ads about Dan on another personals site in which he'd given his home address, phone number, and e-mail address. He asked me where else he could post.

Again, he mentioned the fact that by that point Glenn had been missing for a week and that he was consumed by guilt. I didn't understand what Jonathan had to feel guilty about. What had he done or not done to worsen Glenn's situation? His guilt seemed excessive and misplaced even if he did still care about him.

As far as the state of our relationship was concerned, all Jonathan said was that "the future [would] have to unfold." Although he didn't know what would happen, he did know that the current situation couldn't go on forever. "Something will happen," he concluded. His bland assessment was not reassuring.

In response, I told him that I was willing to do what I could to keep our relationship together. I told him that part of the reason I had bought my new car was so that I could make the trip to Mariah, which was something that my old one wouldn't have allowed me to do. Although we had not explicitly discussed the issue of my moving to Mariah, the assumption for a while had been that if our relationship continued to progress as it should, we would eventually live together. If he were planning to live in Mariah, then we would probably be living together there. I told him, however, that because I was locked into a contract with my job in Hawthorn, I couldn't start another job in or near Mariah and move there until I had fulfilled my obligation. That wouldn't happen at least until the end of the year. Under the circumstances, there was nothing else I could do.

Around 3:00 the next afternoon he replied. In response, he seemed to take a more active attitude toward our relationship than he previously had. He told me not to feel that I was the one who had to assume all the responsibility for what happened between us. He recognized that he, too, needed to make adjustments and that I needed to honor my commitments. He said that he was going to Mariah in the hope that he could make a contribution and that the people at the hospital, and the hospital itself, could be a refuge to him. He knew his health was failing, and on top of it, he was consumed by what had happened to Glenn. He wondered where Glenn was, and how his own life had turned out as it had. He said he felt overwhelmed by it all. He ended his e-mail by telling me that he worried about me as well.

Because of work and other issues, I hadn't written to Jonathan by 8:00 Tuesday evening. He wrote instead to tell me about the interesting events that had happened that day. Apparently, he had spent the afternoon with Miranda, who had told him "a lot of exact, specific, timed things." He restated his position, which he had expressed soon after we had met, that although he wasn't gullible, he did believe Miranda knew things she had no normal way of knowing.

Otherwise, he said he was still negotiating on the house in Mariah and once the deal was made, he would be moving there. He also said that he was scheduled to see the cardiologist on Thursday morning and go to Mariah on Friday morning for pre-employment drug and tuberculosis tests.

When Thursday came, Jonathan wrote to remind me that he would be seeing the cardiologist that morning and told me that later he would be chairing a staff meeting at OutSource. He explained that Mike was in California and had asked Jonathan to chair. He commented that although he was on leave, he was still the COO. I inferred from his remark that his one-month leave had been extended and that he was still performing some duties for OutSource, although his precise relationship to the company at that point was unclear to me.

Later that night, Jonathan wrote to tell me, among other things, that he had spoken to his friend Greg Carroll, who had told him that Dan had called him. Greg had told Jonathan that he had told Dan never to call him again and had hung up on him. Jonathan also said that Laura kept getting hang-up calls from an unidentified number, which he suspected was "that fat old queen," as he called Dan. What Dan was trying to accomplish was unclear, and although Jonathan's postings had surely antagonized him, Dan seemed to be taking an equally aggressive route in responding to Jonathan's revenge, if that was in fact the only motivation behind his actions. I thought that whether or not Dan deserved what Jonathan had done, Jonathan needed to back off, since he was provoking someone who appeared to be troubled and whose behavior was unpredictable.

By the end of that week, Jonathan had managed to make a tentative deal on the backup house. On Friday afternoon, he wrote to tell me that he was happy about the house and that I could start visiting him again on a regular basis, unobstructed, something that I hadn't been able to do for a month. He said that although the house hadn't been his first choice, it was "ok" and he felt it would be a "safe place" for him to be. He was insecure and overwhelmed by the thought of moving to Mariah by himself, however, and pleaded with me to be there, saying, "I don't feel well and get a lot of confidence when you are there." Given the importance of moving to Mariah, for many reasons, nothing would have kept me from being there.

In an ongoing attempt to overcome the "separation thing," we agreed to meet at the bathhouse again that Sunday, although I agreed with Jonathan's sentiment when he said, "What a way to meet." Beyond that, he commented on the chilly, rainy weather that day, complaining, "What a cold damp day toda[y] is." He said that although he had been planning to go to Mariah that day, he wasn't up to the drive and, as an added disincentive, "the little woman," as he called Laura, was wanting to go as well. He said that she was "making sexual suggestions" but that he had "played dumb so far...BUT we sleep in the same bed and all I can say, thank God the lease for the house is ready!" Although he tried to make light of Laura's sexual interest—or, financial interest masquerading as sexual interest—it was obvious that he found the situation disturbing. He wasn't the only one.

By the end of his second week at Laura's, Jonathan's feelings about the sexual, and especially the financial, pressures that she had been exerting on him finally boiled to the surface. On the morning of Saturday, October 6, he wrote to me to vent his frustrations. After telling me that he had been sick enough the day before that he'd stayed inside all day, he went on to say that his experience at Laura's had been good in some ways but bad in others. Apparently, Laura, who didn't "try" as much as he had originally believed, expected him to pay all of the bills, including hers and her sons', for the privilege of living with them. No one in her family worked. I already knew that Laura hadn't worked since spring and Jonathan informed me that her sons kept getting fired from menial positions. His assessment was that they were all just lazy. He estimated that in the two weeks he had lived there, he had spent at least $2,000, part of which included their bills. He was receiving short-term disability and was getting only 60% of what he normally lived on; although that was still a considerable sum, most of it was being funneled into investments, leaving him with much less than he might otherwise have. He said that he didn't want to dip into his long-term investments for short-term expenses and that, unfortunately, he didn't feel it was his place to tell everyone to get off their asses and get jobs. Between Laura's advances and the financial pressures, he felt the need to leave as soon as possible.

In addition, Jonathan told me that Laura had refused to accept a position that paid $12 an hour because that was less than her previous salary of $16 an hour. In my opinion, that was better than her current salary of $0 an hour. Since Jonathan had lived there for less than two weeks by that point, he had been paying more than $1,000 a week for the privilege of staying with Laura and her family. Her true motive for wanting Jonathan to live with her had become blatantly clear.

Jonathan and I had planned to get together in Paladin again on Sunday, but around 8:00 on Saturday evening, he wrote to inform me of a development that would prevent that from happening. After telling me he had a "serious problem," he went on to explain that when he had gone to see the cardiologist in Paladin on Thursday, he had cashed a check for $500. He had put $100 in his wallet and the remainder in a bank envelope, which he'd placed in his dresser drawer. Then, he had bought groceries and paid the cable bill out of the $100 he had in his wallet. When he had gone to take more money out of the envelope that evening, he had discovered that the envelope was missing. He said he didn't feel he could ask or accuse, but he knew where he had put it. He said he could get more money when the bank opened on Monday, but until then he had only $8. Consequently, he couldn't pay for the room or even gas to get there. He said he didn't feel he could or would ask me. He suggested that perhaps we could meet sometime during the week when I wasn't working. He said he was not only very sorry but also very angry, but there was nothing he could do about it.

Frustrated, I wrote back, asking him if he was certain that he hadn't simply misplaced it. Although I didn't say it, I knew he suffered from a certain amount of cognitive impairment from the effects of his illness and wondered if he had simply forgotten where he'd put it. I knew he was living in a nest of shiftless money-grubbers, but would they really resort to stealing? I also knew that Laura wanted to keep us apart and wondered if *she* had taken it, perhaps not permanently, but possibly long enough to interfere with our plans to get together. I raised the possibility in my reply.

In response, he told me that he had searched both of his dresser drawers and the envelope was definitely not in either one. He was convinced that he had actually put it there. He said that if the envelope had been taken, it hadn't been done to keep us from seeing each other, although that was one of the side effects. He said that he had to leave for Mariah on Monday morning, but since he had to leave at 8:30 and his bank in Paladin didn't open until 9:30, he wouldn't be able to cash a check until he got to Mariah, which had a branch. I didn't understand how he didn't have enough gas to go to Paladin, which was closer than Mariah, but I assumed he had meant that he didn't have enough for both trips and needed to make sure he had enough to get to Mariah. Our plans to see each other had been thwarted yet again.

He then expanded on the complications that surrounded living with Laura. Although he was grateful to Laura for having rescued him from the "Old Drunk," as he called Dan, he recognized that she had her motives too. Referring to himself as the "Bank of Jonathan," he said that instead of trying to shift for herself, Laura did nothing but read magazines, eat, watch TV, and visit her parents. He described Laura's house, especially her kitchen, as a "pig sty," comparing it to Daisy's on the British sitcom *Keeping Up Appearances*. I assumed, though, that Laura's wasn't as endearing as the fictional version. Her sons, Jonathan believed, acted the way they did—staying out all night, sleeping all day—because they didn't have role models who could show them a better way to live. Although Jonathan seemed to think that his presence might provide the modeling they needed, I doubted that his brief tenure there would do much to reverse such deeply ingrained patterns.

Turning to his plans for escape, Jonathan said that he was tentatively planning to move to Mariah on Wednesday, the 17th. He was officially scheduled to start his project on Monday, the 22nd, so his plans seemed to be falling into place. Because the house was close to the hospital, he would be able to walk to work and come home during the day if he needed to lie down, let out the dogs, or do whatever else. He said he was hopeful about the job and if it worked out, he might not go back to OutSource.

On Monday, the 8th, Jonathan went to Mariah, but he did not go alone. Around 4:30, he sent me an e-mail in which he told me that Laura had gone with him, so he was "never out of her sight." He said that her sons had bought new clothes and although he was convinced he knew where they had gotten the money for them, he had no proof. He also said that he wasn't able to cash a check that day either because the banks were closed for Columbus Day. "These crazy American holidays," he complained. He ended the message by describing the previous two weeks as "awful" and, in a single, brief sentence, stated that Glenn had now been missing for two weeks.

In the same message, he also mentioned something outlandish that had happened that day. Apparently, while he and Laura were driving, Laura had told him that she thought they should get *married*. Understandably, Jonathan said that her "proposal" had nearly caused him to swerve off the road. Jonathan quipped that he would have to think about that—*not*.

I couldn't believe the ridiculous extreme to which the situation had drifted. Was Laura serious? Did she *really* think Jonathan would say yes? Apparently so, because later, Jonathan told me that his father had called one day to talk to him, and Laura, who had answered the phone, had tried to persuade his father to persuade

Jonathan to marry her. I could only hope that Jonathan *did* get out of her house, away from her, as soon as possible. In their own way, things were just as crazy at Laura's as they had been at Dan's.

The final statement about Glenn, brief as an epitaph, was poignant. There was still no word about where he was, how he was, *if* he was. Jonathan felt guilty that he couldn't do more to find him, help him, but Jonathan's *own* life was complicated enough. The issue weighed heavily on him and only added to his misery. I felt there was little I could do, could say, to make him feel better, although I did what I could.

On Tuesday, the 9th, Jonathan wrote to tell me that Chuck was mad at him because he hadn't felt like going to the bank to get him some money, apparently just to spend. He said that morning, he had written Chuck's dentist a check for $500 to pay for having his cavities filled, but "that [didn't] count." He said that even though Chuck had been in pain, spending his money to go out was more important than spending it to get his teeth fixed. He also informed me that Chuck had gotten fired the day before from his menial job at a restaurant. I assumed that Jonathan would be expected to pick up the financial slack. Even so, Jonathan felt compelled to keep on paying or possibly risk eviction.

On Wednesday, the 10th, Jonathan went to the doctor for more tests. He e-mailed me beforehand to say that he was happy to see the doctor, since he hadn't felt as bad as he did that morning in a long time. Later that day, he e-mailed me again to say that he'd been at the doctors' from 8:30 that morning until 4:30 that afternoon. He said the doctors had finally gotten back a number of results from the tests they'd performed the day he'd left Dan's and had performed other tests. The news was not good. According to the results, the infection had spread to include 35% of his heart muscle, which was an increase from 20% only weeks before. Apparently, whatever treatment they had been administering wasn't doing much good. Despite having planned to meet in Paladin the next day to take care of some unresolved business related to the move, Jonathan said he was exhausted and would have to confirm the next morning. In the end, he determined that he felt too bad to go.

On the morning of Friday, the 12th, Jonathan sent me an e-mail in which he seemed urgent about my calling him and giving him my advice about something important, but unnamed. He told me that because I was levelheaded and had good judgment, I was, in his estimation, able to help him see things that he couldn't. I wondered if the subject involved the situation at Laura's. Without clarifying information, I was curious and concerned.

When I called that morning after class, I learned that Glenn had called Laura's that morning around 8:00. Jonathan had been desperate enough to call Dan after he had escaped and tell him that Glenn had gone missing, asking him to give him Laura's number if he called again; apparently he had and Dan, in spite of his feelings, had cooperated. Unfortunately, the connection had been bad and they could barely hear him, making it impossible to carry on a meaningful conversation. They had, however, managed to gain *some* information about Glenn's condition.

Apparently Glenn had suffered some kind of breakdown, which seemed to have been triggered by something that had happened between him and his stepfather. To make matters worse, his mother had sided with his stepfather, so Glenn could not turn to them for help. After failing to board the plane to England, he had started wandering the streets and had eventually ended up in a homeless shelter. While he was there, he had been robbed and had lost not only his ticket, but also his money. Because he now had no money, he couldn't afford another ticket and had no way to provide for himself. Because of what had happened at the shelter, he was now afraid to return there. Consequently, he was now homeless, penniless, and stranded with no one to help him—except, perhaps, Jonathan. Glenn had said he would try to call back, but he never did.

Jonathan said that he had given Glenn my number with the hope that if he didn't get through to him, he might get through to me. Jonathan said that I had a calming effect on people, which is why he thought Glenn would benefit from talking with me. Jonathan told me, though, that he had told Glenn I was a "friend"—not his *boy*friend—and that if I did talk to him, not to tell him I was his boyfriend. I had assumed that Jonathan had told him who I was—after all, we had been planning to have dinner with him in England, which implied that Jonathan *had* told him—and I didn't know what to think about why he hadn't. Because there seemed to be more pressing issues at hand, however, I didn't ask Jonathan about it and focused instead on doing whatever I could to help Glenn. If it helped not to reveal that I was now Jonathan's boyfriend, then I would keep that information to myself.

Jonathan asked me if I thought it was a good idea to try to wire Glenn some money. His thinking was that if he could speak with Glenn again, he could at least tell him there was money waiting for him. I told him I thought he should. He also suggested making plans to have Glenn flown to my state, where he could receive an evaluation, which I also encouraged him to do. I didn't know exactly what was happening to Glenn mentally, but I did know that if he hadn't been eating and taking proper care, then physically he needed to be checked. With the action plan in place, we concluded our conversation and waited for whatever came next.

I didn't hear from Jonathan again until 6:00 that evening. The text of the e-mail he sent to me was in a discordant mixture of lowercase and uppercase letters and contained numerous misspellings that resulted from clumsily striking adjacent keys. It almost seemed to reflect Jonathan's disorganized emotions. He told me he had been off the computer and phone all day in case Glenn tried to call. He hadn't. He told me he had taken my advice and had wired Glenn some money through Western Union, if Glenn had enough sense to check with them. Unfortunately, given the fact that Glenn didn't know what Jonathan was intending, it seemed unlikely he would. In addition, Jonathan had made concrete plans to fly Glenn to my state, where he could receive an evaluation. Unfortunately, he didn't know about those plans, either. Jonathan hoped that Glenn would still call so he could tell him what he had done. Desperate, he told me to please stay in touch and thanked me for my advice and support. He concluded his message by telling me that my supportive behavior was, however, what he had come to expect from me and why he cared about me.

Later that evening, Jonathan wrote to tell me that Glenn had still not called. Jonathan's appraisal of Glenn's situation was especially dire. Glenn had no place to go or even to turn. He couldn't go back to England or come to the States without help, couldn't go to his stepfather, and was afraid to return to the shelter because of what had happened to him there. Glenn appeared to be "dazed and confused" and Jonathan feared "lost to life." Jonathan also made it clear that he felt his own situation was in some ways dire. He said he couldn't sleep or eat and felt as if he were heading for a breakdown "like [he had] never experienced" over his imagined part in not dealing with the Glenn situation more effectively. As he had expressed before, Jonathan said that he was consumed by remorse and sadness for Glenn. He said that although he wasn't in love with Glenn, he did love him. He concluded his despairing message by saying that it was a difficult time for the both of them.

By the next day, Jonathan had become desperate enough to begin making plans to go find Glenn himself, although in the end he did not.

The next few days were fraught with problems for the both of us. Jonathan was preoccupied now less with his own situation than with Glenn's. In addition, the deal on the second house in Mariah, which had seemed like a sure thing, fell through, so Jonathan still didn't know where he was going to live.

I was preoccupied with both his problems and mine. One of mine was my health. It had never fully recovered after the move, due in large part to the fact that my preoccupation with Jonathan's situation kept me in a chronic state of stress, which not only affected my own ability to eat and sleep, but also left me feeling drained both mentally and physically. In addition, I experienced a constant aching in my joints, which I normally didn't, as well as other peculiar symptoms, such as night sweats. Even my body odor had changed, suggesting some kind of biochemical imbalance. I tried to take care of myself as well as I could, but the constant stress of worrying about Jonathan was like an infection that never went away.

By the weekend of October 20, Jonathan had lived with Laura for almost one month. One very long, very hard month. In the meantime, he had made yet another tentative deal on yet another property in Mariah, this time not a house, but an apartment. Jonathan didn't want to live in an apartment, but the advantage was that he would be able to obtain a six-month lease and would then have half a year to think about where he wanted to live after that. Although Jonathan had originally thought that in spite of the complications, he could tough it out until he could move to Mariah, something happened that weekend that caused him to reach his breaking point.

Around 8:00 Saturday evening, Jonathan wrote to ask me for some advice. He told me he wanted out of Laura's "ASAP." Apparently, Laura had asked him to give her $4,500 to erase her debts, a request that by itself made him feel especially uncomfortable. He thought he could go stay with Art, who was no longer mad at him for not having moved in with him in September, but was afraid that might be yet another "frying pan into the fire" situation. He thought that moving into the apartment in Mariah might be his only real option and wondered if I was available that next week to help him move, if he did. He thought he would be able to get into the apartment by Wednesday. He wanted to escape before then, but with dogs, finding a place to stay for a few days—namely, a hotel—would be difficult. He ended his message by asking me if we could do something the next day. Laura was going to her mother's birthday party but he hadn't been asked. Art had invited him to dinner, but he was stalling him pending my response.

I could *not* believe Laura's audacity. She had finally gone too far. I thoroughly understood why he needed to get out of there as soon as possible and I was heartened to know that staying with Art was now an option. I couldn't believe that he was going to have to move for the *third* time in less than two months. Without question, Jonathan had the worst luck of anyone I'd ever encountered.

In response, I suggested a compromise in which he went ahead and took the apartment in Mariah, despite not wanting to live in one, and went to Art's just long enough to arrange the move then leave. Hopefully, that would take only a few days, a week at most. I also asked him if Laura had said anything about repaying him the money, although I suspected she had not.

Around 9:30, Jonathan replied. He said that Art wanted him to move in, but not just for a few days. Jonathan was concerned that by moving in, there might be "complications," since he didn't want to feel that he was leading Art on. I wasn't sure where Jonathan had gotten the idea that moving in with Art would send him that message, whether Jonathan's concerns were based on something definite that Art had done or on something unfounded that Jonathan simply feared. If it were only the latter, I could understand his reservations, since the run of bad luck he'd suffered in the past two months didn't inspire confidence that the move would make his life better.

In addition, Jonathan told me that Laura had said nothing about repaying him the money. The $4,500 she wanted was *in addition* to the roughly $3,000 he had already spent in the month he had lived there. That was even more outrageous. I wondered if Jonathan had any legal recourse in reclaiming his money. Escaping to Art's, regardless of his motivations, seemed preferable to remaining with the leeching Laura.

Jonathan also mentioned that he had talked to Cliff. They had spoken on the phone for a long time earlier that evening and Jonathan said that since his health had started to decline, Cliff had gone from calling only once a week, as he had begun doing after he had decided to be with Loren, to calling twice a day, something I didn't realize. He said that he and Cliff were finally starting to be able to talk without things becoming too emotional and that like water they were finding their level with each other. He said that although he still loved Cliff, he knew his time with him was past, but he still hoped he could remain friends with him and didn't have to lose him entirely from his life. On the one hand, I thought their relationship had become healthier than it had been in July or even September, but on the other hand, I was sick of hearing about Cliff.

At that point, Jonathan was still trying to figure out what to do the next day. He repeated his desire to escape from Laura's, permanently, if he could. Yet, despite his seeming indecision about leaving the known problems at Laura's for the unknown ones at Art's, Jonathan had already made up his mind about what he needed to do. And, *this* time, *I* would be the one to help him escape.

—16—
GAYMAN

Remember, despite your motives, you have lied and concocted a whole person to someone else.

Throughout the time that Jonathan lived with Dan and Laura, problems aside from those that their behavior caused also emerged. Or reemerged.

While Jonathan was still living with Dan, I decided to save copies of all the correspondence I'd had with Jonathan since I'd met him. I was thinking about canceling my Internet service with the provider I had at the time and knew that if I did, the messages would be deleted. By that point, we had collectively exchanged more than 300 e-mails and I viewed them as a sort of diary of the development of our relationship, which made them important to me. In addition to the e-mails, I decided to obtain copies of the ad through which I had met Jonathan as well as a copy of my reply, both of which were still posted on the *Gayteway* board. The evening of the Wednesday after what in time would come to be called "9/11," I visited the site.

Jonathan had posted the ad under the name "Gayman" (lowercase M). While I was looking at the board, though, I happened to find a series of ads that had been posted between Sunday, August 19 and Saturday, August 25 by someone who also called himself "GayMan" (uppercase M). With my curiosity piqued by the similarity of names, I clicked on the link that would take me to the first posting, an ad titled "Let's Do It."

In the ad, the author stated that he was 41, stood 5′9″, and weighed 165. He said that he had short dark hair and a goatee, was nice looking, and was in average shape. He described himself as a "top" who loved to "fuck, get head" and described his "endowment" as "7+ cut thick." He stated that he was available mornings before 10:00 and afternoons after 3:00. He ended the posting by asking for the reader's "stats."

To my shock, the person who had posted the ad matched Jonathan's description perfectly. Except for the fact that he said he was 41 instead of 44, everything else corresponded, even down to the times that he had been leaving for work and returning.

In reading the remaining postings, I saw that they revolved around "GayMan's" attempts to rendezvous with someone who called himself "Boi" at a Motel6 in Paladin so they could have sex. According to the ads, they had never actually met because of "GayMan's" apparent inability to find the specific Motel6 at which "Boi" was staying, but the exchange had lasted for almost a week.

The "GayMan" ad reminded me of the "GayDaddy" ad from August 10 that I had found on *Gayteway* and that I had suspected—but hadn't proven—had been posted by Jonathan. In any event, it seemed like the same person. The structure of the names, the content, the style of the writing—it seemed too coincidental.

More interesting, however, I also found several other ads on the *Gayteway* board for my state that had been posted under various names and with varying details, but that stylistically all sounded the same and all sounded like "GayMan/GayDaddy." One of these had been posted by someone who called himself "Stiff," who had posted his ad on Thursday, July 5. The message, titled "Maybe," was a reply to another poster's ad. In it, "Stiff" said that he was in fact "stiff" and had a place in Paladin where they could meet. After asking for the poster's "stats," "Stiff" described himself as being a "top," having a goatee, and having "7 cut thick" inches. He also claimed that he was 44 and described himself as "semi hairy," a term that Jonathan had used to describe himself in the ad through which I had met him.

Another had been posted by someone who called himself "GayBear," who had posted his ad on the morning of Friday, July 20. The message, also titled "Maybe," was also a reply to another poster's ad, someone named "Boi." I wondered if it was the same "Boi" with whom "GayMan" had attempted to rendezvous. In the message, "GayBear" described himself as a "top" and a "daddy bear" who lived in Paladin. He also described himself as being 41, standing 5'9", weighing 165, being "semi hairy," having short hair and a goatee, and having "7 cut thick inches." He said that he loved to "fuck, get head" as well as use poppers, an alkyl nitrite-based inhalant used primarily by some gay men to enhance sexual pleasure. He told "Boi," who appeared to live in Hawthorn, that he got there on business a couple of times a month and asked him if he was "worth the drive." As "GayMan" had, "GayBear" ended the reply by asking for "Boi's" "stats."

Then, on Monday, July 23, "GayBear" had posted a clarifying reply in which he told "Boi" that he would be in Hawthorn later that week and asked him if he wanted to "hook up" on Thursday night or Friday around noon. He reminded "Boi" that he loved to "fuck, get head." Then, on Thursday, "GayBear" had posted yet another reply in which he specified where he would be staying and when he would arrive. He said that after getting something to eat, he would be back to his room by 9:00, where he would wait for "Boi" until 10:00; if he didn't show, he would be "off to [the] bar to hook up." He claimed the room would be under a German name. A posting by "Boi" on Friday, the 27th made it clear that they had, in fact, not "hooked up." "GayBear," however, didn't respond.

Yet another ad had been posted by someone who called himself "Top," who had posted his ad on Sunday, September 2. The message, titled "New to Cuomo"—a city near Credence—began by stating that "Top" had just moved to Cuomo and wanted to know where the "action" was. He described himself as a masculine factory worker in his mid-30s who was a "top," stood 5'6", weighed 160, and had "6 cut thick" inches. After stating that he was divorced, having "accepted the fact that dicks are better then chicks," he stated that he liked to "fuck, get head." He mentioned that he liked "experience enhancers," including "weed and poppers." He stated that he planned to start work that upcoming Tuesday and that aside from second shift, when he was scheduled to work, he was available for "daytime fun." The ad was signed "Ian"—a form of Jonathan's middle name.

On the evening that the World Trade Center was destroyed, "Top" had posted another ad in which his "stats" were slightly altered, although the basic story was the same. "Top" still claimed that he was a mid-30s (now specified as 37-year-old) factory worker who was new to the area and worked second shift, but now he had grown from 5'6" to 5'10", gained five pounds, and added one inch to his penis, which he now described as "7" cut thick." This time, he said that he loved to "fuck" but said nothing about "getting head." Apart from not being available during second shift, "Top" said that he was available not only "days and mornings," but also "week ends." Not *weekends*, but *week ends*.

In addition to the similarities, the person who called himself "GayMan/GayDaddy/Stiff/GayBear/Top"—assuming they were all the same person—had stopped posting ads in which he said he was from Paladin almost to the day that Jonathan had left the city, while "GayMan" *et al.* had started posting ads in which he said he was from the Credence area almost to the day that Jonathan had moved to Credence. The pattern was so suspicious that it was difficult to accept as a coincidence.

Needless to say, I became upset when I found the "GayMan" and other ads because I was as convinced as I could be, in the absence of absolute proof, that they had all been posted by Jonathan. In addition, the "GayMan" exchange had taken place during the week that I had spent with him in August. This was the week that Jonathan had told me that he had really begun to fall in love with me, which had culminated in his "proposal" and profession of love the following week. Consequently, the thought that Jonathan was running around Paladin that week trying to "hook up" with someone to have sex with him was deeply upsetting to me. He had led me to believe that he wasn't or wouldn't be sexually involved with anyone else while he was seeing me, at least without telling me. I was concerned because, if Jonathan was having sex with other people and not telling me about it, this meant that I couldn't trust him, not just about that issue in particular, but perhaps in general. I was especially concerned, though, because Jonathan hadn't been using condoms, and if he *were* having sex with other men, then he could be putting me at risk for contracting a sexually transmitted disease, possibly even HIV. For many reasons, I needed to know more.

I e-mailed Jonathan a copy of the "Let's Do It" ad from August 19 and asked him if it was in fact him. In response, he denied it. He told me that in spite of "some" similarities, he wished he weighed 165. He pointed out that there were a lot of men with goatees in Paladin and said that he wished he didn't have to go to work until 10:00 in the morning and got off at 3:00 in the afternoon (despite the fact that was the pattern I had observed). He assured me that if he *were* looking for someone else, I would know. Then, he questioned me about why *I* was looking at the *Gayteway* board. He ended by telling me that he hadn't been on that board in a long time.

I pretended to believe him, but I wasn't convinced. In retrospect, it was stupid of me to take the direct approach, of course, because if it *was* him and he was trying to cover it up, he was obviously not going to admit it. I was emotional at the time, though, and didn't think about the fruitlessness of asking him directly. Because there was no other way to confirm or refute his claim, however, I let the matter drop, thinking that perhaps I was just being paranoid.

On Tuesday, September 18, I visited the *Gayteway* board for my state and found a third message that had been posted by the person who called himself "Top." This one was just a variation on the information he had given in his previous ads. Then, on Tuesday, October 2, I visited the *Gayteway* board for my state, this time because Jonathan wanted me to look at the postings he had started placing there in his attempt to out Dan. In the process, I discovered a fourth ad that had been posted by "Top" earlier that morning. This one was the shortest, least elaborate of his ads, but ended with the phrase "Your stats?"—a phrase that was found in the "GayBear" ad from July 20, the "GayDaddy" ad from August 10, the "GayMan" ad from August 19, and even the "Stiff" ad from July 5.

I also found another ad, titled "New to Mariah," that had been posted by someone who called himself "Friendly." Like Jonathan and "Top," the author had posted his ad on October 2. Since Jonathan was planning to move to Mariah, it piqued my curiosity. "Friendly" said that he was a "[m]id-40's daddy type" who had just been transferred to the Mariah area. After asking what was going on there, he stated that he was single for the first time in five years and was looking for "new friends" and "sex(?)." He described himself as "7+ cut" and was usually a "top" and encouraged people—namely, gay men—to respond. In the ad, "Friendly" not only described himself as Jonathan had in his "Gayman" ad and employed stylistic structures identical to those that Jonathan did, but also gave explicit descriptions of his sexual interests and intentions. In short, the ad was half "friendly" and half sexual and made no reference to our relationship. Indeed, in the ad, he claimed that he was single for the first time in five years. I was 99% convinced it was Jonathan, but not 100%.

To verify it, I posted a response of my own under an alias in which I encouraged "Friendly" to contact me. And he did. As it turned out, "Friendly" *was* Jonathan.

I confronted him about it. He claimed that he was simply advertising for gay *friends* in Mariah and that "there was a possible suggestion of sex, otherwise nobody would probably respond." He claimed that when he and Glenn had been in the process of moving to my state, they had posted ads on the Internet in which they had tried to establish contact with other gay people there but initially no one had responded. He said that it wasn't until he and Glenn had described themselves physically and sexually that people had begun to respond. It seemed plausible, since I knew that gay men were far more likely to respond to sex-oriented ads than friendship-oriented ones. But, even if that were true, the effect it had on me was to resurrect my questions about Jonathan's Internet activities—or, more to the point, his *real-life* activities—especially about whether or not he was in fact the person who called himself "GayMan"—and others—and what that implied.

Because I now realized that taking the direct approach wouldn't give me the answers I needed, I decided to do something more indirect. I decided to contact "GayMan." I didn't like to be devious, but I didn't know what else to do. I was afraid that my life had been placed at risk and I needed to know the truth.

Operating on the assumption that "GayMan" was Jonathan, I decided to post an ad on the *Gayteway* board for my state that directly targeted the Man who was Gay. Around 6:00 in the evening of Wednesday, October 3, I placed the ad under the pseudonym "Chaz"—a name I selected because it sounded like "Chase." I had never seen Chase and Jonathan had never described him to me, but I *had* seen pictures of Cliff, so I described "Chaz" as resembling Cliff. I hoped that both the similarity in name and appearance would attract Jonathan's attention, if "GayMan" was in fact Jonathan. I titled the posting "Where R U, GayMan?" knowing that Jonathan would certainly see it.

Around 10:30 that evening, the infamous "GayMan" replied.

He posted a brief message on the *Gayteway* board that indicated he was the same person who had authored the "GayMan" posts from August. A few minutes later, "Chaz" posted a reply that told "GayMan" more specifically what he wanted. Around midnight, "GayMan" posted a reply in which he asked for "Chaz's" e-mail address so they could continue their discussion in private. After creating an e-mail account in "Chaz's" name, I posted the address and waited.

Around 4:30 the following afternoon, I—or, rather, "Chaz"—received his first e-mail. The sender began by confirming that he was, in fact, "GayMan." He stated that the man he was supposed to have met at Motel6 had never shown up and complained that people often didn't show up when you tried to meet them through the Internet for sex. He explained that he usually didn't have trouble "hooking up" when he felt like it but was tired of the "same people" and wanted to meet some new ones. He said he liked "Chaz's" description of himself and was flexible about *when* they could meet, though not *where*. He explained that he was living with a woman and her three sons and was uncomfortable bringing men home because he didn't want to risk getting into trouble with her ex-husband. He was quick to add that his relationship with his female housemate was "strictly platonic" and described the situation as "very Will&Grace-ish." He told "Chaz" that he lived in a town near Paladin and asked him what he wanted to have happen next. The message was signed "Iain."

Iain. Jonathan's—distinctive—middle name.

I needed more.

I wrote back, giving Iain—whose full name was "Iain Winslett"—a brief biography for "Chaz." I told him, among other things, that "Chaz" had a degree in mathematics, performed data analysis for a company in Paladin, and lived with his brother, sister-in-law, and nephew, who were very religious and who never went out. I thought "Chaz's" living arrangement and family dynamics would throw enough complications into the mix to allay any discussion of Iain's coming to a nonexistent address to have gay sex. In addition, I asked Iain for additional information about his life. I was curious to know what Iain would say about himself and how much of it I had already heard, in some form, from someone else.

I was not disappointed.

Iain wrote back later that night. After thanking "Chaz" for his "quick replies," he went on to tell "Chaz" that while he was growing up, he had lived in a variety of places in the United States and Europe but had been living in the town near Paladin for about three years. He said that he also worked for a technology company "but on the business side." He said that not knowing how he would like his job when he had arrived, he had found out through a friend of a friend about Mary, who had just gotten divorced, had a big house, and didn't want to live in it alone. He said that what had started out as a temporary situation had become "sort of permanent," but that it was generally a good arrangement. He said that Mary's three sons, who were teenagers, had been living with their father, but that summer, their father had remarried and Mary's sons had asked to come and live with her. He reiterated what he had said before about having agreed not to "entertain" with her sons around.

Iain went on to list his interests, which included biking, swimming, camping, hiking, but not going to the gym. He said that most of the interests that "Chaz" had mentioned were his as well. He described himself as a "regular guy who happen[ed] to be gay" and although he didn't hide who he was, he didn't go around "waiving rainbow flags" either. He suggested that they could meet for a drink and said that if they wanted to have sex, they could find a suitable place. Referring to the Motel6 issue, Iain said there was "something about afternoon sex in a cheap motel that [was] kind of fun," but also said he was open to suggestion. He stated that he would be in town until the next Thursday at which point he would be leaving on a business trip for seven to ten days. Iain concluded his message by encouraging "Chaz" to respond.

After replying, "Chaz" received even more information about Iain. After once again thanking "Chaz" for his "fast replies," Iain told him that he had been born in one of the Mid-Atlantic states[1] but had lived in the Midwestern state, the Southern state "twice," Texas,

---

[1] From here, I will refer to this state as the "Mid-Atlantic" state.

Hawaii, and California as well as Germany, Italy, Turkey, England, and Japan. He explained that his father had been a career officer in the Marines and that although it had been fun, it had also been hard to move around so much. He said he had a younger brother who worked for an advertising agency in Los Angeles and said of himself that he had a bachelor's degree in history. He said he had thought about becoming a lawyer, but after spending some time with them, he had decided he didn't want to be like them. He said that he had been living in a Great Lakes state[2] when he had been recruited to his job in my state and that he felt comfortable here.

He assured "Chaz" that he understood about awkward living arrangements and remarked that he couldn't imagine having sex with someone with the boys in their bedrooms nearby. He said that he wasn't happy about that part of his living situation and would find another place to live if Mary's sons stayed permanently. Iain then went on to mention several places where they could meet, adding that Motel6 might be an option too and ending the sentence with a smiley face. After Iain told "Chaz" what he liked sexually, he told "Chaz" that he could either let him know about meeting or, if he preferred, spend more time getting to know him.

In reading the messages, I felt as if I were meeting Jonathan all over again. Iain had said that he worked for a "technology company but on the business side," while Jonathan had said that he was the "COO of a technology company." In addition, Iain had said that he had lived in a variety of states and countries, while Jonathan had said the same, and several of those places overlapped, having been places either that Jonathan had said he'd lived—the Southern state, England—or to which he seemed otherwise connected—the Midwestern state, California, Italy, Japan. Finally, both Iain and Jonathan had described virtually identical living situations involving divorced women with teenage sons and both had even compared them to the situation on *Will & Grace*.

More specifically, Iain had used some of the same phrases that Jonathan had used in his e-mails to me. For example, in Iain's second e-mail to "Chaz," Iain had thanked "Chaz" at the beginning of the message for his "quick replies." In my second e-mail from Jonathan four months before, *he* had thanked *me* for *my* "quick reply." In addition, Iain had said that although he was gay, he didn't "go around waiving rainbow flags"…which was exactly how "Friendly"—who was Jonathan—had described himself to me only two days before. Finally, in a message Jonathan sent to me on Friday, October 5, he opened the message by complaining, "What a

---

[2] From here, I will refer to this state as the "Great Lakes" state.

cold damp day toda[y] is," while in a message Iain sent to "Chaz" the same day, Iain opened the message by complaining, "What a cold icky day." Jonathan's message to me had been sent at 3:47 P.M., while Iain's message to "Chaz" had been sent at 3:58 P.M., only *eleven minutes* later. I wondered just how far Iain would go in continuing this exchange, in going through with his intentions to meet "Chaz."

Meanwhile, I continued my normal exchange with Jonathan as if nothing was wrong, apart from everything else that was wrong.

Throughout the latter half of that week, Iain and "Chaz" refined their plans to meet. Arranging to get together proved complicated, however, because of Iain's busy life. At first, Iain told "Chaz" that he was busy Friday night and Sunday, but that Saturday night he was free. He explained that on Friday, he had a date with a man named "Reg"—a name similar to mine—and said of Reg that "Reg and [he were] friends who occasionally fuck[ed]." Then, on Friday, Iain wrote "Chaz" to tell him that Reg had had him change their date to Saturday night, informing "Chaz" of this when it was too late for the two of them to get together Friday night. Iain eventually said he was available to meet either Sunday evening or Monday late afternoon or evening. Iain said that he preferred Sunday to Monday, so he and "Chaz" planned to meet at Tolliver's—which "Chaz" had suggested—at 6:00 that Sunday evening.

The trap was set.

I contacted my friend Chris, whose boyfriend was co-owner of Tolliver's. After explaining the situation to him, he said that he would tell one of the workers at Tolliver's who was working that night to watch out for him.

I didn't know if he would actually show. Perhaps this was all some kind of elaborate Internet game and Jonathan—if he was in fact Iain—simply enjoyed giving someone the runaround. Iain had been evasive in other ways. "Chaz" had asked for both a picture of Iain and a phone number at which to call him, but Iain had convenient excuses for not providing either.

I also wondered if Jonathan, assuming he was Iain, was on to me. On Saturday morning around 9:15, "Chaz" received an e-mail from Iain in which Iain asked "Chaz" if they'd met before, thinking there was "something familiar" about him but unsure if it was just his imagination. Playing innocent, I, as "Chaz," wrote back, saying that he didn't think they'd ever met before, so he didn't know why Iain thought he sounded familiar. "Chaz" said that in the time Iain had been in the Paladin area, he'd had sex with a couple of men who looked the way Iain had described himself, but neither of them was named "Ia(i)n." He went on to add that they were both one-night stands and that you never knew if people were using their real names in cases like that.

In response, Iain said that he only used his real name and that "Chaz" seemed familiar because of the way he wrote. I hoped that I had allayed his suspicions and that he would show up, proving whether or not he did in fact use his real name.

Unfortunately, that didn't happen.

Sunday morning around 10:00, "Chaz" received an e-mail from Iain in which he explained that they couldn't meet that day after all. Iain explained that he had gone out the night before and had had "too good a time." He said that he had woken up with a bad sore throat and a temperature. He said he was drinking hot tea and had taken some aspirin but still felt "like shit." Telling "Chaz" that he hated to do it, Iain asked him if they could postpone their rendezvous until Tuesday. He assured "Chaz" that he *did* want to meet him and liked how he had found him after two months, but was sick and needed to stay in bed, "unfortunately alone."

I was disappointed in my own way, but I still hoped that Iain would still go through with his meeting with "Chaz." If this really was Jonathan in disguise, I wanted and needed to know that, wanted and needed to know the full extent of his "extracurricular" behavior. "Chaz" agreed to meet Iain on Tuesday to which Iain replied that he would be there "if [he had] to get there in an ambulance."

Whatever Iain's intentions, I decided to start giving him a dose of his *own* medicine. On Monday, "Chaz" wrote to him telling him that he wouldn't be able to meet him on Tuesday after all, since that was his brother and sister-in-law's 14th wedding anniversary and he was the only one available to watch his ten-year-old nephew. "Chaz" suggested getting together on Wednesday instead. Iain agreed, telling "Chaz" that in spite of being sick, he was "incredibly horny" and would "try to save the feeling." Tuesday night, Iain e-mailed "Chaz," telling him that he was still sick and had stayed in bed all day, but that he would be there on Wednesday. Again, he told "Chaz" that he had been "awfully horny the last couple of days" and that you "never know what may or may not happen," adding a smiley face at the end.

Unfortunately, nothing did. On Wednesday, Iain wrote to "Chaz" to tell him that he had "[w]oke[n] up this morning still with a temp and throwing up" and would have to cancel again. Continuing to encourage "Chaz," Iain apologized and suggested that maybe they could get together over the weekend, if "Chaz" was free. Iain signed the message, "Hornily, Iain."

"Chaz" wrote back, telling him that he was disappointed they couldn't hook up but that he understood. He also asked Iain if he'd been to the doctor and told him that he shouldn't still be running a fever after four days. Although the latter appeared to be an expression of concern from "Chaz," it was an indirect questioning of the plausibility of Iain's stories. Iain didn't seem to catch on. In Iain's first e-mail, he had mentioned that he would be leaving the next day on business and would be gone for seven to ten days, postponing the occasion for carnal pleasure until then. "Chaz" asked him if he was still planning to go and told him he hoped they could meet each other "before [they] both die[d] or [were] too old to remember why [they had] wanted to hook up in the first place."

Later that evening, Iain e-mailed "Chaz" telling him that he had just gotten up "after spending all day in bed, mostly asleep, entirely alone." He said although he had planned to go out of town the next day, he was now sending someone else, since he wasn't up to it. He said that he hadn't been to the doctor, but had talked to his father who, interestingly, was himself a doctor and had called in a prescription for him. He said he had no plans for the weekend, since he had originally planned to be in California, so he was open to suggestions, "especially lewd ones."

After a week, I had accumulated enough information to compare Iain and Jonathan. Apart from similar stories that Iain and Jonathan had given about themselves, I had also begun to notice a number of stylistic similarities between Iain's writing and Jonathan's. At first, my impressions were more intuitive than incisive, so I began to compare the similarities in a more systematic fashion.

First, I looked at similarities in spelling. Even with the comparatively limited material that I had gotten from Iain, I was able to derive a list of several misspelled words, which I then compared to a list of words that Jonathan misspelled. For example, Jonathan misspelled the word *suppose* as *supposse*, with two Ss instead of one. He misspelled the word *awkward* as *ackward*, with a C in place of the first W. He misspelled the word *aspirin* as *asprin*, without the I between the P and the R. He misspelled words ending in *-ferred*, such as *transferred*, with one R instead of two. He misspelled, or rather confused, the words *then* and *than*, using the word *then* when he should have used the word *than*. Iain misspelled the same words, and in the same way, but did not misspell other words.

Second, I looked at similarities in syntax and usage. Jonathan's syntax was decidedly British, with the differences between American English and British English readily apparent to someone who had studied the history of the English language and its various dialects in some detail. For example, he split the word *weekend* into two words, writing it as *week end*. He used the word *as* where an American would use the words *since* or *because*. He not only misspelled the word *aspirin*, but also used the plural form *aspirins*, reflecting

British usage. He capitalized the names of titles, writing *Assistant* instead of *assistant*. Finally, he generally wrote the day before the month instead of after ("17 October" instead of "October 17"), which also reflected British usage. Iain did all of the same things.

Third, I looked at similarities in punctuation. I had noticed that both Iain and Jonathan occasionally failed to space after a period before beginning a new sentence. In addition, both Iain and Jonathan usually spaced after a left parenthesis but didn't space before the right one. Oftentimes, they didn't space before typing the left parenthesis, typing the word or number and the left parenthesis as a single unit. Overall, the punctuation was distinctive and it seemed unlikely that two unrelated people would both exhibit the same pattern.

With a background in both linguistics and statistics, I decided to evaluate the similarities in a more numerical fashion. First, I looked at the average length of both Iain's and Jonathan's sentences. Different people would be expected to have different average sentence lengths, since different people expressed themselves with different levels of elaboration. After doing the analysis on an adequate sample of material, I discovered that the average length of Jonathan's sentences was 17.61 words, while the average length of Iain's sentences was 17.48 words. I also computed what I called a "similarity ratio," which simply involved dividing one number by the other number. It didn't matter which number was divided by the other because the only thing that mattered was how close to 1—or "unity," as it was often called in mathematics—the ratio came. A 1 indicated perfect correspondence (e.g., $10 \div 10 = 1$), while a more divergent number, whether higher or lower, would represent greater difference (e.g., $10 \div 8 = 1.2$; $8 \div 10 = 0.8$.). I decided to divide Jonathan's average (17.61) by Iain's average (17.48), which resulted in a similarity ratio of 1.01—statistical variation aside, a perfect correspondence.

Second, I looked at the extent to which both Iain and Jonathan failed to space after periods before beginning new sentences. I calculated the total number of times that both Iain and Jonathan, respectively, failed to space and divided that number by the total number of sentences to derive a percentage of the time each person demonstrated the non-spacing behavior. I discovered that Iain displayed this behavior 32.06% of the time, while Jonathan displayed it 32.44% of the time. Once again, I computed a similarity ratio by dividing Jonathan's percentage by Iain's percentage, which resulted in a ratio of 1.01—once again, a statistically perfect correspondence. Likewise, I had also noticed that both Iain and Jonathan sometimes failed to put a period at the end of the last sentence of an e-mail. Iain did this 15.38% of the time, while Jonathan did it 15.38% of the time. I didn't need to compute a similarity ratio for *that*.

Finally, I noticed a pattern in the times that Jonathan would send his e-mails to me and Iain would send his e-mails to "Chaz." On no less than seven occasions, I received an e-mail from Jonathan, then just a few minutes later, "Chaz" received one from Iain. After a while, it became almost comical because I would receive an e-mail from Jonathan, then switch to the "Chaz" account to wait for an e-mail from Iain that would almost invariably arrive within a few minutes. Two things were striking about the pattern. First, the median amount of time between the arrival of the pairs of e-mails was slightly less than 12 minutes, with the longest separation being slightly more than 16 minutes and the shortest being slightly more than 3. For many reasons, two unrelated people would not be expected to send their e-mails so closely together. A more logical explanation was that the same person was writing and sending one e-mail to one person then, while still at the computer, switching accounts and sending a second e-mail to a second person.

In addition, the sequence in which the e-mails arrived deviated markedly from what would be expected by chance. If two unconnected people were involved, one person should be sending an e-mail before (or after) the other approximately half the time. Therefore, if Iain and Jonathan were in fact separate people, I should have received Jonathan's e-mails before "Chaz" received Iain's roughly 50% of the time. This was not how it worked. Instead, I found that I received Jonathan's e-mails before "Chaz" received Iain's approximately 85% of the time, a marked deviation from what would be expected by chance. In fact, when I later performed a statistical test to measure the likelihood that the result had occurred by chance alone, I found there was only a 3% chance that it had. In addition, I would sometimes receive the pairs of messages at very unlikely times, such as 9:37 A.M. and 9:53 A.M., respectively, 7:50 P.M. and 8:02 P.M., respectively, and 10:38 P.M. and 10:41 P.M., respectively.

Iain was almost surely Jonathan.

Throughout the week that I, as "Chaz," had been corresponding with Iain, who was almost certainly Jonathan, I became increasingly concerned about the financial implications for me. If he were cheating on me sexually, then perhaps he would cheat me financially.

By early October, it had been a little more than a month since Jonathan had left Paladin and the bills for the storage unit and the moving van were still on my credit card, not only unpaid but also accruing interest at roughly 19%. Jonathan had said he would pay them as they came in, but so far, I had gotten nothing from him. I received my credit card statement for September on Thursday, October 4, which indicated that I now owed not only the $229.95 for September rent for the storage unit, but also $311.24 for the moving van, which was twice the original estimate of $160. Since the storage facility was placing the charge for the storage unit on my credit card on the first of the month, I knew that by now I owed an additional $229.95 for October. By October 4, I owed roughly $3,300 on my credit card, at least $770 of which was not mine. Since I had bought a new car only a few days before and had taken out a five-year loan with monthly payments of almost $200, I would now be deprived of that amount that formerly I could have put on my credit card for some time to come. That semester, I was clearing roughly $180 a week and on October 4, I had roughly $450 in my checking account, which was all the money I had to my name. I felt it was time to press the issue with Jonathan.

The day I received my statement, I wrote to him to tell him about it. In response, he agreed that the bill for the van was twice what it should have been, but said that we should see about an adjustment before paying it. I agreed. Because we had already been making tentative plans to meet and spend time together in Paladin that weekend, I suggested that while we were there we go to the facility from which we'd rented the van to see about the bill. Unfortunately, this ultimately proved to be the weekend that most of the $500 he had gotten out of the bank earlier that week had come up missing, a disappearance he blamed on Laura's sons. With no money to buy gas to get to Paladin, we couldn't meet. He told me that perhaps we could meet some day the following week when I was off. I suggested Wednesday, but Jonathan said that he had doctors' appointments on Wednesday and suggested Thursday instead. I told him that although I didn't want to be a nag, Thursday was already the 11th and my credit card payment was due on the 19th. I told him that I had never made a late payment before and that I didn't want to start now. He assured me, "I certainly intend to pay the [credit card] in full as soon as the charges are clear" and, "I always pay my bills." He reminded me that I'd only told him about the charges a day or two before and repeated that he wanted to resolve the problem with the charge for the van before we paid. He reminded me that it was only the 7th, implying that we had plenty of time.

By this point, I suspected he was lying and didn't want to meet with me on Sunday because he wanted to meet with "Chaz." Deliberately being dramatic in response to his story about not having the money to meet with me in order to gauge how sympathetic he was toward me, I wrote to him, telling him that if I couldn't be with him, I would just stay at home and be depressed. I lamented that "[s]o many things seemed to be conspiring against our being able to be together" and that "[a]ll this trouble has been caused not by circumstances, though, but by people's willful decisions to keep us apart for the most selfish of reasons." I told him that I missed him "so much" and just wanted to be with him. I concluded by saying that what was happening was "all so hurtful."

In response, he told me simply that what had happened hadn't been done to keep us from seeing each other but that was one of the side effects. I, however, wasn't convinced that *anything* had been done.

On the evening of Wednesday, the 10th, I wrote to Jonathan to encourage him to meet with me in Paladin on Thursday to deal with the bills from the move. By that point, I had also decided to confront him about the Iain situation. For days he had been complaining about feeling unusually ill, something that he claimed was preventing him from traveling despite the fact that during that time he had traveled to Mariah and Paladin. In my message, I told him I hoped that in spite of his poor health he would come, not only because I wanted to take care of our business, but also because there was a more serious reason that I didn't want to discuss through e-mail or over the phone. Being blunt, I told him that, in my opinion, it was the most important issue that had yet arisen in our relationship and I didn't want to delay in discussing it any longer than we needed to. I hoped these reasons would be compelling enough to motivate him to meet with me.

I didn't hear from him that day. The next morning around 7:45, he wrote to tell me that, once again, he was too sick to meet. He claimed that he hadn't read my message until that morning because he had gone to bed early and had stayed there all night. He then went on to tell me that he was sorry to hear that we had a problem that was so serious we had to meet in person to discuss it, but to be honest, he couldn't deal with any more than he already was without going "over the edge." He reminded me that, in addition to being sick, he was homeless, isolated, and no longer in control of his life. Adding to the list, he said that the Glenn situation was like "a living nightmare" that haunted him whether he was awake or asleep. He told me that if the problem we had was as serious as I suggested, then perhaps I could give him some inkling of what it concerned so we could begin to discuss it and possibly meet in the next day or two—if he was feeling better—to deal with it more fully.

His response left me feeling frustrated and feeling that he was making excuses. I told him that I preferred to see him face to face and that I was asking for only an hour or two of his time. On the business side, I told him that my credit card payment was due the next Friday and that meeting in Paladin the next week was bad for the both of us because I had to work on Monday and Tuesday and he had tentative plans to start moving to Mariah on Wednesday, although ultimately the deal on the house into which he was supposed to be moving fell through. On the personal side, I told him that we also needed to talk, although again I didn't specify about what. I told him that although I understood he was sick and stressed, it was also hard to say when he would feel as well as he thought he needed to feel to meet me. The drive from St. Alban to Paladin was not that far, I reminded him. If he had been able to marshal his strength to go to Mariah and into Paladin, I further reminded him, then he should be able to do it that day for just a couple of hours. I told him that although I didn't mean to sound confrontational, the fact was that I had done a lot of favors for him and that I'd like for him to do this one favor for me. That was all I was asking and it wasn't *that* much to ask. I told him to reconsider.

Around 8:30, he replied. He began by telling me that he was aware of and appreciated everything I had done for him, both practically and emotionally, and in spite of everything that had happened during the past several weeks, he still felt more connected to me than to virtually anyone except for certain members of his family. He stated that he was sick because he had pushed himself too hard that week and could detail how much he had been throwing up and suffering other ill effects. He told me he was so sick, in fact, that when he had tried to get dressed that morning, he had gotten sick and had started crying because he couldn't even dress himself. He asked me if we could meet on Saturday and told me he would overnight me what he owed me, if that was my main concern, and encouraged me to contact the moving company for an adjusted total.

Returning to the undefined issue that I had raised, he told me that if I had been able to keep it to myself as long as I had, then doing so for another day wouldn't do that much additional damage. He implored me to understand that he wasn't in as good a shape, either physically or mentally, as he had been the last time I'd seen him only a week and a half before. He also mentioned that the deal on the house he was looking at in Mariah wasn't definite, so he didn't know if he would be moving on Wednesday. If it was, then I was supposed to help him, but he took it from my messages that I wouldn't be available and, among other things, wouldn't be able to discuss things directly with him then. He reemphasized the fact that he really *was* too sick to make even the short trip from St. Alban to Paladin that day. He ended his message by assuring me that he still cared for me.

In the end, I decided to compromise by talking to him by phone. That wasn't as ideal as talking to him in person, but it was better than communicating with him through e-mail. Late Thursday morning, I called, not knowing how he would react to what I was planning to reveal.

After discussing the moving expenses and what to do about them, as well as the state of his health, which he claimed was poor enough that morning that he was thinking about going to the ER if it didn't improve, I decided, in spite of his condition, to raise the main issue that I wanted to discuss with him. I told him that, using the alter ego "Chaz," I had been communicating with someone who called himself "Iain Winslett," and the two of them had been making plans to get together to have sex. I further told him that Iain bore an uncanny similarity to him, not only in the strange parallels between Iain's life and his life (and middle name), but also in the way he wrote, down to the percentage of the time that both Iain and he failed to space after a period. Finally, I told him outright that I thought *he* was Iain and, by extension, "GayMan."

His reaction was subdued. He asked me, strangely, if I didn't love him anymore. I told him that this had nothing to do with whether or not I loved him, but whether or not he was doing things behind my back that I had a right to know about but that he was refusing to tell me. He steadfastly denied that he was Iain, never giving me any indication that he was anything but innocent. Had I made some colossal mistake, been misled by an incredible set of coincidences? By the time we were through, I was more confused than ever.

Later that day, however, Jonathan had a more intense, well-formulated response to my accusations that he was "GayMan." Sarcastically, he ended each sentence with a word count. He insinuated that I was projecting my experiences with Cole and Henri, the shattering of trust those experiences had caused, onto him. He told me that if I wanted to ignore his past behavior, then I would be ignoring the fact that he had been honest with me about situations that made him look bad, such as sleeping with Chase, that otherwise I would never have known about. He said that he was offended that I had tried to lay a trap for him when we were not in a committed relationship and that we were free to see others—a position that contradicted the one he had presumably held since late August. He told me that if I couldn't trust him, then perhaps we should part friends, but reminded me to ask myself the "Dear Abby" question, which was whether I was better with or without him. He told me that we had cut each other a fair amount of slack in the past and, although he didn't list them, he said that *I* had *my* share of "peculiarities" but had thought the good outweighed the odd. Dismissively, he told me that he was too sick to deal with the matter at that point and that it was up to me to decide what to do next. He ended his e-mail by giving the average word count for the entire message, asking me if there was "[a]ny significance." Then, as if to make me feel guilty for doubting him, he appended a postscript in which he told me that he hadn't gone to the hospital yet and that in spite of everything that was happening, he still loved me.

I didn't know what to do or say in response, so I did and said nothing.

Friday morning, I had to teach, but before I went to work, I checked my e-mail and found that Jonathan had sent me the message in which he alluded to what I would later learn was the desperate phone call from Glenn. He told me that he needed my help and that when the situation didn't involve his "slutful ways," I was levelheaded and had good judgment. He still wasn't acknowledging that he was Iain. In talking to him later on the phone, Jonathan told me that if I talked to Glenn, not to let him know that I was his boyfriend...which made me wonder just how *general* Jonathan's desire to keep this fact secret was. After talking to him, Jonathan wrote to thank me for my help and, almost devotedly, said that in spite of everything that was happening between us, he still cared about me.

Even so, I was still not convinced that Iain wasn't Jonathan. Jonathan's assurances hadn't allayed my suspicions as much as they'd intensified them. So, I, as "Chaz," decided to continue my correspondence with Iain to see what would happen.

Later that evening, "Chaz" wrote to Iain and suggested that they meet at Tolliver's at 6:00 Saturday evening. A little later, however, Iain, who was "feeling better but not perfect, yet," asked if they could meet at another restaurant at 7:00 instead. Iain explained that some of his friends were going there Saturday night at 7:00 and "Chaz" and he could have a drink with them then have dinner alone or eat with them depending on how they felt.

Iain had responded. I was more confused than ever. As if utterly unaware of what had happened between Jonathan and me, Iain later explained that four of his friends, two of whom were a couple and two of whom were dating, were meeting for dinner and drinks at one bar then going to another, telling "Chaz" that they could join them or go off on their own. Iain described what he would be wearing then concluded the message by telling "Chaz" to bring the lube and he would bring the "X" (Ecstasy).

On Saturday morning, Iain e-mailed with yet another change of plans. According to Iain, one of the members of the couple was sick, so they'd canceled, and the other two didn't want to be part of a blind date, meaning that Iain and "Chaz" would be alone. Otherwise,

Iain was still wanting to meet where and when they had already agreed. In response, "Chaz" said that was fine, although he added that he had never been to the restaurant in question and that finding new places after dark wasn't his strong point—a comment that hinted at the fact that, like "Boi," "Chaz" would not be showing up.

By that point, I'd had enough. If Iain was really Jonathan, then this game was becoming sick and had to stop. If Iain was in fact a separate person who, through some incredible coincidence, happened to write and have a life so impossibly similar to Jonathan's, then I was manipulating an innocent person, doing to him what I had accused Jonathan of doing to "Chaz." I decided that the best thing to do was to break off all further contact with Iain and close down the "Chaz" account. "Chaz," whether victim or victimizer, died that night.

By that point, I was also feeling tired, confused, and disgusted with myself for what I was doing, regardless of why I was doing it. In an accurate reflection of my feelings at the time, I finally replied to Jonathan's message from Thursday morning by telling him that although I knew he cared about me and I cared about him, I was very confused about what was happening. I implied that I needed time to think, to sort things out. I told him to take care of himself and to try to feel better now that he knew Glenn was alive. I told him I would take care of myself, too, or would at least try.

In response, Jonathan said that my message seemed to suggest that we were taking some kind of break, if not actually breaking up. In response, I wrote a message that reflected the confusion, the uncertainty, that I was experiencing even more keenly. I told him I wasn't thinking about breaking up but restated that I was confused about things and needed time to sort them out. I told him that Iain wanted to meet "Chaz" and that I was going to their meeting place to see for myself if Iain was really him. I told him that because I had described myself as looking different from "Chaz," Iain wouldn't recognize me if he were in fact a different person, and that if he was, "Chaz" would remove himself from Iain's life. I told Jonathan that if he proved not to be Iain, I would never doubt him again.

I told him, though, that even if he felt offended or hurt, I had to do it. I emphasized again how similar he and Iain were, and that despite Jonathan's displays of honesty and sincerity, his assurance that he told the truth, I couldn't convince myself that he and Iain weren't the same person. I told him that I had to do this because he was asking me to put increasingly greater amounts of trust in him and I had to know that I wasn't being deceived.

Sincerely remorseful over what I was doing, was planning to do, I told Jonathan that perhaps someday I would tell Iain—if he proved to be a separate person—what I had done and why and hope that he forgave me. I also told Jonathan I hoped that *he* would forgive me, someday. And, I said, I hoped that someday I could forgive myself.

Unfortunately, that message provoked an e-mail exchange that made our first fight in July pale in comparison. Throughout the next day, we vented seemingly every grievance that we had accumulated about the other. Around 8:00 Saturday morning, Jonathan sent me a message, titled "Living With Our Actions," in which he excoriated me for my behavior. After beginning with a full paragraph about what was happening to Glenn, he proceeded to address the Iain situation. He suggested that Iain, who *was* a separate person, had "scammed" information he had found in other people's postings, including Jonathan's, which was the true source of the similarities. He mentioned that he had seen Dan do the same thing, "shuffl[ing] facts around like a deck of cards," and when he had asked Dan about it, Dan had rationalized his behavior by saying that "everyone does it." He accused me, in creating my "Chaz" persona, of doing the same thing. He reminded me that, despite my motives, I had lied and fabricated "a whole person" to an unsuspecting man, and told me that no matter how I rationalized my behavior, what I had done was "awful and out of control." He told me that if Iain had been honest with me, then what I had done was worse than what I had accused Jonathan of doing.

He informed me that my devious behavior had damaged his ability to trust *me*. He said that while he thought I was a kind, caring, humane person, my behavior "border[ed] on several areas that [were] really odd." He said that while he would remain grateful to me for what I had done for him, he was now more reluctant to put *his* life in *my* hands. He said that he knew he had behaved "honourably" and that if he weren't an honest person, there were situations he wouldn't have told me about because they would have made him look bad; even so, he *had* told me about them, to his detriment.

He told me that since nothing he said would satisfy my "inner demons," he wished me well in finding someone else. He said that despite some setbacks, he had no trouble meeting people and making friends and no need to create "false personas" in order to "lure" people into his bed. He told me that, while *his* life would go on, in the end, *I* would be the bigger loser because I had thrown away someone who genuinely cared about me, for nothing. He said that *I* would have to live with the consequences of what I had done longer than *he* would.

He concluded by saying that he was "fucking angry," his anger having set in during the past twenty-four hours, and that he had serious doubts about his ability to forgive me. Even if Iain showed up and by doing so resolved the issue for *me*, he told me, it wouldn't resolve the issue for *him*.

In response, I reemphasized what I had already told him, that the parallels between him and Iain were numerous, specific, and striking and couldn't be ignored. I told him that he was expecting me to trust him to the point of leaving behind my life in the United States for a life in England where, as he had explained it, I wouldn't be able to work and would, in effect, be completely dependent on him, at the mercy of him. I certainly wasn't going to do that if I couldn't trust him. I wasn't even sure how I felt about the idea of moving to Mariah, which would involve giving up my stable life in and around Hawthorn for an uncertain one without having some assurance that he was what he said he was. I told him that although he had told me that if there was anything I wanted to know about him all I had to do was ask and he would tell me the truth, he had also made comments—seemingly joking—that perhaps he was giving me just enough truth to lull me into thinking he was being truthful about everything when he really wasn't. I reminded him that I had known him for only four months and that only a fool trusts someone he's just met and that only a fool believes that someone is being honest with him just because he *says* he's being honest with him. I told him there was no other way for me to get the answers I needed. In spite of harboring a certain amount of guilt over what I had done, I didn't apologize to him for trying to learn the truth.

When he replied around 5:30, Jonathan told me that he had no intentions of moving to England, at least with me, anytime soon. Commenting on my reluctance to move to Mariah, under the circumstances, he told me that it didn't compare to *his* moving to the United States, even with Glenn, who had hated living in the States no matter where they had lived. He said that even though he'd had no support system, no idea how to live, no idea where anything was here, he had treated it like an opportunity. Pointing out my deficiencies as a person, he told me that "[n]ew things, situations and change [were] frightening for [me]" and that I liked "guarantees and safety." He told me that I analyzed things, such as the Iain situation, "sometimes past the point of common sense" and, in the end, concluded that even though I was very intelligent, I was also "ignorant of people and afraid to step out." Overall, the tone was condescending, insulting, and self-congratulating.

Now angered myself, I told him that before he started judging me, he should take a long, hard look at himself, especially when it came to being deceptive on the Internet. I told him that what he had done to Dan—posting his name, telephone number, and address on *Gayteway* and other sites within the context of some rather malicious messages—had been incredibly vindictive. I told him that regardless of what Dan had done to him, he could have taken the high road and just dissociated from him instead of making such a concerted effort to expose and damage him. I reminded him that for someone who was so concerned about being honest on the Internet, he had never signed any of the postings he had placed there, preferring instead to hide behind aliases. I told him that if what I had done was wrong, then what he had done was just as bad—the only difference was that in *my* case, it had involved *him*. I told him it appeared that he thought it was all right for him to do something to someone else, but it *wasn't* all right for someone else to do something to him, an attitude I described as "convenient."

I told him that I hadn't made, and *wouldn't* make, any major changes in my life until his *own* life stabilized. I reminded him that in the month and a half since he had first raised the possibility of the two of us living together, he had considered moving back to Paladin, moving to Mariah, moving in with Terrence, and moving back to England, sometimes within the space of a single day. As long as he changed his plans so often, sometimes on an hourly basis, there was no way that I could make plans that coordinated with his.

I reminded him that making plans that coordinated with his was exactly what I would have to do, since he was not the kind of person who would make plans to coordinate with *mine*. My impression was that he expected his boyfriends to follow him wherever he went but wasn't willing to do the same. I reminded him that he had dragged Glenn to the United States even though he had hated it and couldn't adjust to it and his relationship with Cliff was destroyed because he had refused to follow him to California because he didn't want to be what he had once described as an "appendage."

I told him that as far as taking chances was concerned, it was easy to be bold and take chances when you had a safety net underneath you and reminded him that not all of us had been born with silver spoons in our mouths with the resources he had to fall back on if things went wrong. I told him that if he had grown up like some of the rest of us, he wouldn't have the same attitude. I told him that he wasn't in a fit position to judge me and that sometimes I thought it was *he* who had a limited understanding of people.

I reminded him that however he thought I was deficient as a person, I had stayed with him when he had a debilitating and potentially fatal illness. I told him that not everyone would do that for someone he had known for only a few months—only a few weeks when his illness had first emerged—and that not everyone would be willing to stay with someone who was facing a future of increasing debility and, possibly, premature death. I didn't make the comment to be cruel or to seem saintly, but to illustrate my commitment to him, which was genuine.

Jonathan's next message, which arrived around 8:00 that evening, addressed not us, but Glenn. In a brief message only three lines and thirty words long, he informed me that Glenn was in worse circumstances than ever and that he was arranging to go to the Caribbean island where Glenn had last been seen to try to find him. He explained that he was doing it because he couldn't and wouldn't abandon people he loved. Whatever Glenn's condition and whatever Jonathan's intentions, I felt that his message was more an attempt to denigrate my expression of commitment while exalting his own.

Around 9:00 that night, Jonathan finally addressed my message. In his lengthy reply, he began by informing me that I didn't know what had happened between him and Glenn, so I shouldn't even speculate about it. Seeming to reverse, or modify, his previous position regarding Glenn's attitude toward the United States, he said that far from being "dragged" here, Glenn had initially been enthusiastic about coming here and had become unhappy and wanted to return home only after he had seen what life in the United States was like. He assured me that Glenn had had the power to veto any decisions that affected the both of them, that Glenn had never been forced to do anything against his will. He told me that he had stayed on good terms with almost everyone with whom he'd been involved and asked me if I could say the same. He said that in spite of what had happened between him and Glenn, he had forgiven Glenn for what he had done to him and that they both still cared about each other. He said that he would do anything for him, and that whatever else he might be, he was loyal.

As far as Cliff was concerned, he told me that he couldn't follow him to California because he had been committed at OutSource, and because his career was advancing more rapidly than Cliff's, it would have been foolish to walk away. He told me that if he was as selfish as I believed he was, he could have interfered in Cliff's attempt to get the job in California but hadn't because he had known it was what was best for Cliff, even though it wasn't what was best for *him*. He said that if there hadn't been complicating factors, he would have followed Cliff "to the end of the Earth." He told me that he thought Cliff must appreciate what he had done because Cliff still cared about him and stayed in constant contact with him. He said that in spite of what he had done in July, which he described as "not malicious, just dumb," they would always be friends.

Ignoring the effects that his indecisiveness had been having on me, he told me that it was simply his "decision making process" to verbalize his thoughts and receive feedback in order to make the best choice possible. He claimed that he had tried to include me in his decisions in part because of how they would affect me. I was dubious of that last reason because more often than not, he had considered choices or effected decisions that had benefited him far more than they had me. Whatever "feedback" I had given to him had typically fallen on deaf ears, and although I didn't expect anyone to accept my advice if they found it unsuitable, I felt that in some ways his "decision making process" could have demonstrated more consideration toward me.

As far as his illness was concerned, he told me that the people who had cared about him before he had gotten sick still cared. He said that Chase had told him he would do whatever he could to help him, if he would let him. He said that Cliff was only concerned about his getting well and encouraged him to do everything he could to do so. He said that even though it sounded clichéd, he believed in the idea of "in sickness and in health" and that if you loved someone, you didn't abandon him if he was ill.

As far as Dan was concerned, he told me that although he was infuriated with him because of how he had treated him, he was over his anger toward him and was now left with only contempt and pity for "the old drunk." He reminded me that at the time I had found what he was doing to Dan "amusing" and even though I had encouraged him to expose Dan, he had resisted, although that wasn't true. He claimed that he wanted to be done with Dan forever and go forward.

In conclusion, Jonathan said that he was "filled with incredible sadness" at how things between us had turned out. He said that in spite of having genuine affection for me and looking at me as his long-term partner—a notion that contradicted his earlier claim that we were not committed to each other—too much had been shattered by what I had done for him to be able to consider having a permanent relationship with me now. He said that even so, he wouldn't stop caring about me or worrying about my driving home from work at night.

After an entire day of fighting, I was drained and depressed. I was filled with incredible sadness at how things between us had turned out as well and doubted more than ever that our relationship would continue.

We didn't communicate for two days. During that time, my mother was admitted to the hospital because of a possible blood clot in her leg, a special concern because two of her sisters had suffered pulmonary embolisms, which often start in the legs, and one of them had died from one. As it turned out, she didn't have a clot and was sent home on Wednesday evening.

In the end, Jonathan made the first move. On Tuesday, he sent me an e-mail in which he attempted to apprise me of his current situation in spite of everything that had happened. In responding to his request for information about the state of my life, I mentioned that my mother was in the hospital. To that, he sent a conciliatory reply. He said that he was sorry to hear about my mother and wished her a fast and full recovery. He said that she had been a "positive support and influence for [me] and so by reflection to [him]." I had told him I wasn't doing well, although I didn't mention that it was in part from the stress of what had happened between us, and he assured me that caring didn't stop easily for him and, as he had said before, he was quite loyal.

I had restated that I still wanted to talk to him in person and he suggested that before doing so, perhaps we could break the ice by first talking on the phone. Because I had written from work, he suggested that perhaps we could talk later that night. After telling me about some additional matters—Glenn was still missing, the deal on one of the houses in Mariah had fallen through—he assured me that "everything [had] a solution if you want to find it." I wanted to believe that was true.

As far as Glenn was concerned, Jonathan informed me that he had enlisted both Mike's and Cliff's help in obtaining a private investigator through the legal departments at their respective companies try to find him. He was no longer thinking about trying to find Glenn himself, which I thought was an extreme and probably useless move, but he still wasn't sure what to do and still felt guilty for whatever he perceived he had done wrong in taking care of Glenn.

As far as *we* were concerned, Jonathan's attitude and attempts to find a solution to the conflict that had arisen between us made me feel comforted. In the end, I didn't call him that night because I didn't get home until well after 10:00 when I encountered an automobile accident just outside Hawthorn that was blocking traffic, forcing me to take a lengthier route home. When I arrived, my first order of business was to call not Jonathan but my mother, who was still in the hospital, and my sister. By the time I was through, it was after 11:00 and I was exhausted. I had been chronically exhausted for weeks, but I was especially exhausted after my evening...and my week. I wrote to Jonathan, telling him why I wouldn't be calling and, more importantly, that I didn't have any ill will toward him either and that as it had been for him, it had been a bad week for me.

The next morning, I finally spoke with Jonathan. This was the first time we had spoken since the morning Glenn had called and certainly since we had fought. The conversation proved largely a repetition of and expansion on recent events, but in spite of the difficult subjects and feelings we discussed, the conversation left me feeling better than I had in days in part because we were at least talking again. After I brought my mother home from the hospital that evening, Jonathan and I talked again briefly that night, which made me feel even more confident that our relationship had been put back on course.

Even so, if I had done what I should have done, I would have let the relationship end there. In spite of having reconciled, the fact of our relationship was that we had known each other for only four months and even though a certain bond had formed between us, many forces, in some ways less external than internal, in him and in me, seemed to be pulling that bond apart. At that point, the forces pulling our relationship apart had grown so strong that they had almost torn it in half. But, although the relationship should have ended there, it did not.

Perhaps it was partly because, after everything I had done to determine the truth, I still didn't know, for certain, if "GayMan/Iain," was really Jonathan. I was at heart a rationalist who was reluctant to base such an important decision as whether or not to remain in a relationship that seemed to have qualities I didn't know if I would find elsewhere on mere intuition of what *may* be true. It may equally have *not* been true and, in that case, I would have been throwing away the relationship for nothing.

Perhaps it was partly because I was willing to cut him a certain amount of slack because of his sickness and circumstances. I realized that he was under an enormous amount of stress because of events and often reacted emotionally, not rationally. In addition, he suffered from a certain amount of mental confusion, something he had conceded for weeks now, and I had seen for myself how his personality and behavior differed, and seemed to have deteriorated, from what they had been in June. He was not himself, so I tried to consider how he had changed, what he was enduring, in judging his actions.

Perhaps it was partly because, in spite of what was happening, Jonathan still seemed to need me, seemed to view me as the only person who really had his best interests at heart. I did, even though I didn't know what to think about him. I liked to think of myself as a humane person, as a caring person, who wasn't going to abandon someone whose situation seemed so dire. I loved him in some fashion even though I wasn't *in* love with him, felt connected and committed to him by some form of affection, and as he had claimed for himself, I was not going to abandon those whom I loved.

Perhaps it was partly because we had become financially entangled and, although remaining with Jonathan wasn't a condition for repayment, the financial entanglement did add another level of attachment.

Perhaps it was partly because, in spite of his negative qualities—his prejudice, his presumptuousness, his pettiness, his princeliness—I found it difficult not to think of his seemingly positive ones—his intelligence, his interests, his classiness, his caring and concern that he showed me, when he showed it. He had once told me, "You've never met anyone like me before," and that was true. In asking myself the "Dear Abby" question, I still thought he *was* worth it, even if the balance between being worth it and not seemed to be 51 to 49 at that point. For many reasons, I stayed, believing that in spite of whatever difficulties had arisen, whatever doubts I had, I should try to tough it out.

As far as the problems between us were concerned, they eventually blew over. Then, on Friday, Jonathan sent me the e-mail in which he said that Laura had asked him to give her $4,500 to eliminate her debts and that because living with her had become so uncomfortable, he felt he could no longer stay there. At that point, other matters took precedence. I still had my doubts about Jonathan, but perhaps because I didn't know what to do with them, I did nothing with them. They moved into the back of my mind...but they never fully moved out.

—17—
IN THE MIDDLE OF THE WICKEDNESS

Are you my boyfriend?

By the time that Jonathan had escaped from Laura's and fled to Art's, he had started his job at the hospital in Mariah. The hospital posted a story about Jonathan's hiring on their web site, making it official. The position was certainly less prestigious than the one he'd held at OutSource, but it was also less stressful and that was the primary reason he had accepted it. In addition, it would be something of a package deal, since he would not only be working at the hospital, but also be receiving treatments there. The treatment of his endocarditis in the previous two months had been irregular and inadequate at best, so it would help to stabilize his life in more ways than one. I hoped that eventually it would stabilize *ours* as well.

On Sunday, October 21, I planned to go to St. Alban to help Jonathan "escape." In finalizing our plans for the day, he wrote to me around 11:00 that morning to tell me that he'd come back to the "stalag"—his name for Laura's house—after spending a couple of hours at Art's. He said that Laura had called to check on him not one but three times while he was there and once after he'd left to make certain he'd actually gone. The subtler control that Laura was trying to exert over Jonathan was, in its own way, just as detrimental as the blatant control that Dan had tried to assert. He said that once he'd gotten back, he'd gotten sick and hadn't been up to checking e-mails until then. Not surprisingly, he said he wanted to get out of Laura's either that day or the next.

He then went on to say that the deal on the apartment in Mariah had almost been finalized and that it could be available as early as the next week. The apartment was actually the converted second floor of a Victorian-style house that had been fully modernized. The apartment measured about 1,500 square feet, which was about half the size of the house on Millstone Drive. He said he had the lease, which he could sign at any time.

He told me that because of his illness he was "a little confused" and needed my help. He said he had the keys to Art's house in case we decided to go there. He said he had already taken everything he was storing in his car, including *Still Life*, the portrait of his mother with him and his siblings, and a Tiffany chandelier that had been his grandmother's, the day before. He suggested coming to Laura's, picking him up, then going to Art's, where we could decide what to do next.

I thought that was an excellent idea. I was excited to be seeing Jonathan again after not having seen him for three weeks and after having seen him only once in six weeks. I was even more excited because Jonathan seemed to believe that once he moved away from Laura's, he—and we—would no longer be hindered by her inability to accept our relationship. I had come to feel that the enforced separation was in fact damaging our relationship and that we needed to resume a regular pattern of being together to regain the ground we had lost and, hopefully, to move beyond it. For reasons both unselfish and selfish, I wanted to see him, and us, free from those impediments, and I was not only willing, but eager, to help him get away from her.

After making the hour-and-a-half trip, I arrived in St. Alban sometime around 1:00 in the afternoon. Although it was a small town, I had been there only once, and since I had only driven through, I hadn't gotten a good sense of where things were. Consequently, I arrived at Laura's half an hour late.

I saw Laura for the first time in more than six weeks, a six weeks that seemed like six months. She seemed friendly enough to me in spite of the fact that she was jealous of Jonathan's and my relationship. While I was there, I finally got to meet her older son Chuck. Jack, however, wasn't home at the time, so I didn't get to meet him.

I hadn't seen the girls since the day I'd left Credence, and in the ensuing six weeks, both Sweetie and Frizzie had been shorn, their curly, luxuriant locks replaced by a wiry, wavy mat. If I hadn't known who they were, I wouldn't have recognized them. In those six weeks, so many things had changed, almost beyond recognition, and the fact that they, too, had changed almost beyond recognition seemed fitting. Perhaps things would now begin changing back.

We went to the garage, which had become overrun with Jonathan's things. The floor was littered with numerous black trash bags filled with his clothes and other effects. Altogether I counted at least fifteen bags, although there were probably more. We took a few of them but left most of them behind. I assumed we would come back later to claim the rest, but Jonathan left the time of that return unset.

When we got into the car, Jonathan kissed me and thanked me for "rescuing" him from Laura. I was happy and relieved to do it. I hoped that the third time would be the charm, that Art would prove to be better than both Dan and Laura.

I knew little about Art except that he was a friend of Jonathan's who had offered to let Jonathan move in with him when he was leaving his house on Millstone Drive. Art was in his late 40s, a few years older than Jonathan, and lived downtown, not too far from the heart of the city. That environment seemed much more suited to Jonathan's personality, an environment where he could be "in the middle of the wickedness," as he had once described it. In addition, like virutally all of Jonathan's male friends, Art was gay. But, even though Art was gay and lived downtown, he wasn't one of the "gay yuppie scum" that Jonathan despised. Art was, in Jonathan's words, a "[n]ice guy, not a drunk, love[d] dogs," and Jonathan acknowledged that he should have gone to Art's in September, "but who knew." One could only hope that Jonathan's assessment of the situation was accurate and that he was not, once again, jumping from the frying pan into the fire...or from the fire into a conflagration.

When we arrived, Art was at church. Art's house more or less conformed to the stereotypical home of a middle-aged gay man: an older, somewhat musty space overflowing with an "eclectic" mélange of Victorian antiques, chintz, old photographs, tchotchkes, and gay porn. The décor reflected Jonathan's tastes far more closely than had Dan's or Laura's, which made me think he would be more comfortable there.

After we unloaded Jonathan's belongings, we decided to go to the bathhouse. Since he didn't have to be running off to please the "little woman," we were able to stay longer than we had the time before. Later, when we were out driving around, we drove past OutSource. This was the first time in the five months I'd known him that I'd seen his workplace. The building was smaller than I'd envisioned, especially for a concern that employed 350 people, but that didn't necessarily mean they all worked in the same location. Still, the building itself didn't seem as impressive as I'd imagined.

As we drove slowly through the parking lot, which was empty, Jonathan displayed a distinct sense of melancholy. I certainly understood it, but not having the emotional attachments to it that he did, I was thankful that Jonathan was probably leaving it behind.

Later that evening as we were driving back to Art's, Jonathan had an attack of angina. He winced and held his chest for a moment before the pain subsided. I hoped that the job at the hospital and the treatments they would allow him to resume would put an end to that.

On Monday, the 22nd, I had to work, but on Tuesday, the 23rd, I returned. I was now on fall break, and since I didn't have to go back to work until Friday, I had the day free. This time, I finally got to meet Art, who seemed subdued but friendly. He offered me some apple crumb cake that he had just made from apples he had gathered from the apple trees growing in his back yard. That day, Jonathan and I planned to go to Mariah and we remained only briefly before heading out.

Today, I did the driving. After spending half an hour making our way through the Paladin traffic, we spent another hour traveling to Mariah. I had never visited Mariah before and knew little, if anything, about it. I didn't know what to expect.

I was not impressed.

For a city its size, Mariah seemed as oppressively small as a town of 100, far more rural than urban in feel. In addition, the city appeared to have been poorly planned, a jumble of commercial areas lying next to residential ones, stately houses lying next to decrepit ones. Less tangible but no less palpable, the city seemed to exude a backwardness that made me somewhat uncomfortable. I half-expected members of the Ku Klux Klan to appear in their white robes at any moment and gay-bash me. Mariah was certainly not Paladin, and not even Hawthorn, and I didn't know how satisfied—or safe—Jonathan would be living here.

The first order of business was to look at the apartment. We drove to the real estate agent's office, which wasn't far from either the apartment or the hospital. Then again, everything seemed close to everything else in Mariah. The apartment was, in fact, only three blocks from the hospital, which meant that, if he felt up to it, Jonathan could walk to work.

After Jonathan introduced me to the real estate agent and owner, Joan Vogel, and explained, vaguely, that I was there to help him that day, we headed to the apartment. As Jonathan had said, the apartment was located on the second story of a Victorian-style house that had, at some point, been converted into a duplex. Each apartment had its own entrance, but each could also be entered through the garage. We entered through the garage, climbing a set of narrow, somewhat precarious stairs to reach the second floor.

From what I could tell, the upper-story apartment was better than the lower-story one, and although Jonathan would have preferred a house to an apartment, he had been through so much hassle in trying to find a place in Mariah that, after examining the apartment only briefly, he told Joan, without hesitation, that he would take it.

After making the deal, we headed for the hospital. The hospital appeared as antiquated as much of the rest of Mariah did and I fully understood the desire to bring it into the 21st century. I stayed in the waiting room, the décor of which seemed more suited to the set of a 1950s talk show, while I waited for Jonathan to conclude his business with his new boss. As I waited, I saw a young black man enter the hospital and was amazed to see that there were, in fact, black people in Mariah. I had to wonder how comfortable the young man felt in this overwhelmingly white, seemingly conservative environment. I wondered, too, how well *Jonathan* would fare here, being both British and gay.

When Jonathan finally returned, he wore an almost stunned expression and was shaking his head. When I asked him what was going on, he told me that his job had expanded from part to full time, which meant that it would be more intensive than his boss had originally led him to believe. In addition, his boss had described in greater detail Jonathan's role as "designated bad guy" in the struggle to implement the changes his boss felt the hospital needed to make. Jonathan felt ambivalent about the situation, at best. So did I. I could only hope that after his run of bad luck over the past two months, something would finally work out for him.

When we got into the car to leave, he mentioned that the hospital had an opening for a clinical psychologist and wondered if I might be interested. I was neither qualified nor interested, but the implication was that I get a job in Mariah, obviously as part of establishing a life there, with him. Even if I had been qualified and interested, I wasn't prepared to do that anytime soon. Mariah, and Jonathan, were going to have to prove themselves to me more than they had before I would be willing to risk making a serious mistake. I told him I wasn't qualified and left it at that.

Later that afternoon, we ate lunch at the Golden Dragon, a Chinese restaurant in Mariah. Appropriately enough, the message in my fortune cookie read, *Your love life will be very interesting.* That was an understatement.

After returning to Art's, we spent the early part of the evening watching television. The weather had turned progressively grayer throughout the day, and by early evening, we became aware of the lightning that was beginning to flicker outside. I left earlier than I'd planned because I wanted to try to outrun the storm, although given the direction from which it was coming, I would be heading toward—though hopefully not into—it.

Unfortunately, driving back home that night was nightmarish. It poured rain the entire way home, sometimes so badly that I couldn't see where I was going. In addition, every time a semi would drive past—at 60 or 70 miles an hour—it would throw up a huge spray of water that would inundate the car so completely that for several seconds I would be left blinded. It was like going through a car wash every two minutes. At some points after the water subsided, I'd find that I'd drifted dangerously into the middle of the road. There were actually a couple of times when I came fairly close to getting hit, once by a semi. When I got halfway back, I turned off onto a less congested and more manageable state road, but the road was so dark that I couldn't see the wide, deep pools of water that had collected at various points on the road until I plowed into them at 50 miles an hour. By the time I got home, I was stressed and exhausted.

On Wednesday, I spent the day recovering from my ordeal, but on Thursday, I returned to Paladin. Art was gone, so Jonathan and I had the house to ourselves. At one point we were in the kitchen, where Jonathan was fixing something for us to eat, when he told me something that left me stunned.

"By the way, did I tell you about the *murder*?"

The *murder*? "No?"

"The people who moved into my old house were murdered."

The people to whom Jonathan referred were Ted Kanner's niece and her fiancé. I was shocked. "What happened?"

"Someone broke into the house through the sunroom one night and murdered them while they were asleep."

"When did this happen?"

"About a month ago."

Less than a month after he'd left.

"How did you find out about it?"

"My lawyer told me the police were looking for me but couldn't find me because I kept moving."

"Why were the police looking for you?"

"*I'm* not a suspect," he said. "The police don't have any leads and they wanted to know if I had any enemies who might have thought I was still living there at the time and wanted to hurt me."

"Do you have any enemies?" Knowing Jonathan, I could see how he might, since business could sometimes be a cutthroat endeavor—sometimes literally—and since Jonathan, despite his agreeable qualities, could rub people the wrong way.

"No."

"My God. It's a good thing you got out of there when you did." I tried to be philosophical about what had happened. "Perhaps things have happened the way they have so you'd be out of that house and out of harm's way. If that's so, then everything that's happened in the past couple of months has been worth it—*beyond* worth it. Someone must be looking out for you."

For a day or two afterwards, I was unsettled by what I had learned. I couldn't help thinking about the implications not only for Jonathan, but also for me. What if Jonathan had remained in the house an additional month? What if I had been staying with him, sleeping with him, on the night the killer had broken in? We might now be dead. *I* might now be dead. Someone was apparently looking out for *me* as well. Drama seemed to follow Jonathan wherever he went, and if his life could have gotten more dramatic, I didn't know how.

In the days that followed, I went to the library to see if I could find more information about the murders through the Paladin papers. I didn't know the exact date when the murders had taken place, so I looked through papers from mid-September to mid-October. Unfortunately, they didn't contain any stories about the killings. Why not? Were the local police keeping the story under wraps? If so, why? That wasn't the way things normally worked. If they needed leads, wouldn't the police *want* to see the story published with the hope that it would elicit additional information? The situation was bizarre, to say the least, and I didn't know what to think of it. Perhaps because I didn't know what to think of it, I didn't think of it further.

After Jonathan moved back to Paladin, the situation between us became more normal—insofar as it had ever been "normal." At the least, it seemed more familiar and felt more comfortable, since we were once again operating in the city where we had started and had spent the summer and, more importantly, since we could, after almost two months, finally see each other without obstruction. In addition, Art's house lay some 15 miles closer to mine than Jonathan's had, which meant that I was now making a somewhat shorter trip to see Jonathan than I had when he'd lived in Paladin before. I knew, though, that would change once he moved to Mariah, which lay twice the distance from home.

I planned to return to Paladin on Saturday, the 27th. This time, however, I was planning to visit not Jonathan, but Chris. Although we had spoken on the phone just a couple of weeks before, we hadn't seen each other for an entire year. The 27th was Halloween weekend and Tolliver's would be the focal point of some of the festivities. I hoped that after meeting there, Chris and I could go to some of the gay clubs in Paladin not only to view the spectacle, but also to go dancing. Jonathan and I had never gone dancing, something I loved to do, and he didn't seem like the type who would. Chris and I were just friends, so I didn't see anything wrong with going out with him. My entire life couldn't revolve around Jonathan and what he needed. I needed some things myself and I needed to de-stress.

Even so, I did plan to see Jonathan again soon. I had thought about seeing him on Saturday during the day, then going out with Chris later that night, but I wasn't exactly sure how I was going to fit everyone and everything into my weekend plans. I wrote to Jonathan Friday night, suggesting that I see him the next afternoon.

The next morning, he wrote to tell me that he was "awfully tired" and suggested getting together Sunday instead. Jonathan said he had no plans for Sunday and Art was attending church in a nearby town and would be gone until early afternoon, which would allow us to get away without Art trying to tag along. He said that Art wasn't a pest, but he did seem lonely and wanted to be involved in most activities. He told me to come anytime, but also said that he had to leave for Mariah early Monday morning, so he wanted to have an early evening. He also said that he was planning to schedule the move for the end of the week and would be "incredibly happy" to be in his own space again. He ended his message by encouraging me to have fun Saturday night, saying that I deserved "a little outrageousness." I couldn't have agreed more.

On Saturday morning, however, I woke up feeling sick. I had a sinus headache and hadn't slept well. It was also a cool, gray, windy day, which only worsened the way I felt. Since I barely felt like getting out of bed, let alone making a three-hour round trip with several hours of dancing and drinking in between, I decided to cancel my plans. That was especially important if I was going to be seeing Jonathan on Sunday. I wrote to tell him how I felt and what I was planning to do as well as to ask him how he felt.

In response, he told me that he was "not quite quite" himself and had been having a quiet day. More significant, however, he also told me that he had heard from Chase, who had invited him to a showing of the 1925 silent version of *Phantom of the Opera* starring Lon Chaney at which he would be playing the piano. This was the first time in two months that Chase had tried to be involved in Jonathan's life in an obvious way and his reemergence gave me a mild feeling of irritation and concern. Even so, Jonathan seemed to have little interest in seeing him, telling me that he thought it was "better to avoid that whole situation." For many reasons, I had to agree.

He also told me that Jack, Laura's younger son, had e-mailed him asking him if he could live with him when he moved to Mariah. I couldn't believe the audacity. Jonathan's response was that he was "very fond" of Jack but didn't trust Laura and that the situation would be "too complicated." Again, I had to agree. I could only imagine how parasitical Jack, and Laura, would become if they were allowed reentry into Jonathan's life. It was better to keep them, and their money-hunger, at arm's length. Jonathan had suffered enough because of them.

By Sunday morning, I felt much better. I was still wanting to spend some time with Jonathan and e-mailed him around 9:00, suggesting that I could leave Hawthorn around 10:00 and thereby be able to arrive in Paladin sometime between 11:00 and 11:30. Jonathan wrote back, saying that, unfortunately, he was "still under the weather" and was "trying to stay in bed as long as possible." Art had left, so it was quiet, and Jonathan wanted to rest up before making the lengthy trip to Mariah at 6:00 the next morning.

I was disappointed, but I understood the circumstances and I had already seen him three times that week—three times as many times as I had seen him in the six weeks that he had spent in exile from Paladin. I told him that perhaps we could get together sometime during the middle of the week, possibly Wednesday or Thursday when I didn't teach. I assumed he would be preparing to move by that point and could probably use some help. He wrote back, saying the middle of the week would be great and, help aside, it would be nice to see me.

In the same e-mail, Jonathan again raised the issue of Jack's desire to move in with him in Mariah and described the situation as "too weird." I didn't think it was weird, given that Jonathan had insinuated to me that Jack was gay. The day we had met at the bathhouse in Paladin shortly after he had moved to Laura's, Jonathan had stated that although he wasn't 100% certain that Jack was gay, he was "$99^{44}/_{100}$%" certain that he was. If he really was, then it made sense that he would want to live with Jonathan, whom I suspected Jack viewed as some sort of surrogate gay father, and would want a refuge from the mess at home. In response, I asked him if he knew for certain that Jack was gay or merely suspected he was.

In response, Jonathan told me that when he was living with Laura, Jack had actually acknowledged to him that he was gay. Jonathan was quick to add that "nothing did or could happen there for about 10 million reasons," as if I thought it might have. He stated that Jack was only 18, and insisted that although some gay men would be "drooling" over someone that age, he liked men, not boys. He told me that if he and Jack—theoretically—became sexually involved, Laura would "jump off the roof." Sarcastically he added that such a reaction "might make it worth it," but said that the real problem was that Laura refused to face the fact that Jack was gay. Laura's inability to face reality, which had characterized her relationship with Jonathan, was not my problem, however, and I hoped that Jonathan would not let it become his once again, albeit in another form.

Over the next few days, little happened. That was good. Too much had happened and everyone needed a reprieve. This was the most normal that things had been since Jonathan had lived in Paladin before, although normal was, of course, only relative.

One day in early November, we were eating at a Mexican restaurant near Art's when Jonathan told me about a problem that had arisen between the two of them. Problems seemed to follow Jonathan wherever he went, and although things seemed less problematic at Art's than they had at Dan's and Laura's, they couldn't be expected to be problem-free. After two months of the most unbelievable trouble, I cringed, wondering what it was *this* time.

He said that Art was asking him to pay rent for December when it was only the beginning of November and when he wasn't going to be living there in December. He told me about it, not only because he just wanted to talk about it, but also because he said he didn't know if this was an expected thing to do in America. I told him that it wasn't, as far as I knew, and that Art was being unreasonable. Art had another renter and seemed to be able to afford his gayified house only through the help of his boarders. I felt that Art was simply trying to milk money out of Jonathan that he didn't deserve. It almost sounded like the situation with Ted Kanner. Since Art and Jonathan didn't have a contract stipulating that Jonathan pay rent for months he wasn't renting, Art couldn't pressure him legally, and since Jonathan would be getting away from Art soon enough, he couldn't pressure him personally. Although in some sense it didn't matter, I certainly didn't like it and it seemed to be yet another example of someone trying to take advantage of him. It astonished me that there were so many people who were willing to do that in the world and that so many of them had accumulated in Jonathan's life.

By the beginning of November, I had canceled my previous Internet service and, in doing so, had created a new e-mail account through which to communicate with Jonathan exclusively. On Saturday, the 3rd, I sent him a message from my "Jonathan" account in which I referred to myself as his "boyfriend." That e-mail sparked yet another "discussion" of an apparently unsettled aspect of our relationship: my "status." In the message, Jonathan said that Art, who didn't have a boyfriend and apparently wanted one, had asked Jonathan if he was "taking applications." He concluded by saying the reason Art had made the comment was that "he never saw [him] with anybody in particular" then asked me, "*Are* you my boyfriend?" He said that he "didn't think we had decided on that, at least not officially," and concluded by suggesting that perhaps once he moved to Mariah, we could "resume regular visitations, sort of like in prison."

Was I his boyfriend? By that point, I had been involved with him for five months, had been told, "From now on, it's just the two of us," had been told that I was one of the two American men he had considered to be life partners, had been encouraged, indirectly if not directly, to get a job in Mariah and move there with him so we could finally be together, and now he was questioning whether or not I was his boyfriend?

In response, I told him that whether or not I was his boyfriend depended on what he meant by "boyfriend." I told him that for some time I had been operating under the assumption that I was more than "just a friend" or a "fuck buddy," although I was still probably something less than a "life partner" to him. I told him I thought that someone in that position would be considered a "boyfriend." I asked him if "boyfriend" meant something different in England than it did in the United States or, more to the point, how *he* defined "boyfriend." Was I his boyfriend or was I now just "some guy" to him? I told him I was confused and left wondering what his statement meant for me. I signed the message "Your boyfriend(?)" I sent the message sometime around 5:00, thinking that would give him plenty of time to respond, but I didn't hear from him again that day.

We had planned to get together on Sunday, so the next morning, I e-mailed him and told him to call me so we could make definite plans for the day. Around 9:30 he called, but before I raised the issue of plans, I broached the subject that had arisen the day before: whether or not I was his boyfriend. He seemed evasive, not wanting to define what he meant by *boyfriend* and why he didn't think I fitted that definition. Although he hadn't answered my question to my satisfaction by phone, I still planned to go to Paladin that day and raise the issue in person where, hopefully, he would feel more pressured to be specific.

After picking him up at Art's, we went to various places in the city. At one point while we were driving, while he was trapped in the car, I asked him to explain to me what he meant when he questioned whether or not I was his boyfriend. In response, he said, "I asked you to be my boyfriend, but you wouldn't."

I recalled no such discussion. I asked him when he had done that, but he told me to never mind, leaving me mystified as to when he had "popped the question."

Trying to understand, I took a different tack. "So, what does the word *boyfriend* mean in England?"

Seeming more to want to put me off than to clarify something the importance of which I considered to be central, he said, "Watch *Absolutely Fabulous*."

I *had* watched *Absolutely Fabulous*—so much so in the previous seven years that I had practically memorized the script of each episode—and, unless I was missing something, I had never discerned a difference in the way the British interpreted the word *boyfriend* from the way the Americans did. Frustrated, I finally said, "Why don't *you* just tell me?"

Thinking before answering, he said, "It implies a deeper relationship." That was all he said and, once again, not getting a straight answer to an important question, I dropped it.

I wondered, though, how "deep" our relationship was supposed to get before he considered me his "boyfriend." I thought it had already gotten deep enough, in spite of our problems. He had told me that he loved me and wanted us to live together, but did we actually have to be living together for him to consider me his "boyfriend"? Jonathan's thinking and behavior had been erratic for months now, in some ways since I'd met him, and I couldn't help wondering just how far his illness had affected his cognitive processes. It was very disorienting. Sometimes I was at a loss as to how to deal with it.

Something that seemed to get at least partly resolved that day was the matter of the money Jonathan owed me. We hadn't discussed the issue for three weeks and on Thursday, November 1, the storage facility had placed another charge of $229.95 on my credit card. I didn't want it to seem as if money were the most important thing in our relationship—however it might have been defined that day—but his bills were continuing to mount and now amounted to $1,000, minus interest. In addition, I had the new car and the higher insurance and hadn't adequately rebuilt my savings from the summer to cover his expenses as well. And, I shouldn't have had to. In spite of all the other expenses he'd accrued either fairly or unfairly, his expense at *my* expense was no less important. He had, after all, told me to give him the bills as they came in and he would pay them. They'd been coming in for two months now and it seemed like time to start paying up.

I mentioned the issue to him that day, and for the first time since he'd left Paladin two months before, he paid me some of what he owed me. He had apparently taken a substantial amount of cash out of the bank in anticipation of the expenses for the move and ended up giving me $360. I thought it was incredibly foolish for Jonathan to be carrying around that much cash, but his behavior with money was clearly different from that of the average person. He told me that once he got his first check from the hospital, which should happen sometime mid-November, he would pay me the remainder.

Before I left Paladin that day, I took some time to drive past Jonathan's old house. I hadn't seen it since the day in early September that Jonathan's landlord had repossessed it. The house was empty and I tried not to think of what had happened there in the previous few weeks. I tried, instead, to think of what had happened there the previous summer, of the times that Jonathan and I had spent together. I thought especially of the previous June, when things had seemed so simple. They no longer were. I wondered if they would ever be again.

■

On the afternoon of Saturday, November 10, I went to the local university library to work on a project that required the use of software installed on the library's computers but not on mine. While I worked, I occasionally accessed the Internet to check and send e-mail and to check the *Gayteway* site. It had become something of a habit by that point for me to check the site for Jonathan's ads, both actual...and possible. That afternoon, I would not be disappointed.

When I checked the board for my state, I discovered a posting that had been placed that afternoon by someone who called himself "Banzai." Even if I hadn't been able to recognize the author by the style, I would have recognized him by the content. Titled "Fag In Credence," the author mentioned the "nasty old lying queen" in Credence who tried to "lure" unsuspecting men to his "disgusting" house. "You know who it is," he wrote, then for those who might not, he clarified: "DAN."

Obviously something had happened, but I didn't know what. I knew I would be seeing Jonathan the next day and would have to ask him what had provoked the latest posting after a month of peace.

Later that evening, Jonathan sent me what I considered to be an odd and, for more reasons than one, disorienting message. It began by saying that he and Art had gone antiques shopping that day—Jonathan to find a new bed, Art to find a birthday gift—and that Jonathan had purchased a bed in an Art Deco style. He said that the asking price had been $185, but that by flirting with the dealer, who was also gay, he had managed to get him to drop the price to only $120. Jonathan said that when he had concluded his dealings, he had given the dealer a kiss to let him know how much he appreciated his generosity. After relating the story, Jonathan added, "Does that make me a slut?"—a comment that struck me as somewhat neurotic or at least peculiar. I couldn't tell if Jonathan felt guilty about what he had done or, in light of the recently arisen Iain situation, with my intimation of what Jonathan had referred to as his "slutful ways," it was some kind of attempt to gauge my reactions or to be sarcastic.

He continued by saying that in the process of reviewing applications from people who had applied for positions at OutSource, for which he was apparently still doing some work, he had run across an application from someone named Iain who currently worked for the same technology company and lived in the same city that the *other* Iain had claimed he did. Because of the similarities between the two Iains, Jonathan thought they might be the same person. He concluded his message by saying, "Maybe that is your phantom lover." I doubted the plausibility of his story and thought the remark was even more neurotic than the one about his "slutfulness." I wondered if it meant that for him the Iain issue was still unresolved.

Perplexed, I wrote back, telling him I thought his message was odd and to call me the next morning around 9:00. He wrote back and asked me what was odd about it, to which I replied that apparently the Iain issue was still an issue for him and asked him if he wanted to talk about it. He didn't respond that night, but when I spoke to him the next morning and asked him if he wanted to talk about it, he said no. His refusal seemed definite, so I dropped it.

When I saw him later that day, I asked him not about Iain, but about Dan. Jonathan told me that Dan was continuing to accuse him of stealing from him. He also told me, for the first time, that Dan had tried to force him to sleep with one of his partners when he was living with him. I was shocked, but not overly surprised. He said he was considering filing charges against Dan for sexual harassment. If Jonathan's claims were true, then that was a more straightforward way to hold Dan accountable for his actions.

When I heard from Jonathan the next day, his message said nothing about Iain or Dan. Instead, it focused on work, the upcoming move, and some unseemly goings-on at Art's the night before. Writing from work, Jonathan began by telling me that he'd had "the day from hell after the night from hell." His hellish time had started when Art had brought home "this drunk," whom Jonathan described as a "sort of trashy cute, older alchie type," around 10:00 the night before. Jonathan said that the man had been wandering throughout the house, drunk, and had woken him up at one point when the man was "starkers"—naked. Apparently, the man had told Jonathan that having sex with Art was like having sex with a walrus—something that Jonathan did not want to know.

His hellish time had continued into that day when his boss had him chair the "bitch session" with the medical staff at the hospital. Letting his infamous prejudice show through, he made the comment that half of the doctors were Indians or "Pakis" and were only interested in "MONEYMONEYMONEY." He said he had just gotten out of that meeting, seeming relieved.

Finally, he said that in spite of needing to take care of a few details, he was informally scheduled to move to Mariah on Friday, the 16th. He said he knew I had to teach on Friday but said he would manage. He was planning to hire professional movers this time, so even though he had at one point pleaded with me to be with him when the move happened because he felt ill and overwhelmed and my presence gave him confidence, it wasn't as if he wouldn't have help. He said he would like to have moved on Wednesday, but Mike was insisting that he attend a meeting in Paladin with representatives from the company in California, which was scheduled for that day. Jonathan concluded by saying he was exhausted and was not looking forward to the long drive back to Art's that awaited him.

I was relieved that he would finally be getting away from Art, who had proven to be the best of the people with whom he had lived but who still left something to be desired, and would once again have his own space. I wondered, though, what ultimately he would be getting himself into in Mariah.

Our correspondence over the next several days focused primarily on two upcoming events: the move to Mariah and Jonathan's birthday. Jonathan spent much of that week trying to make arrangements with professional movers. Initially, he wanted to move during the week, since it was cheaper than moving on the weekend. He didn't like that idea, however, because he was swamped with work during the week, which would make moving then more complicated. Eventually, though, he was able to arrange to have the movers he had hired move him on the weekend for the same amount. After several weeks of making plans then having them fall through, the move was officially set for Saturday, November 17. That also meant that I would be able to help Jonathan with the move.

That was also the weekend of Jonathan's 45th birthday. My plan was to go to Paladin Friday afternoon, take him out for his birthday that evening, spend the night, then go with him to Mariah the next day.

After wrapping Jonathan's presents and packing for the weekend, I left Hawthorn Friday afternoon around 5:30. Arriving at Art's an hour and a half later, I took Jonathan out for dinner at a local Indian restaurant. The restaurant was located not too far from Jonathan's old house on Millstone Drive. He didn't seem to have a problem with the Indians there, possibly because, like Luella, they were in a servile position. It was just like old times, going out to dinner at a nice place on a Friday night in the old neighborhood. It was very pleasant and very normal. After more than two and a half months of dislocation and separation, I had forgotten what that was like.

Afterwards, we went back to Art's, where we figured out where to stay for the night. We couldn't stay at Art's because Jonathan didn't have his own bedroom there and had been sleeping on the couch, so there was no privacy. We ended up staying at a motel located on the outskirts of the city. Although it was a little noisy, since it was located near a highway, it wasn't too bad for only $40. *Any* price would have been worth it, though, to have our own space.

While at the motel, I gave Jonathan his card and presents. I had gotten him a card that, on the front, had a cartoon of a rabbit that had just stepped out of the shower and had a towel around his waist. He had the towel pulled out in front and was looking down at his crotch. On the front, the card said, "Don't Worry About It," while on the inside, it said, "Gray Hair Is Very Distinguished Looking. Happy Birthday." He seemed to like it. For presents, I had gotten him an amber-tinted glass elephant and had one of the elephant pictures I'd taken on our first date at the Paladin zoo enlarged and framed. He seemed to like both of them a lot and said he would hang the picture up in his office at work. He even liked the paper, which looked like wood, and was careful not to tear it while opening the presents.

Afterwards, we went to bed. It was strange but wonderful to be together in a real bed again in a space that, at least for the night, we could call our own. Perhaps now—*finally*—things would start getting back to normal.

—18—
MOVING TO MARIAH

Just be there when the move happens. Please. I don't feel very well and get a lot of confidence when you are there.

Moving to Mariah was nothing like moving from the house on Millstone Drive had been. Mercifully so. This time, Jonathan hired professional movers. This time, Jonathan paid for the move himself. I had paid for the one from Paladin and, given my limited income, I couldn't have paid for the one to Mariah even if I had wanted. Jonathan had paid me $360 a couple of weeks before, which covered the cost of the moving van and about a fifth of first month's rent on the storage space, but those bills were still mounting and would continue to mount until Jonathan finally received his first check from the hospital and repaid me.

The money, however, was not my primary concern that day. My main concern was getting Jonathan moved, getting him settled into what would be, it was hoped, a better life than the one he had been living for the past two and a half months, than the one he had been living, actually, since before I had met him. I hoped, too, that it would be a better life not only for him, but also for *us* as well.

We awoke and arose sometime around 7:00. I had slept throughout much of the night, although I was occasionally woken up by the rerun game shows from the 1970s that had played on the television throughout the night. I had forgotten that having the TV playing helped Jonathan sleep, and although it had the opposite effect on me, I didn't turn it off because I wanted him to get his rest. Today he would be moving to Mariah and I wanted him to have his strength.

We were scheduled to meet the movers at the storage unit sometime around 8:00. By the time we got dressed and checked out, it was past 7:30. We stopped at a mini-mart where I got some gas, then we drove to Art's, where Jonathan picked up his car. With him driving his car and me driving mine, we drove to the storage unit and waited for the movers to arrive.

That morning, the air was chilly, but the sky was sunny, which, psychologically, helped to offset the chill in the air. While we waited, I became hungry, so I walked to a nearby grocery store and bought a package of pastries for breakfast. By the time I returned, the movers had arrived. After Jonathan introduced me to the small group of men who would be moving his things, we set to work removing his belongings from the place they had patiently waited for the two and a half months it had taken Jonathan to rebuild his life and loading them into the van that would take them to the place that new life would begin.

This time, our primary activity consisted more of sorting than of loading, which we left to the professionals. During the process of sorting, Jonathan found a small watercolor painting that Dan had given to him while he was still living on Millstone Drive. He reacted with disgust and commented on how hideous it was. He asked me if I would throw it into the Dumpster, which, given how terribly Dan had treated him, I gladly did.

The movers took less than three hours to pack all of the things that Jonathan was planning to take with him to Mariah, the things that had taken us several days to pack in the September heat. He planned to leave some things behind that he wouldn't be using right away with the intention of retrieving them little by little at some later date. Before we left for Mariah, Jonathan treated the movers to a meal at a fast-food restaurant that lay across the street, then sometime around noon, we left for Jonathan's new home.

As we drove the distance that separated Paladin from Mariah, the weather slowly deteriorated. In Paladin, the sky had been sunny, but as we approached Mariah, the sun gradually became lost behind ever-thickening clouds. When we finally arrived, we discovered the city itself had virtually disappeared within a thick, smoky fog that gave the impression that illegal leaf burning had gotten out of hand. The fog was so thick that it reduced visibility to only a couple of blocks, which made the apartment seem walled off from the rest of the world. The veils of obscuration made it difficult, almost impossible, to discern what lay beyond. Although I wasn't as acquainted with the vagaries of the weather in the Mariah area as I was with them elsewhere in the state, I thought it was unusual to have such thick fog develop at that time of day. It was the only time that it happened in the time I spent in Mariah, which made me feel it was not an everyday event.

I didn't understand at the time how symbolic, how prophetic, the fog would become for the months that followed.

Over the next few hours, the movers efficiently removed Jonathan's belongings from the van and situated them according to his directions. I was relieved that now I was only supervising. Although most of his things ended up in the apartment, some of the larger items that were difficult to carry up the narrow stairs remained in the garage, including most of the furniture from the bedrooms. The sectional from the sunroom was deposited in the small room at the top of the stairs to form a "den," although the purple chair that Jonathan had favored at the house on Millstone Drive remained in storage. I assumed he would retrieve the rest of his stored things over the next few weeks and we could finally conclude our dealings with the storage facility, which had already cost me $700, before even more was added to the total.

Sometime before 5:00, the movers brought in the last of his belongings and prepared to leave. The cost for the move was $750, which Jonathan paid not by check, but in cash that was drawn from the same stash out of which he had paid me the $360. I didn't understand why he didn't pay by check when it would have been easier and safer. His behavior with money continued to perplex and concern me.

After the movers left, we continued to unpack and arrange Jonathan's things. After a while we decided to take a break and moved into the living room. We sat down on one of the sofas and briefly discussed the events of the day. Eventually, the conversation turned to Glenn.

By that point, Glenn had been missing for almost two months. Despite the fact that Jonathan had become somewhat resigned to the situation, he was still deeply preoccupied and affected by it. I thought I understood why—after all, they had been involved with each other in one way or another for 14 years—but apparently there was more to the story than I knew.

Jonathan said that he wanted me to understand why he was so concerned about finding Glenn. In essence, he told me that Glenn had no one else to take care of him and that he felt responsible for him even though they were no longer involved. He told me more about Glenn's family and how none of them cared about what happened to him. Up to then, I knew only a few scattered facts about Glenn's family, mainly that Glenn's mother, Jeanne, was divorced from Glenn's father and had recently gone back to her second husband, who Jonathan said was the vice president of an important manufacturer and from whom she had previously been separated. I also knew that Glenn's stepfather didn't like him and that his mother had sided with him and not her son in the incident that had precipitated Glenn's disappearance. Now I learned more than those basic facts.

Jonathan said that when Glenn was little, Jeanne had largely abandoned him, leaving him in the care of her mother, who severely abused him. Although he didn't describe the abuse in detail, Jonathan did say it consisted of constant beatings. He said that Glenn eventually became so afraid of his grandmother that he would sometimes wet himself when he heard her coming. In addition, he said that although Glenn had good relationships with his stepsiblings, Glenn's stepfather was cold toward him and didn't want him around. As she had before, Jeanne had apparently asserted her own interests over those of her son's and, in returning to her second husband, she was, in effect, abandoning Glenn all over again. There seemed to be no one left to care about Glenn, to take care of him, except for Jonathan.

In addition, Jonathan told me more about Glenn's previous disappearances, something about which I also knew little. Jonathan stated that on two occasions before they had broken up, Glenn had disappeared for two or three days before reappearing. Jonathan said he wasn't sure where Glenn had gone or what he had done, since Glenn had never said, but he thought Glenn might have gone on what Jonathan described as a "sex binge." I wasn't sure how serious Jonathan was about that, but what Glenn was doing in the present seemed to be qualitatively different from what he had done in the past.

In spite of these new facts, I still didn't understand what was driving Glenn's behavior. He was obviously troubled, but I didn't know how to conceptualize it further. I knew that he had beaten Jonathan up at least twice—that was why they had broken up—and I knew that although Laura had claimed Jonathan had told the members of the Group that Glenn was schizophrenic, Jonathan had claimed he had actually described Glenn's behavior toward him as schizophrenic-*like*—an important distinction—because it had differed so radically from his normal behavior. Jonathan also didn't mention that Glenn exhibited other symptoms associated with schizophrenia: hallucinations, delusions, highly disordered thoughts, or anything else that would indicate Glenn's mind and behavior had deteriorated to a psychotic level. With the information I had available, I concluded that Glenn's background of abuse had failed to provide him with normal coping skills and that his characteristic reaction to overwhelming stress was to flee. I still didn't know exactly what had triggered his most recent flight, although I suspected, knowing what I knew now, that it might not have taken much. Aside from being as consoling as possible, I didn't know what else to do, what else could be done.

By the time evening fell, the fog had grown almost impenetrably thick. Combined now with the darkness, the fog would have made it impossible for us to see our way around had we strayed outside the lighted parts of town. Because there was nothing in the apartment to eat and because Jonathan needed to buy some basic items for his new place, we felt compelled to venture out, confining our activities as closely as possible to the main roads in the middle of the town.

We ate dinner at the Golden Dragon, which was becoming our favorite local restaurant. Afterwards, we drove to Wal-Mart, where Jonathan bought sheets for the bed. Because his bedsheets were packed away—and because he had given Laura his prized Venetian bedsheets as a gift for letting him stay with her—he didn't have any sheets for his bed. He had originally wanted to go to Kmart to buy some Martha Stewart sheets, but since Mariah didn't have a Kmart, he decided to see what Wal-Mart had to offer. He said that he *loved* Martha, and although I thought she seemed cold and unfriendly, in contrast to the homey image she tried to convey, I could see how something in Jonathan might find her appealing.

After Jonathan found some sheets that he found acceptable, we returned to the apartment. After watching some television and generally relaxing after our action-packed day, Jonathan and I—and the girls—finally went to bed. It was the first time in two and a half months that we had all slept in the same bed. The bed was not the one in which he, and we, had slept while he had lived on Millstone Drive, but the Art Deco bed he had bought at the antiques store in Paladin the week before. It was the one he claimed had originally been priced at $185, but by flirting with—then kissing—the dealer, he had been able to buy for only $120. He had also asked me, in regard to his behavior, if that made him a "slut." That night, however, I didn't think about the events surrounding his purchase of the bed and focused not only on the beauty of the headboard, which was richly decorated with lots of intricately inlaid wood, but also on making the bed so we could get some much-needed sleep.

Sunday morning, Jonathan decided to call his parents. Although I didn't eavesdrop on the conversation, I was close enough to the phone when he called to hear the first few lines of the exchange. After calling the number and waiting for several seconds, a woman with a high-pitched voice said "Hello?"

"Mother?" Jonathan asked.

"Jonathan? Where are you?" the woman said, not only with the R-sound missing from the word "are," but also with a tone of surprise.

Jonathan told her that he was in Mariah, and at that point, I wandered downstairs to give him some privacy.

I felt relieved and thrilled that Jonathan would finally again have the privacy, the peace, that he hadn't enjoyed in ten weeks. Although there was a downstairs apartment, it had, according to Jonathan, just become vacant. Even so, Jonathan had managed to speak to the former tenant before he had left, a conversation that had proven to be very interesting. The tenant, whose name was Jim, was a police officer and, coincidentally, was also gay. He commented on how dismal gay life in Mariah was, which was part of why he was moving. Jim did know other gay men in Mariah as well as the surrounding small towns, but his network of gay friends was scattered and diffuse, something that was typical of the social networks of gay men in rural and quasi-rural settings. Jonathan, as far as I knew, didn't try to forge a friendship with Jim, who simply seemed to disappear. Despite the loss of a potential gay friend in Mariah, Jonathan would, at the least, not have to contend with the noisiness or nosiness of downstairs neighbors.

After spending the remainder of the afternoon getting Jonathan more settled in, I left Mariah around 6:30. Two and a half hours later, I arrived in Hawthorn. As I approached my home, I looked at the odometer and saw that I had driven exactly 150 miles. One hundred fifty miles. I longed for the days when I had driven only half that. Mentally, I began to prepare myself for the prospect of making 300-mile round trips for God-only-knew how long. Would I be able to do it? If Jonathan and I remained together, and Mariah was going to be his new home, I had no choice.

After resting a while, I called Jonathan around 9:30 to let him know that I'd arrived safely. We spoke for only a few minutes then said our goodnights. I was exhausted and needed to go to work early the next morning, and so did he. The next day would be the first day that Jonathan would be fully living and working in Mariah. I hoped for the best, hoped the experience would give him what he needed but hadn't yet been able to find. I hoped it was the beginning of a new life for him *and* for us.

—19—
THANKSGIVING

I don't see how we can continue our relationship.

Over the next few days, Jonathan started to settle into his new life in Mariah and I started to settle into a new, and hopefully improved, version of our relationship. For almost three months, our relationship had suffered the stresses of dislocation, separation, and suspicion. Those forces had almost torn it apart. Almost. Somehow, our relationship had endured and, despite whatever damage the months and the events of those months had done, I hoped that now, we could begin anew.

Jonathan, however, did not take the same view. Apart from how the events of the previous three months had affected his attitude toward us, another event that happened shortly after he moved to Mariah enflamed the issue of whether or not he wanted to continue his relationship with me.

Thanksgiving.

That year, Thanksgiving fell on the 22nd. Before we could discuss it, Jonathan had already received invitations from others to have Thanksgiving with them. One of these people was Hope, a woman who worked at the storage facility and whom he had seen the day of the move. I didn't witness the incident, which took place when he was inside the storage unit office and I was outside, but when he came out, he was shaking his head. When asked why, he told me what had happened and was astonished that she had invited a total stranger to Thanksgiving dinner. He wondered, though, if she was interested in him and that was what had provoked her offer. He appreciated her invitation, but since he didn't know her, he had declined. She, however, wasn't the only one who invited.

On Tuesday, the 20th, he sent me an e-mail in which he told me that Chase's parents had also invited him to Thanksgiving dinner. Until then, I had learned very little about Chase's parents, Warren and Joanne Tomlinson, but Jonathan began filling in the missing details. Warren was some type of business executive, although Jonathan never specified what he did and I didn't ask. Joanne was a healthcare worker at one of the hospitals in Paladin, although Jonathan didn't specify which one; presumably, though, it wasn't the one where Jonathan had met Chase. He had met them in August, when they had invited him to come to their home to hear Chase play, although I assumed that invitation hadn't extended to having sex with their son. They seemed to lead a comfortable middle-class life, having a spacious, accommodating house and plenty of money. Although Jonathan had had little to do with Chase and nothing to do with his parents in the three months of his dislocation, now that he was finally becoming settled, those relationships in some way for some reason seemed to be picking up where they had left off.

Before Jonathan told me that he had received the invitation to spend Thanksgiving with the Tomlinsons, we had not discussed Thanksgiving because I had been so focused on more immediate and important concerns—like helping him move to Mariah and reestablish something approaching a normal life—that Thanksgiving hadn't even crossed my mind. In addition, I assumed that for someone who was British, Thanksgiving wouldn't have the same meaning that it did for an American. Because of my living situation, it would be impossible, at least very difficult, for him to spend Thanksgiving with me, especially with his dogs. Without having discussed the matter with me at all, though, Jonathan informed me that he had decided to accept the Tomlinsons' invitation.

I found the prospect of him spending time with the Tomlinsons—with *Chase*—upsetting. I remembered, could not forget, what had happened the *last* time he had gone to Chase's.

In response, I explained why I couldn't invite him to spend Thanksgiving with my family and me. I also got right to the point and begged him not to let a situation like the one that had happened before happen again.

In response, he seemed irritated. He told me that Joanne's offer had been "sweetly presented" and that she had described him as "a stranger in a strange land" to whom she and her family were offering their hospitality. The implication was there as well that *I* was *not*. He also said that Chase's parents were going to be right there the entire time and that he was not going to be sneaking around hopping in beds behind their backs. The issue seemed settled in his mind, but I felt that we needed to discuss it in person, not through the computer.

The next day, I called him at the hospital around 12:15. After telling me that he had resumed his treatments and was already feeling better and discussing how he was settling into his new life in Mariah in general, we got down to discussing Thanksgiving—and Chase. He explained how every year the Tomlinsons had a big feast, spent the day watching football and engaging in other festive activities, and had plenty of room for him and the dogs. They were just trying to do something good for him, which he appreciated, so he had accepted.

Then, the conversation moved into a related, but much more serious issue: the feasibility of continuing our relationship. Jonathan didn't think it would be possible for us to keep on seeing each other now that he lived 150 miles away. He tried to "console" me by assuring me that there must be other gay men in Hawthorn I could see. I couldn't believe how casual he was in dismissing half a year of blood, sweat, and tears, primarily mine. For someone who had accused me of "not fighting for what's important"—something that my behavior in our relationship had thoroughly belied—*he* was the one who no longer appeared to care.

By the time I got off the phone around 1:00, I was deeply depressed. Although the separation of the previous three months had not changed my commitment substantially, it had apparently changed his. From the beginning, Jonathan had complained about the problems inherent in long-distance relationships and not being able to be together on a regular basis, and although I agreed that separation did have a tendency to weaken a relationship, the need to be together was apparently less crucial for me than it was for him. I also knew that the events of the previous three months had taken a serious toll on him, physically and emotionally, and perhaps that, too, had affected his attitude.

But, despite his feelings, I myself had already questioned how feasible it would be for me to make the trip to Mariah on a regular basis. It had been difficult enough for me to make the hour-and-a-half trip to Jonathan's home in Paladin, let alone a trip that involved twice the distance and twice the time. I felt that everything I had worked so hard to keep together was now falling apart and my ability to keep it together had almost slipped away.

That afternoon, I went to school to complete some paperwork. I was grateful that I was able to work in solitude because, upset as I was, I doubted my ability to maintain my composure before others.

The next day was Thanksgiving. On the day when everyone is expected to eat until they become as stuffed as the turkey, I had no appetite. Although I tried to focus on the festivities, I found that I could focus only on what might be happening at the Tomlinsons'.

Jonathan and Chase hadn't seen each other since the middle of August, and while Jonathan and I had endured a tumultuous three months, for which he partly blamed me, he and Chase had enjoyed a period during which nothing unpleasant had happened between them, if only because *nothing* had happened between them. In explaining why he had slept with Chase, Jonathan had said that Chase was stress free and available, something that, by implication, I was not. I did not want the events of August 8 to repeat themselves and was afraid they might.

On Saturday, the 24th, I returned to Mariah. The apartment was still crammed with unpacked boxes and Jonathan appeared to have made little progress. Of course, he'd been busy with work…and with Thanksgiving at the Tomlinsons'.

Saturday evening, we were standing in the kitchen talking. Among other things, we discussed his stay with the Tomlinsons. In the process, Jonathan spoke of Chase as if he were once again someone whom he was considering an involvement with, an issue I thought had died along with his life on Millstone Drive.

"I didn't think you considered Chase to be a potential boyfriend," I said. Then, asking him outright, I said, "Or *do* you?"

With that, we went into the den and sat down. I don't remember the conversation in detail, but I do remember the gist of it. Jonathan told me that over the past couple of months, I seemed to have developed a "cynicism" and a "harshness," that he found dismaying. He told me that Chase, in spite of being "immature" and "bratty," was also kind and caring. He seemed almost disappointed in me. He said that everything that had happened in the past three months had changed him, had changed things, including things between us. He suggested that we see other people and see what happened from there, although it seemed to me that he had made up his mind that other people were *all* he wanted to see.

After hearing everything he had to say, not just for that night but for days, I'd had enough. I just wanted to leave, to get away from him and his thoughtlessness, but by that point it was dark, and the 150 miles of gloom that lay between me and home seemed like too great an obstacle to overcome in my state. Later, we went to bed, but I was too agitated to sleep. Sometime in the middle of the night, I got up and went into the den, where I sat alone for a time in the dark. Finally, around 3:30, I decided that I *was* going to leave even if it *was* in the middle of the night. I thought that instead of driving all the way back to Hawthorn, I could drive to Paladin where I could get a motel room for the rest of the night, then complete the trip home the next day. All I knew was that I didn't want to stay *there*.

Given his attitude, I didn't feel Jonathan deserved the politeness of a good-bye. Quietly, in the darkness, I started getting dressed and packing up my things. Jonathan would wake up to find me gone.

Unfortunately, Jonathan, who tended to be a light sleeper, woke up. He asked me what I was doing and I told him I was leaving. He asked me why and I told him, in so many words, that I wasn't going to stay somewhere that I wasn't wanted. I told him that if he preferred Chase over me, then he could have him. I kept on packing.

Jonathan then told me that if I felt our relationship was important, then I should stay and talk about it, fight for it, instead of running away. He insisted that he didn't want to sleep with Chase and hadn't made any decisions about what he wanted to do. Although I wasn't happy about his vagueness, about his implicit assumption that *I* was the one who should do the fighting, I stopped packing and tried to listen.

Despite the fact that earlier in the evening he had enumerated Chase's strengths and my flaws, Jonathan now enumerated my strengths and affirmed that of everyone he had encountered in the past several months, I was the only constant, the only true source of help. That softened me somewhat and, after finally venting and calming down, I decided to stay.

I left the next afternoon, in time to avoid having to drive in the dark. As I left, Jonathan reiterated the theme that had emerged during the last few days, telling me that he couldn't make any promises about the future of our relationship and that we would "just have to see." Exhausted and depressed, I left.

Although that was what *he* wanted, that was not what *I* wanted. I was not yet willing to throw away almost half a year of effort, of suffering and sacrifice. In spite of Jonathan's accusation that I didn't fight for what was important, I thought our relationship, damaged though it was, *was* worth fighting for.

I wondered if I hadn't been clear enough about why I thought we shouldn't see other people. I felt that seeing other people would confuse rather than clarify the issue of whether or not we really wanted to be with each other. At our ages, I didn't know why we needed to be "playing the field" to figure out what we did and didn't want in a partner when we should have already done that. I decided to discuss the matter further with him, to make certain he understood what I wanted and why I wanted it.

Because I was preoccupied with teaching on Monday, I decided to wait until Tuesday to raise the issue with him. Tuesday morning, I sent him an e-mail in which I told him there was something I wanted to discuss with him and to give me a call.

I was not expecting his response.

—20—
REVERSAL OF FORTUNE

I…wish we could spend all our time together.

Jonathan replied to my message almost at once. In his message, he told me he couldn't call me because his phone wasn't working properly and he was waiting for someone from the phone company to come and service it. That, however, was minor compared to what he told me next.

In the sentence that followed, he announced, "I am probably not staying in Mariah." He went on to explain that after a Monday full of meetings, he had lost a "huge huge political battle." He said that his boss had reversed his formerly progressive position and had decided to maintain the status quo. Jonathan said that continuing with the job appeared to be "too much aggr[a]vation" and that he was hoping to be able to move back to Art's and decide what to do from there. He said that he had been too upset to write to me the night before and was "so so so distressed." He ended the message by telling me we would have to e-mail until the phone was fixed.

When I finished reading his message, I wanted to scream. Once again, my needs had, albeit unintentionally, been swept aside by yet *another* of Jonathan's seemingly endless crises. Apparently, my needs would have to be addressed at another time, if at all. My frustration was compounded by the fact that, from the wording of his e-mail, Jonathan seemed to be through with the hospital not because he had been fired, but simply because, in his words, continuing with the project would be too "aggravating." He had had the job for only a month and wasn't even going to fight, to try. After all the trouble that he—and *we*—had gone through to settle him in Mariah and begin to put his—and, hopefully, *our*—life back on track, he was abandoning it all for what appeared to be capricious reasons. *So much for the idea of fighting for what's important*, as Jonathan had claimed that I did not do. I was aggravated myself, beyond measure. Indeed, I wrote an e-mail to my sister immediately afterwards telling her what had happened and describing Jonathan as "that fucking Brit."

Before I could respond, I got another e-mail from Jonathan, this one even more pleading. In it, he begged me to write to him as soon as I could and stated that he had learned the phone company wouldn't be able to service his phone until the next day, leaving him without a direct way to contact anyone. He said that he wasn't handling what had happened very well, saying that he had been certain that the job in Mariah would be ideal, but now, everything had "blown up in [his] face." Distraught and confused, he said that he didn't know what he was going to do next.

Even so, I contained my frustration and tried to be sympathetic. In response, I tried to calm him down and assure him that we would figure something out. It seemed to work, but I had no idea what to tell him beyond that because I was overwhelmed in my own way by this unexpected turn of events. At that point, I had barely begun to process what had happened, what it meant, and was at an utter loss.

That evening I had to teach in Viridian. Once I arrived, I sent Jonathan an e-mail letting him know that I had arrived "safely." The term "safe" appeared to have clarified a feeling that Jonathan had been experiencing, but had been having difficulty defining. When I checked my e-mail before leaving work, I found that Jonathan had written me a message in which he said that he didn't feel "safe." He also said that he missed his family, with an implication being that he felt unable to turn to them now for support because he couldn't bring himself to tell them what had happened, how he had failed.

Unable to help him directly, I did the best I could from half a state away. I told him to do whatever he could to keep from feeling isolated and becoming too focused on his darker thoughts. I didn't know what else I could do. I went to bed that night and, somehow, managed to sleep.

Wednesday morning around 9:00, Jonathan sent me an e-mail in which he said that he wasn't doing well and asked me if I could e-mail him as soon as possible. I did, asking him if he had some way to instant-message. He wrote back, saying no, then wrote again a few minutes later asking if we could meet. I suggested that perhaps we could meet somewhere between Hawthorn and Mariah.

When I asked him what he thought, he wrote back, saying that he didn't know then begging me to tell him what to do. He said he couldn't think straight and needed help. He ended the abrupt message with a desperate "please."

Before I could begin a reply, he sent me another e-mail only one minute later in which he told me he was having "some disturbing thoughts." He said he was "sort of unraveling" and begged me again to tell him what to do.

I didn't know what *I* should do. I tried my best to calm him down, however, and dashed off a supportive message that I sent within minutes of receiving his. It seemed to work. Minutes later he replied, repeating that he didn't know what to do and telling me that his nerves had been on edge as it was, but since he hadn't slept or eaten, his anxiety had only grown worse. Again, he repeated that he didn't know what to do next, that he was in the middle of nowhere, where he didn't know anyone and it was difficult to get anything done. He said that he was feeling better and, after thanking me for everything I had done to try to help him, he told me that I had been "as solid as a rock" since he'd known me and that he hadn't fully appreciated it until now. With that comment, I felt that I had made some kind of breakthrough in his attitude toward me.

After he had calmed down, he wrote back later and asked me what I had wanted to talk to him about. He must have assumed the worst because he concluded his message by saying, "[t]hings can only get so bad and then it stops." At first, I had decided not to raise the issue of our relationship, given what had just happened, but since he had asked, I decided in the end to address it. Under the circumstances, though, I decided not to be as "direct" as I had originally intended to be, choosing instead to send him a gentler, if equally firm, message about what I did and did not want for us.

A while later, I received his response. He said that he thought I saw the issue more clearly than he did and that the *real* reason he had suggested we see other people involved something that had happened—or *not* happened—when he had been with Chase. He said that, although he had been presented with "several easy opportunities" to reenflame his relationship with Chase, he had found that he couldn't do it because he had started "feeling a commitment even though one hadn't been made." He said that feeling had made him nervous and that perhaps by seeing other people, we might be better able to decide if we really wanted to spend our lives together. He said that although his life had been more fluid over the previous months, mine had been more solid and that he didn't want to uproot me from my life until we were absolutely certain. He said that he "miss[ed me] and wish[ed] we could spend all our time together," even asking me about job opportunities in Hawthorn. I felt that the real issues had finally been addressed, that I had finally gotten what I thought was best.

On some level, though, I was suspicious of his sudden change of heart about us. The day before he loses his job, he is telling me that he wants to see other people, then the day after he loses his job—only *two days* later—he is telling me that he wants us to be together all the time and that, although he'd had plenty of opportunities to rekindle his involvement with Chase, he hadn't been able to do it because he'd felt a commitment to me even though we hadn't formally made one. I didn't know if the experience of losing his job and having everything collapse on him had simply shaken him up enough to put things in perspective for him or if he merely felt the need to cling onto someone convenient and I just happened to be there. I liked to think it was the former, but the timing seemed suspicious, and it made me feel cautious. Consequently, I thought it prudent to keep some kind of distance, not necessarily physical but practical and emotional, and see how things materialized once the shock wore off.

Thursday morning, I made arrangements to miss class on Friday so I could go to Mariah that day and stay for the next several days. After doing some packing, I left Hawthorn sometime around 1:00. I drove to Mariah, not knowing what I would find when I arrived. It had been three days since Jonathan had lost his job, and the e-mails I had received throughout that time had drawn a picture of someone who was deeply depressed, physically deteriorated, increasingly agoraphobic, and fleetingly suicidal. I was not looking forward to what awaited me, but I needed to see him for myself, help him myself

When I arrived, Jonathan was seated in the den watching television. The girls, which had been curled up next to him before I'd arrived, went into their usual frenzy when I knocked, but settled down once Jonathan opened the door and they saw who I was. After I entered and Jonathan closed the door, we hugged. He looked depressed, but seemed functional. He did have something of an odor, indicating that he hadn't bathed in a while. It wasn't offensive, but it was indicative of his mental state.

After getting settled, he repeated and expanded on the events of the previous week. Apparently, his boss had decided not to implement the changes that he had hired Jonathan to make, having decided instead to maintain the status quo. Although Mariah wasn't a small town, it seemed to have a small-town mentality that didn't accept change and that mentality had ultimately swayed his boss. Since his boss had decided to keep things the way they were, Jonathan's services were no longer required. Therefore, he hadn't quit in frustration, as I had originally believed, but had been let go. Jonathan said, however, that he had gotten the impression that some of the people at the hospital didn't like him because he was British and suspected, but couldn't prove, that their dislike of foreigners had somehow figured into his firing. Although he didn't mention it, I wondered if they knew he was gay and, if so, if that had played a part as well. In any event, after Jonathan had gone to all the trouble he had to get the job and move to Mariah, after all the hope the job had held out for restoring his health, his life, everything had been pulled out from underneath him. In some strange way, his situation mirrored my own two years before. I could empathize, fully, with what he was experiencing.

I asked him if he had told his parents what had happened. He said that he hadn't and, although he knew he was going to have to do it eventually, he was afraid of how they would react. They already thought he had messed up his life enough during the past few months and the latest turn of events would only be the *coup de grâce*, the final blow that would confirm for them that Jonathan was incapable of managing his life.

When things had gone wrong for me in Paladin, at least I'd had my family to lean on. He didn't have his, for more reasons than one. I felt more than ever that I needed to be family for him.

Jonathan told me that he hadn't changed his clothes for three days. I suggested that he would feel better if he took a bath, but he resisted, saying that he didn't feel like "getting all wet." Although I felt he needed to take care of his hygiene, I also knew what it felt like to be depressed and how something as simple, and usually pleasurable, as bathing could be uncomfortable.

The surroundings were as depressing as Jonathan was depressed. The apartment was in shambles. Although the movers had arranged the main pieces of furniture and Jonathan had organized some of what remained, the process of setting up the household had progressed only partway before the events of the past week had brought it to a screeching halt. Several large boxes partially blocked the short hallway that led to the back rooms and the living room had turned into an unofficial storage room. The bedroom was strewn with Jonathan's clothes, including a giant mound of ties that were piled up on my side of the bed—refuse, it seemed, from an aborted career. Most poignant of all, Jonathan had set up a child's toy rocking chair near his side of the bed and seated in it was what appeared to be a stuffed toy moose wearing a hunting cap and a kilt. I had never seen it before, but I felt he was trying to comfort himself with reminders of a simpler childhood. Indeed, Jonathan seemed to have become somehow childlike, reminding me of a five-year-old who had lost his mommy in a shopping mall and didn't know what to do.

I wasn't much of a cook, but I felt that Jonathan, in spite of his stomach problems and general loss of appetite, needed to eat. So, I went to the local Wal-Mart and bought a good frozen pizza, garlic bread, and pasta salad. To round out the Italian-theme meal, I thought I would buy spumoni for dessert, but finding none, I settled for mocha almond fudge. Apparently, that was, unbeknownst to me, one of Jonathan's favorite flavors of ice cream and I was pleased that I had, albeit inadvertently, chosen that "comfort food."

The comfort it provided, however, was short lived. That weekend, Jonathan informed me of another complication—one that, if not resolved, would rip our relationship apart. Jonathan reminded me that he had been granted permission to come to and live in the United States specifically because he had obtained a position here. Therefore, he was in the United States not on a residence visa, which did not require him to work, but on a *work* visa, which *did* if he expected to stay here. Having never lived or worked in another country, I knew very little about the particularities of visas, but Jonathan explained that if he became unemployed, he had 30 days from his last day on the job to find other employment or be in violation of the Immigration and Naturalization Service's (INS) policies. In other words, if he didn't find another job by the end of the year, he would be deported.

Further complicating the situation was that, according to him, it couldn't be just any job, but a job that required special skills that were especially desirable but difficult to find among the native and naturalized residents of the United States. A job as a COO of an information technology company would qualify; a job as a hamburger flipper would not. Because the former were far less prevalent than the latter, finding a job would be that much more difficult. And, the 30-day clock was ticking, more loudly with each passing moment. If Jonathan didn't find another job within the grace period and was deported, it would, under those conditions, be highly unlikely that he would be able to return to the States for some time to come.

One solution to the problem would be to fully resume his position at OutSource, but because he felt he no longer had the physical ability or the mental acuity to perform such a demanding and unrelenting job, he felt that was not a viable option. Another, but less certain, solution involved his disability. Jonathan was receiving short-term disability, which, he informed me, would cease at the end of the year, but he had been considering applying for long-term disability, which would last indefinitely. Jonathan told me that if he applied for long-term disability and it was awarded before the grace period expired, that would freeze his visa status, since the ruling would indicate that he had a legitimate reason for not working. In that case, he might be able to have his visa amended so that he could remain here for "humanitarian" reasons, specifically, so he could receive medical treatment for his condition. But, the insurance company would have to approve his claim before the grace period expired, and neither having the claim approved nor having it approved before the deadline was certain. It would be a race against time with no certainty that it was even possible to win.

On top of everything else, that was the weekend of Glenn's birthday. By that point, it had been almost two months since he'd called Laura's in October and no one was any closer to finding out what had happened to him than they had been two months before.

I returned home late Sunday afternoon. I had missed class on Friday and didn't want to miss it again on Monday. I felt that I had done all I could do, which was more than anyone else seemed to be doing. I was very reluctant to leave Jonathan alone, but I had no choice.

Before I left, Jonathan hugged me and, with tears in his eyes, told me there was something he needed to say. He told me that I was a "very good man" and that he loved me, which was not something he often said. He told me that I was "the most compassionate person [he'd] ever met, apart from Marcus," which I found extraordinarily flattering, since I knew how much Marcus had meant to him.

In addition, Jonathan kept telling me not to worry about him because he had a "plan." I didn't know what that plan was.

I waited in my car for several long minutes before I left, worried about what would happen once I did. Jonathan didn't seem suicidal, but he was decidedly emotional, and I didn't know what he might do once he was alone again with his tormenting thoughts.

I arrived home sometime around 8:00. I was exhausted, not only from the drive, but also from the events of the past several days. In addition, I hadn't slept well at Jonathan's, which only added to my exhaustion. In spite of everything that was happening, I looked forward to putting everything aside and getting a good night's rest.

That, however, was not what happened.

As soon as I got home, I called him to let him know that I'd arrived home safely. We talked for only three minutes and when we concluded, he thanked me somewhat formally for the call. He sounded fine in spite of the state in which I'd left him and I tried to relax after my draining weekend.

Later that evening, I checked my e-mail to see if Jonathan had written. When I did, what I found was tantamount to a suicide note. He didn't explicitly state that he was thinking about killing himself, but the implication was there. In the message, Jonathan told me that he was a "burden" and enumerated his faults, telling me that I was "so good to [him] in spite of [his] arrogance and bad temper." His message ended by telling me that I had a "wonderful future ahead of [me]" and that I should "be of good cheer." I was left feeling upset and desperate by the finality the message implied, by my inability to do anything directly.

I replied, telling him not to do what he was thinking about doing and assuring him that he was not a "burden." I told him that he had enhanced my life, not detracted from it, and that I was a better person for having known him. I told him not to do what he was thinking because of what it would do to me. I started thinking about calling the police in Mariah if the situation got too far out of hand.

His second message was more subdued than the first. He was still in a self-pitying mode, stating that he felt that he didn't have what he used to have and, therefore, felt like a burden. In response, I restated my opinion that he *wasn't* a burden and that I was a better person because of him. I didn't know what else to say, to do. I went to bed, wondering what I would find upon awakening.

The next morning, I woke up to find that Jonathan had not killed himself during the night. In checking my e-mail, I discovered that he had sent me a message in which he thanked me for staying in touch but also told me that he was "already having a hard time" without my presence. He said that he'd called the hospital and left a message for his former boss, which he was following up with an e-mail. He complained that he hadn't slept much the night before and had a sore throat. Later that evening, he wrote to tell me that after having trouble getting warm enough throughout most of the day, he finally had after putting three duvets on the bed. He said he had tried to drink some ginger ale but was having trouble swallowing because of his throat.

I wrote back, telling him that although part of how he felt was probably psychosomatic, part of it was probably physical. I implored him to return to the hospital and resume his treatments, but he insisted that he didn't want to "ever go there again." I understood his feelings, but I was worried about what the lack of medical attention was doing to him. I tried to drawn his thoughts away from ones of self-destruction and toward ones of self-preservation.

Over the next couple of days, Jonathan continued to complain about not being able to sleep, not having an appetite, and being constantly cold in spite of the unseasonably warm weather. Although it was the beginning of December, the daytime highs were ranging between the mid-50s and mid-60s, and I was still seeing insects that should have disappeared weeks before. I suggested he was cold because he wasn't eating and urged him to get a prescription for

Compazine, an anti-nausea drug he'd taken before. He told me, surprisingly enough, that he wasn't nauseated; he simply had no appetite. He had, however, tried to eat some coconut patties that someone he knew from the Southern state had sent to him, which proved to be a mistake. He said they had tasted good, but had made him "barf" because they were too rich. For the most part, he seemed to be subsisting on ginger ale, then when that ran out, Coke. At least he was staying hydrated, if not nourished.

On Tuesday, the 4th, Jonathan wrote to tell me that he had finally heard from his original doctor, who had to examine him and review his records before he could make a determination about Jonathan's condition. Jonathan said he needed him because he was "the one the insurance company [had] listened to in the first place." I hoped that now that he would be seeing this crucial doctor, it wouldn't be long before Jonathan was awarded the long-term disability he needed for more reasons than one.

Later that night, I went to Viridian to teach. Before I left, I e-mailed him to remind him that I would be home by my usual time of 10:00. When I failed to e-mail him after I'd returned, I got an e-mail from him at 11:00 telling me he was worried that he hadn't heard from me. I wrote him back, assuring him I was all right. Earlier that day, he had thanked me for my constant messages, saying that they "really ke[pt him] going at this point." I seemed to be his only lifeline, even if that line was stretched 150 miles thin.

On Wednesday, the 5th, Jonathan e-mailed me begging me to please come back soon. He said he was "frightened and not feeling well." He apologized for the inconvenience, saying that he knew I would have to make a long trip, and for being "so much bother," but he was desperate to have me with him. I told him I could come back on Friday, the 7th and stay through Sunday, the 9th at which point I would have to return to Hawthorn to teach. I told him that after teaching on Monday and Tuesday of the next week, I could return on Wednesday, the 12th and, by canceling my class in Hawthorn on Friday, the 14th I could stay until Sunday, the 16th. I didn't like the idea of canceling the same class for the second time in two weeks, but I felt torn between my responsibility to my class and my responsibility to Jonathan and Jonathan seemed more important.

Later that day, Jonathan finally ventured out after more than a week of seclusion. He told me, though, that he was "hiding" in the apartment and had no intention of going out again until I got there on Friday. To add to his troubles, Jonathan told me that he'd gone to Wal-Mart that day to return an unneeded item he'd recently purchased there, but for some reason they wouldn't accept it. He had been counting somewhat on the reclaimed money, little though it was, but even that was denied to him. In addition, the dogs were being "very barky" and Jonathan said that he "just want[ed] to strangle them."

On top of it all, he had received an e-mail from Laura stating that Chuck's father wouldn't help Chuck with his truck payments and they were hinting that Jonathan should. He said that in spite of the fact that Laura was a "leech," he feared that he might have to go back to her, since, apart from Art's, he had nowhere else to go. I couldn't image what life would be like for Jonathan if he *did* move back to Laura's. That, to me, was worse than being trapped in Mariah.

Later still, Jonathan wrote to tell me that earlier that day, the phone had rung but he hadn't answered it. He wondered if it was me, which it wasn't. He was afraid that it was actually his parents, whom he was still avoiding. He said they "[had] a habit of calling [him] at work during the week because of the time difference" and if they had, he was sure they'd been told he was no longer there. He said that he was "just not up to dealing with them on any level." When I suggested that *I* call him, he said he didn't want to talk on the phone. He said that "there [was] just tomorrow then [I'd] be [t]here Friday night" and assured me that he could "hold on til then." I hoped he could.

On the morning of Thursday, the 6th, he told me that he hadn't fallen asleep until 6:00 in the morning and at 9:30 had just gotten up. He described himself as a "nervey wreck" and said that "[e]very little noise spook[ed him]." He said he "[did] not plan on moving from [the apartment] today" and appeared to have gone back into his agoraphobic mode.

Later that day, he received what he described as a "snotty" e-mail from Chuck, wanting money. "If they only knew," he remarked. I told him what I thought Chuck could do to himself. Why should Chuck's behavior be any surprise, though, I thought, with people like Laura for role models? Otherwise, he said, everything was "status quo," although he was "[j]ust very nervous."

Later still, Jonathan wrote to me to tell me that he had finally heard back from the hospital. The news wasn't good. He told me that the hospital had informed him that because they had spent more transferring his visa than he had earned in the month he had worked there, they were going to apply his wages, which he had not yet received, to the cost of the visa. He said that depending on the difference between the two, the hospital would either reimburse him or bill him for the remainder. He said that it hadn't been in his contract to reimburse them for his visa, so he didn't believe it was legal for them to do what they were planning. He said that he had c-mailed a friend who had worked with him at TekNetium who had told him she knew it was illegal in the Southern state, but wasn't sure about my state. He said that even if it was illegal, it would still take the hospital "forever" to pay. The hospital had also informed him that they had notified the INS the day he had lost his job that he was no longer employed there, which meant that "the clock [was] now ticking." Needless to say, Jonathan was very upset.

I wasn't surprised by the news, but I was concerned. What was Jonathan going to do? The clock *was* ticking and time was running out rapidly. Although Jonathan was hardly a threat to national security, the government's attitude toward foreigners appeared to have changed since September 11 and the government seemed to be finding any and every excuse to deport whatever foreigners they could. At least that was Jonathan's impression. If the situation unfolded as Jonathan predicted, then the New Year might be one without Jonathan in it.

Jonathan also told me that he'd received what he described as a "rather cryptic" e-mail from his father, which made him believe that his father knew something wasn't right. If Jonathan's pattern of communication with his parents had changed, then that would eventually lead them to suspect that something was wrong. He knew he needed to tell his family what had happened, but he was still afraid of their reaction. He said that his father "might help, but he could also let [him] drown." As for his siblings, he said that his brothers and sisters "[would] help [him] to come home but not to stay here." In other words, they would help him, but only on *their* terms.

My feeling was that Jonathan needed to tell his parents what had happened as soon as possible. My reasoning was that if they proved sympathetic and decided to help him, then he would receive their help, if they decided to provide it, sooner rather than later. If they proved unsympathetic, however, and decided not to help him, then at least he would be no worse off than he was now and nothing would, in the end, really change. I felt that he had nothing to lose and possibly something to gain by coming clean. Jonathan still resisted, however, saying that his father could give him "all kinds of hell" that he preferred to avoid, which was why he didn't want to tell him what had happened until the related issues were resolved or he was forced to do it. He told me he hoped I understood. I *did* understand, but I also still thought that he was just postponing the inevitable.

As the weekend approached, Jonathan grew increasingly nervous. He began to fear that I wouldn't return. On Wednesday, he had implored me to "please come back soon," and on Thursday, he had asked me what time I might be arriving the next day. He said that he didn't want to be "peeping all day and catastrophizing about [me] not showing up" and guessed that he was "in full neurotic mode." He was. On Friday morning, he wrote to tell me that he had woken up after only two hours of sleep feeling "very anxious" and added that he would be "very happy to see [me] today, more even then usual." I had originally planned to leave for Mariah around 11:30, which would have put me at Jonathan's around 2:00. When I got delayed and wrote to tell him that I wouldn't be arriving until later, he wrote back thanking me for letting him know and telling me that he was "neurotic enough without wondering if [I was] having car problems, had [had] an accident, [had] changed [my] mind and [was] not coming." Then he added, "[a]nd those are just off the top of my head." I hoped that my presence would do something to temper his anxieties.

Before I left, my mother decided to give Jonathan $100. Although my mother was still working full time and was receiving Social Security, she netted only about $16,000 a year, so that was a considerable sacrifice for her. Still, my mother had always been "generous to a fault" and routinely gave family, friends, and even strangers money and possessions, sometimes to her financial detriment. Even so, I had observed her model throughout my life and emulated it because I believed there was a purpose greater than the obvious for doing it, which was part of why I continued to help Jonathan financially in spite of the effects. I was uncomfortable with her helping Jonathan, however, when Jonathan was *my* responsibility and *I* was the one who was supposed to help him. Even so, I respected her wishes to help him and took him her money.

After I arrived and settled in—or, rather, hunkered down—for my second post-disaster weekend in Mariah, Jonathan and I got caught up on recent events. Among other matters, Jonathan told me he was scheduled to see the doctor in Paladin on Monday for more tests. So many doctors seemed to be involved in his case that I wasn't sure which one it was. I was concerned about him driving to Paladin by himself in his "wonky" car, as he described it, which hadn't been properly repaired in September and was backfiring. Unfortunately, he didn't have the money to have it fixed. And, unfortunately, I couldn't take him because I had to work on Monday.

He also told me that his prized Blue Willow china, some of which he had used as a child and which, therefore, gave him a sense of security and connection to home, had come up missing. He couldn't understand what had happened to it and neither could I. We had stored it at the storage unit during the move in September and it had, as far as we knew, remained there. We reviewed the possibilities, realizing that the only time something could have happened to it would have been during the move in September. The main possibility was that someone had stolen it, either someone who saw it sitting out, unattended, at some point during the move, or... *I* certainly hadn't taken it, which left only Greg and Laura. I couldn't imagine Greg taking it and, despite my feelings toward Laura, I couldn't imagine her taking it, either. The most likely explanation was that the movers had simply left it behind in the move to Mariah. Jonathan planned to check the storage unit when he went to Paladin.

Before I left on Sunday, Jonathan took some time to write my mother a thank-you note for the money she'd given to him. He let me read it, wanting to know if it was "all right." I wasn't sure what he thought might be wrong with it or why it might be inappropriate. I assumed it was another example of his uncertainty about how to deal with Americans. The note was actually more than all right. In it, he thanked my mother for her generosity and commented that he now understood where I had gotten mine. He also described our relationship as "special and close." I was reluctant to leave, but given my need to hold my own life together even as Jonathan's had fallen apart, I was forced to go. Jonathan was again alone.

When I finally got home, I e-mailed Jonathan to tell him that I'd arrived safely. In response he told me that he was "kind of weepy" but that he always was after I left. He thanked me for arranging to come that weekend and, touchingly, told me that he'd had a good day that day because of me. I was happy to know that my presence had made a difference, but I was unhappy that I couldn't do more. I was only one person, though, and it was impossible to be in two places at once, live two lives at once. To maintain my relationship with Jonathan, to help him maintain his well-being, I would have to return to a pattern similar to the one I had sustained during his tenure on Millstone Drive, but with double the distance and more than double the duress.

■

Through the events of the preceding two weeks, the balance of power in our relationship had discernibly shifted. Until he had lost his job, Jonathan had always seemed to be the more dominant one in our relationship and I didn't take charge of things or assert myself as much as he did. Now, that had changed. Now, *I* was the dominant one, the one who took care of things, got things done, took care of *him*.

■

On the afternoon of Monday, the 10th, Jonathan sent me an e-mail in which he updated me on the events of the day. He said that he had just gotten back from Paladin, where he'd gone for tests. He reported that he hadn't gone to the storage unit to see if his china was actually there, as we'd discussed, because he was too exhausted. He said he would try to go sometime that week.

More significant, though, was that Jonathan had received a letter from Glenn's mother, Jeanne. She reported that Glenn was not on the Caribbean island where she lived and he had last been seen. She thought, however, that he might have gone to the Southern state where he and Jonathan had previously lived, but since she hadn't heard from him, she really didn't know where he was. From what little she did seem to know, the last time that anyone had seen him, he was very sick and wasn't sleeping or eating. Apparently unwilling to do anything herself, Jeanne had begged Jonathan to find him. Jonathan was distraught and frantically trying to figure out what to do.

He ended his message by begging me to come to Mariah on Tuesday night after class. He said that between what was happening to him and what now seemed to be happening to Glenn, he was beside himself.

I tried my best to comfort him by telling him that even though the situation seemed desperate, it did sound as if Glenn was in fact still alive. I wondered, though, how Jeanne knew he was no longer on the island? Why did she think he had gone to the Southern state?

In response, Jonathan stated that no one had seen or heard from Glenn for seven weeks, so there was really no proof that he was in the States or even still alive. He said that the situation was "breaking [his] heart if it [could] be broken anymore then it [was]." He then informed me that he had received an e-mail from Cliff, which had served to upset him even more. He told me he was looking forward to seeing me the next day but pleaded with me to write before then. He ended the message by saying that he was "bathed in tears."

I was overwhelmed by everything myself. I couldn't imagine how Jonathan must have felt. His misery seemed to be compounding exponentially, like interest on some kind of karmic bank account. Cliff's timing was perfect, as usual. I myself was beyond sick of hearing about Cliff and Jonathan's masochistic relationship with him, which had now endured for half a year, but I didn't tell Jonathan how I felt. Instead, I did what I always did, which was to take Jonathan's side and express my disapproval of Cliff's selfishness, his seeming lack of awareness of anyone's feelings but his own.

Around 6:00 that evening, Jonathan replied. He began with an update on Glenn before moving on to Cliff. Jonathan told me that he had written to friends in England, who had told him that Glenn was definitely not there as of Monday. Apparently, Glenn was receiving payments of £650—roughly $1,000 US—at the beginning of each month, which were direct-deposited into his account in England; since he could access those funds worldwide, he had money available to him—at least $2,000 from November and December that had so far gone untouched—if only he thought to access it. He said that he had passed the information on to the private investigator who was searching for Glenn but had not yet received a reply.

The monthly payments to which Jonathan referred came, he explained, from a small trust fund that Glenn's stepfather had established for him. I thought the amount he received was also a measure of his stepfather's feelings toward him. One thousand dollars was a minuscule amount for the vice president of a major manufacturer. Although it was something, it was, in fact, nothing. Even so, it was something, but even if Glenn realized the money had been deposited, I doubted that, in his condition, he would be able to make good use of it. I didn't know what to suggest.

As far as Cliff was concerned, Jonathan said simply that he was who he was. He said it was difficult knowing he was so close but he couldn't see him. That knowledge, he feared, could be the last straw that might send him "over the edge." He almost seemed to excuse Cliff's selfish behavior by expressing the opinion that we were *all* self-centered, but that Cliff was simply more obvious about it. He told me he knew I would understand, but he still loved Cliff even if he had been forced to give him up. He said that Cliff was in the same category that Glenn was. Jonathan might have given them up physically, but emotionally, they were all too present.

Throughout that evening, Jonathan sent me several more e-mails in which he expressed various thoughts about the Glenn situation as they occurred to him. For instance, he wondered why, if Glenn had come to the United States, he hadn't come to my state to find him. He pointed out that Glenn had Laura's number, so he could have contacted him through her, even if he didn't know exactly where Jonathan was living. He feared that Glenn "could as easily be dead as in any location." He concluded by saying he was "flummoxed."

In response, I pointed out that although Glenn may have been thinking about *calling* Jonathan, he may not necessarily have been thinking about *coming* to him, even if he had come back to the United States. After all, the former was much easier to do than the latter, and if Glenn wasn't well, which apparently he wasn't, then the prospect of coming all the way to my state might have seemed too daunting. My state was, after all, hundreds of miles farther away from the Caribbean Islands than the Southern state was. I also pointed out that Glenn might have thought that if he did come to my state, he might not be able to find Jonathan. I tried to reassure him by telling him that there were a number of possibilities that didn't involve something bad.

I was still curious to know why Glenn's mother thought Glenn might have gone to the Southern state. Where had she gotten that information? Also, why would Glenn have gone there when he no longer lived there? Instinct? Indeed, if Glenn didn't have access to money, how could he have even gotten there? I wondered if it was simply wishful thinking on her part.

In response, Jonathan said that Jeanne had told him that people on the street had told her they had seen Glenn wandering around and he had told them that he was going to the Southern state to find Jonathan. He said that if Glenn was looking for him, though, he knew he was now in my state. Jonathan was overwhelmed by the latest twists in the Glenn situation, but felt powerless to do anything about it.

I planned to return to Mariah on Tuesday, the 11th. I was planning to do it anyway, but after the news about Glenn and Jonathan's pleading, my presence seemed especially crucial. That night was the last night of my Tuesday class before finals week the next week. I didn't have much material left to cover, so I decided to dismiss my class around 7:00. Afterwards, I would head for Mariah, arriving sometime around 9:30.

I woke up that morning feeling queasy. Since I didn't have to leave until 5:00 that afternoon, I remained in bed much of the morning. Jonathan wrote to tell me about his own morning, saying that he'd woken up after only three hours of sleep. He said he was "very nervous," predominately, it seemed, because of Glenn. He said that Jeanne's version of events differed from Glenn's, so he didn't know what had really happened. Feeling overwhelmed, he said he was going to hide out in his apartment until I got there later that night.

Later that morning, Jonathan wrote to tell me that his doctor in Paladin had just e-mailed him wanting him to go to Winford, a nearby larger city, for an EKG. He said he would be leaving around 11:00 that morning and returning later that afternoon. As if I needed an explanation, he added that it was "part of the insurance thing." He wrote again that afternoon to report that he was back and that the drive had been nice, but his only comment about the procedure was that it had been "no big deal."

As the day had progressed, I had started feeling better. That was good because I had a long evening ahead of me.

I made the shorter trip to work then, after dismissing my class around 7:00, I made the much longer trip to Mariah. The Christmas music playing on the radio was my only companion as I drove mile after mile through the darkness. I arrived sometime between 9:30 and 10:00, not too far off schedule.

I had arranged to miss my class on Friday, the 14th. Because I had to cover the same amount of material in my Friday class that I'd had to cover in my Tuesday class, which was very little, I felt justified in simply leaving study guides for my students. Consequently, I felt less guilty than I might otherwise have for canceling the class twice in two weeks. By missing Friday, that left me free to stay in Mariah from Tuesday night through Sunday evening, when I would have to return in time for finals, which I would be giving on Monday and Tuesday.

While I was there, I saw an envelope sitting on the kitchen counter which, on closer inspection, proved to be the letter from Jeanne. The return address was in a town in the Caribbean Islands. I might have asked Jonathan if I could read it, but I felt that I had gotten the basic point from him and that whatever I could glean from the letter would probably add very little.

The five days that I stayed in Mariah were fairly nondescript. I recall spending much of my time grading the 50 term papers I had received the week before and planned to return the week to come. Although Jonathan and I certainly spent some of our time discussing his situation and possible solutions, we also spent a considerable amount of time taking care of the basic necessities of life and actually trying to enjoy ourselves a little in spite of, or perhaps because of, everything that was happening. Overall, Jonathan seemed to be improving, overcoming the initial shock of what had happened to him and adapting somewhat to his new reality.

My impression proved to be short lived. On Monday, the 17th, Jonathan received an e-mail from Art, who informed him that he had gotten a new boarder. Jonathan described him as a "pot head friend of the guy who live[d] up stairs." Jonathan was upset about the turn of events for two reasons. First, he had left several of his most valuable possessions there—the portrait of his mother, the Tiffany chandelier, the Cubist painting—and he was afraid of what might happen to them with such questionable people around. Second, since Art had gotten another boarder, there was no longer room for Jonathan. Returning to Art's, which had been the least unattractive possibility, was no longer an option. The loss of his job, his entrapment in Mariah, his loss of Glenn—everything was conspiring to raise his level of desperation to an all-time high. He suggested that the best thing for him to do might be to return home, a suggestion that selfishly I resisted.

In response to my suggestion that his situation could still improve, he told me that he felt immobilized, isolated, and alone. He reminded me that while I had my family, he was totally alone with no prospect for change. He explained that he wasn't unloading on me as much as he was trying to make me understand the extremity of his situation. He said that his situation couldn't continue forever and even the door to going back to Art's, which had been open, was now closed.

I didn't know what was going to happen next.

—21—
X-MAS

This is the worst holiday of my life.

As Christmas approached, Jonathan made little mention of the holiday. Whenever he did, though, his opinion seemed to be that because his life had become so miserable, so much the opposite of merry, he had no desire to celebrate Christmas, even to think about it. At one point, he told me that he didn't want to exchange presents, since he didn't have the money to buy gifts and would feel obligated to give me something if I gave him something. More philosophically, however, Jonathan took the position that Christmas was for families, and explicitly told me that even though he couldn't celebrate it with his, there was no reason that I shouldn't celebrate it with mine.

Even so, I wanted to incorporate him into some version of festivities. Because it would be impossible to have him spend the holiday with me because of accommodations, as it had been at Thanksgiving, I had half-thought that I would go to Mariah and spend Christmas with him there. Otherwise, because of his seeming desire to forget the holiday and because of my preoccupation with my end-of-the-semester work, I didn't seriously raise the issue of what to do for Christmas until he raised it for me.

On Thursday, the 20th, Jonathan wrote me a lengthy message in which he expressed how he felt about the fact that I hadn't invited him to spend Christmas with me. He began by enumerating everything that I had done for him, the extraordinary lengths to which I had gone to help him when no one else was doing anything for him. He even included my mother in his praise, expressing his amazement at her generosity and her desire to help him when no member of his family had or would. Then, he got to the point. He said that although we had been seeing each other for more than six months, he had feelings for me "beyond the norm," and he believed I did for him as well, this was now the second major holiday that I had left him alone. He said he understood that I didn't have a space of my own and that Hawthorn was far away, but this Christmas was "the worst holiday of [his] life." He was sick, broke, and isolated, and this was the first Christmas that he had ever spent on his own. He said that although we hadn't discussed him and the holiday, I knew his circumstances and he was hurt that I would leave him alone. He said that *he* would never do that to someone he loved.

He then admitted that what had provoked his message was prodding not only from Colin, but also—and more significantly—from Chase and his family, who had invited him to spend Christmas with them. Apparently, they had invited him the week before, but he had declined. Because he felt committed to me, he didn't feel comfortable going there, especially since it would involve spending the holiday with Chase. Although Chase knew that Jonathan was committed to me, Chase and his family still cared enough about him to try to include him in their Christmas festivities only a month after they had included him in their Thanksgiving ones. He reiterated that he cared about me and wouldn't expect me to include him in my family's celebrations at that point, but the fact that I had ignored the situation had hurt him a lot. He said that he wasn't saying what he had to make me feel guilty or to gain sympathy, but he did feel the need to get his feelings off his chest so they wouldn't fester and poison the progress of our relationship. He ended the message abruptly by telling me to stay warm.

I was stunned. I felt caught off guard by his sudden change of attitude and felt that it was yet another example of how he flip-flopped on so many issues, that yet again I was left with the feeling that I never knew where I stood with him, except perhaps on a constantly shifting expanse of emotional sand. Most galling of all, however, was the implication, despite his claims to the contrary, that I wasn't, that I hadn't been, doing enough for him when I had, in fact, done more for him, and put up with more out of him, in the previous several months than anyone else had. This was turning into another Thanksgiving, something I did not want to repeat.

In response, I vented my frustrations over his seeming lack of appreciation for everything I had done, over the implication that with their single invitation, their single act, the Tomlinsons had somehow done more for him than I had done for him in the previous six months. I reminded him that while the Tomlinsons had invited him to spend a day or two with them, they had otherwise ignored him. I, on the other hand, had been there for him every day, in whatever capacity I could be, even when it had sometimes seemed as if I was the only one who cared if we even stayed together. I reminded him that while Chase was comfortably and obliviously nestled away at school playing his piano, I had become emotionally and even physically sick from the unrelenting stress and worry that everything that had been happening to him in the previous several months had caused me. I reminded him that in the previous three months, I had put some 6,000 miles on my new car, roughly half of which had been from driving to Paladin and especially to Mariah to see him, to be there for him. I reminded him that I had rearranged my work schedule for him and informed him that, despite what I had led him to believe, I had gotten into a certain amount of trouble over it. I expressed my resentment at how the Tomlinsons' one little gesture at Thanksgiving had apparently been enough to call our entire relationship into question and how it seemed to be happening in some form all over again.

I told him he took me for granted. I told him that nothing I did ever seemed to be enough for him, that it seemed that unless I continued to offer up an endless supply of altruistic acts, then that invalidated everything I had done. One sin of omission, real or perceived, and everything started collapsing for him. I told him that sometimes I felt that I gave and gave and gave and it just went down a black hole. I told him that *I* needed something back from time to time, that *I* needed someone to take care of *me* from time to time— not my mother, not my sister, not my friends, but *him*. When was *my* turn? *I* counted for something, too, I told him. Because of everything I had done, was having to do, I was drained emotionally and physically, and needed someone to take care of *me* for a while— namely, *him*. I told him that perhaps because our relationship had grown up around the fact that the quality of his life had deteriorated so precipitously over the last few months and *I* had been the one doing everything for *him*, he had come to feel that it was right and natural when *I* was the one giving and *he* was the one receiving— which, I told him, it was *not*.

I asked him that as far as Christmas was concerned, why was it any more *my* place to invite him to *my* house than *his* place to invite me to *his*? I reminded him that only a month before, he had been enumerating my faults, as he perceived them, and telling me that he wanted to see other people, which had made me feel unimportant and unworthy. I told him that I was still recovering from that blow and that maybe I would feel flattered and touched to have *him* ask *me*, of all people, to spend Christmas with *him*. I told him that maybe it would make *me* feel important and special, make *me* feel that he really wanted me. I told him that if he actually wanted to have Christmas instead of turning it into a funeral, then I would gladly come and be with him. But I asked him, did he want me to? He may have mixed emotions about how I had addressed the issue of Christmas, I told him, but he had given me mixed signals, and he needed to be definite about what he wanted. I ended by telling him that it wasn't all my fault.

In response, he began by questioning his ability to express himself clearly, given the effects of his illness, and assured me that he *did* appreciate everything I had done. He said that he cared for me and knew that I cared for him. Under normal circumstances, he said, *he* was the one who would be taking care of *me*, which he had Glenn and to a lesser extent Marcus. The point, he clarified, was simply that we had never discussed the issue of Christmas, at least that he could remember. We had, but his memory for certain things seemed bad. He said that he didn't want to turn Christmas into a funeral, that he had loved Christmas his entire life, but that after Marcus had been killed, Christmas had become a difficult time. He reiterated the fact that this was the first time he had ever been alone at Christmas, burdened not only with the memory of Marcus's death, but also with all of the misfortunes that had befallen him in the past several months.

He said that Chase and his family were only trying to show him some compassion. There was, however, no contest or comparison between us: I had always come through for him no matter what. He said that after Thanksgiving, he had been anxious about the commitment we seemed to be approaching, which was why he had suggested that we see other people to make sure, for both our sakes, that we were doing the right thing. When I had become upset at the suggestion, he had immediately withdrawn it because he hadn't wanted, and didn't want, to lose me.

He said, though, that he didn't know how our relationship could progress if he couldn't tell me something that upset him without my overreacting. He reminded me that I had been prepared to leave at 4:00 in the morning when I had become upset over his suggestion that we see other people. He reminded me that sometimes you had to stand your ground and clear the air instead of letting things continue to bother you.

He concluded that I should spend Christmas with my family, stating his belief that Christmas was for families. After he repeated his sentiment that his illness and isolation were making his feelings of loneliness at Christmas especially acute, he repeated his assurance that he *did* understand and appreciate everything I had done for him, telling me that no matter what happened he couldn't forget any of it, and that it bothered him to no end that he couldn't do anything similar for me. He apologized for having upset me, but told me again that he thought it was better to tell me how he felt than to keep it to himself. He ended his message by telling me that he still loved me.

Softened somewhat by his seeming show of appreciation, I apologized for getting as upset as I had but told him that it did seem as if he were saying that I wasn't doing enough for him when I was doing more than anyone else was. I explained that the reason I had gotten so upset by his suggestion that we see other people was that he seemed to be conspiring with the people who had been making destructive decisions about our relationship, like Dan and Laura. I told him that I didn't want to lose him either and that when he had suggested we see others, I had felt that I had no power, that no one cared what I thought, that I didn't matter. It seemed as if all the hard work I had done to try to sustain things between us throughout an adverse time had come to nothing, that all my blood, sweat, and tears had been for naught. I told him that I kept racking my brain to come up with some kind of brilliant solution to his problems but that a solution kept eluding me. I admitted that I didn't know what to do for him. I told him I was afraid that in another month, he would be in England, having been forced to return, and I wouldn't be able to see him again. I told him I wasn't in the best condition either, both emotionally and physically, and it was intensifying my own need to be taken care of.

In response, he apologized for making such an issue over Christmas and suggested that it was just a surface issue related to more fundamental concerns. He said that he was all too aware of the INS deadline and that unless he got a job, he would be forced to go home, making it very difficult if not impossible to return under the circumstances. He reverted to his previous position that I should spend Christmas with my family and that he would be okay. He said he felt as if he had the flu and was tired, so he needed to go back to bed. He concluded by suggesting that we write the next day. I agreed. The exchange had left me exhausted and I was already exhausted enough.

On the morning of Friday, the 21st, Jonathan wrote to tell me about the intensified interest his family and friends had taken in his plans for Christmas. He said that he had received a number of e-mails from friends wondering where he was as well as one from his parents on Wednesday. He said he had called them on Thursday night instead of e-mailing them because he had "just wanted to hear something familiar." He said that his family was having Christmas in London that year instead of Eiseley, where they normally had it. He said that his parents had asked him how and what he was doing and in response he had lied, telling them he was all right and would be spending Christmas with some American friends in Paladin. He said that his mother had seemed especially sad that he wouldn't be home for Christmas, but he also said that he doubted with the crowd that would be there he would be missed.

Moving away from the issue of Christmas, Jonathan also mentioned that the night before, he'd had a dream about Glenn, who had come home wearing a shirt that he had given to him two years before. He said that he'd woken up with wet eyes, but tried to dismiss it by saying that "maybe it's just the flu." I wondered where Glenn really was, how he would be spending Christmas.

Later that afternoon I replied, telling him that I had several things I needed to do but that I couldn't find the energy to do them. I also repeated and expanded on why I hadn't addressed the issue of Christmas—my preoccupation with work, my belief that he wanted to avoid the issue—and what I might do to bridge the gap between spending Christmas with my family and spending it with him. I particular, I told him that in my family the activities were usually over by 3:00 in the afternoon and that perhaps I could come to Mariah later that day, allowing me to spend at least some of Christmas with him. That way I could spend Christmas with everyone. At the end, I mentioned Glenn, expressing my wish that he could be home for Christmas too.

Later that afternoon, Jonathan wrote to tell me about his wasted day in which he'd done nothing but spend the day in bed, getting up only to feed the dogs, check the computer, and throw up. The otherwise mundane message ended, however, on a thought-provoking note. Mentioning Stonehenge, which we were supposed to have visited during the trip to England, he said that today was the winter solstice and that the Druids had practiced human sacrifice there. Then he asked me, "Do you think that I've made enough sacrifices this year?" In response, I told him that I didn't think he'd sacrificed as much as he'd been sacrificed.

In his reply, Jonathan told me that Laura had e-mailed him, telling him that she wanted to come to Mariah to see him on Christmas Day. To my knowledge, Jonathan had never told Laura exactly where he was living, hoping to thwart the oppressive, if not obsessive, involvement in his life that he feared that knowledge would unleash. He also told me that Jack was still pitching to move in with him, something that he had steadfastly believed would cause more problems than it would solve. He mentioned that Jack had applied to the school at which I worked, although he didn't mention what he was planning to study. Although I worked there, I didn't plan to offer my help with admission, however, not only because I hadn't been asked, but also because they would do fine without me and I didn't want to be involved in their lives any more than Jonathan seemed to want to be. Jonathan mentioned that he was feeling a little dizzy and would probably go back to bed, where he'd been watching TV, after he finished his mailing.

The day before Christmas Eve, a storm front moved through the state, bringing snow, sleet, and freezing rain to much of the region. Although the snow provided most of the state with a white Christmas, it also made driving hazardous, especially in the vicinity of Mariah.

Around 10:30 in the morning on Christmas Eve, Jonathan wrote to tell me about the effects of the weather, but more importantly, about the effects that the weather, and the holiday, were having on him. He told me that the day was proving to be harder on him than he had anticipated. After mentioning the weather and the numerous accidents it had caused, he bemoaned the fact that he couldn't turn on the television without "the Christmas thing" being on "every bloody channel." He said the girls were keeping him company and, as usual, followed him wherever he went, so he never felt entirely alone. He berated himself, however, for not being able to cope with the day better than he could, commenting that he was supposed to be made of tougher stuff.

He mentioned that he had a craving for hot chocolate, so he thought he might walk to the local deli to get some if it wasn't too windy. He said that he had left his down jacket and gloves at Laura's, so he would layer sweaters under his leather jacket if he did go. I hoped that small pleasure would help to comfort him.

He concluded by imploring me to write, as if I wouldn't. He told me how isolated he felt and repeated how he wasn't doing as well as he'd hoped. He said that he couldn't handle the thought of my driving in icy weather, especially at Christmas, because of what had happened to Marcus. Trying to be humorous, he said that perhaps we should wait until the spring thaw for me to come to Mariah. He ended the message on a poignant note, saying that he had prayed for Glenn and hoped he was okay. Trying to keep a stiff upper lip, he told me he was going to stop being a "sad sack" and "get on with it."

In response, I told him that I suspected the next few days would be more difficult for him than he had expected. The holidays, I reminded him, had the effect of bringing out fairly intense emotions in people, whether positive or negative, and regardless of the mental preparation people made in advance, it usually wasn't until the time actually came that they really knew how they were going to react. Often they weren't prepared for those reactions. I told him that if a person had had a bad year, as he had had, then all the bad feelings he had accumulated throughout that time could end up imploding on him during the holidays, sometimes with considerable force. That, I explained, was why I wanted to come on Christmas Day because I knew it wasn't going to be an easy time for him and I wondered if he really realized just how difficult the day might actually be.

I told him that no amount of effort on his part was going to convince me that he was all right because I knew he wasn't. I told him that I would call him later that evening, if he was answering his phone, so I could see how he was doing and make more definite plans to come. Trying to be encouraging, I reminded him that the next few days would be over before he knew it and perhaps then he could begin to put them, and the whole awful year, behind him.

In response, he admitted more baldly that he wasn't doing well and couldn't pretend that he was. He said that he had gone out at one point, but with the wind chill in the single digits, it had been so bitterly cold that he had come back after walking only two blocks. He said he wished I was there but the conditions were too bad, in his opinion, for me to make the trip. He said that he was going "slightly crazy" by himself and wished he'd made a better plan about Christmas, one that involved being with other people. He concluded by assuring me that he would be all right, but I wasn't convinced.

Later that afternoon, he wrote to tell me of further trouble. He informed me that the heat in the office and the bedroom had gone out. Joan Vogel and her husband, who owned the house, were out of state until after the first of the year, but since it was Christmas Eve, no one was available to fix it anyway. He said, though, that he had a space heater and was using it to heat the office. He said the den was warm, so he and the girls were spending most of their time there, watching TV. Although it was a minor inconvenience on a list of major problems, his situation seemed to intensify its impact.

As seemed to happen every Christmas Eve, I was rushing around at the last minute trying to finish my Christmas shopping. Consequently, I wasn't able to read Jonathan's messages until later that afternoon. When I read that his heat had gone out, I wrote to him and offered to bring up one of my space heaters when I came. I wanted to reassure him that I *was* coming, despite his belief that I wasn't or shouldn't. The temperature had dropped from the upper 40s the day before down to the upper 20s, but even though the wind had picked up and it was flurrying, the conditions were far from treacherous. I wished that day that either Jonathan was with me or I was with him, but it wasn't possible. I felt sad and somehow guilty that he was alone that night of all nights. I told him I would call him later that evening to see how he was doing. It had been a while since

I'd heard the sound of his voice. I missed him a lot, that day even more than normal.

In response, he said that he would move the space heater from the office to the bedroom later, indicating that he would manage. More poignant, however, he repeated that he had never been alone on Christmas before, let alone in a foreign country. I didn't plan to let him be alone for any more of Christmas than I had to.

After taking some things to my sister's later that evening, I returned home around 9:00 and called Jonathan a little before 9:30. We spoke for about twenty minutes, and in that time, he encapsulated all of the problems and feelings that the events of the past month in general and the holiday in particular had presented and provoked. At one point, he broke down a little, then regained his composure. I tried my best to console him from 150 miles away and although he had insisted that I spend Christmas with my family, I still felt guilty that I was here and he was there.

Later that night, he wrote and apologized for having gotten emotional, telling me, though, that "when you are alone so much and have so many things staring you in the face it becomes hard to gloss over all of the issues one is trying to deal with." I wasn't sure how to help, what to do.

A little after midnight, I e-mailed Jonathan to be the first person, at least on this side of the Atlantic, to wish him a Merry Christmas. I went to bed sometime around 2:00, knowing that the next day would be full, not only with festive activities, but also with ambivalent feelings about being with my family in Hawthorn when Jonathan was alone in Mariah.

The next morning, I didn't wake up until after 10:00. I discovered that we'd received a light dusting of snow during the night, but it was already starting to evaporate. In checking my e-mail, I found that Jonathan had responded to my Christmas wish that I'd sent him the night before, wishing me and my family "*Happy* Christmas"—the standard British greeting—as well. He said his bedroom had been a little chilly that morning but the rest of the apartment was tolerable. Apart from the Christmas wish, there was no mention of anything that might indicate it was Christmas.

I replied, and later that morning he wrote, telling me that the apartment was warming up and that he planned to stay inside and watch TV. He concluded by telling me to enjoy my holiday. I tried, despite the circumstances.

Around 2:00 that afternoon, my mother and I went to my sister's, where we celebrated Christmas. Although I tried to focus on the festivities, I frequently checked my e-mail to find out if I'd received messages from Jonathan. My body was in Hawthorn, but for the most part, my mind was in Mariah.

The first time I checked, I found that Jonathan had sent me a message in which he was more obviously morose, similar in tone to the ones he had sent to me the day before. He told me he had tried to call his parents but couldn't get an international line, so he'd resorted to sending them an e-mail. He said it was evening in England and they were having Christmas dinner, which was why he had tried to call when he had. "Oh well," he concluded forlornly.

He told me that he had been flipping through channels on TV when he had come across the video for the song "God Gave Me Everything" by Mick Jagger. He commented that the next line was, "then He took it all away," which it wasn't, leaving me to wonder what he had actually heard or seen, but it certainly said something about his state of mind. In any event, he said he thought he would adopt it as his personal theme song.

He told me he had a bad headache and was planning to lie down. Worse, he admitted that he had been "on the verge of tears all day," saying that Christmas used to be fun, which now it wasn't, and mentioned that Boxing Day, the day that Marcus had suffered the accident for which he felt he was partly to blame, was "looming." He concluded by saying that he would get through it the best that he could and thanked me for my family's and my kindness. I hoped it would help to sustain him until I could get to him.

We didn't stay very long because my mother wanted to visit one of her sisters, who was spending Christmas in the hospital. "What a way to spend Christmas," I told Jonathan. With my aunt's and Jonathan's health problems on my mind, I quipped that "Crappy Christmases seem[ed] to be going around, like the flu."

Later that afternoon, Jonathan wrote to tell me that his day had been "like the rest." He said again that he had been "weepy" throughout the day, attributing it more to thoughts of Marcus than to being alone on Christmas. He also attributed it to thoughts of Glenn, wondering if "he [was] even alive and [knew] that it [was] Christmas." He described his unhappy thoughts as "ghosts coming back to haunt." He said that if there was any good news, the heat had suddenly started working again. He also said that his father had responded to his e-mail, asking Jonathan if he wanted him to hold on to his presents or send them to him. Jonathan said that he felt like telling his father to give them to Oxfam, which he described as the British version of Goodwill, since he felt there was little chance that he would ever see them, let alone use them. Otherwise, he said he had been watching a chronological cut of *The Godfather*, something he described as "the highlight of [his] day." He concluded by saying it was turning icy again, a comment I felt reflected his thoughts about Marcus.

I replied, trying to be as comforting as possible. In response, he sent me a message that was even more despondent than the previous one. He began by saying that the evening was proving to be harder than the day had been. He said that he'd had a "crying jag," but that instead of feeling better, he felt worse. He said there were "so many cars on [the street in front of the apartment] and we"—he and the dogs—"could hear all the people going into the houses," which made him feel even more isolated. He said he didn't mind solitude but repeated that he had never been alone on Christmas before and "[didn't] like it very much." He said he should have gone to Laura's or Chase's or "anywhere" to avoid being alone. He said that he hated not knowing anyone in Mariah and that the people at the hospital had "dropped" him as soon as the project was canceled. He said he didn't know where to go to meet people, since he wasn't a bar person, but didn't want to spend his time hanging around at straight bars and wasn't supposed to drink with his heart condition anyway. Eventually he said he knew he was rambling and needed to lie down since, as he put it, "[c]rying makes one very tired." He concluded with Scarlett O'Hara's famous line from *Gone with the Wind* that "Tomorrow is another day," but added that "in this case a worse one." After reading the e-mail, I knew that I needed to call him.

Around 9:15 that night, I called. Even if his e-mails throughout the day hadn't mentioned it, I still would have known that Christmas had been a difficult day for him, that he had spent the day feeling isolated, excluded, and depressed. Although I had done what I could to convince him that I wasn't excluding him, and had by that time decided that I was going to go to Mariah the next day and spend as much of the rest of my vacation with him as I could, I still thought I needed to reinforce my concern about and commitment to him by speaking to him directly. We talked for about half an hour, during which time Jonathan broke down more than once. I told him not only that I was planning to come to Mariah the next day and stay as long as I could, but also that I had been formulating a plan that would allow him to begin to put the pieces of his shattered life back together. I hoped that not only my words, but also my actions, would comfort and encourage him. Jonathan had said that the next day would be worse, but I was determined to do what I could to make it better.

The next morning he wrote to tell me that after tossing and turning all night in spite of having been exhausted, he had finally gotten out of bed "out of boredom." He said that the apartment had stayed warm throughout the night, which was good, but that at 7:30

in the morning, it was still dark. He concluded by apologizing for being so emotional when we'd talked but said that "[his] nerves were shot."

I wrote him back, telling him that I was still planning to come. He wrote back to ask me if I was sure, warning me that it was cold and icy out, but I assured him that the conditions weren't as bad as he feared and that I *was* coming. I had no intentions of repeating the Boxing Day disaster of 15 years before, but I was also not going to leave him alone. I prepared to leave for Mariah and to remain there, with him, as long as I could.

—22—
Unusual Jonathan
I think I'm in trouble.

The day after Christmas—or Boxing Day in England—proved to be cold, but clear. The sun was shining brightly, if ineffectively, and the driving conditions proved ideal for making the 150-mile trek to Mariah. I didn't know how long I might be gone, but I was prepared to be gone as long as Jonathan needed me, possibly until the end of my winter break almost three weeks away.

The night before, I had formulated a plan to help Jonathan not only in the short term, but also in the long term. The plan was as specific and detailed as I could possibly make it, given that I had wanted to have a workable plan completed before I went to Mariah the next day.

We would begin by making certain that Jonathan's most immediate needs were met. The day I arrived, we would buy whatever groceries and get whatever other items he needed. In addition, we would clean the apartment. After losing his job at the hospital, Jonathan had retreated into his apartment, venturing outside as little as possible. That included going outside even to take the dogs into the yard to "make," which meant that they had resorted to "making" in the unused areas of the apartment, especially the living room. Jonathan seemed too depressed or overwhelmed or indifferent to make much effort to clean the apartment and didn't seem that troubled by the state into which it frequently fell. I, however, was, especially by what the dogs did. I tried to clean up the messes they made as often as I could, but an absence of only a few days would undo any progress I had made. Since I had been away longer than usual, I knew the situation would be worse than usual by the time I returned.

In addition, Jonathan preferred to keep the temperature in the apartment as warm as possible, since he seemed to have difficulty staying warm. An unfortunate side effect of this practice, however, was to intensify the stale odor in the apartment. Because it was winter, it was difficult to open windows to air the place out. Since Jonathan spent virtually all of his time inside, he had become acclimated to it, but I had not. Therefore, one of my principal immediate tasks would be to get the living room as clean as possible.

That same week, we would make a trip to Paladin to retrieve Jonathan's belongings that he had left at Art's. While we were there, we would also go to the storage unit, not only to check on the condition of the items he had left there, but also to see if he had, by chance, left his missing china in the unit. After taking care of these more important matters, we would then go to the stylist who had given Jonathan the buzz cut in late July, since he had done such an excellent job and since Jonathan hadn't had a haircut in weeks.

I also thought that while we were in the Paladin area, we would drive to St. Alban to retrieve the items he had left at Laura's. These included his winter jacket, gloves, and other clothes as well as the printer for his computer. Retrieving Jonathan's things from Art's and Laura's was a part of a larger plan to recollect all the items he had deposited in the different places he had lived throughout the fall and, therefore, not only have everything back in his possession for its own sake, but also more symbolically begin to regain some semblance of order in the chaos that had ravaged Jonathan's life.

I also planned to make a concerted effort to persuade—implore, pressure, even beg—Jonathan to resume his medical treatments at the hospital. From what I understood, Jonathan still had medical coverage that would pay for his treatments, as well as any other medical expenses, in full, so the issue of how to pay for his medical needs did not appear to be an issue. In spite of how the hospital had treated him, and his resulting—and understandable—desire never to return there, I felt that he was being incredibly foolish not to resume some kind of treatment for his condition when he lived within walking distance of a hospital and apparently had no difficulty funding such treatment. The only halfway viable alternatives were in Paladin and Winford, the closest an hour's drive from Mariah. Given that if he were going to resume his treatments in earnest, he would require treatment on an almost daily basis and, given that his only mode of transportation, when I wasn't available to drive him, was his "wonky" car, going elsewhere wasn't feasible. In my opinion, the only thing that was preventing him from returning to the hospital was his stubborn pride, a quality that, under the circumstances, was literally killing him. He did not have a cold, after all, and to go without some kind of medical treatment to arrest the progression of a disease that was slowly, and irreparably, damaging his heart was foolish in the extreme.

In the meantime, I continued to urge him to go to the doctor to get a prescription for Compazine, something he had failed to do. In addition, I thought he should get a prescription for some type of antidepressant. I realized that an antidepressant wasn't going to solve his problems, but it might at least put him into a better frame of mind so he could deal with them more effectively.

Once these matters were addressed, we would then turn our attention to solving the longer-term problems of restoring Jonathan's cash flow and resettling him in Paladin. Jonathan still wanted to sell *Still Life*, a plan that had gotten put on hold because of the preoccupying events of the previous several months, and I thought that now we should proceed with trying to sell it. He had told me that the painting had been appraised—conservatively—at $750,000, and after the auction house had deducted their standard commission of 20% and the federal government had collected an additional 50%, that would leave him with around $225,000, enough money to live on comfortably for several years. This would also obviate the need to work for money and allow him to concentrate fully on regaining and maintaining his health, insofar as that was possible. Jonathan told me that he could enter *Still Life* into the spring auction at one of the major auction houses, which would take place sometime around the middle of February. After the sale was made final, he would collect the profits sometime around the end of February or the beginning of March.

That, however, was still two months away. In the meantime, we would have to find a more immediate, and more certain, source of income. In discussing the possibility of selling some of his art or antiques, Jonathan had raised the possibility of selling his two signed lithographs by the American artist. Jonathan had told me that the larger of the two had been appraised at $15,000, while the smaller of the two had been appraised at $2,000. If he sold both of them for the prices at which they had been appraised, he would, after commissions and taxes, net around $5,000. Unlike *Still Life*, which needed to be entered into one of the major auctions, the lithographs could be entered into one of the weekly ones. In other words, they could be entered at any time and the money from their sale would be available almost immediately. Five thousand dollars would be more than enough money to allow him to pay his rent, get his car fixed, and pay his other bills until *Still Life* sold two months later. My opinion was the sooner, the better, so I decided that, if possible, we should go to the auction house, which was located in a major city in a nearby state, sometime during the next week to have the lithographs entered.

Then there was the messy issue of Jonathan's visa. That was one aspect of Jonathan's situation over which I had absolutely no control. It was a toss-up whether the insurance company or the INS would have its way first—and there was no guarantee that the insurance company would rule in his favor. Consequently, there seemed to be only one sure alternative: Warren.

Several days before, Warren had offered to put Jonathan on his payroll, even though he couldn't pay him a salary, because in doing so, that would at least give the appearance to the INS that Jonathan was employed. Doing this was obviously a risky venture because if Jonathan and Warren were caught, Warren would be fined and Jonathan would be deported. If he were deported, Jonathan would not be eligible to return to the United States for at least ten years. Although I wasn't in favor of the idea for lots of reasons—not the least of which was the fact that Jonathan would then become further enmeshed in what he had described as a "very sticky web" in which Chase was, indirectly, one of the threads—desperate times called for desperate measures. Filled with reservations and reluctance, I told Jonathan that if he hadn't heard anything from the insurance company by the week of January 14—the week the INS deadline arrived—he should proceed with Warren's plan. In spite of the complications, at least then he could remain in the United States and try to rebuild his life here without having to return home in defeat and without tearing our relationship apart.

Once *Still Life* sold and Jonathan received the money, he could then proceed with his plan to leave Mariah and return to Paladin. In the meantime, he, or we, would look for a house in Paladin. I would encourage him—strongly—to put the money into some type of account where he would have unfettered access to it and thereby avoid running out of available funds again, which was the primary reason he had gotten trapped in Mariah. Once he had resettled in Paladin, he would pay off the lease on the apartment in Mariah as well as his expenses from the September move, which basically meant repaying me. In addition, he could resume his medical treatments in Paladin and possibly hire someone to look after him at home until I could see my way clear to move in with him and look after him myself.

That was my plan.

This is how things really went:

After helping Jonathan take care of some smaller problems at home that he had apparently been unable to remedy himself, we went to Wal-Mart to buy a hose for the washer. In the six weeks that he had lived in Mariah, Jonathan had been unable to wash his clothes because the washer hose, which had been stored in his washer during the move from Millstone Drive, had disappeared. In addition, Jonathan didn't know what type of hose he needed or how to hook it up himself. Although Jonathan had "more clothes than anyone I know," as he said Cliff had once remarked, and could go for months before he was forced to wash, he couldn't go forever. Since he refused to go to the laundromat, saying that he was "past that," getting the washer into working order seemed crucial.

As expected, I discovered that Jonathan had made no effort to clean up after the dogs in the week and a half that I'd been away. After only six weeks the living room carpet was officially destroyed, reminding me of the one in the house on Millstone Drive by the time he had moved. I spent at least half an hour cleaning up the piles of feces that the dogs had deposited on it. Curious to know how many piles there were, I started counting them, but in the end, I never got an exact count, since I stopped at 90.

On Friday, we drove to Paladin to retrieve Jonathan's things from Art's. We had intended to go the day before, but Jonathan had said he didn't feel up to it. Ever since Jonathan had learned that Art's latest boarder was a "pot head," Jonathan had feared that his expensive belongings would be either damaged or sold for drug money. I didn't know how realistic those concerns were, but I appreciated Jonathan's nervousness. In addition, I knew that *Still Life* would be crucial to the realization of the plan to restore Jonathan's life, so I was anxious myself to see it reclaimed.

We left Jonathan's around 12:30 and arrived at Art's around 2:00. We went when Art was at work, which is how Jonathan preferred it. I didn't understand why Jonathan wanted to avoid Art when there didn't seem to be anything wrong between them, but I didn't question it because it didn't seem important. Jonathan still had the house key that Art had given to him, so Art didn't have to be home to let us inside. When we went upstairs to the room where Jonathan's things were stored, we found that everything he had left was present and intact, which was a great relief. Over the next half-hour, we carefully removed the paintings and the chandelier and delicately packed them into my car. The paintings were carefully maneuvered into my back seat, while the chandelier was wrapped inside my long wool coat and nestled in my trunk. I had already brought some of Jonathan's lesser things with me from home, where I had been tending them since he had left Paladin the first time, and now my new car reminded me of the way my old car had looked the fateful day that Jonathan had said farewell to the house on Millstone Drive. After Jonathan made sure he had removed everything that was his, he left his keys on the kitchen table and we left.

I asked Jonathan if he wanted to get his hair cut, but he declined. In addition, I asked him if he wanted to go to the storage unit to see if his china had, in fact, been left there, but he declined to do that as well. Most important of all, I asked him if he wanted to go to Laura's to retrieve his belongings he had left there, but he declined to do that. I understood why he didn't want to deal with Laura, but I still felt that he needed to reclaim his things and be done with her once and for all. Instead, we simply stopped in Paladin for lunch before heading back to Mariah.

Even so, I felt that we had already made substantial progress in only two days. I hoped we would be able to accomplish something even greater next week, namely, taking the paintings to the auction house, where they could be appraised and entered into an auction.

Unfortunately, that didn't happen. Because of various circumstances, but mainly because of Jonathan's lack of motivation to pursue the matter while I was there, we never took the paintings to the auction house.

In the end, I spent more than two weeks in Mariah. For the most part, my stay was uneventful and stultifying. In a semi-rural city like Mariah, there was little to do that was stimulating, and the nearest cities where there might be were at least an hour away. Our outside activities mainly consisted of forays to Wal-Mart and the grocery store to buy food for ourselves and the dogs and occasionally going out to eat at one of the limited selection of local restaurants. We also visited the one antiques shop in the city as well as a thrift store run by one of the local churches.

Our indoor activities mainly consisted of watching endless hours of television, primarily the shows that Jonathan favored. These included British comedies, such as *Keeping Up Appearances* and *Are You Being Served?*, numerous cooking shows, *The Antiques Road Show* (both the American and the British versions), *Jeopardy*, *Sex and The City*, *Queer As Folk*, and *The Jerry Springer Show*. Indeed, Jonathan planned his day around watching *Jerry Springer*, which aired three times a day five times a week, insisting, "I can't miss Jerry!"

While he sat mesmerized by the shameless spectacle of humanity at its worst, I tried to find something more constructive to do, such as *be elsewhere*. Given the lack of activities, though, I often found myself doing what Jonathan came to call "drifting," wandering aimlessly throughout the apartment in search of something, anything, to do to pass the time, no matter how minor.

We also watched news programs, and at one point, one of them aired a story about the child sex abuse scandal that was shaking the Catholic Church at the time. In response to the allegations that the children involved were coerced into sexual activity with priests, Jonathan vehemently reacted. Virtually shouting at the screen, he exclaimed, "Nobody forced us to do anything! Nobody held a gun to our heads!" I didn't say anything in response to his outburst because I didn't know what to say. I didn't know if his reaction came from a genuinely positive perception of what had happened to him in school or if he was actually traumatized, more than he realized, and was trying to convince himself more than anyone else. Either possibility was disturbing to me, but because his reaction to the story was fleeting and he didn't mention it further, neither did I.

On December 31, we rang in the New Year by staying at home. I suggested that we go somewhere to celebrate the arrival of 2002, such as one of the gay bars in Winford, but Jonathan said he was too fatigued and, after considering the idea myself, I thought better of making a two-hour round trip through unfamiliar territory in the dark. Instead, we passed the evening mainly watching the "Dame Ednathon," a 24-hour marathon of actor Barry Humphries's talk show as the irrepressible Australian housewife turned megasuperstar, Dame Edna Everage. Early that evening, Jonathan had turned to CNN to watch the thronging celebrants crowding Trafalgar Square in London as they welcomed the New Year to the booming of Big Ben several hours before it arrived in the American Midwest. Jonathan's longing to be in London instead of Mariah was evident, if not spoken, and I would have settled for Hawthorn instead of the dismal surroundings in which I found myself.

Later in the evening, he spoke with his parents, who had just returned from a night of dancing and celebrating at the Savoy Hotel, just around the corner from their flat in London. He expressed amazement that two people their age, one of whom had suffered from colon cancer only six months before, could still evince such energy and strength. Around midnight, he took the phone and went into the office to call Colin and other friends in England, who were just returning from a full night of partying at various gay nightclubs in London. I hoped that next year, he could do the same.

By the beginning of the year, the hospital had finally decided that Jonathan had made only enough money in the month he had worked there to cover the cost of transferring his visa. Although he wouldn't have to reimburse them, they wouldn't be reimbursing him. Because almost all of his remaining money was tied up in investments, he was, in effect, close to penniless with no prospects for money in sight.

I didn't understand why Jonathan didn't keep more of his assets liquid in case of emergencies. His financial behavior had always perplexed me. Jonathan had told me that around the beginning of September, he'd had somewhere between $15,000 and $17,000 in available cash, all of which he'd spent in the ensuing four months. I wasn't certain what had happened to the £10,000 that his father had promised to send him while he was living at Dan's. I thought it was ridiculous that he kept so little on hand when he had been making $850,000 a year. Although he was on short-term disability and was receiving only 60% of his salary, that still amounted to $144,000 a year, if only his base salary of $240,000 a year was considered. Even so, almost all of that money was still being dumped into his investments, primarily his retirement fund, and none of it was available for use. According to Jonathan, withdrawing money from his investments or even lowering the amount going into them would cause him to incur penalties that would prove even more ruinous in the long term than short-term poverty would. For someone who was so intelligent and interested in money, Jonathan's financial behavior was sloppy, almost stupid.

Although Jonathan was planning to sell some of his paintings, that plan would take some time to come to fruition. He had also talked about selling some of his belongings at the local antiques shop, although he knew he would be getting less money for them in Mariah than he would elsewhere, since the shop owner there didn't, in his estimation, seem to know the value of things. In addition, he had mentioned that although he was deriving some money from the rental of his former home in the Southern state and those funds were being routed into a retirement trust, he thought he could have that money redirected from the trust to him without penalty. Although that amounted to only a few hundred dollars a month, it was better than nothing, and I encouraged him to pursue that avenue of help. Getting money from his family and friends in England was utterly out of the question, since his family had made it clear to him that they refused to support him in a situation they deemed ridiculous and detrimental, and his friends, because of their respect for his family's, his parents', opinion, felt compelled to do the same.

Jonathan had paid the rent for the second half of November and all of December, but he had not paid the rent for January. By the first week of January, the rent was not just due, but overdue, and Jonathan had no way to pay it. In addition, he needed money for other bills and, of course, for food, both for himself and for the girls.

Jonathan had told me that the primary reason he was staying in the United States was to be with me. In addition, he had told me that I was the only person whom he could trust and on whom he could rely. Consequently, I felt responsible to do whatever I could to help him, to help us, get through this difficult time and reestablish a normal, or at least better, life than the one that he, and we, presently had. Since Jonathan had no immediate prospects for obtaining the money he needed, I felt that the only option was for me to give it to him.

Although I didn't have the cash to give to him, I told him that I could take out a cash advance on my credit card. That way, I could get the cash immediately and I—we—could then repay it in small, manageable installments, in spite of my high interest rate. Initially, he was reluctant to accept my proposal, but driven by desperation, he finally accepted. I asked him how much he thought he needed and eventually he settled on a figure of $900. He needed $650 for the rent and said that an additional $250 would help him meet his other expenses.

On the afternoon of Friday, the 4th, we went to the bank, where I took out the cash advance. While I completed the transaction, Jonathan waited at the door, seemingly reluctant to get any closer to what was transpiring. When I finished my business and gave him the money, he thanked me profusely and assured me that he would repay me. I was certain that he would, since he had already repaid me $360 in November. I viewed what I had done as an investment in our future.

■

The two weeks that I spent in Mariah, although largely uneventful, were not entirely untroubled. During my stay, a couple of things happened to Jonathan that were unsettling.

One took place one morning when Jonathan checked his e-mail. After he had been in the office for a while, I went in and sat down. He then told me about an e-mail that he had just received from one of his relatives—a disquieting one.

"I just got an e-mail from my brother Terrence, who said that someone tried to take a credit card out in my father's name." After explaining the details, he said, "They wondered if I was the one who did it."

I didn't know what to think. As if to allay any suspicions that I might have had, he quickly added, "I hope you know me well enough by now to know that I would never do something like that."

As I looked at him, a feeling of—uncertainty—went through me. Although I had no solid proof that he was lying to me, my intuition told me that perhaps he was. I wanted to take his word for it, wished I *could* take his word for it, but I found that a part of me simply could not. Given Jonathan's situation, the nature and the timing of the incident were too...convenient. Jonathan had run out of money, had no prospects for money, and at that particular moment, someone had *just happened* to target his father in their attempts to fraudulently obtain a credit card. Unfortunately, as with the Iain issue, I had no way to verify or refute my feeling, which caused me to assume my default position of giving him the benefit of the doubt.

Around the same time, something even more significant, and upsetting, happened. One afternoon, Jonathan went to check his e-mail, and when he returned some time later, he said, "I think I'm in trouble."

Taken aback, I said, "What's wrong?"

"I just got an e-mail from Charmaine. She said that my father has been talking about having me declared diminished."

"Diminished?"

"My father says that he's seen a pattern of poor decision making over the past several months and feels it indicates that I'm no longer capable of taking care of myself. He's talking about going to the British court and having me declared diminished. It's not the same as being declared incompetent, but it would give them the right to have a guardian appointed to administer my affairs. It would also give them the right to come here from England and take me back home."

I was shocked. To me, that sounded almost like a marginally legalized form of kidnapping. "I can't believe our government would allow them to do something like that."

"Your government has a policy of cooperating with us in legal matters, so they probably would."

"Do you think your father could actually have you declared diminished?" I asked.

"The laws in England are different than they are here," he explained. "In America, you're considered innocent until proven guilty, but in England, you're considered guilty until proven innocent. The belief is that it's better to err on the side of caution."

Jonathan decided that he needed to talk to someone at home. He said that he needed to "try to sound normal," to make his family believe he was doing well.

He called Charmaine, but she wasn't home. He then called his nephew Alcuin and spoke to him for fifteen or twenty minutes. While he spoke upstairs, I stayed downstairs, out of earshot, out of respect for his privacy. When the talking stopped, I went back upstairs and asked him how he thought things had gone. He seemed to think that they had gone well, that he had convinced his family that he was in fact all right.

Later, Jonathan's parents convened a family meeting at their home in Eiseley, which included his parents and sisters. After discussing the matter until 2:00 in the morning, they decided that, for the time being, they would not pursue the idea of having Jonathan declared diminished and dragged back to England. Instead, they would simply leave Jonathan alone, letting him "twist in the wind," as he described it, until his situation in the States became so intolerable that he would realize the futility of remaining there. Their version of "care" was interesting indeed.

Once that crisis had passed, another one, concerning me, arose just a few days later. On Wednesday, January 9, I received an e-mail from my sister, who told me that one of my cousins had died. Later that night, I spoke to my mother, who told me the visitation would be on Sunday and the funeral on Monday. I couldn't go to the funeral because that was the first day of the spring semester, but I could at least go to the visitation. I decided to come home on Friday. By that point, I had been in Mariah for two weeks and, even if my cousin's death or my need to return for work hadn't provided an incentive for going home, I just needed to leave. I had spent two weeks in that hellhole and I felt that I had served my time. I needed to escape. I knew and was saddened that Jonathan could not, at least right now, but I held out the hope that he would be able to do so, soon, and resume some kind of normal life, for both our sakes.

■

While I was there, Jonathan mentioned someone whose name had arisen once the previous summer then only rarely in the six months that had followed: Andy. From what I could gather, he and Andy had recently been corresponding, although it was only as friends. He said that he "liked" Andy, saying it, though, in a strange, far-off way that left me feeling odd, but unable to explain why. He had used that tone before, when he had first told me about him. All in all, he said little about Andy, merely mentioning him and the fact that he "liked" him, before moving on to other things.

■

When the issue of having him declared diminished and dragged back to England arose, Jonathan told me that his family didn't understand him. He told me they didn't understand why he had ventured to the

United States when he could have stayed in England and continued to lead a comfortable, fulfilling life. They certainly couldn't understand why he was choosing to remain in a God-forsaken place like Mariah when he could return to England and resume a cushy, upper-crust existence. They had always thought he was strange, he said. Indeed, his predilection for doing things beyond the range of normal English "dottiness" had earned him the nickname "Unusual Jonathan." I thought he had his share of peculiarities, too, but I wasn't sure how much of that came from cultural differences, from his condition and circumstances, or from something deeper. His "unusualness" made him interesting, but it also made his behavior unpredictable and often incomprehensible. Sometimes his behavior seemed more like that of a child or an adolescent than like that of an adult, with the egocentrism, immaturity, and instability the former displayed. I often felt that I didn't know where I stood with him, what to expect from him. Sometimes I felt the more I knew him, the less I knew him.

■

Once, Jonathan said something funny to which I said, "You're insane." To that he said, "You have *no* idea."

As it turned out, I didn't.

—III—
—The Other Flies—

If I lie some on the internet I don't think that I am the first or only person to ever do it. Stop being so fucking judgemental. In the end, where is the harm?

—Jonathan

—23—
GAYBOI

Didn't you realize something snapped when things got so bad?

During the two weeks I spent in Mariah, I frequently used Jonathan's computer. For the most part, I used it to check my e-mail as well as to work on some files that I needed for the upcoming semester. By that point, I had learned that I would be teaching three classes again: one in Hawthorn on Monday and Friday mornings, one in Viridian on Tuesday afternoons, and another in Hawthorn on Thursday afternoons. I was going to be as busy that spring as I had been the previous fall and I hoped that 2002 would be the year that everything would fall into place for Jonathan and for me.

In the process of using his computer, I discovered from viewing his browser history that Jonathan had been visiting a number of gay web sites, ones that contained both pornographic material and personals ads. I wasn't concerned about his interest in pornography, but I was concerned about his interest in the personals.

One site that he frequented was *Gayteway*, the site through which we had met. At one point, I checked to see which specific pages he had been visiting and discovered that he had been visiting the travel page, which focused on flight information. I thought it was odd because, as far as I knew, he had no intentions of traveling, at least by plane. I knew that his family and friends in England had been encouraging him to return home where he could received the social and medical support that he needed and, although he seemed unwilling to do it, I wondered if he was beginning to think along those lines. Even so, I didn't know why he would use the *Gayteway* site to find out about flights when logically he might be expected to use a regular travel site. Ultimately, though, I didn't give it further thought and didn't raise the issue with Jonathan.

On the morning of Thursday, January 3, I went to use the computer to check my e-mail. While I was online, I took a look at the sites that Jonathan had been visiting. Another site that he seemed to visit with some frequency was called *Sex Now*. The site was a personals site for gay men who were interested in having casual sex. When I went to review the specific pages that Jonathan had visited that day, I found that he had visited one on the *Sex Now* site that gave the contact information for someone who called himself "Sucker." A user could send another user an e-mail by clicking the e-mail link provided in the ad. This would launch the default e-mail application on the computer the respondent was using. Curious, I clicked on the link. When the e-mail program opened, it displayed the number of messages in each folder. I saw that the outbox contained three. When I opened the outbox, I saw that two of them were messages to potential employers, while the third was not.

The third message bore the rather unprofessional title "Suck My Dick." I clicked on the message title and read the message. It said, "43, 5'9", 7"+ cut thick, poppers. Interested?" According to the time stamp, the message had been sent at 3:00 that morning.

Later, I told Jonathan that I had read one of his e-mails. He told me in a neutral tone that what I had done was "not nice." I told him that maybe it wasn't but that I had discovered a message titled "Suck My Dick" and wanted to know what it was about.

He explained to me that he had been opening all sorts of files and that it was probably an old message of Glenn's. I told him that, according to the time stamp, the message had been sent *that morning*, so it couldn't possibly be an old message of Glenn's. He told me that he couldn't explain why it had that date but that it wasn't his. I didn't believe him, but instead of arguing about it, I moved on to the larger issue of why he had been visiting so many different personals sites. He explained that he enjoyed reading the ads because he found them "entertaining." For someone who loved *Jerry Springer*, I wasn't surprised that he considered that "entertainment."

On the evening of Thursday, the 10th, the last evening that I spent in Mariah before returning to Hawthorn, Jonathan and I planned to go out to eat at a local Asian restaurant called Gobi, which specialized in Mongolian grill. That evening, I was using Jonathan's computer and, out of curiosity, decided to visit the *Sex Now* site. To use the service, new members had to complete a profile in which they were required to give basic information about themselves. Jonathan had not logged out of the site, which gave me access to the personal information he had given in his profile. The home page contained a link through which a member could access his profile information if he were logged in. Curious about what Jonathan had said about himself, I clicked on the link.

I didn't expect to find anything revealing, since I had, after all, been involved with him for seven months and knew the essentials about him. As I read down the profile, I found that most of the information he had given about himself was not only unadorned, but almost disappointing. The information was so spare that, at first, the only thing that seemed to be significant about it was that there seemed to be *nothing* significant about it. At first, it appeared that he had filled out the profile in haste, providing only the barest amount of information necessary to gain access to the site. As I read the profile, the only piece of information I found that deviated from what he had led me to believe about himself was that he had given his age not as 45, but as 41.

Then, I reached the end of the profile and saw the e-mail address he had given—one that I had seen before.

Iain's.

My heart began racing. There was no longer any doubt.

Jonathan was "Iain." Jonathan was "GayMan."

Shaking, I slowly stood up from the seat. I tried to steady myself as well as I could before doing what I needed to do next.

Heart pounding, I walked into the den, where Jonathan was sitting in his favorite spot. He looked up at me, but before he could say anything, I said, "Could you come in the office for a moment? There's something I want to show you."

"What is it now?" he said, exasperated. From my tone, he knew I was about to confront him with something he'd done wrong.

"Just come here," I said, my tone making it clear that I was in *no* mood to countenance his resistance.

He stood up from the sofa and I turned to lead him into the office. Once there, I gestured toward the *Sex Now* profile still burning on the screen.

"What?" he said impatiently.

"Look at the e-mail address."

When he did and realized he'd been found out, Jonathan became enraged. In the seven months that we had been together, I had never seen him have an outburst of temper, but now, he gave vent to his anger with gale force. Shouting at me, he told me to ask myself the "Dear Abby" question—whether I was better with him or without him. He made no effort to explain anything to me, merely expected me to accept it. I didn't. I didn't want to be close to him and the office, which was cramped, was too close for comfort. Upset, I hurried out of the office, away from the computer, away from him.

As I went, he yelled something at me that made me feel as if I'd fallen though a crack in the earth.

"Stay out of things you don't understand!"

Things I didn't understand? I *didn't* understand what he meant, but I *did* understand that his comment was only the tip of an immense iceberg that was floating in a very deep, dark, stormy psychological sea. The feeling that washed over me at that moment was the same one that had assailed me at the zoo when I had looked at him and had been flooded with the feeling that there was much more to this person than met the eye. I didn't understand what he meant, but I did understand that whatever lay behind his comment, it was bad. I was more unnerved than ever.

I retreated into the bedroom, where I began sorting through and organizing my clothes in preparation for the trip back home the next day. I considered leaving that night and would have had it not involved a 150-mile trip in the middle of a Midwestern winter night. I didn't know what to do.

After a while, Jonathan came into the bedroom. His voice thick with anger, he told me that he'd e-mailed Colin and told him that he'd decided to come home. Then, he stormed back into the den. I followed him partway, but I don't remember what I said in his wake. Whatever it was, it made no difference. He wasn't even willing to discuss what had happened, what he was planning to do. His deception was more important to him than I was.

I headed back to the bedroom. As I headed toward the room, which lay adjacent to the office, Jonathan yelled at me to "stay off that damned computer" to which I yelled back that I was *not* getting back on it. I had *no* intention of using the computer again, not because of his orders, but because of my inability to handle any more revelations. I had seen enough for one night—too much—and I did *not* want to see any more.

After a while, I had calmed down enough that my stomach reasserted its need for food, so I decided to go out for something to eat. I got my coat and told Jonathan what I was planning to do and that if he wanted to go with me to get his coat and get down to the car. He didn't respond, so I left the apartment—through the front door instead of the side one that opened into the den so I could avoid him.

Instead of going to Gobi for Mongolian grill, I went to McDonald's for a cheeseburger and fries. I brought the food back to the apartment to find Jonathan still seated in his favorite spot. I didn't want to be anywhere near him, so I sat in the kitchen, on the side farthest from the door that connected the kitchen with the den, and ate my food while half-watching the television on the kitchen counter. After I finished, I decided to start unpacking the remainder of Jonathan's items that I had brought with me to Mariah. I continued to use the front entrance instead of the side one, and at one point, Jonathan finally spoke to me, but only to tell me to stop sneaking around and use the door in the den. I ignored him and continued to bring his things in through the front door.

A couple of hours after the argument and the ensuing silence had begun, I had finally calmed down enough and sensed that Jonathan had calmed down enough that I decided to approach him in an attempt to talk about what I had found in a more constructive manner. He was still sitting in his favorite spot when I went to stand in the door that separated the kitchen from the den. I began by saying, "Jonathan, I am willing to admit that I could be wrong about all of this, and if I am, then I am sorry," but before I could finish the rest of what I had to say, Jonathan jumped up from the sofa and, with tears in his eyes, began repeating, "It doesn't matter; it doesn't matter," before kissing me hard on the lips. He assured me that he would never cheat on me—my implication being that he might have been—then pulled me over and onto the sofa, where he held me against his chest.

Regardless, I had a number of unanswered questions. In particular, I asked him how he had Iain's information if he wasn't Iain. In response, he claimed that when the Iain issue had first arisen in October, he had performed a web search to see if he could find more information about him so he could prove to me that he wasn't him. He said that, in the process, he had discovered a directory containing Iain's *Sex Now* profile and password, had downloaded it onto his computer, and had started accessing the site through it. That explanation was implausible in the extreme, but I pretended to accept it. I was going to be leaving the next day and I just wanted to keep things calm until I could get out of there and figure out what to do in peace.

I didn't sleep well that night. I was up and down as much as Jonathan usually was, although *he* seemed to be sleeping unusually well. At many points, I thought about getting dressed and just leaving, but the thought of driving the 150 miles to Hawthorn or even half that distance to Paladin in the middle of the night was too much. I felt trapped. Finally I became exhausted enough that I returned to bed and, in spite of Jonathan lying beside me, I managed to go to sleep.

The next morning, the Iain issue arose once again. Jonathan brought it up, not me. At one point, he looked at me and, shaking his finger at me, said, "I don't care what you think—I'm *not* him." He was half-laughing as he said it, as if he were at once trying to persuade me and mocking my presumed gullibility.

I still didn't know if Jonathan was Iain or merely had a connection to Iain, but I didn't get into it with him because I didn't want to have another fight.

Then, almost offhandedly, he added, "Anyway, I just hope that Iain doesn't use the name of one of his pets as the password to his e-mail account because that would make it too easy to get into it." Somewhat confused by the tangential remark, I simply replied that I hoped not too because it was stupid to use such an obvious password. Then, the issue was dropped.

Around noon, we went to Gobi, where we had planned to go the previous evening before the fight. Then, wanting to make sure that I got home before dark, I left Mariah around 2:00.

As I drove the 150 miles that separated Mariah from Hawthorn, I began to think of some way of proving to myself, beyond any doubt, that Jonathan was not simply using Iain's information but *was* Iain. I *knew* he was lying—that was obvious—but I wanted, needed, to be unerringly certain of what was really happening before making further accusations or, more importantly, possibly throwing away a relationship that, despite its complications, seemed to have some positive qualities. My previous attempts had failed, and at first, I couldn't think of a more effective way of doing it.

As I drove, however, I began to think about the strange remark that Jonathan had made about the password to Iain's e-mail account, that he hoped it wasn't the name of one of his pets. Why would he think that Iain's password was the name of one of his pets unless he suspected...or knew? Had *he* been accessing Iain's e-mail account? If so, had he been using it to masquerade as him? Or was it simpler than that? If Jonathan *was* Iain, then he certainly knew the password to his *own* account. If it *was* his account, had he been encouraging me to guess the password and use it? Why else would he have made the remark? I wondered now if it had been as incidental as it had seemed.

But if he *had* been encouraging me to access the account, why? Did he plan to delete all its contents so that if I did access it I would find that it contained nothing, nothing incriminating? If he wanted to maintain an illusion that he wasn't Iain, then he couldn't just *give* me the password, since that would be the same as an admission. This way, however, he could perhaps feel that he was throwing me off the trail that led to him, and unless the Iain account contained information that said, in effect, that Iain *was* Jonathan, I still wouldn't have absolute proof, but I might let the matter drop. I didn't know what to think, but I *did* know by now that Jonathan liked playing games and I wondered what kind of game he was playing now.

Coming home after spending two weeks in an environment quite different from my own was like coming back to Earth from another planet where things operated very differently than they did here. On Friday, I was preoccupied with taking care of the business that had accumulated in the two weeks I had been gone, but on Saturday, I decided to see if I could gain access to Iain's—or *Jonathan's*—e-mail account.

Following Jonathan's "suggestion," I tried to access the account by trying the names of Jonathan's dogs. The first one, Frizzie, proved unsuccessful, but the second one, Sweetie, proved to be the key.

I could not have been less prepared for what I found.

Among other things, I found all of the e-mails that Iain had received from me as "Chaz" as well as copies of the ones that he had sent to "Chaz." From what I could tell, it appeared that the account had been created specifically to correspond with "Chaz," since the date the account appeared to have been created—Thursday, October 4 of the previous year—was the date that Iain had answered the ad that I, as "Chaz," had posted on *Gayteway*. I even found one that Iain had sent to "Chaz" the Saturday night they were supposed to have met in downtown Paladin for dinner and sex. Since I had deactivated the "Chaz" account before he had sent the final message, it had been sent back to him, where it had remained in his inbox for the previous three months. In the message, Iain claimed that he had gone downtown, in the rain, where he had waited for an hour, only to have "Chaz" not show. He told "Chaz" not to contact him again and that he was just like the guy in the original "GayMan" ad—a "no show."

More shocking, however, I discovered several e-mails that Iain had sent to Cliff, starting around the time that Jonathan had moved to Mariah, in which he had claimed that Jonathan was staying in a hospice where he was being cared for by nuns. The implication was that Jonathan had become so gravely ill that he not only required hospice care, but also needed someone else to send and receive e-mails for him because he was too sick to use the computer. There was also a plaintive message from Cliff in which he asked Iain, "Can't I even speak to him?" suggesting that Iain was preventing direct contact between Cliff and Jonathan. Cliff appeared to believe Iain's story, which made me wonder what Cliff had tried to do to verify it and what had *really* been going on between him and Jonathan.

At first I was disoriented. I didn't understand if Iain was actually Jonathan in disguise or, more disturbingly, if Iain and Jonathan were separate people who were conspiring to perpetrate an elaborate set of manipulations and lies. The first explanation was simpler, more plausible, however, which somehow made the magnitude of what Jonathan had done far greater.

As it turned out, however, the messages to "Chaz" and to Cliff were trivial compared to the remainder—the majority—of what I found.

Most shocking of all, I discovered an elaborate series of correspondences between "Iain"—whom I now understood to be Jonathan in disguise—and someone who called himself "Gayboi." The inbox contained between 70 and 80 messages and roughly half of them were from "Gayboi." The oldest message dated from around the middle of November, from shortly before the time that Jonathan had moved to Mariah, while the newest one dated from Wednesday, January 2—only ten days before. At first, I thought that "Gayboi" was someone with whom Jonathan, as "Iain," had established some type of cybersex relationship that didn't involve physical contact. I had found a couple of other messages from various people with whom Jonathan, as "Iain," had established cybersex connections and I thought he might have established a more elaborate one with the person who called himself "Gayboi." Curious, I opened one of the messages and, to my shock, discovered who "Gayboi" was.

"Gayboi" was Andy.

I read more. Although the e-mails didn't tell the full story, only pieces of it, it appeared that Andy was in love with Jonathan and that Jonathan had led Andy to believe that he was also in love with him. This was disturbing enough, but even more disturbing was the story that Jonathan had led Andy to believe about his situation. Instead of telling him the truth, it appeared that Jonathan had told Andy that, because of his illness, he had been forced to return to England in order to receive the medical care that he required. Jonathan's condition had grown so grave, in fact, that he now appeared to be on his deathbed—a story that was similar to the one he had told Cliff—and Jonathan otherwise appeared to be the focal point of an extremely intricate scenario in which he was referred to as "Lord Jonathan" and that involved a variety of characters, including Colin, Alcuin—and, of course, "Iain"—all of whom were playing a variety of roles the e-mails only hinted at.

But most disturbing of all was Andy's intentions to go to England to be with Jonathan—not just temporarily, but permanently.

From what I gathered, Jonathan had apparently told Andy that he wanted them to be together and had promised Andy that if he came to England, he would take care of him. With that enticement, Andy had begun making plans to leave behind his life in the United States for the fantasy life that Jonathan had led him to believe awaited him in England. At some point, however, Jonathan had apparently come to his senses, at least partially, and realized that the fantasy had gotten out of control. He had realized that he needed to do something to stop Andy from acting on his intentions. Instead of dealing with what he'd done in a more direct fashion, however—by telling Andy the truth—Jonathan had decided to take the devious approach.

Specifically, he had decided to pose as "Iain," who was no longer working as a businessman in Paladin, but as a travel agent in England. Jonathan presented "Iain" as a friend of Jonathan's whom Jonathan had placed in charge of making the arrangements for Andy to fly to England. "Iain" would arrange flights for Andy, then always come up with some excuse for why those plans didn't work out, thereby preventing him from going. One time, the reason was that events forced a change of plans, while another time, the reason was that "Iain" had inadvertently given Andy the wrong flight number. I now understood why Jonathan had been visiting the *Gayteway* travel page: to acquire plausible-sounding information about flights to incorporate into his lies. At the same time, "Iain" worked to instill in Andy a feeling of suspicion and mistrust toward Jonathan with allusions to the fact that Jonathan was somehow not all he seemed to be. At least *that* was the truth.

I had never encountered anything like this in my life, at least outside of a psychiatric textbook. I couldn't begin to process it, understand it. Certainly there were pieces missing, important pieces that might have made what I had found more comprehensible, but even with those missing pieces fitted into the puzzle, the picture would have still been insane.

I began to wonder about Andy, who he *really* was. Jonathan had told me that he and Andy had dated for a couple of months before we met and that although things hadn't worked out between the two of them, they had remained friends. I began to wonder, though, if that was all there was to the story or if that was the story at all. Had he actually met Andy at the Stress Center? Andy appeared to have fallen for this elaborate, preposterous story without reservation and I began to wonder if Andy was mentally ill. Were they *all* mixed up in some kind of shared delusion, a *folie à plusieurs*?

Had Jonathan *wanted* me to see this? If so, *why*?

"Stay out of things you don't understand!" I hadn't, and now, I understood things, understood Jonathan, less than I ever had. Everything had changed. Everything.

Whatever the truth, I knew that I could no longer trust Jonathan. He had deceived me about being "GayMan," had deceived me about being "Iain," had deceived Cliff about the true nature of his health, and now had deceived Andy in the most extravagant fashion, to the point that Andy had come perilously close to throwing his real life away for a fantasy life that Jonathan had led him to believe awaited him in England. What had I gotten myself into?

On a practical level, I became concerned that Jonathan wouldn't repay me the money he owed me. My concern was even greater now than it had been in October. By this point, he owed me more than $2,000, and for someone who was now netting only $150 a week, not recouping that money would have a damaging financial impact on me. I decided then that I needed to do something to try to ensure that I would.

Sunday morning, I wrote to Jonathan telling him that I had been discussing his situation, his health, with my mother, who had voiced her concern that if something happened to him, I wouldn't recoup my money, which would have a detrimental impact on me. That was true, but exaggerated, since *I* was the one who was more concerned. I told him I thought that, "just in case," we needed to have some kind of legally binding agreement that would ensure that I would get my money back in the event that something happened to him. I suggested that I take the smaller of the two lithographs as collateral, which was worth enough that it would allow me to regain some, if not all, of my money. Jonathan had actually suggested doing that before, so I ran with the idea. Trying to come across as businesslike as possible, I reinforced the idea that not recouping the amount he owed me with my income level would be financially devastating and, given the uncertainty of his situation, I wanted to be protected. It was nothing personal, I explained, just business, although after what I had learned, it had become *very* personal.

That message precipitated an e-mail exchange that lasted until late in the evening. In his first message, he explained that he had continued to accept money from me because the alternatives were either to accept money from the Tomlinsons or to go home, neither of which he wanted to do. He thanked me profusely for my generosity and agreed to signing an IOU for the amount he owed me, minus the $360 he had paid me in November, and giving me the smaller lithograph as collateral. He told me to send him the IOU, which he would sign and send back to me.

Then, he went on to reveal that even though he wanted and needed to see me, he could no longer afford to host me. He stated that he hadn't gotten his hair cut while I was there, as he had planned, because he had spent that money on buying us lunch the day I had returned from Mariah. He further stated that when I was there, he shopped for two when normally he shopped for one and spent money on things he wouldn't if I weren't there. He said that although I hadn't asked him to do it, he didn't want to feel like a "total leech and slug" by expecting me to pay for everything when I had already paid for enough. Because of his inability to pay his fair share, he suggested that I not visit him again until he could.

Further emphasizing his impoverished condition, he mentioned that he wouldn't have any money until he sold the lithographs in February. In addition, he now claimed that he wouldn't be able to sell *Still Life*, his only source of substantial income, until June. If that were true, then he would have to live on the profits from the sale of the lithographs—a few thousand dollars—for four months. Although he didn't state it, he seemed to imply that by taking the smaller lithograph as collateral, I would be further depriving him of what was already a paltry amount. In addition, his revelation that *Still Life* couldn't be sold until June suggested that "the plan" I had formulated would have to be substantially modified.

I didn't know what to think about the message. By stating that he couldn't sell *Still Life* until June and would have to live on the profits from the larger lithograph for four months, was he trying to discourage me from taking the smaller one? If I couldn't see him, how was I supposed to acquire the smaller lithograph if I did accept it? If I sent him an IOU, would he sign and return it to me? Perhaps I was being paranoid, but after what I had learned, I couldn't help wondering if he was trying to evade my attempts to make him take responsibility for his debt to me.

Before I could respond, Jonathan wrote to inform me that he had spoken to his father. When his father had discovered that he had accepted money from my mother and me, his father had become furious. Accepting money from others, especially from people at our income level, was considered "bad form" and was *totally* unacceptable in his social circle. His father had insisted on repaying my mother and me at once. (My mother didn't want her money back, considering it a gift, but if I could reclaim it for her, I would.) Then, when he had asked Jonathan for my address, which Jonathan didn't know, his father had gone "really ballistic," as Jonathan described it. His father also took Jonathan's borrowing as an indication of just how dire his situation had become. Consequently, he had given Jonathan an ultimatum: He had one week to decide if he was going to stay in the United States or return to England; if he decided to return, his father would help him, but if he decided to stay, his father would cut him off. Jonathan was beginning to think that his only choice was to return home.

I didn't want him to return home either—at that point not so much because of any feelings I might have had for him as because his return would put him out of reach both physically and legally, reducing or eliminating my ability to reclaim my money. Even though Jonathan had said that if he returned his father would repay me, I didn't know what might happen if he slipped back to England.

I tried my best to contain the situation. I asked him if I could visit him on Wednesday, when I didn't have to teach, in spite of his reluctance to have me. I told him I would pay him for lunch as well as for my food while I was there so that my visit wouldn't be a financial burden. I made it seem as if I wanted to see him for the sake of seeing him, but my *real* intention was to get him to sign a notarized IOU, obtain the smaller lithograph, then confront him about the Andy situation and leave. I had no idea what the fallout would be. I knew it was a risk, but it was one I had to take.

I waited for his response, but he didn't reply.

By Sunday afternoon, everything that I had learned that weekend finally began to have a more emotional impact on me. The betrayal, the deception, the potential financial damage, the feeling that I did not know the person with whom I had been involved for more than half a year—*everything*—collapsed in on me, crushing me beneath its weight. Although I am not a crier, let alone an uncontrolled one, I began crying uncontrollably. After spending fifteen or twenty minutes crying, I would manage to pull myself together for a while, only to have thoughts of what had happened assail my mind, like flashbacks from a disaster, and trigger another episode of uncontrolled sobbing. Sunday afternoon, I went to the drug store to buy an item, only to have to leave almost immediately upon arriving because I was overwhelmed by yet another wave of crying. Sunday was also the day of my cousin's visitation, but in my fragile emotional state, it would have been impossible for me to maintain my composure, which kept me from going. Although crying is not only permitted but expected on such occasions, I would not have been crying for the *right* reason. The next day was also the first day of the spring semester and I was burdened with the prospect of having to face a classful of students and try to teach for well over an hour when I didn't seem to be able to do anything but fixate on what had happened and cry.

Sunday, January 13, 2002 was one of the worst days of my life.

Later that evening, he finally responded. Between two different replies, he said several things that I found disturbing because they suggested an intention not to repay me. First, he now questioned the need to sign an IOU if his father was going to be doing the repaying. The suggestion, of course, was that he was going to allow someone else to be responsible for his debt. Second, he expressed his regret at having accepted money from me and my mother, commenting that it had turned what was a relationship into a "business arrangement." The suggestion was that by overlooking the money issue, it would restore our relationship to its proper status. Third, he explicitly questioned the sincerity of my mother's generosity and implicitly questioned mine. He remarked that "everything has its price" and that although she had *given* him money, which she had insisted was a *gift* and not a loan, she was now wanting it back. He commented that since he had suffered financial setbacks, he had noticed that people were "funny" about money, implying that their "generosity" was inauthentic. The suggestion, again, was that by forgetting about the repayment issue, it would restore his faith in my mother's—and my—motives.

And, finally, he said that although he loved me and I had been kind, thoughtful, and helpful to the best of my ability and beyond what anyone could reasonably expect, he would probably return to England in the near future. He said that he needed to be with people but that his current circumstances didn't permit it. He pointed out that we lived far apart and that even if he moved back to Paladin, I would still be far. He said that although he had accepted some help from the Tomlinsons, he wasn't comfortable accepting any more. He felt that he had accepted more from me and my family than he should have and that it had "blown up in [his] face" with me, my mother, and his parents. He explained that he wasn't making decisions for me but for himself because he needed to take care of and be responsible for himself.

He ended his final message by quoting the title of The Brains/Cyndi Lauper hit "Money Changes Everything" and added, "That is a true statement." For me, though, it wasn't the *money* that had changed everything.

I didn't know what to think about any of what had told me, about the implications that lay behind it. By late that evening, I was exhausted from the stress, the disorientation, the crying, the shattering of my conception of who Jonathan was. Because of my exhaustion, I slept soundly that night, but not peacefully.

By the next morning, two days after I had discovered the contents of the "Iain" account, my feelings had spanned the emotional spectrum from the darkness of confusion to the blue of angst to the yellow of fear to the red of anger. By that point, I had half-decided that I would contact Andy and tell him how Jonathan had deceived, manipulated, and exploited him. Andy deserved to know the truth for the sake of knowing the truth, if not now to prevent him from making a disastrous decision that would destroy his life. In addition, I was insulted by what Jonathan had done, since his "relationship" with Andy had made no mention of his relationship with me. To this end, I decided to show Andy the contents of the "Iain" account as proof not only that "Iain" was Jonathan but also that the entire scenario that Jonathan had presented to him was nothing but a lie. So that Jonathan couldn't get back into the account and delete its contents, if he planned to do so, I changed the password to a string of ten random digits, which meant there was only a one in ten billion chance of his being able to guess it, even if he knew it *was* a string of ten random digits.

At first, I didn't know how to approach Jonathan regarding what I had found. I had intended to wait until Wednesday, when I planned to return to Mariah, but I found that in my anger, I couldn't. In retrospect, what I did was not the best way to do it, but after spending an entire day crying uncontrollably because of everything he had done, I wasn't feeling sympathetic toward him. Monday morning, before leaving for work, I accessed the "Iain" account, with the intention of sending Jonathan a message...as "Iain." I wanted not only to shock him, as the messages to "Iain" and everything they implied had shocked me, but also to let him know, in no uncertain terms, that his attempts to deceive me, if that had been his intention, had failed.

Because the password was "Sweetie" and because she had recently injured one of her feet, I sent Jonathan a simple, one-sentence message in which I told him I hoped she was doing better. Then, I signed it "Iain." I sent it and left for work.

I finished with class around 9:45. Afterwards, I went to the computer and checked to see if I had received a response. At that point, Jonathan had normally been checking his e-mail around 9:00, so I thought he should have responded by then. When I accessed my account, I discovered that he had. His response was shocking.

In it, he condemned me for having "push[ed] too far." He asked me if I didn't realize that "something [had] snapped" when things had gotten so bad for him and that the only thing that had helped him to maintain "even a bit of sanity" was to "retreat into fantasy periodically since reality was so awful." He accused me of having "finished destroying [him] more thoroughly then any illness or lack of funds or anything else could ever do" and told me that he hoped I had gotten enough satisfaction from what I had done to "keep [me] warm all winter." Reviving a charge he had made before, he accused me of not understanding people because I was so isolated myself and, therefore, of not understanding why he had done what he had done. He went on to state that he was "starting to pull back to something that could enable [him] to put [his] pieces back together" and that I didn't know what I had done to him. He ended his message with the almost childlike statement that whether I contacted him again or not I would get my money because "Papa promised."

At that particular moment, the money was the *last* thing on my mind. I was too confused, too stunned. This was the most bizarre, shocking message that I had ever received from him, from *anyone*. I didn't understand how what I had done had "destroyed" him or what he had meant when he had said that he was "starting to pull back to something that could enable [him] to put [his] pieces back together." As for the idea that "something [had] snapped" when things had gotten so bad, I certainly knew that Jonathan had suffered emotionally because of the events of the previous several months, but until that point, I *hadn't* known that he had deteriorated to the point that he felt compelled to engage in such maladjusted behavior. Jonathan had done such an excellent job of presenting the façade of someone who was handling the extreme stress that he was suffering that I had never suspected that psychologically he had crumbled to such an extent.

As soon as I got home a half-hour later I did call. I needed to talk to him *directly* about what had happened. Initially, his reaction was defensive, telling me that I had had no right to look into "his" account—something he had formerly denied it was. In response, I asked him why he had hinted at the password to me if he hadn't wanted me to look into it. He insisted that he had never said anything like that, which I found stunning. How did he think I had gotten into it? Was he suffering from mental confusion or had he conveniently "forgotten" what he had said to make it seem as if I had done something wrong, worse than what *he* had done? Given his message to me—and given his messages as "Iain"—I realized more than ever that his thinking wasn't rational, so I didn't know what to think about his denial. Having finally had enough of his deflections, manipulations, and deceptions, I snapped that he *had* hinted at the password hoping I would guess it and asked him, point blank, what the hell kind of game he was playing with me and everyone else.

Evading my question, he told me, sarcastically, that I was "just too good" for him—a refrain he would begin using to deflect my criticisms of his unacceptable behavior. Focusing on the situation between him and Andy, I asked him if he was really in love with him, since the e-mails from "Iain" had stated that he was "besotted" with and "very mooney" over him. Jonathan told me that he wasn't, to which I replied that I didn't think you should tell someone you were in love with him when you really weren't. He countered my comment with the idea that I was being "self-righteous" and "judgmental"—something that, like the "you're just too good for me" refrain, he would use in the future to maneuver the focus away from his wrongdoing.

I was more concerned, however, about the most disturbing aspect of the whole situation: the idea that Andy was planning to throw away his life in the United States for the fantasy life that Jonathan had led him to believe awaited him in England. Jonathan assured me that Andy had no intentions of going to England, that he had taken adequate measures to contain the situation, and that Andy was safely back at work and at home. Since I had seen only the e-mails that Andy had sent to "Iain" and none of the ones that he had *knowingly* sent to *Jonathan*, I could only take Jonathan's word that the situation was in fact under control and that Andy was no longer in danger of doing something impulsive and ultimately self-destructive.

Somewhat validating that idea, though, were the impressions I had received from a message that "Iain" had sent to Andy on New Year's Day, just two weeks before, in which "Iain" had been attempting to instill in Andy a feeling of suspicion and mistrust toward Jonathan in addition to his attempts to prevent Andy from flying to England through his (allegedly) bungled travel arrangements. That thought did offer me some measure of comfort in an otherwise profoundly disturbing and potentially disastrous situation.

I asked Jonathan why, when he saw that the situation was getting out of control, he didn't try to stop it in a more direct fashion—for example, by telling Andy the truth. In response, Jonathan told me that he was "from a different culture and that [he handled] things differently." I did believe that the British of the upper class from which he came placed a strong emphasis on saving face, on dealing with social matters in such a way as to avoid embarrassment, and thought that his explanation was plausible, even if I didn't approve of the approach.

I didn't ask him directly about the bizarre e-mail that he had sent to me earlier that morning—I didn't know *what* to say about it—but I did ask him how he could have allowed something like this to happen. He said that "the restraints that would have normally been there had been removed"—reinforcing my belief, which he had seemed to express in his e-mail, that this sickening situation had somehow been induced by the stresses he had suffered during the past several months, which had driven him to escape into a fantasy world that, unfortunately, the people he had involved did not realize *was* fantasy.

In looking through the e-mails, I had noticed several that had seemingly been sent by Colin. When I asked Jonathan how Colin had become mixed up in the fantasy, which suggested that he was just as unscrupulous or unbalanced as Jonathan appeared to be, Jonathan told me that the e-mail account through which the messages had been sent was actually one that he and Colin shared and that *he* had sent the messages pretending to be Colin. I asked him if Colin had seen the e-mails and what Colin thought about what he had been doing in his name. He claimed that Colin had encouraged him to stop what he was doing, but hadn't taken any direct action. He further claimed that Colin hadn't told Andy what was really happening because he didn't want to "embarrass" Jonathan, so the situation had continued.

Although that sounded plausible, given what I believed to be the British upper crust's need to save face, I didn't believe that Colin knew anything about what was happening. The idea of two best friends sharing a personal e-mail account was unlikely. What was likelier was that Jonathan had simply created an e-mail account through which to masquerade as Colin. That meant that he was pretending to be not only the fictional character of "Iain," but also a real person—his best friend—which was even worse. Unfortunately, I didn't have any way to contact Colin to tell him what was happening, so I was powerless to do anything to let him know what his "best friend" was doing in his name, doing in general, and have him help me stop him.

As the conversation progressed, the subject shifted away from the Andy situation in particular and the "Iain" issue in general to more fundamental questions about us. I asked him why he hadn't told me the truth about being "Iain" and what he had been doing through the Internet in general. He explained, tearfully, that he had been reluctant to do so because, when I had discovered the *Sex Now* account and had thought he was "Iain," I had been so angry at him that he had become afraid of losing me. That, of course, didn't explain why, among other things, he had hinted about the password to the "Iain" account, creating the possibility that I would guess it and find out that he was "Iain." In addition, he still wasn't admitting to me that he was the author of the "GayMan" postings from August even though he had admitted it to "Chaz." On the surface, what he said *sounded* good, but it didn't ring true, leaving me to believe that he hadn't told me he was "Iain" simply because he hadn't wanted me to find out what he was doing.

Even so, his comment did begin to soften me somewhat because it was now clear to me that Jonathan was far more ill emotionally than I had previously realized and I tried to sympathize with the mindset of someone who had been engaging in some kind of maladjusted behavior that had grown out of suffering extraordinary stress. Whether knowingly or unwittingly, Jonathan only reinforced my feelings by raising the issue of how his family, especially his parents, couldn't understand how his life had become diminished by his illness and how he couldn't rely on his own family for emotional support.

He claimed that aside from Marcus and Glenn, I was the only other person he had ever truly loved. He didn't mention Cliff, but I assumed he figured into that select group. That, I suppose, softened me even more. Although I had lost some of the edge of my anger, I had not, however, lost my profound feeling of concern over Jonathan's emotional condition and the disaster that had been narrowly averted.

Finally, we discussed my coming to Mariah on Wednesday. Under the circumstances I felt ambivalent about seeing him, but the part of me that needed to see him face to face was stronger than the part of me that wanted to avoid him.

After about an hour, Jonathan told me that he needed to conclude our conversation because the telephone connection was going bad. Whether he was telling the truth or simply looking for an excuse to conclude an undesired conversation, I don't know, but by the time I got off the phone, I had begun to feel better, if not good. I still didn't know what to think about various aspects of the situation, but I did feel that some aspects of his behavior had become more comprehensible and, therefore, emotionally more manageable. In addition, I felt better thinking that, regardless of what had driven it and what had ended it, the situation between him and Andy *was* ended and Andy had been placed out of harm's way.

Even so, my feelings were tempered by the realization that Jonathan was in far worse shape, mentally, than I had ever suspected. That by itself was troubling enough, but far more disturbing was the particular way in which he had chosen to deal with his problems. Retreating into fantasy—reading a novel, watching a movie, playing a role-playing game—was normal and healthy, but the way Jonathan was doing it—indulging in fantasies that others took, or *mis*took, for reality and that consequently led them to take *real* actions that altered their lives in *real* ways—was not only pathological, but dangerous.

I was also disoriented by his behavior regarding my having accessed the "Iain" e-mail account. On the one hand, he had deliberately hinted at the password, doing everything but giving it to me, then had denied doing it and had become hostile when he had discovered that I had guessed and used it. Perhaps the way I had gone about letting him know what I had done had shaped his response, but after admitting his need to retreat into fantasy to maintain his mental stability, I knew it wasn't that simple. What was happening in his mind? His behavior had the characteristics of a defense mechanism. It was as if he were crying for help, wanting someone to discover what he was doing and stop him when he couldn't stop himself, but at the same time, it was as if he couldn't handle someone discovering what he was doing, perhaps because if someone *did* try to stop him, that would deprive him of the main psychological crutch on which he had come to lean. That was the only explanation that made sense to me. I didn't know, but I *did* know that whatever was happening in his mind, it was bad and I had the disturbing feeling that I had only gotten my feet wet in the stormy ocean that was Jonathan's psyche.

I became extremely concerned, not only for Jonathan, but also for the people who were being snared by Jonathan's lies. Someone had almost gotten hurt, had almost been permitted to destroy his life because of Jonathan's pathological need to indulge in stress-reducing fantasies, and someone could still get hurt. I hoped, for everyone's sake, that the disgusting, potentially disastrous situation had in fact ended, for good.

I hoped, but I also knew that what had happened once could happen again.

—24—
DESPERATE MEASURES

You are the primary and really only reason that I'm still here.

In December, Jonathan seemed to have recovered somewhat from the shock of losing his job and all that implied. He seemed to maintain a relatively optimistic, or at least functional, state of mind throughout much of December and into January, but by the middle of January, he started becoming depressive and pessimistic once again. Whatever else may have triggered the change, certainly my leaving him alone in Mariah after having spent two weeks with him—not to mention the revelation of the Andy situation and the resulting upheaval it caused—were contributing factors. And, I understood now just how fragile, how psychologically ill, Jonathan was, that whatever stability I thought he had was largely an illusion.

The day after we discussed the Andy situation over the phone, Jonathan sent me several messages in which he told me that his situation had become so desperate that he was having to give up his dogs. He asked me if I knew anyone who would take them. He said that he had actually spoken to Cliff, who had agreed to take Prissy, the one he thought would be the hardest to place. He said that he was waiting to hear back from people with whom he thought he could place Sweetie and Frizzie, which he wanted to keep together. He told me that if I had any leads, "the girls would appreciate it."

I sent him an e-mail from my "Jonathan" account, but apparently, he didn't receive it. Three hours after he sent his e-mail—an adequately long time for me to have responded, he seemed to feel—he sent a second e-mail in which he displayed an even greater sense of desperation. He told me that he had written to me several times in the previous twenty-four hours but that I hadn't responded, making him wonder if I had stopped communicating with him. He told me that if I didn't want to talk to him anymore to let him know and he wouldn't bother me again. He then went on to repeat what he'd told me about the dogs and asked me if I was still coming the next day. Finally he told me that although it was "very late days," a company in Mariah had contacted him and wanted to talk to him. He said that under the circumstances he didn't know what to do and wanted my advice, if I was willing to give it. He ended the message by telling me to please reply even if it was only to tell him that I didn't want to reply.

In spite of everything, I *was* replying, but apparently, none of my messages were getting through. I sent him yet another one from the "Jonathan" account, hoping this one would. In the meantime, Jonathan sent me another e-mail on a totally unrelated and unexpected subject. In this message, he told me, with considerable excitement, that *Jeopardy* was holding tryouts in Chicago the first week of April and that they'd given him an appointment. He said that he'd sent the required information to them a few weeks before but they were just now getting back to him. He said that he knew it was silly, but even if he didn't go or wasn't chosen, it was still nice to have been asked.

Mixed into the middle of his messages of desperation and despair, the *Jeopardy* message came across as odd, but if it were true, then perhaps it would give him something to look forward to. Jonathan loved *Jeopardy* and rarely missed a question. He would be an ideal contestant and, if he did become one, perhaps it would give him some much-needed money, even if the tryouts were still three months away.

Since my messages didn't seem to be getting through, I decided to call him. I did so around 3:45, but he didn't answer. I did, however, leave a message, hoping he would get it. Later, I decided to send him another message from my regular e-mail account, thinking the problem might lie with the "Jonathan" account from which I had sent the others.

Finally, late that afternoon, he sent me an e-mail in which he told me that perhaps the problem with the e-mail was on his end. He said that he'd been around when I'd called but had been lying down and possibly hadn't heard the phone, since he had been feeling drowsy and the TV had been on. He told me he would call, but wasn't going to "run up bills that [couldn't] be paid by [himself] and [he didn't] want to leave them for others to clear up..." He ended the message by saying that he "[wouldn't] be around much longer so this particular thorn [would] be removed from [my] side, one way or the other."

I wasn't sure what he meant when he said he wouldn't "be around much longer." I wasn't sure if he had decided to return home…or worse. Around 6:30 that evening, I called him and talked to him directly. He didn't seem suicidal, but he did seem desperate. By this point, however, he was no longer talking about giving away the dogs. We talked for about forty-five minutes and not knowing how else to help, I assured him that, in spite of everything that had happened in the previous few days, I would come to Mariah the next day.

Since I wasn't working on Wednesdays that semester, I planned to spend Wednesday afternoon through Thursday morning with him, at which time I would return to Hawthorn in time to teach my class on Thursday afternoon. Around 9:00 Wednesday morning, I sent him an e-mail confirming my plans and assuring him that in spite of current problems, I still loved him. I still wasn't sure, though, what I meant by "love." I left around 10:30 and arrived in Mariah around 1:00.

I was not looking forward to the conversation that was coming.

The primary topic for discussion was, of course, Andy. I asked Jonathan if he had anything else he wanted to tell me about him, but he said no, as if that was that. Then, turning on me, he insisted that I had had no right to access the "Iain" account. Having had enough, I reminded him that he had done everything but give me the password and asked him to explain how else I could have gotten into it. Ignoring me, he said he didn't know, but he was sure there were ways. Sarcastically, I told him that perhaps I had gotten it by doing an Internet search using "Iain's" name and had found a directory that had contained "Iain's" account information. He said nothing in response. I still wasn't sure if he had actually forgotten what he had done or was just playing another game, but I was sick of it.

When he realized he wasn't going to turn things back onto me, Jonathan finally cooled down and became more compliant with my desire to know more about Andy. One thing I wanted to know was how they had met. Jonathan told me they had met through a mutual friend of theirs named Ryan. According to Jonathan, Ryan had lived and worked in Paladin before being transferred elsewhere. Apparently Ryan had a paternal attitude toward Andy and, as Jonathan described it, had "put Andy in [his] care." He said that Andy was young and socially isolated and that Ryan had felt that Andy needed someone to watch after him. For whatever reason, Ryan had felt that Jonathan would be the perfect foster father to Andy.

Jonathan had certainly done an excellent job of "caring" for him all right. He had nearly destroyed Andy's life through his neurotic need to retreat into fantasy, through the manifestations of his maladjustment. I didn't say any of this to Jonathan, however, and the *only* thing that gave me even the *slightest* sympathy toward him was the fact that I knew he was mentally ill. Otherwise, that would have been that.

I gave him the password to the "Iain" account and he went and deleted its contents. He said that he would delete the entire account, but I told him I didn't know how to accomplish that. Not using the account further would be good enough. The fact that he did this made me feel better, if not exactly good.

The next morning, I left Mariah around 9:30. Jonathan's father had sent him some produce, and before I left, Jonathan gave me some to take with me. It had arrived in a large box, which he kept sitting on the kitchen table. At one point, I looked at the label on the box. Curiously, they had been sent from an address in the Southern state. I didn't ask Jonathan about the incongruity, though, because I assumed that his father simply had friends in that state who had sent the produce to Jonathan in his father's name.

I arrived back in Hawthorn around noon and e-mailed Jonathan to let him know I had gotten back safely. Around 12:30, I left for work, thinking I had plenty of time to get there. I had never been to the building where I was teaching my Thursday class and the directions I had been given used a specific street as an orientation point. As it turned out, though, the street was closed for repairs, which made finding the building almost impossible. By the time I managed to find the small, secluded building, I was half an hour late. It wasn't exactly the best introduction or the best impression I could have made, despite the fact that I was a victim of circumstance. Little did I know that the messiness of that day—that week—was only a foretaste of even greater messiness to come.

When I finally arrived home around 4:00, I found that Jonathan had sent me an e-mail that was at once encouraging and discouraging. He said that he had mainly been playing the online version of *Jeopardy* all morning and had managed to get his score up to 400,000 but that he had also sent out four résumés. Even so, he said he didn't know what to do. He said he feared that if he didn't get a job and didn't let his father know that he was returning home, he would eventually become homeless. He said that was why he was thinking about giving away the girls even though it was killing him to do it. He said he was glad we had cleared the air regarding the Andy situation and thanked me for making such an effort for us yet again. He ended the message by saying, as had been true too many days already, that there was "nothing to [g]o for and no place to go anyway." His message was filled with both positive and negative and I wondered which would ultimately win out.

In response, I told him that our conversation had done a great deal to clear the air and had finally answered several crucial questions that had gone unanswered for several months now. I told him that what he had told me had put a lot of things into perspective and had allowed me to understand certain things that otherwise had been incomprehensible. I told him that I wanted to put what had happened behind us and move on to whatever awaited us. In truth, I really didn't know what to say and this seemed to be the most positive spin I could put on the otherwise disturbing situation.

Later that evening, I wrote a lengthy message that carefully delineated the pros and cons of returning to England or remaining in the States. In response, he told me there was so much in my message that he didn't want to answer it offhandedly. He said he was very confused and had cried from 7:00 until 9:00, causing him to miss a favorite show. He said his parents had called that evening and had "applied the usual headlock." Then he told me that I was "the primary and really only reason that [he was] still here" and thanked me for everything I had done for him. Disturbingly, he told me again that he was very confused and sometimes thought that Malcolm, whom he called "Michael," was talking to him and telling him why things could get overwhelming. He said he still had a couple of days before he had to tell his parents whether he was going to return or stay and planned to use those days to think. He said that if he could get even one interview he would have hope and said that he always got the job if he wanted it. He ended the message by telling me not that I was "too good" *for* him, but that I was "too good" *to* him.

I was very worried about his state of mind. His comment that he thought his dead brother, Malcolm—whom he was now confusing with his live brother, Michael—was talking to him was deeply troubling. In response, I told him that I thought he needed to be taking antidepressants for the clinical depression from which he was obviously suffering. He resisted the idea, but despite the fact that I had always let people make their own decisions and run their own lives as they saw fit without my interference, I had come to feel that his well-being was *my* responsibility and that in his state of mind, he no longer had the ability to decide for himself what was best for him. I refused to let him spiral down any further and I planned to do what I could to stop it.

In order to help Jonathan, I did something that I had never done before and would never do again. Around the end of January, I made an appointment with my doctor and told him that *I* was suffering from depression with the hope that he would give me Prozac—which

I could then give to Jonathan. My doctor agreed and gave me enough samples of Prozac to last for at least two months. I felt incredibly guilty about what I had done, not only because of the questionable legality, but mainly because I had lied to a man whom I respected and who had done so much to help me. I felt that I had somehow taken advantage of his goodwill and I found it difficult to accept my deception. Perhaps I was rationalizing my behavior, but I reminded myself that I was trying to help another person overcome a debilitating disorder and possibly prevent him from killing himself, something he had alluded to doing.

The Prozac came in six bottles of ten pills. Because a clinical psychologist who had once treated me for depression had told me there were two ways to use the antidepressants to cure my problem—"take one a day or take them all at once"—I was careful to give him only one bottle at a time. As it turned out, Jonathan took only four of the pills before refusing to take more, which made me feel extremely frustrated after what I had done to get them.

I didn't return to Mariah that weekend because I had just been there on Wednesday and I saw no point in running back. In retrospect, I should have avoided the mid-week trip and waited until the weekend because I had off not only the weekend but also Martin Luther King Jr.'s birthday the following Monday, which meant that I could have gone to Mariah on Friday afternoon and stayed until Tuesday morning. But, although that arrangement would have worked better logistically, it wouldn't have worked better emotionally, since my need to see and speak to Jonathan face to face about Andy and associated issues as soon as I could after I had learned the truth about them was much more important.

On Friday, Jonathan wrote to tell me that he had heard back from one of his résumé submittals for a position as the vice president of human resources for a company in Paladin. His résumé had passed the first cut and had been sent to the selection committee. Apparently, they had received approximately 85 résumés and had forwarded only 10. From those ten, they would select three to go through the entire interview process. Although they had, of course, made no promises, Jonathan had at least made the first cut.

I told him I thought that was wonderful news and although nothing was set in stone, the news should give him cause for hope. I told him I would keep my fingers crossed and maybe his luck was finally changing. I tried to be as optimistic as possible.

In response, Jonathan was pessimistic and desperate. Although he thanked me for the words of encouragement, he also reminded me that the other companies that had contacted him had done so quickly, but that in the end nothing had come of it.

He then went on to ask me when I thought I would be coming back to Mariah. He claimed, though, that he was doing all right and commented again that the last time I had visited we had "cleared a lot of shit out of the way" and were in good stead. He also said that he knew the weather was uncertain and that he worried about my driving so much and putting so many miles on my new car. He further said that he understood that I hadn't been home much in the previous several weeks and would want to take care of whatever business had accumulated. Jonathan's attitude toward having me return was sufficiently conflicted that I was left feeling unsure about what he wanted me to do.

He concluded the message by telling me that he and Warren had decided to go ahead with the plan to make it look as if Warren were employing him and that he had finally received the papers that Warren had submitted to the INS. Apparently it was only a note of sponsorship and Jonathan and Warren had 22 days to send in the completed forms, which Jonathan also had to sign. He said that now he was "semi-legal," which was fortunate because the deadline for obtaining a sponsor was that day; without one, an order of deportation would have gone into effect. I took from his decision that he was trying either to stay in the States or not to damage his chances of coming back by being deported.

Jonathan's message left me feeling ambivalent for lots of reasons. Although someone needed to be taking care of him—and I seemed to be the only one who was able and willing to do it—the very thought of returning to Mariah so soon left me feeling drained. I had just made the 300-mile round trip only two days before, and now, Jonathan was wanting to know how soon I was going to do it again. I needed some time to myself to rest and recoup. In the previous month, I had spent only one week at home, and most of that time, I had been preoccupied with work—or with Jonathan. I was exhausted. After teaching that morning, I had spent much of the afternoon running errands, and by the time I had gotten home, I had become so worn out that when I had lain down on the couch, intending to watch TV, I had fallen asleep for two and a half hours—something I rarely did. I needed to be with Jonathan, but I also needed to be by myself, do things for myself. I felt very guilty, very torn.

I told him that although I would be busy on Saturday, I might be able to come on Sunday and stay until I had to teach in Viridian on Tuesday. That was actually the last thing I wanted to do. In response, he told me, mercifully, to take the weekend for myself. He told me that because the weather was unpredictable and because I had been "under so much pressure because of [him] and all of [his] goofiness,"

I should wait until the following weekend to return. He told me that he was probably not going back home immediately, if he did, and that there were many reasons, "but mostly you, us, the girls."

I didn't need much encouragement to stay home.

Later that night, Jonathan sent me another e-mail in which he asserted his need for reassurance from me that if he refused to go home, he could continue to count on me. He said he had gotten "the usual bash e-mail from [his] father" and wondered if his father could "make the screws any tighter." He told me that if he stayed, he would be "jumping off a cliff" and that I was his only safety net. He said that it took "a lot of faith and courage to do that relying so much on one relationship" and that once he told his father no, he would have nothing to fall back on if he couldn't rely on me.

I tried to reassure him that if he decided to stay, I was behind him 100%. I reminded him that we had a plan that would allow him to begin to get back on his feet and take care of the most pressing of his short-term problems. I told him I knew that, in spite of the problems that had arisen in the previous few days, I was still committed to our relationship and making it work, to helping him in any way that I could. I assured him that if he decided to stay here, I would do whatever needed to be done to help him be here. I concluded by telling him, adamantly, to "go tell [his] father no."

Saturday morning, he wrote to tell me that he'd had an "awful" night, saying that he hadn't fallen asleep until after 6:00 in the morning and had just woken up after three "rather bad" hours. He said he had a sore throat and was congested, and although he knew that part of it was from being run down and from the cold weather, he also knew that part of it was psychosomatic, from his worries over how his parents would react to his refusal to return home. He said that according to the last two e-mails he'd received from them that morning, they were planning to call the next morning. He thanked me for my encouragement and told me he would let me know what happened. He concluded by telling me that he was going to make some strong coffee, "the last of that," and try to wake up and summon up some energy. Telling me he would write more later, he again thanked me for everything.

If he *was* going to stay, then it was crucial that we put the plan that we—mainly I—had formulated into action as swiftly as possible. When I had stayed with Jonathan during my winter break, we had taken photographs of *Still Life* with the intention of submitting them to the auction house through which he was trying to sell it so they could begin to appraise it. I felt it was important to submit the photographs as soon as possible, so to that end, I sent him a package containing $20 as well as a photo mailer and some stamps so he wouldn't have to bother with getting them himself. That afternoon, I wrote to him, telling him what I'd done, as well as reminding him that we had discussed the possibility of his having the rent on his property in the South temporarily redirected from his retirement account to him. I hoped this would help the plan to progress.

Around 2:30 that afternoon, Jonathan sent me an e-mail that began on a poignant note. After thanking me for my message, he confessed that he was bothered about how quiet it got around the apartment, "especially when you can't go out, even if there was some place to go and you wanted to." Then, he apologized for the fact that I had felt compelled to send him money once again and said that he didn't want money to intrude into our relationship any more than it already had. He said that he would look into having the rent money rerouted from his retirement trust to him. He said it would be only a few hundred a month, but given his situation, it seemed like a million. He said, though, that a request to do that had to be in writing, which unfortunately meant that "[l]ike everything else," he would have to wait.

On a more hopeful note, he said that he'd had an e-mail exchange with his former boss at TekNetium, who had told him she was looking for someone to fill a vice president/human resources position working for one of their clients in Winford. Although she was asking in general, Jonathan had told her *he* might be interested. Surprised by his interest, Jonathan had explained "some but not all" of what had happened to him in recent months. He said the job emphasized recruitment and planning but was also high-stress and a step down from what he had been doing at OutSource, so he didn't know if it was desirable or feasible. Even so, he commented that he had been "thinking of working at Dollar General, so..." he thought it wouldn't hurt to look into it. He said that in addition to learning about the TekNetium client position, he had learned that, unfortunately, there were no positions currently available at TekNetium Corporate, thinking that might be a possibility. I assumed he wasn't wanting a position as COO, since that had led, in part, to his undoing

As far as the *appearance* of jobs was concerned, Jonathan informed me that the Tomlinsons had invited him to dinner on Sunday and that Warren wanted him to come to his office on Monday morning to sign the papers that would give the INS the impression he was working. He said that Chase had moved into a condominium, which Jonathan said was "a problem eliminated." He said that someone would come to get him on Sunday and take him back on Monday. He told me he knew I had been thinking about coming to Mariah on Sunday but said that although he wanted and needed to see me, I did so much driving the way it was and had just visited a few days before that he thought it was better that I waited until next weekend to come. He also said he thought he was coming down with something and didn't want me to catch it. Wanting my input about what he should do, he asked me, "What do you think, my dear?" He ended his message by telling me he was glad that I was having a normal life.

Was he joking? My life hadn't been normal for months.

I assured him that I didn't mind sending him the $20 for the photos, so he shouldn't feel uncomfortable about accepting it. It was hardly anything at all, I said, and it was serving what I felt was an important purpose. I also assured him that I didn't feel money was intruding into our relationship—although that wasn't entirely true. I told him I thought the position with the client company sounded interesting, although I wondered if he had the stamina to assume such a position. Perhaps if he were receiving treatments, though, he might be able to manage it, although it was difficult to tell.

I encouraged him to take the Tomlinsons up on their offer to have dinner the following night. I told him I thought it would allow him not only to take care of some important business, but also to do some much-needed socializing. I thought it would also allow him to get out of "Hooterville," as he sometimes called Mariah, for a while and spend some time in a different, and better, environment. I told him I was glad to know that if he did go, someone would be taking him to and from Paladin because I had my concerns about the reliability of his car. I told him I thought it would help him feel more invigorated and less isolated.

I also confessed, however, that my motives for having him spend the weekend with the Tomlinsons weren't entirely about him. I acknowledged that I had been feeling exhausted and could use the weekend to gather my strength. I assured him it wasn't that I didn't want and need to see him too—in fact, I felt better when I was there and could see for myself how he was—but that I needed to recharge and not do anything too strenuous. I admitted that I was having trouble staying awake for extended periods, that my body seemed to be telling me something. I told him I might be able to come to Mariah sometime during the coming week—late Tuesday afternoon through early Thursday morning, perhaps—or, if not then, possibly the following weekend.

Something in his message, though, bothered me. There was something about his use of the phrase "What do you think, my dear?" that gave me an odd feeling. Perhaps it was the fact that he rarely used terms of endearment, which made me think he was in an unusual frame of mind. I knew, of course, that there was something wrong with him—the revelation of the Andy situation had made that obvious—and I was now sensitized to oddities in his writing and behavior. Even so, I didn't know, rationally, what to make of it…or if I was perhaps making too much of it. I didn't dismiss my feeling, but ultimately I decided not to question him in some way about the issue.

Around 7:00 that evening, he replied. He began by telling me that he was having one of his "neurotic episodes." He said that once he told "Papa" that he wouldn't be coming home, he would cut him off and refuse to help him later. He said that he would then be marooned in the United States, in Mariah, with no fallback at all. He said it was either "victory or death, just like the Knights of Malta."

He mentioned the TekNetium client job again, saying that it seemed to be intense and that for roughly the same effort and money he could return to OutSource, so it didn't seem to be much of an option. Jonathan said that since he was still receiving disability, which he apparently still was, Mike couldn't fire him unless he was deemed fit to work and didn't. He said that under the Americans With Disabilities Act (ADA), Mike was compelled to give him the same or a similar position, although I didn't know how the ADA rules might apply to a foreigner. He said that what he ultimately did depended on what the insurance company did regarding his claim for long-term disability. He complained that everything was getting "so confusing." I knew *I* was confused.

Jonathan said that since he had last written, he had accepted Joanne's "kind invitation" to visit. He said, though, that what he and Warren were planning to do made him nervous, since they were "circumventing the law in spirit if not in fact." He also mentioned the "Chase Factor." As far as I knew, Jonathan hadn't seen Chase since Thanksgiving, and he wasn't the only one who wondered what would happen if they saw each other. He said, however, that if he was going to stay with them, he had no choice. He told me he was sure I needed a break from him and his problems—which I did—and told me to enjoy my "Jonathan free" vacation.

In response, I assured him that he was not flying without a net if he remained here, as he seemed to feel. I reminded him that we had a plan to put his life back onto solid footing and that there were other people who were both able and willing to help him get on top of his current situation. I reminded him that I had been there for him and assured him that I would continue to be there for him. I told him that things could, and would, be all right if he just availed himself of the help around him. I hoped for the best, but I was also prepared for the worst.

I had difficulty sleeping that night. I wondered how Jonathan's parents would react to the news that he had decided to stay in the States in such abysmal conditions. Early that morning, I wrote to him to find out if he had delivered the news to his parents and had gotten their reaction. I also tried to encourage him, knowing it was especially important that morning.

In response, he told me that they hadn't called yet, which they usually did somewhere between 10:00 and 11:00 our time. He also said that he had gotten some clothes together to take on his overnight trip to the Tomlinsons' but admitted that he felt "very nervey" and that he might go another time, depending on how things went with his parents.

Later that morning, he finally spoke to his parents and told them about his plans to sell *Still Life* and remain in the States. Around 11:30, he sent me a message with the alarming title "Nuclear Meltdown." Apparently, things had not gone well.

According to Jonathan, he had just gotten off the phone after speaking to his parents, mainly his father, for forty-five minutes. When Jonathan had told his father that he was planning to sell *Still Life* to remain in the States, his father had gone "nuclear." He forbade Jonathan to sell it, reminding him that it was a legacy from his grandfather, and to think carefully about doing something so outrageous. Drawing on the book of Genesis, Jonathan's father had compared him to Esau, who had sold his birthright to his brother Jacob for a mess of pottage. Although Jonathan owned the painting and didn't need his father's permission to sell it, his father had told him that if he did, he would never speak to him again. His father told him that his behavior was "out of proportion" and that he just needed to come home. His father had said that he would call him that Wednesday to see if he had changed his mind. Needless to say, Jonathan was beside himself. The line had been drawn and now it was up to Jonathan to decide if he had the courage to cross it.

He ended the message by telling me that he had to get ready for his overnight trip to the Tomlinsons' and that Chase, who would be chauffeuring him, would be arriving in about an hour. He told me he would be back the next day but would try to check e-mails from Paladin.

I wasn't surprised at his parents' response. I knew how much the members of Jonathan's family valued their "things," seemingly at the expense of other considerations. Although the painting could be viewed as a "legacy," I felt, as Jonathan did, that a work as significant as *Still Life* belonged to the public. I still felt at odds with myself for keeping the scarab, which I felt belonged in a museum. Even so, I was more concerned about his father's attitude toward *him*, about what seemed to be important to someone of the British upper crust and what did not.

In response, I suggested that Jonathan simply tell his father that he had decided not to sell *Still Life* after all even if he did decide to go ahead and sell it. The painting was his and he had the right to do whatever he wanted to do with it. Although I knew that his father would eventually learn that the painting was gone—hopefully under better circumstances—he could tell him that he'd sold it not because he needed the money, but because he'd thought it belonged in a museum or done it for some other "acceptable" reason. I suggested that in the meantime, he could tell his father that he'd decided to reroute the money from his property in the South or that he had promising job leads here. I told him that although it probably wasn't my place to say it, I didn't understand how his father could expect his children to be independent, yet not allow them to run their own lives.

I didn't expect a response until Monday, when he returned from the Tomlinsons'. Around 6:00 that evening, he finally wrote. He told me that Chase had picked him up around 12:30 Sunday afternoon and that they'd gone to Paladin. According to Jonathan, Joanne and Warren were the consummate hosts. Joanne had made Bangkok Chicken, which was apparently covered with peanuts that Jonathan carefully ate around, and a four-layer cake, since Joanne apparently knew how much Jonathan loved his desserts.

At one point, Joanne had taken Jonathan aside and given him a "motherly" talk. Although Joanne was only six years older than Jonathan, she told him he seemed much younger to her and, therefore, she felt maternal toward him. She suggested that what Jonathan should do was to come back to Paladin, stay with Chase until he got back on his feet, then decide what to do next. Joanne had also offered him money, which he was too embarrassed to take, especially in light of the conversation he'd just had with his father.

On Monday morning around 11:00, he and Warren had gone to Warren's attorney's to sign the papers that would make it appear to the INS that Jonathan was gainfully employed, something that made Jonathan "about…choke." Afterwards, Chase had taken him out to lunch and had shown him his condo, which was a graduation present from his parents. It was, conveniently, located behind one of the gay nightclubs in Paladin. Later, they had gone back to the Tomlinsons', where Jonathan had gotten his things, then they had gone back to Mariah. Chase was supposed to buy groceries for Jonathan, which he had done once before, but Jonathan refused to let him do it. He said he wasn't going to be anyone's "charity case" and would starve first.

Given his increasingly desperate situation, I wondered how long he would maintain his resolve.

As far as my suggestion that he sell *Still Life* and not tell his father was concerned, Jonathan said that he refused to lie to him "for many reasons." I wondered if feelings of remorse over what he had done to Andy, to Colin, to Cliff, to me figured in any way into his reluctance. I hoped.

He concluded by telling me he was going to lie down, having found the experience emotionally draining. He repeated that he would be speaking to his father again on Wednesday and was now dreading it even more. I knew that whatever he chose to do, it wouldn't be easy on either of us.

Because I had a teachers' meeting the following Saturday, I wasn't going to be able to spend the following weekend with him, either. I told him, though, that I would come to Mariah from Viridian on Tuesday and stay until I had to return to Hawthorn on Thursday.

Around 9:45 that Monday evening, he replied, more morose than ever. Although he seemed to look forward to my coming on Tuesday, he said that he used to look forward to our "week ends" together, a pattern that seemed to be changing "just through life going on"—or, rather, through everyone *else's* life going on while his had come to a standstill. He said that even if he sold the lithographs, no one would rent him a place to live without a job or income, which meant that he was stuck in Mariah. He said that he didn't want to become the Tomlinsons' "pet project" and needed to be careful about how enmeshed he became with them. He said that his visit to Paladin had only emphasized how wretched his life in Mariah was, which was making him think his father was right. He told me we could discuss it more when we saw each other, but he was beginning to think that he should admit defeat and go home. "We'll see," he ended uncertainly.

To try to offset his sorrow over the loss of our "week ends," as well as his feelings of isolation and despair, I decided to return to Mariah on Tuesday. Although Jonathan expressed his reluctance to have me make the long trip, he told me I was welcome to come if it wasn't too much bother. He said that Joanne had told him that he could stay with them anytime if things became too hard for him, so I wasn't his only source of support. In spite of what the Tomlinsons were doing for him, however, I felt that *I* needed to be there for him.

I stayed with him from Tuesday afternoon through Thursday morning, when I returned to Hawthorn to teach the second week of my Thursday afternoon class. Our conversations while I was there involved rehashes of the latest information that he had already given to me, reexpressions of the growing feelings of hopelessness and desperation that increasingly weighed on him. I tried to comfort him, but aside from the suggestions for improving his lot that I had already made, I could think of little of practical value to add. By the time I got home from work Thursday afternoon, I was physically, mentally, and emotionally exhausted from driving, from teaching, from worrying.

On Friday morning around 11:30, Jonathan sent me an e-mail in which he was painfully direct about the extremity of his circumstances. He said that he was overwhelmed by everything that was happening: no replies to his résumés, no money to pay his bills, the landlady demanding to be paid... He was extremely agitated that morning and didn't know what to do.

Around 1:30, he sent me another e-mail that was heartbreaking. He told me he was feeling better, having gone for a second walk that day to try to relieve his nervousness then having gotten his hair cut. He said that he had scrounged together six dollars in quarters that he'd found in his car and since that was the price of a haircut, he had taken it as an omen. He said as well that it was still too early to worry about Joan trying to evict him. Raising the subject of repayment, he assured me that he would give my phone number to his father, who he knew would repay me and my mother what we had given to him as soon as possible. He thanked me for everything I had done to help him, telling me, though, that he loved me not because of my help, but in spite of it. He expressed his hope that he could see me the next weekend. As if he were trying to bribe me with a tempting offer, he told me there would be an all-you-can-eat "pig fry" at one of the local churches and perhaps we could go. That would give us something to do when normally in Mariah there was nothing.

This was no way to live.

For several months, Jonathan and I had discussed the possibility of living together not simply in Paladin or somewhere else in my state, but eventually, in England. He had told me, though, that it was difficult for foreigners to get visas to work in England and that my ability to work, at least legally, would be limited. That had always bothered me because by not working, by not having my own income, I would be dependent on Jonathan's goodwill to survive and, in some ways, to control my own life in a foreign country, totally cut off from my familiar sources of support. Consequently, I had always had reservations about following him to England.

Even so, we had discussed certain job possibilities there and he told me about one that involved his family. He had told me that his family owned a company called VeraMed, which produced aloe-based skin care products. He explained how the aloe, which was grown in South America, was harvested, the aloe removed, and the leftovers fed to the cattle. He said that the extraction process was simple and inexpensive and that the products themselves yielded a 700% to 900% profit. Jonathan's parents had been enticing him to come home by offering to buy him a small business to run and they thought letting him run VeraMed might be an option. Knowing that I knew how to design and maintain web sites, Jonathan told me that if he accepted their offer, I could design and maintain the company's site, which currently didn't have one.

In some ways it was an appealing option, but I still didn't know about the idea of going with him to England where my life would be expanded in some ways but diminished in others. It seemed unlikely that if Jonathan returned to England, I would be returning with him. If his situation became too dire, then the only reasonable alternative would be to give up and return home, which would bring an end to our relationship. Even after everything we had been though, *I* had been through, it was difficult to accept, but the possibility seemed to be looming larger with each passing day.

—25—
THE ONE TRUE HONEST PERSON

I always enjoyed talking to you and felt that you were really the one true honest person in that circle.

Although Jonathan had deleted the e-mails in the "Iain" account and had promised to stop using it to masquerade as the business executive/hospice worker/travel agent/Internet cruiser, I wasn't convinced. His need to retreat into stress-relieving fantasy was too compelling and I doubted that the unmasking of "Iain" would stop anything. Jonathan had retained the password to which I had changed it and was allowing me to access the account, but I took his "openness" less as an attempt to prove to me that he really had desisted than as an attempt to pacify—or mislead—me. If he had created the "Iain" account, he could have easily created another through which to continue playing that character. Although he had assured me that the situation between him and Andy had ended, I wasn't foolish enough to take his word for it. So, I continued to monitor the account, thinking that even if Jonathan, as "Iain," didn't send further messages to Andy, *Andy* might send one to *him*—one that I might be able to intercept—which would then give me some indication of the actual state of things between the two of them.

On the morning of Tuesday, January 29, I checked the "Iain" account. I had been checking the account sporadically throughout the previous two weeks and had found nothing. I didn't know if this was because Jonathan had been managing to intercept, and delete, the e-mails going into that account before I managed to find them or if

"Iain" had, in reality, not been receiving any. Whatever the case, that Tuesday morning when I checked the account, I did find an e-mail—from Andy.

In it, he regretfully informed Iain that he and Jonathan were no longer involved with each other. According to Andy, he had failed Jonathan in his ability to believe that any of what Jonathan had promised him actually existed. He said that he'd had plenty of help "casting the shadow of doubt," but in the end, it was he who had chosen to disbelieve. He lamented that "us commoners" were not meant to be with what he described as the "true princes of the world." He told Iain that he had always enjoyed talking to him and felt that he was the "one true honest person" in Jonathan's circle. He ended the message by wishing Iain well and thanked him for everything he had ever done or said to him.

One of the "true princes of the world." The "one true honest person" in Jonathan's circle. If Andy only *knew*. The outrage over what Jonathan had done to both Andy and me that had been seething beneath the surface for two weeks finally boiled over. Over the next hour, I composed and sent Jonathan an ultimatum that defined the situation and expressed my expectations in *no* uncertain terms:

First, I told him that I had checked the "Iain" account and had found the latest message from Andy. Although the message seemed to indicate that Andy knew he had somehow been misled, he still had *no* idea just how far. He still had no idea that "Iain" was an invented person, was Jonathan in disguise, and he deserved to know. Indeed, he deserved to know the truth, the *whole* truth, and not just convenient bits of it. I told Jonathan that if he had *any* respect for Andy, then he would recognize his right to know the truth, especially about someone for whom he was willing to throw his life away. What he had done to him was awful. Andy was apparently in love with Jonathan, but all Jonathan had done was to exploit and manipulate those feelings, the most positive and profound feelings that one person can have for another, for no better reason than to satisfy some neurotic need of his to retreat into a fantasy world or to entertain himself when he'd grown tired of watching *Jerry Springer*.

I reminded him that, unfortunately, he had affected Andy's life on the level not of fantasy, but of reality. I told him that although he congratulated himself on how he had managed to prevent him from abandoning his real life in the United States for some imaginary life in England, he needed to remember that *he* was the one who had created the problem in the first place. He had told me that he was always going to have to live with the consequences of his actions, but I informed him that he was living with them without actually having taken *real* responsibility for them. I told him that if he *did* take real responsibility for what he had done, he would tell Andy the whole truth and bear the brunt of whatever followed, even if that meant losing him from his life.

I told Jonathan that he was going to tell Andy the truth about where he had *really* been, what he had *really* been doing since the previous summer. He was also going to tell him that the entire scheme to bring him to England so the two of them could be together was nothing but a fantasy. And, he was *certainly* going to tell him that he wasn't "besotted" with him, if in fact he wasn't. If he *was*, then he was going to tell *me* the truth. Either way, I told him, we *both* deserved to know the truth.

I told him that by pretending that our relationship, that *I*, didn't exist, he had devalued our relationship, *me*, and I was deeply offended by it. I told him the only way I would begin to feel better about what had happened was if he told Andy the truth about us. I told him that he deserved to know the truth and I deserved to be shown basic respect and that we *both* deserved better than what we'd gotten.

In the end, I told him that I had taken all that I was going to take of "this Iain shit" and that it was time for him to clean up the mess he had made. I told him that what he had done had damaged my ability to trust him and, more importantly, had nearly destroyed Andy's life. I told him that it was time he took some *real* responsibility for what he had done and that if he didn't, our relationship would never be right again—or perhaps not be at all.

Throwing his own challenge back in his face, I told him to ask himself the "Dear Abby" question: Was I worth it or not? Was perpetrating and protecting his lies more important than being with me? I told him to decide.

Infuriated and disgusted, I went to work.

Jonathan's response, which he sent around 1:00 that afternoon, was defensive. After pointing out that Andy's e-mail had only confirmed that he had indeed ended the "Andy thing," as he called it, he parroted my position that the situation had been sick and had gotten seriously out of control. Yet, in spite of his seeming acceptance of responsibility for what he had done, he spent much of the message attacking me. He told me that if I wanted to punish him for being a "terrible person" by telling Andy the truth, I certainly had the ability to do that. His rationale for not doing it himself was that since Andy was not directly involved in the mess that his life had become, he didn't want to hurt him further by telling him the truth. He claimed that if he had planned to continue using the "Iain" account, he would have changed the password to bar me from accessing it, as I had done to him. He told me that he hadn't checked it since he'd emptied it and had just wanted to close it, but since he didn't know how to do it and neither did I, he had left it active.

He then told me that if he didn't think I loved him, I should end our relationship. Condemning me for my seeming sense of superiority, he told me that it was easy for me to be "judge, prosecutor, and jury." He claimed that Andy knew that he wasn't "besotted" with him and pointed out that if he were, he could have easily let him know that he was nearby and could have been seeing him, since he had plenty of time to do it. As he had before, he accused me of overreacting, telling me to "take a deep breath" and calm down. He told me that if I chose to end our relationship over the "Andy thing," he would be "extremely upset and sad for an extremely long time." He told me that I was the only one on whom he relied, as if this were supposed to make me feel better or perhaps to make me feel guilty.

After reaffirming that the situation between him and Andy had ended and wouldn't be reenflamed, he implored me to drop the issue because in his fragile state, he was unable to deal with the repercussions, both from Andy and from me, for what he had done. Again, he told me that he knew he couldn't stop me from getting my "pound of flesh" by telling Andy the truth, but asked me to ignore the issue, at least until he could find the strength he needed to face it.

Because I was at work and couldn't respond, Jonathan had time to send me another, somewhat angrier version of the same message an hour later. Stating that he would attempt to express himself more clearly than he had the first time, he largely repeated the positions he had assumed before. Andy already knew that he couldn't trust him, he said, and since their relationship had ended, that should be sufficient for me. He told me that *our* relationship could end because of it, but he hoped it wouldn't. He stated that *I* was the main reason he was trying to rebuild his life in the United States, under difficult circumstances, when it would be much easier for him to go back to England and resume a decent life. He added that if he did, ironically, he would be where Andy thought he was and, therefore, could make most of the lies that he had told him true.

He asked me what I would gain from telling Andy the truth apart from hurting a stranger further than he had already been hurt and to "debase" him (Jonathan). He asked me who *I* was to decide when enough was enough regarding something that affected me, yes, but that affected others more. Trying to minimize what he had done at my expense, he revived his accusation that I had "hacked" into the "Iain" account, which was bad enough, but going to Andy and telling him the truth was going too far. If *he* was guilty of wrongdoing, then so was *I*—perhaps even more so—and implied that morally I had no right to take a superior attitude, let alone act on it.

He went on to inform me that if I raised the issue again, he would go home. He said he was having a difficult enough time maintaining even a semblance of a normal life the way it was, but without my emotional support, it would become impossible. He stated that he had written to his father, informing him that he might be returning, and could be back in England as early as the following week. He concluded by telling me that once I got over my "fit of indignation," as he called it, I should decide if that was what I wanted. If so, he said, then it would be done.

I was astonished at the way he had rationalized his behavior, evaded any responsibility, and in some ways, suggested, if not outright stated, that he thought *my* behavior was irresponsible, unethical, and unreasonable. I was especially astounded by his comment that if he returned to England, where Andy thought he was, he could make most of the lies he had told him true. The way his mind twisted reality, rationality, in order to avoid the consequences of his actions was disorienting and disturbing. In the end, I was even more upset and sickened than I had been in the beginning.

In response, I sent him a lengthy message in which I told him that if he had in fact gone to all the trouble he had to stay in the States just to be with me, then he should at least make it worth his while by knowing what the issues were that needed to be resolved. There were at least two. I told him, first and foremost, that every time I took issue with something he did that I considered wrong, he usually overreacted, sometimes to the point of threatening to end our relationship and return to England. I told him I felt that he was more interested in shutting me up than taking me seriously and discussing the issue rationally and respectfully. I told him that his angry, dismissive, even threatening reactions were a definite impediment in our relationship and that if our relationship was going to continue, then that was going to have to change.

Second, I reminded him that he had repeatedly stated that the only reason he was remaining in the United States was to be with me, but if that was true, then how did his plans involve me? I told him that if he was serious about us living together, having a life together, then we needed to make a specific, concrete plan to make that happen. Even though I *had* made such a plan, he had done little to further it, which left me wondering what he wanted. Without those two issues addressed in some meaningful way, nothing could progress. *We* could not progress. I concluded by telling him that after spending all afternoon teaching and driving I was exhausted and telling him to write to me, if he would, or at least write to me to tell me that he didn't want to write to me.

When he responded around 9:00 that night, his tone was much more subdued, much more reasonable. He explained that because of his situation and condition, everything seemed intensified, which caused him to overreact. He said that Andy had written to "Iain" to do what he needed to do to move on with his life. He said that he was ashamed of what had happened but promised that it wouldn't happen again. He reminded me that I overreacted sometimes as well—for example, when I had intended to leave in the middle of the night when he had suggested we see other people—and that we all have emotional reactions to things that then pass.

He said that his threat to return to England had been triggered by my expression of doubt about our future. He stated that I was the only one who was providing him with the help he needed to be able to remain in the country, and that if I withdrew my support, he would have no choice but to go back. He said that the Tomlinsons had helped him in some ways, but that he was reluctant to become too entangled in their "sticky web" from which he felt it would be difficult to extricate himself.

He said that as far as our future was concerned, he needed to obtain some kind of income—from working, from disability, from selling the paintings—before he could offer me a definite plan. He expressed his desire to return to Paladin, which he said he liked and didn't find overwhelming the way he did cities like New York or Chicago. He lamented that he didn't have the strength that he'd had six months before, which was difficult for him to accept, but that he was trying to adjust. He predicted that he probably had one difficult month left, by which point he should have a job, have his long-term disability approved, or have the lithographs sold, any of which would give him enough money to live on until *Still Life* sold later. He reminded me that was the plan that I had largely created and that if he overcame the final hurdle of obtaining the funds he needed, he could make it come to fruition. He told me he had a job interview in a city located between Mariah and Paladin that Thursday, which meant the job would be an easy commute from either city. Although he knew he was qualified, however, he also knew he had to appear healthy and coherent and was nervous about doing well, since he felt desperate to get it.

Otherwise, he stated that he couldn't deal with any more serious issues at that point, reminding me again that I overreacted then calmed down, as he did. He also expressed his concerns about how tired I was, how much driving I did, and how I didn't seem to be taking care of myself. He concluded by telling me he knew he was rambling but was glad that I had answered him. He told me he hoped to hear from me soon and maybe see me soon.

With that encouraging note, with his increasing concentration on making his life better in *reality* and not in fantasy, on making things better for *me*, I felt relieved and even a little hopeful. Perhaps if Jonathan got the job or *a* job, sold *Still Life*, moved back to Paladin, resumed his treatments, returned to some semblance of normality, his need to retreat into stress-reducing fantasies and their damaging effects on other people would vanish, becoming a footnote in an unfortunate chapter in his life. At least that was what I hoped.

■

Aside from the last message that Andy sent to "Iain" on January 29, I found no further activity on the account and assumed that Jonathan had stopped posing as "Iain," which I thought was a step in the right direction. Even so, I was still confronted with a much larger, much graver, matter: Jonathan was not only physically ill, but also mentally ill and I was now afraid that what had happened before could happen again—this time, with disastrous results. His behavior was manifestly not that of a rational person, and whatever other reasons I might have had for staying with Jonathan, I was now staying with him, staying close to him, in part to monitor his behavior and prevent him, I hoped, from truly harming someone. The complications in my life that I was suffering because of Jonathan seemed to be growing exponentially with each passing day and I was growing equally uncertain what I should do.

Yet, despite Jonathan's and Andy's assurances that the "Andy thing" was indeed over, I did decide that if I saw *any* evidence that it wasn't, I was going to tell Andy the truth. I wasn't planning to do this to hurt a stranger further than he had already been hurt, as Jonathan had described it, but to *stop* him from being hurt further. *Jonathan* was the one who was concerned about being hurt. I didn't want to "debase" Jonathan, but preserving his upper-crust pride was not paramount when someone else seemed in danger of destroying his life because of it. Jonathan had accused me of being "judge, prosecutor and jury" and asked me who I was to decide when enough was enough in a matter that affected others more than it affected me, but *someone* with the knowledge, the rationality, the conscience, the responsibility—something that I alone among everyone involved seemed to possess—needed to take an appropriate action. Unlike Cain, I had always believed that we *were* our brother's keeper, were obligated to help someone avert disaster. This had very little to do with feelings of "indignation," as Jonathan had dismissively described my reaction, but with doing the right thing, with keeping someone from getting hurt, and I was prepared to do it.

To that end, I composed a letter to Andy in which I outlined, in great detail, where Jonathan had *really* been and what he had *really* been doing in the eight months that I had known him. It also included numerous ways that Andy could find out for himself that I, unlike Jonathan, was telling the truth. The "one true honest person" was someone Andy had never met, but the truth he had to tell him was only an e-mail away. I hoped I would never have to send it, but I was prepared to do it. I was not going to allow Jonathan's need to retreat into fantasy to destroy Andy's reality.

—26—
STRANGE DAYS

i think i'm having a nervous breakdown.

By the beginning of February, my physical and emotional health had grown considerably worse. In February, I often suffer from depression, presumably the type called seasonal affective disorder, but this February was especially rough. The unrelenting strain of trying to take care of Jonathan from afar, the continuous 300-mile round trips between Hawthorn and Mariah as I tried to hold down not one but two lives, and the unremitting preoccupation with Jonathan's myriad problems were all beginning to take their toll.

Whenever I mentioned how bad I felt, however, Jonathan usually managed to upstage me with his own, more extravagant problems. On Tuesday, February 5, I e-mailed him and mentioned that I wasn't feeling good. In response, he e-mailed me to tell me that he didn't feel good himself and was having "a lot of problems about some emotional things." He said that Glenn had been on his mind so strongly that evening that he was convinced he was alive but in trouble. Unfortunately, he couldn't do anything but wait. In addition, he'd gotten an e-mail from Cliff, which he always found upsetting. Given what Jonathan had been leading him to believe, however, I couldn't imagine what Cliff had been reacting to. Finally, a phone interview he'd done that day was "hard to read," leaving him feeling uncertain. He concluded by telling me that it hadn't been a good day and that things were getting "harder and harder."

As I had tried to do practically from the beginning, I ignored my own problems and focused on his. In response, I wrote a lengthy, supportive message in which I tried to comfort him. In the message, I told him that I had had a dream about Glenn the night before in which Glenn called me to let me know what had happened to him. He was definitely alive in the dream; he just hadn't had any way to contact anyone until he somehow got my number. I told Jonathan that although I didn't know what it meant, it was, at the least, an indication of how prone I was to absorb other people's situations and problems.

When I finally received his reply around 12:30 the next afternoon, Jonathan appeared to be both apologetic and appreciative. Even so, he spent most of his message focusing on his own situation. He began by telling me that he had been up since 5:30 and had been crying on and off throughout the morning. He mentioned Glenn again and how tormented he felt over the situation. He expressed how much he hated living his marginalized life in Mariah. He stated that he was receiving disconnect notices and Joan was becoming demanding about his unpaid rent. He lamented how days went by with no one even to say hello to. He said that his latest job interviews had not gone well and stated that no one else was responding. He described himself as feeling as if his head were in a vise, as if he were in the cul-de-sac of his life.

He told me, though, that he didn't expect me to fix things; he told me that I had already done enough and hated the fact that money had "bolloxed up" our relationship. He reported that if he got the lithographs to the auction house by Wednesday, February 20, the profits from their sale would be available no later than Sunday, March 10. As far as the sale of *Still Life* was concerned, he said that the art dealer with whom he had been working had forwarded the materials he had provided to him regarding *Still Life* to an expert on Cubism and that the dealer would be getting back to him with their verdict soon.

He ended his heartbreaking message by telling me that he would continue to do the best that he could for as long as he could and, again, thanked me for everything.

Concerned for him, I wrote back, telling him I was planning to come on Friday. In response, he told me how glad he was that I was coming. He told me he missed me a lot and said, sweetly, that even if other people were around, it wouldn't be the same as it was when I was there.

Reporting on events back home, he told me that it was Accession Day in England, which commemorated the day that Queen Elizabeth II had succeeded to the throne. This year was special, however, because it was also the Queen's Golden Jubilee, marking her 50th year as monarch. Yet, in spite of the special occasion, no one seemed very excited. Jonathan said that Colin had reported that "bloody" cannons had been going off all day all over London and that at one point when he had been on Oxford Street, they had performed a 42-gun salute, which had nearly knocked him down. He also mentioned that Heaven, the gay-oriented nightclub that Jonathan and his friends had frequented, was going to be featuring a drag salute to the Queen, which he assumed would be "wickedly funny and mean."

Returning to more serious matters, he apologized, as he had many times before, for causing me so much worry. He said that his situation was overwhelming to him and that some days it affected him worse than others; that day had been a particularly rough day. He told me to have a good day and urged me not to be too concerned. He assured me he would be all right in the end. I wasn't convinced.

On Thursday, the 7th, he wrote to tell me that he planned to go to the park "after Jerry [Springer]" and "watch the river for a while." There was little else to do. He considered taking Sweetie and Frizzie, but then decided against it because he "[couldn't] seem to manage them anymore." That was unfortunate because, except for one time when Frizzie had briefly escaped one day in December, the dogs hadn't seen the outside for more than two months.

Later that evening, he wrote to tell me that he'd gotten *four* e-mails from his parents that day. "That was unusual," he commented, because "it [was] 3 most days." Most of the messages appeared to have come from his father, and the increase had occurred because "[his] mother [had] taken to writing on her own." Although he didn't discuss the content of the messages, I surmised they were not supportive.

Before I left for Mariah on Friday, I had already decided that I would try to stay there until I had to teach in Viridian on Tuesday. I was planning to give my Monday morning class a test, which someone else could proctor for me and which, therefore, did not necessitate my being there to do it. That way, I could spend the better part of four days with Jonathan. I sent my boss's secretary an e-mail informing her that I needed to be out of town Monday and asking her if she would proctor the test for me.

That Sunday, Jonathan and I went to Paladin. On Wednesday, Jonathan had asked me if we could spend the day there, and although I told him that we could spend the whole weekend there, for which I would pay, he vetoed the idea, telling me that I was "very sweet and kind," but that he "[couldn't] afford it and [he wouldn't] keep allowing [me] to keep paying."

In the end, we spent what proved to be a chilly, rainy, and generally nasty day there that only grew chillier, rainier, and nastier as the day progressed. Since it had been several weeks since we'd checked the status of Jonathan's things, I suggested that we pay a visit to the storage unit, but he said he didn't feel up to it. Instead, we stopped at a thrift store in a strip mall across from the units, where we both bought pullover sweaters, what Jonathan referred to as "jumpers." Later, we made our way downtown to one of the big antiques malls that we had visited before, but not for some time. I thought this was the store at which Jonathan had bought the new bed and had flirted with the owner until he had dropped the price, but I wasn't sure.

After looking around for a while, Jonathan asked me if I would wait in the hallway for a moment. I did, and a few minutes later, he appeared. After we were finished at the mall, we decided to call it a day and return, reluctantly, to Mariah.

When we did, I learned why he'd had me wait in the hallway at the mall. He handed me a card that he'd bought while I was waiting. I opened the envelope and saw it was a Valentine's Day card. It was an old-fashioned card that reminded me of one from the 1920s and on the front was a boy wearing an outfit that reminded me of the one that Jonathan was wearing in the portrait of his mother and siblings. When I opened the card, I found that it read, "You are too good to me. I would be lost without you." It was signed "V-Day #1."

I was deeply touched and flattered. I hoped that "V-Day #2," if there was one, would be far different, far better, than V-Day #1.

Unfortunately, my plan for Monday did not go according to plan. Monday morning, I received an e-mail from my sister in which she told me that the school had called my mother that morning, wondering where I was. In spite of having e-mailed the secretary the Friday before to inform her that I would be missing Monday, she hadn't checked her e-mail before students had inquired as to where I was. Once she did check her e-mail, she found that I had indeed done the right thing, which seemed to smooth things over. Even so, I was rattled and concerned about how the incident would reflect on me.

I left Tuesday morning to go teach in Viridian. Tuesday and Wednesday were filled with additional stresses, and by Thursday, I had reached the breaking point.

On Valentine's Day morning, I finally collapsed under the weight of everything that had been piling up on me not just for weeks, but for months. I had been doing everything I could to keep my relationship with Jonathan together at great personal cost and I felt that I had no one to talk to about my stresses, even Jonathan. Especially Jonathan. With everything that had been going on in his life, it seemed almost selfish of me to force my own problems onto him, so I kept silent. On the morning of Thursday, February 14, I found I could no longer do that.

After waking up early from an upsetting dream that reflected my emotional state, I composed a message to Jonathan. My pent-up feelings came flooding out in a lengthy stream of consciousness that was very uncharacteristic of the controlled way that I normally wrote, thought. After revealing that I felt as if I were having a nervous breakdown, I told him that I felt so overwhelmed that I had been afraid to get out of bed and didn't know how I was going to summon the courage to leave the house and go teach. Because of my background in psychology, everyone expected me to be their personal therapist and constantly bombarded me with their crises and dramas when some days I could barely deal with *my* problems. No one listened to *me*, including Kathryn, who was always focused on herself, and my mother, who only half-listened. Although I had been trying to hold everything together for months now, I couldn't do it anymore. Now, *I* was the one who needed help.

I hadn't heard from Jonathan since 11:00 the morning before and demanded to know where he was. I told him that when I didn't hear from him, that could mean anything from the possibility that his Internet service wasn't working to the possibility that he had been evicted to the possibility that he had killed himself. I told him that one of my greatest fears was that some day I would come to the apartment to find that he *had* killed himself. He had once said that he wouldn't kill himself because of how it would affect "the girls," but he had never said anything about not killing himself because of how it would affect *me*. Was I less important to him than a dog? I reminded him that it wasn't just about *him* anymore; now, it was about *us*.

Then, I asked him if I hadn't heard from him because he had found someone on the Internet who was more interesting than me. I knew he did plenty of looking. I reminded him, however, that there was a *real* person in the *real* world whom he said he loved and who needed him. I told him that perhaps he was being narcissistic, as he claimed gay men were, and was thinking only of himself. I told him, however, that *I* was *not*. I told him that all I had done was think about him, worry about him, but now, I needed something back, needed *him*.

In response, Jonathan wrote what was one of the first truly supportive messages he had written to me in months. In it, he apologized for being such a burden and explained that because he had been so preoccupied with his situation, he hadn't given me the attention I needed and deserved. He said that he was "hanging on by [his] fingernails [himself]" as his situation seemed to grow more dire with no solution in sight. He was waiting to hear something definite from the auction house about selling the paintings, which he had not.

He was waiting to be evicted from his apartment with nowhere to go and no way to rescue his possessions, something that seemed imminent. He was waiting to hear about a job, any job, so he could make some money and survive, which he had not. He was waiting to restart his medical treatments so he could physically get through his day, something that seemed unlikely in the near term.

As far as his Internet activities were concerned, he explained that it was the only outlet for social interaction he had. He said that even if his car were working properly, there was nowhere to go. He said that he "scanned" the ads on the Internet because he was so bored, but had reined in his behavior because it had gotten out of control and had caused problems between us.

He ended his message by telling me he thought I should stay home that weekend and try to recuperate rather than make another wearing trip to Mariah. I felt relieved and somewhat comforted that someone had actually listened to my darker thoughts, had actually tried to help.

In response, I told Jonathan that I had decided not to return to Mariah that weekend—not because I didn't want to, but because I didn't have the strength to. I felt that I did need to stay home and rest—or at least try, as preoccupied with and worried about Jonathan's problems and life as I usually seemed to be. Even so, I felt that, perhaps for once, I would be just a little bit selfish and do something that was good for *me*.

Again, Jonathan seemed understanding and supportive. In response, he told me that he understood about the weekend, recognizing that I spent enough time with him and needed to attend to my own life. He expressed his regret that Kathryn, whom he described as my "only outlet," seemed too self-centered to notice my condition. He apologized for being "so many problems" and said that it wasn't a position in which he usually found himself in life. He said that he felt responsible for what had happened to me at work on Monday and was sure that I wasn't giving him a full description of the consequences, implying—correctly—that I was trying to shield him from additional stress.

With the impending eviction, having nowhere to go, and the remaining problems that confronted him, he said he was being forced to make decisions that he didn't feel prepared or want to make. He described his difficulties in obtaining enough money to sustain him, mentioning his attempts to sell the paintings and some of his belongings. He said that although he had e-mailed the art dealer who was trying to help him sell the paintings, he hadn't heard back from him, so his attempts to proceed with the sale appeared stalled. In addition, he said that even though it would be a simpler matter to sell the lithographs, he couldn't afford to insure them and said that the auction house wouldn't accept liability for them anyway regardless of what happened to them. He also mentioned the possibility of selling his prized Blue Willow china—if it ever reappeared. He said that no one in the backward city of Mariah seemed to know how valuable some of it was, although he had learned that he could get at least $800 for what he knew he had, which included a large serving platter from the 19th century valued at $250.

Finally, he stopped himself, realizing that what he was telling me was doing little to ease my stress. He told me not to worry about him any longer, that he would figure out what to do without my help. He apologized for relinquishing more to me than he should have but said that it was easy to do so when he was so sick, "perhaps more then [I knew]," and had difficulty even deciding to get dressed, let alone do anything else. He lamented the bad decisions that he felt his illness had caused him to make, that had destroyed his former life and had left him in "terrible water." He told me that he felt I needed a break from his troubles, and that, under the circumstances, he probably needed a break from mine, since although I could be "very sweet," sometimes I could also be "a bit touchy," a criticism he tried to ease with a smiley face. He told me that he was continuing to have computer problems as well as cable problems, but that the cable company didn't seem to care, both of which increased his feelings of disconnection. He described the situation as "hell" and voiced his need to escape. He ended his message by telling me that without his problems to worry about, I should now concentrate on mine, and that he was deciding what to do. Unfortunately, I couldn't abandon my concern for him that casually.

Valentine's Day had already gotten off to an unlovely start, but things became even less lovely later that day. That afternoon, I gave the students in my Thursday afternoon class their first exam. The test was a 50-question, multiple-choice test and I gave them 75 minutes to work on it. That was standard procedure in all my classes and everyone seemed able to complete the tests within that time. That day, however, I had one student who, when the time was up, had answered only 30 of the 50 questions. When I told her that I needed her test, she started resisting me and told me that she hadn't been able to complete it because other people in the class had been talking and distracting her. I had left the room from time to time during the test, but the secretary, who was in the room next door, said that she hadn't heard anything through the thin wall that separated the two rooms. In addition, everyone else seemed to be able to complete the test within the allotted time, so if there *had* been talking, it hadn't affected *them*. Even so, the student started demanding to know who my boss was and ended up calling her to complain on me. She was very melodramatic and no student had ever done anything like that to me before. I was stunned and upset. Although we got the situation straightened out, I was still a nervous wreck because of the mess that had happened on Monday and how I feared it would reflect on me as well as because of my condition in general.

After I got home around 4:00 that afternoon, I checked my e-mail and found a message from Jonathan. In its own way, it was just as upsetting as what had happened earlier that day, perhaps more so.

After telling me that he had written me a long e-mail only to lose it when the system had malfunctioned, he informed me that, as far as he knew, Joan had only *threatened* to evict him. The last time she had done so had been the previous Wednesday and even though he had been checking every few hours to see if she had left another eviction warning, she had not yet done so. If she did choose to initiate eviction proceedings, the process would take about two weeks. Jonathan was extremely stressed, since if he was evicted, he had nowhere to go and no way to take anything with him except for some clothes and small valuables. Otherwise, he was out of options.

He told me that the money he'd gotten by selling a watch was now gone except for two dollars. The dealers to whom he had spoken were willing to give him far less for his other items than what he knew they were worth. He was of the opinion that they knew he was in desperate straits and were trying to take advantage of him using "all of that Midwestern American charm" that seemed to be so plentiful in Mariah. I didn't know if that was true, but I did know that, at the least, his comment reflected his discouragement, his despair over having lost control of his life.

As if he anticipated my reaction, he repeated his refusal to accept more financial help from me than he already had because of the complications it had introduced into our relationship. He said that he hated being a "mooch" and said that he had tried to give back by taking me out to eat a couple of times and cooking the others when I had visited. There was a sense, though, that he felt these shows of reciprocity were inadequate and pathetic.

He told me that I had been wonderful to him and that he appreciated everything I had done or had tried to do for him, but he told me that under the circumstances perhaps it was better that we took a break. He said that he wasn't asking to end our relationship, but for me to consider whether or not I would be better off without him and his problems. My outburst that morning had made it clear to him that I had been neglecting myself, so perhaps it was better to give each of us the chance to do what we needed to do for ourselves. He said that whatever I decided he would be supportive of me as he hoped I would be supportive of him. He ended his message by telling me that he hoped things were easier for me now, a statement that implied he felt no choice but to end our relationship.

The thought of Jonathan being evicted, returning to England, was unbearable. I was already in an emotionally fragile state, which made an objectively desperate situation seem exponentially worse. I had gone to such lengths to keep our relationship together, and to think that it was now on the verge of being torn asunder primarily because Jonathan couldn't afford to pay his rent was more than I could handle. Therefore, I did the only thing I felt that I could do, that could be done, to keep the end, in more ways than one, from coming: I decided to pay Jonathan's rent.

The February rent, which was already two weeks overdue, was $650. By that point, I had amassed at least $2,300 in unrecovered debt to help Jonathan, which meant the debt would now be pushing $3,000. The actual figure was certainly greater, however, because of the interest that had accrued on the total in the previous five months. In some strange way, though, I felt that if I didn't pay Jonathan's rent, with the aim of helping him to remain in the States and keeping us together, that $2,300 would have been wasted, even if he eventually repaid it with interest. My decision to pay February's rent was not rational, but emotional. Purely emotional. And, the fact that it was Valentine's Day only intensified the emotional pressure.

I had already half-considered paying his rent several days before and had actually gotten Joan's phone number from the Mariah phonebook when I'd been there the previous weekend. I'd done this secretly, however, because I didn't want Jonathan to know what I was tentatively planning. I found the number and, around 4:30 that afternoon, I called her.

Our conversation proved very interesting.

Feeling no need to go into detail, I told Joan, who didn't appear to remember me from the showing in October, that I was a "friend" of Jonathan's and knew that he was having trouble paying his rent. I told her that I wanted to pay it for him and asked her where to send the check. Despite the fact that Jonathan had portrayed her as someone who was concerned only with money, a perception undoubtedly shaped by his feelings of desperation, I found her to be a surprisingly compassionate person. She told me she believed that God would bless me for what I was doing.

Our conversation was interesting, however, not because I learned that she was more compassionate than expected, but because I learned what Jonathan had told her about why he couldn't pay her the rent he owed her.

Jonathan had told her that he didn't have the money to pay her because he was having to spend his money to pay for a private investigator to find his missing *son—Glenn*. According to this story, Glenn had disappeared several months before and Jonathan was desperately trying to find him. There had been some kind of friction or falling out in the family, which had prompted Glenn to run off. Jonathan was supposed to be divorced and his ex-wife, who didn't care as much about Glenn as Jonathan did, wasn't motivated to help. Therefore, the financial burden of trying to find Glenn fell totally onto Jonathan.

I was caught off guard by this unexpected story—Jonathan had never told *me* that he was telling Joan something like this—but I tried not to react. This was apparently some kind of cover story that Jonathan had concocted in order to soften Joan's attitude toward him and I didn't want to blow it. If Joan learned that he had been lying to her, then she might have tried to evict him at once, in spite of her compassion. I wasn't going to be responsible for that, especially when the whole purpose behind my paying his rent was to achieve the opposite. So, I played along, pretending that it was the truth. I didn't know what else to do.

After we said our good-byes, I wrote Joan a check and placed it in the mail that day. It would reach its destination in a couple of days and, even if Joan initiated eviction proceedings when she didn't receive March rent, those would take at least two weeks. That, combined with the two remaining weeks of February, meant that I had now bought Jonathan at least four or five weeks, if not a little more. That would be just enough time to receive the money from the sale of the lithographs or at least figure out some other way of getting the money he needed.

Later that day, I e-mailed Jonathan, telling him what I had done. I told him that I didn't do it to make him feel further indebted to me or to further complicate our relationship, that I did it because I loved him and was the only one who seemed able and willing to help him. I told him not to be angry with me and to just accept what I had done in the spirit in which it was intended: the spirit of Valentine's Day. I told him that if he *did* feel the need to be angry with me, though, then he would at least be doing it with a roof over his head.

I didn't hear from him until 12:30 the next afternoon. He said that he hadn't written because his Internet connection had become unreliable, that he had sent e-mails that hadn't arrived and couldn't get online half the time. Addressing the issue of what I had done, he told me that he wasn't angry, only embarrassed and feeling powerless. He told me I was far kinder and more generous than I should be under the circumstances. He told me that since he couldn't stop me from doing what I had already done, he would accept my show of "love, support, and concern" with as much grace as possible. He was sorry that I had done what I had, but admitted that it did relieve the pressure that was bearing down on him, pressure that had been driving him to consider things "best left unsaid." He said he loved me, not because of what I had done, but because of the kind of person I was that would do what I had done. He told me he would miss me that weekend, but looked forward to seeing me soon. He ended his message by saying once again that he loved me.

In response, I told him that I wasn't doing well but that I had started taking the Prozac that was originally intended for him and was hopeful that it would help me as it had helped me two years before. I had five bottles of ten pills, which would last me until the beginning of April. Because my depressions seemed as tied to the environment as to events, the coming of spring would undoubtedly pick up where the Prozac would leave off.

In response, Jonathan told me about the latest developments in his life, none of which was good. He told me that he was still having trouble with his Internet connection in general and his e-mail in particular. He said that he had received three e-mails from me at once, all of which had been sent at different times. He informed me that he had relinquished his telephone service because he could no longer afford it. Something had to go, and he felt that it was more important to maintain his electric and cable service than his phone. He said he didn't miss it, since it seemed to be more of a hassle for other people who wanted to talk to him than it was for him. Unfortunately, it deprived not only him, but also me, of another way to stay connected.

He also informed me that four of the companies to which he had applied had decided not to consider him further. That left two major companies, along with a handful of lesser positions, as possibilities. After two months of searching, his prospects for employment seemed as uncertain as ever.

He further reported that Joan had been showing the downstairs apartment to potential tenants throughout the day. He said that he could hear them every time they made a move and assumed they could do the same with him. He said the dogs, which reacted to every disturbance, had become agitated from the noise. He expressed his hope that he could leave before it was rented, but if it were rented soon, that seemed unlikely.

The most interesting thing that he reported, however, was a "very involved" dream he'd had the night before about Glenn. He said that in the dream, someone had told him that Glenn was in a care facility and that a balding man with sandy colored hair had given him the phone number. He said that when he had woken up, he could remember part of the number. The area code was 65* with the numbers 755 following it. He said that he had written to Miranda, who was trying to intuit the dream for him, to determine if it was a message or just wishful thinking. He also said that Miranda had told him that she had been thinking of him very strongly lately and felt that he had entered a "dangerous" time. He said that she had even invited him to come and stay with her and her son for a few days, but he said that he didn't feel up to making the trip and didn't know if he wanted to be in what he described as "that supercharged atmosphere."

He ended his message by telling me to take care of myself and expressing his hope that the "bad stuff," as he called it, passed for me soon. I hoped it did, for all of us.

On Sunday, I spent much of the day in bed. I didn't officially get up until almost 2:00 in the afternoon, which was unusual for me. I had gotten up before then to have some breakfast, but I ate it in bed. Otherwise, I spent much of the afternoon watching television and trying to rest. My thinking had cleared up somewhat, but I had little motivation, energy, or enthusiasm to do anything. Even small efforts seemed to require more from me than I could give. I felt as bad now as I had two Februaries before, but at least then, I'd had only myself to worry about. A person could push himself only so far before he burned out and I had reached my limit.

Later, I felt rested enough to use the computer. Intrigued by the possibility that the telephone number in Jonathan's dream might prove to be some kind of lead, if not a psychic perception then at least an unremembered fragment of information Jonathan knew about Glenn that had surfaced in the dream, I decided to do an Internet search for a possible connection. In the process, I discovered that the parameters of the number fitted those of a convalescent facility in California. I wrote and told Jonathan about my discovery and asked him if Glenn had ever been in California. In response, he said that Glenn had spent time there as a teenager, but otherwise the connection was unclear. He said that since he no longer had a phone, Miranda would call the facility for him, although he wasn't sure they would give her any information. I myself thought the dream was just a product of Jonathan's wishful thinking with no real meaning, but I hoped the information offered him some kind of comfort.

Later, I wrote and told Jonathan more about my day. I also told him that I would see how I felt by the end of the week. I wanted to return to Mariah then, since by that point, I would not have seen him for almost two weeks. With his telephone gone and his e-mail unreliable, face-to-face contact seemed more crucial than ever, even if it meant a 150-mile drive to achieve it. My plan for the week was just to go to work and not push myself too hard while I was there, then do nothing but rest while I was home. I told him that what I needed was a good rest from everything.

In response, he expressed his wish that we were together and not 150 miles apart. He said that if we were, he would make me some "really good chicken rice soup with lots of carrots and make [me] eat some of the boiled chicken for strength." He agreed that I needed a break from everything, adding "probably [him] most of all," and advised me to rest up and relax. The truth was that I was too tired to do anything else.

He also reported that Leandra had written to him, which had made him "almost [fall] out of the chair" because, aside from Charmaine, none of his siblings had regular contact with him. He said, though, that it was more "propaganda" that attempted to make him feel guilty for not having visited in so long. Jonathan said, though, that "the guilt stuff [didn't] work anymore" and reasonably countered by saying that "[i]f they were that concerned they could damn well do something to help [him] dig [his] way out." He said that if it weren't for me and the Tomlinsons, he would probably be "in a Deportation Camp in the Everglades." Given that he had lost the job at the hospital three months before and the INS deadline was well past, he would probably be not in a deportation camp, but in England. He ended the message by stating his hope that it got through, as his last one had, since e-mail appeared to be unpredictable.

It angered me that Jonathan's family and friends in England weren't willing to do more to help him than they had. Any one of them could have easily given him a few hundred pounds and not even missed it, but they had decided to let him dangle. *My* family and friends, with much less money, would have never done that to *me*. In addition, if they wanted to see him so badly, then why couldn't they come to the States instead of expecting him to go to England? Any one of them could have easily flown here to see him. Obviously, though, they expected everything to be done on *their* terms, regardless of the effects their behavior was having on Jonathan.

Throughout everything, I continued to check the *Gayteway* site to see whether or not Jonathan had, in fact, altered his Internet behavior because of the damage it was doing to our relationship. Although his postings on *Gayteway* seemed trivial in comparison to the Andy situation, which hadn't involved the site, I was still curious to know if he was continuing to use it as an "outlet." By mid-February, I hadn't found any postings that I could firmly attribute to him for more than two months except for one posting he had placed on the board for my state in mid-January that was directed at Glenn. Naming Glenn by name, it was a straightforward message in which Jonathan encouraged Glenn to let either him or his mother know where and how he was and urged him to come home so they could "take care of [him] and make [him] feel well again." Unfortunately, a month had passed since Jonathan had posted the message and four had passed since he had last heard from Glenn, but still nothing. The message had proven to be yet another futile attempt to find someone who had seemingly vanished from the face of the earth.

By that point, my mother was starting to notice that something was wrong with me. I had been in fairly bad shape on Saturday and I couldn't hide my depleted condition any longer. My mother said that she knew there was something wrong with me because she had noticed that I seemed unusually forgetful and didn't seem to remember certain things she'd told me, which was true. I told her that I was clinically depressed and was having a lot of difficulty but that I was also taking Prozac and was doing what I needed to do to take care of myself. It was a relief to feel that I didn't have to be putting on some kind of act anymore, which by itself helped.

After telling Jonathan this, he replied with encouragement before telling me about a disturbing, but perhaps not unexpected, development. He claimed that he had received a "weird" message from Laura in which she had told him that Dan had called her and was trying to find him. He said that Laura had told him that Dan had "really pumped her for information" and had told her that he had driven to St. Alban and had staked out her house for several hours to see if Jonathan was there or would show up. Apparently, though, Laura had told him she didn't know where he was, which Jonathan said was technically true, since she didn't have his address in Mariah and hadn't directly spoken to him in months. He told me that Laura had described the incident as "very creepy," which I could only imagine. Reverting back to thoughts that had occupied him in the aftermath of the disaster he'd suffered at Dan's, Jonathan said that he wished he knew how to expose him to the residents of Credence but then wondered what good it would do.

I didn't know what to think. I didn't know when Jonathan had last heard from Dan, but I assumed it hadn't been since mid-November. I wondered what had provoked Dan to do what he had, seemingly out of the blue. God only knew what had been percolating in Dan's brain in the ensuing time. At least Laura had used *her* brain in the situation. Dan knew that Jonathan had moved to Mariah and I only hoped that he didn't go there and try to find him. What was Dan thinking?

I warned Jonathan against the idea of continuing to try to expose Dan. It was tempting, given all the hardship he'd put him through, but if Jonathan actually did it, Dan would surely know who was behind it and do God-knew-what to him if he found him. We were dealing with an unstable personality in Dan, I believed, *especially* when it came to his sexuality, and Jonathan needed to be careful. In writing back, I expressed my concerns not only about the situation in general, but also about the idea of outing Dan in particular.

Around 10:30 Monday morning, Jonathan replied, saying that he was "hanging on by [his] fingernails" because the thought of "the fat fag drunk," as Jonathan called Dan, "lurking outside waiting to pounce [was] ridiculous but worrying." He said that Dan had stalked Laura and now he was stalking him. Dan was continuing to claim that Jonathan had taken from him, a charge that Jonathan continued to deny. He described Dan as being "the one who [was] really imbalanced."

Beyond his concerns about Dan, Jonathan said that he'd finally received an e-mail from the art dealer, but the text was garbled and unreadable. He said that he'd sent him a response and hoped it got through. He went on to say that a major airline was interested in talking to him about a divisional job, but the catch was that it was in Alabama. He said that he'd never been to Alabama and that all he knew about it was that "the Klan [was] very popular there and gays [were] not." He said they wanted to do a preliminary phone interview with him, but he was reluctant to pursue it "for lots of reasons"—one of which was that it would take him away from me.

In his message, Jonathan had expressed his concern for my condition and his hope that teaching that morning hadn't been "excruciating." Teaching wasn't excruciating; it was what happened afterwards that was. After class, I went to the computer lab to check my e-mail. The lab was located next to the General Education department main office, and while I was reading my e-mail, my boss, who was elsewhere, happened to call, wanting to talk to me. She started off by asking me if I'd gotten the problem with my student worked out. I told her that I had. Then, she asked me if I had been starting classes late or letting them go early. I had, but I didn't understand why that was a problem. College teachers didn't punch time clocks like people in other professions and it wasn't unusual for them to show up to class a few minutes late or let class out early if they were finished with their scheduled activities. At least that was the pattern to which *I* had become accustomed while in college and I assumed it was acceptable. Apparently, it wasn't. My boss explained to me that the students were paying for a certain amount of class time and that it was important to keep them the entire time. I thought that was ridiculous, although, of course, I didn't say that. Who had told her I had been doing that? I suspected the student who had complained on me the week before was the culprit, but I didn't know.

Whoever it was, I was stunned and shaken. I had been working for my school for two years and had never received any serious criticism of my performance. Suddenly, I seemed to be getting bombarded with it. I wasn't threatened with being fired or anything like that, but I had been warned. This all came on the heels of everything that had happened at work the previous week. It rained but it poured and it was pouring a slow, steady, depressing drizzle. It was hard to take.

It was especially hard to take, not only because my depression magnified everything that was negative, but also because my depression was the reason that I had been acting as I had. I had been suffering from chronic fatigue and cognitive problems to a significant degree, both of which had been interfering with my performance. Some days I was so tired that I couldn't teach for the entire time and had no choice but to dismiss my classes early. That was especially true of my three-hour classes. It was exhausting enough to teach for three hours under normal circumstances, but to do it when some days I barely had enough energy to get out of bed was practically impossible. In addition, my thinking had sometimes been so muddied that I couldn't think clearly enough to continue teaching for the full time. It was hard to concentrate and remember things and sometimes I seemed to reach a point, usually after two hours, where I started becoming incoherent, at least to myself.

I was especially discouraged by the fact that I was trying hard to do a better job that semester because I felt I'd done a poor one the previous semester. No one had said that, but that was how I felt. It was one of those days when I hated teaching because, not being at my best, I felt as if I was simply making a fool of myself in front of thirty people.

I told Jonathan what had happened that morning and told him that I was thinking about calling my boss later that day and trying to explain to her what had been happening to me. It wouldn't be the easiest thing to do, but I wanted her to understand that I hadn't been acting the way I had because I'd suddenly turned unprofessional or uncaring. In response, Jonathan advised me not to tell her that I was having psychological problems, since he believed that people were more understanding of physical problems than psychological ones, which was probably true. He tried to relieve my fears of being fired and receiving a bad reference by assuring me that they could only confirm dates, titles, and duties, otherwise they could open themselves up to a lawsuit. The rational part of me, insofar as one seemed to remain, knew that I was overreacting, but the emotional part of me made my concerns seem justified.

Otherwise, he reported that he'd just gotten back from Wal-Mart, where he had bought dog food then had left as fast as he could. He said that he was "getting paranoid about that old fat fart" but knew that if he allowed himself to be cowed, he was letting him win. Everything else, he reported, was "status quo"—whatever *that* meant under the circumstances. Then, showing concern for my welfare, he advised me to "rest up and...eat properly" and told me that if we were living together, he could "make sure that [I was] OK and watch out for [me]." Hopefully he added, "[m]aybe later down the road."

In the end, I decided not to talk to my boss, hoping everything would just blow over. I told Jonathan not to be so concerned about Dan, since even if he did come to Mariah looking for him, it was unlikely that he would actually find him not knowing his address. As far as I knew, I was the only one connected to him who knew it. I didn't expect him to contact my "too obviously gay" self, however, in an attempt to get it. After writing, I retreated to my bed for a while. It had proven to be an exhausting, upsetting day.

Tuesday, the 19th, was equally miserable. The weather was cloudy and cool, drizzly and depressing. I had fallen asleep around 10:00 the night before and had woken up around 2:30 in the morning. Unfortunately, I hadn't been able to get back to sleep until almost 7:00 and had slept sporadically and fitfully until I finally got up, unrefreshed, around 10:00. I had to teach my Tuesday class in Viridian and, apart from having to make a two-hour round trip in the rain, I was apparently going to have to keep my students the entire three hours or risk, I feared, getting into further trouble. I hated my life.

Around 10:00 that morning, Jonathan sent me an e-mail in which he displayed his heightened concern for my condition. He told me that he wasn't "bombarding" me with e-mails, since he thought I wanted the chance to escape from my stress and recoup. Even so, he said that he wanted to keep me informed about what was going on so that "when our lives ever [got] back to any sort of normal pattern, there [wouldn't] be any surprises."

He told me that he still hadn't heard from the art dealer but commented that it was still early in the day and the art business didn't start at 9:00 in the morning, as other businesses did. He told me that he had sold one of his smaller paintings locally and had gotten "screwed royally," since he had gotten only $120 for a painting that was worth $750. He said, however, that he had been "down to a buck," so he'd had no choice.

Turning to the issue of employment, he said that Warren had insisted that he do a phone interview with the airline and would arrange for him to talk to them at either his office or his house. He said that although he didn't want to move to Alabama, he thought the airline might have something suitable in the immediate area. He commented on the rain and concluded by stating that he doubted he would go out.

When I replied, I began by telling him I was sorry that he'd felt pressured to sell the painting he had sold, since I knew he liked it. I tried to make him feel better, though, by telling him that Joan should have received my check for the rent, so at least he didn't have the threat of imminent eviction hanging over his head. I encouraged him to do the interview and told him to let me know what was happening in that regard, since if it meant he might be moving away, that would obviously have a major impact on our relationship.

Already exhausted, I went to work around noon in the 45-degree drizzle. Somehow, in spite of my fatigue, I managed to get through my two-hour round trip and my three-hour class. While I was at work, I checked my e-mail when I had the chance, but didn't find replies from Jonathan. After I finally got home around 5:00, I continued to check my e-mail to see if he'd replied. Nothing. I felt abandoned.

Things had been bad for weeks, months.

And they were about to get worse.

—27—
CLIFF@JONATHAN.CON
We both love you.

Sometime around the beginning of December, I noticed a posting that had been placed on the *Gayteway* board for my state by someone who called himself "Naughtyboy." The posting was in response to an ad from someone who was looking for "discreet encounters" in the Mariah area. Although it wasn't clear who had written the response, it described the region as "deadly dull as far as cock was concerned." *Deadly dull* was an unusual phrase, one that I had rarely heard. It was, however, a phrase that Jonathan had used on occasion and I recalled one evening around the beginning of December that Jonathan had described Colin's home town as "deadly dull." His use of the phrase made me cringe, because I had already seen the "Naughtyboy" ad and, because of peculiarities in the ad that I had seen before, I was already suspicious that "Naughtyboy" was actually Jonathan. In addition, the username of the e-mail address that "Naughtyboy" had given through which to respond to his ad was *xxcliff*—and given that the letters represented by *xx-* referred to *Cliff's* home state, it made my suspicion that "Naughtyboy" was Jonathan even stronger. As with "GayMan," however, I didn't have absolute proof.

On Tuesday, February 19, I didn't hear from Jonathan throughout most of the day. He e-mailed me around 10:00 that morning, then didn't contact me again until 8:00 that evening. After telling me, offhandedly, that he hoped I wasn't too exhausted after my day, he proceeded to focus on himself. In his message, he informed me that he had spent a "very quiet day" at home, having stayed inside all day watching TV because of the rain. He said he was concerned that he hadn't received any mail, even junk mail, since the middle of the previous week, which suggested there was some kind of problem with his mail delivery. He said that he hadn't heard anything from Joan, which made him think she was now placated, and thanked me again for having paid his rent, since he said it had been "so terrible just waiting for the ax to fall." He mentioned that it was supposed to rain all day again the next day, too, then turn cold and icy, which he quipped sounded "lovely." He ended the message by saying that he was going to scrub out the tub and have a good, long soak. Otherwise, he asked me nothing about my condition or showed any real interest in me and what I was suffering. His desire not to "bombard" me with messages, it appeared, was really just an excuse not to deal with me.

Although I didn't discover e-mails from Jonathan, I did discover that sometime that afternoon, the person who called himself "Naughtyboy" had posted another message on the *Gayteway* board for my state and had once again given the *xxcliff* address as the contact address. From the style of the writing in addition to the contact address, I was more convinced that ever that "Naughtyboy" was in fact Jonathan. I was still curious—and concerned—about the nature and extent of his sexually oriented Internet activities, but now, after learning about the situation with Andy, I was more curious—and concerned—than ever.

I decided to answer the ad.

After creating an alias, I sent an e-mail to "Naughtyboy" at the *xxcliff* address as it was given. Just as quickly, however, it was bounced back to me because, apparently, the *xxcliff* address didn't exist. At first, I thought it might just be a false address, one that, if Jonathan were in fact behind it, had been given in an attempt to further the legitimacy of the ad, to encourage potential respondents to make contact, but that actually led nowhere. So, I posted another message on the *Gayteway* board in which I told "Naughtyboy" that I couldn't get through and gave him an e-mail address at which *he* could contact *me*.

About half an hour later, I—or, rather, my alter ego—received a response. The sender said that he didn't understand why I hadn't been able to get through, since he had been getting other e-mails at that address. Then, after telling me that I sounded like fun, he informed me that he had lived in the Mariah area for only a couple of weeks and was still adjusting. He said that he loved "good head" and a number of other acts and was also "p&p friendly"—an abbreviation for the phrase "party and play," which meant doing drugs and having sex. He said that if I was interested in "hooking up" to let him know.

Apparently, my previous e-mail had not gone through because the sender had given an incorrect address. Instead of ending in the suffix -*.com*, the correct address ended in -*.co.uk*. A *U.K.* address. But even if the address had been the non-U.K. version, the username by itself would have told me who it was. The response itself was far less interesting than the name of the person to whom the account claimed to belong: *Cliff*.

"Naughtyboy" *was* Jonathan. And *Jonathan* was posing as *Cliff*.

I was upset and angry for more reasons than one. First, I discover that Jonathan—as "Iain"—is telling Cliff that he is in a hospice on his deathbed, and now, I discover that he is masquerading *as* Cliff. Jonathan had not only told someone with whom he claimed he was once passionately in love that his health had declined so drastically that he had been forced to acquire hospice care—indeed, so drastically that he was forced to relay messages through "Iain" because he was too ill to do it himself—but also created a fraudulent e-mail account through which he was pretending to *be* him. This was also the *second* instance of which I knew in which he had pretended to be not a fictional persona but a *real* person without his knowledge. I was dumbfounded. Why was he doing this? *If he would do this to someone he says he loves*, I thought, *what would he do to someone he hates?* I had seen what he had done to Dan, but I wondered if I had seen everything he had done.

I could no longer restrain myself. The emotional dam burst and my feelings about Jonathan's deceitful, exploitative, deranged behavior spilled out in a flood of accusation and anger.

I began by informing him that while he had spent the entire day ignoring me, I knew he had been posting sex ads on *Gayteway* under the name "Naughtyboy." I also told him that I knew he had been using that alias, as well as several others, to post ads all over *Gayteway* for months. I told him that I was sure he'd had another e-mail account through which he was posing as someone else and now knew he was posing as *Cliff*. Although he had never admitted it, I told him that I knew he was the same "GayMan" who had posted the "GayMan/Boi" ads in August. I reminded him that he had lied to me about that as he had lied to me about being "Iain." I told him that even if those ads were nothing but fantasy, it still sickened me to think that he had spent practically the entire week I had stayed with him after the England trip was canceled doing what he had done behind my back, especially when he had displayed almost no sexual interest in me or even physical affection toward me that week. I told him that although he had promised me that he would refrain from posting ads because of the problems it had caused between us—and others—he obviously hadn't. I asked him why he couldn't find some other way of connecting with people if all he wanted was basic social contact. I asked him why he needed to escape from reality in this particular way, why everything was so *sexualized* with him.

I asked him if he knew what his Internet behavior did to me. I asked him if he ever thought there was anything questionable, at best, about what he was doing. I told him that *I* should be the focus of his sexual life, that if he should be directing those feelings toward anyone it should be *me*. I told him that sexually he seemed to think that I was pretty much interchangeable with everyone else, that there was nothing special about me. I questioned him about his sexually selfish behavior in which I was the one who always had to make the first move and how he always seemed more concerned about being satisfied than satisfying me—if he even thought of it. I told him that even if he didn't think there was something special about *me*, I had been thinking there was something special about *him*, which was why I had put forth all the effort I had to help him and be there for him.

As far as the loneliness he claimed was at the root of his behavior was concerned, I told him that if *he* was lonely, then so was *I*. I reminded him that I had no gay friends in Hawthorn, let alone a boyfriend, so I was just as lonely as he was; even so, I didn't resort to cybersex to deal with it. I told him that when he did that, he was totally forgetting that he *had* a boyfriend—one who really needed him. I told him that I had just had one of the worst weeks of my life and that less than one week before, something inside me had snapped. I needed him more than ever, but he conveniently pretended that I didn't exist.

I reminded him, too, that I had snapped because of all the pressure I had been under for months because of *him*. He had driven me to it. For months, especially the previous three, I had been doing everything I could to help him through his dislocations, dramas, and disasters, which was more than I'd ever done for a boyfriend. At Thanksgiving and at Christmas, he had indicated that I wasn't being a good boyfriend, so I had turned my life upside down in an attempt to prove that I was. After three months, enough was enough.

I made certain he knew what I had done. I told him that I had put more than 6,000 miles on a new car that I had bought less than five months before and that more than half of those miles had been to help and be with him. I had been making a 300-mile round trip practically every week—sometimes twice a week—just so he wouldn't be lonely even though it exhausted me physically and mentally more than I had led him to believe. I told him that by that point I had spent at least $3,000, and probably more, on him to pay for storage and moving and rent and other things when that semester

I was clearing only $150 a week. I told him that I had neglected my own life to the point that it had turned into a shambles. I told him that I had gotten into trouble at work because of him. I told him that I had ignored my family because of him. I told him that I had practically destroyed myself emotionally and physically because of him. I told him that I had been so depressed during the previous couple of weeks that I had actually thought about killing myself just so I could stop the pain I felt.

I asked him how he could just lie and lie to someone he said he loved. I asked him if he had even a shred of respect for me. I asked him if his lies were more important to him than our relationship was, if he cared how his behavior had damaged my ability to trust him. I told him it was time to stop lying and start caring. I told him to tell me the truth, especially about what had *really* happened between him and "Boi" in August. I told him to stop thinking about how everything affected *him* and start thinking about how it affected *me*. I told him that *I* mattered just as much as he did and that he was going to have to start thinking about what *I* wanted and needed. I told him that if he *really* loved me, he was going to have to *show* it by doing things to make things better for *me*. I told him that if he didn't, then that said it all. I told him that *I* needed something back and that I needed it *now*. I told him that he could start with the *truth*.

In response to my anger, Jonathan simply rationalized his behavior, growing more irate as he wrote. He started by saying that he was isolated and alone with no one to interact with and in a town where there was nothing to do. He said that days went by without his hearing "another live human voice" and that even if I visited that weekend, it would have been two weeks since he'd had a real conversation. He said that maybe something had snapped inside him that day too. He said that the only human contact he'd had that day had been with Colin, who had just written to say hello, and with me, who had just written in the morning. He said that he was going crazy. He claimed that he never met with anyone he met through the Internet, that it was always mental, never physical. He claimed that if I were with him, he wouldn't resort to cybersex. He claimed that he was simply so lonely that he craved any form of human contact and that he was also hoping to feel sexual again. He claimed that he hadn't felt sexual since he'd starting taking "those little poison pills"—the Prozac—despite the fact that he'd taken only four, far from enough to have any ill effect. He claimed that he hadn't met anyone in August and hadn't slept with anyone since we'd become involved in June. He said that if I saw cybersex as cheating, then that was up to me.

Continuing to hold me semi-responsible for his behavior, he said that in spite of everything I had done for him, my feelings for him, I had never invited him to stay with me and had left him to "rot" on every holiday, despite the fact that I had explained to him more than once why it wasn't possible to have him come. He told me it was easy to criticize him when I was in my normal environment, surrounded by my family and leading a relatively normal life, and asked me how well I thought *I* would do, how *I* would react if *I* became marooned like him. He reminded me that he was staying in the United States, forced to sell his possessions for a pittance just to be able to afford to live, mainly to be with me when it would be easier to go home. He told me that if I was so unhealthy for him, then I should do what I felt I had to do—namely, end our relationship.

Becoming angrier, he sarcastically told me to forgive him for being "a naughty" one wet afternoon and said that he'd had it too. Rationalizing his behavior further, he told me that if he lied sometimes on the Internet, he didn't think he was "the first or only person to ever do it." He told me to stop being "so fucking judgemental" and asked me "[i]n the end, where [was] the harm?" He said that most of what was online was "bullshit," which meant it didn't matter. He told me that I wasn't the "sex police" and to "[g]o set [my] traps for someone else."

Playing the Chase card, he told me that he would have Chase help him get the rest of his things out of storage that weekend, something that we had planned to do. He told me that he hoped I felt better soon, now that the pressure of dealing with him was gone, and wished me well in finding someone who was "worthy" of him.

Dragging my sister into the fray, he said that at least he wasn't like Kathryn and "juggled real people" although that was exactly what he had done. He ended by telling me again that he hadn't slept with anyone since we'd met—Chase presumably not counting—and telling me to believe it or not.

In the message, he did something that stunned me: He gave me the password to the *xxcliff* account. He claimed that it was an old e-mail account of Cliff's that they had shared but that Jonathan no longer used. Sarcastically, he told me that he was giving me the password so I could monitor what was going on through *that* account, as I had the "Iain" account, claiming that he had "nothing to hide." I doubted that, but given everything else that was happening that night, checking the account, for whatever good it might do, was one of the last things on my mind.

When the exchange was over, I suffered a scaled-down version of the emotional collapse I had suffered on Valentine's Day. I responded, and my response betrayed my fragile state. Although I was a 35-year-old adult, the outpouring, in retrospect, seemed more like that of an articulate adolescent caught in the throes of raw, unrestrained emotion born of insecurity and fear. The dominant theme of the message revolved around my fears "of losing my job, of losing my mind, of losing my life, of losing you," as I distilled it for him. Although parts of the message were somewhat dramatized in an attempt to penetrate his defensiveness, to inspire sympathy, to be heard, most of what I wrote was unfortunately close to the truth.

In response to my outpouring, Jonathan was understanding in a way that he had rarely been before. He began by telling me that his current situation was the most difficult one that he had ever suffered except for when Marcus had died. He assured me he knew I loved him and told me he hoped I knew he loved me. He told me that I had done more for him than anyone ever had and that it wasn't an exaggeration to say that if it weren't for me, he would probably be dead. He said he was acutely aware of everything I had done for him and had tried to let me know that.

He said that what had seemed like good decisions over the previous few months had been disasters and that he was desperately trying to work his way out of his mess. In my message, I had asked him about moving to Mariah, but he told me that he didn't want me to do that because he himself wanted to get out of Mariah and back to Paladin, back to life. He repeated that he hadn't wanted to interview for the job in Alabama because if he got it, it would take him away from me, from us. He promised that although he was very self-absorbed because of his circumstances, he would pay more attention to and be more supportive of me. He said that I deserved it, I had earned it, and he wanted to do it.

Even so, he insisted that I stop trying to trap him. Again, he swore that he had not met nor had sex with anyone since June (Chase notwithstanding). He explained that if he wasn't as interested in sex as he normally was, it was because he was physically sick, depressed, and unemployed. It wasn't me; it was him, he assured. He was confident, though, that when his life improved, so would his sex drive.

He restated his new attitude that I now had his total attention, although he said it was hard to know what to do or say from so far away. Even so, he advised me to "rein in the hysteria" and "not to go off of the deep end," suggesting that I soak in a hot bath and drink some brandy, as he just had. Since I was off the next day, he also suggested that I sleep in, eat well, and relax. He ended by assuring me that he loved me.

By the time the exchange was over, I was exhausted. I did feel better that I had finally vented my feelings and that Jonathan had, in the end, responded sympathetically to them.

I did *not*, however, feel better about the fact that he was masquerading as Cliff. Did Cliff know what he was doing? I couldn't imagine it. Who would allow his old boyfriend to go around pretending to be him in order to solicit sex from strangers on the Internet? That was ridiculous. In addition, wasn't Jonathan supposed to be so sick, so close to death, that he couldn't use the computer himself and, therefore, was forced to have "Iain" send e-mails for him? I was certain that Cliff knew *nothing* about what Jonathan was doing.

I also knew that something deeper, more devious, lay behind his use of Cliff's identity than simply playing sex games through the Internet. That didn't seem compelling enough. Because Jonathan had gone from using the fronts of invented personas to using the façades of real people without their knowledge to perpetrate his fantasies, something that could have damaging consequences for the one whose identity had been stolen, I needed to find out what.

Because I was so exhausted after our exchange, I didn't try to access the Cliff account until the next morning. When I did, I discovered the password that Jonathan had given to me was correct, allowing me to access it. The account, however, was empty. I wasn't surprised. At that point, I felt that Jonathan had beaten me to the punch, had granted me access to the account to "prove" that he had "nothing to hide," but had deleted whatever incriminating messages it might have contained beforehand so I would have nothing to hold against him. If that was true, then I fully expected him to give me access to the account for only a limited amount of time, just long enough to feel that he had satisfied my curiosity, before changing the password and denying me further access. I also wondered if he had just abandoned the account, only to create another one in Cliff's name that I didn't know about. Whatever the truth, I planned to continue checking the account as long as I could.

I checked the account throughout the rest of the morning. Nothing.

Sometime that afternoon, I checked the account again. This time, however, it was *not* empty. The inbox contained a single message from someone I would have never expected to find a message from, someone I knew.

Jack.

Addressed to "Cliff and Jonathan," Jack was seeking "their" advice about an urgent matter that had recently arisen. Apparently Jack's car was going to be repossessed either that day or the next, but he was also receiving a tax refund of $250 that could allow him to stall the repossession, at least for a while. Laura had suggested that he use the money to make the appropriate payments for the car so he could keep it for at least another month. He wasn't sure what to do, though, because the tax refund was all the money he had, so if he used all of it for the car, he would be left broke. The message contained numerous misspellings and instant-messaging abbreviations and, overall, had an almost childlike quality to it. The message was signed, "luv, jack."

Jack. Laura's son. *My God*, I thought. *Jonathan is pretending to be Cliff to* Jack.

But *why*?

Later that day I checked the account again. This time, I discovered that "Cliff" had replied. In an almost fatherly tone, "Cliff" told Jack that he was sorry he had to deal with adult problems at his age. "Cliff" advised him to negotiate with his mother, possibly using half of his funds for the car and keeping half for himself so he would have money for gas. He also asked Jack if he had to "forage" for food, suggesting that he wasn't getting adequately fed at home, and telling him that having money for food was another consideration. "Cliff" told Jack that if he wanted to see "them"—Jonathan and him—"they" could get him in St. Alban or Laura could bring him to Mariah. Apparently, "Cliff" and Jonathan had already invited Laura to spend a weekend—which "Cliff" had spelled *week end*—with "them." "Cliff" said that he was going to Paladin on Friday to look at houses but that Jonathan wouldn't be coming with him because he was too sick with a lung infection to make the trip. "Cliff" also mentioned that Jonathan was in bed that day and that his temperature was too high for him to take his inhalation treatment, which he was allegedly receiving.

The most shocking statement in the message, however, amidst a number that were shocking enough, was that the reason "Cliff" was looking at houses was that purportedly "Cliff" and Jonathan were planning to move back to Paladin sometime in the next four to eight weeks and that once they did, Jack would come to live with them. "Cliff" ended the message by telling Jack, "We both love you," and signed it "Cliff."

"We both *love you."* Jack had *no* idea that there was no *both*, only *one*.

The level of deception and manipulation revealed in the half-page message was indescribable. Although it was only a single message, not forty, it was just as awful in kind if not in number as the messages to Andy had been. I knew, though, that as with Andy, this was only one thread in a much larger web of deceit.

I tried to understand what I had found. Jonathan and "Cliff" had invited Laura to spend a "week end" with them? If she accepted, what kind of excuse would Jonathan offer to explain why Cliff was not there? Or, would Jonathan simply try to weasel out of his invitation in the same way that he, as "Iain," had weaseled out of his promise to bring Andy to England with an endless string of excuses?

And, what about the "plan" to have Jack move in with Jonathan *and* Cliff? What would make him offer to have Jack come and live with "them" and how would Jonathan weasel out of *that*, more significant invitation? Jonathan had mentioned that Jack had been angling to live with him, but now I realized that originally it had probably been *Jonathan's* idea, not Jack's.

I didn't know what to do except to keep following what was happening, gather as much information as I could.

I checked the account several more times that day. Later in the day the messages from earlier in the day had been deleted, lending weight to my belief that Jonathan was trying to delete them before I could read them, thereby leaving me with nothing incriminating. If that had been his intention, however, he had seriously failed. But, given his behavior in the "Iain" situation, I was beginning to doubt his stated reason for allowing me into the account. I couldn't help wondering if it was really just another manifestation of some desire to have someone see what he was doing and try to stop him when he couldn't stop himself coupled with his powerful opposing need to keep others from discovering what he was doing and remove his crucial psychological crutch. Unfortunately, I didn't know.

I checked the account again the next morning. This time, I found that "Cliff" had received an e-mail from *Laura*. Jonathan's "condition" was still an issue. In her brief message, Laura asked "Cliff" how Jonathan was doing and if his temperature was still up. She also asked "Cliff" if he was still coming to Paladin the next day.

That afternoon, I had to teach my Thursday class—the class with the student who had complained on me the week before. I didn't look forward to seeing her, but the issue seemed minor compared to what was going on in my personal life.

While I was at work, I checked my e-mail...and "Cliff's." I discovered that by then, "Cliff" had responded to Laura's message. In his reply, "Cliff" told Laura that Jonathan's temperature was a little over 100° and that the medications he was taking seemed to be working despite the fact that his breathing still sounded like a "freight train," as he described it. "Cliff" went on to tell Laura that he would indeed be going to Paladin the next day to look at three houses—two downtown and one near Jonathan's old house on Millstone Drive—then coming right back. "Cliff" told Laura that he would invite her and Jack to lunch, but that he wouldn't have enough time to meet with them. "Maybe next week," he offered.

Here was direct proof that Jonathan was pretending to be Cliff not only to Jack, but also to *Laura*. From what I could gather, he was telling Laura and her family that he and Cliff were together and that Cliff was taking care of him. Why was he doing this? How long had this been going on? Why was he *doing* this?

Was there some part of Jonathan that could not accept the fact that he and Cliff were no longer together, could no longer be together, and he was able to deal with that fact only by acting out a bizarre fantasy in which he and Cliff *were* together again? Or, was this some perverse form of revenge that he was exacting on Cliff for the emotional damage he perceived that Cliff had inflicted on him, as the "Iain" messages to Cliff could also be construed? Or was it an equally twisted revenge against Laura and her family for their thievery and other leeching behavior? Or was it some combination of the three? Or something unfathomably different? I didn't know. What I *did* know was that Jonathan's pathology was even deeper, even more unrestrained, than it had seemed before. The situation was only getting worse.

Later that day, I found that Laura's message and "Cliff's" reply had been deleted. Jack, however, had responded to "Cliff's" message from the day before in which "Cliff" had given him the fatherly advice about what to do with his money and had assured him that he would be living with "them" in Paladin in the next few weeks. Jack informed "Cliff" that he had made the car payment and that Laura had agreed to pay for the insurance, having told him that she would give him gas money until he moved in with them. Excited by the prospect, Jack told "Cliff" that he couldn't wait and was anxious to meet him, feeling, however, that through his messages he already knew him. He asked "Cliff" how Jonathan was doing and told him to "send him [his] best." As before, he signed the message "luv, jack."

Manipulating Andy had been bad enough, but manipulating Jack, a vulnerable, susceptible 19-year-old, was somehow even more despicable.

I thought of Cliff's e-mail to Jonathan in July titled "Little White Lie" in which he had told him that he had been living not 2,000 miles away but only 100 miles away for the previous two months, something that had left Jonathan devastated. Jonathan, however, was doing a similar thing to Jack. *When other people deceive him, that's reprehensible*, I thought, *but when he does it to others, that's completely acceptable.*

More personally, I was shocked and hurt for more reasons than one. As I had reminded Jonathan only a couple of days before, I had done more for him than I had ever done to help a boyfriend, to help *anyone*, in my life, wrecking my mind, my health, my life in the process, and *now*, I discover that he has been giving all the credit for his care not to *me*, but to *Cliff*. I was insulted, injured, and infuriated. This was too much, too much.

I felt a sickening sense of déjà vu that I did not want to feel. The events of only one month before were repeating themselves, and although I was painfully aware of Jonathan's basic problem, I was even more disturbed by its latest manifestation. The problem was even worse than I had previously suspected, hoping, as I had, that the worst of it had been confined to Andy. Now I knew I was wrong. How many others were involved in one of his deranged fantasies, and where would it end?

I checked the account later that night only to find that the latest message from Jack had been deleted and that the account was empty. When I tried to access the account the next morning before I went to work, I found that I couldn't. Whatever game Jonathan thought he was playing with me, whatever manifestation of mental illness it might have been, it had come to an end. In a sense.

Friday afternoon, I made the 150-mile trip to Mariah. I was not looking forward to the conversation, the confrontation, that was coming. In my exhausted condition, the second to last thing that I wanted to do was to make a 150-mile trip, and the *last* thing that I wanted to do was to discuss what I had found. If I could have called him, I would have, but since his telephone service had been suspended, I couldn't do it by phone. In addition, I thought that, given the importance of what we needed to discuss, I needed to do it in person.

After I arrived, I sat down with him on the sofa. He asked me how I was doing, and I told him that, physically and emotionally, I was exhausted. I also repeated that I had started taking the Prozac I had intended for him and hoped it would help. In addition, I told him that I had injured the muscles on one side of my jaw when I'd bitten down on something hard in some cereal I had eaten a few days before and couldn't open my mouth all the way because it hurt too much. He had no idea, however, just what was *really* wearing on me.

To my complaints, he offered his opinion that I was "delicate"— an opinion he had been expressing since the previous June whenever I would mention feeling depleted—and that I would have been better suited to life in a monastery during the Middle Ages than to life in the hustle and bustle of the modern world, since it was obvious that I was constitutionally incapable of dealing with the stresses it brought. His condescending tone made me want to tell him that *he* should try making a 300-mile round trip, sometimes not once but twice a week, and try to hold together not only his life but also another person's life for months then see how well *he* coped…but I held my tongue. I didn't want to argue about it because I knew there were more important subjects to discuss, one in particular that would spark argument enough.

Finally, I decided to raise the issue I dreaded, but needed, to raise. I said, "There's something I need to talk to you about."

"What is it?"

"I found out that you've been telling Laura and Jack that Cliff has been taking care of you."

He was expressionless for a moment until the impact and implications of what I had said sank in. Then, with eyes widening, he bellowed, "You weren't supposed to see that!"

I wasn't supposed to see what? Did he mean that I wasn't supposed to access the account, even though he had given me the password, or that he had failed in whatever game he had been playing with me? Or did it mean something entirely different that I couldn't begin to fathom?

When I reminded him that he had given me the password, he countered by saying that even when Glenn and he were having problems, he had never even *thought* about looking through Glenn's things because he had too much respect for his privacy. Was this, then, some strange test to see how "ill-bred" I was in regard to his privacy? I had become painfully aware that Jonathan's thinking was not only irrational in many ways, but also idiosyncratic in a way that I didn't fully understand, so I didn't know *what* to think.

He stood up from the sofa, prepared to storm out of the room.

"Why have you been *telling* them this?" I asked, desperately trying to understand why he would tell something to Laura and Jack that was just as bizarre as what he had told to Andy and Cliff.

Flustered, he said, "Laura wanted to come and take care of me. I didn't want her to come here. You have no idea what it was like to live in that house. She was overbearing. I couldn't get away from her. She monitored my every move."

At that point, I didn't ask him the obvious question of why he felt he owed her an explanation at all or why he didn't just tell her that he was being cared for adequately at the hospital and didn't need her help. Instead, feeling insulted by the fact that I had run myself ragged for three months to take care of him only to have all the credit go to an ex-boyfriend, I said, "Why didn't you tell Laura that *I* was taking care of you?"

"She knew you were far away," an explanation that addressed the question tangentially at best, that did not answer the question at all.

"I also see that you've been telling Jack that you and Cliff are planning to move back to Paladin and that when you do, he'll move in with you."

Again, addressing the deception obliquely, Jonathan said "I think having Jack live with me would be good for me." I distinctly felt that behind that statement was the implication that *I* would *not*. He continued: "Jack is a good kid. Laura doesn't take care of him. She doesn't even feed him. He has to eat at friends'. Jack is very bright, but he has no direction. I think that having him live with me would be good for him."

I asked the obvious question. "If the two of *us* are living together and Jack moves in, how are you going to explain why you and Cliff aren't together?"

He didn't have an answer to that question any more than he'd had an answer—a *real* answer—to any of the others. He started to walk away.

Yelling after him, I said, "You think you should be able to do anything you want and get away with it. I know how you were raised. I know you were raised to think that you're better than everyone else."

He stopped and with a look of pure condescension, emphasized by his upper-crust accent, he said, "We *are* better!"

Having had enough of his arrogance, I said, "This—*this* is better?" gesturing to the shit-covered shambles around me.

"At least I'm not like *you*," he yelled. "I don't just wallow in it. When I needed to make a change, *I* actually *did* something about it."

I reminded him that if I hadn't made the changes he thought I ought to make, it was only because I had been waiting for *him* to find a job in Paladin and return there, as we had been discussing for months. I was *not* going to change a single thing, give up whatever stability or security I felt I had, until I felt that things had finally stabilized in Jonathan's life—not just financially, but psychologically. *Especially* psychologically.

He stormed off into the office and was gone for some time. After my 150-mile trip—and especially after our exchange—I was exhausted. I went to the bedroom and lay down. I stayed there for about an hour, trying to recover from what had just happened. In the meantime, Jonathan started dinner. Finally, I got up. Jonathan seemed to have cooled down and seemed more amenable to having a rational discussion.

We sat down at the table to have dinner. Somewhat in the tone that an adult would use with a child who had been naughty, Jonathan said that although I didn't deserve it, he wanted me to have something good to eat. Overlooking the remark because I didn't have the energy or the desire to fight, I took my food and tried to eat as well as I could with my injured jaw. At least now that Jonathan was in a more congenial mood, perhaps I could extract additional information from him.

I asked him about the Cliff account. He told me again that it was an old e-mail account of Cliff's that Cliff never used and claimed that it was a "shared" account to which he had Cliff's password and that he had permission to access. He had previously told me that Colin's e-mail account through which he had been e-mailing Andy pretending to be Colin was also a "shared" account, which meant that he "shared" e-mail accounts with at least *two* people. I found that highly implausible. I didn't believe him and knew that Cliff had *no* idea that Jonathan had created an account in his name and was pretending to be him any more than Colin did.

First of all, I had discovered that the account had been created on Thursday, October 25, only four months before, which refuted the notion that it was an "old" e-mail account, regardless of who it belonged to. In addition, the account had been created only a few days after Jonathan had left Laura's, which suggested that Jonathan had created it *specifically* to deceive her and her son. That also suggested that the deception had been going on for at least four months.

Second, although the date on the account was actually the last date the account had been *updated*, not necessarily created, the evidence strongly suggested that October 25 was in fact the date that it had been created. The username of the Cliff account, *xxcliff*, was identical in structure to that of the username of Jonathan's "legitimate" account, *xxjif*, in which the *xx-* represented the first letters of states and the remaining letters referred to the person's name. I knew that Jonathan had created the *xxjif* account on Thursday, September 6 of the previous year and had derived the structure of its username from one of Dan's, *xxdan*. Therefore, the *xxcliff* address couldn't be older than six months at most, well after Cliff was out of the picture and would have been creating any "shared" accounts with Jonathan. Therefore, October 25 was almost certainly the date it had been *created*, not merely updated.

Third, why would Cliff, an American, be inclined to create a U.K. account? It seemed more likely that *Jonathan* would create one than the American Cliff would.

But the most obvious indication that Cliff knew nothing about the *xxcliff* account, let alone had access to it, was simply that, at the same time that Jonathan was using the account to convince Laura and Jack that Cliff was taking care of him, he was telling Cliff—as "Iain"—that he was in a hospice on his deathbed. Although Jonathan had apparently been deleting the messages in the account as quickly as they arrived, he couldn't have risked the possibility that Cliff would access the account at some random time and intercept undeleted messages from Laura or Jack that indicated what Jonathan was telling them, which would have destroyed his story to Cliff. That by itself was proof to me that Cliff was totally ignorant of how Jonathan had been using his identity for his own deceitful purposes.

By the time I left two days later, I still hadn't learned why Jonathan was doing what he was doing to Laura and her family. His answers to my questions had been evasive, tangential, not answers at all. Perhaps *Jonathan* didn't know. Jonathan, it appeared, was driven by powerful unconscious forces over which he seemed to have little understanding and little control.

■

By the time I left Mariah on Sunday afternoon, our relationship had fundamentally changed. I didn't know *how* it had changed, only that it *had*. I didn't know what to think, didn't know how to feel, didn't know how to react. I was totally disoriented. Jonathan's apparent need to retreat into fantasy had grown far more consuming than I could have ever imagined and I didn't know the best way to counteract it. I thought about telling Laura how Jonathan had been deceiving her and her family, but ultimately I decided not to do it, mainly because I didn't know what kind of effect that would have on him. By that point, I had also decided not to tell Andy how Jonathan had deceived him in part for the same reason. Would bringing everything out into the open force him to stop...or would it drive him over the edge?

In retrospect, I realize that I should have consulted with some of the psychologists I knew from college about what to do, but I had come to feel detached from them, from that part of my life, and somehow I didn't know how to reapproach them. I was also embarrassed about the state of my life and didn't want to deal with the uncomfortably probing questions and high expectations I thought they would have. Neither my family nor my friends would have known what to do, so I didn't "consult" with them. *I* was the one with the psychology degrees, so *I* was the one who should have known what to do. But I didn't. I had never encountered anything like this in a psychology book, and never in real life, and I didn't know how to handle it. I was alone in trying to understand, to contend with, something, someone, who was becoming increasingly incomprehensible. I didn't know what to do.

—28—
THE MOTHER OF VICE

La conscience est la mère du vice.
(Conscience is the mother of vice.)
—Georges Braque

I hoped that proceeding with the plan that I had created to restabilize Jonathan's life would also restabilize his mind. Part of that plan involved selling the paintings.

Around the end of February, I decided to see if I could find more information about *Still Life* because I thought I might be able to help verify its provenance as well as to fill in some of the details about what had happened to it between the "missing" years when it was completed in the 1930s and 1955, when it came into Jonathan's grandfather's possession. I found a *catalogue raisonné* of the painter's works at the local university library in which *Still Life* was included. What Jonathan had thought was an insect was actually a part of another object. The information given in the book seemed to corroborate Jonathan's story that the painting had been acquired within the time period he had claimed, which would help to authenticate it and, hopefully, to help it sell for a fitting price.

I wondered, though, if Jonathan's estimate of its presumed worth of $750,000 was overly optimistic. Although it was a "lost" painting by an influential Cubist, the painting was hardly in pristine condition. Painted in the 1930s, it had accumulated a fair amount of grime in the more than 60 years that had passed and now had a dirty orange-brown tint. In addition, a considerable amount of the canvas had been trimmed away, reducing the painting to approximately half the size it had originally been. I didn't know how much the alterations might diminish its value.

By the beginning of March, it had been more than two months since we had planned to go to the auction house to sell Jonathan's paintings. For various reasons, however, that hadn't happened. Among others, Jonathan had led me to believe that the auction house wouldn't accept the paintings unless he insured them, which he couldn't afford to do. In addition, Jonathan had led me to believe that the auction house preferred to see all of the paintings together, and since the Cubist expert still wasn't available to render his judgment about the authenticity and value of *Still Life*, there was no point in going to the auction house until he was. I didn't know what I could do about the appraisal, but I decided to see what I could do about the insurance.

On the evening of Monday, March 4, I e-mailed Jonathan to ask him how much it would cost to insure the lithographs. When I didn't hear back from him that night, I decided to take matters into my own hands. I e-mailed the art dealer from the auction house and explained that it was my understanding that the lithographs had to be insured before they could be accepted for auction and, if that were the case, how much would the insurance cost.

The next day, I received an unexpected reply. The dealer informed me that lithographs by the artist in question usually sold for $500 to $1,500, well below the price that Jonathan had hoped, or had led me to believe, he could sell them for and apparently below the price the auction house could accept for auction. The dealer wasn't aware of the insurance issue and had actually referred Jonathan to another auction house that would be willing to handle a smaller sale. Jonathan had never said anything to me about any of this and I was confused.

I forwarded Jonathan a copy of the message and asked him if I was missing something. In response, he said that the dealer didn't know about insurance, how or from whom to get it, and wasn't able to recommend a particular company or plan, since it would be a conflict of interest. As far as the lithographs were concerned, Jonathan said that the dealer was referring to the prices that large-edition lithographs by the artist tended to garner, not to the pieces he had. His pieces were hand-painted stencils, and while there were several dozen in the series, there were variations among them, making each unique. That meant that his would bring higher prices. Even so, he reminded me that after taxes and commission, there would be little left, although he didn't say if that was discouraging him from selling them. He ended the message by thanking me for trying to help, but also telling me that he preferred to handle the matter himself. He explained that it was confusing to the people with whom he was negotiating and embarrassing for him if I got involved, since it made it seem as if he couldn't handle his own business. I had unwittingly touched a sore spot when he was already touchy enough, so I backed off.

I wrote back, telling him that I was sorry if what I had done had caused embarrassment or confusion and explaining why I had written. In response, Jonathan began by repeating what he had said before, that he appreciated what I was trying to do but that my involvement made things complicated. He then went on to explain that the auction house would in fact probably accept the lithographs for auction, since they were worth more than the dealer seemed to realize, but also to repeat that they would have to be insured if they were to be accepted. He said that he had some other smaller items to sell, which the auction house wouldn't accept and to which the dealer had apparently been referring. Although there may have been some confusion on my part, there also seemed to be some on the dealer's. I was beginning to wonder if my involvement would hinder or help.

Jonathan did confirm that the dealer had directed him toward three or four smaller auction houses, two of which he had contacted. The sale conditions were always the same: 20% to them, 50% to the government. That meant that after commission and taxes, Jonathan would net only 30% of the sales price. That didn't seem to be any different from what he had already told me. For the lithographs, that would leave him with very little. If the larger one sold for $15,000 and the smaller one for $2,000, then he would earn only around $5,000. Although that would help in the short term, $5,000 was well below the prices for which he had purchased them and now he seemed to be having second thoughts about selling them. He said, though, that if he decided to remain in the States, he would do whatever he had to do, no matter how financially unsound or personally distasteful he found it.

The e-mail clarified some things but left me confused about others. I asked Jonathan if the only reason they hadn't wanted to see the lithographs before now was that they preferred to see them and *Still Life* together and had just been waiting for the Cubist expert to become available to look at *Still Life*. I asked him if they would be willing to see the lithographs sooner than *Still Life*.

In response, Jonathan said that they *would* see them separately, but that it would be easier to do everything at once, since otherwise it would require two trips instead of one. Therefore, it had actually been *he* who hadn't wanted to take them separately. He reminded me that the lithographs could be entered into one of the smaller weekly auctions at any time, since they weren't big-ticket items, but since *Still Life* had to be authenticated before it could be entered and was considerably more valuable, it would be entered into one of the major auctions for big-ticket items that took place only a few times a year. He concluded by asking me why I wanted to know.

I explained that if they would see the lithographs sooner than *Still Life*, we could arrange to take them to the auction house now and take *Still Life* later, if necessary. I knew it would mean making two trips, but I told him I was willing to do it if it meant that he would have the money sooner and if he was up to making two trips. I told him I wished I had understood that they would consider them separately because if I had, then I would have been much more insistent than I had been about taking the lithographs to the auction house and "the plan" might have proceeded more quickly than it had.

I told him that as far as the insurance was concerned, I was willing to loan him the money for that and that he could pay me back later along with everything else. I told him that I knew the idea probably made his hair stand on end, but I told him that if it would mean getting the money, and things back on track, more quickly, then I was willing to do it.

In response, he explained that the holdup was based in part on his reluctance to leave the lithographs at the auction house without insurance. Apparently, it *was* possible to leave them there without insurance as long as he signed a waiver releasing them from responsibility in the event that something happened to them. He adamantly refused to let me pay for the insurance, however, stating "there [was] too much there already," which made him uncomfortable. In addition, he said the auction house preferred to see everything at once, but even if they did agree to see the lithographs by themselves, there was always the possibility they wouldn't accept them for sale, in which case we would have to go to the other auction houses and do more travel. The devil was in the details, it seemed, and the situation was becoming increasingly devilish.

In response, I told him that I was fully aware of what would be required and that I had been prepared to make the trip ever since we had come up with the plan to sell the paintings back in December, that I had just been awaiting his word. I reminded him that he seemed to be operating under a definite time constraint and the sooner things got done the better. I told him that if he finally had some money to work with, then perhaps he wouldn't feel that he was being blown about by circumstances and making choices he didn't want to make. I told him he would finally have some real control over his life for the first time in months. I told him that if he could get an appointment on a Wednesday, when I was off, I could go to Mariah from Viridian on Tuesday afternoon, then we could go to the auction house and come back late Wednesday before I had to go to work in Hawthorn on Thursday. I also reminded him that I was on spring break the last week of March, but that it was still two and a half weeks away, which seemed like a long time to wait when things could be underway before then. I assured him that I was willing to do what needed to be done.

He wrote back, saying that he would ask for an appointment for the following Wednesday. That, however, was the last time I heard about the two of us going together to sell the paintings.

Joanne had been encouraging Jonathan to spend more and more time with her family so that Jonathan wouldn't have to be alone. Although Jonathan relished the opportunity to spend time with people in general, he also felt obligated to spend time with the Tomlinsons in particular, since they had not only taken such an interest in his welfare, but also "cooperated" in keeping him in the country. Over time, the Tomlinsons had become more influential in persuading Jonathan to do what *they* thought was best for him. Around the time that I became more insistent about his selling the paintings so he could get his life back on track that much faster, Jonathan decided that instead of having me go with him, he would have Chase go. He made tentative plans to go to the Tomlinsons' on Sunday, the 17th from which he and Chase would leave on Monday, the 18th.

I was dismayed. Jonathan never explained why his plans to sell the paintings, a plan that I had helped to create, had now changed not to include me when for two and a half months they had. I suspected, however, that after everything that had happened between us in recent weeks, it was born partly out of a desire to spend less time with me and more time with Chase.

His relationship to Chase, however, was secondary to a far greater issue that had slowly arisen throughout the previous several weeks, a fundamental issue that, by the middle of March, I felt I could no longer ignore.

—29—
FOUNDATION OF SAND

[Without truth]… any relationship is built on sand and can't stand for long.

By the middle of March, I was feeling well enough again to make an occasional mid-week trip to be with Jonathan. After teaching my Tuesday afternoon class in Viridian on the 12th, I made the trip to Mariah instead of the trip back home. As I usually did, I arrived around 6:00 in the evening, intending to stay until Thursday morning, when I would make the 150-mile trip back to Hawthorn.

My main intention during this trip was to speak with Jonathan about an issue that I could no longer avoid, which was the foundation upon which all meaningful relationships are built: trust. Over the previous two months, my ability to trust him had drastically deteriorated. The foundation of rock—soft though that rock might often have been—on which our relationship seemed to have been built had been slowly eroded by the revelation of his lies to Andy, his lies to Cliff, his lies to Joan, his lies to Laura, his lies to Jack, his lies to me. Jonathan lied to lots of people about lots of things, it seemed, and his word no longer carried much weight. He had claimed that he was staying in the United States solely to be with me, but if that were true, then he was going to have to understand that either he was going to have to rebuild the foundation of our relationship by being truthful, not only with me but also with everyone else to whom he had lied, or he might as well leave. Because I knew how crucial his fantasy life appeared to be to his psychological stability, I didn't expect him to do it all at once, but I *did* expect him to do it. And, I certainly expected him to seek some kind of psychiatric help for a form of maladjustment that had gotten perilously out of control. I would have to see *some* evidence that he was committed to restoring the trust in our relationship, the truthfulness in his relationships with others, because the last thing I could do was have a relationship with someone who was not truthful, whom I could not trust.

Things did not, however, go as planned. After I arrived Tuesday evening, my long afternoon and long drive had left me drained of the mental clarity and emotional strength that I felt I needed to have to raise such an inflammatory issue. On Wednesday, I developed a sinus headache that grew progressively worse throughout the day and left me feeling too sick to deal with the matter again that day.

On Wednesday, before I grew sicker, I checked Jonathan's computer to see where he had been, what he had been doing. I checked the default e-mail program on his computer on which I had found the message he had written to "Sucker" titled "Suck My Dick" two and a half months before. Today, I was also not disappointed. Today, I found a message he had written not to a faceless cruiser on the Internet, but to a familiar name from his past—a message that was just as fictitious as any he had ever sent.

Addressed to "David," the message began with Jonathan describing himself as "a voice from the distant past." He then wished David a happy birthday. Jonathan said that he had been thinking about him lately and had found his web site, which was where he had gotten his e-mail address. After he told David he hoped he was doing well and was happy, Jonathan told him that he himself was doing well and was happy. He went on to tell him that he had been with the same—unnamed—man for 14 years and of their relationship said that although some of it was "excellent" and some of it was "shitty," it was "mostly good." That reminded me of how he had described his relationship with Glenn, stating that the first five years had been "excellent," the next two years, "okay," and the last two years, "shitty." He said that he and his partner were now living in the Midwest, having moved from the Southern state, but said that he still spent a lot of time in Europe on business, naming London, Milan, Brussels, and Frankfurt as destinations. He expressed his wish that he and David could be friends, "even casual ones." He ended the message with an X that represented a kiss and signed it, "Jonathan" with his second middle name "Joshua" beside it in his odd parentheses.

"David" was David Garrett.

David now belonged to the not-so-exclusive club of people Jonathan had deceived in the most pathological way. One way or another, this had to stop.

By Thursday morning, I felt better. Because I had to be back in Hawthorn by 1:00 that afternoon to teach class, I had to leave by 10:00. I didn't want to raise the issue I'd planned to raise, then just leave, but I also felt that I needed to discuss it face to face and I didn't know if I would have the chance to discuss it in person before Jonathan made a final decision to stay or to return, which by that point he seemed on the verge of doing. So, I decided to say what I had to say and see what happened.

I began by telling him that I didn't know if what I had to say would make his decision about whether to stay in the States or to return to England any easier or harder, but that I wanted him to be aware of certain realities that would be attached to either choice. I told him that if he returned to England, I couldn't go with him. A decision to return to England, then, would effectively end our relationship. Then, I told him that if he did find some way to stay and wanted to continue with our relationship, he would have to do certain things to make things better between us, to begin to restore the level of trust I once had in him. I reminded him that he had once told me that any relationship not based on the truth was built on sand and couldn't stand for long and I told him that over the past couple of months, the foundation of our relationship had become awfully crumbly. I told him that in December, my level of trust in him had, on a scale from 1 to 10, been somewhere around 8, but because of the events of the past couple of months, it had dropped to somewhere around 4. That was actually a generous rating. Although unvoiced, my true feeling was that it had dropped to at least 2—possibly lower.

I pointed out how he had tried to cover up his Internet behavior and had lied to me about what he was doing even when I'd had the evidence in front of me, when I'd caught him red-handed. I told him how I had seen him tell one person one thing, a second person a second thing, and a third person a third thing and it made me wonder about what he had been telling *me*.

I told him it was wrong to continue using the fraudulent e-mail accounts through which he had been pretending to be Colin and Cliff. I told him that posing as someone fictional was one thing, but posing as someone real was something entirely different. The results could be extremely damaging to the person involved, whether one intended to do harm or not, and he didn't have the right to appropriate another person's identity and use it as he saw fit. I asked him to consider how Colin and Cliff would feel if they knew what he'd been doing. We were, after all, talking about his best friend since childhood and an ex-boyfriend with whom he had said he was once passionately in love. I turned it around and asked him how *he* would feel if *I* went around posing as *him*?

As I spoke, Jonathan slowly rolled his eyes upward, giving me the dismissive look of someone who couldn't look the truth in *its* eyes but who wanted to make *me* out to be wrong. In his now-familiar refrain, he sarcastically told me that I was "just too good" for him and that he was "unworthy" of me. He accused me of being judgmental and self-righteous. I told him to stop it and listen to me, but it was clear that he was closed to anything I had to say. He reminded me that the only reason he had been staying in the United States was to be with me and that if I didn't feel I could trust him, then there was no reason for him to stay. I was disheartened by his reaction because it told me that his lies were more important to him than I was. At that moment, I knew that our relationship was over or, at the least, in serious trouble.

Disappointed, I went and got my things. As I was leaving, I asked him if he could do me a favor. Having turned morose, he said sure, and I told him that if he was going back to England, we needed to make some arrangement to have him repay the money he owed me. He had told me that if he returned to England, his father was still willing to clear his debts, including the debt Jonathan owed to me. I asked him to give me his father's e-mail address so I could communicate with him directly. He said he would and said he didn't know why he hadn't gotten it to me before. Then, I left, not knowing what would happen next.

I left around 9:30 and arrived home around noon, which gave me enough time to check my e-mail before going to class. When I did, I found that Jonathan had sent me a message about half an hour before. In it, he told me that he had been very emotional when I had left that morning, which had been obvious. He said he didn't want to go back to England but felt his options were narrowing. Apparently, though, Joanne wanted to talk to him before he made definite decisions, since she and Warren had come up with some ideas that she thought might be helpful. He mentioned that Joanne had offered to pay for the insurance on the lithographs, that he and Chase would probably be going to the auction house the following Monday, that the lithographs, if accepted, would be sold the following week, and that he would finally have the profits the week after.

He acknowledged that he was "not normal right now" and had probably suffered some kind of emotional breakdown. There was no "probably" about it. He said that his condition had gone largely untreated and that he was trying to heal himself. In truth, it had gone *completely* untreated and the way he was trying to "heal himself"—by retreating into stress-relieving fantasies that involved real people—was sicker than the disorder he was trying to treat. I wasn't sure if he genuinely recognized the seriousness of his condition and the side effects for everyone around him or if he was simply telling me what he thought I wanted to hear.

He claimed that he understood the efforts and sacrifices I had made on his behalf and appreciated everything I had done, perhaps more than I realized. That was becoming a familiar refrain, casually tossed out when the situation seemed to demand it, but unfortunately having no real substance. His expressions of "gratitude" were wearing thin and growing increasingly meaningless.

In addition to everything else that was happening, he informed me that two companies, one in Paladin and one in Hawthorn, wanted to interview him. He was confused about what to do. Getting the job in Paladin would allow him to move back into that environment, while getting the one in Hawthorn would allow him to be near me. I didn't know how *I* felt about either possibility should either materialize.

He went on to inform me that he still had electricity, at least for that day, and that he would probably be having a new neighbor in the near future, which in spite of his isolation he didn't want. Then, he apologized for having wreaked so much havoc in my life and said that our relationship had reached the point that it had because of "events in [his] life." His "apology," however, rang hollow because once again, he was blaming circumstances, not himself, for how he had behaved. He ended his message by expressing his hope that my trip home had been easy and, assuming that I wouldn't be reading his message until later that afternoon, that work hadn't been "too awful."

I didn't have time to respond before going to work and after I returned home I was so tired from traveling and teaching that I couldn't compose a response, not that I would have known what to say anyway.

Around 7:00 that evening, he sent me another e-mail titled "Silence Speaks For Itself." In it, he lamented that I had always used to let him know that I'd gotten home safely, which I hadn't done this time. He said he understood why I hadn't written (although he didn't) and expressed the opinion that perhaps it was better that way, if painful for him. He said that he was now going to go to the Tomlinsons' the next day instead of waiting until Sunday, as he'd originally planned, because Joanne was concerned that he had too many negative things to deal with and spent too much time alone. On Monday, he would go to the auction house with Chase.

He concluded by telling me to stay well and expressing his hope that things worked out well for me. At the very end, he told me, emphatically, that I deserved a better boyfriend than him. This statement stood in stark contrast to his previous position, which was

●

that *I* was the one who hadn't been the good boyfriend. I certainly deserved better than what I had suffered.

After that, I didn't hear from Jonathan for several days. I didn't expect to, not because I felt that he would have no further contact with me—at the least, we still had business to conclude—but because he rarely e-mailed me from the Tomlinsons'. Under the circumstances, I was more dismayed than I might otherwise have been, given what Jonathan was planning to do. I was very uncomfortable with the idea of him and Chase going to the auction house together. They would be spending the night together and I felt that was asking for trouble. Chase was persistent and Jonathan, I had come to understand, did not have the same degree of self-restraint that I had. With the stability of our relationship now called into question, this might give Jonathan an extra level of permission to turn to Chase in ways that were more than purely emotional. It was, in a way, Thanksgiving all over again and I was disturbed.

In addition, I couldn't help feeling cheated out of a trip that rightfully belonged to me. The trip to sell the paintings was, after all, part of "the plan which [I] had so much to do with," as Jonathan had once described it. The whole point of selling the paintings was to give Jonathan the money he needed not only to restabilize his life, but also to restabilize *our relationship*, and I felt that I should have been part of that. I had also been looking forward to the trip for almost three months simply because I felt it would be a much-needed diversion from the stress that had come to characterize my life. If I couldn't have London, then perhaps I could at least have a night in some major city. Now, not only had I been denied that, too, but someone whom I disliked, who had been the source of so much discord in my life, was going in my place.

Over the next couple of days, I composed a letter in which I repeated and expanded on what I had told Jonathan on Thursday. I wanted the opportunity to express my thoughts more clearly and completely so that he would fully understand my position and the implications of his decisions. I sent the letter on Monday, expecting it to arrive by Wednesday. It did.

That afternoon, Jonathan sent me the first e-mail that I had received from him in almost a week. In it, he began by informing me that he had just returned to Mariah and confirmed that he had received my letter. He said that although he couldn't disagree with much of what I had said, he wasn't sure how we should proceed. He criticized me for spending two days with him then raising the issues that I had with him right before I had left. He told me that if it was that important to me, I could have tried to rally on Wednesday and he congratulated himself on how *he* managed to do it when it was important, in spite of not having many good days. He then went on to accuse me of being "preachy and self-righteous," telling me that although that might not be my intention, that was how I came across. He listed all of the burdens that were weighing on him—his health problems, his isolation, his lack of family support, his inability to function in a foreign country—all of which had conspired to make him suffer an emotional collapse. He said, however, that he knew he was a good person who had been successful personally and professionally throughout his entire life but that his circumstances had changed everything, had changed *him*. He said that he wasn't prepared for the effects they'd had on him and that the choices he had made had proven to be bad.

He told me that, in his opinion, we needed to take a break. He told me that he would repay me what he owed me in the next few days. He alluded to the ideas that Joanne and Warren had come up with to help him, one of which would provide him with "a big block of cash" that would allow him to repay me and do other things he needed to do. He said that he was returning to the Tomlinsons' that weekend and that while he was there, they would get his things out of storage so the cost would no longer be added to the total. He said that he had been looking at places to live in Paladin and was starting to get job interviews, expressing his desire to do something constructive that would eliminate the isolation and inactivity that had, he believed, led to his breakdown.

In my letter, I had told him, bluntly, that he was obsessed with Glenn. He informed me that if he was in fact obsessive, that was my definition, not his. He repeated his position, which he'd first expressed during our second major fight in October, that he wouldn't abandon the people he loved and would continue to try to find Glenn. He said that Glenn was basically a good person and that the bad he had done at the end of their relationship didn't negate the good he had done. Sarcastically, he told me that perhaps I had never loved someone outside of my family enough to forgive people for the wrong they had done and that his two long-term relationships had probably made him more tolerant of people's imperfections than I was. His statement was just another example of his now-infamous habit of evading criticism, since forgiving people for their mistakes had nothing to do with his obsessiveness over Glenn. In any case, I felt that in spite of his professed love for me, he was, in his own way, abandoning *me*.

Again, he stated that he didn't know what was going to happen between us. He said that if I didn't feel I could trust him, then perhaps I needed to find someone I could. He said that in any event he didn't seem to be capable of having a serious relationship until his other problems were resolved. He held out the possibility that once they were, perhaps we could try again, since he said that the things that had initially attracted him to me were still there. He reiterated his stance that once he loved someone he always loved them, even if it was in a different form. He concluded by telling me that he had only "good thoughts and hopes" for me.

His good thoughts and hopes, his love, for me were difficult to discern in a message that was, fundamentally, all about him. Although I knew that he was going through a difficult time, I also knew that much of it was self-created and I had grown tired of his excuses for treating me as if I didn't matter. I wrote him yet another message in which I found myself repeating my complaint that in spite of everything I had done for him, he had done nothing for me, for us. He had taken only a handful of the Prozac that I had lied to my doctor to obtain for him. He had refused to stop posting his sex ads in spite of the problems his behavior had caused between us. He had refused to seek any kind of medical and especially mental help in the months he had been in Mariah despite the damage it was causing him and especially others. And, in spite of the fact that he had once told me that I had "saved [his] life, literally," he had given all the credit for my life-saving effort, which had come at tremendous personal cost, to an ex-boyfriend. I told him that although he had forgiven Glenn for what he had done to hurt him, *I* had forgiven *him* for the things he had done to hurt *me* and had remained with *him*. I told him that if all he was going to do was not to take us, take me, seriously, then I didn't see how our relationship could progress.

His response was predictable. After suggesting that my inability to understand what he was trying to express was the result of cultural differences, he claimed that he had in fact listened to me and had modified his Internet behavior accordingly. He stated that he understood it was self-destructive and didn't reflect who he really was. He said the problem was not what I had said but how I had said it. He told me that while I often reminded him that he was a snob, I also failed to see my own smugness, acting as if I were the "moral arbiter" for the whole world. He expressed his opinion that my experience of the world was limited and indirect, implying that someone with a broader perspective would find his behavior acceptable. He reminded me that when things had fallen apart for me in Paladin, I had run home to recover instead of toughing it out, which suggested that my emotional stability wasn't perfect either. He challenged me to consider how well *I* would do in his isolated circumstances with no one to rely on.

As far as getting medical or mental help was concerned, he stated that the nearest help outside of Mariah was at least an hour's drive away, which meant that getting the help he needed hadn't been a viable option for months. Although the only thing that had kept him from getting help in Mariah for his endocarditis and his emotional problems had been his upper-crust pride, his "reason" for refusing it appeared valid to him, his position, final.

Then, he explained to me, as if I were ignorant of the fact, that sometimes relationships "[were] not all 50 -50 due to events." After "apologizing" for not giving me more time and attention, he informed me that sometimes he had shouldered more of the burden in his relationships than his partners had, but he had always understood that everything would eventually balance out. He told me that when Glenn had developed problems and he had tried to take care of him, the last few months of their relationship had been 95% Glenn and 5% him. In addition, he told me that when Marcus had suffered problems with his father and stepmother, their relationship had become focused on Marcus, but that later, when Jonathan was switching to a career in business, their relationship had become focused on Jonathan. He informed me that since I had never been in a "true" long-term relationship, I might not understand how it worked in real life as opposed to how it worked in a book or a school course. In other words, everything I had been doing for him had been not only reasonable, but also expected, and the implication was that I was being selfish for wanting something back.

After stating that he didn't want to get into a "pissing contest" because of his strong feelings for me and his feeling that further arguing was unproductive, he told me that he was planning to look for a small house either in the trendy area of Paladin where we had eaten several times the summer before or downtown and wanted to move back within the next two to four weeks. He mentioned that within the next week to ten days he would have somewhere between $10,000 and $20,000 and that even after repaying me he would have enough to live on until he acquired even more within the next month. He didn't clarify, but I wondered if he was referring to the "big block" of cash to which he had referred previously that he would obtain by implementing one of Joanne and Warren's ideas for helping him. He said that finally having the money he needed was a huge weight off his shoulders and would allow him to concentrate on other things—presumably, us. Even so, his resentment was still evident when he suggested that while I should feel happy for him now that his circumstances were improving, I didn't. He ended his message by asking me what else I wanted him to do or say and saying himself that he was at a loss.

I was at a loss as well. Once again, he had resorted to all of his familiar tactics to deflect criticism and disown responsibility. He had rationalized his behavior without really addressing it. He had continued to invalidate my criticisms by expressing the opinion that I didn't understand relationships, people, and life in general, a criticism that he had been leveling against me since the previous July. He had accused me of being self-righteous, judgmental, and morally superior, an accusation that he had added to his arsenal of psychological weapons more recently. Despite what he had said about having listened to me and taken what I had said to heart, he hadn't listened to me at all, had only pretended to do so.

I knew that our relationship was dying, although it lived on for a little while longer.

—30—
EASTER

I have been invited to the Tomlinsons for Easter as they do not want me to be alone.

In 2002, Easter fell on the last day of March. Another holiday was approaching, and it was yet another holiday that I could not invite Jonathan to spend with me. As had been the problem at Thanksgiving and Christmas, my house was too small to accommodate Jonathan and his dogs. If he could have left them with someone else, then he might have been able to stay with me, but there was no one to leave them with. Even so, I didn't know how I felt about having him visit me under the circumstances. I knew he was mentally ill, something for which I was prepared to give him some sympathy, but his behavior had left me largely alienated. But, even if I had invited him, I was sure he wouldn't come, since in the ten months that we had been together, I had only gone to him and he had never come to me.

By Friday, March 22, we hadn't communicated for two days. After our e-mail fight a couple of days before, I wasn't eager to speak to him. On Friday morning around 10:30, however, he e-mailed me to tell me that he had decided to keep me apprised of his situation, "at least until we either disengage or figure out what comes next."

He stated that he had come back to Mariah on Wednesday, which I knew, but was going back to Paladin that afternoon for the "week end." One of the companies to which he had applied and that had initially turned him down now wanted to talk to him because their other candidate hadn't worked out. In addition, he was planning to look at four houses in Paladin on Saturday, two in the trendy area and two downtown. While he was there, he was, of course, planning to stay at the Tomlinsons' and Chase was the one who was planning to take him to see the houses.

Then, for the third time since Thanksgiving, I learned that the Tomlinsons had beaten me to the punch. Jonathan informed me that they had invited him to spend Easter with them because, as he stated, Joanne felt that the main cause of his emotional problems was his persistent isolation and she had taken a genuine interest in alleviating that problem. Apparently, Joanne had told him that he was like a member of her family and that he didn't have to be alone anymore. He said that he had cried when she had told him that. Although unexpressed, the implication was that he felt that *I* hadn't been doing enough to alleviate his loneliness in spite of all the time I had spent with him in Mariah. I wondered how he had portrayed the situation to the Tomlinsons, what they thought of me.

Moving on to practical matters, he told me that they would be getting his belongings out of storage that week. According to him, they couldn't do it that Friday because Warren had an important meeting and Chase was working. With more than a hint of sarcasm, he "apologized" for the delay but promised that his things would be out of storage soon. The Tomlinsons were graciously allowing him to store his items in their spacious garage, where he would be able to leave them until he moved back to Paladin in the next few weeks.

Broaching the subject of his Internet activities, he assured me that he was staying "completely" off the Internet. He compared his condition to that of being a "drunk," stating that you didn't dare take that first drink. I wanted to believe him, but couldn't. His need to use the Internet to retreat from reality was too compelling.

He ended his message by emphasizing how difficult it was to keep in touch. He repeated that his cable connection, which affected both the Internet and the television, was unreliable. I felt, though, that the main obstacle to staying in touch was Jonathan.

I was on spring break from Saturday, the 23rd through Sunday, the 31st. Before the problems of the previous week had arisen, I had planned to spend most, if not all, of my vacation with Jonathan. I was planning to spend the time not only keeping him company while he waited out his sentence in Mariah, but also helping him do whatever he needed to do. Now, he didn't want to do that. The Tomlinsons were snaring him ever more strongly in their "very sticky web" and he no longer seemed to mind. In addition, Chase had given him an electronic passkey to his condo, providing further encouragement. Jonathan had previously shown me the passkey, and although he rolled his eyes, he didn't seem *that* dismayed. On the one hand, I praised the Tomlinsons for wanting to help Jonathan, but on the other hand, I was ambivalent about the way in which they seemed to be doing it.

By that point, our relationship was disintegrating at an accelerated rate. As time had passed, our ability to stay in touch had diminished until it had practically vanished. Because Jonathan lived 150 miles away, had no phone service, and had irregular e-mail service, the only ways to stay in touch with him were either through regular mail or through direct contact, which seemed increasingly hindered by various forces. Early in our relationship, Jonathan had sometimes signed off his e-mails by telling me to "email, smoke signal, [use] tom-tom drums"—in short, do whatever I could to keep in touch—and now, I felt that I needed to be innovative in finding ways to keep the lines of communication open.

In the end, Jonathan didn't go to the Tomlinsons' until the morning of Saturday, the 23rd. While he waited for Chase to pick him up, I decided to post a message on the *Gayteway* board for my state, where I assumed he would see it. He did. The message told him that we needed to talk about everything that was going on, that somehow we needed to resolve things. Over the next hour, we took our turns posting messages to the other, trying to be as private as the public board allowed. Finally, he told me that Chase had arrived and that he needed to leave. The exchange left things very uncertain, very *un*resolved, but now that he was gone, I wouldn't be able to communicate with him for several days.

Still, I needed *some* way to communicate with him. Since I knew that he was going to be going to the storage unit that weekend, I decided to write him a letter and leave it there. On Sunday, the 24th, I made a special trip to Paladin to the unit, where I slipped the letter under the door and attached another one to the door telling Jonathan to look for the one in the room. I hoped he would find it.

In addition, I decided that if he was able to go online, even if he couldn't always access his e-mail, then perhaps I could post messages on a personal web site where he, but only he, could read them. By giving the pages with the messages file names that only he would know, that would function, in effect, like a password, allowing him to read them but not allowing others. To that end, I acquired web space with a hosting provider and posted several messages to him through it. I was also given a new e-mail address along with the pages and hoped the new "message" account would be immune to the technical problems that my regular and "Jonathan" accounts, which were with another provider, had displayed. I e-mailed him to tell him about the pages and how to access them, but I received no response.

By Wednesday, the 27th, we had been out of touch for four days. The average length of time that was now passing without communicating was growing longer, which was bad. I e-mailed him early that morning and asked him what was going on with him and what his plans were for the rest of the week because I wanted to see him at least one day that week. I told him that I felt we needed to work things out and not dealing with what had happened was just going to make things worse. At the least, it wasn't going to allow them to get better, I thought, and I, for one, wanted them to get better, even if "better" involved parting as friends.

That morning around 11:00, he finally responded. He told me that he had just returned from Paladin that morning. Because of the bad weather we'd experienced during the previous several days, including several inches of snow on Tuesday, he had spent those days at the Tomlinsons'. He commented, almost offhandedly, how nice it was to be snowed in "with everyone in the house." I knew, however, that there was nothing offhanded about the remark.

Moving on, he told me that he had been offered a job in Asia, which would start the first week of May. He also informed me that he'd had two interviews while he was in Paladin. Another company that had seemed interested in him had needed an immediate response, which he didn't feel he could give, so he had "let it go." He said that while he was in Paladin, he had looked at some housing, but was planning to wait and see how things materialized before making final decisions.

As far as the upcoming holiday was concerned, he reiterated that he was spending Easter with the Tomlinsons, who didn't want him to be alone on holidays anymore. This was the third stab that he had taken at me regarding the holidays and I didn't appreciate it. In addition, Jonathan, who stated that he was going back to Paladin on either Thursday or Friday, offered his opinion that given the bad weather and the limited time remaining until he left, he didn't see how it was possible for us to see each other that week. Dismissively, he ended the message with an abrupt "Stay warm."

To me, that wasn't acceptable. I felt that even though he didn't seem motivated to do it, we needed to talk, in person, about what had been happening between us. The situation seemed to have reverted to the way it had been the previous fall, when we were having problems but couldn't deal with them directly because other people—apart from hard feelings—were getting in our way. Since he had said that he would be going back to Paladin on either Thursday or Friday, I decided to go to Mariah later that day.

Earlier that week, I had written Warren and Joanne a letter. This would be the first contact we would have and, despite my feelings toward Chase, I didn't have similar feelings toward Warren or Joanne. Indeed, I appreciated the fact they could help Jonathan in ways I could not. In the letter, I introduced myself and told them I was Jonathan's boyfriend. I thanked them for taking an interest in him and his welfare and for everything they had been and were doing to help him. I explained that I had been trying to help him insofar as I could, but because of financial and practical limitations, I could only do so much. I explained in some detail what those limitations were, so they would hopefully understand that I had really been trying to help him. In particular, I explained to them that I lived in a small house and had what I described as an "awkward living arrangement" that made it impossible, or at least very difficult, to have Jonathan stay with me.

After mentioning that Jonathan and I were having difficulty staying in touch because he currently had no phone service and irregular e-mail service, I asked them if they would give me some way of contacting them, of contacting Jonathan, while he was staying with them. I told them that I hadn't asked Jonathan for their telephone number or e-mail addresses because Jonathan had strong feelings about matters of privacy and I knew he would be unwilling to give me this information without their permission. Because I had no other way to get it to them, I had originally intended to leave the letter at the storage unit, where I knew they would find it, but if Jonathan was going to be spending Easter with them and I was going to be seeing him beforehand, I decided to give it to him to give to them.

When my mother found out that the Tomlinsons had invited Jonathan to spend Easter with them, she decided to write him a note in which she explained, herself, that she would have invited him for Easter, and would have invited him for Thanksgiving and Christmas, but that her house was too small to accommodate him and his dogs. She made sure he understood that it wasn't because she didn't *want* him to stay with us, but simply because he *couldn't* stay with us. He had heard that from me, more than once, but I hoped that, coming from my mother, it would carry additional weight and he would, perhaps, finally stop holding it against me, which he clearly still was.

After getting my hair cut, I left for Mariah Wednesday afternoon. Because I didn't want resistance, I decided not to tell Jonathan I was coming. I knew he didn't like surprise visits, but I felt I had no choice. I took a change of clothes, but under the circumstances, I thought it might be overly optimistic of me to do that, since I didn't know if I would be welcome to stay. I didn't know what was going to happen, which way things were going to go. But, I knew I had to do *something* to resolve the stalemate.

When I arrived, Jonathan was naturally surprised. After allowing me somewhat uncertainly inside, I explained why I was there. We sat down in the kitchen and discussed what had been happening, or had *not* been happening, between us. As we talked, Jonathan kept saying, "I can't believe you came." It was difficult to interpret his tone as an indication of pleasure or dismay, but I hoped that he viewed my making the trip to Mariah as an example of how I was indeed trying to "fight for what's important," despite his past accusations that I didn't.

I asked him if he had gotten the letter I'd left at the storage unit. He told me that because of the bad weather, they had decided not to go. My trip to Paladin to deliver it, then, had been wasted effort. Driving all the way to Mariah seemed justified.

While I was there, I happened to notice that one of the lithographs he had been planning to sell was still propped up against the back of the loveseat in the living room, where it had been sitting for some time. I asked him if he and Chase had gone to the auction house and he said no. I actually felt good to know that, even though it meant the paintings were still unsold. Jonathan then explained that the reason they hadn't gone involved not the bad weather, but one of the ideas that Joanne and Warren had come up with for helping him, which, I now learned for certain, would give him the $10,000 to $20,000 within the next few days and additional money within the next month that he had mentioned earlier.

He told me that Joanne had suggested that instead of selling *Still Life* in June when he could make more money by selling it in the fall, Jonathan could have the money he needed now by "syndicating" it. I was certainly familiar with the syndicating of media, but not art. Jonathan explained that interested parties would buy shares of the painting—giving him the money he needed now—and that when the painting finally sold, the shareholders would not only recoup their initial investment, but also make a profit that was a certain percentage of the selling price. Joanne and Warren together, as well as Joanne's mother, would be among the shareholders. The buy-in price was $10,000, which would give Jonathan around $20,000. That would be more than enough money for him finally to move back to Paladin and be enough, if he were frugal, to live on until *Still Life* sold in the fall.

It was an ingenious idea, I had to admit, although it was also one through which the Tomlinsons would benefit. If they were so wealthy and concerned for his welfare, though, I wondered why they couldn't just *loan* him the money he needed to get back on his feet. *I* had given him plenty to keep him going when I didn't have it to give, and even though they weren't involved with him the way I was, neither was my mother, who had also given him money she didn't have to give. Their generosity, as much as Jonathan might have been pulled into it, had its limits, and they were obviously just as interested in helping themselves as they were in helping Jonathan. My feelings about them were beginning to change.

That day, we talked about the issues that had arisen throughout the previous two weeks. I tried to be conciliatory, as conciliatory as possible without relenting on my main points. I told him that I felt I had been too harsh with him about some things, especially about the issue of trust, but I remained firm in my insistence that if he were going to continue to have a relationship with me, then certain things were going to have to change. I told him I understood that much of his behavior over the past several months had stemmed from a maladjusted way of coping with the stresses he'd been forced to endure, but even though that explained it, it didn't excuse it. He was going to have to tell *everyone* he'd deceived the truth and I was going to have to see proof that he had. In addition, he was going to have to tell everyone that we were involved and I was going to have to see proof of that, too. I was still deeply offended that, after almost ten months, no one seemed to know that we were involved with each other, *especially* after everything I had done to try to keep our relationship together, after everything I had done to try to keep *him* together.

His response was more subdued than it had been two weeks before, but otherwise little different. He had no intention of telling them the truth. Indeed, he seemed to feel justified in having done what he had because he claimed that when he had been in Paladin the last time, he had seen a psychiatrist who had told him that his behavior over the past several months—including the elaborate, potentially damaging lies he had told numerous people—had been a "normal" reaction to the stress of his isolation and illness. I didn't know what to think about his claim. Either his psychiatrist was just as crazy as he was or he had misled her as much as he had misled so many others. Or, most likely of all, he was lying yet again and was attempting to use the air of legitimacy that he thought a psychiatrist's judgment could provide to justify his pathological behavior.

Perhaps because we had reached an impasse on the issue, I tried to focus on other things. That did not mean, however, that I was going to drop the issue forever, only set it aside for a while. An unresolved issue of this magnitude was a major stumbling block for many reasons and ultimately it could not be ignored.

Instead, we talked about the opportunities for change that had arisen over the past several days. Although Jonathan had been offered the job in Asia, he didn't know if he was going to take it. I reminded him that taking the job would mean being alone in a foreign country with no one to take care of him. I told him that at least if he stayed in the United States, preferably in my state, he would be in a familiar environment surrounded by people who could and would care for him, but he was unsure what to do. He didn't seem to be having any luck finding a fitting job in the States in general or in my state in particular, and although he would be getting money from the syndication and sale of the paintings, working for money was not the only reason he wanted to work. If he took the job in Asia, in the same way that if he returned to England, I wasn't sure that I wanted to follow him, especially with the stability and quality of our relationship in serious question.

In the end, I spent two days in Mariah. While I was there, I used Jonathan's computer to check my e-mail. In addition, I checked his Internet history. In the process, I discovered something that didn't make sense.

Jonathan had told me that he had stayed with the Tomlinsons from the afternoon of Friday, the 15th through the afternoon of Wednesday, the 20th. I saw from the history, however, that while he hadn't used the computer on Saturday, the 16th or Sunday, the 17th, he *had* used it on Monday, the 18th and Tuesday, the 19th. *Someone* had, at any rate, and apart from Joan and Chase, Jonathan and I were the only people who had set foot in the apartment since the middle of November. I checked to see if the clock had been reset, but it had not, thereby failing to explain the discrepancy that way. Even if it had, though, that wouldn't have explained why there was a *two*-day gap instead of the expected *four*-day gap, since resetting the clock wouldn't have affected the apparent *pattern* of usage, just offset it. Had Jonathan come back from the Tomlinsons' earlier than he'd indicated, but had told me otherwise? If so, why?

In addition, I found a letter on Jonathan's computer that Jonathan had sent to Cliff the previous May. The brief letter, which had accompanied and addressed a gift he had sent to him for his birthday, contained a postscript in which Jonathan told Cliff, "I love you madly and I always will." Otherwise, the letter was unremarkable except for two things. First, Jonathan had sent the letter during the time that Cliff and he were allegedly avoiding contact with each other because contact was too painful. Second, the letter was dated May 30—the night that Jonathan had placed his ad that I had answered. I didn't know what to think about the timing of the letter, either as it pertained to Jonathan and Cliff or as it pertained to Jonathan and me. With Jonathan, nothing was straightforward.

After spending half of Wednesday and all of Thursday in Mariah, I left around noon on Friday. Chase was supposed to be picking Jonathan up sometime around 12:30 and I didn't want to be there when he came. At first, I thought about hanging around and surreptitiously getting a look at Chase without Chase's or Jonathan's knowing—Chase had, after all, gotten a look at *me*, so it seemed only fair—but in the end, I decided not to do that.

The next three days were strange. The winter was ending and the weather was warming, and in the same way that nature was becoming unfrozen, Jonathan's situation also seemed to be unfreezing, admitting movement and maneuvering that had been denied to it throughout the long, difficult season. Circumstances were changing so rapidly now that it was difficult for me to keep up with them emotionally. Our relationship had frequently been wracked by various forms of instability, but this was a new kind of instability I had not previously experienced. With Jonathan on the threshold of returning to Paladin and regaining a modicum of his former life, it felt good to think that things might be returning to some version of normal, but if they did, it certainly would not be the same version that had distinguished it the summer before. Too much had happened in the intervening time for it to return to the carefree state that had graced it the previous June.

On the first day of April, I sent Jonathan a message asking him if I could come to Mariah on Tuesday. I had planned to be in Hawthorn that Tuesday evening for a relative's birthday, but as it turned out, she had to work, which left me free. Later, he wrote back, informing me that Tuesday wouldn't be a good day, since he had interviews in Paladin with two companies. He also added that he was using Chase's computer and, therefore, communicating would be difficult. I felt that even if he hadn't had interviews or been otherwise impeded, he still wouldn't have been interested in getting together.

My feeling was emphasized by the fact that the same day, Jonathan posted yet another sex ad on *Gayteway* under the name "Tough." Titled "Want To," the ad was a reply to one placed by "Rough Rider," a frequent advertiser on the board. In the ad, "Tough" said that although he was usually a "top," he wanted to be fucked by a "masculine hot dude," which he told "Rough Rider" he thought he was. Surprisingly, "Tough" described himself as looking the way Jonathan actually looked, although he added that he was in "decent shape" and had a "firm ass," which was certainly not true. After listing several sexual acts he said he allegedly enjoyed, he asked "Rough Rider," "Want to?"

Apparently, he didn't feel he could use Chase's computer to communicate with *me*, but he *did* feel he could use it to communicate with total strangers through one of his insipid sex ads. By that point, I had come to believe that Jonathan never intended to "hook up" with the men he targeted through his ads, that if he got off on anything it was on giving people the runaround, but even though I wasn't concerned about that, I'd had enough.

Exasperated and insulted, I posted my own ad in which I took aim at Jonathan. In it, I made several provocative comments about the inadequacy of my sex life and encouraged men who were "up" to the job of satisfying me to respond. I ended it with the phrase "Let's do it," the catchphrase that Jonathan had used in the "GayMan" ads from August and in several additional postings. I described myself in enough detail that Jonathan, who would inevitably see the ad, would know it was me. Maliciously, I signed it "Andy" and gave "Iain's" e-mail address as the contact address.

I knew that my reaction was juvenile, but it was also cathartic. I'd had enough of being made to feel that I was second best, if in fact I ranked even that high, that I wasn't worth as much as some nameless, faceless stranger on the Internet appeared to be. I didn't know what kind of reaction I would receive, but by that point, I wasn't sure that I cared. I was beginning to realize that I'd had enough, not just for that day but also for the previous ten months. Unconsciously I had been asking myself the "Dear Abby" question and was beginning to sense that what I had to endure, what I had to accept, to be involved with Jonathan was no longer worth it. The strain of the past ten months had finally built to the point that something would have to give.

The next day, it did.

—31—
THE BREAKING POINT

...I have nothing further to say to you.

My relationship with Jonathan had rarely been easy, and as time had worn on, it had only grown harder. Yet, in spite of the turmoil that seemed to define it, I had felt compelled to keep it together. The reasons had changed as the relationship had continued, but by the beginning of April, I was remaining in the relationship, more than anything else, by sheer force of habit. I had been living my life a certain way for so long that I didn't know how to live my life any other way. In addition, I didn't want to admit defeat, admit that after investing almost a year's worth of blood, sweat, and tears in our relationship, that after toughing it out through the most trying of times, I had ultimately failed. Further, by remaining in the relationship, I felt that I could maintain a certain amount of control—over the reclaiming of my money, over the damage that Jonathan was doing through his deceptions, over a situation that was growing increasingly out of control. And, finally, I was restrained by fear—fear that I would never again find someone who possessed in one place all of the positive qualities that Jonathan possessed, had displayed when I had first met him. I still held out a tenuous hope that things would change, that *he* would change, for the better, but I also knew that without an incentive, people didn't change and Jonathan had *no* incentive, expecting others—me—to change. In reflecting on the situation, I find it ironic that our weaknesses are often stronger than our strengths.

The tensions in our relationship, however, had built up to the point that, like two tectonic plates butting against each other with maximum pressure, something eventually would have to give. An earthquake that would alter the topography of our relationship was inevitable.

On the morning of Tuesday, April 2, our relationship finally reached the breaking point.

That morning around 10:15, Jonathan sent me an e-mail in which he told me, in no uncertain terms, not only what *he* was going to do for himself, but also what *others* had *not* done for him that had driven him to his decision. He began by telling me that he was about to go to Paladin for his two job interviews and had spoken to a third company by phone that seemed interested in him. In addition, he had spoken to Greg Carroll, who had been transferred to California in February. Although Greg was American, he had also worked in Europe and knew how business operated in both the United States and abroad. In spite of his interviews, Jonathan complained that Paladin looked "sort of dead" to him as far as career options were concerned and Greg had remarked that business was conducted differently in Paladin than it was anywhere else that he and Jonathan had worked. Although the job in Asia was still an option, Jonathan didn't know how feasible it would be to take it because of the difficulties involved in moving overseas. Therefore, if nothing arose in Paladin within the next week, Jonathan had decided, he would go to live with Greg in California.

Greg's reasons for wanting Jonathan to live with him were not entirely professional. Although one of the reasons was that he didn't know many people in California and relished the idea of having a familiar face to keep him company, another, perhaps greater reason was that Greg was dismayed by the fact that, in his estimation, Jonathan hadn't been getting the day-to-day help that he had needed. Jonathan appeared to agree. To make his point, he reviewed his experiences over the previous seven months. Living with Dan had been disastrous. Living with Laura had been better, but her money-grubbing and sexual advances had done more harm than good. Living with Art had been the best, but after he had moved to Mariah and Art had gotten another boarder, returning to Art's was impossible. The Tomlinsons had been helpful, but they had their own agenda and their help always seemed to have strings attached. And, Chase, who was in love with him and had offered to take care of him in Mariah, was too young, in Jonathan's opinion, for him to allow him to disrupt his life to do so.

Then, there was me. Although he acknowledged that I had done a "tremendous amount" to help him in the months that he had lived in Mariah, he also remarked that I hadn't always been able to provide him with the day-to-day help that he had needed. Although I had been prepared to help and commit, I had done so only to what he called "that indefinable point." He said that although I would be able to do more if I moved in with him in Paladin, he had needed the help in Mariah and I hadn't given it. The result was that he had been alone in Mariah for six months (although he had, by that point, been there for only four and a half). Therefore, Greg also wanted Jonathan to live with him so he could provide him with the ongoing care that no one else, including me, had given to him. Jonathan said that he understood my issues but needed to be selfish and think about what was best for *him* because it was, after all, *his* life on the line. He reminded me that, unlike me, he wasn't living in a safe environment surrounded by his family and told me that without him, my life would go on, but without the regular trips to Mariah and Paladin.

He concluded his message by telling me that he needed to go. He said he would throw on his "business drag" and try to appear healthy for his interviews. He was, of course, planning to stay with the Tomlinsons that night and possibly longer, since it was "great to be in a normal environment and around people." That was that.

By the time I finished the message, I felt as if I had been slapped hard across the face. I had turned my mind, my health, my life, inside out for months to help him, to be there for him, when everyone else had turned their backs on him, wanted to use him, or tried to harm him, and now, he was claiming that I had helped and committed to him only to "that indefinable point"? What more was I supposed to do for him, to have done for him? I couldn't *believe* him. He seemed to be a bottomless pit, a black hole of insatiable need. I couldn't believe how he had just dismissed everything that I had done for him for months in one fell swoop. And, now, he had decided, nonchalantly it seemed, to end our relationship. He hadn't explicitly stated that, but he might as well have. In what I had come to understand as typical Jonathan fashion, he had made a major unilateral decision without my input, one that would affect my life in an overwhelmingly significant way, and didn't seem interested even in discussing it. I couldn't believe his selfishness, his callousness. He was throwing me out of his life like a piece of trash after everything I had done for him, tried to be to him, and I was just supposed to accept it.

By the time I absorbed his message, insofar as I could, I had only an hour before I had to leave to teach my Tuesday class in Viridian. Jonathan had always had a talent for dumping emotionally loaded information onto me at the most inopportune moments and this was in some ways the worst of those occasions. There was no way that I was going to be able to concentrate on teaching for three hours without somehow responding, somehow unloading my thoughts and feelings about what he had said. In addition, I felt I needed to send my reply before he left for Paladin, for the Tomlinsons', so that, hopefully, I wouldn't have to wait until he returned to continue the discussion.

Over the next hour, I composed what proved to be a lengthy message in which I tried to explain to him why it had been impossible for me to live with him in Mariah and for him to live with me in Hawthorn, as if he didn't already know. I also reminded him that he had never explicitly invited me to live with him in Mariah and that, whenever I had even hypothetically raised the possibility, he had rejected it, stating that he didn't want to upturn my life nor want me to live in such an awful place from which he himself was trying to escape. I told him that, at some points, I hadn't been certain that my help was even wanted, although I had tried my best to provide it. I told him that if he moved to Paladin, I would be able to take care of him on an ongoing basis and maintain my life in the Hawthorn area—if he were willing to cooperate.

I reminded him of everything I had done to try to change the conditions that had made it impossible for us to live together and told him that I didn't appreciate the way he seemed to be putting the burden for everything that had happened onto my shoulders, since *he* had played *his* role in the disaster that had been the previous several months by making things difficult for me through the decisions he had made.

Moreover, I told him that his unilateral decision to do what was best for him was thoroughly self-centered. Although he had said that it was his life on the line, the fact remained that *I* was going to be powerfully affected by what he was intending to do. It was a little more complicated than not having to make further trips to Mariah or Paladin, something to which he seemed oblivious or indifferent. I told him that in making his decision, he was wadding up and throwing away almost a year's worth of history and effort—mainly mine—which was *very* difficult to take. I reminded him that my life had become entangled with his and that he didn't have the right to make decisions that affected me without taking me into consideration.

I concluded my message by informing him that I was planning to come to Mariah that weekend to discuss the matter in person and that I expected him to be there. I told—actually ordered—him not to make plans to be in Paladin—especially at the Tomlinsons'—or anywhere else. I ended the message by telling him that I wished he could see my point of view but that, I supposed, he would see only what he wanted to see.

I went to work, not knowing when I would receive a reply. I *hated* the fact that Jonathan had left me with no simple way to communicate with him. That seemed to be by design.

I checked my e-mail at work, only to find that he had not responded. Either he hadn't gotten my message before he'd left or he was thinking about how to respond. The former was more likely because he was very good at thinking on his feet, responding fully off the cuff. When I got home, I checked my e-mail again, again to find no response.

I decided that, regardless of when he read it, I needed to emphasize the importance of his being home that weekend so we could discuss what he had said, what he was planning to do, face to face. So, around 6:00 that evening, I wrote him a message in which I emphasized this point in no uncertain terms. I told him that I was planning to come to Mariah on Friday and I expected him to be home. I told him that we needed to have a face-to-face discussion about what was happening and we couldn't do that as long as he was at the Tomlinsons'. I ordered him to cancel or not make plans for the weekend and emphasized once again that I was coming to Mariah on Friday and I expected him to be there when I arrived. I told him that I deserved a say in what was happening, that I deserved to be heard.

Later that evening I checked my e-mail. This time, I found that Jonathan had responded. His message was brief, but it said far more than its words conveyed. In two abrupt sentences, he told me, angrily, not to yell at him or order him about, then told me he was not in the mood to be "brow beaten" by me again in one of my "self-righteous" moods. That was it. But, that was enough.

Jonathan and I could fight like the best of them, and his dismissive comment triggered an e-mail fight that raged for the next two days and vented, it seemed, every hard feeling we had ever harbored toward each other. In our exchanges, the dominant theme I expressed was how his self-centeredness had undermined our relationship and the dominant one he expressed was how his self-centeredness was justified. In the end, we merely rehashed the same themes that had dominated our arguments for months, just with more hostility and less civility. The things we said either heal a relationship or kill it, depending on how they are delivered and received, and this time, it was clear that our fight was a fight to the death.

If there was one difference between our previous fights and this one, it was the way in which Jonathan decided to drag my mother into the fray. In one of his messages, he stated that he had let Joanne read the letter that my mother had written to him in which she had explained why he couldn't stay with us. According to Jonathan,

Joanne's only comment had been to dismiss my mother's position as "self-serving." He claimed that Joanne had remarked that if someone important to her and her family was alone, sick, or in trouble, as he was, then she would allow him to sleep on the floor in her house rather than leave him on his own. He claimed that he had told her that he thought her comment was unfair, but added that "it was interesting to see another American's reaction," making it clear that he didn't find it *that* unfair.

I was angry enough about the things he had said about me, but I was even angrier about the things he had said about my mother. Jonathan had already made plenty of comments about my sister, accusing her of being self-absorbed and "juggling men," but my mother, who hadn't done anything but support him, both morally and even financially, had done nothing to deserve his reproach.

In the process of needing to vent to someone about what he had said and with my mother as the closest person at that time to whom to do it, I told her what he had said about her. Angered herself by what Jonathan had done and said, my mother wrote him another letter in which she expressed her displeasure over his letting Joanne read her first letter, which she had meant only for him. In it, she reminded him of the scheme that Joanne had concocted to make money off *Still Life* and how that was "self-serving." She took issue with Jonathan's use of his illness as an excuse for his behavior, telling him that she had suffered from depression for years but didn't use that as an excuse for her behavior. Putting the lie to his perception of his superiority, she remarked that although we weren't as "good" as he was, at least we didn't let our dogs dirty on our carpets. She concluded by saying that she was glad that her ancestors, some of whom were British, had left England. Her final comment was not aimed at the British in general, but at Jonathan in particular, who had been routinely insulting Americans for months. In any case, my mother had tolerated enough of his behavior as well and had earned the right to vent her own feelings.

Since my mother didn't know how to use the computer, including e-mail, she had me send the message for her through an e-mail account that I had set up for her but that she never used. Shortly thereafter, Jonathan responded with a message written in the bluest blood. He claimed that he took full responsibility for his bad decisions and blamed nothing but his bad judgment for his situation. Later in the message, however, he reverted to his standard position of blaming his "chronic and debilitating illness," as he described it, for his behavior. He said that since they had never met, she had no way to judge how he was managing, despite the fact that much of her opinion derived from my firsthand experiences with him that had led me to believe that he did use his illness as an excuse when he found it advantageous. He dismissed her by stating that since she wasn't his mother, he didn't have to listen to her "poor manners and poor communications" and that if she viewed herself as inferior, then it was merely a reflection of *her* feelings, not his, despite the fact that he constantly implied—and had outright declared—that he was "better."

Not content to stop there, he went on to attack her success as a mother. He accused her daughter of not being able to "stay in one bed or relationship" and her son of "having difficulty facing life and having relationships," implying that poor mothering skills were to blame for her children's alleged failures. After "thanking" her for what she had done for him in a tone that couldn't have been more thankless, he offered his standard dismissal by telling her to calm down and go on with her life. He concluded his assault by telling her that it was probably good that her ancestors had left England "for many reasons."

I was infuriated by his attack on my mother and began composing a counterattack of my own. Before I could finish it, however, he sent me another message in which, strangely, he began by berating me for discussing our relationship with my mother. He said that he didn't discuss me with the Tomlinsons and had only done so to explain to Joanne, who had questioned what I had meant in my letter to them about having an "awkward living arrangement." Apart from thinking that his comparison between my discussing our relationship with my mother and his discussing it with the Tomlinsons wasn't exactly parallel, I didn't understand why he thought I shouldn't be discussing our relationship with my mother. It was almost as if he didn't think I should be discussing it with *anyone*, not just my mother. Beyond that, he reminded me that he had told Joanne that he thought her comment that my mother's letter was self-serving had been unfair, although he had made it clear that he agreed. Stating that we had reached an impasse, he suggested that instead of allowing the situation to turn uglier, we "let it cool" and go on with our lives.

Yet, despite his seeming desire to disentangle, he continued to keep me updated about his life. Because of all the holdups in getting his remaining things out of storage, I had finally suggested that he leave them at the storage unit until he moved back to Paladin. Now, however, he reverted to his previous position that it would be better to get them out and store them at the Tomlinsons' as soon as possible, despite the difficulty in arranging the move on such short notice. I didn't care, though, because the storage of his belongings had been my problem for long enough—too long.

He also told me that he had decided not to take the job at one of the companies at which he had interviewed, stating that it "didn't feel good"—a juvenile comment that I had also heard, more than once, in reference to his health when he wanted an excuse for not doing something he didn't want to do. As far as his health was concerned, he said that he was seeing the doctor for the insurance company the following Monday, which would be the last time he would be seeing a doctor before the insurance company made a decision about whether or not to grant him long-term disability. At that point, I felt little interest in the details of his life that didn't affect me.

Returning to us, he told me he had strong feelings for me and appreciated everything I had done for him more than he had apparently been able to express to me. He apologized for being so much trouble and not being able to satisfy me or live up to my expectations. Again, he claimed that his failing health had been the cause of it all. He expressed his belief that if he hadn't gotten sick, things might have worked out between us, since things had seemed to be going well the previous summer. "Who knows," he commented. I was beginning to believe that *I* knew, that the events of the intervening months hadn't changed him as much as they had revealed him for who he really was.

After telling me that he was once again throwing up all the time, attributing it not to his health but to his nerves, he wished me well and assured me that I would be happy. What he did next, however, did little to further my happiness.

While I was composing my reply, Jonathan sent yet another message to my mother in which he said that he had let Joanne read her e-mail to him. He said that Joanne had been just as disgusted with it as he had been and had referred to it as "drivil" (as he spelled it). In spite of his claim that he had told Joanne he had thought her comments about my mother's Easter letter had been unfair, he agreed with her and, far from "letting it cool," he only seemed to want to keep the fight enflamed.

After absorbing all of the attacks that he had aimed at my family and me, I shot back. My reply addressed and countered all of the criticisms, rationalizations, and cheap shots that Jonathan had leveled against us. I was still angrier about what he had said about my family than I was about what he had said about me and much of my response revolved around defending my mother and sister. I told him that before he accused my mother of bad parenting, he should look at his own family. None of his siblings seemed to be shining examples of successful parenting. According to Jonathan's own descriptions, Reginald was a "slug" who led a useless, stress-free life in a backward town in England; Bettina had totally retreated from the stresses of life as well, earning her the nickname "Strange Bettina"; Leandra was a nasty, conniving bitch; Charmaine still hadn't dealt in any meaningful way with her husband's death after three and a half years and avoided trying to establish any new relationships; Malcolm had killed himself, apparently because of his failure to live up to his parents' expectations. I told him that although my mother wasn't perfect and had made her share of mistakes, at least she supported her children instead of letting them "twist in the wind" and allowed them to live their own lives instead of still expecting them to do exactly what she said when they were mature adults. I told him that if my parents had failed, then so had his.

I pointed out, as I had in July, that as far as my sister was concerned, she had been married for 10 and 12 years, respectively—longer than he had been involved with Glenn—before she was forced to divorce her husbands. I told him that before he saw fit to judge her for separating from people who were mentally ill, perhaps he should remember that he had gotten rid of Glenn when he had become threatening even though he was an abused child and was mentally ill. I also told him that before he accused my sister of bed-hopping, he should remember that, unlike him, she hadn't had *three thousand* sex partners, had sex with half her teachers, and had relationships with married men. I told him that if he was going to accuse someone of being a whore, then he should look at himself first. I ended by telling him that although he had accused my mother of being "ill-bred," he wasn't above firing off cheap shots himself.

Jonathan's reply, which I didn't read until Thursday, again attacked not only me but also my mother. In spite of making sarcastic comments about my family's "perfect and classy background," he referred to my mother as an "old bat" and told her to take a "flying leap," showing true classiness himself. He said that her comments about English people were stupid and that we would be "happier sticking to what [we knew], which [was] not much." He assured me that he would return the $100 the "old bat" had given to him because, as he described it, he did not want to "ever feel beholden to [me] or any member of [my] family again." He claimed that he had been reluctant to accept money from me because he knew that, particularly with people "like [me] and [my] family," everything would change and it had. In my opinion, he hadn't been *that* reluctant to accept my money, especially when he now claimed that in November, Warren had offered him the money to "pay [me] off" and get rid of me, opining that I wasn't much of a boyfriend if I would leave him alone and sick on holidays. Jonathan seemed to have forgotten that at the same time, he had questioned whether or not I *was* his boyfriend and whether or not he wanted to continue our relationship.

True to form, he rationalized his selfishness by saying that if I viewed his behavior as a "me thing," then that was okay with him. As if he were having some kind of mental hiccup or simply running out of ammunition, he accused me, once again, of not understanding how relationships worked and how all of my relationships had failed because of my unwillingness to accept people's imperfections. I had heard all of these accusations before and he seemed to have nothing new to add.

His strongest reaction, perhaps predictably, was reserved for my comment about Glenn. He said that my remark that he had gotten rid of Glenn even though he was mentally ill had been "unknowing, shallow and cruel" and had "stopped any feelings that [he] had for [me]." He stated that after Glenn had turned violent, it had become dangerous for him to stay with him. Even so, he said that he had continued to help him after he had gone back to England and would continue to try to find him.

After reading his tirade, I still had a few things left to say. I told him that in spite of liking to think of himself as worldly and sophisticated, there was a lot he didn't understand not only about Americans, but also about people in general. I told him that his own experience had been fairly limited, confined mentally if not physically to that "little clod of dirt in the middle of the ocean" that he called home. I told him I thought that he was one of the most bigoted, intolerant people I had ever met and that it was obvious that his alleged exposure to the rest of the world had done absolutely nothing to make him more sensitive to or respectful of the differences among people. I told him that he had said some pretty stupid things himself about entire groups of people, but supposed it was all right to do that as long as *he* wasn't the target.

In the final paragraph, I summarized why our relationship had to end. I told him that he had too many problems, too much emotional baggage, and too little ability to focus on anyone but himself to be capable of having a serious relationship with me or anyone else. I told him that our relationship had been *all* about him. He had told me that I had committed to him to "that indefinable point," but I told him that he had done the same to me. He seemed to want all of the benefits of a relationship without having to do any of the work required to have one. He wanted me to be totally involved in his life while he pushed me away. He had implied that when the going had gotten tough, I had abandoned him, but I told him that, in his own way, he had abandoned me. I told him I regretted the fact that he couldn't see things from my perspective, that he didn't have the slightest inclination to do so. I told him that what troubled me the most, however, wasn't so much his selfishness as the nastiness that had come from it, and the nastiness that it had, in turn, provoked in me. I told him that at least now I could go back to a saner life than I had known in the past year, since the only problems I had suffered in that year had come from him.

He didn't respond. I didn't care. It was over.

■

On Thursday, I e-mailed him to remind him that I still had some of his belongings, some of which had been in my possession since he'd left the house on Millstone Drive. It wasn't much—his copy of *Make Way for Lucia*, a 2′ × 3′ rug coated with poodle hair and poodle piss, a guidebook to London for the England trip that never took place, some assorted odds and ends—but I wanted them gone. I told him that if he wanted them, though, he was going to have to come to Hawthorn to get them because I was *not* going to do any more driving on *his* account. I told him that he had two weeks from that day to get them or they went. I also told him that while he was at the house, he might see for himself how small and unaccommodating the house was so that he might finally understand how impossible it would have been for him and his dogs to have stayed there. I added, though, that doing so might force him to revise his opinion, although I knew how important it was for him to be right.

Jonathan didn't reply that day, although it was clear that he *was* using the Internet. Instead of replying to me, he posted yet another sex ad on *Gayteway* on Thursday afternoon. The elaborate, rambling ad revealed practically the entire life history of his latest alter ego. He began by saying that he and his wife—"Yeah, I'm married"—had just moved to Winford from Maine. They were both bisexual and had a relationship that was "completely open" in which he could see men and she could see women but not "the other way around." He described himself as more than ten years younger, several inches taller, and much more slender than he actually was as well as having sandy-colored hair and green eyes, which he didn't. He described a number of physical types and sexual acts that he claimed to like, none of which he had ever mentioned to me. He listed various possibilities for getting together and complained that since he had lived in Winford, he had been to only one bar where he'd met a man who'd had to "suck [him] off" in his car because they didn't have enough time to get a room. None of this had ever happened. The Internet had allowed him to create yet another façade, yet another lie.

On Friday, he finally replied. He expressed his desire to "clear the decks" as much as I did as soon as possible, although I doubted he could have wanted it more than I did. He requested a list of his belongings that I still had as well as an itemized bill of his debt to me minus the $360 he'd paid me in November. I replied, telling him that although I knew how much I had loaned him, the interest that had accrued would have to be calculated and figured into the total, something that would take a little work. I told him that my mother did not want her $100 back. She continued to insist that it was a gift, not a loan, and, therefore, he didn't need to repay it. In spite of everything, my mother still had a generous spirit and expected nothing in return. I told him that the only reason *I* was asking for *my* money back was that it would severely hurt me financially if I didn't. I told him I knew he thought I was being petty, but I reminded him of how, over the past few months, he had gotten a taste of what it was like to have little money and how even a small debt could have a huge impact on one's life. I told him that, otherwise, I would have just *given* him the money without reservation because all I had ever wanted to do was to help him.

Around 11:30 that night he responded. He told me that he had never wanted to accept money from me and had always expected to repay me, saying that after being so generous, it wouldn't be right for me to suffer for it. He also said that he would repay my mother what she had given to him whether or not she wanted it back. His opinion that people "like us" were being petty for wanting to have loaned money repaid appeared to have changed.

Beyond that, he told me that his recurring flu had returned and he was trying to rest up in anticipation of a hectic week in Paladin the following week. He said that while he was there, he would be seeing doctors and settling on a place to live and would arrange for "us"—presumably him and Chase—to come to Hawthorn to collect his things. He said that since he would be with either Chase or Greg, the easiest way would be the best way—something with which I fully agreed.

In the message, he said something that I found ludicrous—something that only emphasized how unable or unwilling he was to see the true cause of our relationship's demise. In his opinion, a "large part" of our breakup stemmed from "culture clash" and "semantics and meanings of the same words to different ears." Returning to the tangential issue of his description of my mother as an "old bat," he claimed that he often referred to his own mother the same way and that it was a common British term. He said it was okay with him, though, because he had fought all he was going to fight.

In response, I told him that since Chase had lived in Hawthorn, they should have no trouble finding my house. Privately, I wondered if Chase would try to vandalize it if he finally learned where I lived. I told him to give me a day that he would be coming and I would be sure to have his things ready. I reminded him that he knew my schedule, so if he wanted to avoid me—in reality, I wanted to avoid *him*—it might be best to come when I was at work.

I also told him that I didn't want fight anymore either, but that I *did* want to clarify some things. In particular, I countered his ridiculous assertion that our breakup was mainly the result of misunderstanding differences between American and British English. For whatever good it did, I reminded him that the problem went a little deeper than my saying "toh-may-toh" and his saying "toh-mah-toh" or not agreeing on what the word "boyfriend" implied. I reminded him that the *real* reason our relationship had ended was that he had always come first and I had always come second, if not last. I told him that I was genuinely sorry that things had ended up the way they had, but that I couldn't continue to be in a relationship where I didn't count. I mattered too, I told him.

He didn't respond. I didn't care.

With that, I felt an enormous sense of relief, felt that an onerous burden that had become increasingly insupportable as time had passed had finally, mercifully, been lifted from me. For the first time in ten months, I felt free.

■

That Saturday night was the first Saturday night that I had either not spent with Jonathan or regretted not spending with Jonathan since the previous June. And I loved it. I could do whatever I wanted with my time, with my life, without feeling I should be doing something that revolved around *him*. That night was all about *me*. I spent the evening shopping, enjoying being home, enjoying being alone…but not *lonely*. While I was out, I bought a book and, after a couple of hours, I went home. I remember lying in bed, reading my book, enjoying the simple, satisfying, subdued pleasure that gave to me. I also remember later watching a program on television that I enjoyed, but of which I had seen very little in the previous ten months because I was usually with Jonathan, who always watched something else. This time, the drama was only on TV. My life would go on, *was* going on, and I was already feeling better than I had for…too long.

On Monday, the 8th, I sent Jonathan an e-mail in which I told him I was interested to know what he had found out lately about his health. In spite of everything, I was still concerned about him, though now in a much more detached way. Whatever health problems he had, he would now have to worry about them himself.

I didn't receive a reply to my message. Perhaps because I was now more interested in settling up with him and cutting the last cord that connected him to me, my correspondence to him switched from personal issues to practical ones. On Tuesday, I sent him a message in which I gave him a revised list of his items I still had. In addition, I told him I had finished calculating the loan amount—$3,642.44—and would be sending him spreadsheets in the mail that broke down the figures more finely. I printed out and mailed the spreadsheets the same day.

I didn't receive a reply to *that* message. By Friday, I'd had it. It had been a week since I'd last heard from him and it had become apparent that he wasn't interested in dealing with any of the issues that had arisen in the previous week. I knew he didn't want to deal with me—the feeling was mutual—but he *did* need to deal with the business we needed to conclude. I sent him an e-mail in which I told him I knew he was ignoring me, which was fine on a personal level, but not on a business one. I told him that I wanted to know if he'd gotten the spreadsheets I'd sent him three days before, and I threatened that if he didn't respond, I would go directly to his father.

My threat to contact "Papa" worked. Later that afternoon, he sent me a terse e-mail typed in capital letters—the written equivalent of shouting. He began by claiming that he hadn't gotten the spreadsheets as of that day. He told me that if I wanted to speak to his father to go ahead, although he didn't think I would get much of a reception if I did. He claimed that he wasn't ignoring me, just that he had nothing to say to me. He told me that I could not possibly want to be done with things more than he did, although I had to disagree. He said that some positive things had happened and that he "[did]n't want to dwell on negative things."

His statement that he still hadn't received the spreadsheets three business days after I'd mailed them when Mariah was only 150 miles away was absurd. He had stated before that the mail in Mariah was unreliable, but everything else I'd sent to Mariah had arrived without delay—especially money. In addition, I felt that his statement that he "[did]n't want to dwell on negative things" was childish, selfish, and irresponsible. I had observed—*endured*—enough of that behavior to last me a lifetime and I was *not* going to accept his excuses any longer. So, I decided that on Saturday, I would deliver the spreadsheets myself. Then, he could no longer claim that he hadn't received them and he could no longer avoid dealing with me, no matter how "negative" he found the experience.

I prepared myself for yet another trip to Mariah.

—32—
ALL'S WELL THAT ENDS

*You have your perspective on things and I have mine. The two
are now so divergent that it is better just to clear things up and
go on with our lives.*

On Saturday morning, I left for Mariah around 9:30. This trip, however, was unlike any trip to Mariah that I had made before. I was not going to "rescue" Jonathan, to help him pick up and put back together the pieces of his life when it had fallen apart yet again. I was not going to do any of the innumerable, menial things for him that he refused to do for himself because he was too princely or too lazy to do them. I was not going to confront him with the latest revelation of how his need to retreat into stress-relieving fantasy had disrupted, damaged, and almost destroyed even more lives. I was not going to stay with him anymore while he waited out his sentence in Mariah. I was not going to do *anything* for him in *any* way, only to be told that what I had done was *still* not enough. I was certainly *not* going with the intention of trying to reconcile, because I had reconciled *myself* to the fact that our relationship was beyond repair. I was not going for *him*. I was going for *me*.

Even though I was going for myself and not for him, I still couldn't help thinking of the endless miles I had traveled throughout our relationship to be with him. In the ten months I had been involved with him, he had never come to me, despite the invitations he had falsely claimed I hadn't offered, so I had always had to go to him. Later, I estimated that in those ten months, I had driven at least 6,500 miles on our behalf—mainly *his* behalf—compared to the zero miles that Jonathan had driven. I had put nearly 4,000 miles on my new car during the Mariah phase of our relationship alone. This was after deducting the mileage that I had saved by having some of my visits coincide with my travels to and from my work in Viridian. I was thankful that I'd had fuel-efficient cars that got anywhere from 24 to 30 miles to the gallon and that gas prices had been averaging around $1.30 a gallon for regular during that time—$1.10 during the Mariah phase—otherwise I couldn't have afforded it. As it was, I had spent at least $300 in gas, which I didn't figure into the total he owed me. He had never offered to help me pay for gas. Although $300 was low compared to what I could have been paying in later years when gas prices rose to record levels, I felt that I had paid enough in other ways.

I arrived in Mariah around noon. Jonathan's car was in the driveway, so he was not at Wal-Mart or with the Tomlinsons or with Chase or somewhere else doing God-knew-what with—or *to*—God-knew-whom. I parked alongside it, in what had unofficially become "my" spot, then went into the garage and up the stairs, something I had done too many times.

I knocked at the door, which immediately set the dogs to barking. When the door opened, I was surprised to see not Jonathan, but a young man whom I had never seen. Appearing to be in his early 20s, he stood about six feet tall, had a medium build, and was clean-shaven with short, sandy blond hair. From the look of the ashtray that sat on the arm of the sectional and from the smell of the air, he smoked profusely. Jonathan had complained about Glenn's smoking and the smoke couldn't have been good for Jonathan's health, but apparently he was tolerating it.

I told the young man that I wanted to see Jonathan. He said sure, and called to Jonathan, who had, by that time, come to the kitchen window to see who was there. When he saw it was me he said hello with a tone that seemed to be a mixture of formality and uncertainty. He invited me inside and the three of us went into the kitchen.

I told Jonathan that I had come to bring him the spreadsheets and wanted a moment to talk. He looked at the young man and, without bothering to introduce us, dismissed him—a little too much like a servant for my taste. We then went into the half-finished living room, which added yet another level of strangeness about the setting, since in neither his house in Paladin nor the apartment in Mariah had we ever sat in the living room, except for twice: when we had sat in his living room in Paladin when he had offered me the Surrealist vase and when we had sat in the living room in Mariah when he had explained to me why he was so preoccupied with finding Glenn. Sitting in the living room seemed to have become something we did when an old chapter in our labyrinthine story ended and a new one began.

As soon as we sat down, Frizzie jumped into my lap and flopped backward against my shoulder, encouraging me to rub her stomach. I began by handing Jonathan the spreadsheets, which he took. At least now he could no longer use the excuse, which I knew to *be* an excuse, that he hadn't yet received the spreadsheets in order to avoid dealing with the issue, with *me*.

Next, Jonathan and I briefly engaged in some idle pleasantries before we moved on to more important matters.

The first thing I asked Jonathan was if the young man who was staying with him was Chase. Jonathan said no, that it was someone who was helping him with the move. I thought he might be either a friend of Chase's or someone the Tomlinsons otherwise knew and whose help they had enlisted. As if to allay any suspicions on my part, Jonathan hastily added, "It's not romantic." Given that we had officially ended our relationship a week and a half earlier, I felt I had no right to question it further.

Jonathan said that he didn't realize how much stuff had been in storage. I wasn't sure what he meant by "storage," since it hadn't looked as if anything had been brought up from the garage and it didn't look as if any of the things in the storage unit had been retrieved. It didn't matter, however, because all that mattered to me was that *I* would *not* be involved in any way in the move back to Paladin—the *fifth* move that Jonathan would be making in less than eight months and the third that—if circumstances had not intervened—would have included me. *This* time, someone *else* would have to bear the burden of helping him move and it would have to be *his* problem because it would *not* be *mine*.

As far as the money he owed me was concerned, Jonathan informed me that 25% of *Still Life* had been put into syndication and that the money was now in escrow. The syndication offer period was almost up, which meant that the money would soon be released. When it was, he could repay me. *The sooner, the better*, I thought. Once I got my money, snapped the last thread that bound us, I could go on with my life. Instead of having him come to Hawthorn to pick up his things and send me the money he owed me separately, we tentatively planned to meet in Paladin sometime in the next few weeks to effect the exchange. I didn't mind the idea of making a trip to Paladin, not because it was closer, but because I felt that in spite of how he might benefit, I would be doing it for *myself*, not for *him*.

Eventually, the conversation turned to more incendiary issues. I mentioned the fact that I thought he should apologize to my mother for the insulting things he had said to her. His nostrils flaring, he affirmed that he was *not* going to apologize to her for what he had said. I had become well acquainted with his stiff-necked, upper-crust pride and, therefore, expected nothing different. I said something to the effect that my mother didn't plan to apologize either because most of what she had said in her letter was true. I also felt that he should apologize to my sister for the things he had said about her, but I didn't raise the issue because I knew he would react in exactly the same fashion in which he had reacted to my insistence that he apologize to my mother.

I further told him that I thought he had expected too much from me, had expected me to rescue him from his situation when it was neither my place nor in my power to do so. He told me that I had done far more for him than anyone could have ever expected, although I felt as if he still thought I had not done enough. Finally, I asked him to tell me, specifically, what I should have done. I had *no* intentions of doing more; I merely wanted him to give me, for once, a concrete answer. He said he didn't know, then said that to discuss it further would just be to "replough the same field." With that, we dropped the issue. Forever.

Eventually, I excused myself to go to the bathroom. As I went, I cut through the bedroom. In the process, I discovered that *both* sides of the bed had been slept in, with the nightstand on "my" side holding a bag of Fig Newtons—a food I had never seen Jonathan eat. That, of course, didn't mean that Jonathan and the young man had been sleeping together in the euphemistic sense, but I couldn't help feeling that was precisely the case. Considering we had ended our relationship ten days earlier, perhaps it didn't matter, but I thought it was awfully quick work for him to have already taken a lover. Seeing what I saw, I began to doubt Jonathan's story that their relationship was "not romantic." I began to suspect that the young man had been in Jonathan's life for more than ten days.

By now, I knew that Jonathan was a liar, but he was also so good at lying that it was difficult to know when he was lying or telling the truth.

When I was finished, I came out into the kitchen where Jonathan was waiting. It was approaching 1:00 and he told me that he and his guest were going to be leaving. I took the opportunity to make certain he understood why our relationship had ended. Although I had explained my perspective quite forcefully in my messages, I needed the opportunity to tell him in person. I told him that I could not have a relationship with someone who put me second and, more importantly, I could not have a relationship with someone whom I could not trust. He said something to the effect that perhaps it was just as well, though significantly offering no further explanation or apologizing for his behavior. What he did *not* say was even more telling that what he *did* say and that was that.

He escorted me to the door, telling me that he would see me when I returned his things and he paid me my money. I bid him farewell and the door closed behind me. Another door closed as well, though one not so tangible.

When I got home and checked my e-mail, which I hadn't since the previous day, I found a message that Jonathan had sent to me the evening before. Mainly addressing the repayment of the money he owed me, it would have done nothing to preclude my trip to Mariah had I found it the previous night. Much more interesting, however, were his comments about the ending of our relationship. He told me that I had my perspective on things and he had his and since the two were now so disparate and irreconcilable, it was better to separate and go on with our lives. He still accepted no real responsibility for what he had done, not just to me but to so many others. I was astonished by the way his mind worked. It was indeed better that we go our separate ways.

Around that time, I e-mailed one of my best friends and told her about the breakup. In response, she told me that she wasn't surprised to hear about it, since she could tell that I was growing tired of the situation the last time we had talked. She agreed that Jonathan had a lot of problems and couldn't be trusted. She reminded me that I was a straightforward person and that I deserved to have someone who said what he meant and meant what he said without the "drama, and BS." I couldn't have agreed more.

Humorously, she told me that her dream for me was for me to find a nice gay man with simple American values, then settle down together in a mid-size town where we could buy a two-bedroom house, paint it mauve or powder blue, and put in a koi pond. At that point, that actually sounded appealing.

Turning serious, she told me that the hardest thing I would have to deal with now was loneliness. I had gotten used to having a relationship, even if it was a crazy one. It sounded to her, though, as if I was taking care of myself, and she encouraged me to keep it up.

It was true that I was *alone*, but I was not *lonely*. It was through my aloneness that I was taking care of myself.

■

When I had been at Jonathan's, I had noticed something that I couldn't understand. In the five months that Jonathan had lived in Mariah, the painted table had gone uncovered, but now, it was covered with a lace tablecloth that he said had been his mother's. In addition, the walls in the bathroom had gone unadorned, but now, they were decorated with several small pictures. A number of tchotchkes had been unpacked and set about and, in general, the apartment looked as if Jonathan were settling in rather than moving out. If he were going to be leaving in only a few days, then why were things being *un*packed? Jonathan had once said that as long as he lived in Mariah, in such wretched conditions, he refused to hang a single picture, and now that he was leaving, now that the apartment seemed like less of a prison, had that mentally freed him to complete the task of moving in, even though he would soon be moving out? I understood the need for completion, for "closure," and perhaps this was his way of achieving that. I also understood, though, that even after knowing him for almost a year, there was much I *didn't* understand about Jonathan. His behavior had always been erratic, eccentric, and during the past three months, I had discovered that his "dottiness," as he had once described it, was only the most superficial layer of a much deeper pathology. Sometimes I wondered just how deep that pathology went.

—33—
LOOSE THREADS

The big news is that Greg tracked down Glenn…

Although our relationship was officially over, Jonathan and I still had our share of loose ends to tie up. In addition, Jonathan, by himself, had his share of loose ends that had gone untied for months. These included his long-term disability claim, his need for some kind of income, and his plan to move back to Paladin, all of which stretched back to November, as well as his uncertainty and torment over what had happened to Glenn, which stretched back to September. Around 4:30 on the afternoon of Monday, April 22, Jonathan sent me an e mail in which he told me that, almost miraculously, all of these loose threads had simultaneously become woven together.

After expressing his hope that the spring weather wasn't wreaking havoc with my sinuses, as it notoriously did, he commented on how his life had become busy, which, even though it was exhausting, was nice after the months of inactivity and boredom. Then, he told me something extraordinary. According to Jonathan, Greg Carroll had tracked down Glenn and had him brought back to my state. Apparently Glenn had ended up in Texas and was in bad shape. When he had been found, he was disheveled and confused and had gone through hell in the previous seven months. Fortunately, he was currently receiving the evaluation that Jonathan had been hoping he would receive. According to Jonathan, Greg had found Glenn using a computer program he had written that had checked the phone numbers for all of the facilities in the United States where Glenn might be to see if he was at one of them, a program using numbers that Miranda had provided. The facility in Texas had proven to be a variation on those numbers. According to Jonathan, Greg had known Glenn from England and had arranged his return and evaluation. Greg was in Mariah but would be leaving the following Monday. Jonathan said it was a huge load off his mind that Glenn had finally been found and even if he wasn't in great shape, he could at least now be cared for.

Otherwise, Jonathan said that the money from the syndication of *Still Life* would be out of escrow on the 26th. He told me that he would be busy moving over the weekend and Monday but could meet with me in Paladin to repay me what he owed me any day after Tuesday. He added that his claim for long-term disability had been approved, which meant that he would be receiving payments beginning in May and back payments for the previous six months.

He ended the message by telling me to let him know how I was. In spite of telling me that my comment about his having gotten rid of Glenn when he was mentally ill had stopped any feelings he had toward me, he told me now that his feelings didn't "go on and off like a light switch." He told me to drive carefully and to eat properly.

In more ways than one, it was an odd message, one that I didn't quite know how to take. The oddest part about it was his explanation of how Glenn had been found. I remembered his story from February about the dream he'd said he'd had about Glenn in which a balding man with sandy colored hair had told him that Glenn was in a care facility that had a telephone number with 65* as the area code and 755 following it. He had claimed at the time that he had contacted Miranda, who was supposed to have intuited the dream, and I wondered if he meant that she had supplemented those numbers based on her perceptions. Whatever the case, the story sounded like something more out of science fiction than out of actual fact. I knew by now that Jonathan had a powerful need to retreat into fantasy, some of which had been bizarre indeed, and I wondered if that was what he was doing again.

Had Glenn *really* been found? Or was this simply more wishful thinking on his part? Without direct proof, it was difficult to tell, though I suspected the latter. Although I was no longer monitoring his behavior—not, I felt, that what I had learned about it had ever done anyone involved any real good—I was still concerned about his mental state and how it might affect others.

I didn't know how much of the rest of the message to believe, either. The idea that so many significant, long-standing problems had suddenly been resolved sounded suspiciously neat. Perhaps I was personalizing, but under the circumstances, I couldn't help wondering if he was trying to make it seem as if, in spite of all of my efforts, his life had finally fallen into place now that I was out of it. I wondered if he was trying to take some kind of stab at me while pretending that he wasn't.

In my response, I pretended to believe him and be happy for him. I didn't know what else to do and was tired of trying to figure it out, so I took the simplest way out. Mainly, however, my correspondence with him over the next few days concentrated on making plans to meet him in Paladin to have him pay me the money he owed me and have me return his things. At that point, that was all that mattered.

Because he would have the money by then and because it was a Wednesday, I sent him an e-mail on the evening of Wednesday, April 24 asking him if it would be convenient for him to meet with me on Wednesday, May 1. The next morning he replied, telling me that would be okay and to pick a place to meet. He said that his house wouldn't be good because Chase, Warren, Joanne, Glenn, and a couple of friends would be there. He claimed that meeting there wouldn't be good because with the unpacking and setting up of the house things would be hectic, but I suspected that it was really because he didn't want us mingling. If that was so, then that was fine by me, since I had no desire to see anyone who would be there.

Later that day, I wrote back and told him that I wanted to meet at the storage unit at 3:00 on the afternoon of Wednesday, May 1. I checked my e-mail again that evening, but by the time I turned in, I had still received no reply.

That was the last time that I would be able to check my e-mail for more than two weeks—a two weeks that, more than anything in my relationship to Jonathan ever had, would change everything.

—34—
THE PRETENDER
Whoever it was did an excellent job of impersonating you.

Sometime around the middle of April, about a week or so after Jonathan and I had officially broken up, I started to notice that something peculiar was happening to my e-mail. There would be times that I would check my regular and "Jonathan" accounts, find messages in my inboxes that I would decide to wait until later to open, then log out of the account. Later, when I would log back into the accounts, I would find, on occasion, that one or more of the messages had been opened or deleted. At first, I thought it was just my imagination—perhaps I was just so preoccupied with other matters that I had inadvertently opened or deleted the messages myself and had forgotten that I'd done so—but as I began to pay closer attention to the alterations, I quickly realized that I was *not* the one who was causing them. It *seemed* as if someone else was accessing the accounts, although I couldn't imagine who or why.

Around that time, however, I received a message from my e-mail provider informing me that I was approaching the storage limit for one of my accounts and that if I didn't delete some of my messages they would have to delete them for me. That message pertained to only one account, however, so it didn't explain why the alterations were happening to *both* of them. Even so, both accounts were with the same provider and I assumed that it was behind all of the changes, possibly as some kind of general housecleaning, so I didn't think much about it.

In the meantime, I continued the process of disentangling myself from Jonathan. The only piece of unfinished business that stood between connection and separation was the return of the things that I had been keeping for him since he had left Paladin in September and the repayment of the $3,600 he now owed me. I wanted our business to be concluded as quickly as possible so I could move on with my life.

On the morning of Friday, April 26, I tried to check my e-mail, in part to see if I had received a confirmation message from Jonathan about meeting on Wednesday. When I tried to log on to my primary e-mail account, however, I found that I couldn't. I also tried to log on to the "Jonathan" account, but I found that I couldn't get into that one either. Every time I would enter the required information, I would get an alert telling me the information was incorrect. I could see that the username I had entered was correct, but because I couldn't see the password, which appeared only as a string of asterisks, I couldn't see if it was correct. At that time, I had started having trouble with the key for one of the letters in the password, which didn't work half the time, and I half-wondered if it had finally stopped working entirely. At that time, I didn't think to check the key using another application, thinking instead that I would check my e-mail at work.

When I did, I found that I couldn't access it there, either. Since I was using a different keyboard, it seemed unlikely that the problem was a malfunctioning key. When I got home and checked the key using another application, I found that the key did in fact work about half the time, as it had been. When I typed the password into a word-processing file and verified that it was complete, I copied then pasted it into the password field on the login page. Still nothing. At that point, I half-thought that my e-mail provider was doing something that rendered my accounts temporarily unavailable, possibly as part of the housecleaning they seemed to be doing. If that were the case, then I would just have to wait it out.

Over the weekend, I tried to access the accounts a number of additional times, always with the same result.

I might have been more concerned about my inability to access the accounts and more active about doing something to fix it, but the e-mail associated with the "message" account still worked and I could send and receive e-mail through it. In addition, I wasn't expecting any important messages to come to the affected accounts, except perhaps for a message from Jonathan about meeting on Wednesday. If he had confirmed, I couldn't access the message, but if I didn't have access to my accounts by the first of the week, I would e-mail him through my accessible one, apprise him of the problem, and try to get a response through it. Of course by then, Jonathan would be in the midst of resettling in Paladin and I didn't know if he would have the ability to check his e-mail. Therefore, I didn't know what to do about Wednesday. Unfortunately, e-mail was the only method I had for communicating with him.

Otherwise, I had entered into a busy time and the e-mail problems seemed secondary to everything else that was happening. First, it was now the end of the semester and I was embroiled in grading term papers, preparing finals, and generally trying to finish the semester in one piece. Actually, now that the burden of my relationship with Jonathan had been lifted, I had an energy, a clarity, that I had not had for months, so my ability to do what I wanted and needed to do was immeasurably improved. Several people commented on how engaged I had suddenly become with everyone and everything around me, telling me that for some time I seemed to have been walking around in something of a fog. It wasn't just the Prozac or the coming of spring that had affected the change. At last I began to realize just how much my relationship with Jonathan had detracted from the rest of my life, how much it had destabilized and diminished it, doing precisely the opposite of what a *good* relationship is supposed to do. I was becoming my old self again, someone I hadn't been in months, and I loved it.

I was busy in other ways. I had entered the "rebound" phase and was now seeking the social and sexual satisfaction that my relationship with Jonathan had never given to me. I was beginning to realize, again, that there *were* men out there who didn't think only about themselves. It was an exhilarating and reinforcing time, one that did much to compensate for the damage that Jonathan's self-centered behavior had done to me.

By Tuesday afternoon, I was still unable to access my regular and "Jonathan" accounts. I sent Jonathan an e-mail through my functioning account, apprised him of the problem with the other ones, and asked him about meeting the next day. By Wednesday at noon, however, I had still not received a reply. I wondered if he couldn't reply because he didn't have any way to access his e-mail. If that were true, then he might be expecting me at the storage unit, thinking I had read but not responded to his confirmation, so I decided to take a chance that he would be there and go to Paladin.

In addition, I was anxious for our business to be concluded, so we could finally disentangle and go on with our lives. If there was a half a chance that we could do it that day, then I wanted to do it. That afternoon, I boxed up his remaining belongings, including the scarab, which I wasn't sure I wanted to keep, and left Hawthorn around 1:30. I arrived at the storage unit sometime shortly before 3:00.

Jonathan wasn't there, so I wandered around the parking lot for a time, occasionally returning to the car to sit, before wandering around some more. I thought of the times I had spent in Mariah, of the times I had "drifted" about his apartment. I thought of the times I had been left alone to drift while he checked his e-mail—while he had written flowery messages to Andy as "Iain," fatherly messages to Jack as Cliff, fraudulent messages as a multiplicity of personas to a legion of unsuspecting recipients who unreservedly believed that he was who he pretended to be. I felt grateful to have relieved myself of a relationship that had become nothing but a burden.

Around 3:30, I grew tired of wandering around the lot and decided to go to a fast-food restaurant across the street to get something to eat. It was the same fast-food restaurant at which Jonathan had treated the movers to a meal the day they had moved his things to Mariah. After braving, on foot, the seemingly endless, swiftly-moving traffic that sped along the busy street in front of the facility, getting to the restaurant, and ordering my food, I sat down at one of the tables that gave me the most unobstructed view of the entrance to the lot. I assumed that if Jonathan were coming, he would be arriving in his own car, so I wanted to keep on the lookout for it. While I watched, I didn't see him arrive.

Around 4:00, I finished my food and decided to return to the storage unit. It had been raining on the way over and after a bit of a reprieve it was starting to storm in Paladin. After once again braving the traffic that raced along the street, I ran back to the lot, without an umbrella. Still no sign of Jonathan. I didn't know what to think. I had waited an hour past the designated time and I felt that I had waited long enough.

Since I didn't know where Jonathan now lived, I couldn't go to his house. Even if I had known, however, I would *not* have gone there, given what I thought of as the "cast of characters"—Chase, Warren, Joanne, Glenn, and God-only-knew who else—that would be there. I had never seen these people in the flesh, had never had them be a part of my life in a concrete way, and given that they were all connected, and negatively, to a life that was now coming to an end, I saw no reason to meet them, even to *see* them. I assumed they felt the same way toward me. So, with the weather deteriorating and my frustration mounting, I made the hour-and-a-half trip back to Hawthorn.

After I arrived home sometime after 6:00, I tried, once again, to access my primary e-mail account and once again I failed. The problem had persisted now for almost a week and I was getting aggravated. I finally decided to contact my e-mail provider to inform them of the problem or obtain some kind of answer. In addition, I checked my functioning account but still didn't find a reply from Jonathan. The next day, I sent him an e-mail asking him why he hadn't shown up at the storage unit, but I didn't get a response to that message either. I had no idea what had happened to him and given my limited options for making contact, I could do little but wait for him to contact me.

On Thursday and Friday, I concluded the lecture portion of my two Hawthorn classes. The following week was finals week and after grading finals and submitting final grades, the semester would be finished. It had been a complicated semester, a complicated year, mainly because of Jonathan's drama, and now that both were over, I looked forward to having some peace. By Friday night, however, I still couldn't access my two affected e-mail accounts and had still not received a response from my provider regarding the problem.

The next morning, however, I finally learned the truth about why I had been unable to access my accounts.

When I got the mail Saturday morning, I found among the pieces a white, business-size envelope with my address typed on the front in capital letters. There was no return address, but the envelope was postmarked in Paladin. Because of the postmark, I thought it might be a letter from Jonathan, perhaps even a check, or at least an explanation for why I hadn't heard from him for over a week.

When I opened it, however, I found that I could not have been more wrong.

Typed in capital letters, like the address, was an unsigned letter that threatened my family and me. The sender said that he was going to "hurt [my] entire family," starting with my "slut sister" and "working [his] way out from there." He said that he had already figured out a way to hurt both me and my "bitch mother" that involved that "queer from England." He claimed that he had been working on that plan "for some time now," then hinted at what it involved. He told me "[t]here [was] a reason why [I hadn't] been able to get into [my] e-mail accounts for the past two weeks," thereby implying that he had gained access to my accounts and had changed the password. He said that he had been having a "pretty fun time reading all that sickening queer bullshit and making good use out of it," although he didn't say how. He concluded by saying that, "[we] queers ma[de him] sick and [we] all deserve[d] to be wiped off the face of the planet," but adding that, "keeping you alive so you [could] be made to suffer [was] a lot better."

At first I was shocked and shaken, but as my emotion subsided, my reason took over and I began to try to figure out who had sent it. Whoever it was knew not only my family, but also Jonathan. At least they knew *of* him, possibly only from e-mails. The sender, however, seemed focused primarily on my sister, while the rest of us appeared simply to be in the way—collateral damage. Consequently, I tried to think of people who might want to target Kathryn.

Initially, two possibilities came to mind: a longtime male friend who had become sexually obsessive toward her and whom she had rejected or her now-ex-husband. Both of them had the technical skill, intelligence, and motivation to do something like this. In thinking about it more carefully, however, I eventually discounted the former because, even though he had the computer skills to access any e-mail account he wanted, the message had been extremely homophobic and, as far as I knew, he had no antipathy toward gay people. In addition, he had no antipathy toward my mother or me of which I was aware, and if he weren't targeting Jonathan because he was gay, then he would have had no *personal* reason to try to harm him, since he didn't even know him.

That left Kathryn's ex-husband. For the previous year, my sister and he had been going through what had proved to be a messy divorce after what had proved to be a messy marriage. As time had passed, her ex had begun to manifest what appeared to be antisocial tendencies and had tried to exert progressively more control over Kathryn and her children. Toward the end, he had started conducting frequent inspections of my sister's and her children's belongings, had repeatedly hacked into her e-mail, believing that she was having an affair, and had possibly bugged the phone lines, which resulted in my sister and my having some very surreal conversations that were conducted in code. Just weeks before, the divorce had finally been granted, removing what he might have perceived as his last bit of control over her.

In addition, he was supposed to sell their house and split the profits with my sister as part of the divorce agreement, but after an extended period of dragging his feet on the matter, he was now being pressured to give up his "castle." Further, my sister had taken back her previous married name, which he must have seen as an additional form of rejection. Finally, he considered my sister to be a "slut," my mother, a "bitch," and me, a "queer," which were the words that had been used to describe us in the letter. Therefore, he had ample cause, at least in his mind, to hate my sister, to hate my mother and me, and to wreak the havoc he seemed to be causing.

The use of the Internet through which to effect his revenge also seemed to fit. He worked only three days a week, four at the most, and spent much of his free time doing nothing but sitting at home, alone, using the Internet. In the months before my sister and he had separated, he had become so addicted to the Internet that he was spending eight to ten hours a day online. In addition, he had the history of hacking into my sister's e-mail. Further, the method of attack was anonymous and indirect. My ex-brother-in-law, who loved to play chess, had the attitude that "life is a chess game," an endless series of moves and countermoves, of calculation and manipulation. The person behind this wanted to make a game of it and the game-playing approach fit my ex-brother-in-law's personality perfectly.

Later that day, I was finally able to speak with my sister. She was shocked by what had happened, but hadn't received any similar threats. She did agree with my assessment that it was probably her ex-husband, however, since so much of what the letter embodied fit his personality. In discussing the matter, she also claimed that at least one of her friends had received an e-mail from "her" that she didn't remember sending, which suggested to her that someone had compromised *her* e-mail account and was sending e-mails from it pretending to be her. Since her husband had hacked into her e-mail in the past, it seemed plausible that he was behind it. Although he lived in Hawthorn and the letter was postmarked in Paladin, it was possible that he had sent the letter from Paladin to throw us off his trail. Kathryn didn't seem overtly anxious about what had happened, although she often had suppressed reactions that left her true feelings unclear. We agreed to monitor the situation, however, and not to tell our mother, whom we didn't want to overreact. Although she probably would have been more likely to react with hostility than anxiety, we both hoped that whatever animosity was driving my ex-brother-in-law to do what he appeared to be doing would soon burn itself out and he would leave everyone alone.

Because the sender of the letter hadn't provided me with the password to which he had changed it, I was still unable to access my accounts. Consequently, I still had no idea what the sender might be doing with the information he had found in them and I needed to find out. I also needed to find out more than ever why I hadn't heard from Jonathan for at least a week and a half when he could have at least called me. Although I thought I knew who was behind the disruption and had some sense of the threat he actually posed, I didn't have proof and I was now acutely concerned about what had happened to Jonathan.

After I spoke to Kathryn, I sent an urgent message to Jonathan. Suspecting the sender had done the same thing to me that it appeared he had done to my sister, I explained the situation to him and asked him if he had received any messages from my blocked accounts in the previous week and a half. I made it clear that if he had, *I* was not the one who had sent them. I told him that if he had to send them to me so I could see what they said. I was especially concerned to know if the sender had said anything about my sister and mother. Since I wasn't getting any help through my provider, I asked him if Greg Carroll or someone at OutSource could help me in trying to access my accounts or finding out who was behind it. After commenting on how he hadn't shown up at the storage unit on Wednesday, I asked him again why he wasn't there and if he was all right. Partly motivated by the need to physically see him, to see for myself that he was all right, I ended the message by telling him that we needed to meet so we could discuss what had happened.

I didn't receive a response. I didn't know what to think. When I seemed to be getting my life back on track, it was getting derailed again by even more insane behavior, although this time from a tangential and unexpected source.

Although I didn't think that Jonathan was in any physical danger, I still needed to find out what had happened to him, why I hadn't been hearing from him. Perhaps it was just because of the disruption of the move…or perhaps it wasn't.

To try to quell my concerns, I decided to contact some of Jonathan's friends or possibly family who I thought might know where he was. There was no point in contacting Dan or Laura, since they didn't know where he might be, and even if they did, I didn't want to talk to them. I thought about contacting Cliff or Art, but was sure they didn't know anything either. After all, Cliff had been led to believe that Jonathan was on his deathbed in a hospice and God-only-knew what Art had been told. The e-mail account in Colin's name was fraudulent, and since I didn't know the address to his legitimate one, I couldn't contact him. I didn't know how to contact any of his other friends whom I'd met. I didn't know how to contact his family in England, and although the "Terry Frazier" site I had found a year before provided information for contacting him, I wasn't certain that Terrence would talk to me, given that I was a lower-class American. In the end, the list of options narrowed to two people: Greg Carroll and Miranda West. I hoped that one of them would respond and could help.

I wasn't sure how to contact Greg. After visiting his company's web site, I eventually found contact information for someone I believed was him as well as two e-mail addresses through which to contact him. To try to verify that it was really him before revealing more, I sent him a message in which I told him that I needed to speak to him about something important that involved Jonathan but that before I did that, I needed to know I had the right person. I told him to verify his identity by giving me the names of Jonathan's dogs, which I thought he probably knew. Unfortunately, I never received a response.

I *did* know how to contact Miranda. She had an online presence that contained plenty of information about how to get in touch with her. I composed a detailed message to her in which I explained what had been happening and urged her to get in touch with me if she could help me in any way. I sent the message on Thursday, May 9, hoping for an answer.

On Friday, the spring semester ended and, in spite of what was happening, I tried to relax. There was little else I knew to do. By that point, I hadn't heard from Jonathan for two weeks.

On Saturday morning, I went to the mailbox. For the second time, I found a business-size envelope with my address typed in capital letters and postmarked in Paladin. I hurried inside and, nervous, I opened it.

In this letter, the sender gave me the changed password to the e-mail accounts from which he had kept me barred so I could, in his words, "see what [he'd] done to [me]." He also gave me the changed password to my *mother's* account—which I didn't even know had been affected, given that he hadn't mentioned it in his previous letter and the account hadn't been used since I'd sent my mother's message to Jonathan almost six weeks before—and ordered me to "start there." The new password to the accounts was *heilhitler*.

The password the sender had selected convinced me more than ever that he was my ex-brother-in-law. He was a history buff who had actually studied to become a history teacher and his favorite period of history was World War II. More specifically, his favorite personage from World War II was Adolf Hitler. He constantly, almost obsessively, read books and watched programs about Hitler and his interest was far from simple historical fascination. My sister had told me that he had once said, "Hitler had the right idea"—which said it all. The fact that the real estate agent who was putting the pressure on him to give up his "castle" was also Jewish must have only fueled his resentment. Even so, I still had no *solid* proof that the sender was my ex-brother-in-law, although the circumstantial evidence seemed to be mounting.

Immediately I checked my mother's e-mail account. I found that the password I'd been given was correct, so I was able to access it. When I did, I was shocked by what I found. On the afternoon of Wednesday, April 17, someone, pretending to be my mother, had sent several messages to Andy in which "she" had told him the truth about Jonathan. "Her" stated reason for doing so appeared to be to "keep a young person from ruining his life." "She" also stated that "she" had taken it upon "herself" to tell him the truth to protect me, "her" son, from the repercussions I might suffer if Jonathan found out that the truth about him had been revealed. The most feared repercussion was that Jonathan wouldn't repay me the money he owed me in order to punish me. The exchange ended with my "mother" making Andy promise that he wouldn't tell Jonathan what he had learned until Jonathan repaid me, which was supposed to happen in about a week. Andy appeared to agree and after that, there was no further communication between "my mother" and Andy.

The style of the messages was similar, but not identical, to that of my mother's, as if someone who had access to samples of her writing was trying to promote the illusion that it was actually her by imitating her style. There were several e-mails and the style of the later ones was different from that of the earlier ones, as if the sender were trying to perfect her character. The e-mail exchange was quite a feat for someone who couldn't even turn on a computer.

Next, I checked my primary e-mail account, and there, I also found several messages that revolved around Andy. The first was a message that had been sent to Andy on Friday, April 19 in which the sender was now pretending to be *me*. I was stunned by the date because at that point I still had access to the account but hadn't seen the message. I didn't normally check my sent messages, however, but the sender presumably didn't know that, which made me wonder if he had originally intended for me to see it before deciding to change tactics.

In any event, the message said essentially that now that my mother had taken it upon herself to tell him the truth about Jonathan, I thought that I would tell him the truth in more detail. The e-mail also indicated that the sender knew the "relationship" between Jonathan and Andy had *not* ended in January, that it had continued in some form throughout the next three months. If that was true, then Andy had somehow been pulled back into the situation and Jonathan had lied to me about *that* for three months while God-knew-what had been going on between them. This was like mid-January all over again.

The e-mail also contained a link to the web site on which I had been posting messages to Jonathan and stated that a complete account of our relationship, as well as Jonathan's actual whereabouts during the past ten months, was posted there. When I clicked on the link, I found that the letter I had written, but not sent, to Andy after finding his "farewell" message to "Iain" in January had somehow been acquired and posted there for Andy to see. The file name, which functioned like a password, was unfamiliar to me, however, which meant that I wouldn't have seen the message when I checked the account. It was like the Purloined Letter, hidden in plain sight. Apart from using the e-mail portion of the account, I hadn't checked the file directory since early April, when I had stopped posting messages to Jonathan, so I hadn't discovered that there was anything wrong. Once again, I didn't know if the person behind it had hoped I would find it or had simply blundered in keeping what he was doing secret. I also didn't understand why he hadn't just locked me out of this account as well when he had the others. That, however, seemed a minor point.

The next e-mail I found had been sent to Jonathan from my primary account a week later, on Friday, April 26—the day after I had been locked out. This message told him, explicitly, that "I" had told Andy the truth about him and how despicable "I" thought he was for what he had done. "I" had told him that it must be easy for him to live with himself when he had no conscience and that "I" wanted him gone. The message contained a forwarded copy of a message that "I" had sent to Andy that was supposed to be "my" reaction to his apparently not having believed anything that he had been told regarding the fact that everything Jonathan had been telling him was a lie. The sender had indicated that he had gained access to the fraudulent Colin account and had read a message that Andy had written to Colin in which Andy had described the information he had received as part of a "smear campaign" against Jonathan. It also suggested that he had gotten the idea that someone had been sending messages from the e-mail accounts of the different characters involved pretending to be them in an attempt to wreak havoc.

In response, "I" had written to Andy and informed him, angrily, that Jonathan had been deceiving and manipulating him for months. "I" told Andy that "I" thought that out of pure self-interest, if nothing else, he would want to check out the facts for himself—for example, by going to Jonathan's apartment in Mariah and seeing for himself that he was there—but if he didn't want to admit that "I" could be right, then there was nothing else "I" could do. "I" told him that "I" didn't understand how he could believe what Jonathan had been telling him when he had *no* direct proof that any of it was true. Harshly, "I" told him that if he was too much in denial or too stupid to check out the facts, then he deserved what he got.

In what seemed like a blatantly forced attempt to affix responsibility, "I" told Andy that he could tell Jonathan *exactly* who had been communicating with him. "I" told him my full name and told him that Jonathan would recognize the name, since "I" had been his boyfriend for almost a year. "I" also told Andy that he could refer Jonathan to the web site that "I" had created so he could see the materials for the "smear campaign" himself and encouraged him to forward a copy of the current message to Jonathan.

The message also contained Jonathan's reaction, which had been swift and harsh. He told "me" that he wanted "me" to be gone as well. He also informed "me" that he had reported "my" hacking activities to the webmasters and had filed an appropriate report. He reminded me that Greg Carroll worked for an IT company and knew what to do in such circumstances. He informed me that my actions also had consequences. He told me not to contact him again and that his attorney would deal with me from that point forward. He ended the e-mail by telling me to give my regards to my "dear sweet mother," whom he described as being just as "fucked up" as I was.

I was horrified, but suddenly, everything made sense. Jonathan had thought that *I* was the one who had contacted Andy and had tried to destroy the elaborate web of lies that seemed to be so crucial to his mental stability. To me, however, that was just as insane as the fantasies into which he periodically retreated. Apart from believing that the "Andy thing" had ended three months before, I had, in the months that had followed, decided that I wouldn't tell Andy the truth because I was afraid of how it would affect Jonathan. I was afraid that exposing the fantasies on which his "sanity" seemed to depend would either drive him over the edge or drive him to commit suicide and I was *not* going to be responsible for either. I had decided not to tell Laura the truth for the same reason. Even though it would have been the right thing to do, to reveal the truth, however it was received, would have been to open a Pandora's box and revealing the truth to Andy had accomplished precisely that.

The chaos didn't stop there. Most outlandish of all, however, was a series of e-mails that the imposter had sent to Jonathan that night again pretending to be me. According to these messages, I had broken down under the strain of everything that was happening and had decided to kill myself. The messages contained "confessions" of how I had lied to him about certain things myself and how inferior and unworthy I felt because of what I had done. They then described how I had taken an overdose of sleeping pills and, as the messages were being written, I was in the process of dying. The messages then stopped, giving the silent suggestion that I had succeeded. Significantly, Jonathan hadn't responded to any of these messages and he certainly hadn't tried to contact me that evening in some other way to try to stop me. Did he believe that I deserved to die—literally—for what "I" had done?

As an indication of how concerned Jonathan was that I might actually have killed myself, the day after he had received the "suicide notes" from "me," he had posted one of his fraudulent ads on *Gayteway*. Using the name "DoIt," he had described himself an attractive biker who was interested in an extensive list of sexual activities. Because "DoIt" didn't resemble Jonathan at all, I knew it was one of his runaround ads. "DoIt" claimed that he was visiting from Los Angeles and would be staying in a city in another part of the state until Thursday. Later that evening, the ad had attracted the attention of someone who called himself "doittome" and had initiated a lengthy exchange that had lasted until the next Wednesday. Between Saturday evening and Monday evening alone, "DoIt" had posted no less than 13 messages on the board in which, true to form, he had offered one excuse after another for why they couldn't actually meet. Although "DoIt" claimed he was trying to find "doittome," something always prevented it from happening. In the end, he had actually begun to blame "doittome" for giving *him* the runaround. Ironically, "DoIt" had complained that he didn't have time for "bullshit games." Finally, after a break of two days, "DoIt" had told "doittome" that he was leaving for L.A. and, after expressing his hope that they could finally get together when he returned in the fall, he had assured "doittome" that he was a "nice guy."

For all Jonathan knew, I could have been dead, but instead of trying to find out for sure, instead of showing the slightest hint of compassion and concern, he played sex games on the Internet. Did he really value his lies over my life?

With this new information, I contacted Jonathan and attempted to reason with him. First, I tried to make him understand that I had *no* motivation to contact Andy because he had, after all, told me in January that his "relationship" with Andy had ended—something that Andy himself had confirmed at that time. Since I had believed that Andy was no longer in danger of doing something self-destructive and that the situation between Jonathan and him had ended, contacting him would have not only been purposeless, but also potentially done more harm than good. Although I *had* expected him to tell Andy—and everyone else—the truth, I had expected *him* to do it, not me, and had expected him to do it as part of rebuilding the trust and truth in our relationship, which had ended. I didn't tell him, however, that I was afraid that if Andy learned the truth before he was psychologically prepared to deal with the repercussions, he might have a breakdown or even kill himself, although I should have. In short, I had nothing to gain by doing what it had been made to look as if I had done and what risked causing tremendous harm.

Second, the e-mails suggested that I had been planning to tell Andy the truth all along but hadn't because I was afraid that if Jonathan found out, he might retaliate by refusing to repay me. If that were true, then why hadn't I waited until I had my money before I told him? Although my "mother" had made Andy agree not to tell Jonathan what he had learned until I had my money, would my mother, who was so concerned about protecting me, have been foolish enough to expect Andy, whom she didn't know, to keep such an important promise? Wouldn't she have considered and been concerned about the possibility, the *probability*, that the *first* thing Andy would do would be to run to Jonathan and tell him everything? Whoever did this, I asserted, appeared to have done it because that was *precisely* what he had been hoping would happen.

Third—and most nonsensical of all—if I had been so afraid that he wouldn't repay me if he believed that I had told Andy the truth, then why would I have blatantly *ordered* Andy to forward a copy of the April 26 message to him as well as to inform him about the web page that detailed the truth about him? None of this made any sense and I implored Jonathan to be rational and to consider the logical flaws in what he had been led to believe. I urged him to meet with me so we could figure out what to do.

On the evening of Sunday, May 12, Jonathan finally responded. This was the first contact that the *real* me had had with him in almost three weeks. I might have been relieved to hear from him, but the message he sent proved far from relieving.

He began by describing what I had told him in my message as "too complex" for him to absorb, which seemed to indicate that he refused to do so. He informed me that he had spoken to his "shrink," who had suggested that the person behind the e-mails was actually *me*—or, more accurately, an *alternate personality*. According to him, she had suggested to Jonathan that I was suffering from dissociative identity disorder—what used to be called multiple personality disorder. He claimed that he had shown her an e-mail he had received from "me," which had been sent under the name "Heorshema." The message not only indicated that the sender was "quite ill," but also had threatened his safety. He informed me that Warren had wanted to turn it over to the police. Jonathan had been reluctant to do it, however, because he felt that I was mentally ill and didn't want to cause me further trouble.

Refusing to listen to me in any way, he reasserted his accusation that I had hacked into not only his e-mail account but also those he "shared" with friends. He informed me that *he* had permission to use their accounts, but *I* did *not*. He further insisted that I *was* the one who had contacted Andy, then him to tell him that I had. He said that if it wasn't me, then whoever it was had done an excellent job of impersonating me. He then went on to say, however, that he didn't care if it was me or not. He did know I could be vindictive and he would never know if it was me or not, so he had decided not to pursue finding out who it really was.

He told me that as far as meeting was concerned, he was in England and wouldn't be back until the 23rd. He told me that if I insisted on returning his things I should leave them in the hallway at the storage unit or, better yet, with Hope, the woman who worked at the facility who Jonathan had said had invited him to spend Thanksgiving with her. He said that he had already lost so many things, so it didn't matter and I should do whatever I wanted. He saw no reason to meet with me since nothing would ever be resolved, so there was no point in our prolonging our entanglement. He told me that his attorney would deal with me regarding any unsettled issues. He ended his message by informing me that he just wanted to move on, had in fact done so, and now felt freer and less anxious because he had.

I was floored. This was one of the most bizarre messages that Jonathan had ever written to me, one of the most unexpected, disorienting, and upsetting. Jonathan had made damaging claims about me, had even mentioned getting the law involved, and seemed to have no interest in hearing my side of things. Apparently he saw fit to believe what he wanted to believe, regardless of how that affected me, and the message made it abundantly clear that he couldn't have cared less what happened to me now.

The message was bizarre in other ways. Although it didn't impress me at the time, Jonathan seemed to have assumed a very nonchalant attitude toward someone his "shrink" had suggested was suffering from dissociative identity disorder in which one of the personalities had apparently threatened his safety. Although he claimed that Warren had wanted to take the message to the police, Jonathan also claimed that he himself hadn't wanted to get the police involved, allegedly because he didn't want to cause me further problems. If *I* had thought that *I* was in bodily danger from someone, *especially* if he were mentally ill, *I* would have contacted the authorities, regardless of the problems it caused him. He also stated that he didn't care if it was me or not and was out of the situation. Once again, if *I* had been in his position, I would have cared *very much* if someone who was mentally ill were physically threatening me and would want to have him stopped instead of just walking away. Finally, after raising such an inflammatory issue, he almost as abruptly dropped it and began focusing on purely practical matters. It was almost as if two different messages intended for two different people had somehow gotten spliced together, as if the message itself suffered from its own form of dissociation.

Beyond that, I was very skeptical about his claim that he was in England. Even if he did have more money now than he'd had for the previous several months, or if his family or other parties in England had finally paid his way there, his claim that he was there didn't ring true. I suspected it was just an excuse to avoid me, just another of his many lies.

In some ways, though, the most bizarre aspect of the message was that instead of having sent it from his own e-mail account, he had sent it from the fraudulent *Cliff* account, which, we both knew, he most certainly did *not* "share" with Cliff.

Tired, upset, and angry, I sent him a lengthy message in which I countered his charges and vented the full measure of my frustration. Addressing the message to "Cliff," I told him that he could believe whatever he wanted about what had happened. I told him that if I knew anything about how he liked to present himself, he was going to accept the version of the truth that made him look the best and made me look the worst, no matter how much he had to distort the facts to accomplish that. I told him that his arrogance and his belief in his own superiority made him incapable of acknowledging that he could be wrong about anything, which made it impossible to reason with him.

I countered the ridiculous notion that I had dissociative identity disorder by informing him that no one had ever noticed any symptoms of something like that, especially the many psychologists with whom I had associated over the years. I told him that if his "shrink" wanted to make an armchair diagnosis of someone she had never met, then it had as much validity as her belief that what he had done to Andy and so many others was normal. I told him, however, that because she had heard only his carefully crafted version of the truth, what else should she believe? I told him that if she had the opportunity to hear *my* side of things, she might end up having a *very* different perspective. As many different people as he'd been over the Internet, as many different stories as he'd told people, starting with Andy and going from there, I told him, *he* seemed to be the one with the multiple personalities.

I explained my belief that "Heorshema" was actually my ex-brother-in-law and, given his fixation on World War II, the fact that he had used a name that referred to the nuclear attacks on Japan only strengthened that belief. I told him that my ex-brother-in-law was no physical threat, but I was upset to think that he was defaming and damaging me and that Jonathan had bought into all of his sickening crap without reservation. I told him that obviously he *wanted* to believe it was me for some reason, given that he had no desire, it appeared, to hear anything I had to say.

In several lengthy paragraphs, I told him exactly how my relationship with him had affected me, how it had damaged me. In the process, I remarked on his comment that I was vindictive, reminding him that he had done some incredibly vindictive things himself. I told him I didn't trust him at all and wondered what he would do to me now that he was enflamed at me. I told him that if he *was* in England, then he should stay there, since all he had done was damage me and the farther away he stayed from me, the better. I still wanted my money, but I never wanted to see *him* again.

I received no response.

After I was allowed back into my accounts, there were no further intrusions that I was able to detect and no further threats to do me or anyone else connected with me further harm. More important, however, no harm was ever inflicted on anyone in my family, apart from some needless stress. Whoever was behind the manipulations apparently felt that he had accomplished whatever he had set out to achieve, making further attempts at wreaking havoc unnecessary.

At first, I thought that the hard drive of my computer had been hacked, since I didn't know where the imposter could have gotten some of the information he had used, but later, I realized that everything he had employed in his game could have come from my e-mail accounts. For example, I found evidence that the e-mail from April 26 to Andy that "I" had forwarded to Jonathan had apparently been spliced together from at least two and possibly three e-mails that I had sent to my sister and a friend in February. The amended message had been edited to include the more recent information that I didn't know. In addition, I had also forwarded to a friend a copy of the letter to Andy in which I had detailed Jonathan's true situation, so it was also available in my e-mail. Further, several of the lines from my Valentine's Day message in which I had told Jonathan that I felt as if I were having a nervous breakdown had been incorporated into one of the "suicide notes."

The origin of the remaining messages was more difficult to discern, but the e-mail accounts that had been accessed contained among them hundreds of examples of my writing, some of which were quite lengthy, that could have easily been sampled and spliced together into convincing-sounding messages. Whoever was trying to impersonate me did indeed do an excellent job because, having used my writings, in some sense he had *become* me.

In time, I came to call the person who had wreaked the havoc "The Pretender," not only because he had pretended to be me, but also because he, like a political pretender who tried to seize authority without the right to do so, had presumptuously taken, without my permission, the identity that was rightfully mine.

■

In spite of the damage The Pretender inflicted, it was, in retrospect, a blessing in disguise. If I had not felt driven to contact those of Jonathan's friends whom I did out of concern for his safety, I never would have stumbled onto the path that ultimately led me to discover that the person I thought I knew, I did not know at all—indeed, that the person I thought I knew was not a *person* at all.

—IV—
—U*ntangling*—

People aren't that devious, or at least ones that I've known have not been able to maintain facades long term and the truth will always emerge...

—Jonathan

*If circumstances lead me, I will find
Where truth is hid, though it were hid indeed
Within the centre.*

—Lord Polonius, *Hamlet*, 2.2.157-59

—35—
A Woman With Insight

He is not *from England...*

Several days went by without my receiving a response from Miranda. I began to wonder if I would receive a response at all, not knowing anything about her or her level of interest in what was happening. After receiving Jonathan's message on Sunday in which he had accused me of having dissociative identity disorder and, as one of my "alters," having threatened him, I half-wondered if he had told Miranda that I was insane and dangerous and she was avoiding me.

Then, on the Tuesday night following the Thursday on which I had sent her the e-mail, the phone rang. I was reading in bed, and at 9:45, I was beginning to doze. When I saw that it was Miranda, however, I came fully awake.

"Richard? This is Miranda West. I'm not calling too late, am I?"

When I told her she wasn't, she said, "I got your e-mail." Then, she said something that opened the door to another reality that, to that point, I would have never suspected: "I think the person behind this is Jonathan."

Stunned, wondering what would cause her to arrive at that conclusion, I simply said, "Really?"

Over the next forty-five minutes, Miranda told me a number of things that I wasn't certain I believed. I didn't believe she was lying, but I did believe she might be misinformed. What she had to tell me was so different, so disconnected from what I knew, or thought I knew, about Jonathan that I couldn't assimilate it. Even so, I kept an open mind as I listened to what she had to say.

First of all, she told me that Jonathan was mentally ill. I already knew that *something* was seriously wrong with him, had assumed that it was stress related, but Miranda indicated that his problems actually ran far deeper than I had suspected. She described him as "borderline," a term that technically refers to a type of personality disorder characterized by extreme fluctuations in identity, attitude, and emotion as well as generally erratic behavior. Apparently, his psychological problems had started long before the previous fall, long before I had met him.

She told me she had learned that Jonathan had stolen a substantial amount of money from his former employer. She told me that she and Jonathan had met through a woman named Cassandra, a former coworker of Jonathan's who was also a client of Miranda's, and it was Cassandra who had informed her of the theft. According to what Cassandra had told her, Jonathan had stolen at least $25,000 and probably much more.

She told me that his employer had hired a private investigator and, in the process, the investigator had learned a number of interesting things. For example, Jonathan had apparently told his coworkers the story he had told me about his family's involvement in VeraMed, the line of aloe-based skin care products, but the investigator had learned that his family was not involved in the company in any way.

To my shock, Miranda told me that she had also learned from Cassandra that Jonathan had been telling people at work that he and Miranda were involved in a passionate love affair. Miranda was stunned to learn what he had been saying about her—about *them*—since, of course, *none* of it was true.

I also told Miranda about the Andy situation and how Jonathan's pathological need to retreat into stress-reducing fantasy had almost led Andy to abandon his real life in the United States for a fantasy life he thought awaited him in England. Jonathan had never mentioned an Andy to her, so she was unable to add anything to what I knew, or thought I knew, about him. In some ways, Andy remained as enigmatic as ever.

Perhaps most intriguing of all, Miranda told me that she had actually met Glenn. She told me that Jonathan had brought Glenn to her for a reading, and when he had, Jonathan had tried to pass off Glenn as his *son*. This was not the first time I had heard the "Glenn is my *son*" story, since I had also heard it from Joan Vogel. It became clear to me that Jonathan, who claimed that he was "glad to be gay" and harbored no reservations about revealing his sexuality, was in fact deeply concerned about maintaining a façade of heterosexuality, seemingly as deeply as he claimed Dan was.

Miranda also told me what she knew about Glenn. Since she had actually met Glenn, she was in a position to give her own firsthand appraisals of him. As with Jonathan, I already knew that, psychologically, there was something seriously wrong with Glenn, although with the limited amount of information I had about him, I couldn't conceptualize his condition any more specifically than as a highly deficient ability to cope with the stresses of life that resulted from his background of childhood abuse. Laura, of course, had said that Jonathan had told people at the Stress Center that Glenn was schizophrenic, but Jonathan had told *me* that Laura was mistaken, that he had actually characterized his violent behavior as schizophrenic-*like* because it differed so radically from his normally subdued behavior. According to what Miranda told me, however, *schizophrenic* seemed closer to the mark.

Although Jonathan had told Miranda certain things about Glenn's behavior before he had brought him to see her, Glenn himself had not only confirmed what Jonathan had told her, but also expanded on it. Miranda described a number of hallucinations and delusions that Glenn had related that were decidedly religious and paranoid in nature. She also described what appeared to be fugue states in which Glenn would get into a car and drive to another state, then come to and not know how he'd gotten there. Jonathan had already told me how Glenn would disappear for days at a time before reemerging, but there was apparently more to *that* story than he had ever made clear. Finally, she told me that Jonathan had told her the same story that he had eventually told me (and others) about how Glenn had started beating him up and had threatened to kill him, which had caused Jonathan and Glenn to separate.

She also asked me if Jonathan had ever discussed any of his paranormal experiences with me. He had not, since presumably that would have damaged the façade of normality he had tried to maintain, so I was *very* interested to know what he had told *her*. One experience involved the antique rug with the torn border that had lain in the living room of his house in Paladin and that now resided at the storage unit. She said that Jonathan had told her that one morning, he had woken up to find that the border, which had previously been intact, was now torn. Instead of thinking that something mundane had happened to it—for example, that the dogs had torn it—he believed that it was actually the work of spirits.

Another experience involved the purple chair that had sat in the sunroom in his house in Paladin and that, with the rug, now resided at the storage unit. She said that Jonathan constantly talked about the chair and believed that it possessed some type of paranormal energy or functioned as some type of psychic amplifier. He had said that when he sat in it, he sometimes received inspirations or impressions that he would not otherwise receive. I knew the purple chair had been his favorite place to sit—I had rarely seen him sit anywhere else when he was living on Millstone Drive—but Miranda's revelation brought a whole new dimension—in more ways than one—to his favoring of that spot.

Miranda also asked me about my physical health. She was concerned that through my involvement with him I might have contracted a sexually transmitted disease, even HIV. I acknowledged that our sex had not always been safe, but added that our activities had been only marginally unsafe and that although I hadn't been tested, I had experienced no symptoms that would indicate I was sick. I asked her if she perceived anything medically wrong with me, but she said that she didn't. On the whole, however, the issue of my physical health now seemed the *least* of the issues.

One thing she said piqued my interest perhaps more than anything else. In my e-mail, I had mentioned that Jonathan was British, something I restated in our conversation. To that, she said, "He is *not* from England." She said she didn't know where he was from, but she thought he might actually be from the Southern state in which he had previously lived. Briefly, I thought of the produce he had received from his father around Christmas, which had been sent from there. Even so, this was perhaps the most difficult piece of information to accept. Everything I had seen pointed to the fact that Jonathan *was* British, that what he had told me about *that* was true. His accent, his possessions, his elaborate, detailed stories about his family, his friends, his past, his life in England... He couldn't *possibly* have deceived me in such an extravagant fashion for so many months. On this point, I thought—I *knew*—Miranda was wrong. I thought her information was only partially correct, although it was clear that Jonathan was *not* everything he had said he was and *was* things he had not said he was.

Contrary to thinking that *I* might be dangerous, Miranda felt that *Jonathan* might be dangerous and wanted to speak to me further about him because she felt I needed to know as much as possible about him. We arranged to meet at her home in Paladin around 11:00 Thursday morning. I asked her if I could bring a tape recorder to record our conversation because I didn't want to rely on often-unreliable memory to record what she had to say. I needed to hear, and recall, every word.

In the meantime, I tried to find out more about Andy, who he *really* was. To that end, I entered his name into a search engine, hoping to find something tangible about him. What I found was not only perplexing, but also disturbing. I discovered that Andy's name was an anagram of the name of a character from one of Shakespeare's plays. That made me wonder if Andy's parents had named him in honor of Shakespeare…or if Andy was exactly what he now appeared to be: a character. I still had no way of knowing. I had been accused of e-mailing damaging information to him when I hadn't, but did *I* dare go to him now and find out if he was in fact a real person at all? Perhaps because I found the possibility disconcerting and knew how Jonathan had reacted in thinking that I had contacted him, I decided against it. More than ever, I needed to talk to Miranda.

Two days later, I left for Miranda's around 9:30 in the morning. Ironically—or significantly—Miranda's home lay only a short distance from Jonathan's home on Millstone Drive, in the same region of Paladin where so many significant events had happened to me in the previous three years. It had always taken me about an hour and a half to travel from my home in Hawthorn to Jonathan's home in Paladin, but since Miranda's home lay somewhat farther beyond, I arrived about fifteen minutes late.

When I did, Miranda was waiting for me in her well-shaded front yard. I had seen the photograph of her on her web site, so I already knew what she looked like. In her early 50s, she was tall, blond-haired, and blue-eyed and carried herself with a stateliness that was somehow even more impressive than her appearance, which was impressive enough. She was dressed in a somewhat unconventional outfit that lent her an exotic air, making me think of an updated version of the attire that a priestess of one of the ancient, female-oriented religions might have worn. She was surrounded by an eclectic assortment of garden decorations, many of which bore a metaphysical or mystical motif. Wind chimes tinkled soothingly in the light spring breeze. The atmosphere, far from being "supercharged," as Jonathan had once described it, was actually peaceful and calming, and despite my anxiousness over being late, and perhaps over hearing what I was about to hear, I began to feel at ease.

We greeted, then stepped inside. After spending a few minutes getting settled, I started my player to record what proved to be one of the most fascinating, and unsettling, conversations that I have ever had.

Miranda immediately got to the relationship between Jonathan and Glenn. "The reason I'm going to jump right ahead and then I want to get back to [Jonathan is that] this just came to me [so I want to mention it] before my brain forgets about it… Did he ever bring up stuff to you about how Glenn—and I've met Glenn, by the way…"

"Okay, so he's a real person?" I said because, at that point, I no longer took for granted what was real and what was not.

"Yeah, I know!" she said, fully appreciating my attitude. "Yeah, because [Jonathan] brought him to me for a reading and it *blew* [Jonathan] out of the water. I was kind of shocked that he brought him in, but he did...as a matter of fact, I think I saw him twice...[Jonathan] couldn't stand it. I guess this guy, really—and he is *very* odd, trust me. Oh, my God..."

"Glenn is?" I said, wondering if she was referring to Jonathan.

"Ooh. *Scary.* Do you know what I'm saying? Serial-killer type scary, in a way..."

"Yes."

"I mean, like, a really scary type person, in a way..."

I repeated the story that Jonathan had finally told me about how their relationship had ended because Glenn had started beating him up, the story that he had also told her. This time, I gave her more details about the abuse, telling her that Jonathan had told me that Glenn had blacked his eye and that he had been forced to go to work wearing sunglasses to hide it. In addition, I told her the story that Jonathan had told me about the two of them getting into a fight in the guest bedroom during which Glenn had bloodied his nose and the blood had splattered onto the walls, which had stained them. Finally, I told her that Jonathan had told me that when he had decided they couldn't be together anymore, Glenn had threatened to kill him and that when they had gone to the airport when Glenn was going back to England, Glenn had shoved him down the escalator.

"Back to *England*?" she said, perplexed.

"Yeah."

"What is this *England* obsession?"

"Well, the thing with, you know, I don't [know], I've thought [about it and]..."

"He is *not* from England," she insisted, "and he is not—*no.*"

I still didn't know what to think about her assertion that Jonathan wasn't from England. Everything I had seen indicated that he was, so I found it difficult to believe that her assertion that he wasn't was correct. Although all of his stories about his life in England *could* have been lies—I had, after all, seen how he had created and maintained such elaborate, detailed sets of lies online to so many different people—could he have faked a British accent and maintained such a convincing British persona *in person* for *ten months*? It was difficult to believe to the point that I wasn't willing to believe it. On that account, something somewhere was wrong.

She changed the subject. "Let me fill in the Glenn piece that I know of, too. [Jonathan] was *obsessed* with Glenn and was constantly trying to track him down. Glenn was trying to run away from him."

"Really?" I said, taken aback.

"Oh, *hell* yes."

Stunned by this sudden change of perspective on the Glenn situation, I said, "So Glenn was trying to *get away from him.*"

"Oh—my—*God*. That's why he would just take off. And [Jonathan] was crazy, too, but in a different way. See, I told you for a long time, [Jonathan] tried to present it to me—he came right in here and told me that Glenn was his *son*."

"Uh-huh."

"And, I was like, you know, 'Don't lie to a psychic.' And I'm sitting there, like, 'Okay?' And then he starts telling me this wild-ass story about how it was his sister's—his sister had married into this family—I wish I could remember the whole story because it's *wild.*"

"Yeah."

"'Cause he finally admitted, 'No, my wife and I...'—he told me he used to be married—and his wife and he, right—adopted Glenn."

"Okay."

"That this was his *adopted* son, okay?"

"Okay."

"Mmhmm. 'Cause I would just get right in his face—I wasn't mean, but I would just say, 'I just don't feel like he's your son,'" she said, laughing at the absurdity of Jonathan's claims.

"Yes!"

"*Please*. You know?"

In an attempt to understand why Jonathan would make such a bizarre, and blatantly transparent claim, I said, "Well, do you think he was lying to you because he didn't want to acknowledge being gay?"

"Partially, yeah. Oh, yeah, yeah, yeah, I think that piece at first."

"Yeah."

"'Cause he was telling people at work the same thing, that this was his *son.*"

"Well, I know that when he was living in Mariah, he told his landlady that one of the reasons he couldn't pay her his rent was because he was having to spend all of his money on a private investigator to find his *son* Glenn. So it was the same thing again."

"Is that the same...who was the one...he told me some wild story the last time I saw him he was living with this woman and having sex with her, [whatever], and her son lived with her...? That they were in this big affair and she was in love with him...is this the same landlady?"

"No."

"That's another woman, right, in…?"

"Yeah. Her name is Laura…"

"*Yes.*"

"She lives in St. Alban."

"*St. Alban.* Yeah, he lived there for a while."

I told her when he had lived with Laura then when and where he had lived with Art and that during this time he had gotten the job at the hospital in Mariah.

"It just blows you away, doesn't it?"

"Yeah."

"That he was in a *hospital* setting?"

"Yeah, I know."

"And that they *hired* him."

"I know."

"And how he keeps *getting jobs*. They were blown away here—they were just blown away researching all this stuff with him."

"Yeah, and he'd gotten a job there—I mean I know this was a legitimate thing because I went with him to the hospital."

"Oh, yeah. No, he showed me a bunch of stuff about that, oh, yeah."

"And I saw stuff from the hospital, so I know that was definitely legitimate."

"What was he doing there?"

I explained the job insofar as he had explained it to me and Miranda told me that he had told her the same thing. I also told her when he moved to Mariah and that I had helped with the move, so I saw where he was, what he was doing, with my own eyes.

"Sure. I'm glad to hear this," she said. "I probably wouldn't have believed it."

"[*I*] probably wouldn't have believed it, no."

"*God.*"

"So I saw all of this. And he had this job for about a week and a half [after he moved to Mariah] before he said they decided to end the project, that they weren't going to go ahead and continue with it."

"No. And you know what my suspicion is—again, this is totally going on my intuition—*I* feel—and it ties in with some other things…—I bet anything that some of whatever was going on with him here with, you know, the investigation, with trying to pursue him and pursue legally whatever they were trying to do…"

"Yeah."

"…caught up with him. Or somebody made a phone call, found out, you know, 'Oh, he's working in Mariah…' Maybe he made the mistake of putting somebody down as a last [employer]—I would love to see his résumé—he put down his last person that he worked for, I bet somebody made a [phone call] ... *Something* happened."

"Yes."

"Because they were having him investigated—you know, what's interesting about the private investigator—I know for a *fact* that they had hired a private investigator."

"Yes."

"So that would be my suspicion, is that something [happened] because they don't end projects after a week and a half."

I told her I had accepted his story because it fit with the small-town mentality that seemed to prevail in Mariah in which they didn't want someone to come in and upset the status quo, especially a foreigner. I told her, though, that afterwards, he was stuck in Mariah.

"God, what a weird place to end up," Miranda said, rolling her eyes.

I agreed. I also told her I could verify that he had been there from mid-November through at least mid-April because I had been there with him throughout that time.

I offered more detail about Jonathan's life in Mariah. "I do think his ability to travel was somewhat limited because his car was in bad shape and needed to be fixed and he said he didn't have any money to do that."

"Did he ever tell you the white Jaguar story?"

I thought a second. "No—I'd love to hear it," I said, laughing.

"*Okay*. One day, he blew in here..."

"Yeah."

"And it was this whole story...again about his family, about how supposedly his great-grandfather or grandfather or somebody came up with this whole [aloe-based line of skin-care products]—and there *is* a holistic, or there is an herbal—there *is* a company that exists, but apparently from what the investigator [found], he's not connected with them in any way... But anyway, he was telling me about his father—that [Jonathan] had a leased car or something, that his car was *leased* with his dad's company, and that his dad had just called him and told him to get rid of the car he had. And, he was so excited; he was going to get this new white Jaguar."

"Uh-huh."

"And it just never made sense to me. And, I'm like, 'Well, I've never heard of that; that would be, like, a really extravagant kind of thing for [someone in his position]...' And, he was always telling me about how he had $30,000 and Glenn had taken $15,000—you know, like, one time, Glenn disappeared, 'Oh, Glenn got into my money...' He was always telling me about all this *money* he had around his house."

"Yeah."

"That he kept all this money in his house."

"Yeah."

"And I *do* think he had that because he took—I know of one sum he took from that place was twenty-five [thousand]. But then I think they found a whole bunch more that was missing."

"I actually saw a bunch of cash one time."

"Yeah."

"It was last summer when he was still living here…"

"Yeah. Exactly."

I told her the story about the evening he had taken the wad of cash out of the backpack he kept locked in the trunk of his car and had told me it was $2,000. I told her he said that he'd gotten it out for the weekend but that I couldn't understand why he would need $2,000 for only two days.

"*Yeah.* He would come in *here* with this big wad of money; it was, like, *weird.*"

Miranda then asked me if I had ever seen Jonathan take medications, felt that he was doing drugs, or felt that he was "self-medicating." When I told her I didn't know, she asked me if I had seen prescriptions, which I had. When he had lived in the house on Millstone Drive, I had seen a script for Phenergan, the anti-nausea drug, and a bottle for Paxil, an antidepressant, but the bottle was empty. Now that I thought about it, however, I realized that I had never actually *seen* him take either of these drugs or *any* prescription drugs, for that matter. Aside from that, I had never seen any evidence of non-prescription or illegal drug use, apart from the relatively harmless poppers. I had rarely seen him even drink alcohol and could remember only a couple of times in the ten months we'd been involved that he'd had even a social drink. Miranda suggested that his pattern of drug use—or non-use—reflected an attempt to stay in control, an opinion with which I fully concurred.

Changing the subject, I restated that I could verify where he had been staying in the ten months we'd been involved. Miranda asked me how long he'd gotten trapped in Mariah and I told her I could verify it was at least until the middle of April, the last time I'd actually seen him, which was not long after we'd broken up at the beginning of April.

She asked me why we'd broken up. I explained some of the reasons for the breakup, telling her about the e-mail from Tuesday, April 2 in which Jonathan had told me that he was reviewing his options about what to do and that one of those options involved returning to Paladin. Miranda was surprised to hear that he was thinking about returning to Paladin when he was under such intensive legal investigation there. I commented that I wasn't sure he had actually returned, however, remembering, as I did, the oddity of seeing that many of his belongings that had remained packed since he'd moved to Mariah had been unpacked. Miranda said she had been trying to tune into his location and felt herself that he wasn't in Paladin. I also mentioned his saying in the e-mail that he was also thinking about taking the job in Asia, which made sense to her, since she believed the only real option left open to him was to get out of the country.

I told her more about my efforts to keep our relationship together, to help Jonathan while he waited out his sentence in Mariah, which included making 300-mile round trips not just once but sometimes twice a week just to make sure that he wasn't lonely and that someone was taking care of him.

"Which is fascinating," Miranda said, "'cause see, that's typical, too, of the problems he has." She paused, then said, "His whole presentation to me and to the people at work [was that] he's this great rock to this Glenn; he's the steady [one], he's the father figure, he's the nurturer..."

"Exactly, exactly. That's how he's presented his relationship with Glenn to me—that things were fine for years and years, then all of a sudden, Glenn fell apart and he's been trying to track him down and get him together and, you know, just take care of him."

"He was just *frantic* when he couldn't find Glenn and didn't know what was going on."

"Exactly."

"And he kept seeing Glenn dead—he kept telling me, 'I just know he's dead, I just know he's dead.'"

"He kept telling me that too."

"And I read that just through the psychosis that there was some part of him that *wanted* him dead. See, he scared me at one point, really... I mean, I hate to even say this on tape, but I'll just go ahead..."

"I could shut it off."

"No, that's okay. I... What creeped me out about the both of them..."

"Yes."

After a long pause, she finally said, "There was something really scary about the combination of the two of them."

"Yeah."

"It's the kind of stuff, you wonder if there's dead bodies somewhere. I'll be honest."

"Really."

"Or you wonder... Do you know what I'm saying?"

"Yes."

"Because Glenn would get into these visions of Jesus on the Cross—I mean, he told me. I had heard about some of this from [Jonathan]. And into this white supremacy stuff?"

At that point, I became *very* interested. "Really? Really?"

"You don't know this angle? Yeah, this white supremacy stuff. Oh, *yeah*."

I thought of *heilhitler*, the altered password. "That's very interesting; that's very interesting," I said, "because I think there's a tie-in with this."

"And homophobic stuff?"

"Oh, God, *yes*."

"Yeah."

I thought of the threatening letters I had received, the homophobia they had expressed. When I told Miranda about the changed password, she suddenly recalled that Glenn had told her that he believed that either he had been Hitler in a previous life or at least he was able to channel Hitler's spirit. Because of his homophobia and fixation on Hitler, I had suspected my ex-brother-in-law, but now, I realized that if *Glenn* had the same feelings and fixations, then they could just as logically have come from *him*...or from someone who had been *influenced* by him.

"I think it's got to be Jonathan... I don't think Glenn is smart enough to do it. But it's almost like Glenn and Jonathan are symbiosed," she said. "They're not separate from each other; they're ego extensions of each other."

"They're fused together somehow."

"They are. It's very weird. It is the oddest thing I have ever seen. I mean, it really is. And, I think that... When Jonathan first told me stuff about how Glenn was homophobic and he was this and this and this and he was, like, into this white supremacy stuff and he would, like, open up his windows and he would see visions of Jesus and he would yell things out, I thought, 'Oh, my God, this can't [be true].' But when I met him and he started telling me some of his own stories, he said he would just get into a car and drive and he would end up in [another state] or he'd end up in...he wouldn't even know how he got places."

"Yeah, yeah."

"I mean, there's a bunch of stuff that's really...scary."

"It sounds like either he's schizophrenic or has a dissociative disorder." I thought about Jonathan's assertion that *I* had a dissociative disorder. Now that I knew that *Glenn* appeared to have one, the connection between Jonathan's idea that an alternate personality had written the messages and the idea that Glenn might somehow be involved or influential seemed obvious.

"Oh, yeah. See, and I think they met, from what I can remember from what this place of business was telling me, they found that they *do* go way back, that they met in an institution in [the Southern state]."

"Really. Really. Okay." I was nonplused.

"Which makes total sense."

"It *does* make total sense."

"I mean, it really does."

I didn't know what to think. I certainly knew that Jonathan was disturbed and was now open to the possibility that his disturbance went back further than just a few months, but now to find out that he had actually been institutionalized at some point was difficult to take. How much of our relationship had been real and how much had merely been the acting out of his pathology—or worse?

I went on to describe some of the content of the letters I'd received. Since they had been mainly focused on my sister, I mentioned what Jonathan had said about her, how it seemed to tie together. "He's described her as my 'slut' sister; he thinks that my sister's a whore, basically, because she's been going through this divorce, but yet she's been seeing other people. I mean, she and her husband have been separated for a *year* now."

"*Please.*"

"He thinks she's a slut. And he hates my mother. Or has come to hate my mother."

"Why did he hate your mother?"

"Well, he seemed to like her okay up until..."

"He doesn't like *women*, is what it is."

"Yeah."

"He *uses* women. And, I think that it's under the guise of liking women, but he really doesn't."

"The only people he seems to want to be friends with are other gay men."

"Right, *right.*"

"He doesn't want to be friends with women, he has no interest in them."

"He *uses* them."

"He *uses* them."

"Well, he uses *everybody*, but he uses women in a different way."

"Uh-huh. And [gay men seem] to be the only kind of person he wants to be friends with."

"That makes total sense."

"Yeah, it does."

Even here, though, he always seemed to have something disparaging to say about most of them, generally commenting about their superficiality or silliness or selfishness and seeming to have something positive to say only when he was sexually interested in one of them or using such comments to create jealousy or otherwise manipulate.

In talking further about the dynamics of our relationship, how I had gone to such lengths to help him, Miranda said, "And he always finds good people."

"Oh, yeah."

"Except for the Glenns. I think Glenn is a matching picture to his dark side…"

"I think that's true."

"And it's also someone he can feel superior to."

"Oh, he *loves* to feel superior to others."

"And control, try to control."

"Right."

"And then he finds really good people, from what I can understand from the pattern, he does, he's very good at attracting in very nurturing, good people. Very *pure* people."

"And I don't mean to sound like I'm Mother Theresa, but I take care of people."

"No, but you're a good person. I mean, you have my identical numbers. I mean, that's what's even freakier to me."

I chuckled.

"We have identical numbers, in numerology."

"Really?"

"Yeah. There's some kind of real big tie-in. If I'm remembering right, too, the woman that connected him to me, I think she might have been born on my birthday. The same thing. This whole thing is karmic. There's something about the whole thing…"

"Yeah, there has to be."

"…that's wild."

"There has to be."

"I don't think this has all happened…"

"No."

"…for no reason."

"There's a reason. And good will come out of it."

She wanted me to continue my story about why we'd broken up and asked me if Jonathan had ever gotten physical with me. He never had, and being much shorter, heavier, and more out of shape than me, I had never felt physically intimidated by him. I had put up with a lot from Jonathan—too much—but if he *had* ever hit me, it would have been the *last* thing he would have done.

Miranda wasn't surprised. She felt that Jonathan was actually masochistic, the abused rather than the abuser. I had trouble believing that Glenn's violent behavior had come out of the blue, as Jonathan had described, and believed that it actually went back further than the period shortly before their breakup. Although I couldn't prove it, I felt, based on my understanding of the dynamics of abusive relationships, that the violence had gone on for a long time.

Miranda returned to her experience of seeing Glenn. In the process, she said something small but interesting that tied in with comments that Jonathan had made to me the summer before. "He dyed his hair red," she said, implying that the color held some special significance. *I* thought about Jonathan's comments about my "peachy" hair and, more to the point, Chase's comment about my being "red-haired," a comment that was meant as an insult. I was beginning to wonder if Chase had said anything to that effect at all, if it was in fact *Jonathan's* opinion expressed in Chase's name. Perhaps my hair had reminded him of Glenn and whatever else that implied.

"Interesting person," she said, referring to Glenn. "I mean, he was. I kind of felt sorry for him."

"Mmhmm."

"But the weird thing was—I'll never forget this as long as I live—'cause [Jonathan] sat in there," she said, pointing toward the hallway, "He was shocked. When he came in, I think he was really under the impression... He put on this big front, 'Oh, you know, I really want you to talk to Miranda.' And [Jonathan] told me in private, 'Oh, he'll never talk to you by himself.' [But Glenn] didn't want Jonathan in here."

"Interesting."

"And it freaked [Jonathan] out. I could feel it from the other room."

"Yes."

"I could just feel him, like, run the gamut of, like, fear, jealousy...the whole thing. And [Glenn] was, like, whispering, he was telling me, 'I've got to get away from him...'"

Continuing, she said, "But I saw definitely when I talked to [Glenn] there were, like, four or five personalities. Very street type of person, which you can imagine. Kind of a hustler. Street hustler. And I was shocked; he did verify some of what Jonathan had told me... 'Cause also he went into this thing about how he had this vision and how he just *knew*... He was in this hotel room and he saw Jesus on the Cross... I mean, this whole thing."

"Okay?"

"*God.*"

"And talking about, you know, queers—I mean, he used that term..."

"Really?"

"...talking about 'queers,' talking about 'faggots,' 'black people'...I mean, [whatever], just, oh, my God..."

"Well, see, Jonathan is very bigoted himself, too," I commented.

"Well, of course."

"I mean, he says he doesn't have a problem with gays, of course, but he has a problem with everybody else."

"He has a problem with *everybody* else."

"He does, he does—it's *everybody* else."

"I mean, look at the things he was saying about *me*."

"I know, I know."

"I mean, just the denigrating way..."

The phone rang, which she answered. When she was through, she expanded on her comment about "the institution."

"[Glenn's] the one who told me more, until I found out more from the people at the work situation, something about [the Southern state] and the institution. And I was shocked. And I *know* that's why [Jonathan] was freaking out. He was like, just, see, 'cause he never...I think he thought he was going to drag him here...'cause he was still trying at this point to present him as his *son*, okay? And so you can *imagine* how freaked out he must have been when he wasn't in here to control whatever. And [Glenn] told me later, he goes, 'I was so shocked that he took to you because he does *not* like women.'"

She returned to the subject of Glenn's disappearances. "Did [Jonathan] tell you something about Glenn disappearing and he found him, like, at the Y or something or with this group of people and they were doing drugs or some kind of story like this? Or did he tell you about something I had predicted and I had said you're going to find him, something about this bridge... Did he ever tell you any of these stories?"

I hadn't heard that before. "The only thing he told me about Glenn disappearing before was—before this last time he was supposed to have disappeared—was something about how there was a couple of times before they broke up that he disappeared for maybe two or three days at a time and then came back and he wasn't sure where he went and he thought he went maybe on a sex binge or something like that. He wasn't real specific about it, but that's what he told me."

"Sex binge," she repeated under her breath, laughing a little.

"Yeah, that he went..."

"Probably."

"Probably."

"Probably trying to get away from him. He would say, he said, 'He's driving me [crazy]. I mean, I'm telling you, at one point, I was ready to go out that door and just *scream* because I was freaking out. But, I've done this for [years] so I've heard it all."

"Exactly."

"But at one point I had to keep myself from laughing because I was just, like, 'Fuck *Survivor*—put a camera in *this* guy's life...'"

"That's right!"

"[He's] whispering. And then one voice is telling me about niggers, queers, [whatever], and then he looks at me and goes, '*He's* crazy.'"

"Oh, my *God*."

"I know! And I was sitting here going, "Oh, *no*—this is *nuts*."

"Oh, my God."

"Yeah."

"Oh, my God."

"At one point he just rotated energies and was just like...it was all coming out. And it was, like, just *wild*."

She paused. "See, [Glenn's] not in England. I do wonder what happened to him, though."

"Yeah, so do I."

"Now, did you ever see blood on the wall in that [bedroom]?"

"No, I actually never did... I wasn't in that room too much until he finally moved out."

"Did he ever go into any of this psychic stuff about that he felt that spirits were in that house and they attacked this rug? Remember I told you the rug story?"

"Yeah. No, he never said that to me."

"Did he ever tell you about any of the alien stuff?"

The day that he'd met Kathryn, we'd briefly discussed our beliefs about extraterrestrial life, but we'd never discussed them after that.

"I kept picking up this reptoid thing with him," Miranda said. "Very reptilian. And before I ever told Jonathan that, he was telling me how [Glenn] saw him turn into this reptile." By *reptile*, she meant a Reptilian, one of a group of militaristic aliens that some believe are secretly visiting Earth.

"Really?"

"Yeah. So there was another added—and I don't want to freak you out—there was another added thing with all that."

It *didn't* freak me out because, apart from the fact that I had a background in psychology and was well aware of different mental disorders, what I was hearing simply fitted neatly into the picture that was now emerging of someone who was suffering from a psychotic disorder, something that Jonathan had tried to hide.

Miranda commented on how she and others were amazed at how Jonathan, regardless of what he did, always seemed to be able to evade any responsibility or repercussions for his behavior. That had led Miranda to wonder if, apart from the fact that he was so brilliant, he had actually been some kind of government operative, with special skills or connections that helped keep him out of trouble. I didn't know if that was true, but her perception intrigued me because I remembered a comment that Jonathan had once made to me to the effect that he thought he would like to be a secret agent who slept with people to get information out of them, like Mata Hari.

Miranda was stunned that her perception had so closely mirrored something Jonathan had actually told me. She also mentioned that, like Jonathan, Mata Hari had been a Scorpio.

"Oh, God!" I said. "I feel like *I'm* the one getting stung here!"

"You poor thing!" She then went on to explain that "there's always a receptivity between the water signs, especially Cancer and Scorpio. It would have been very easy to get pulled into this." Interestingly, Miranda herself was a Scorpio and I had felt an instant rapport with her.

"I think in some ways you couldn't have avoided this," she assured me.

"Yeah."

"The good news is, you'll never go through this again," she explained, "but not because you're going to be bitter. I think your lesson is—look at your whole life—anything you can find out about your conception, gestation, birth, [infancy], childhood, what your parents' relationship was like, your early life—and then look at your history with relationships—what's been the same, what's been different, what's the [consistent theme]."

"Yeah."

"Where have you encountered a Jonathan, where have you encountered this before. Does this remind you of your father, your mother, what is the familiar hook, what was the same, what was different. It's really going to give you an opportunity to get a big picture and see what there really is about this, of why you attracted the drama."

Given my background in psychology, I certainly could appreciate and accept the fact that something within me, some kind of weakness, negative tendency, or damage, had drawn me into the situation and had kept me trapped there, like a fly in a web, until some force that was strong enough to counteract the ensnarement had pulled me free.

In helping me to understand why I had become ensnared in the drama that was Jonathan's life, Miranda went beyond my present life. "I feel it's very past life; I feel you've known him before. I think that you were like a matching picture to a higher part of himself; this Glenn had been a matching picture to his…dark self. And I think that when that started to break up—because I do believe that was a very long-term relationship from what I can gather from people, that they had been around together for quite a while…"

"Yeah."

"…when the dark part of him that, I think, for a long time he could control got *out* of control…"

"Mmhmm."

"See, 'cause I've often wondered, too, if there wasn't some type of violent… I don't know; it worries me. I felt it at the time. You know, I wondered if this Glenn hadn't hurt somebody or killed somebody, if there hadn't been some kind of weird thing that Jonathan…I don't know—some really… But I think that when that started to fall apart, then what he did, or does, he found *you*. You were like a matching picture to a higher part of himself and you brought out *good* things and stabilized him for a while."

"Yeah."

"And it's the same thing with, like, the Lauras or the people—he finds people that can, like, for a while, keep that [under control for him]. He was just devastated; I mean, he just sat here and cried on the floor at one point with this Glenn thing."

"Really."

"And I knew it wasn't about what it appeared to be."

"Yeah—that it was more about him than about Glenn," I offered, meaning that his relationship with Glenn was critical to his psychological stability.

"Yeah."

"It makes a lot of sense."

In the end, the image of Glenn that Miranda painted, someone who had actually seen him and had no reason to present him in a particular light, differed markedly from the image of the upper-class Englishman that Jonathan had given to me. I still didn't understand if Glenn had schizophrenia alone or a combination of schizophrenia and dissociative identity disorder, but it was obvious that Glenn was severely mentally ill and that while one of them alone would have been bad enough, the combination of both Jonathan and Glenn *was* indeed "scary."

Miranda then tried to remember what, if anything, Jonathan had said about me. "And...I'm trying to remember if he brought up [your name]..." After a pause, she said, "Your birthday sounds familiar to me. See, I think... I'm going to have to grab my other [appointment] book and I'll call you back and tell you when he was here exactly that last time. I probably have a bad check."

At the time, the "bad check" comment didn't register the way it should have, but later, I learned that Jonathan had written Miranda a bad check for a lengthy reading, something that cost almost $200. That, I assumed, was for the reading he'd had with her at the beginning of October—the last time he had seen her.

Miranda returned to the relationship between Jonathan and Laura. "Did he tell you that story, too, about that woman in St. Alban, that he was, like, involved with her?"

"No, he made it sound like it was a very *Will & Grace* kind of situation where he was Will and she was Grace and even though they were sleeping in the same bed they weren't doing anything."

"Okay."

"[But] she was trying to seduce him and she was saying she wanted them to be together and this whole thing even though she knew he was 100% gay. And he was trying to say that he was having to pay for everything around there and all this..."

"Yes, he told me that story. And he called me panicked one time, actually, about the sex. [He said,] 'Look, I don't know what I'm going to do 'cause just all she wants is all this sex.'" Laughing, she said, "And I was like, '*What?*'"

"*God.*"

"But I almost felt like he was trying to make me jealous. And, see, all of it was just *insane*. I mean, it was just—got more bizarre..."

Then, under her breath, she said, "I wonder if I still have that..." and got up from the couch and went to a shelf that stood behind me.

As she went, I said, "He tries to make people jealous."

"*All* the time," she said.

"He tried to do that with me." And, unfortunately, sometimes he'd succeeded.

"And, see, I don't get that because I'm not a jealous person; I don't think that way."

"No."

"I mean, I don't want to live [like that]."

"But that's just part of the manipulation."

"I'm going to show you this too. I just thought about this. This is something he gave me."

While I stayed seated on the couch, I watched her remove a small white box.

I gasped. I recognized the box all too well.

"This—supposedly, he had three scarabs that this guy…"

"I *have* one."

"I knew it. That's why I [wanted to show you this]."

"Do you want me to show it to you? I've got it in my car."

"Yeah."

"Okay. I'll be right back."

I hurried out to my car and retrieved the box containing the scarab from the box of Jonathan's things I still carried in the trunk of my car then hurried back in.

Once I'd returned, she compared hers and mine. "I think I showed somebody mine and they said that they didn't think it was old."

"Uh-huh."

"Because they do reproduce [them]."

"Yeah."

"*But*, at the same time, it's like the same thing… That's why people that are, like, pathological are so good—a lot of what they tell you is *true*."

"That's true."

"They weave it…"

"They weave it [together]."

"It's all weaved in. And, for some reason, when he told me *this* story, I kind of believed it."

"Yeah, yeah."

"Not because I *wanted* to, I just thought, 'I don't know'."

"Right. Well, the story he told me about it was that he got it from his friend Harald…"

"Right."

"…who is an antiques dealer in England, that it came from the funeral wrappings of a mummy that had recently been acquired by a…"

"Something to do with a museum…"

"…a museum in Berlin."

"Right. Yeah, yeah, yeah, it was. That's what he told me, too."

"…this person, he was a scribe or some kind of bureaucrat…"

"Yeah?"

"…from the Middle Kingdom…"

"Yeah? Okay."

After absorbing that, she said, "The only thing that was weird to me about that, though—and I think he's tapping into past-life stuff because one time when I was doing a reading for him I got this real Egyptian—I do think we probably knew each other in Egypt; I think there's tie-ins with past-life stuff, too—but the thing is that's weird is when they do that, they don't usually *sell* things."

"Hmm."

"I mean, why would the guy have them is weird."

"Yeah."

"*But*, it happens."

"Yeah. I mean, I know there are artifacts that get through."

"Oh, yeah, there are lots because I have some stuff."

"Yeah."

"But it's an odd story. That makes sense—the Berlin stuff, that makes sense…I remember that too."

"So, yeah, I knew that there were three; there was one he gave me for my birthday last year. And then when…he was moving out of his house last summer, he had two more in his stuff that he showed me. So I know there were at least three altogether."

"See, that's what I'm trying to remember—when he gave this to me."

"Because this was first week of September, last week of August, first week of September, and he still had two in his possession at that point."

"Mmhmm."

"At least that *I* knew about."

"That's interesting to me, too, that he did name three, that there were three."

"Yeah."

"Hmm."

"Who knows?"

"It's *wild*."

"It is."

We returned to the reasons for the breakup. In the process, I told Miranda how my mother had been dragged into our final fight when Jonathan had claimed that he'd shown the letter she'd written to him explaining why he couldn't stay with us at Easter to Joanne and that Joanne's reaction to it had been to call it "self-serving." I asked Miranda if he'd ever mentioned the Tomlinsons, which apparently he hadn't, although she thought—but couldn't be certain—that he'd mentioned Chase.

When she wanted to verify that the Tomlinsons actually did exist, I said, "Presumably. I'm taking [Jonathan's] word for it…which is not good, but still. I've never had any direct contact with them at all, [so] I don't know." She then got the phone book and tried to find out if they existed *there* and I told her that I'd looked up numbers, but that I couldn't find anything. The Tomlinsons, despite their influence in Jonathan's life, remained in some ways as distant as ever.

Later, we discussed the events of the previous weekend that had culminated with Jonathan's claim that he had received the message from "Heorshema" that had threatened his safety, which he had used as an excuse for not meeting me, and that he'd shown the message to his psychiatrist (whom neither Miranda nor I believed he was seeing) who had allegedly told him that she thought it was me and that I had a dissociative disorder. Miranda was quick to point out that he was actually "telling it on himself."

In mentioning that the changed password to the accounts was *heilhitler*, Miranda suggested that I might have mentioned something to Jonathan at some point about my ex-brother-in-law's interest in World War II, in Adolf Hitler, and that Jonathan had seized on my ex-brother-in-law's persona to misdirect me away from him. In the almost year that I had known him, I had shared numerous details about my sister, my ex-brother-in-law, and the problems between them with Jonathan. In spite of his supposed mental confusion, he had never lost his ability to play a perfect game of *Jeopardy* or to remember hosts of minor details, especially if it proved advantageous. Until then, I hadn't considered the possibility that someone might be *pretending* to be my ex-brother-in-law, but now that my mind had been opened to the possibility, and to the possibility that it could have been *Jonathan*, it seemed plausible. After all, it wouldn't have been the first time that he had appropriated a real person's identity to manipulate or mislead. And, the fact that certain elements of my ex-brother-in-law's personality appeared to dovetail with those of Glenn's or Jonathan's—or "Jonathan-Glenn's"—may have made posing as him seem natural.

But if it *were* Jonathan, why would he do something like this? I knew that Jonathan was disturbed—and now Miranda had suggested that he was even more disturbed than I had ever suspected—but even so, that didn't mean his motives were incomprehensible, only unknown. To paraphrase Lord Polonius in *Hamlet*, although it was madness, there had to be method in it. Even the most bizarre psychosis had its own "logic." What was it here?

The messages that had been left in my mother's and my e-mail accounts suggested that the repayment of the money Jonathan owed me was the issue—and now, Miranda had informed me that he had stolen a substantial amount of money from a former employer. If that were true, then had this all been an elaborate scheme to create a "legitimate" reason for not repaying me? Although I had never expressed the concern to *Jonathan* that he wouldn't repay me if he turned against me, anyone reading my e-mails would have learned that I had been expressing that concern to friends as far back as January, when I had first begun to appreciate his deceitful side. By making it appear that I had divulged the truth to Andy, had tried to interfere in the fantasy that Jonathan had seemingly felt the need to perpetuate, a powerful motive for turning against me, for having nothing further to do with me, had been created. Indeed, one of the e-mails had stated that *I* was the one who didn't want to have further contact with Jonathan because he was such an awful person, making it look as if it were *my* wish when—as far as my money was concerned—nothing could have been further from the truth.

When hard feelings alone didn't seem to be sufficient reason for not repaying me, however, "Heorshema" had appeared, making his blatant threat of physical harm against Jonathan. Insisting that *I* was "Heorshema," an even more compelling motive for avoiding me had emerged. His intention to have no direct contact with me seemed emphasized by what I believed to be his bogus claim that he was in England, thousands of miles away, and wouldn't be back for two weeks. Although Jonathan had told me that his attorney would deal with me regarding any unsettled issues, including the repayment of the money he owed me, my requests for his attorney's name and contact information had so far gone unanswered—which suggested there was *no* attorney. I found it suspicious, too, that I had been locked out of my e-mail accounts on April 26—the day that Jonathan had claimed the money from the syndication of *Still Life* would be out of escrow and he no longer had an excuse not to repay me—and that after April 22, Jonathan hadn't contacted me again until May 12—the day after I had gotten back into my accounts and after the imposter had fully accomplished whatever he had set out to do. I wondered if an unrelated person would have conformed to such a "convenient" schedule. And, I still found it interesting that for someone who claimed his safety had been threatened by someone he believed had a violent alternate personality, Jonathan's reaction had been so nonchalant, almost indifferent—very different from the reaction he might be expected to have if he had genuinely believed the threat had been real.

Beyond that, Jonathan may have had other motives. Even though Andy didn't seem to believe what he had been told, viewing it as part of a "smear campaign" against Jonathan, perhaps that was, contrary to the purported aim, the desired effect. Because Andy didn't believe "me"—a reaction that he might have been manipulated into having, as he had been manipulated into so much else—I now appeared to be nothing more than a discredited slanderer who would not be believed if the *real* me *did* attempt to tell Andy the truth. I had threatened to do that as far back as January, and even though I ultimately hadn't, I wondered if Jonathan still feared that I might. If so, what he had done was a preemptive strike, destroying my credibility while bolstering his own. Of course, that assumed that Andy was a real person and not a figment of Jonathan's imagination which, if "he" *were*, then Jonathan could make "him" do whatever he wanted, serve whatever purpose he desired.

In addition, the letters I had received might have been, in part, a tool for Jonathan to vent his animosity toward me and my family with unrestrained force. The letters had referred to my "slut" sister and Jonathan had been referring to Kathryn in similar, if more subdued, terms for months. In addition, he had finally turned against my mother, whom he had previously seemed to like, because she had dared to question his belief in his superiority and had made other valid criticisms that had cut too close to the bone. I knew, however, that his animosity toward them ran far deeper than his insults to me would suggest. I still had many unanswered questions, but I was now beginning to see what had happened in the past month—the past year—in a different light.

In discussing Andy, Miranda said that Jonathan had never mentioned him. In response, I told her that in searching for information about him on the Internet, I had discovered that his name was an anagram of the name of a character from one of Shakespeare's plays...which made me wonder if "Andy" was even a real person. When I commented that maybe his parents had named him in reference to Shakespeare, Miranda disagreed and told me that Jonathan had actually told her about visiting Shakespeare's birthplace and generally seemed fixated on the Elizabethan era. I already knew that "Iain's" messages to Andy certainly suggested an even more princely and important background than the one that Jonathan had presented to me. She concluded that "Andy" was in fact a character that Jonathan had invented or one that his mind had invented for him.

If that were true, then that raised the frightening possibility that Jonathan was actually communicating with *himself*. As Miranda said, "That's even scarier! His personalities are *e-mailing* each other! *God!*" I didn't know, but I had found it interesting that one of Jonathan's aliases on the Internet had been "Gayman" (or "GayMan"), while Andy's was "Gayboi"—suggesting a desire to play out the father/son relationship he had tried to play out with Glenn.

We talked for a few more minutes about other details of the Andy situation, trying to understand it, trying to understand Jonathan, but when we were finally through, an hour and a half after we'd begun, I felt that I'd received all the information I could absorb for one day. Or longer.

Before I left, Miranda performed an aura cleansing on me and prayed for me. Whether it was purely psychological or something more, I was left feeling "supercharged," to use Jonathan's term for Miranda's environment. What happened that day was one of the most fascinating, memorable, and life-changing experiences I have ever had.

Miranda had said that something good would come out of my experience with Jonathan. I liked to believe it would. I didn't know what form that good might take, but I did hope that something good, constructive, positive, useful could be salvaged from the pieces left behind by the storm named Jonathan that had swept through my life.

■

When I left that day, I didn't realize that I had just embarked on an odyssey every bit as fascinating, unsettling, and life-altering as the one on which I had embarked almost a year before to the day when I had first encountered the person who called himself Jonathan.

—36—
STALKING JONATHAN
You never know who's sleeping next to you...

In the days that followed my conversation with Miranda, I replayed the recording of the conversation again and again in an attempt to assimilate the new, and radically different, information about Jonathan that I had received. Emotionally, the new knowledge produced a paradoxical effect within me, proving at once disorienting and liberating. The person I thought I knew I did not know at all, but my intuition that he was something other—worse—than what he appeared to be seemed vindicated.

Sometime shortly after I spoke with Miranda, I contacted the INS office in Paladin. Despite Miranda's insistence that Jonathan was not from England, I still believed he was—after all, if he selectively deceived different people about different things, then he might have told me the truth about where he was from, but deceived Miranda about it. I contacted the INS not simply to seek some kind of revenge—although I *did* relish the thought of getting both Jonathan and Warren into trouble in one fell swoop—but mainly to try to stop someone who was running amok with no restraints on his destructive behavior. If Jonathan *was* from England, I was going to do whatever I could to see him deported and delivered into the hands of his family, never to return to the States again.

I also decided to take a more direct approach in letting his family know what was happening. I didn't relish the thought of talking to them, though, because of the condescending, upper-crust attitude I expected to receive from them, but they needed to know how Jonathan was behaving and do something to stop him. To that end, I tried to find an "Edward Frazier" in Eiseley, but couldn't. I did find several "Edward Fraziers" in *London*, but none of them seemed to fit the profile of his father. When that failed, I wrote to my doctor, who not only was a physician, but also had gone to school in England. I thought he might know how to locate an English doctor. Kindly taking time out of his busy schedule, he called me and told me how I might be able to do it. I planned to do what he suggested, if nothing else worked. I still felt guilty about having lied to him about needing the Prozac for myself, even though I was the one who had ended up taking it, and I hoped that I could use his information to help stop the person on whose behalf I had needlessly lied.

Around the end of May, I tried to contact Joan Vogel to see if she could tell me where Jonathan had gone. We had already talked and she knew I was a friend, so I assumed she might be willing to help. When I called, I learned that she and her immediate family were on vacation in another part of the state and I was given the number. I called, but she wasn't there. I left a message, but she never returned my call. I didn't know why, but she proved not to be of help. I decided not to contact her again.

Around the same time, I did what I could to reclaim my money on my own. I e-mailed Jonathan to make him a deal. I told him to send me a cashier's check for the full amount that he owed me within two weeks and I would never bother him again. I received neither a response nor a check. Silence spoke for itself.

Once it became clear that Jonathan had no intention of repaying me, I decided to sue him. I had never sued anyone in my life and didn't want to start now, but I felt that I had no choice. I contacted a lawyer and spoke to his paralegal. She told me that I would need Jonathan's current address so an officer of the court could serve him papers. Since I didn't have it, I couldn't proceed until somehow I got it.

Over time, I slowly began to suspect that Jonathan had not actually left Mariah. First of all, when I had gone there to give him the spreadsheets, he had appeared to be *un*packing instead of packing, something that didn't make sense if he was preparing to return to Paladin in just a couple of weeks. Second, in his sex ads throughout the previous several months, Jonathan had usually said that he lived not *in* the place he actually did, but *near* the place he actually did, and the ads he was posting largely revolved around the Mariah area. For example, on Tuesday, April 16, he had posted an ad under an alias in which he had said that he was living in a small town just outside Mariah. In addition, on Friday, April 26—the day that I had allegedly contacted him to tell him that I had contacted Andy— he had posted a response to his April 16 ad under another alias.

Everything taken together suggested that Jonathan was in fact not only in the Mariah area, but also still in Mariah itself.

To verify this, the simplest thing to do would have been to drive to Mariah and see for myself. I was *not* going to do that, however, primarily because I now had an emotional resistance to making the drive that I had made far too many times. So, I decided to take a different tack. By that point, I had downloaded some e-mail tracing software that, using the Internet Protocol (IP) address that was included in the header of every e-mail, would allow me to determine a sender's general location, if not his street address. I had already started comparing the IP addresses of some of the e-mails Jonathan had sent to me and had discovered they had not always been sent from the places he had said he was. I already knew, from checking the Internet history on his computer, that he had actually been in Mariah on March 18 and 19, when he had said he was in Paladin with the Tomlinsons. Later, he claimed that he had spent Easter with the Tomlinsons and had been there when the fight that had ended our relationship had erupted, but using the tracing software, I discovered that he had actually been in Mariah during that time. His stories about his job interviews and undoubtedly, much of the rest of his activities in Paladin during that time—and probably others—had been fabricated.

Without hard proof, I had no way of knowing if he had, in fact, left Mariah, but the circumstantial evidence was mounting that he had not.

Around the time I was looking into filing the lawsuit, I decided to answer one of his ads, which he seemed to be posting with increasing frequency. My primary purpose in doing so was to obtain the IP address from which he was *now* sending e-mails so I could trace it. Although it wouldn't allow me to obtain his street address, it might at least give me a better idea of where he was located. And, to be honest, I wanted to see how well I could deceive him into believing I was someone else. I had deceived him as "Chaz" and less elaborately as two other respondents, but I hadn't tried to do that since I had answered the ad through which I had discovered that Jonathan was posing as Cliff. The thought of conning the con—especially if I could get useful information that I could use against him in the process—was irresistibly appealing.

On Tuesday, May 28, Jonathan posted an ad in which he stated that he and his boyfriend were looking for men with whom to have group sex. In the ad, he described himself as looking very different than he actually did, making it clear that he had no intention of meeting anyone. At first, he said that "they" lived *near* Paladin, but in a subsequent posting stated that "they" lived *in* Paladin, suggesting "they" did neither. He resurrected the factory worker persona that he had used on occasion since September, claiming that he and his boyfriend preferred to meet during the day because "they" both worked second shift. He ended the message with the fraudulent promise that "they" were "real."

Pretending to be a man named "Darin," I responded to the ad using an e-mail address he didn't recognize. He replied and we began an exchange. The exchange proved interesting for more reasons than one.

First, he replied as "Alcuin," using the e-mail address that I had believed was a legitimate one belonging to Jonathan's favorite nephew. Now, I knew it was just as fraudulent as the ones that he had created through which to pose as Colin and Cliff. To see how Jonathan would react, I wrote back, commenting that his name sounded British and asking him if he was.

When he responded, he told me that Alcuin was a "friend"—not a nephew—of his whose e-mail account he had "permission" to use. That now raised the number of accounts Jonathan claimed he "shared" with others to *three*. His explanation for *why* he was using his "friend's" account instead of his own was even more interesting. He claimed that he had recently had problems with someone he'd met on the net—a "psycho" named "Richard." He claimed that Richard had been "stalking" him, had hacked into several of his friends' e-mail accounts, had been harassing him and them, and had generally been wreaking havoc in his life. He apologized for all the "cloak and dagger shit," as he called it, but warned that "you never know who's sleeping next to you" and that you had to be careful. I had to agree.

I didn't know how to take his response. The story that he had begun to develop about me a few weeks before had grown worse. I didn't understand, though, what was happening in his mind. Miranda had suggested that it was actually Jonathan, not my ex-brother-in-law, who was the person I would in time come to call The Pretender. But if that were true, was Jonathan now spreading his story about me to others as yet another way to wreak havoc in my life? Or did he know, or suspect, that "Darin" was actually me? He knew that I had the ability to identify his sex ads and had tricked him as "Chaz" and and two other respondents. If he believed it *was* me, was this his way of letting me know that and attacking me in the process?

But what if he *didn't* know or suspect it was me? What did *that* mean?

Did he actually *believe* what he was saying? That thought was more disturbing. I already knew that the fantasies he created about his life became half-real to him, that he half-believed them, if not more. He seemed to believe them in a way that a normal person wouldn't, possibly couldn't. We all had the ability believe "truths" about ourselves, our lives that on some level we knew weren't true, but with someone like Jonathan, the process seemed to work much more efficiently, even ruthlessly. Whether consciously or semi-consciously he fabricated self-flattering or satisfying fictions about himself or others that he knew weren't true, but over time, he came to believe them so completely that through self-reinforcement and the unwitting reinforcement of others they acquired the force of truth. They *had* to in order to fulfill their ego-gratifying function. And, the time it took for fantasy to become reality could be shockingly short. Within just a few weeks, I had been recast as a dangerously psychotic villain who was trying to destroy his life. His *fantasy* life, it seemed. Whatever his original motive for contriving his story about me—whether it was to create a legitimate reason, in *his* mind, for not repaying me the money he owed me or something else—it now appeared to be serving other purposes.

On a practical level, however, Jonathan's psychological problems didn't matter. It didn't appear that I would be able to reclaim my money without legal intervention.

On the evening of May 30, the night was warm, but it was also veiled by storm clouds that hid the stars from view. The Scorpion lay beyond, unseen. By then, Mars had traveled to the other side of the solar system, but Pluto, moving far slower, had barely budged. Like Jonathan, it was out there, somewhere, invisible but still exerting its influence.

Around the same time, I received my credit card statement for May. Because of all the drama that I had endured throughout the month, I had completely forgotten that the storage facility would charge me another month's rent at the beginning of the month. Now, with interest, Jonathan owed me at least $4,000. Minus the $360 he had paid me in November, I now owed for the cost for the moving van ($311.24), the cost for nine months' of storage for his things ($2,119.55), January and February rent ($1,300) and miscellaneous expenses ($250). Except for February rent, which had been drawn from my checking account, all of the charges had been placed on my credit card and, throughout the previous nine months, had been accruing interest at an average rate of more than 20%. His $360 didn't even pay for the interest, let alone any of the balance. I now owed more than $6,000 on my credit card, the most I had ever owed. When I got my statement for May, I immediately called the storage facility and told them to stop charging my account. In the process, I found out that Jonathan had still not gotten his belongings out of storage. I didn't know what would happen to his things now that no one was paying to store them and I didn't care. That day was the day that I officially stopped paying for Jonathan, although I had paid far more in other ways.

Partly because I needed more information and partly because I was angry, I later decided to answer an ad that Jonathan had posted under the alias "2Hot" on June 10. In this ad, he claimed he was from a small town near Winford that he had also mentioned in an ad from mid-April. Pretending to be a young man named "Kevin"—or "Kev," for short—who was interested in the three-way "2Hot" had proposed, I answered the ad on June 11. The same day, Jonathan responded.

Actually, it wasn't "Jonathan" who responded, but "Colin." Jonathan wasn't replying from the address that he had used to pretend to be Colin to Andy, but from yet another e-mail address that I didn't recognize. Neither did I recognize the IP address from which the message had been sent. When I entered it into the tracing program, however, I discovered that the message had originated in the Mariah area. That did not mean, though, that he was *in* Mariah— he could have been somewhere different, if nearby—but it suggested, strongly, that he had *not* returned to Paladin.

This time, he—or, rather, "Colin"—revealed none of the paranoia that he had previously displayed over Richard, the psycho. So, I continued to play along. I, as "Kev," wrote back and asked "Colin" if he wanted to meet in Winford. He said that he did and added that he had a "friend" who also wanted to join in. The name of this "friend" was *Glenn*. For the next several days, we engaged in a salacious exchange that clarified specifically what we would do and where we would do it. We eventually agreed to meet at a motel in Winford on the 16th—Father's Day, or "Daddies' Day," as "Kev" suggestively called it. I knew that "Colin" would come up with some excuse at the last minute to get out of making good on our plans and I waited to see what it was.

True to form, around 1:00 Sunday afternoon, "Kev" received an e-mail from "Colin" in which he told him that he couldn't meet. Until then, "Colin" hadn't mentioned what he did and explained that he couldn't meet because of something that had come up at work. Apparently, he had gotten paged to come to the *hospital*, where one of his oldest patients had been taken after she had suffered an accident. It wasn't serious, but she panicked easily and "Colin" had to be there to comfort her. "Colin" explained that although he had done rounds early in order to leave him free for the rest of the day, he had felt compelled to take the page even though he wasn't on call. He told "Kev" that if starting later was a problem, he was off on Thursday that week, wasn't on call Saturday, and had third call the next Sunday. Glenn, apparently, was willing to be flexible as well, since both of them really wanted to have sex with "Kev." "Colin" urged "Kev" to let him know what he wanted to do, telling him that he could check e-mails from the hospital.

So. "Colin" was a doctor. Just like his father.

"Kev" wrote back and, seeming disappointed, told "Colin" that he understood. *I*, however, wasn't disappointed at all. I had managed to determine that Jonathan was probably still in the Mariah area and to have a little fun deceiving the deceiver. I didn't plan to continue the exchange and didn't expect to hear from "Colin" again.

I was wrong.

On Wednesday, the 19th, "Kev" received another e-mail from "Colin." In it, "Colin" said that he knew "Kev" was angry about the previous weekend but assured him that he and Glenn were "real" and still wanted to meet. Jonathan didn't seem to have the faintest notion that *I* was "Kev," and since I found the idea of deceiving Jonathan just a little more irresistible, "Kev" responded. "Kev" assured "Colin" that he wasn't mad, just disappointed and still wanted to get together too if "Colin" was in fact "real." "Kev" also complained that "a lot of people online [were] just full of bullshit and just [gave] you the runaround." "Colin" wrote back, saying that he had been "messed with" before, too, and had "show[n] up with nobody to meet." He again assured "Kev" that he was "for real" and added that "Kev" was the kind of guy that "I(we) like to have fun with"—a slip-up that Jonathan had made before, but never corrected, when he temporarily forgot that others were supposed to be involved in the scenario. "Colin" concluded by saying, "I want to do this, for real."

"Kev" wrote back, telling "Colin" that after things hadn't worked out between them on Sunday, he had answered another ad from someone who had wanted to meet at the bathhouse in Paladin to have sex. Unfortunately, after "Kev" had driven to Paladin and spent quite a bit of money on a room, the man had never showed. "Kev" told "Colin" that he didn't want the same thing to happen again, not that week, because he wasn't in the mood. "Kev" added that he hoped "Colin" was "for real" because he wanted "real, not bullshit."

In response, "Colin" did something stunning: He gave "Kev" his phone number.

"Colin" claimed that it was his cell phone number "through our clinic in…"—of all places—"Mariah." He said "Kev" could call him "to confirm or just to check up" and again assured "Kev" that "they" were "real."

At first, I didn't know if that was Jonathan's real number or just one he'd fabricated to placate "Kev." His phone had been disconnected for the last six weeks of our relationship, but perhaps he had finally acquired the funds to have it restored. If that *was* his real phone number, then perhaps *it* could be traced. I had to find out.

I thought briefly about asking a gay friend of mine to call the number and, if it proved to be valid, to pretend to be "Kev." I thought that in doing so, he might be able to find out, specifically, where Jonathan was living. Ultimately, though, I decided against it because I didn't want to get my friend involved in my mess. I decided to call myself.

I didn't call from home because I didn't want my name and number appearing on Jonathan's caller ID. That summer, I was once again teaching the psychology class that met in Viridian on Monday and Friday afternoons, so after teaching the class on the afternoon of Friday, the 21st, I drove to a town near Viridian that had no connection to me and called the number from a pay phone. Unfortunately, I received a message telling me the phone was currently unavailable.

Frustrated, I finally decided to call him from home. I wasn't going to keep going out of my way to call him from phones whose numbers couldn't be connected to me. I decided that I didn't care whether my number showed up on his caller ID or not. If it did, then perhaps it would also make him wonder how I had gotten *his* number. Would he make the connection between giving "Kev" his number, then receiving a call, only two days later, from me?

I *had* to know if the number Jonathan had given to me was "real." So, when I got home later that afternoon, I called the number Jonathan had unwittingly given to one of my multiple "personalities."

After several rings, a breathless voice with a British accent said, "Hello?"

A voice I knew all too well.

The sound of his voice left me feeling as if I'd received a mild electrical shock. Immediately, I hung up. I was stunned and sickened, but also exhilarated. Although I still didn't know where he was, I did know that at least the number he had given to "Kev"—me—was "real."

After I settled down, I sent "Colin" an e-mail in which "Kev" complained that he had tried to call him several times, but that every time he had, he had gotten a message that said the phone was unavailable. "Kev" insisted on knowing if that was "really" "Colin's" number and stated that he wouldn't meet unless he could talk to him first. *I*, however, already had *my* answer to that question.

The next day, "Colin" wrote back and lamely explained that *was* his number but that sometimes he forgot to turn his phone on. He explained that if he was "on duty," he left it off. He assured "Kev" that if he gave him a time when he'd be available, he would be sure to leave it on. "Kev" wrote back and suggested sometime between 7:00 and 10:00 that evening.

Around 7:00, however, "Kev" received an e-mail that was a perfect abstract of Jonathan's tactics. He began by telling "Kev" that although he knew they had settled on a time to talk, there were two other men who were ready to meet him and Glenn at a nightclub that night to "hook up" if they liked each other. "Colin" assured "Kev" that he was their first choice, but on the off chance they didn't connect, they wanted to meet up with the other two, who seemed to be a surer thing. "Maybe in the future," "Colin" offered. He told "Kev" that other men had stood him up but assured him that he and Glenn were "real people" and *did* show up. He comforted "Kev" by telling him that he had been stood up before but that you got over it and found someone more reliable. He then reaffirmed that he had done the right thing the Sunday before by being there for a longtime patient whom he cared about. He told "Kev" that if he still wanted to get together to let him—them—know. Reminiscent of what "Iain" had told "Chaz" in October about going away on business in a few days and not being available for more than a week, "Colin" told "Kev" that he would not be available Tuesday through Saturday of the upcoming week. Reminiscent of the compliment that "DoIt" had given to "doittome" at the end of their lengthy exchange, "Colin" ended the message by telling "Kev" that he was sure that he was "hot and fun" and hoped they did get together.

I was touched by his concern for "Kev's" feelings and, especially, for the moral rectitude he had displayed in choosing to care for a sick, scared, elderly patient rather than be led astray by the promise of carnal pleasure.

"Kev" had no further contact with "Colin." "Kev" had gotten a kind of satisfaction that was far more gratifying than anything sexual.

As soon as I determined the number "Colin" had given "Kev" was "real," I contacted a private investigator to see if he could trace the number. After several days of waiting, however, the private investigator's secretary informed me that the number was untraceable because it had gone through a reseller. Unfortunately, that made the number useless to me as a way of finding Jonathan.

I didn't want to make the 150-mile drive to Mariah to determine whether or not he was actually still there, but given my lack of alternatives, I was beginning to suspect that was exactly what I was going to have to do.

During the last week of June, a man named Dwayne responded to one of my personals ads. Although he lived in another state, he occasionally came to Hawthorn and thought that perhaps we could meet. Because I didn't want him to drive all that way, we eventually decided to meet somewhere in-between. Our mutual destination, as it happened, lay only 40 miles from Mariah. In the previous months, I had driven that route more times than I had cared to count and, therefore, I would have no difficulty finding the spot where he wanted to meet. We planned to meet on Saturday, the 29th, the weekend of my birthday.

Saturday afternoon, I left for the place where we had arranged to meet. My itinerary took me through Paladin, and as I drove along the miles of streets, past thousands of houses, I wondered if Jonathan was living in one of them. I had no way of knowing. On this evening a year before, I had known exactly where he was: the house on Millstone Drive, with me. Now—possibly—he was lost, on the loose, in the midst of a vast metropolis.

I arrived at our meeting place sometime around 7:00. I met Dwayne, who was pleasant and friendly, and we became comfortable with each other almost at once.

Knowing that it was my birthday, he thought it was only right that he treat me to dinner, so we went to a nearby restaurant. It was during the conversation over dinner that the events of the previous year spilled out.

I concluded by telling him that I didn't believe Jonathan had actually left Mariah. He suggested that since we were only 40 miles away, we go and see for ourselves. I agreed.

We left around midnight. On the way to Mariah, I let him listen to the tape of my conversation with Miranda, which I had been keeping in the car and to which I listened on occasion while driving so I could continue to absorb it. He was even further astonished and dumbfounded by the complexity of the insanity into which I had unwittingly been drawn.

We arrived at the apartment sometime around 1:00. The garage was lighted, which Jonathan hadn't done while we'd been involved. His car was gone, but the belongings that he had stored in the garage were clearly visible from the street.

So it *was* true: Jonathan had *not* left Mariah.

He *had* been here all the time and had lied to me about having returned to Paladin. I felt triumphant. I had found him at last, and now that I had confirmed his current address, I could continue with my case against him.

I wondered where he was at 1:00 in the morning. Was he with the Tomlinsons? With Chase? With the guy who had greeted me at the door? *We* had certainly never stayed out until 1:00 in the morning on a Saturday night while *we* had been together. It was hard telling where he was, what he was doing, to whom he was doing it.

Since he wasn't home, Dwayne and I took the opportunity to snoop around, to see what we could see. I parked the car about two blocks away, out of sight, then we walked back. I looked into the garage and confirmed again that the things inside were indeed Jonathan's. I went around to the front door, which he rarely used, and peered into the shadows. Vaguely illuminated by the nearby streetlight, I saw the larger of the two lithographs, which he was supposed to have sold at auction, sitting on a table in the foyer. I felt like breaking in and stealing it then selling it myself to recoup my losses, but of course I didn't. I also wondered if the glass elephant that I'd given him for his birthday, which he'd never set out, was still sitting in its box in the foyer where he'd left it in November. If I had been able to get into the apartment, that *was* one thing that I would have taken, since he didn't deserve it.

I wondered if anyone was watching us. Although we weren't doing anything illegal—a little trespassing notwithstanding—I was afraid we looked suspicious. I was more concerned for Dwayne, who, despite having a Ph.D. and a respectable position, was still a black man prowling the streets of a backward town in the middle of the night. I was also afraid that Jonathan might return at any moment, so I thought we should keep our visit short, if not exactly sweet.

Before we left, I decided to leave Jonathan a "calling card." I wanted to let him know that I knew he had lied to me about having left Mariah and having returned to Paladin. I was still carrying his unclaimed belongings in the trunk of my car, including the rug that was coated with poodle hair and poodle piss as well as the boring, pretentious *Lucia* book he so understandably loved. I placed the book in the mailbox and spread out the rug in front of the front door. I knew he wouldn't find them at least until Monday, assuming he checked his mail, but he *would* find them nonetheless and know that he had been found and found out.

I went back to the hotel where Dwayne had rented a room buzzing with a feeling of exhilaration. Although it was 2:00 in the morning, I wasn't tired at all and spent an hour walking around in the parking lot and the adjoining area enlivened by the feeling that suffused me.

The next morning, Dwayne said that he knew I had been really hurt by Jonathan and that I didn't deserve it. I appreciated his understanding and kindness and really needed to hear that.

After Dwayne and I said our good-byes, I drove back to Mariah to see if Jonathan had returned. He had. I drove past quickly enough not to let him see my car but slowly enough to let me see *his* car parked in its usual spot in front of the garage. Apparently he wasn't away, as I had thought he might be, and was in fact very much in the area. I wondered where he had been the night before. Satisfied, I drove off and headed for home.

On the way back through Paladin, I stopped at Miranda's. I felt that I was being intrusive, since she wasn't expecting me, but I felt that I had to tell her what I had found. She was the only person I knew who not only knew the truth about Jonathan, but also had been caught up in the drama of Jonathan's life. Her intuition, as well as my suspicions, had proven correct and I wanted her to know this. In addition, I had information that I thought she might find helpful if she decided to file suit against him for the bad check he had written to her. The first words out of my mouth were, "He never left Mariah."

Since it appeared that she was about to go out and since I still had a long drive in front of me, I tried to keep the conversation short. We spoke for about half an hour, then I headed for home.

By the time I arrived, I was exhausted. Yet, I was also exhilarated because I had confirmed an important piece of information about Jonathan that helped me not only practically but also somehow psychologically. Knowing where he was made me feel more in control of a situation that was growing increasingly out of control. In more ways than one, that was a far better birthday present to me than a scarab could ever have been.

—37—
A VERY DANGEROUS MAN

The situation with Jonathan was as bad as it gets without it turning violent.

By the first week of July, more than six weeks had passed since my initial conversation with Miranda. At that time, Miranda had told me that her assistant would get me Cassandra's number, the woman who had informed her about the investigation, so I could speak with her myself. By the beginning of July, that hadn't happened. Miranda had made some provocative statements, to say the least, and I didn't want to believe them if they weren't true. I certainly didn't believe that Miranda was lying to me, but I *did* wonder if she might have been misinformed, either unintentionally or deliberately. I didn't know anything about Cassandra's credibility or motives and needed to speak with her myself to determine how solid her information was.

I also thought that whether or not the claim that Jonathan had stolen a substantial amount of money from an employer was true would have a definite bearing on whether or not I would be able to reclaim my own money. If it wasn't true, then perhaps I could do something, possibly with the help of a mediator, to break through Jonathan's hostility, irrationality toward me and make him listen to reason. Given what I had seen and suspected, I knew the hope was small, but I felt that if I could get him to talk to me, then maybe I could marshal my knowledge of psychology to penetrate his madness, in more senses than one.

But if the claim *was* true, then the chances of my reclaiming my money were slim. After all, if he didn't have any compunction about stealing tens of thousands of dollars from his company, then he wasn't going to have any compunction about not repaying a comparatively paltry $4,000. In addition, it appeared that he had gotten away with the crime he had committed. If the claim that he had stolen the money was true, then I wasn't dealing with a disturbed narcissist in pure form, but one in which the sense of entitlement that was central to the narcissistic personality had veered off into criminality. That would make things trickier. For more reasons than one, I needed to know.

Miranda had told me there were warrants out for his arrest, presumably in the county in which Paladin is located and presumably for his (alleged) criminal activity at work. Therefore, I decided to contact the police there to see if there was, in fact, a warrant out for his arrest in Paladin. On the morning of Monday, July 1, I called and spoke with one of the officers. After doing some searching, he could not, however, find any warrants that had been issued for Jonathan in Paladin.

I didn't know what to think about the results. There were at least two possibilities that occurred to me, given the information I had. First, there were no warrants for Jonathan's arrest and what Miranda had told me was wrong. Second, there *was* a warrant, but the officer simply couldn't find the record. Whatever the case, I wasn't getting the answers I needed, so I decided to take a more direct approach: I decided to contact Mike Harmon at OutSource and talk to him myself.

I had never had doubts that OutSource was a legitimate company or that Jonathan had actually worked there because Cassandra had confirmed that both were true. That was, after all, where she and Jonathan had met. I did have doubts, however, about the nature of the company or at least about its prestige. I had tried to find it listed in the Paladin Yellow Pages under various IT-related keywords, but had found nothing. Eventually, though, I found it listed in the *White Pages*. If it were a prestigious IT company, then why was it listed in an almost inconspicuous entry in the White Pages? I was beginning to have my doubts that it was even an IT company, although Miranda seemed to believe it was.

Shortly after I'd spoken to the officer about the warrants, I called OutSource. The secretary answered and I asked to speak to Mike Harmon. She put me through. That meant that a Mike Harmon did in fact work for OutSource and, therefore, might actually know something about Jonathan.

After a couple of rings, Mike answered. I introduced myself, then told him my reason for calling. I explained that I had heard that Jonathan had been accused of stealing money from his company and wanted to know if that was true.

At first, Mike seemed careful in the way he spoke to me. His answers were meticulously phrased. I knew that employers ran the risk of being sued if they said anything negative about former employees, especially if it implied criminal activity, so I thought I understood his reticence.

"He was involved in an insurance fraud scheme," he explained. "There were accounts in [the Southern state and the Midwestern state]. That's a matter of public record. He didn't collect any money. The insurance company is pursuing him."

I was confused. "So, he didn't steal money from your company?"

"No, I didn't say that," he said, as if he were under oath and trying not to misrepresent the facts.

I was still confused. Cassandra had told Miranda that Jonathan had stolen money from the company, but Mike denied it. I might have thought that Cassandra had mistakenly, if genuinely, believed that Jonathan had gotten away with money from his insurance fraud scheme, but Miranda had said that Cassandra had told her, specifically, that *cash* had come up missing. Had *both* happened?

"A woman named Cassandra told a friend of mine that Jonathan had stolen money from your company," I explained.

In response, Mike said something that stunned me. "That was the name on one of the accounts."

My God, I thought. Did Cassandra know about this? Was *she* somehow complicit in the fraud? It seemed more likely, though, that she was just another innocent victim whose identity Jonathan had appropriated to further his deceptions. Speaking to Cassandra became more urgent than ever.

Thinking the insurance company hadn't been able to catch up with Jonathan because he kept moving, I told Mike I knew exactly where he was living. Mike told me, though, that the insurance company had traced him to Mariah and knew he had worked for the hospital. By that point, seven months had passed since he'd lost the job at the hospital and I wondered how long the insurance company had known he was there. At any rate, they did. Mike's information lent weight to Miranda's speculation that Jonathan had lost the job because his criminal activity in Paladin had caught up with him in Mariah.

I wanted to know more about Jonathan's position at OutSource. "He told me he was the COO of your company," I said.

"No," Mike said. "He was a general manager."

General manager. Not COO.

I told Mike that Jonathan had told me that OutSource was an information technology company. Mike explained that OutSource was actually a human resources company. The company did help employers find workers for IT positions, but it wasn't an IT company itself. Therefore, Jonathan's position at the hospital, which their web site had described as a human resources position, was just a continuation of what he had done at OutSource. Now that I knew what he had *really* been doing at both the hospital and OutSource, Jonathan's work history made more sense—*much* more sense that *his* version did.

I told Mike some of what Jonathan had told me about his experiences at OutSource—being COO, making three-quarters of a million dollars a year, raising OutSource's profits 40% over expected each year, leaving the company because he had developed incurable endocarditis and could no longer handle the demands of his prestigious position...

Everything was a lie. Everything.

"You can believe only about ten percent of what he says," Mike said, beginning to let his personal opinions show through. Then, he added, "And you can't be sure about that ten percent."

When I mentioned the circumstances under which Jonathan had left, Mike told me that Jonathan hadn't even worked for him since March 2001, when he had terminated Jonathan's employment. Apparently, Jonathan wasn't fired because his fraud had been uncovered, which didn't happen until later, but because of something simpler. Mike explained that in February 2001, Jonathan had taken a leave of absence under the Family and Medical Leave Act because of an alleged medical condition—presumably, the *heart* condition. Under the provisions of the Act, Jonathan had to report back to Mike within 30 days or be terminated. He didn't, so Mike fired him.

I asked Mike how long he had worked for him. He couldn't remember exactly when he'd hired Jonathan without looking at his records, but he thought he'd hired him sometime in the summer of 2000. In other words, Jonathan had worked at OutSource for only six to eight months, not for almost two years.

In discussing his employment history, Mike confirmed that Jonathan had indeed worked for TekNetium in the Southern state in which he'd said he'd lived before coming to my state in the fall of 1999. He did *not* come, however, to work at OutSource, which he didn't start doing until months later. In reality, he had come to work at another company, one whose name I had heard before: *Intellex*.

I remembered the web site that I had found when I had tried to find a picture of Jonathan a few days after we met. Although I'd found the page out of context, the domain name contained letters that didn't relate to OutSource—something that, at the time, hadn't registered as it should have. I also remembered that after I'd told Jonathan I'd found the page, it had mysteriously disappeared—presumably at his behest. In addition, I remembered the day the previous July that we had gone to look at the penthouse. When the woman who had shown us the penthouse had asked him where he worked, he had said "Intellex." At first I had been confused—hadn't he told me, in some detail, that he worked at *OutSource*?—but then I had concluded, vaguely, that OutSource might be a division of "Intellex" and hadn't questioned it further. *Intellex* was the *information technology* company. Now I realized that Jonathan had simply taken elements of his jobs at both Intellex and OutSource and had fused and inflated them into a single grand affair in which he was second only to the CEO.

I also realized then that Cassandra had actually worked for *Intellex*, since Mike knew her not as an employee, but only as a name on a fraudulent insurance claim. Therefore, Jonathan had stolen the money from *Intellex*, *not* from OutSource, which was why Mike had denied that Jonathan had stolen money from *him*. To my shock, I realized that Jonathan had committed crimes at *both* places.

I thought about Miranda's contention that Jonathan was not really from England. I said to Mike, "He told me that he was from England. Do you think that's true?"

"I think he may have dual citizenship," Mike said. "The investigator found a piece of property in his name on a [certain street] in London." That was all he knew. The issue of whether or not Jonathan was actually British was still unresolved, although I still thought he was.

As far as property was concerned, Mike mentioned the fact that Jonathan had had "problems with landlords"—which I took to mean that he'd been failing to pay his rent. Knowing now that his "illness," his untreatable endocarditis, was just another lie, I began to question why he had *really* left the house on Millstone Drive. If he hadn't left because he could no longer live alone due to his illness, as he'd claimed to me, then perhaps he'd left because he'd been *forced* to leave—because he'd been *evicted*. Knowing, too, that he didn't have the funds he'd claimed he had, knowing that by the time he'd left he hadn't worked for months, and figuring that he might not have paid his rent even if he'd had the funds, it seemed more likely than ever that he'd been evicted. Yet *another* lie.

At some point, I mentioned Glenn. In response, Mike said, "Glenn actually worked for me."

"He did?" I was surprised to hear that Glenn had worked at all, let alone at OutSource. Jonathan had told me that Glenn hadn't worked while he had lived in the United States and that he had supported him because he didn't have a work visa that would have allowed him to do so.

"He did data entry," Mike explained. "Jonathan hired him as part of his team."

There were only two ways that Glenn could have legally worked at OutSource: Either he did have a work visa or…he was *American*.

I asked him if Jonathan had told him that Glenn was his son. He said that he had. I corrected him by telling him that Glenn was not his *son*, but his *boyfriend*. I received some satisfaction from exposing *that* lie. I also mentioned what I had learned from Miranda, that Glenn was intermittently psychotic and violent. Mike said nothing in response. Then again, what *could* he say?

Interestingly, Mike had his *own* stories about Jonathan's e-mail behavior. Mike said that in trying to straighten out the mess that Jonathan had created for him, he had found himself communicating with people by e-mail who he thought were real people, but who actually turned out to be Jonathan in disguise. I told Mike that Jonathan had been doing that on a personal level as well, pretending to be various people for deceitful purposes. Obviously, this behavior wasn't the pathological result of overwhelming stress, as I had come to believe, but part of Jonathan's modus operandi.

Mike described Jonathan as "deeply disturbed." Off the record, he told me that he had tried to help Jonathan with his "issues," as he called them. It became apparent to everyone after a while that he had "issues." I told Mike that I knew he had been going to the Stress Center, but Mike didn't comment or say specifically what he had done to help Jonathan. He did add, though, that it hadn't done any good. Obviously not.

I thought of the story that Jonathan had told me the summer before about "Ben," the troubled employee who had been siphoning off small amounts of money from the company but who had finally been caught. It was obvious now who "Ben" *really* was. I also thought of his e-mail to me in mid-October in which he had claimed that Mike was trying to help him obtain a private investigator to find Glenn as well as his story to me in November about how the police had been trying to find him to question him about possible enemies in the alleged murder of Ted Kanner's niece and her fiancé. It was obvious now, too, where the idea of a private investigator and a criminal investigation had *really* come from.

Mike said something that I found absolutely chilling, something that echoes in my mind to this day: "The situation with Jonathan was as bad as it gets without it turning violent. And I think it could turn violent. He is a very dangerous man."

In mentioning my intentions to reclaim my money, Mike said that by the time he was done trying to clean up the mess that Jonathan had made at his company, he had lost $57,000. *Fifty-seven thousand.* That made my relatively paltry *four* thousand pale in comparison. Knowing this, and knowing about Jonathan's indifference to the effects of his actions, I now realized that the chances of his repaying me were slim.

Mike told me that although he knew losing the money would hurt, I should just walk away from the situation. He also intimated that if I pushed Jonathan too far, I might push him to "turn violent," to use Mike's phrase. I had never seen Jonathan become physically dangerous, but I was certainly aware by now of how dangerous he could be in every *other* way.

After about twenty minutes, I thanked Mike for taking the time to speak with me and he politely told me it was no problem. Then we hung up.

My mind was left reeling, trying to recast the past year of my life in light of this new and *true* information. I thought of the incredibly elaborate, detailed stories that Jonathan had told me about his experiences at OutSource throughout the first several months that we were involved. In truth, by the time I met him at the end of May the previous year, he hadn't worked for several months. Everything Jonathan had told me about his experiences at work, about working, period, had been a lie. *Everything.*

I thought of the timings of the e-mails that Jonathan had sent to me on days when he had led me to believe he was working. He had sent them in the mornings, before he was supposed to have left for work, and in the afternoons, after he was supposed to have returned. If there was any deviation from this pattern, he was always careful to explain it. He had done the same thing with "Chaz" as "Iain." Whenever I had stayed with him on weekdays, he was always gone from mid-morning to mid-afternoon, telling me what he was going to be doing that day at work before he went and telling me what had happened that day when he had returned. If he hadn't spent his days at work, then where had he spent them? I knew he had been going to the Stress Center—that was, after all, where he had met Laura and "fat" Greg, who had confirmed that themselves—but was that the only place he had gone? Had he sometimes rendezvoused with men for sex? None of his sex ads from that summer seemed to indicate that he had, but those ads weren't the only ones through which he could have arranged to have casual sex. Or had he just been whiling away his days doing nothing of importance, all to give the impression that he was working?

Likewise, I thought of the Saturday night the previous July when Jonathan had claimed that Mike had called him to a late-night meeting at his home and had left for an hour. Obviously, he hadn't gone to Mike's. Where *had* he gone? Had he gone to rendezvous with one of the men he'd met through the Internet but to whom he was *not* going to give the runaround, as he normally did? Or was it merely another element in the charade that he had been enacting for me? I would never know, but I knew enough.

Finally, I thought of the incredibly elaborate, detailed stories that Jonathan had told me about his "illness," which had started three weeks after I'd met him and had continued throughout the remainder of our relationship. Indeed, his "illness" had largely defined our relationship and it was because I had believed he was seriously, perhaps terminally, ill that I had gone to such lengths to help him—loaning him thousands of dollars to pay his expenses, making 300-mile round trips to take care of him, tolerating behavior that, under normal circumstances, would have been intolerable, and generally turning my life upside down, *myself* inside out, for him. Everything that I had done for him, everything that I had done to myself, had been done for lies.

By that point, I had heard enough. Jonathan's pathology ran far deeper and his behavior was far more destructive than I had ever suspected. And he was running amok, wreaking havoc, and no one seemed to be able to stop him.

I knew what I had to do.

—38—
JOHNNY

His real name is Johnny.

After talking to Mike, I decided that I had to do something to try to contact Jonathan's family to make certain they knew what he had been doing and what had been happening. Jonathan had explicitly told me that he was keeping his family from knowing more about his actual condition than they wanted to know so they wouldn't intervene—*interfere*—in his life, but *I* felt that given everything I had learned and experienced, they needed to know as much as possible because other people were being harmed by his pathological and criminal behavior and perhaps they could do something to stop him.

Because I didn't know how to contact his parents or siblings in England, I decided to contact the one relative I did know how to contact: Terrence.

Jonathan had told me that Terrence was an artist who lived in the Northeast and I had found his web site not long after Jonathan and I had met. I recalled how the site had made the discrepant claim that Terrence was not from England, but from the Midwestern state, something that at the time I couldn't understand. Insofar as I had thought about it, I had eventually concluded that either it represented some kind of "artistic license" that he was taking with the facts of his life in order to project a persona that somehow gave him more credibility as an artist working in an American style or it was some kind of mistake. In addition, I recalled that when I had told him that I had found the site, Jonathan had criticized me for using the Internet to find information about his family, citing my lack of respect for his family's privacy, as he saw it, as "ill-bred." I knew now that his reaction had been that of someone who had something to hide. The same day I spoke to Mike Harmon, I called Terrence's professional number, using the information I had found on his site.

A woman answered and, after confirming that she was his assistant, I asked to speak to "Terrence." She asked me if I meant *Terry*. Terry? Confused, I simply repeated my request to speak to *him*. She asked me why I was calling. *If she only knew*, I thought. I explained that it was a personal matter. I mentioned that I was contacting "Terry" because his family lived in England and he was the only member of his family, aside from Jonathan, who lived in the States. In response, she said that his family lived in *the Southern state*.

The *Southern state*? I was even more confused.

She wasn't sure that we were talking about the same person, but eventually we confirmed that "Terrence" and "Terry" were one and the same. I explained that Jonathan had told me that he was from England and told her some of the other things he had told me. I acknowledged that Jonathan was mentally ill and running amok, but was hiding his condition from his family. I told her I thought his family needed to know the truth so they could do something to stop him.

She said she would give "Terry" the message. I hung up, not knowing what to think.

Terry. The Southern state.

Afterwards, I wondered if I would hear back from "Terry." I assumed that "Terry" looked down on Americans, especially lower-class ones like me, and I wondered if he would dismiss talking to me as "unworthy" of him. If I did hear from him, I didn't expect the conversation to be easy, and I wondered if he would even care about what his brother was doing to a clutch of lower-class Americans.

I didn't hear from him that day or the next. I did, however, hear from someone else—someone from whom I didn't expect to hear.

On Tuesday, the 2nd, I checked my e-mail and was startled to find a message from Jonathan. I had not received a message from him for almost two months, and to receive one now, after everything that had happened, was a shock.

The message was titled "Good For You??"—an ambiguous title I didn't quite know how to interpret. Was he asking me if I found some kind of satisfaction in leaving some of his things at his home, which by now he would have found, or was he congratulating me, sarcastically, on my discovering that he had lied to me about having moved back to Paladin? I steeled myself for the emotional blow I feared the message would deliver.

As it happened, the e-mail was an automated message that Jonathan had sent from a job search site that contained a link to information about a research position in Washington D.C.

I didn't know how to interpret his attempt to "help" me. Did he view my returning some of his things as a sign of goodwill on my part, which had, as improbable as it seemed, provoked a reciprocal response? Or was he just trying to get me out of his hair by sending me to Washington D.C.? I didn't know what to make of it.

I wrote an equally neutral, but inquisitive, response in which I thanked him for the information about the job and told him that although I was committed throughout the summer, who knew about after that. I ended the message by asking, "By the way, does this mean you're speaking to me again?"

I didn't receive a response, but perhaps being optimistic, I interpreted his e-mail as a sign that his feelings against me had softened somewhat. If that were true, then perhaps there was some hope that I could reclaim my money. He had, after all, repaid me some of the money he owed me, so perhaps he would repay the rest. He didn't know that I'd spoken to Miranda or Mike and didn't know that I knew what I did about him. I was prepared to play dumb, get my money, and get the hell away from him.

I wondered, though, what would happen if he learned that I was the one who had told his family he was mentally ill, had revealed the secret he had tried to hide from them.

Thursday was the Fourth of July, the holiday that Jonathan had said was a "sore point with us" [British]. I was home that day, and with the heat index hovering around 100°, I was staying inside. Around 1:00 in the afternoon, the phone rang.

The caller ID told me it was "Terry Frazier." I felt unprepared to talk to him but knew I had to. After taking a few seconds to calm myself down, I answered.

When I said hello, the man on the other end asked if I was Richard. When I confirmed that I was, he told me that he was Terry Frazier.

Terry pronounced the Rs at the ends of his syllables as distinctly as I did. Far from being British, his accent was as *American*, as *Midwestern*, as mine. Jonathan had told me that his youngest brother had been in the States for 15 years—was that long enough for his accent to have changed?

After we engaged in small talk for a couple of minutes, Terry told me that he'd gotten my message. Then, I told him some of what Jonathan had been doing and that I thought his family needed to know so they would take action to stop him. I told him I had contacted him because I had no way to contact his family, in England.

Before we continued, Terry corrected me about two things—two of the most fundamental things I thought I knew about the British Jonathan: "His real name is *Johnny* and he's from [the *Midwestern* state]."

Johnny. The *Midwestern* state. Although Miranda had told me he was not from England, and Mike had suggested he might be American, neither of them had known where he was really from and neither had known his real name. With one simple sentence, Terry had snapped perhaps the thickest thread in—*Johnny's*—web of lies.

"*Really*. He was telling *me* that he was from *England* and that his family lived in England."

"Johnny is a pathological liar," Terry stated matter-of-factly. "You can't believe anything he says." Terry reiterated what Miranda and Mike had already learned and what *I* was slowly learning. "He did live in England for a long time, but he's not *from* there. He's from [the Midwestern state]."

The discrepant information that I had found about Terry's birthplace wasn't discrepant at all. It was the truth. *Johnny* had lied.

I understood now why "Jonathan" had repeatedly referred to the state. He had talked about having friends there, going on business trips there, and "Iain" had told "Chaz" that he had lived there. And, most recently, the fraudulent insurance account in that state. "Jonathan" had been fixated on the state not because he had indirect connections to there, but because he was *from* there.

I also realized now that "Jonathan's" British accent had been fake. Except for one time when he blamed the change on fatigue, "Jonathan" had faked a British accent continuously for *ten months* without slipping up. I was stunned, not only by the magnitude of the deception, but also by the level of control he had managed to maintain in order to perpetrate his charade. His accent, like so many things, had simply been another tool of manipulation, especially useful on Americans, given how easily so many of them were swayed by British accents.

Returning to the issue of getting his parents to do something to stop his brother, Terry said he didn't know what his parents could do. He said they were old and in poor health and, although they were comfortable, they weren't rich. I told him that I didn't expect them to do anything, now that I understood who his parents *really* were. I was more interested in Terry's description of his parents, which was diametrically opposed to the one that "Jonathan" had given to me. The image of the wealthy, indomitable, almost godlike people who were born and bred to lead the British Empire had been wiped away and replaced with a more realistic one of two people who were not only mere mortals, but also suffering from the ultimate effects of that mortality.

Wondering what else *Johnny* had lied about, I asked Terry if I could ask him some questions about Johnny. Unexpectedly, he turned defensive, saying, "I don't know you or know what your intentions are."

I was confused by his reaction. Was he trying to protect Johnny? What did he think I was going to do with the information he gave to me? Cautiously, I said, "I just mean, like, how old is he?"

"Oh," Terry said, calming down once he realized I didn't want to know anything *that* sensitive.

"He told me he was 45."

"No. *I* turn 45 this year and he's about seven or eight years older than me."

"So, then, he's more like 50?"

"A little older than that."

"He also said that your father was a doctor."

"Now *that's* true, so if you talk to him, it *is* Dr. Frazier."

"Do they live in England?"

"No, they live in [the Southern state]."

I thought about the produce his father had sent to him in January. "Sometimes I would see packages around his house from an Edward Frazier who lived in [the Southern state]," I said, more to myself than to him. I also thought about the coconut patties that "someone" had sent to him in December from the Southern state—someone, who I was now certain, was his father.

I failed to ask him if his parents were *from* England. I remembered the phone call the weekend "Jonathan" had moved to Mariah in which he had spoken with a woman whom he had called "Mother" and who had sounded as if she had a British accent. If she wasn't from somewhere in the United States where people dropped their Rs, then the woman with whom he had spoken was *not* his mother.

I asked him about his siblings. I ran down the list of names that "Jonathan" had given to me.

"Do you have a sister named Charmaine?"

"No."

"Leandra?"

"No."

"Reginald?"

"No."

"Sarah?"

"That's *close*."

In the end, I deduced there were only two Frazier children. The rest were either based on real people Johnny knew or fabricated from his pathological mind. What, then, of "Jonathan's" prized portrait allegedly of his mother, himself, and his two youngest sisters, the latter now revealed not to exist? Were the girls in the portrait other people or, more bizarre, had Johnny commissioned the portrait to further his charade that he was British and his invented siblings were real?

In addition, Terry told me that his family had relatives in one of the Mid-Atlantic states—the same state in which "Iain" had told "Chaz" that he had been born. Either way, except for a few scattered facts about his father and "Terrence," *everything* that "Jonathan" had told me about his family had been a lie.

Eventually, we returned to the issue of Johnny's pathological behavior. Terry told me about some of the things his brother had done to *him*. "Last year he took a credit card out in my name and ran up a couple of thousand dollars of charges before I caught it. I'm still trying to straighten out that situation."

The *credit card*. The one that, back in January, "Jonathan" had told me someone had tried to acquire in his *father*'s name, a situation that "Terrence" had informed "Jonathan" of. In reality, *Johnny* had managed to acquire a credit card in *Terry's* name—without his knowledge, let alone his permission—and his family had suspected *Johnny*.

I hope you know me well enough by now to know that I would never do something like that, "Jonathan" had told me. Obviously, I *hadn't* known him well enough, but now—too late—I was learning.

Terry continued. "He's been pulled over by the police and told them that he's me."

I thought of "Jonathan's" concerns about getting pulled over and not having an American driver's license. Obviously, there was more to that fear than I could have imagined. If he were pulled over and gave his own name, the police would probably discover that he was wanted.

"I could give you a list a mile long of things he's done over the past thirty years."

I knew some of what he had done in just the *three* that he had lived in my state and I shuddered to think of what he had done in *thirty*.

"He was kicked out of a foreign country," he said, naming a country in northern Europe, "and in fact I think he did some time there."

I thought of "Jonathan's" story about working for a bank in that country. I also thought about another story he had fleetingly told me about a youthful indiscretion that had supposedly taken place while visiting Turkey and that had involved what he had mysteriously referred to as "currency," the result of which was that he was no longer allowed to go to Turkey. I wondered now if it was really the country in northern Europe that Terry had named and the "currency" issue had actually involved stealing money from the bank. He had stolen from employers before, so it would have been perfectly consistent with what I had already learned about his more recent activities.

Terry explained that Johnny's modus operandi was usually to commit lots of smaller crimes instead of one big one. By stealing or swindling only a couple of thousand here or a couple of thousand there, many people didn't feel it was worth their trouble to go after him. That was part of why he had gotten away with taking so many people and had managed to remain a free man. It also reminded me of "Ben's" modus operandi and Miranda's comment that when "Jonathan" attributed pathological, criminal, or otherwise unacceptable behavior to others, he was really "telling it on himself."

"Johnny is a deeply troubled person," Terry said. "He actually saw a psychiatrist once, but it didn't work because you have to tell the truth, which he doesn't."

I thought of my accusation, in response to his claim that the psychiatrist he was allegedly seeing in the spring had told him his behavior toward Andy was "normal," that she was obviously getting a grossly distorted version of the truth. No psychiatrist in *her* right mind would say something like that and I had been convinced for some time that he had never seen one.

"Johnny's always been like this," Terry said. "He leaves a wake of destruction wherever he goes. Ever since I was a kid I've warned people away from him, told them he's nothing but bad news. I don't understand why he's like this. Our parents gave him everything, but he still turned out like this."

Terry did add, however, that if he had one problem with the way his parents treated Johnny, it was that whenever he messed up, they bailed him out. This kept him from having to take responsibility for his actions. I found it difficult to believe, though, that this had *caused* the problem, even if it did appear to play a role in perpetuating it.

Terry also described his brother as a "bully." I had already seen examples of his bullying behavior. "He knows not to mess with me," he added. "Whenever we're in a room together he knows to give me a wide berth. Sometimes I've felt like beating him up, but that would just bring me down to his level."

I thought about the times that Glenn had beaten him up. For the first time, I felt that Johnny had gotten *some* of what he deserved.

At some point, I asked Terry if he knew Glenn. He didn't. In fact, he didn't know anything about any of Johnny's relationships with other men.

He did, however, know that Johnny was gay. "He's never come out to our parents, but everybody knows; it's pretty obvious."

In one of his first e-mails, "Jonathan" had said, *[My family] all know that I am gay and know Glenn and some other of my friends. No one makes a big deal out if it and [it] is just considered part of life.* Apparently not.

Then, Terry said something that stunned me. "He was even married a couple of times, but those marriages failed because he was gay; that's just not where he was at."

Married. I knew that some gay people tried heterosexual relationships, even married, before they realized or accepted they were gay, so that wasn't what stunned me. Neither did the realization that all of his elaborate stories about his freewheeling, sexually uninhibited youth in England were also lies. Realizing now that Johnny had grown up not in the sexually liberated England of the 1970s, but in the sexually repressed Midwest of the 1960s, and realizing that he had attempted to fit into a heterosexual mold, both in the past and, in some ways, in the present, I suddenly gained an entirely different understanding of his sexuality. Sexually, he had never really related to me the way that well-adjusted gay men generally did, and not simply because he had related to me selfishly. Sexually, he was apparently more troubled than I'd previously realized.

By that point, I was so overwhelmed with information that I hadn't begun to assimilate that I failed to ask obvious questions, such as when he had been married, how long he had been married, and whether or not he had children. I thought of his attempts to convince Miranda, Joan, Mike and others that Glenn was his son. I could only *hope* that he *didn't* have children.

I knew I would have more questions once I'd had the chance to absorb what he had told me, so I asked Terry if I could speak to him again. He said yes, but thought it would be better for me to do so by e-mail. He gave me his e-mail address and I knew I would be using it.

Altogether, we talked for about forty-five minutes. At the end, I thanked him for taking the time to talk to me, to tell me what he had about Johnny, and he wished me luck. Then we hung up.

Strangely, I felt exhilarated. I should have felt overwhelmed or upset or something unpleasant, but instead, I felt, as I had in speaking to Miranda, that my intuition about *Johnny* had been correct. I realized that *I* wasn't the one who was crazy, that my feelings about and my reactions to Johnny's behavior had been those of a relatively normal person dealing with a mentally ill person whose behavior was far more ill than he had realized. I had once commented to "Jonathan" that his life—and mine with him—seemed to be taking place in some kind of "disorienting parallel universe" that was governed by laws that were very different from the ones that governed ours. I realized now that the universe he inhabited, into which I had been pulled, was simply the universe of lies where nothing, ultimately, made sense, the sense that only the truth can make. Now, my world was starting to make sense again and I was starting to feel a sense of stability, solidity that I had not felt almost from the day that I had run afoul of the person who had called himself "Jonathan."

■

Later that day, I told my family what I had learned. After everything that had happened, after everything that we'd learned, no one seemed as surprised as one might have expected.

That evening, I went to my sister's. While I was there, I placed Terry's screen name, which was the username of his e-mail address, on my younger niece's instant-message contact list, hoping to catch Terry online. I couldn't do that at home because I didn't have the proper instant-message program. Unfortunately, I didn't catch him online, although I could still contact him through e-mail.

Although I had planned to remove his screen name from the contact list before I left, I forgot to do so. In forgetting, something would happen that allowed me to see a side of Terry that I had failed to appreciate.

■

After I had gotten home from my sister's, I e-mailed Terry one of the pictures of "Jonathan" that he had sent to me the day before he had left Dan's to verify that we were in fact talking about the same person. The next morning, I checked my e-mail and found a message from Terry. I assumed he was writing to confirm or deny that the person in the picture was his brother. He was not.

In the message, he claimed that people who said they knew me had been contacting him wanting to know more about Johnny and that he was "not happy." He told me, in no uncertain terms, that if it didn't stop, he would have to "look into [his] legal options."

I was stunned. He didn't specify who the people were who had contacted him, so I didn't know who they might be. The only people who knew I had spoken to him were my family and none of them would have any reason to contact him. I was even more shocked by his threat of legal action, which seemed outrageously overreactive.

At first, I suspected the message had come not from Terry, but from Johnny. It actually seemed more like his style. In addition, if Johnny was the one who had broken into my e-mail accounts in the spring, then perhaps he had also been accessing Terry's account in order to monitor his activities and, possibly, to masquerade as him. If so, then Johnny would have found the message I had sent to Terry and realized that I had been learning the truth about him from his own family, his *real* family. The pathological liar, con man, and control freak that he was, Johnny's greatest fear was to be unmasked and I already knew how he reacted when his deceptions were exposed. Finding the message to Terry would have sent him over the edge and provoked the kind of hostile, bullying response I had received.

In telling my family about the message, I learned that one of them *had* contacted Terry—accidentally. When my younger niece had used the computer after I had placed Terry's screen name on her instant-message contact list, she had found it. She hadn't recognized it, but since the screen name contained most of Terry's name, she had thought it might be him. She hadn't been sure, however, because my sister also had a friend whose name, by coincidence, was almost identical to Terry's. Innocently, she had instant-messaged Terry and asked him who he was. When she didn't get a clear response, she had asked him if he had a brother named Johnny. With that, he had wanted to know who she was and, in the process, she had mentioned my name. That was when all hell had broken loose. Apparently, Terry had replied by threatening her, telling her that if she didn't leave him alone, he would take legal action. Immediately she had stopped, feeling more confused than threatened. Afterwards, he had sent me the message in which he threatened *me* with legal action.

Once I found out what had happened, I called Terry. I explained what had happened, that it was all a misunderstanding. Although I thought he had overreacted, I told him I understood why he was sensitive about people finding out that Johnny—the pathological liar, the con man, the criminal—was his brother. He agreed that he *was* sensitive about it, but explained that his feelings came more from wanting to have a reputation for being associated with honest people, whether they were family members or not. I understood the power of guilt by association, and although it was irrational and unfair, people still made those connections. That was just another burden created by Johnny's behavior that Terry had to endure.

After concluding my conversation with Terry, after learning the essential truth about his brother that until then had been denied to me, I realized that the person I had been involved with for almost a year was not a person at all but a *persona*, a character named "Jonathan" that Johnny had created and acted out for me. Of all the cast members in Johnny's *dramatis personae*, he was the greatest. I realized, then, that I hadn't had a relationship with another, if disturbed person, but had, instead, been an audience member in a play that had cost me $4,000, a year of my life, and an uncountable amount of my emotional and physical welfare to attend. His self, his life, was nothing but a lie.

I thought of the day I had met him, of how I had thought he resembled Ash, Ian Holm's character in *Alien*. Like Ash, Johnny looked like a normal human on the outside, but on the inside, he deceived and manipulated at the expense of others. His "humanity"—certainly his humaneness—was as much a masquerade as everything else.

I also recalled his words to me when I had revealed to "Jonathan" that I was "Chaz": *Remember, despite your motives, you have lied and concocted a whole person to someone else. You can rationalize it any way you want to but this is awful and out of control. If [Iain] has been forthcoming to you, you are worse then what you have accused me of being.*

"Iain" had *not* been forthcoming to me…and neither had *Johnny*, not only "Iain's" creator, but also the creator of countless personas with countless purposes both trivial and substantial, but always deceitful. The level to which *Johnny's* behavior had been, continued to be "awful and out of control" was beyond description. I knew, now, that I had fallen not merely into the trap of a disturbed narcissist whose sense of superiority led him to believe that he was entitled to have, do, and pretend to be what the normal person never would, but into the very sticky web of a classic psychopath whose lack of conscience ravaged every life it touched. And, like a fly in a web, I didn't know the best way to free myself.

What I did next, though intended to free me, only further entangled me.

—39—
CONFRONTATION

Now it's my *turn.*

The Saturday after I had spoken to Mike Harmon and Terry, I went to Mariah to confront Johnny directly about the money he owed me. Regardless of who or what he was, I still wanted and needed my money. I was hoping we could have a rational discussion about the matter and achieve some kind of resolution because I did not want to have to proceed with a lawsuit against him. I knew what a mess that would be and that it would only cost me more money that I didn't have. Although I knew that if he didn't have any compunction about doing what he had done at his places of business, not to mention to his own brother, he wouldn't have any compunction about refusing to repay me, but I decided to try. In addition, I went there partly because Terry had described Johnny as a "bully" and, if that was the case, then the only way to deal with him was to stand up to him and assert my rights. After everything I had heard, I was now somewhat concerned for my safety, but I felt prepared if there were problems.

When I arrived in Mariah, I decided that rather than just showing up at the apartment unannounced, I would first try to call him. Because I didn't have a cell phone, I went to a local supermarket and used a pay phone instead. The phone rang several times but no one answered. I was convinced he was home, though, since he rarely seemed to leave what I had come to think of as the "shithole."

I left the supermarket and drove to Johnny's neighborhood. As I had the Saturday before, I parked a couple of blocks away. I didn't want him to see me coming because I knew he wouldn't go to the door if he knew it was me. I *wanted* him to come to the door.

When I arrived at the apartment, I saw Johnny's car in the driveway. The windows were rolled down, which suggested that he had been outside that day; it seemed unlikely that he had left the windows rolled down all night. In addition, if he had left the windows rolled down, it seemed unlikely that he was gone. Therefore, he must be in the apartment.

I decided to enter the way I had always entered, through the garage door. The door was closed and when I tried to lift it, I discovered it was locked. That was unusual. Johnny had always left the door unlocked, even though it contained things he considered valuable. Obviously, something had changed. In more ways than one, it seemed, I was no longer dealing with the same person.

Frustrated, I went around to the front door. Because Johnny spent almost all of his waking time in the den, which lay about as far away from the front door as possible, I doubted he would be able to hear me knock, but I tried. I knocked several times, but received no response.

When I couldn't raise anyone, I checked to see if he had gotten his mail that day to verify that he was actually home. In the process, I discovered what appeared to be a summons to appear in court on Wednesday, August 7 in the county in which Mariah is located because he was being sued for $3,350. I couldn't tell from the summons who was suing him or why, although I suspected that Joan Vogel was suing him for not paying his rent. I had paid his rent for January and February, but unless he had either stolen or scammed money from someone else, the rent had remained unpaid for at least four months, five if July were included. Since his rent was $650 a month, that meant he owed $3,250, approximately the amount listed on the summons. I thought of Mike's comment about "Jonathan's" problems with landlords. I put the summons back and decided to return to the garage door.

In the three months that had passed since I had seen Johnny in person, someone had moved into the downstairs apartment. Since the apartment had remained unoccupied throughout the entire four months of the Mariah phase of our relationship, the fact that it was now tenanted added another level of strangeness. The neighbor appeared to be home, so I went to the apartment and knocked on the door. A dark-haired, well-dressed man in his 30s answered. I explained that I wanted to see the person who lived upstairs, but since the garage was locked, I couldn't use the garage entrance. He said he had thought it was unlocked and told me he would unlock it. I thanked him and after he came around and raised the door, I walked inside and headed for the stairs.

Although normally I would have felt nervous about doing what I was about to do and was concerned about what Johnny might do, strangely I felt energized. I was certainly functioning in a very efficient, businesslike mode—after all, I *was* there to conduct, and hopefully conclude, business—but I also believe that part, perhaps much, of my lack of nerves came from feeling that somehow I now had the upper hand. As far as I knew, Johnny had no idea that I had spoken to Miranda, Mike, and Terry and had learned as much of the truth about him as I had.

When I reached the top of the stairs, I knocked on the door. The instant after, I heard the "girls" start barking on the other side. They were in the den, and because, like Mary's little lamb, they followed Johnny wherever he went, that meant that Johnny was in the den as well. Now more nervous, I waited.

A few seconds later, the door opened. Before me stood not "Jonathan," but *Johnny*. In more ways than one, I was beholding a different person...and I was shocked by what I saw. He looked as if he had aged ten years in the three months since I'd last seen him. Given that he *was* almost ten years older than he'd claimed to be, it seemed fitting. His hair was shaggier and the salt and pepper saltier than I'd remembered. He looked haggard and disheveled, reminding me of a mentally ill person who had been wandering the streets.

I told him that I wanted to talk to him and asked him if I could come inside. He said, "*No*," in what I now knew to be his *fake* British accent. I then asked him if he would come outside. Instead of responding in word, however, he responded in deed. He slowly shut the door in my face, careful not to close the door on the "girls," and refused to speak with me further.

For a moment, I stood at the door, thinking about just leaving, but finally, I decided that wasn't good enough.

Turning back toward the door from which I'd half turned away, I shouted, "You might want to look in your mailbox. Apparently I'm not the *only* one you owe a substantial amount of money to." I paused, then added, "And, by the way, I know your *real* name is *Johnny* and you're from [*the Midwestern state*]. And I'm not the *only* one who knows the truth about you. And I know what you did at OutSource. And if you're in this position, it's only because you've *put* yourself in this position. You've got no one to thank but *yourself*." Then I stormed off.

As I left, I decided on what I would do next—*where* I would *go* next. I decided not to return to Hawthorn, at least directly. I decided that, on the way, I would make a little detour. Through St. Alban.

It was time that Laura learned the truth. I was so infuriated by Johnny's arrogant attitude that he should be able to do anything he wanted, to me and to others, and get away with it, that I finally decided to tell her how he had been deceiving her. I realized that I should have done it long before then because she, and her family, didn't deserve to be deceived any more than Andy or Joan Vogel or Cliff or David Garrett or I or anyone else deserved to be, but it took that incident, that insult, to serve as the straw that broke the camel's back. I remembered "Jonathan's" threats to destroy Dan's façade of heterosexuality in Credence, to expose him for what he really was. Destroying façades could work both ways, and now, *I* was determined to destroy *Johnny's* façades.

I arrived at Laura's about an hour later. Unfortunately, no one was home, so I left a message on her door telling her that I needed to talk to her about "Jonathan" and to call me.

On my way back to Hawthorn, I drove through Paladin, to Miranda's. Although I had seen her only a week before and felt that I was pestering her, she had been involved from the beginning, and I felt that she might be interested to learn what had happened. I told her what I'd done and she seemed pleased that I'd confronted him and gotten my feelings out of my system. She expressed her hope that now I would have a new direction and could begin to put what had happened behind me.

Before I could do that, though, Laura at least needed to know the truth.

I arrived home later than afternoon. When I did, I found that Laura, having gotten home and found my note in the meantime, had called. Immediately I called her back.

My throat was dry and tight from dehydration and stress, which made it difficult to talk. Even so, I tried my best to tell her everything I needed to say, everything she needed to hear.

"Jonathan has been lying to you about Cliff taking care of him," I began. "Cliff has *not* been taking care of him. If anyone has been, *I* have."

"Really," she said, seeming stunned.

I proceeded to tell her what had *really* happened between the time "Jonathan" had left her house at the end of October and the time I had discovered he was still in Mariah at the end of June. I told her that I had discovered the "Cliff" account in February and had learned that, for some incomprehensible reason, "Jonathan" had been using that account to pretend to be Cliff to her and her family. I told her about the other fraudulent e-mail accounts he had created under various guises and told her about the situation that had developed between him and Andy. I added to what I had learned myself by telling her some of what I had learned from Miranda, Mike, and Terry.

In response, she told me that "Jonathan" had mentioned that I'd been contacting his friends. I told her that was true and told her that I had done that because when I'd received the letters that implied he might be in some kind of danger, I was trying to find out if he was all right. I also told her that he owed me $4,000 and that I had gone to Mariah that day to get my money or, if not, to sue him.

When I mentioned the money, she told me that *Dan* had sued him for check fraud in the amount of $642.59. I thought that amount sounded suspiciously close to the $645 that "Jonathan" had told me he had paid for the repairs on his car, for which Dan had written the garage a check and for which "Jonathan" had written Dan a check to reimburse him after the garage hadn't accepted his own.

Laura didn't say, though, if she knew what the circumstances were, but apparently the matter was unresolved. In addition, she told me there was a warrant out for "Jonathan's" arrest in the county in which Dan lived, presumably for not appearing in court. *That*, it seemed, was where the warrant had been issued, which was why the officer in Paladin couldn't find it. Now, I realized that in having received a bad check from Johnny, neither Miranda nor Dan was alone.

I told her about "Jonathan's" claim that Dan was stalking him and at one point had lain in wait for him outside her house for several hours. Laura said that wasn't true, that Dan had simply driven by one day to see if "Jonathan" was still there but hadn't waited outside the house, as "Jonathan" had claimed. There was obviously more to the story, but Laura didn't seem to know it.

When I told her about the fraudulent Cliff account, she told me that "Jonathan" had said that he and Cliff shared e-mail accounts and that they knew each other's passwords. He had given her the same story that he had given to me about "sharing" e-mail accounts with "friends," which was ridiculous.

"Did you know his real name isn't Jonathan?" I asked her. "It's actually Johnny."

"Now that you mention it, his father called here one day when he was here and asked for 'Johnny'." I failed to ask her if his 'father' had had a British accent, probably because I assumed that if it was his *real* father, he hadn't.

"Did you know he's really from [the Midwestern state]?" I asked.

"Yes, he told me that."

I was stunned. "He *did*?"

"Yes."

"He told *me* he was from *England*."

"Isn't that funny," she said, strangely.

Not really, I thought. I also thought she was taking all of this a little too lightly...but maybe what I was telling her hadn't yet had a chance to sink in. "Then how did he explain his British accent?" I asked.

"He said he *lived* in England." Obviously, then, Laura wouldn't have found it odd that his father didn't have a British accent.

"Where did he tell you he went after he left your house?"

"He said that he went to a hotel for a few days before he and Cliff moved to Mariah."

I told her that he had *really* moved back to Paladin to live with Art before he had moved to Mariah—*without* Cliff.

"Did you know he was working at the hospital?"

"He told me he didn't take that job."

I assured her that he *had* taken that job, although he'd lost it only a week and a half after moving to Mariah. I also told her about the story on the hospital's web site about "Jonathan's" hiring and told her to look at it as proof.

While on the subject of Johnny's employment, I told her that in talking to Mike, I had learned that he had been not the COO of OutSource, as he had led us to believe, but a general manager. I also told her that I had learned that he had been fired early the previous year for failing to report back to Mike after taking a medical leave for an alleged health condition. I also told her about the insurance fraud scheme that Johnny had tried to perpetrate and how Mike's attempts to clean up the damage he had wrought had cost Mike $57,000. Laura's reactions gave me the impression that she didn't know what to think about what I was telling her, which was understandable, but she seemed increasingly willing to consider what I was saying.

In telling her how "Jonathan" would be gone for hours during the day and had been leading me to believe he was going to work, I wondered openly where he *had* been going. In response, Laura told me something that should have been obvious, which was that he had been spending all day at the Stress Center. That explained that, but I asked her how he had explained how he was the COO of a company, yet was able to spend all day at the Center. She told me that he had told her, simply, that he was on medical leave from work. Apparently, "Jonathan's" "leave" had started sometime before he and Laura had met, a month or more before it had begun in the version he had presented to me. No wonder Johnny had been so nervous when Laura and I had begun exchanging information the Saturday we had helped him to move and why he had worked so hard to keep us from doing so again.

"Did he tell you why he left your house?" I asked.

"No, he never really gave a reason," she said.

I told her his story to me and to Miranda that he had felt driven to flee because she was expecting him to pay for everything there and, worse, because she was constantly pressuring him for sex. In response to that revelation, she acted subdued, but dismayed.

Curious, I asked her who he had said *I* was, how *I* fit into his life. I had told her that we had been in a relationship, but she said that he had told *her* that, although I was interested in *him*, he wasn't interested in *me* "in that way." He said that I wanted the two of us to move in together, but he didn't want to do that. He said the reason he wasn't interested in me was that I was "too gay" for him. I thought that was an interesting comment because that was what he'd claimed *Dan* had said about me.

I asked her if she knew about the plethora of sex ads that Johnny compulsively posted under a variety of guises. She seemed to know about some of them, but not most of them. I explained to her that in finding out about all of the lies he was telling different people, his sex ads had actually put me on the trail. In particular, I told her about our exchanges in which I had posed as "Chaz." That was one set of ads she *did* know about. Apparently, when Johnny had learned that I was "Chaz," that I had deceived him, he had become enraged. I knew that he had vented his hostility in his subsequent messages to me, but he had also done the same to Laura. She didn't specify what he had done or said, but I got the impression that the ire he had expressed in his messages to me was only a fraction of what he had conveyed to others.

After absorbing to some degree what I had told her, Laura raised the issue of Johnny's mental stability. In particular, she asked me if I thought "Jonathan," which she was still calling him, was "bipolar." I told her that I didn't know everything that was wrong with him, but I *did* know he was a pathological liar and appeared to have narcissistic and psychopathic traits. At least she seemed to believe that Johnny was mentally ill, however it was defined, and that she shouldn't accept everything he said as the truth.

At the end of our conversation, Laura suggested we keep in touch and we exchanged e-mail addresses. By the time we were finished, an hour and a half after beginning, I was exhausted.

Later that evening, I sent Laura an e-mail containing a link to the story on the hospital's web site about "Jonathan's" hiring. I hoped this would serve as further proof of the truth of what I'd told her. In addition, I gave her Johnny's address in Mariah in the hope that she would see for herself where and how he was truly living.

I knew, of course, that the first thing Laura would do would be to contact "Jonathan" and tell him what I had told her. I didn't know how much of what I had told her she had believed—after an entire year of indoctrination, *I* had found it difficult to accept what *Miranda* had told *me*—but Laura seemed receptive, or at least interested. I also didn't know how Johnny would react when he discovered what Laura knew, what *I* knew. I had told him only a fraction of what I knew and had told Laura much more. I did know, though, that what I had done would not pass without comment.

It did not.

■

The next day, in checking the "Jonathan" account, I happened to find a message titled "Your Turn," from "jonathan iain," from an unfamiliar address. Later, I checked the public profile associated with the address and found that the account had been created on Wednesday, July 3, just a few days before. This made at least three new e-mail accounts that "Jonathan" had created within the previous month—and these were just the ones I knew about. Interestingly, he had sent—or had tried to send—the message to my regular and "message" accounts, but had misspelled their addresses, so they didn't go through. Although he had gotten the "Jonathan" address correct, the message had gone not into my inbox, but into my junk mail, which I thought was appropriate. The message confirmed that he had found out that I had been spreading the truth about him. The message was extremely vicious and caused anything I had ever said or done to be "vindictive" to pale in comparison.

"jonathan iain" told me that I had failed in my "attempt" to expose him. He claimed that his friends I had contacted—he didn't specify, but I assumed he meant Andy and Laura—thought I was "way off" and were "afraid for [his] safety with someone like [me] around." He also claimed that "Terrence" was planning to file a harassment complaint against me for what "Jonathan" described as my "insane" phone call. He insisted that I had "broken into" his garage and insinuated that he was planning to file a restraining order against me. He insisted that if I had "put the same energy into establishing a life of [my] own that [I had] into harassing [him] and [his] friends, [I] might have by now established some kind of normal life and relationships instead of working for nothing, living with [my] mommy, talking over the details of [my] pathetic life with [my] whorish sister, and obsessing over someone who view[ed me] with nothing but contempt and pity." He concluded by saying, "Now it's *my* turn."

I was stunned by the vehemence of his psychopathic rage. Did he *really* believe I was obsessed with him? Was he *that* deluded? The truth was that after everything he had done, after everything I had learned, *I* had nothing but contempt for *him*—but *no pity*. After I had discovered that he had been masquerading as Cliff, I had asked myself, if he would do this to someone he said he loved, what would he do to someone he hated? Now I knew. And, in the same way that the victims of his identity theft knew nothing about what he was saying through them as them, I knew that the message represented only one slender thread in the web of lies he was undoubtedly weaving about me. I remembered his comment to "Darin" about his perilous encounter with the "psycho" named "Richard" and all the mentally ill things that "Richard" had done to him. To what extent would Johnny go to destroy me?

What, I wondered, had I gotten myself mixed up in? I wasn't prepared for any of this, didn't know how to begin to deal with it.

Although I had already contacted Terry twice that week and—especially after Johnny's claims that Terry perceived it as harassment—I was reluctant to contact him again, I decided to contact him for a third, and final, time to ask him if Johnny's claims were true. The idea might not have carried much weight were it not for Terry's reaction to my niece's innocent attempt at contacting him. He seemed extremely sensitive when it came to his brother and I wondered if he, in his defensiveness, were really planning to do something like that. I was genuinely concerned and wanted to know the truth.

That afternoon, I called his workplace, but he was unavailable, so I left a message in which I told him what Johnny had claimed. A little while later, Terry returned my call. The first thing he told me was, "Don't fall for this," and told me that he "[didn't] have a problem with [me]." He also said that he had told his parents what I had told him and that they had probably spoken with Johnny about the issue. I still didn't know what Laura might have told him. After talking with Terry a little while longer, I felt assured that Johnny's claims were just more of his lies, just more of his pattern of using other people's personas as his mouthpieces without their knowledge. Terry did say that he was tired of the whole issue, which I understood, and was officially "out of it." He also informed me that he wasn't going to get his parents further involved, since they were old and in poor health and didn't need the stress. In concluding the conversation, Terry reiterated his belief that in the aftermath of my disastrous encounter with his brother, I needed to "heal and move on" and wished me luck. After hanging up, I realized there was nothing more he could or would do to help and, not wanting to bother him further, I decided not to contact him again.

The same day, I also contacted Laura again to see if she had spoken with Johnny. When I called, I got her answering machine as well and left her a message asking her to call me. Some time passed, but when she didn't return my call, I decided to call her again. Under normal circumstances, I would have been more patient, but after everything that had happened, I was agitated and wanted answers, reassurance, as soon as possible.

The second time I called, Laura answered. This time, she seemed very different than she had the day before. This time, she seemed nervous and evasive. When I asked her if she'd spoken with "Jonathan," she told me no. In mentioning what I'd told her about Johnny's pretending to be different people, she responded that she thought "Jonathan" probably *did* pretend to be different people—"to lovers." To *lovers*? Hadn't she understood what I'd told her? Or was she simply unable to accept the truth? Whatever the case, she seemed particularly concerned about my attempts at contacting "Jonathan's" friends, family, and him. She warned me that "Jonathan" had "powerful friends" and that he could "destroy" me if I antagonized him. I insisted that he didn't, but she remained convinced that he was in fact as powerful as he claimed to be. Finally, when I told her to find out the truth for herself, she said, with an attitude strangely echoing Terry's, that she was "tired" of the situation and wanted to "go on with [her] life."

After twenty minutes of what had proven to be an unexpectedly disorienting conversation, I ended by emphasizing the fact that the *only* reason I'd gone to Mariah was to try to get back the money Johnny still owed me. I wanted to convince her that was my *only* motivation, which it was. I didn't know, could only imagine, what "Jonathan" had told her about me, so I tried to remain as rational and matter-of-fact as I could under what were proving to be less-than-rational circumstances.

I knew that Laura wasn't telling me the truth about not having spoken to Johnny and I assumed that his reaction toward me was in response not to what he had learned from his parents, but to what he had learned from *her*. Whatever the case, I fully realized that I was now enemies with a deeply disturbed psychopath who would stop at nothing to discredit, to destroy, me.

I didn't know what to do.

—40—
ENTR'ACTE
...heal and move on...

For days following my encounter with Johnny and the repercussions it wrought, I felt emotionally and physically sick. I felt disgusted, disoriented, damaged, drained. I felt as if through my contact with Johnny, I had been infected with a virus—a psychological virus—and was now suffering its pathological effects. For the first time since I had known him, I had *finally* seen the *real* Johnny in all his psychopathic fullness, and apart from wondering—worrying—what he would do to me next now that he had been provoked, I was horrified to think that, for an entire year, I had been utterly oblivious to the monster that had lurked behind the façade that had called itself "Jonathan." I felt like an uncomprehending insect that had been snared in a spider's web, unaware of the danger it was in until it was too late. I was not an idiot and I was not naïve. I had a bachelor's and a master's degree in psychology and I knew about psychopathic behavior. Most of all, I had lived for 35 years and knew full well what people were capable of being and doing. What had I done wrong?

I decided that the only way to deal with what had happened to me was to take Terry's advice to "heal and move on." Although I had thought that his attitude was simply a rationalization for passivity, for unwillingness to deal with the disaster that was his brother directly, I also wondered if perhaps he knew something that I didn't. As much as it tore me up to acknowledge it, I had to admit that Johnny was right: Through his elaborate, convincing lies, through his thorough, year-long indoctrination, Laura and Andy and anyone else whom he thought I might seek out and tell the truth about him had been, it seemed, unshakably persuaded that *I* was the monster, that *I* was the lunatic, that *I* was the liar and poor, innocent, *honest* "Jonathan" was the victim. I didn't know how to break through the seemingly impenetrable fog of lies that had descended over them. I felt like a prisoner who had been falsely convicted of a crime but who couldn't convince anyone of his innocence. His family wouldn't help, the law wouldn't help, *nothing* would help. Johnny had won. I had lost. As long as I held out hope that something would change, that *I* could change something, there *was* no hope, for *me*.

I decided that I had to put the past in the past and move on with my life.

I realized that, throughout the previous year, I had lost myself. My first order of business, then, was to find the person I had lost. I needed to recenter myself by finding things in life that brought me happiness, fulfillment. The previous year had been about nothing but "Jonathan." The present would be about *me* and making myself whole again.

When I was around eight, I developed an interest in entomology. That interest supplanted my previous interest in dinosaurs and captured my attention for the next several years. By the time I reached adolescence, my interest had begun to wane, if not disappear, but in the previous three or four years, my childhood interest had started to reassert itself. This reemergence was prompted, in part, by my work on a personal web site. I had decided that in order to give people some insight into my personality, I would devote several sections to significant interests that I'd had throughout my life, which included entomology. I thought about having several pages dealing with the insects that were native to my state and I wanted to include photographs of representative species. I wanted to avoid using other people's photos because of copyright issues, however, so I decided to take some of my own.

The Christmas before, my sister had given my younger niece a digital camera. Because I somehow always got the job in my family of figuring out how to use all new technology, I had experimented with the camera the previous December and was amazed at the quality of the photos and the ease of its use. I had always marveled at the close-up photographs of insects in nature books and films and had always wished that I could produce some of my own. Now, I would finally have my chance.

In mid-July, I borrowed my niece's camera and began taking photographs of the local insect fauna. I started with the butterflies that came to take nectar at the phlox that bloomed along the back of the property in midsummer before discovering in mid-August a butterfly garden at one of the local parks that attracted a wider variety of species and in greater numbers. I will never forget the first time that I approached what I later learned was a butterfly bush to find it covered with four tiger swallowtails that had been magnetically attracted to its rich nectar. I was overwhelmed not only by the beauty of the sight, but also by a feeling of wonder and happiness that was almost childlike in its quality. I felt as if after rummaging around for an uncountable length of time in the dusty, forgotten boxes of memories in the attic that was my mind, I had finally stumbled upon a keepsake that on finding it, immediately reconnected me to my childhood, placed me back onto a path that I was supposed to have taken long ago but had forsaken because of the intervening and interfering events of life that had come later.

For the next six weeks, I spent much of my free time losing—or, rather, finding—myself in the natural world at the local parks and photographing the insect life that surrounded me. Slowly, I began to feel more and more like my old self—not the self I had been immediately before I had met "Jonathan," but the self I was supposed to be starting in childhood. In the same way that the insects I photographed had undergone a metamorphosis, I, too, began to undergo a transformation of my own.

Yet, in spite of my newfound form of relaxation and fulfillment, the summer of 2002 proved difficult for reasons beyond those that involved Johnny. Around the middle of June, my mother's second oldest sister died. She had suffered from congestive heart failure for many years and was frequently hospitalized for the condition, as she had been at Christmas. Then, around the end of July, my mother was involved in an automobile accident when she was driving home from visiting her oldest sister, who was staying in a nursing home in a nearby town and was suffering from an inoperable aortic aneurysm. A truck whose driver had failed to stop at the red light at the intersection she was crossing struck her car. The accident totaled her car and left her with a subdural hematoma—brain bleeding. Although she wasn't hospitalized, she suffered from severe headaches and disorientation for days afterwards as well as residual effects for months to come.

Then, a week after the accident, my mother's oldest sister died. Although she wasn't as close to this sister as she was to her second oldest one, the death still had its impact. When she went to the visitation, she had barely begun to recover from the accident and my sister, who went with her, told me that her behavior at the funeral home was noticeably disoriented.

Within a period of less than two months, my mother was in an automobile accident that had left her brain injured and her car totaled and had lost two of her sisters. In addition, what Johnny had done had affected her, mainly indirectly, but also directly. Terry had conveniently decided to shield his old, sick parents from the effects of Johnny's actions, but what about *my* aged, grieving, injured mother?

Around the beginning of August, I spoke again with Miranda. I had been trying to arrange another official meeting with her for some time, but events seemed to conspire against me. One time, I drove all the way to Paladin, only to be slowed by road construction near the city to the point that I arrived half an hour late, just as another client was arriving for a reading. Another time, I drove to Paladin, only to become trapped in a traffic jam during rush hour. When I arrived, I found that she had been called out. Frustrated again, I returned home. Finally, on Saturday, the 3rd, I managed to make it to her house and we continued our discussion of the person we now called "Johnny."

I showed her the e-mail that "jonathan iain" had sent to me on July 7. She noted his use of the word "we," which puzzled me because it wasn't clear whom he was referring to. She thought "we" referred to his multiple personalities, which she believed he had. I told her that I had been keeping up on his sex ads and that in most of his more recent ones, he had been referring to himself as part of a couple. In the four months since we had broken up, Johnny had posted at least nine ads on *Gayteway*, five of which had made references to having a partner, and privately, he had been bringing Glenn into his fantasies. She expressed her opinion that Glenn would *always* be in the fantasies because he was obsessed with him. She had emphasized that before, but I had seen it for myself, in distorted form, while I was involved with "Jonathan."

I also showed her the first of the threatening letters that I had received in the mail in May. When she read it, however, she wasn't certain if Johnny or Glenn had written it because it sounded more like Glenn. I didn't know if Glenn even knew about me, but I knew she had told me—couldn't forget, in fact—about Glenn's psychotic fascination with white supremacy and his equally virulent homophobia.

"It was just some of the most bizarre stuff I've ever seen, actually," she commented. "He hates 'queers'—I mean, he uses that term all the time"—a term that, along with the Nazi allusions, had figured prominently in the letters from The Pretender. Although I still had questions about the true identity of The Pretender, the idea that it was actually Johnny, or "Johnny-Glenn," increasingly made sense.

Otherwise, Miranda repeated much of what she had said in May about the relationship between Johnny and Glenn and Johnny's behavior when he had brought Glenn to see her. When I mentioned how she had previously described the two of them as having some kind of bizarre symbiotic relationship in which they didn't seem to function as two separate people, Miranda said that it "was hard to know who was whose keeper." She also restated how nervous Johnny had been when he had been forced to leave Glenn alone with her because of his inability to control what Glenn told her—for example, about the institution. Miranda repeated that Johnny had been "disturbed" to leave the two of them alone and that when he was waiting for them to be done, she could hear Johnny nervously pacing in the hallway while Glenn spoke to her in whispers about how he had to get away from him. Miranda said that the experience was "like a frickin' movie."

She also described her impressions of Glenn in further detail. She said that Glenn was "not a bright light" and said that she had to explain things to him in very simple ways because his level of intelligence seemed to be fairly low. She also said that Glenn looked like "[a] pure white trash street [hustler]—somebody you'd see standing on the corner, [trying to pick up people], hiding in the bushes in the park—that whole lifestyle. And hustler—but not *smart* hustler." That image stood in stark contrast to that of the upper-class British gentleman that "Jonathan" had painted for me.

At one point in our conversation, I told Miranda that I had learned from Terry that none of the siblings "Jonathan" had claimed he had, except for Terry, were real. I wondered openly where Johnny had gotten the histories he had presented to me, whether they were derived from real people or merely products of his pathological mind. Later, after reading the threatening letter, she addressed the question.

"Can I tell you something that creeps me out?" she began.

"Mmhmm."

"Because I think you need to know it, especially after I read this."

"I need to know as much as possible," I said, concerned.

"*Creeps me out*. Something that when I read this just snapped me 'cause it was already something I had thought... Like I said, I've been doing this for [many] years and I have a background in psychology and there's just too much... It started when you asked me that question about are these people people he really knew or are they [not]...what is it? And I think there's two answers—like I said, I feel like..." She hesitated before continuing, then said, "I find this highly disturbing to even verbalize this, but I'm going to have to... I feel like somewhere along the line—and again, I don't know if he did it or if Glenn did it—I feel like somebody was murdered. The hair is raising up on my arms. I just *feel* it; I think I alluded to this to you before, but boy, is it here strong now. I mean…and I think it may have been somebody that they took over, an identity…it may have been somebody from England."

"Yeah."

"I just *feel* it." She continued. "And they become people. Some of those people, it's like—if you study anything about people who are like this, a lot of the time they don't kill people—that sounds *terrible*; I don't want to term him a serial killer; I don't think he's a serial killer—but I do think something has happened like that; I really do."

"Yes."

"I really do. And these people, what they do, because they're so…because there's no division, there's no boundaries, there's no nothing, they become that person. If you read anything about the serial killers, for example, actually there was something they liked about the people and they consume them."

"Yes."

"It's like the guy that ate the people…"

"Jeffrey Dahmer."

"Jeffrey Dahmer. Oh, yeah."

"[Some] say that's the reason that he ate [his victims]."

"Yeah—it's the *opposite* of what people think. They want their essence; they want their…"

"Yeah."

"And it's actually a primitive thing; it's not something that people think [it is]."

"Oh, it is."

"Oh, it's like, 'Our society's so screwed up'… *No*—there's been cannibalism from [the beginning]."

"Right, right."

"There's ancient stuff about this—this is not a new story; this is not new stuff. And a lot of people who kill people, it's not what people think; it's not this evil [whatever]—it's a whole different thing. And there's something about *this*," she said, referring to the letter, "because what would flip me out the most with Johnny…let's call him Johnny now…"

"Yeah," I said, glad that she had finally made the transition to using his *real* name.

She continued. "…was when he was telling me this whole Glenn story—and this is when he was missing, had gone missing—he would intersperse it with these weird stories about how this guy would be like sitting and he'd look out and see these visions of these crosses and this *Nazi* stuff…"

"Yeah."

"It'd be Nazi, KKK crap... But there'd be times, especially the second or third time I saw him, I couldn't tell if he was talking about... He would say it was how *Glenn* felt, but I felt like he was talking about how *he* [felt], a division within *himself* about gay people or about this or that, okay?"

"Yeah."

"So then, when I finally met Glenn... I think I just confronted him—I think at one point, I just thought, you know what, I've got [enough of] this crazy shit, so I said, 'Do you have some kind of visions about, you know, crosses?' I didn't know *what* to say; it was just kind of creepy..."

"Yeah."

"He goes... It just, like, *flipped* him," she said, snapping her fingers. "Okay? *Flipped* him. And you could see it—his face changed..."

"Mmhmm."

"It was, like, okay—it was like possession; here comes this other personality out. It was like *Sybil*—I swear to God, if I had a camera going, anybody in the psychiatry field would have gone, '*Hello*, let's study *this* one—*this* is wild.'"

"Right."

"It was not an act—I mean, it was not an act."

"No."

"And his voice changed, and he started talking about, 'I had to dye my hair a different [color]' or—he went into this weird thing about his [hair]...I don't know, but anyway... He was talking about 'those goddamn queers,' you know, and 'Mexicans' and [whatever]..."

"Mmhmm."

"...just this *creepy*..."

"Oh, God."

"...*creepy* stuff. And then that's one of the things that Johnny would say was, like, 'I'm afraid he's going to kill somebody' or 'I'm afraid he's going to harm [someone]...' After, I think, [Johnny] realized [that I didn't believe Glenn was his son]—'cause I'd said enough to him without insulting him to let him know that I didn't believe the [story]..."

"Right."

"Yeah. That I knew..."

"Right."

"I just didn't... I'm not a mean person and there's nothing to be gained even from a therapeutic sense to just [be mean]."

"Right."

"So gradually, you know, he started telling me things, and it was kind of, like, 'He's probably holed up in some hotel, you know, with some guy in this wild, drug/sex weekend...'"

"Jonathan" had told me the same thing and Miranda and I had already discussed in May what Johnny had told her. Glenn had made it clear to her that he was not interested in Johnny and wanted him to leave him alone.

"I think that whatever had gone on between them was probably over a long time ago, in a sense," Miranda said. "And I think that—how can I put this into words?—and I think some of the violent stuff that Johnny would talk about between the two of them—and I think what happens sometimes with sadomasochism and all that kind of stuff that people get into—I think that probably took the place of sex with them where I think [Johnny] would try to control and repress [Glenn]—and I think that's why legitimately in [Johnny's] mind he could think of him as his son, child."

"Yes, yes."

"Because I think that *had* changed. And I think then maybe [Glenn] *would* get violent, but not to the degree that Johnny was saying. Yeah, I do think they had [that kind of relationship]...because I think the guy was physically trying to get away from him 'cause he was saying stuff to me like 'I'm a prisoner' and 'He's trying to [control me]...'"

"Yes, yes. Because he's a control freak; Johnny's a total control freak."

"Oh, yeah."

"I mean, if things get out of [control, he can't handle it]... I think that's what freaked him out when I went ... to his apartment the other day..."

"Oh, my *God*."

"He just can't handle that."

"No."

"He's got to be in control of *everything*."

"Anytime people want to control, it comes from a fear-based reality."

"Of course."

"This is one thing I learned a long time ago—I don't want anyone to control me, but I don't want to control other people—it's too much work!"

"It is!"

"If you don't learn anything in this level, you don't control *much*. And the best way to get the results you want is to *let go* of control and let things *come to* you. So when you see people like that, it's just frightening."

"It *is*."

"Oh, he's so good at projecting—'I've got all this *power* and *money* and I'm going to take care of you...'"

"Exactly, exactly," I said enthusiastically because she had him *totally* pegged.

"...and I'm the big person that can help everybody..."

"Right."

"...when in essence that's not...he's a little frightened child."

"He is, exactly. And that comes out in him sometimes."

"Very childlike."

"Yes, he is, he is; it's very interesting."

"I saw that a lot."

"I would see him go into these modes where it was like he would turn into a seven-year-old."

"Oh, yeah."

"It's weird."

Miranda was convinced that Johnny had been sexually abused when he was a child, although there was, unfortunately, no way to prove it. Even so, she was convinced that the kind of fragmentation or manifestation of behavior Johnny exhibited came from some form of childhood sexual abuse. I told her the stories that "Jonathan" had told me about the priests at the boarding school having sex with the students and his adamant reaction to the story about the sex abuse scandal in which he had insisted that it was a lie, that the priests at his school hadn't forced the students to do anything they didn't want to do. Miranda had never heard *those* stories and found them very bizarre, if very interesting.

I thought that if Johnny *had* been sexually abused, his reactions were consistent with a type of defense mechanism called a *reaction formation* in which a person develops on a conscious level the opposite, and acceptable, thoughts or feelings from the unacceptable ones he harbors on an unconscious level. Another hallmark of a reaction formation is the forced quality with which the person who experiences it expresses his consciously held beliefs, something that "Jonathan's" vigorous denial of the coercive nature of the priests' behavior seemed to belie. Then again, Johnny's behavior could have been just another of his many acts, performed for some reason known only to him.

I told Miranda that I'd managed to speak to Laura. I told her, among other things, what I had learned about what Johnny had been telling her and her family about his relationship with Cliff. Miranda was flabbergasted. Unfortunately, I didn't have any answers for her about why Johnny had done what he had. I asked Miranda if Johnny had ever mentioned Cliff to her and, after thinking a moment, she remembered he had, since Cliff's full name was unusual. After verifying that Cliff was in fact a real person and not just another figment of Johnny's twisted imagination, I told her the story he had told me about his and Cliff's almost supernaturally intense love affair that ultimately was torn asunder. Miranda said that even though Johnny had mentioned Cliff to her, he had never told her any of what he had told me, which left me wondering what had *really* happened between him and Cliff.

She asked me if Johnny's things were still in storage. I told her that I didn't know, but that in June, I had contacted the storage facility and told them to stop placing the monthly charges on my credit card. I also told her that I had more recently gotten a letter from the facility informing me that if the belongings weren't claimed soon, they would be auctioned. Since the letters were being sent to me, not Johnny, he didn't know what was happening unless he himself had been checking. At the time, I had thought that I might let them auction off his belongings behind his back and buy them myself for next to nothing, reselling them at a profit to recoup some of my otherwise lost money. In the end, I had decided not to do that and, when I had gotten the letter, I had given the storage facility his address in Mariah so their correspondence could be sent to him. I didn't want to get into some kind of trouble for being underhanded, although the contract was in *my* name, but I also felt that to buy his belongings and resell them would maintain my entanglement with him. I wanted nothing further to do with him.

Even so, Miranda thought that there might be stolen money hidden in his belongings, including the purple chair about which Johnny was so obsessed, and that I should buy them and tear them apart. Her main concern, however, was that Johnny had placed the responsibility for the stored items in my name because they *did* contain stolen money and he was setting me up if the items came to the attention of the authorities. At that point, I wasn't putting *anything* past Johnny, but I still believed the main reason he had manipulated me into taking financial responsibility for the storage of his belongings was simply that he didn't want to do it himself. Although I had gotten stuck with $4,000 of his debt, that was, however, as far as it would go.

The first time I had visited her, Miranda had mentioned that higher forces had orchestrated my experience with Johnny. Her emphasis was on the astrological and the karmic. This time, I showed her a copy of my natal chart and she became even more strongly convinced of the inevitability of Johnny's and my meeting. "He's Scorpio and you have Scorpio Ascendant. It hit right in your chart. He hit right in your Twelfth and First House and your Ascendant. It's past life; you shouldn't feel stupid at all. You could never have avoided this. His sun hit right on your Neptune, which is delusion—you don't see things clearly. Twelfth House is always past life, hidden things, secrets… South Node, it's past life, big time. Just *big* time, past life. I mean, you didn't have a *chance*. It just hit right on your stuff. *God*. Oh, no, you could *never* have avoided this; it's *all* over your chart."

She then added a more numerological interpretation. "Your top number is his bottom number; your bottom number is his top number. Each of you owed the other person a karmic debt. Each of you had a missing piece of a puzzle."

Before I left, Miranda performed a healing ritual on me to break up the blockages that were preventing my spiritual energy from flowing freely and hindering my healing from my experience with Johnny. Whether it was psychic or psychological, I did leave feeling energized. I felt relieved of some more of my emotional baggage and I felt renewed.

That was the last time I saw Miranda, whose purpose in that chapter of my life seemed to be fulfilled. I recalled the first time "Jonathan" had mentioned her to me, more than a year before, and at the time, I could not have envisioned the twisting, winding path that would ultimately, but perhaps inevitably, lead me not only to her but also through her to a greater understanding of my life, myself.

■

During the third week of August, the week before the fall semester started, I waited to be contacted about teaching classes that fall. As the week wore on, however, the phone didn't ring. I began to wonder what was going on. Near the end of the week, I contacted the campus in Hawthorn to ask if they needed me to teach psychology that fall. To my shock, they said no. Apparently, someone else would be teaching the class that I had taught for the previous two and a half years. I also contacted the campus in Viridian to ask if *they* needed me to teach psychology that fall. Again, to my shock, they said no. Apparently someone else would be teaching the one psychology class they were offering that fall, despite the fact that I had been the *only* person who had taught psychology there for the previous two years. I didn't understand what was going on and was given no explanation for the change.

I started to become paranoid. Had Johnny contacted them and poisoned them with his lies about me in order to damage me? I knew how convincing he could be. Had they believed him? Had I lost my job because of his lies?

In the end, however, I was offered three classes: an introductory psychology class on Monday nights in a nearby town, an advanced psychology class on Wednesday nights in Hawthorn, and a basic math class on Thursday afternoons in Viridian. Since I didn't have a permanent contract and, therefore, the school was not obliged to give me further work, the classes were up for grabs by whoever was qualified and apparently other people had simply beaten me to the punch to teach them. The fact that they had was just a coincidence. The fact that I was eventually offered three classes without comment allayed my fears that Johnny had gotten to them with his lies, but I couldn't help wondering, sometimes worrying, what he was out there doing to damage me. I knew he would stop at nothing to damage me for the crime of having tried to expose his lies.

—41—
UNDUE INFLUENCE

...he had told me that you were stalking him...and that you might be dangerous. I just didn't know which one of you to believe. I think I know now.

Through the second half of July and the entirety of August, I attempted to pick up the pieces of my broken life in earnest and move on. With each passing day, I felt better, freer, stronger. Johnny was well on the way to becoming an unfortunate footnote in my life, but a footnote nonetheless.

On the first day of September, that all changed.

That Sunday afternoon, I went to check my e-mail. I was stunned, not because I wasn't expecting what I found, but because, in some strange way, I *was* expecting it: a message from Laura.

She began by telling me, ironically, that she knew she was probably the last person I expected to hear from, then told me that she had a big favor to ask of me. She said that she had thrown away "his" address that I had given to her, but now she needed it. She said that she was in the process of finding out some things on her own, in addition to what I had told her in July, regarding Johnny and was willing to share what she learned with me, but she had to verify some things before she did. She asked me if I was still pursuing him or if I had given up. Then, she told me she had one more thing to ask me and told me it was "very important" and to "please, please answer truthfully." She asked me if I had actually seen "him" the day I had gone to Mariah then had spoken to her or if I had just gone to his "house," as she referred to it. She promised that she would explain why she was asking me everything she was but needed the information first. She said she knew that she had told me she'd moved on, but she had changed her mind. She told me to get back to her as soon as I could, since it could benefit the both of us.

I was curious but cautious. I knew that Laura hadn't believed what I'd told her the day I'd confronted Johnny and I wondered why she was contacting me now. Knowing how devious Johnny was, my first thought was that he had manipulated her into believing him and was now using her to gather more information for him. He knew that I had spoken to his brother and, when he had shut the door in my face, I had yelled to him, "There are a lot of other people who know the truth," so I couldn't help wondering if he was now using Laura to find out whom I had spoken to and what I had learned.

After some careful thought, I composed a somewhat cautious message. In it, I told her that I was no longer trying to reclaim my money because doing so would just involve further entanglement with Johnny and I never wanted to have any kind of contact with him again. Even so, I told her, I was still interested in learning as much of the truth about him as possible because knowing the truth about him was far more precious to me than my $4,000. I assured her that the day I had gone to Mariah, I *had* seen him with my own eyes and explained precisely what had happened. I gave her his address and told her I thought he was probably still there. I told her that if we could help each other, I was more than willing to do my part.

Later that day, I received a response—one that not only confirmed what I had suspected Johnny had done in reaction to my telling Laura the truth, but also revealed some of what had happened after.

Once she thanked me for getting back to her, she acknowledged that she had been communicating with "whatever his name is," as she called Johnny, all along—something that didn't surprise me. She admitted the reason she didn't tell me that was that he had told her that I was stalking him and calling his family and friends and that I might be dangerous. She said she hadn't known which one of us to believe, then said, "I think I know now."

She told me that "he" had promised her and Jack a number of things that he was supposed to have delivered the previous weekend, but that when the time had come for him to make good on his promises, "he" had "conveniently" dropped out of sight, having failed to answer any e-mails or phone calls since the previous Sunday. Suspicious, she had decided to see if he was still around, so she had created a phony e-mail account under the name "Trevor," a gay man from England who was supposed to have found "Jonathan's" ads on the Internet, and had sent him a gay e-card. "Being the idiot that he is," she remarked, "he replied within an hour." At that point she realized that he had some "serious mental issues" and was more inclined to believe that *I* was the one who was sane. She said that afterwards, she had gone through the items he had left at her house and had found some "interesting things," although she didn't elaborate. She said that some of her friends were pulling in favors to dig up whatever "dirt" there was on him and that she should know more by that Wednesday.

She also said that "he" had told her that about a month before, I had shown up at the storage unit with a forged letter that gave me access to his things but that the manager had sensed trouble and had called him, scaring me off. That was ridiculous, since the rental contract had been in *my* name and *I* had had more right to his things than he had, but this *would* have been around the time that I had had his correspondence from the storage facility rerouted to him. I suspected he had been infuriated to learn that his belongings would be auctioned—or had been—and his accusation was just a pathetic attempt at retaliation.

Finally, she revealed why she had wanted to know if I had actually seen "Jonathan" at his house (as she still thought it was) the day I had confronted him or had merely gone there: He had told her that at the time, he was in *Italy*. The fact that he had lied to her about that only strengthened the case that *I* was the one telling the truth and *he* was the liar.

She concluded by asking me if I knew where his sex ads were and if they said anything she could use in fleshing out her alter ego, "Trevor"—which she planned to continue using.

Instead of writing back, I decided to call.

This time, Laura seemed *happy* to hear from me. This time, her tone was *very* different from what it had been the last time I'd spoken to her. She was just as eager to tell me everything that had happened as I was to hear it and she held nothing back now. A year to the day that we had begun it, Laura and I resumed the revealing conversation that "Jonathan" had interrupted.

Laura began by expanding on the events that had taken place the previous weekend. She explained to me that Jack had decided to attend school that fall and that "Jonathan" had promised to pay for his schooling. "Jonathan" was supposed to come to St. Alban that weekend to give them the payment in person, but when the time had come for him to do that, he had disappeared. After not getting a response from "Jonathan," Jack had contacted "Cliff" to find out what had happened to him. Shortly thereafter, "Cliff" had responded, explaining that "Jonathan" had suffered a massive nervous breakdown. "Cliff" had described "Jonathan" as a "pleaser for people" and apparently, the strain of trying to do everything for everyone had gotten to be too much. "Cliff" had described "Jonathan" as a "shattered man" and had said that he feared that he might be "gone to all of us."

The message was so dramatic and implausible, though, that Laura's reaction had been to call it "bullshit." That was when she had decided to find out what had *really* happened to "Jonathan."

Realizing as I had that she wasn't going to get the answers she needed by taking the direct approach, Laura had chosen to do something devious—something after my own heart. Posing as "Trevor," she had contacted "Jonathan." When he had made the fatal mistake of answering, she had known then that he was lying, had been lying, about his breakdown—and perhaps much more.

After deciding to go through the numerous bags of belongings that "Jonathan" had left at her home and that had remained untouched since he had fled her house the previous fall, she had found a number of documents that verified much what I had told her in July and highlighted "Jonathan's" deceitful and criminal behavior. At that point, she had decided to contact me.

In speaking with Laura, I learned more about the "interesting things" she had found. Among other items, she had discovered a number of unpaid utility bills from when he'd lived in the house on Millstone Drive. Some of the bills were in the name "Jonathan," while others were in the name "Johnny"—thereby verifying my claim that he was also (and accurately) called *Johnny* and was using at least two different names. In addition, she discovered a letter stating that "Jonathan's" COBRA insurance had been discontinued in February 2001—thereby verifying my claim that Johnny wasn't on leave from work the summer before, which is what he had told Laura, but had, by the time she'd met him, been unemployed for months.

Furthermore, she had found two W-2 forms from 1999 and 2000 with income totaling around $100,000. Assuming that he'd worked throughout most if not all of those two years, that meant he was making, on average, around $50,000 a year, a figure in line with the salary of a general manager or the head of a human resources department and certainly much less than the salary befitting a COO of an IT company. Since the forms that Laura had found included the ones that were supposed to be submitted with a filer's federal and state returns, and since online filing hadn't yet generally caught on, this suggested that Johnny had failed to file taxes for both years, making him guilty, not surprisingly, of yet another crime.

Of greater interest to me, however, Laura finally told me what had *really* happened in the aftermath of my telling her that everything "Jonathan" had been telling her was a lie. She said that after she had spoken to me that Saturday, she had e-mailed "Cliff" wanting to know who he was. She had also indicated that I was the one who had told her that what "Jonathan" and "Cliff" had been telling her was a lie. That had provoked an intensive e-mail exchange that had lasted through the next day.

During that time, "Jonathan" had sent her not one but several lengthy e-mails in which he had claimed that I was obsessed with him and was stalking him. He had claimed that I was harassing his family and friends and had repeatedly broken into not only his e-mail accounts, but also those of his friends. He claimed that in order to get back at him for not wanting to be with me, I was spreading lies—or, as he had called them, "half-truths"—about him. In the same way that Johnny had used his talent for manipulation to convince Laura and her family that Cliff was taking care of him and that "they" wanted Jack to live with them, he had also used it to convince Laura that I was insane and should not be believed. The story he had begun concocting about me in May was proving to be convenient and effective in discrediting me. By early July, he'd had more than two months to build on his story, and at that point, I could only imagine what those e-mails had said.

I told Laura that some of what Johnny had told her *was* true—but twisted. I *had* contacted some of his "friends"—Miranda and Greg Carroll—to try to find out what had happened to him because I was concerned about him. I *had* contacted some of his family—Terry—to tell them what their relation had been doing with the hope they would help stop him. And, I *had* gained access to two of *his* e-mail accounts—with *his* help. Laura herself had found it difficult to believe that I had actually hacked into all of the accounts that "Jonathan" had claimed I had and expressed her opinion that I would have had to be a "technological genius" to do it. Johnny had done exactly what people like him do, basing their lies on some kind of truth, then carefully twisting that truth to suit their needs.

Laura finally admitted that the reason she had warned me that "Jonathan" had "powerful friends" who could destroy me if I antagonized him was that she was concerned for me and was trying to help me. Thinking I might be mentally ill but rational enough to listen to reason, she thought she could frighten me into leaving "Jonathan" alone, for *my* sake. Later, I would find out more about *Laura's* experiences with "Jonathan's" "powerful friends."

Laura told me that one of the people "Jonathan" had mentioned whose e-mail account I was supposed to have hacked was Andy. She didn't know who he was, though. I told her that I wasn't sure that Andy was even a real person, that he was anything more than a figment of Johnny's imagination, if not an alternate personality that Johnny didn't know existed and, therefore, viewed as a separate person. Laura wanted to send an e-mail to "Andy" to see what kind of response we would get, but I advised against it. If Andy were really Johnny, then I had no idea how he might react or how much of that reaction might be directed at me.

I learned from Laura that "Jonathan" was claiming that he and "Cliff" were no longer together, despite the fact that "Cliff" knew what was happening to him. He and Glenn, however, were. Although having Glenn around certainly would have proven an obstacle to having Cliff around, "Jonathan" had told Laura that the main reason he and Cliff were no longer together was that "Cliff" couldn't "keep it in his pants." That seemed as convenient an excuse as any for getting "Cliff" out of the way.

In the messages I had seen in February, I knew that "Cliff" had stated that he and "Jonathan" were planning to move back to Paladin and that Jack would then come to live with them. Although "Cliff" was now out of the picture and the plans to have Jack come and live with "Jonathan" had stalled, Laura told me that "Jonathan" had told her that he had found a house in Paladin and either was planning to return or had returned. He had actually given Laura an address, but when she had checked it out, she had found that it didn't exist. If Johnny was still worried that the overbearing, money-grubbing, sex-obsessed Laura would hunt him down and take care of him, he was still doing an excellent job of keeping her from finding him. As it turned out, however, Johnny had more practical reasons for keeping Laura from tracking him down.

Laura finally told me what had *really* happened between "Jonathan" and her family when he had lived with her. Laura said that, far from pressuring him to give her $4,500 to eliminate her debts, as he'd eventually claimed, it had been *"Jonathan's"* idea to take care of her and her family financially. When "Jonathan" had first gone to live with her, she had told him that she wanted to make sure he understood that because no one in the family was employed, money was tight and he was going to have to pitch in. In response, "Jonathan" had told her to make a list of everything she and her sons needed and he would give them the money for it. The final total was $4,500, which was apparently the origin of that figure. Laura said that she still had the notebook in which they'd drawn up the list.

As far as Laura and her sons being shiftless leeches was concerned, it was apparently *Johnny* who had told them that they didn't need to worry about working because he would support them. Indeed, while "Jonathan" was telling me that Chuck and Jack spent their time stealing his money, Laura told me that he was handing them twenty-dollar bills "like candy" until she finally had to tell him to stop.

Laura told me that "Jonathan" had planned to buy her sons expensive new cars. He had even gone so far as to go with her sons to test drive cars and had actually gotten approved for a loan, knowing full well that he would never buy them. I was astonished that Johnny had actually managed to pass the credit check, although I was sure that he had used the "good" version of his—or someone *else's*—financial information. With that door opened, it was no wonder that Chuck had later expected "Jonathan" to help him make his truck payment—if in fact "Jonathan" hadn't promised him that he would.

Especially worrisome was the fact that, in the process, Johnny had gotten Jack's Social Security number. I didn't know what he might do with it, but I told Laura that I was concerned he might use it in one of his cons and that she should look into having it changed if possible. I knew what Johnny had done to his own brother with the information he had about *him* and I feared that he might do something similar, or worse, with Jack's, leaving Jack to deal with the resulting damage.

Laura told me that it was actually *"Jonathan's"* idea for her and her family to move to Mariah, not hers or Jack's. "Jonathan" had wanted them to take a two-week, all-expense-paid vacation to his home in the Southern state before they all moved to Mariah. That, he knew, was never going to happen, so conveniently, he used the idea that he and Cliff were together and that Cliff, who, in this version, didn't like Laura, was inconveniently in the way.

Most bizarre, however, was Laura's claim that *"Jonathan"* was the one who had mentioned marriage to *her*, not the other way around. She told me the day they had gone to Mariah to look at houses the previous October, "Jonathan" had turned to her at one point and had said, "We've been together for a while now, so when are we going to get married?" That reminded me of the wording of "Jonathan's" "proposal" to *me*. I remembered Laura's story about how "Jonathan" had told her he wasn't *completely* gay, and knowing something now about his *real* sexual history, I had to wonder if Johnny *did* have feelings for Laura...or if he simply wanted to cement his hold on her in the same way that he had apparently used his "proposal" to me to accomplish the same end.

Laura told me that eventually "Jonathan" had written her some $2,200 in checks to pay for the expenses he had told her he would. That, apparently, was the origin of "Jonathan's" claim that he had spent "nearly $2,000" after living with Laura for two weeks. Not surprisingly, the checks were bad, just as the ones he'd written to Miranda and Dan around the same time had been. By the time the bank had notified her that the checks were bad, however, Johnny was long gone. *That*, then, was the *real* reason Johnny had felt such an urgent need to leave: He knew that he needed to get away from her before she discovered what he had done.

When Laura was notified that the checks had bounced, she had contacted "Jonathan" to have him rectify the matter. That was when "Cliff" had appeared. She didn't elaborate as fully then as she would later about what had happened, but apparently, "Cliff" had bullied her into not filing suit against "Jonathan," stating that if she did, *he* would file suit against *her* for having "undue influence" over a chronically ill and confused man. Believing that "Cliff" had the power to destroy her if she pressed the issue, Laura had relented. The positive tone she had displayed in her e-mails to "Cliff" had been born not of liking, but of fear.

Laura told me that ultimately she had had to file for bankruptcy and Chuck had lost his truck because of how she and her family had believed "Jonathan's" lies and had counted on him to make good on the promises he had made to help them. Because she had filed for bankruptcy, she had forfeited her legal right to reclaim any of her lost money. Laura said that after everything that had happened, she had become suicidal. She had already been through enough that year with losing her job and being a single mother with two sons to support, the stress of which had driven her to the Stress Center and into Johnny's web.

Apparently, though, Laura wasn't the only one whom Johnny's behavior had driven to thoughts of suicide. Jack seemed to have gotten even more caught up in "Jonathan's" promises than the rest of Laura's family had. After continually disappointing him by never making good on any of those promises, after keeping him on an emotional roller coaster for months, Jack had finally suffered an emotional breakdown from the strain. Laura told me that in July, Jack had taken an overdose of sleeping pills and had almost died. I will never forget Laura crying on the phone to me as she told me what had happened. She made it clear that the main reason Jack had felt driven to suicide was Johnny. I was especially sickened to learn that "Jonathan" had actually had the gall to call Jack when he was in the hospital, again presenting himself as the caring, concerned father figure, when *he* was the reason Jack had tried to take his life. I had lost $4,000 because of Johnny, but *Jack* had almost lost his *life* because of him. It seemed that I had gotten off light.

After a lengthy and enlightening conversation—the conversation I wished we could have had in July that could have saved her, her family, and me two additional months of needless suffering—Laura and I said our good-byes. Even so, we continued to stay in touch and our conversation that day was in some ways only the beginning.

After we concluded our conversation, Laura sent me the e-mails that had gone back and forth between her and "Cliff" that week, starting with the first—and fatal—e-mail from "Cliff." In it, "Cliff" told Laura that Jack had contacted him letting him know that something was wrong with "Jonathan." According to "Cliff," "Jonathan" had suffered a "total collapse; physically, emotionally and mentally." He explained that although "Jonathan" had been trying to take care of everyone and everything throughout the past year, he had been in a fragile state the entire time and *he* was the one who had needed the care. Glenn's return had been a mixed blessing; although "Jonathan" had been obsessed with him for months and was now relieved to know after all that time that he was alive and well, Glenn was too much for "Jonathan" to handle alone in his depleted condition. In addition, "Cliff" described "Jonathan" as a "pleaser for people" he cared about, as someone who couldn't say no. Consequently, the pressures to do everything for everyone who asked him for help had only compounded his stress and he had become like a "drowning man." "Cliff" reminded Laura that he had called "Jonathan" every day when he had lived with her and had tried to help him make decisions and alleviate his burden, but after they had separated, no one had been doing that for months. Although normally, "Jonathan" could "run rings around everybody," he could no longer do that, despite the fact that he still acted as if he could. Finally having broken under the strain, "Jonathan" had gone "over the edge" on every level and was now a "shattered man." "Cliff" was left with the fear that "Jonathan," as he put it, "may be gone to all of us."

"Cliff" informed Laura that he would do anything he could to help, but that "Jonathan" was a proud man and was profoundly ashamed of what had happened to him. In his shame, he didn't want to see or speak to anyone. "Cliff" said that he would respect "Jonathan's" wishes but also try to keep an eye on him from afar, intervening if he could. "Cliff" assured Laura that "Jonathan" cared about her and Jack and that he had just wanted Laura to know what had happened to address Jack's concern.

In reading the message, I now understood for myself why Laura had considered it "bullshit." It was so melodramatic, so "over the edge," as "Jonathan" would have said, that it strained the thread of credulity to the point that it snapped it.

Seeing what kind of response she would get, seeing just how far "Jonathan" would go in playing his game, Laura responded with a message to "Cliff" that hinted that she knew it was all a lie. After telling "Cliff" that "Jonathan" wasn't the only one who was shattered, she told him that she was worried about Jack, since he loved "Jonathan" so much, and was devastated to hear what had happened to him. She then said that she knew something *must* have happened to "Jonathan" when he didn't come, since she knew he wouldn't "intentionally deceive" them, adding that she *hoped* that was true.

Although there was nothing funny about it, I could only laugh—at Laura's cleverness in perpetrating what was now *her* charade, at Johnny's stupidity at not realizing that now, *he* was the one who was being duped.

In response, the melodrama didn't end. Instead, "Cliff" only intensified it. "Jonathan's" condition had now grown far worse, with "Cliff" describing it as "really bad." Now, "Jonathan" refused to let "Cliff" see him—which, oddly, mirrored "Iain's" insistence to the *real* Cliff that "Jonathan" was too sick even to talk to him. "Cliff" asked Laura when the ever-considerate, ever-responsible "Jonathan" had simply not shown up when he'd promised to do so or had at least not let you know that he wasn't coming; "Cliff" assured her that it had never happened to *him*. "Jonathan" was now completely incapable of taking care of himself and "Cliff" informed Laura that he was worse now than when he'd given up his house the summer before because of his declining health. "Cliff" ended the message on an uncertain note, telling Laura that he didn't know what was going to happen next.

Unfazed, Laura replied, suggesting that if "Jonathan" was indeed so "shattered," then perhaps she should do something to help—namely, to notify his parents. She said she had their phone number and address and asked "Cliff" if he needed them.

In response, "Cliff" told Laura that "Jonathan's" parents were "old and sick" and that he would talk to "Jonathan's" brother.

Old and sick. That was closer to the truth than what "Jonathan" had told *me* about his fantasy parents, closer to the truth that Terry had told me about their *real* parents. So, while urging her not to trouble "Jonathan's" old, sick parents, "Cliff" would call "Terrence" instead—someone whose number Laura did *not* have. Ingenious. I marveled at how Johnny managed to find a way to work himself out of *every* corner.

Almost.

Ultimately, however, he had failed. Eventually, people like Johnny always go too far and that is always their undoing—and with Laura, he had finally gone too far.

■

In communicating with Laura, I discovered just how Johnny had been attempting to discredit me in the previous two months. He had spared no expense in painting me in the worst possible light. It was worse than I had imagined and thoroughly reflected the extent of his hatred toward me.

He had launched his assault in earnest on the evening of Saturday, July 6, the day that I had confronted him then contacted

Laura to tell her that much of what "Jonathan" had led her to believe to be true was a lie. In his first message, he not only repeated the themes that had originated in May and had been reflected in his messages to both me and "Darin," but also expanded on them in light of more recent events.

He informed Laura that I appeared to be suffering from dissociative identity disorder, which his "shrink" had suggested I had. He told her that I had broken into his e-mail accounts and had "harassed" his friends, then had denied that I had, claiming that "other people" had done it. My denial was proof that I had multiple personalities. His "shrink," warning him that I was dangerous, had told him to stay as far away from me as possible.

He complained that he couldn't understand why I wouldn't leave him—*them*—alone and go on with my life. He bemoaned the fact that although he was somewhat happy now, doing things, feeling better, I wouldn't let go. He claimed that I was fixated on him and that whenever he ignored me, I tried to get him to pay attention to me by doing "crazy things."

He then went on to catalogue the legal actions that he and his brother were planning to take against me. He was planning to file charges against me for violating his e-mail. His brother was planning to file charges against me for my harassing phone calls. They—presumably he and his brother, although he didn't specify—were planning to file restraining orders against me to keep me away.

He told Laura that I thought I had "scored" by discovering that he was still in Mariah in July and hadn't moved in the spring, which he had told her he had been planning to do. He expressed his hope that she hadn't told me that he would be moving in a few weeks, as he had told her he would now be doing. He stated that he didn't want me to know where he was, who he was with, or what he was doing.

The most interesting part of the message, however, was not the message itself, but the e-mail he had attached to the message. He said that it was one of the "many" "insane" e-mails that I had sent and was the "scariest." He urged her to read it then to decide for herself whether or not I was crazy.

I was stunned to find that the attached message had come from the infamous "Heorshema." The message was dated Sunday, May 5, the day after I had received the first of the threatening letters in the mail. At least that was the date it *appeared* to have been sent, although aside from Johnny's having alluded to such a message and its contents in his e-mail to me a week later, there was no clear evidence that it had existed before July 6. Whatever its origin, the writing style and content were identical to those of the letters I had received—everything capitalized with thoughts separated by long strings of periods and with a chilling, semi-psychotic tone. It was clear they had come from the same hand...the hand that had also belonged to The Pretender.

"Heorshema" began by telling "Jonathan" that he was bored with him now, calling him a "stupid 'bloody' fag." He said that he'd had a "helluva lot of fun over the last few weeks pulling everybody's strings and making them dance [his] dance but now that it look[ed] like everybody [was] going to do exactly what [he] want[ed] them to do [he was] bored now." He said that what he had accomplished had been "too easy" and lamented over what he would do now to have fun. "Heorshema" then said, as The Pretender had said to me in his second letter, that he was going to give my mother and me back our e-mail accounts so I could see what he *had* done. He then went on to make some incredibly vulgar sexual comments about my sister and warned her that "her time [would] come," suggesting, as had the sender of the letters to me, that my sister was a main target of his antipathy. He then went on to refer to me as a "fucking queer" and made equally vulgar comments about my mother. The content, the sentiments, were consistent with the letters I had received in May.

Most interesting—and perhaps most telling—of all was the "threat" that "Heorshema" had leveled at "Jonathan." The threat was directed not only at "Jonathan," but also at *me*...and it revolved around *the repayment of my money*. Specifically, the message said that "[i]f you pay Richard a single dime of what you owe him I'll hunt you down and break your goddamn neck...and his too." The threat was reinforced by "Heorshema" reminding us that "Paladin [was] not that big and Hawthorn [was] even smaller" and that he would find us. He ended by saying that if we didn't do exactly what he said, we had both "had it" and that we had been warned.

Those statements made it transparent, if nothing else had, that the main—or *a* main—reason The Pretender had done what he had was to try to make sure that I didn't recoup the money I had loaned to "Jonathan." The fact that nothing had ultimately happened to my sister, who was supposed to have borne the brunt of "Heorshema's" wrath, while *I* was the one who had been harmed, strongly suggested that "Heorshema" wasn't my ex-brother-in-law. The person who had the strongest motive of anyone for not repaying me was, of course, *Johnny*.

The threat against *me*—which made no sense if it were me or even an alternate personality, whose purpose, presumably, would be to *protect* me—could be seen as either an attempt to make it appear that the message came from a third party or an expression of Johnny's anger at me for expecting him to repay me, among other possibilities. It was interesting to me that Johnny had completely glossed over the threat against *me*, as well as those against my sister and mother, when he was trying to make me appear crazy to Laura and to me (assuming the message, and not just the sentiment, existed at the time), when it didn't suit his agenda. Although the message was in black and white for any literate person to read and interpret, Johnny tried, as he always did, to make people see what he wanted them to see.

Johnny's attacks against me and attempts to discredit me didn't stop there. Over the course of the next day, he sent Laura several additional messages that got worse as his story about me grew. In the second e-mail that Laura forwarded to me, "Jonathan" began by describing me as "obsessed and obsessive," then went on to explain to Laura that I was behaving the way I was because I was unable to accept the fact that he had "dumped" me. He told her, though, that our relationship was all in my mind because I was *never* his boyfriend. Because of my inability to accept the fact that he didn't want to be with me, I was now seeking a "twisted revenge" by harassing and hurting him, his family, and his friends. He told Laura that the only reason I had "dump[ed] this shit" on her was to hurt him through her; otherwise, I didn't give "2 shits" about her or Jack except as a tool to get to him.

He expanded on his previous claim that "Terrence"—whose name was spelled two different ways in the message—was filing a complaint against me with the telephone company. He told Laura that I called him "incessantly," and that at first, "Terrence" had let me ramble because what I was saying was "all so goofy," but eventually it had become "sick" and had crossed the line into harassment.

In addition, he repeated his claim that he was filing charges against me for breaking into his e-mail account, but now, he amplified his story by stating that I had broken into not only his account, but also Cliff's, Colin's, Andy's, and Alcuin's. Parroting what I had told him about my experience with The Pretender—or "telling it on himself," as Miranda had described it—he claimed that I had "sent them emails purporting to be from [him and had] sent [him] phony emails supposedly from them," which had caused an incredible amount of disruption until they had gotten the matter sorted out. He added that the only reason I knew that he and Laura were in contact was that I read his e-mail. He claimed that even though he changed the password regularly, I always managed to hack in.

Finally, he claimed that some of the fraudulent and harassing e-mails that I had authored had been written and sent from the computers at my workplace; consequently, his attorney was planning to contact the school, inform them of their liability, and have me fired.

Reminding me of the claim he had made in the May 12 message to me in which Warren had wanted to turn the "Heorshema" message over to the police but "Jonathan" had resisted because of his compassion for me, he now claimed that he had told me that if I ceased and got psychiatric help, "they" wouldn't press charges against me. Even so, he claimed that he only had my word that I was getting such help and now that I had gone "way over the edge," he would have to resort to legal means to restrain me.

Jonathan said that he feared for his safety, stating that after having reviewed the "Heorshema" e-mails, of which there were "literally hundreds," his psychiatrist in Paladin—who was now a man—was concerned that I could become violent. He also expressed his fears for Laura and Jack, now that I had chosen to target them. He assured them that he loved them, but also suggested that they should protect themselves from me by distancing themselves from him. He expressed his sadness at having to do that, since he cared about them so much, but thought it might be better for them if they didn't have the stress the situation was causing in their lives, since they already had enough to deal with. He lamented the fact that he already had enough stress himself taking care of Glenn and trying to maintain his own health and sanity without my insane behavior disrupting his life. He concluded by stating bluntly that I was "nuts" and implored Laura to believe him, for her own welfare. He told Laura that he loved her, but that she needed to do what was best for her and her son.

In the third e-mail that Laura forwarded to me, "Jonathan" told her that he had just spoken with Glenn's attending physician, who was more accessible than his psychiatrist, and had shown him some of the "Heorshema" e-mails, had described my behavior toward Laura, Colin, Andy, Terrence, and others, and had told him about my breaking into his house through a locked garage door and then going to Laura's. He said Glenn's doctor could only give him a superficial evaluation and some general advice. He believed that I was "sick, confused, very angry and [felt] rejected," and that the more I was allowed to talk about "Jonathan," the more empowered I felt and the more self-worth I gained when in fact I possessed very little. Referring to my setback in Paladin and the resulting reduction of my life, he told Laura that I couldn't make "a real life in the real world"—a statement I found ironic coming from someone who lived his life through the computer under a variety of guises. The doctor had advised the people I contacted to tell me, "'I am not interested in any of this, whether it is true or not. Please do not call or email me again or I will file a complaint' and then hang up or block his email." The implication was that it was crucial not to listen to me because "the more [I talked] about it the more the story [grew] and the more

[I] believe[d] what [I was] saying"—a statement I found especially interesting because that was precisely what *he* did and seemed to be a perfect example of Johnny's neurotic habit of "telling it on himself."

Again, he tried to understand why I was harassing him when he had done nothing to provoke it. Then, revealing his true feelings through the guise of others, he suggested a solution to the problem that he believed would be more effective than legal action or psychological treatment. He told Laura that Cliff wanted to kill me, "literally," and asked her where a homicidal patient from the Stress Center was when you needed him. And, again, he expressed his profound fear of me, stating that if I sank far enough into my feelings of frustration I might turn into "Heorshema" and "act," leaving it up to Laura to imagine what I might do. He said he was glad he was moving and never wanted me to know where he was. He ended the message with the melodramatic phrase, "The storm is passing."

There were more, but that was enough.

I was sickened and infuriated. I knew that Johnny had gotten to Laura with *some* kind of story to discredit me, but I had *no* idea how elaborate and detailed and horrible that story had been. Like all his other lies, it was so complex, cohesive, and complete that it was no wonder Laura had been convinced of its truth. It was no wonder she had been afraid to talk to me. *I* would have been, if *I* had believed what Johnny had said. Was there no depth to which he would not stoop to damage those who crossed him?

I was especially unnerved to think that in claiming that I had repeatedly broken into his and his friends' e-mail accounts and had sent "hundreds" of messages through them pretending to be them—a cast of characters that included the main players in the Andy fantasy and the "Cliff" messages—Johnny was planning to disown responsibility for most, if not all, of the "insane" e-mails that *he* had sent in the previous months. I had already wondered if he had created a fraudulent e-mail account in *my* name through which he pretended for whatever reason to be me, but the thought that he might try to blame *me* for what *he* had been doing—and that he might be believed—was especially upsetting.

The most interesting part of the e-mails, however, was the "advice" that Glenn's attending—who I believed didn't exist—gave to those to whom I tried to speak about "Jonathan": If I did, they were supposed to say, "I am not interested in any of this, whether it is true or not. Please do not call or email me again or I will file a complaint," then hang up or block my e-mails. *Whether it is true or not.* Even if he really *is* a psychopathic con artist, you should ignore it. That "advice" was no more rational than the alleged "advice" that his nonexistent psychiatrist in Paladin had given to him about Andy, but was endlessly revealing about his attitude toward the truth. Lies, truths...they were all the same, all morally equivalent, as long as they proved useful in achieving one's ends. I hated him now more than ever, and if he had been standing in front of me at that point, I might *have* become violent.

In addition, my phone call to him in June had not passed without comment. On Monday, June 24, "Jonathan" had sent Laura an e-mail in which he had asked her if I had been in contact with her, telling her, for the first time, that I had been "trying to get [his] attention and [had] been harassing a couple of [his] friends." He told her that the phone had rung "a little while" before—actually, *three days* before—but that he hadn't gotten to it in time to answer it. Even so, my name had appeared on the caller ID, so he knew it was me. He said that very few people had his number, so he wondered if I had gotten it from her. "Oh well," he wrote nonchalantly, saying he would be moving soon anyway. Then, leaving the issue abruptly behind, he asked her how she was doing and told her he was looking forward to hearing from her. He ended the message by asking her if "we"—it wasn't clear if he meant Cliff or Glenn and he—could see her the following Wednesday.

The e-mail revealed the same strange mixture of concern and nonchalance that his e-mail to me in May, in which he had accused me of having a dissociative disorder then had gone on to talk about the return of his things, had. *A psycho is stalking me, is harassing my friends, has gotten my private phone number...but "oh, well." So...ya wanna get together?* My impression was that he wasn't *that* concerned and I viewed his comments as part of some kind of preemptive strike to discredit me if I chose to tell Laura the truth about him. Although I hadn't threatened to tell Laura the truth as I had at first threatened to tell Andy, he undoubtedly feared the possibility that I might and be believed. I did find it amusing, however, that apparently he hadn't made the connection between having given his phone number to "Kev" only the day before and having received the call from me when "very few" people had the number. Johnny was smart, but not *that* smart, and occasionally he missed things—some more important than others.

After Laura had sent me the e-mails in which "Jonathan" had warned her that I was insane and dangerous, I asked her if I could read the "Trevor" e-mails. I was very curious to know what that exchange included. When I received them, I was not only fascinated, but also delighted to discover that Laura's and my minds worked so amazingly alike...to Johnny's detriment.

After "Trevor" had sent "Jonathan" the e-card, "Jonathan" had responded "within an hour," as Laura had said—proving that, far from having had a "total collapse" and being a "shattered man," he was perfectly fine. Continuing the exchange to see what else he would say, Laura, as "Trevor," offered "Jonathan" an abbreviated autobiography. He told "Jonathan" that he had been born and raised in London and had been in the States for about ten years. He said that he now lived in Los Angeles and, like "Jonathan," was involved in business. "Trevor" said that he had recently ended a long-term relationship and was lonely. He said that he had seen "Jonathan's" name around and thought that he had also lived in London. "Trevor" said that he wanted to hear more about "Jonathan," ending the message by thanking him for the response to the e-card and telling him that his day now seemed brighter.

Although the message lacked Briticisms that might have made it more convincing, the language was educated, if informal, and "Jonathan" didn't appear to take note of the lack of British grammar that he incorporated, whether consciously or not, into his own writing. Overall, the writing style fitted the character of "Trevor" perfectly.

I couldn't help noticing the first line of "Trevor's" e-mail, which read, "I appreciate your quick response." That reminded me of the first line of *"Jonathan's"* second e-mail to *me* and the first lines of two of *"Iain's"* early e-mails to *my* alter ego, "Chaz." Laura didn't know that and I found it not only ironic, but also strangely fitting.

Far more interesting, however, was "Jonathan's" reply. Something in "Trevor's" e-mail had aroused his suspicion and had made him wary. He went on to say that he was curious about where "Trevor" had found his name and, after apologizing for being so cautious, explained that someone he had met through the Internet and with whom he had had a "dating relationship" for a while had proven to be "psycho"—"really psycho"—and, in a now-familiar story, enumerated what he had done: hacking into his e-mail accounts, sending e-mails to people whose names and e-mail addresses he had found through them, calling and harassing his family and friends after he had stopped seeing him, breaking into his locked garage...which had made him hesitant about meeting people through the Internet. Changing the subject somewhat, "Jonathan" told "Trevor" that he had a strong connection to the U.K.—although he didn't tell him, as he had told me, that he was actually *from* there—and said that he would allay his suspicions so they could begin the process of becoming friends.

"Trevor's" response was even more brilliant. In it, he sympathized with "Jonathan" over the trouble he'd encountered, telling him how horrible he thought it must have been for him to have had someone invade his privacy the way he had. He then went on to tell "Jonathan" that he wasn't certain where he had seen his name, then explained that several months before, when his relationship had begun to deteriorate, he had gone online for the first time and had found several gay personals sites. He said that he had made a list of men who seemed interesting, of whom "Jonathan" was one, but had forgotten about the list when his partner and he had decided to work on their relationship. "Trevor" said that his former partner and he had been separated for only a few weeks and that morning he had found the list, which he had put away in his desk drawer. He said that online dating was new to him and he had hesitated to write but thought that he had nothing to lose and possibly much to gain.

Returning to what "Jonathan's" unnamed former partner had done to him, "Trevor" said that he couldn't imagine anyone being so cruel as to do what his partner had done and understood if "Jonathan" didn't want to continue communicating with him. Even so, "Trevor" assured "Jonathan" that he was a "truthful person, to a fault, actually" and could really just use a friend. He then ended the e-mail by saying that he hoped "Jonathan" was more at ease with him now, but if not, he appreciated "Jonathan's" response and wished him the best.

"Jonathan," however, not only did respond, but also revealed the identity of the "psycho." After telling "Trevor" that he was willing to take a chance and trust him, Jonathan went on to tell him that if he allowed "that Richard person" to destroy his chances of making new friends then Richard had won. He told "Trevor" that he wouldn't call Richard his partner—he had been in "real relationships and this was not one of them"—but that his experience with Richard had made him more cautious about meeting people through the Web. He concluded by saying that he had never been shy or unfriendly before and was willing to continue his exchange with "Trevor."

In reading "Jonathan's" second response, I was struck by three things. First, although Johnny's comments to "Trevor" were nowhere as detailed as those to Laura, they further revealed just how far the process of his believing his own lies about me had gone. Four months after they had first taken shape, they had become a permanent fixture in the way that Johnny thought of and reacted to me. The process I had observed at work in Johnny's mind, where lies became truths, fantasy became reality, was incredibly disturbing.

Second, I realized that part of what had raised Laura's suspicions about "Jonathan" wasn't just the obvious fact that the "nervous breakdown" story had been exposed as a lie, but also "Jonathan's" admission that we had had a "dating relationship" when he had previously told Laura that he wasn't interested in me "in that way" and that I was *never* his boyfriend.

Third, I thought it was interesting that "Jonathan" had commented that he had been in "real relationships and this was not one of them." I thoroughly agreed. *Real* relationships are based on mutual respect, trust, reciprocity, and truth—things that I never received from Johnny, who was completely incapable of giving them.

After sympathizing with "Trevor" about his failed relationship, "Jonathan" claimed that he was "about a year out of a long term relationship [himself]"—which I took to be some kind reference not to me but to Glenn. He then assured "Trevor" that they could move on with their lives because they were "strong men"—a portrayal very different from that of the "shattered man" that "Cliff" had claimed the very next day that "Jonathan" was. Otherwise, "Jonathan" claimed that although he was living in the Midwest, he still owned a "small mews house"—a fashionable, converted stable house that only the wealthy can afford—in London and visited as much as possible. All in all, he painted a picture similar to the one he'd painted for David Garrett in his e-mail to him in March—and, in some ways, similar to the one he'd painted to me when I had first met him.

The exchange between "Jonathan" and "Trevor" ended the day before Laura contacted me. Laura had thought about continuing the exchange and had asked me where his sex ads were so she could incorporate information from them into her messages, but in the end, she decided not to. She had gotten what she had wanted out of her charade, so she allowed "Trevor" to disappear back into cyberspace from which he had come.

Switching to other issues, I was curious to know what Johnny had told Laura about Glenn and how it differed from what he had told me. On Wednesday, I e-mailed Laura a list of questions about Glenn. In answering them, Laura confirmed that Johnny had told her that he and Glenn had separated sometime in the spring of 2000 and that the immediate cause of the separation was that Glenn had started beating Johnny up. I was beginning to suspect *that* part of Johnny's story was actually true. What I knew was *not* true was that Glenn had returned to *England*. Shedding some light on the question of what had happened to Glenn, Laura told me that "Jonathan" had told her not only that Glenn was *American*, but also that he had eventually gone to one of the Great Lakes states—the one where "Iain" had told "Chaz" he had worked before coming to mine. In looking through the unpaid phone bills Johnny had left behind, Laura found calls Johnny had made to a small town in that state. I had never heard of the town, but later, in performing an online search, I discovered that someone having Glenn's exact full name and presumed age was listed as living or having lived there. Since the town had a population of only a few hundred, it couldn't have been anyone else.

I knew, however, that if the chronology of events that I'd been given was correct, Glenn hadn't left the Paladin area immediately after he and Johnny had separated in the spring of 2000. Mike Harmon had told me that Johnny had hired Glenn to be part of his team, but Johnny hadn't started working at OutSource until sometime in mid-2000, after he and Glenn had separated. I didn't know how long Glenn had worked at OutSource, but it appeared likely that he had remained in Paladin throughout much of 2000.

Indeed, it was possible that he had still been in or near Paladin when I had started seeing "Jonathan." In an e-mail that he sent to me on Thursday, June 21 of the year before, "Jonathan" had told me that he had mentioned his health problems, which had emerged the day before, to "the ex"—Glenn—who had felt guilty enough about "Jonathan" being alone that he had offered to "come over" to comfort him. Given the casual nature of what he claimed Glenn had said, it seemed unlikely that "Jonathan" had meant come over from *England* but, rather, from somewhere much closer. Only in retrospect could I fully appreciate the truth that "Jonathan" had carelessly suggested.

I told Laura the story that Johnny had told me about Glenn's disappearance the previous September and asked her what kind of story he had told *her*. She said that she would have to think about it, but that the story he had told *me* "wasn't right." I was sure it wasn't. She did confirm, however, that she had actually spoken to Glenn when he had called in October as well as the story about the bad connection making it impossible to communicate with him. I had seen the letter—or at least the *envelope* in which *something* had come—that "Jonathan" had received from one of the Caribbean Islands the previous December, presumably from Glenn's mother. I didn't know, though, how the island really figured into the Glenn drama, if it did at all.

I *did* learn the truth, however, about the "trust fund" that "Jonathan" had told me Glenn's stepfather had set up for him that paid him £650 a month and that "Jonathan" had mentioned the day he was supposed to have received the letter from Glenn's mother begging him to find her son. The 650 *pounds* a month was, in reality, 1,000 *dollars* a month that Glenn received in *psychiatric disability*. "Jonathan" could not, of course, have told me the truth about the "fund," since that would have destroyed the façade of normality that he was trying to project. Once again, he had presented the "truth" to me in a way that didn't allow me to see the truth at all.

■

At some point in our correspondence, Laura and I stopped referring to *him* as "Jonathan" or "Johnny" and started referring to him simply as "J," since that seemed simpler. The resemblance between the letter J and the shape of the constellation Scorpio, the arachnid that stung and Johnny's sun sign, didn't escape me.

■

By Wednesday, September 4, several days had passed since the events of the previous weekend had led Laura to realize that Johnny had in fact been deceiving her and her family. In that time, she had passed from disbelief through suspicion through tentative acceptance to certainty, and by Wednesday, she had assimilated the truth to the point that she felt prepared to confront Johnny. At the conclusion of her message about Glenn, Laura said that she had been writing a letter to "J" telling him what she thought of him and what he'd done. She said she wasn't sending it yet, but it made her feel better putting her thoughts and feelings in writing. She told me, "You know."

I *did* know because by that point I had begun to write about my own experience with Johnny and it had helped. I told her, though, not to mention to him that we had been in touch over the past few days or what we had discussed. Johnny hated me enough and this would only provide further fuel for the fire of his psychopathic rage. I wasn't scared of him because I knew he had no real power to harm me, but emotionally I wasn't equipped at that point to deal with more retaliation.

On Wednesday evening, Laura e-mailed me. Attached was the letter she had written to Johnny in which she revealed that she knew the truth about how he had deceived her and her family and detailed how his lies had affected them. The letter was damning and devastating.

After expressing her hope that through his "fog of mental illness and fantasy" Johnny would understand how his lies had affected their lives, Laura told him that she finally knew the *xxcliff* e-mails had been written by *him*. She said that his pretending to be Cliff upset her the most because the "Cliff" e-mails were so horrendous that she couldn't imagine anyone writing them, let alone someone she thought she knew and loved. She accused him of preying on an unsuspecting family with limited resources whose only mistake was "rescuing" him from Dan and wanting to take care of him. She told him that in response to their hospitality, he had lied then left, leaving her with $2,200 worth of bad checks, then had had the audacity to e-mail her, pretending to be Cliff, and accuse her of having "undue influence" over a sick man. She told him she thought he was "sick all right" and that he made *her* sick.

Then, she told him that what *really* made her want to come to his apartment and "beat the life out of [him]" was how his endless promises and endless excuses for not fulfilling them had led Jack to attempt suicide. Shouting with capital letters and exclamation marks, she told him that Jack had almost *died* and asked him if he could get out of his "psychosis" long enough to realize what he had done. She also told him that because of him, she had been forced to file for bankruptcy and Chuck had lost his truck. She told him that none of these things would have happened if it weren't for him, that *he* was the one who had caused them.

Playing on his fear of having his whereabouts exposed, she told him that her boss had a good friend who was a private investigator and that he had found out where Johnny lived and had been watching him. She also told him that now that she had it, some of her family members would love to know his address so they could send some "big thugs" there and "beat [his] brains in." She expressed her feeling that, given the "pathetic" life he was living, they would be doing him a favor by killing him. She also told him about the W-2 forms she had found and how she had contacted the IRS's fraud department, giving them his address. She also told him that she had given Dan his address and taunted him by telling him that Dan had "said something about stopping by for a visit." She also told him that Chuck, who was no longer living at home, was coming home to visit at the end of the next week and had been wanting to "murder [him] for months now," since he had known what Johnny was from the beginning.

She told him that she finally knew the *real* reason he had stopped going to the Stress Center—they had kicked him out for not paying his bill—and that she was kicking *herself* for not figuring everything out before. She told him that she'd had her doubts, especially when she had learned that I had gone to his apartment and had found him there when he had told *her* that he was in *Italy*. "Quite a trick," she called it. She asked him how many other people he had conned. She told him the only thing that made her feel better was knowing that he was living in worse circumstances than she and her family were.

She asked him if he knew that when the bank had informed his father, whose name was also on the checking account from which Johnny had written the bad checks, that they had bounced, his father had signed an affidavit stating the checks had been stolen. She told Johnny that since that now made it appear as if his father was lying, his father could be accused of fraud. She told him she was composing a letter to his parents informing them of what he had done to them.

She told him that to try to recoup some of her lost money, she was going to have a garage sale and sell some of the things he'd left behind. She said it probably wouldn't bring in much but it would at least be something.

She said that now, she and her family could go on with their lives after having wasted an entire year because of him. She told him he should consider himself *very* lucky that Jack was still alive because if he had died, *he* would now be dead too. She told him that sooner or later he was going to antagonize the wrong person and said that now she understood why he always complained that he didn't feel "safe."

She told him that she hoped he was sane enough to understand the seriousness of his lies. She told him to check himself into an institution because he shouldn't be allowed to roam free.

She ended her rebuke by telling him that "Trevor from L.A." had told her to tell him "hi." Referring to her year-long ignorance about who was really behind the "Cliff" e-mails, she concluded by asking him, "You just don't ever know who is sending emails you receive, do you?"

I was ecstatic. For an entire year, Laura and her family had been deceived, manipulated, and exploited to the point that one of them had almost died. Now it was over. She had won. *We* had won.

We knew that Johnny would try to weasel out of what he had done and it was not long before Laura received the predictable response. As if resigned to his fate, he told her to do as she liked. He told her that she had no idea how difficult and horrible his life had become, how terrible it was to "be on top then gone." He told her he had tried to get out of his situation the only way he knew but unfortunately he didn't have what it took. He told her that he was at the end of his rope and that at least she had some rope left. He told her that he couldn't explain to her what he was experiencing, that he couldn't explain it to himself. He insisted that he hadn't meant to let the events of the past year happen, that everything had gotten out of his control a year before and he couldn't get that control back. He said he couldn't take anymore and ended his e-mail by saying, "There is no escape."

Unmoved by his attempts at further manipulation, Laura shot back, confronting him, among other things, with the fact that it wasn't Cliff but *I* who had been with him, taking care of him in Mariah. In response, he tried, once again, to come up with a plausible-sounding lie to explain away the revealed truth. He told her she was wrong, claiming that Cliff and I were "sort of simul[ta]nious" and that I had been around only occasionally—a half-truth at best, since Cliff hadn't been around at all. Continuing his attempts to discredit me, he told Laura that I was at least as sick as he was, if not sicker. Unfortunately for him, his own behavior had proven who was sick and who was not and, therefore, who should be believed.

Continuing to evade responsibility for his behavior, he told her that no one could understand what he was going through and described himself as a "spectator," able to observe what was happening but unable to do anything about it. He stated that he hadn't been himself for over a year and asked her why he had been going to the Stress Center if he had been well. He told her that taking care of Glenn had not been easy and the strain had only worsened his condition. He said that he didn't want to speak to or see anyone, that he just wanted to hide because he felt so ashamed of what he had become, and voiced his opinion that he should have killed himself the summer before, when he was on the verge of doing so. He told Laura that if she had seen his W-2 forms, then she had also seen that he made a good living when he was able to work, implying that if he weren't sick, he could have made good on the elaborate promises he'd made to Laura and her sons. He described himself as being at the "cul de sac" of his life and told her it was worse to have been well then gotten sick than it would have been to have never been well at all.

Pretending to be confused, he asked her if he was making sense and said that sometimes he wasn't sure, that sometimes he didn't make sense even to himself. The confusion excuse was familiar, and whether he used it to "explain" the inconsistencies in his lies, to achieve some kind of gain, or to evoke sympathy, it was just another of his many forms of manipulation.

In her response, Laura attacked Johnny's claims that his "sickness" explained his lies, pointing out that even if he was as sick as he claimed, he still had moments of clarity when he should have been able to see that what he was doing was wrong. She told him to go back to the Southern state, where he had once been institutionalized, and get some help, if it was true that things were really as bad as he claimed. She ended by telling him, though, that she now doubted that *anything* he told her was true.

In Johnny's overly dramatic response, he continued to weasel out of responsibility for his lies. Again, he said that seeing and being able to take action were two different things, comparing himself to a "rabbit who sees the wolf but freezes and can't hop away." And, again, he told her she should have let him kill himself the summer before instead of trying to help him and convince him to start over. Then, he reminded her of his experience with Dan, whom he described as "a predator and a drunk," as having a heart that was "black," and as "evil"—someone who was so awful that his own son had turned against him. He claimed that if he hadn't been ashamed to let his friends see how bad he was, that if his judgment hadn't been so impaired, he never would have "hooked up with friends like him or Richard," whom he implied were pathological substitutes for healthy friends. He told Laura that he had hoped to have recovered enough by then to be able to help Jack but that nothing had worked and he was in even worse shape now than he had been a year before. He told her that some of what he owned was worth a lot of money and that he would sell some of it, finally providing Jack and her with what he had promised to them. He concluded by assuring her that he wasn't "saying this to say it" and that she would "see when [she got] it."

Johnny's sincerity can perhaps be measured by the fact that at the same time he was groveling to Laura, he was posting sex ads on *Gayteway*. On Thursday, the 5th, the very next day, he posted an ad in which he revived a version of the blue-collar laborer persona he had employed before. In this ad, he stated that he was looking for partners along a broad swath that stretched north and south of Mariah. At the end, he complained that although he had heard that the message board was "dead," he thought he would try it anyway.

Then, only fifteen minutes later, he responded to his own ad by posting a reply under another alias in which the second persona also complained about the lack of action on the board. The second persona stated that he couldn't "party" with the first persona because he lived too far away, but told the first persona that if he did "hook up with some nice dick" to let everyone on the board know that people did actually meet through that board. True to form, Johnny was far more interested in playing games and reinforcing his ego than he was in anything else.

By the time I had read all of the defamatory e-mails that Johnny had sent to Laura, I was infuriated. I wrote to her, venting my fury toward him to her, then ending by telling her that I hoped she and her family didn't fall for any more of his lies so they wouldn't get hurt again.

In response, Laura tried to be consoling, telling me that she had thought long and hard before sending me those e-mails but had believed I could handle it. She also reminded me of what a "pathetic little man" he was, which was true. She assured me that she wouldn't fall for his lies again. She said that she had written to him again that day during lunch and had told him that if what he was telling her about his situation was true, then he should do the right thing and sell a couple of his valuables so he could repay her what he owed her. Not surprisingly, she hadn't heard anything more from him.

She never did.

I had told Laura that I would send her a copy of the tape of my conversation with Miranda in May. Although I didn't need to do that now as further proof that I was telling the truth, I still felt that Laura deserved to know what he was saying about her and what else he was doing not just from me but also from another knowledgeable victim. I sent the tape early the next week and she finally listened to it the following Saturday. She wrote to me later that day, telling me that she'd listened to the tape, and adding, "I hope he rots in hell." She said that neither of her sons had asked her about "Jonathan" and that she wasn't going to raise the subject. She had decided, wisely, that "[w]e just need to go on with our lives and know we are much better off without him." *Everyone* seemed to be much better off without him.

After the beginning of October, I didn't have any further contact with Laura for almost a month. Throughout that time, I decided to compose my own letter to Johnny. In the letter, I detailed what I had learned from Laura, not only about what he had been saying to her about me, but also about what he had done to her and her family through his psychopathic behavior. Around the end of October, I sent Laura an excerpt from the letter that pertained to her to make certain the information I had included in it was correct. I also asked her if she would send me a copy of the e-mail in which "Cliff" accused her of having "undue influence" over a sick man. She sent it, and several more. For the first time, I was able to see, clearly, what Johnny had attempted to do. Laura had said the e-mail was "awful" and, after reading it, I thought that "awful" was an understatement.

The e-mail had been sent in the late afternoon of Sunday, October 28, one week after Johnny had left Laura's. In it, "Cliff" began by telling Laura that *he* would consider paying her the $2,200 that "Jonathan" had promised to her, but that anything beyond that would have to be verified by "Jonathan." He then went on to question Laura's behavior toward "Jonathan," suggesting that she had manipulated him into giving her money by taking advantage of the mental confusion he was suffering. "Cliff" expressed his dismay at the "whiff of undue influence" over a sick person that Laura's behavior implied. He said that he would work with Laura because that was what "Jonathan" wanted, but that he himself was still disturbed by her questionable behavior.

"Cliff" also said that "Jonathan" had mentioned the promised trip to the Southern state but stated that he didn't feel that "Jonathan" was capable of managing it, something that should have been obvious to her. Otherwise, "Cliff" reported that "Jonathan" was thinking clearly that day but had overdone the day before and was now exhausted. "Cliff," with his ability to access "Jonathan's" e-mail through their "sharing" of accounts, had seen that Laura had sent "Jonathan" a couple of e-mails but that neither "Jonathan" nor "Cliff" had opened them. Overall, the animosity expressed in the e-mail was fairly subdued and was only a shadow of what was to come.

After not having heard from either "Cliff" or "Jonathan" for several days, Laura, who was still deeply concerned about "Jonathan's" health, sent "Cliff" an e-mail on Halloween in which she told "Cliff" that she cared about "Jonathan" and pleaded with "Cliff," who seemed to be ignoring her, to give her some kind of response.

On the day that was designed for hiding behind masks, Laura received a terse response in which "Cliff" told her that Jonathan hadn't been on the computer since the "week-end" and that he had been keeping him in bed resting after he had suffered some minor health problems from which he would soon recover.

Laura's response displayed not only her concern for "Jonathan," but also her fear of "Cliff." She thanked "Cliff" for apprising her of Jonathan's condition, but told him that even though she was glad that he was taking care of him, she wished "Cliff" wouldn't be so harsh with her. She asked him what was going to happen to the job and the house in Mariah now that "Jonathan" seemed too sick to work. She mentioned that in an e-mail that "Cliff" had sent to her sons, "Cliff" had stated that he had taken Jonathan to the hospital on the Monday before Halloween and she asked him why he had. She asked a number of other questions about "Jonathan's" condition, for which she apologized, but said that "Jonathan" wasn't available and she was concerned about him.

The response she received from "Cliff," which was the last in the exchange, was the most sickening of all for numerous reasons. In it, "Cliff" explained that he had taken Jonathan to the hospital because the infection in his heart had spread to his lungs and he was having trouble breathing. "Cliff" said that it had been frightening to "hear his chest rattle and see him turn almost blue trying to catch his breath," which had made him afraid that Jonathan was going into heart failure. "Cliff" said that Jonathan had stabilized, however, and after receiving some inhalation therapy, Jonathan had talked the doctor out of admitting him; altogether, they had spent 13 hours in the emergency room.

Turning to his feelings about Laura, "Cliff" said that regardless of what he thought of Laura and her behavior, Jonathan was "crazy" about her and her sons and claimed that when they had been in the emergency room, Jonathan had talked about them and had said that he was upset that he couldn't see them. "Cliff" offered his opinion that if Jonathan were straight, he would have said that he was in love with Laura and that perhaps in some way he was. "Cliff" claimed that Jonathan had asked him to "play nice" with her but said that he became aggressive if he felt that Jonathan was being manipulated and would do anything to protect him.

To emphasize the point, "Cliff" said that his attorney was a full partner in one of the "Big Six" law firms and that he had told him they had actionable cause for "undue influence" over a sick person—a felony. He explained that his attorney had looked at the checks that Jonathan had written from two different accounts while he was living with Laura—an old one he was planning to close and a new one into which he was transferring the funds—and had concluded that, in his opinion, both checkbooks looked identical except for the check numbers. Because money was still being transferred from the old account to the new one when Jonathan had written his check to Laura, the check would have cleared were it not for the fact that Laura's bank had held the check beyond the date when the old account was finally closed. Consequently, given the facts that there had been funds present in the old account when the check had been written and that Jonathan had not been informed about the lack of rollover—and, coupled with the mental confusion that resulted from his illness—there was no intent to defraud, hence little chance of prosecution.

"Cliff" warned her that he could easily move Jonathan out of jurisdiction and file charges against her for undue influence. "Cliff" asked her if she really wanted to face that. He reminded her that since he wasn't the one who had signed the checks, Jonathan was the one she would have to go after. "Cliff" claimed, though, that he would pursue the matter "to the max" if Laura provoked him, but told her that because he didn't want to put Jonathan through the stress of a legal case, he had chosen not to pursue it...yet. "Cliff" claimed that he had Jonathan's e-diary, which recorded that Laura had brought up money the first day that Jonathan had lived with her and that she had asked for a lot. "Cliff" concluded that he would try, for Jonathan's sake, to get along with her, but especially for Jack's, whom "Cliff" described as "the apple of [Jonathan's] eye."

Johnny's fingerprints were all over the message: his misspellings, his Briticisms, his peculiar punctuation, his overdramatized style... If Laura had only seen the similarities between "Cliff's" writing and Johnny's writing and figured out the truth when she'd originally received them, things might have turned out very differently. I couldn't help wondering how the previous year might have been different for all of us.

In addition, the fact that Johnny would go to such elaborate, grandiose lengths to keep Laura from trying to reclaim the money he owed her, to keep her from holding him accountable for what he had done to her, was further proof to me that The Pretender, who also appeared to be "Heorshema," had in fact been *Johnny*.

There were more, some to Laura, some to Jack. On Tuesday, November 27 of the previous year—the day after Johnny had, in reality, lost his job at the hospital—"Cliff" wrote to tell Laura that he and Jonathan were in Mariah but that Jonathan wasn't doing well and wouldn't be able to take the job at the hospital. "Cliff" said that he didn't think they would be able to stay there and that for the first time since he had started taking care of Jonathan he wasn't sure what to do. He concluded by asking Laura if she wanted to give her input into what was happening before they decided how to proceed. The e-mail, though tinged with uncertainty, was very businesslike and controlled, betraying none of the blatant, even suicidal desperation that Jonathan had displayed toward me the same day.

Two months later, on the morning of Monday, January 28, "Cliff" had written to Jack to apprise him of Jonathan's and his situation. He told Jack that Jonathan had suffered a flare-up of the lung infection that had plagued him since the end of October and that he was running a temperature, which was forcing him to remain in bed. In addition, "Cliff" said that he and Jonathan were still discussing what would happen next between them. "Cliff" said that Jonathan was still angry with him over "some imagined slights and things that [he] did or didn't do," which was causing friction. "Cliff" said, though, that if he left, no one would be there to take care of Jonathan except for paid help, which wasn't the same as "someone who love[d] you and [was] concerned for reasons other then a paycheck," a sentiment that revealed "Cliff's" devotion.

"Cliff" was quick, however, to counter any ideas that Jack might have about coming to Mariah to take care of Jonathan himself. "Cliff" told Jack that he thought he was too young take care of someone who depended on him for everything by himself and was afraid that if Jonathan saw him, he would insist on having Jack stay. Even so, "Cliff" said that Jonathan asked about Jack every day and said that as soon as Jonathan was well enough, Jack could visit. He said that Jonathan had also asked about Laura and Chuck, belying Johnny's true feelings toward them.

Then, he told Jack that they were hoping that Jonathan's health would improve enough to let Jonathan "move up the list for a transplant." Apparently the damage to his heart had reached a critical level. "Cliff" ended the e-mail on a sweet note, telling Jack that "the dogs look[ed] really cute now that their hair [was] growing back and [they] spen[t] nearly all of their time with Jonathan."

It was interesting to compare what Johnny, as "Cliff," had told Jack that day with what he, as "himself," had told *me* the same day. About half an hour before "Cliff" sent Jack the rather dramatic e-mail about "Jonathan's" medical condition, "Jonathan" had sent me a comparatively tepid one in which he complained that he was trying to figure out what to do with himself that morning but that he planned to go out to get dog food, which he would do between episodes of *Jerry Springer*. The next one I received that day, around 9:00 that night, was equally bland, informing me that aside from going out to get the dog food, he had mainly been lying down throughout the day watching TV. Apparently, he *had* found something to do with himself that morning beyond buying dog food and watching *Jerry Springer*, something that he had failed to tell me.

Like some insidious shape-shifter from science fiction, Johnny had the ability, the facility to assume almost any persona for almost any purpose he desired. The mixture of deception, manipulation, narcissism, cool malevolence, and unbridled self-centeredness that the messages to Laura and Jack collectively revealed was beyond description. To Johnny, the rest of us were simply tools to be used for his personal gain or pleasure. We were simply *things*, not beings with rights and feelings, with selves or lives that *mattered*. We were *nothing*. I already knew what he had done to others, but it wasn't until I read the e-mails that Johnny had sent to Laura and Jack as Cliff that I fully began to appreciate the horrifying potential for evil within someone who functioned without a conscience.

The day after "Cliff" had sent the reprehensible e-mail about "Jonathan's" condition to Jack was the day I had intercepted the unsuspecting message that Andy had sent to "Iain" in which Andy had regretfully informed Iain that he and "Jonathan" were no longer seeing each other. At the time, I had assumed, less because of what "Jonathan" had said than because of what Andy had said, that Johnny had in fact ended the "Andy thing"—something that, since May, I had known had *not* ended.

■

That September proved to be an eventful month. As it turned out, Laura was not the only one of Johnny's victims who would seek me out during the waning days of summer to learn the truth about "Jonathan."

—42—
MEETING CHASE

I am going to say that I am Chase.

I am not a "religious" person, meaning that I do not follow the tenets of a particular belief system, but I am a "spiritual" person, meaning that I do believe in a spiritual reality and strive to understand and connect to it. To this end, one thing I have always done is pray. Sometimes I pray little, sometimes I pray much, but I only pray when I have something meaningful to pray. As I have grown older, I have come to understand that some of the prayers that have the greatest chance of being answered seem to be the ones that are the most selfless, the ones in which the petitioner has the least to gain and another has the most. When I pray these prayers, ones in which I remove myself as much as humanly possible from what God, as I understand God, can do for *me*, I am never disappointed.

By the middle of September, Laura had learned the truth about how she and her family had been deceived by Johnny and she had begun the process of putting the damage and pain that Johnny's lies had caused her behind her. She was not his only victim, but at least she knew the truth. Others, however, did not.

During this time, I thought of Andy. I still didn't know if Andy was a real person or merely a product of Johnny's pathological mind, although I was slowly coming to believe that he was probably real. That idea was simpler, though somehow worse. If he *were* real, then he was yet another of Johnny's many victims who had unwittingly become entangled in his complex web of lies. I had been led to believe that the "Andy thing," as "Jonathan" had once described it, had ended in January, something that Andy himself had confirmed at the time, but I also knew that, according to the messages The Pretender had left behind in the spring, the "Andy thing" had been reenflamed sometime in the weeks that had followed. It was obvious that Andy hadn't believed what The Pretender had told him about "Jonathan," much of which appeared to have been accurate, and I didn't know what Andy did or didn't believe. It was possible that, five months later, he was still trapped in Johnny's web of deceit. Whatever he knew, I still couldn't accept the fact that for months Andy, if he were a real person, had been deceived in the most extravagant fashion and had almost thrown away his real life in the real world for a fantasy life that existed only in an ill mind. Andy deserved to know the truth if for no other reason than because it was *right*.

Aside from Andy's e-mail address, which I'd found through the "Iain" account, I had no way to contact Andy. Even if I had, I doubted he would believe anything I had to say. After all, he hadn't believed The Pretender, who he had thought was me. In addition, I was still partly laboring under the possibility that Andy might *not* be a real person and that if I e-mailed him, I might actually be e-mailing Johnny. I wasn't going to risk it. I didn't know what to do, so I did the only thing I could do.

I prayed.

On the afternoon of Monday, September 16, I was at one of the local parks photographing insects and escaping into nature. While I was there, I began to feel what some Christians call a "burden," an especially strong need to pray for someone or something. As I walked along a path that led me from the dense, dark woods back into the light, I began to pray that Andy would know the truth. I told God that I didn't know if Andy was a real person or not, but if he was, he deserved to know the truth. I prayed that Andy, wherever he was, would somehow learn the truth. Then, I left it to God.

■

The next morning, I turned on the computer and went online. When I did, an alert box appeared on the screen, informing me that I had received an e-mail in my "message" account. I assumed it was nothing out of the ordinary, since the only e-mail that got sent to that account was junk mail. When I checked the account, however, I could not have been more stunned by the message I found.

Short and to the point, the sender said that he was sure I was surprised to hear from him and told me that if I received his message to let him know that I had so we could talk.

The message was signed *Andy*.

Surprised wasn't *quite* the word.

At first, I didn't know what to think. First, I still wasn't convinced that "Andy" was a real person, that he wasn't, as Miranda had suggested and I had suspected, either a figment of Johnny's imagination or—even more disturbing—a separate personality with whom he had been communicating through e-mail. Second, I couldn't understand how "Andy" had acquired that particular address. I knew that *Johnny* had that address, but if Andy were in fact a separate person, why would Johnny have given it to him? Finally, I found the timing odd—suspiciously so: Answered prayers or not, I found it "convenient" that I was hearing from "Andy" only *two weeks* after hearing from Laura. Johnny knew that Laura and I had communicated in July, that I had told her much of what I had learned about him in the previous several months, but she had told him only a fraction of that at best and now the flow of information from her had been turned off. If Andy were just a figment of Johnny's imagination or even an alternate personality, then that persona or personality was trying to find out what I knew…which was a chilling thought. If Andy were a real person, however, then I suspected that Johnny had manipulated him in such a way that he was now using him to extract more information from me. I suspected a trap…and proceeded with caution.

After overcoming my initial shock and deciding on the most prudent way to proceed, I replied. I told "Andy" that although in one way I was surprised to hear from him, in another way I was not, and that I was eager to speak to him as well, already knowing what the subject would be. The message revealed nothing while prodding "Andy" to reveal *himself*. I sent the message, then waited.

Later that afternoon, "Andy" replied, saying that if I gave him a phone number and a time he would call. I gave him my number and told him to call me that evening. If I were actually communicating with Johnny, then I was giving him no new information and having Andy call me would actually work to my advantage, since I would at least learn whether or not Andy was a real person. I sent the message sometime around 5:30 that afternoon and told him to call me sometime after 7:00.

Because I was too full of nervous energy to wait by the phone, I went back to the park where I'd prayed the day before to finish watching a red-spotted purple emerge from its chrysalis, which I had discovered when I'd visited earlier that afternoon. When I returned home an hour later, I checked my e-mail, only to be disappointed when I found a reply from Andy in which he told me he would not be able to call me that evening because he had to get up for work early enough that he would have to be asleep by 7:00. He wanted to know if he could call me the next evening. I wondered if I was getting the runaround—one of *Johnny's* tactics. I told him that because I had to teach on Wednesday evenings, I wouldn't be available, although I would be available throughout the day on Wednesday.

By mid-afternoon the next day, I hadn't heard from him. I wondered if I would. Then, at precisely 3:00, the phone rang. After answering, a very official, efficient-sounding voice said, "Richard, this is Andrew Black."

Instantly, four months of wondering about whether or not Andy was a real person came to an end. Andy was *real*. I felt a strange sort of relief. The next question was, what had prompted him to contact me *now*?

Andy had an incredible story to tell me. About a week before, he had been driving through—of all places—Mariah. At one point, he had become tied up in traffic, which had given him some time to survey his surroundings. In doing so, he had spotted a familiar car— a champagne-colored Cadillac. And, inside the car, he had seen someone who should have been in London or Eiseley or Paladin or Hell or *anywhere* but Mariah: "Jonathan."

Andy said that he had been so angry that he had wanted to kill him. Instead, he had later e-mailed "Jonathan," asking him for concrete proof of the truth of what he had been leading him to believe about himself and his situation. "Jonathan" didn't respond.

By that point, though, Andy had already become suspicious of "Jonathan"—not so much because of anything anyone else had said or done as because of what "Jonathan" himself had said and done. First, Andy had called the hospital in Mariah, where The Pretender had told him "Jonathan" had worked, and confirmed that "Jonathan" had in fact worked there in November, placing him in Mariah when he should have been in England. Second, Andy couldn't verify certain pieces of information that "Jonathan" had given to him about himself for which there should have been public records if they were true. And, third, Andy had grown suspicious of "Jonathan" in general because of his endless series of promises that never materialized. In that respect, he had apparently followed the same pattern with Andy that he had with Laura's family and me.

When he mentioned the information that "I" had sent him in the spring, I informed him that I was not the one who had sent it. He wasn't expecting *that* twist in an already twisted situation. I explained what I believed to be true about what had happened and why it had happened. I told him that although I had seen the information about "Jonathan" that The Pretender had posted on the "message" site as well as the associated e-mails, I didn't know what other kinds of information he might have been given about "Jonathan's" actual identity and whereabouts. Eventually, Andy told me that he needed to go back to work, but I emphasized the fact that we needed to talk further.

After a week, I still hadn't heard from Andy. I didn't know if he was busy or overwhelmed or reluctant to learn more, but I still felt that he needed to know the truth. On Friday, the 27th, I e-mailed him and told him that I still wanted to speak to him. I emphasized the fact that "Jonathan" was dangerous and that he needed to know as much of the truth about him as possible, not only for its own sake, but also for his own protection. I also emphasized that, unlike "Jonathan," I had proof of the truth of what I had to tell him.

Later that day, he wrote back and said that he had intended to call me but had lost my number. I gave it to him again and told him to call. I had sent my last message from the public library around 5:00, and by the time I got home about half an hour later, I found that he had already called. Not getting me, he said he would call back.

Around 7:00, the phone rang. It was Andy. I told him that I had a lot of things to discuss with him and a lot of things to show to him and asked him if he wanted me to come to Paladin so we could meet. He said that he didn't get out much and that actually he wanted to come to Hawthorn. Andy suggested that we meet at 8:00 that evening, ironically, just across the street from the park where I had found myself praying less than two weeks before that Andy would know the truth.

I spent the next hour hurriedly assembling as much documentation as possible of the truth of what I had told and would tell Andy. The storage unit contract in "Jonathan's" and my names, credit card statements that placed "Jonathan" and me in my state when "Jonathan" should have been in England, the canceled check to Joan Vogel for my payment of "Jonathan's" February rent, the hollow Valentine's Day card that "Jonathan" had signed, e-mails from "Iain" both to Andy and to "Chaz," all the e-mails that "Jonathan" had sent to me regarding the "Andy thing"...anything and everything that seemed useful in proving the truth. Then, I hurried to the prearranged location, where I found him waiting. Andy *was* real and finally he was here.

When I first laid eyes on Andy, I was struck by his resemblance to Johnny. Like Johnny, Andy was short, had a stocky build, and had closely cropped black hair. Although Andy differed in having blue eyes, being clean shaven, and being in better shape, the similarities were striking. Indeed, Andy could have passed for Johnny's younger brother. Seeing Andy added even greater weight to my hypothesis that Johnny was particularly attracted or attached to men who, like Glenn and Greg Carroll, whose pictures I had seen, superficially provided a narcissistic reflection of himself. *I* didn't look like Johnny, but I had played another role in satisfying his narcissism. I recalled "Jonathan's" comment about homosexuality being a form of narcissism, of loving one's own image, and although I disagreed with what I considered to be an outdated Freudian belief, I had to believe that a significant component of *Johnny's* sexual makeup did in fact revolve around a desire to possess an externalized reflection of himself.

I suggested that we go to a nearby fast-food restaurant to talk. Andy told me that while on his way to Hawthorn, he'd been called in to work later that night and, therefore, wouldn't be able to stay as long as he'd wanted. Even so, he would be able to stay long enough for us to begin the process of replacing Johnny's lies with the truth.

After we got to the restaurant and got settled, I pulled out the documents I had brought with me. Seeing it, Andy asked, "What's all this shit?" I told him this "shit" was proof of the truth of what I had to tell him, of where *Johnny* had really been, of what *Johnny* had really been doing. He no longer had to take anyone's word for anything because here was tangible proof. As I watched him look through it, I was suffused with a feeling of intense satisfaction.

In the process of talking to Andy, I finally learned the full story that his e-mails to "Iain" had only hinted at. I also learned that I had misunderstood certain aspects of the scenario "Jonathan" had presented to Andy—not surprising, given the incomplete information on which I had to base my interpretations. Andy was very forthcoming and, on that night and in the days that followed, he answered every question I had ever had about his entanglement with "Jonathan."

According to Andy, "Jonathan" and he had first met around the beginning of July 2001, about a month after "Jonathan" and I had met. (This was also around the time that "Jonathan" and Chase were supposed to have met.) He was initially introduced to "Jonathan" through a friend of his—the Ryan who "Jonathan" had told me had put Andy in his care—who had contacted him one evening and had told him he wanted him to meet someone named "Jonathan" with whom he thought Andy might be compatible. All Andy had known at that point was that "Jonathan" was 41—an alternate age he'd frequently given in his sex ads at the time—and British. Andy had contacted "Jonathan" and the two of them had begun an online correspondence that had eventually culminated in a meeting at Half-Time, the gay-oriented restaurant in downtown Paladin, sometime in mid-July. (This was also the night that "Jonathan" was supposed to have gone out with Chase the week of our first fight and explained why "Jonathan" had mentioned Andy's name to the waiter when we went there a few days later.)

Apparently, though, things had not gone well between them, at least from "Jonathan's" perspective. "Jonathan" had left "somewhat disgusted," as Andy described it, having gotten the impression that Andy wasn't interested in him because of his age, his looks, or something else. Even so, they had continued their online correspondence and the relationship didn't progress beyond simple, perhaps somewhat sexualized, friendship. Andy said the two of them never had sex and he never went to Johnny's house in Paladin.

Then, sometime around the end of August, the same time that Johnny had moved out of his house on Millstone Drive, "Jonathan" had told Andy that, instead of having gone to Credence, he had gone back to England. At first, everything had seemed fine. Then, one day not long after "Jonathan" had returned "home," Andy had received an e-mail from Logan and Nigel, two of "Jonathan's" close friends, who had told him that "Jonathan" had suffered a terrible accident. According to them, "Jonathan" had climbed up on a ladder to change a light in a chandelier when he had lost his balance and had fallen, hitting his head on the fireplace mantel. He had lain on the floor, unconscious, until he was discovered by his maid eleven hours later. For the next five weeks, "Jonathan" had lain in a coma, hovering precariously in the netherworld between life and death.

During this time, at least three different people had appeared *en scène* and had begun vying for "Jonathan's" affections. One was Andy. The second was Logan, who had been interested in "Jonathan" for some time. (It was also at this time that *I* had first heard of Logan, who was presented to me in the guise of an emergency room doctor.) The third was a young man named Jack. In one of the e-mails that "Iain" had sent to Andy, "Iain" had made a fleeting reference to a Jack, assuring Andy that "Jack would never be anything more than eye candy for Jonathan." Knowing the *real* person on whom the character of "Jack" was based—the young man whom Johnny's machinations had nearly killed—I asked Andy who Jack was supposed to be. Andy said that "Jonathan" had initially begun seeing "Jack" as a "trick" and that "Jack" had been jockeying for position as "Jonathan's" boyfriend, primarily because "Jack" was a "gold digger" and had wanted a piece of "Jonathan's" millions. (Interestingly, that seemed to mirror "Jonathan's" complaints to me that Laura and her sons were money-grubbing leeches, comments that he was making around the same time.) Andy said that while Logan and "Jack" had both seemed more aggressive in their attempts to become the chosen one, he had tried to be a "gentleman," saying that "Jonathan" should be the one to do the choosing, should he regain consciousness.

Then, around the middle of October, "Jonathan" had awoken. Slowly he had recovered, although the fall had damaged his autonomic nervous system, the branch of the nervous system that controls the body's muscles, organs, and glands. The damage created unpredictable physical effects. One of these effects was occasional difficulty breathing, which required focused medical treatment.

By the end of October, "Jonathan" had recovered enough to be able to call Andy, the first direct communication they had had since before "Jonathan" had returned to England. This, however, was where Johnny had made his first mistake. The caller ID revealed that the number from which "Jonathan" was calling had not the expected prefix for London, but the prefix for the Mariah area. Andy's friend Ryan, who worked for the phone company, was actually the one to point out the discrepancy. Although "Jonathan" had explained it away by saying that the phone he had used belonged to Cliff—who was also included in the scenario as one of "Jonathan's" many suitors—that incident had planted the first seed of doubt about the truth of what "Jonathan" was telling him in Andy's mind. Unfortunately, it would still take many months for that seed, further nourished with the food of inconsistency and implausibility, to sprout and blossom into the flower of truth.

It was also at this point that "Jonathan" had first proposed the idea of seeing Andy in person, either by "Jonathan's" returning to the States or by Andy's coming to England. Eventually, it was decided that Andy would come to England.

At this time, "Iain Winslett" had appeared. The timing coincided with the first e-mails I had seen that Andy had sent to "Iain," which dated from the middle of November. This also coincided with the timing of the strange e-mail "Jonathan" had sent to me in which he had referred to "Iain," saying that an "Iain," who claimed to live in the same city and work at the same company that the "other" Iain did, had applied for a job at OutSource and that maybe the former "Iain" was my "phantom lover."

For Andy, though, "Iain" had undergone a career change. Now, he was no longer working in technology, but in travel. "Iain," who was supposed to be involved with "Jonathan's" best friend Colin, had been asked by Colin to make the arrangements to have Andy fly to England to be with "Jonathan."

Unfortunately, one mix-up after another had prevented that from happening. For example, Andy told me that "Iain" had made reservations for him to begin his journey to England from the airport in Winford. When Andy had tried to verify the reservation, however, he had found that the airline had no record of it. He had then contacted "Iain" to find out what had happened. "Iain" had replied, telling him that he had checked himself and had discovered that the computer file was blank. Somehow, the contents had mysteriously disappeared. (This reminded me of "Jonathan's" claim that his first heart test results had been lost and that all that had remained was an empty file.) Another time, "Iain" had simply told Andy that he had made reservations with one airline when in fact he had made them with another. "Iain" had apologized for the mistake, and although

"Jonathan" was supposed to have been furious with him for having made it, "Iain" had continued his (ultimately bungled) attempts to make travel arrangements, the result always being that Andy never got to England. "Iain" sounded very incompetent, I thought, and should have stayed in technology or hospice work.

By the time I intercepted the "Iain" e-mails around the middle of January, the situation between "Jonathan" and Andy had started to cool, and by the end of January, it appeared to have ended—something I believed mainly because *Andy*, not "Jonathan," had said it had.

Andy, however, then told me something that came as an utter shock to me. Although the e-mails that had been left behind in my account in April had suggested that either Andy or "Jonathan" had reenflamed the "Andy thing" sometime after the January "breakup," it was unclear to me what had actually happened. As it turned out, the "Andy thing" not only had not ended in January, but also had continued *in person*.

While "Jonathan" had been leading me to believe that he was trapped in Mariah and unable to travel because his car was in bad shape or because he was too sick to get out, he had started making at least semi-regular forays to Paladin to visit Andy. The visits had begun sometime in January, only days before I had discovered the final e-mail from Andy to "Iain." According to Andy, "Jonathan" had by that time recovered enough from his accident to resume a fairly normal life...which included his work for OutSource. The requirements of his job had sometimes brought him back to the United States...which included Paladin. Apparently, Andy had actually given "Jonathan" an electronic passkey to his apartment so he could come and go as he pleased. I told Andy that in March, "Jonathan" had shown me a passkey, but had told me it was a key to *Chase's* apartment. Andy confirmed that the passkey was actually to *his*.

Andy and I were able to determine specific dates and times when "Jonathan" had said he was in Paladin, allegedly with Chase's family, that he was actually with *him*. In January, "Jonathan" had told me that while he was spending the afternoon of the 20th in Paladin with the Tomlinsons, he had gone out to lunch with Chase. As it turned out, he had *really* gone out to lunch with *Andy*. He had, I now realized, intimated that he was planning to do something behind my back. I recalled that when "Jonathan" had asked me, in an e-mail to me from the 19th, whether or not he should go, he had said, "What do you think, my dear?" At the time, the term of endearment struck me as odd, although I wasn't sure why. Now I knew. His seeming sweetness had been nothing but a façade, a pretty face masking his true intentions.

Andy and I were also fairly certain that one of the e-mails that "Jonathan" had sent to me on Sunday, January 27, allegedly from the Tomlinsons' computer, was actually sent from *Andy's*. Indeed, much of what "Jonathan" had told me about Chase seemed to be true for *Andy*. I had suspected for some time that Chase—at least the Chase that "Jonathan" had presented to me—did not exist and now I was coming to believe that he was actually Andy in distorted form. As Andy said, "I am going to say that I am Chase." Later, I learned that Andy had a brother named "Chase," which suggested that was the origin of that character's name. Ironically, it was *Chase*, not Andy, who was the character.

Andy also told me about the circumstances that had led to his and "Jonathan's" "breakup" around the end of January. I had always assumed that "Jonathan" had succeeded in breeding a sufficient level of suspicion in Andy to cause him to become disillusioned and end the relationship, but there was apparently a more concrete reason that the relationship had ended.

Andy told me that the weekend before he had sent his final e-mail to "Iain" on Tuesday, January 29, he had been asleep in his bedroom around midnight when he had woken up to find "Jonathan" looming in the bedroom doorway wanting sex. Andy said that "Jonathan" had "scared the hell out of [him]," but he had recovered enough to allow "Jonathan" to stay. "Jonathan" had told him that he had been to Boston on business and had decided to make a stop in Paladin to see Andy before heading to California on business. He said that "Jonathan" had taken off his clothes and had gotten into bed, but Andy hadn't wanted to have sex, so they had just "sort of rubbed around on each other." Eventually, "Jonathan" had put his clothes back on and had left, but the incident apparently caused a rift in the relationship, leading to its dissolution. So much for "Jonathan's" tears, I thought, when he had told me he would never cheat on me when I had found that he had given "Iain's" e-mail address on his *Sex Now* profile only two weeks before.

I had come to wonder what Johnny had actually done Easter weekend, which he had allegedly spent with the Tomlinsons. Obviously he hadn't, but I wondered if he'd spent time with Andy. Apparently, he had not. According to Andy, "Jonathan" had told him that although he would normally want to spend Easter with his family in Eiseley, he wished to stay in Paladin to be near Andy, since he wasn't getting along with his parents, who wanted "Jonathan" to live in seclusion. Consequently, he had tried to spend Easter with a man named Chester, who lived in Paladin. ("Jonathan" had mentioned a friend named Chester, one of the few gay men in Paladin he seemed to like, but I had never met him and now doubted he existed.) "Jonathan" had gone to Chester's on the Saturday before

Easter but couldn't stay with him because Chester had to go to be with his family in another state. He then said that he had spent Easter with a man named Mike Carlson, who was ("strangely enough," as Andy put it) also from England. "Jonathan" explained that Mike was an old friend of Glenn's who ("just happened," as Andy put it) to be involved in a project at, of all places, *the hospital in Mariah*.

While "Jonathan" was staying with Mike, he had apparently begun feeling ill with the flu. Andy had wanted to be with him, so he had told "Jonathan" to tell him where he was so he could visit him. "Jonathan" had said, however, that it would be considered an imposition and because he was already sick and a guest in someone else's house he could hardly invite Andy over, if only to visit. This had gone on for a week. At the end of the week—which was the week that, in reality, we had broken up—"Jonathan" had started to feel better, but had decided to stay with Mike for a while longer to ensure that he didn't relapse. Given the severity of his neurological condition, it had seemed only right that "Jonathan" stay put until he was healthy. Although Andy hadn't argued with "Jonathan," he had let him know that he was unhappy about not being able to see him.

On the following Wednesday, "Jonathan" had claimed that Sarah's children, who were supposed to be doctors, had come to the United States and had taken him back to England. Andy said that after his face-to-face encounters with "Jonathan" earlier in the year, that was the last he had physically seen of him until the day in September when he had seen him in Mariah.

I had never heard "Jonathan" mention a Mike Carlson. The only Mikes that "Jonathan" had ever mentioned to me were his brother Michael (who didn't exist) and Mike Harmon, the CEO of OutSource (who did). Although "Mike Carlson" might have been an actual person, I assumed he was probably just another of the many fictional devices Johnny employed in his deceptions. It did seem terribly coincidental to me that a friend of Glenn's (the British version) had "strangely enough" ended up at an obscure hospital in an obscure city in the United States that "just happened" to be only an hour-and-a-half drive from where "Jonathan" had used to live.

In the five months that had passed between the beginning of April and the beginning of September, "Jonathan" had allegedly remained in England, where his brother Reginald had taken control over most of his life. According to Andy, they were supposedly putting together an "agreement" in which "Jonathan" would take care of Andy. Andy said, however, that because of one holdup after another the agreement was never delivered—a story that fitted neatly into Johnny's pattern of making grandiose promises then using one excuse after another for never making good on them.

Andy said that eventually he had become so frustrated that he had decided to stop talking to "Jonathan" and his family. Several weeks later, though, he had decided to resume contact. He had told "Jonathan" that after he'd learned the agreement had been held up once again, the stress had caused him to suffer a nervous breakdown. That wasn't true, Andy said, but it was at that point that he had decided to starting telling "untruths," as he called them, in order to make his personal situation seem worse than it actually was and to evoke sympathy that he hoped would move "Jonathan's" family to take some kind of definite action.

Andy told me that eventually, "Jonathan's" brother Reginald, along with his sister Sarah, had forced "Jonathan" to sign over his wealth to a trustee, claiming that "Jonathan" was of diminished capacity. Unable to tolerate the loss of control over his life in England, "Jonathan" had decided to move back to the United States and, using the limited amount of money he had secreted away here, begin a new life free of his family's control, though also devoid of their wealth. Once again, "Jonathan" was able to weasel out of making good on any of his material promises to Andy, since "Jonathan's" financial status had now been reduced to that of the typical commoner.

By the time Andy contacted me, "Jonathan" was supposed to be in the process of resettling in Paladin. Allegedly, he was splitting his time between staying with Chester and staying at his own place. Andy said that he had asked "Jonathan" where he was living, but "Jonathan" had never been specific. "Jonathan" had told Andy where *Chester* lived, however, but when Andy had investigated, he had found the house vacant—a ruse similar to the one he had tried with Laura. By then, Andy had accumulated enough doubts about "Jonathan" to question his veracity, but I wondered how long Andy would have continued to be snared in Johnny's web of lies had he not had his fateful encounter with him in Mariah that had confirmed his suspicions once and for all.

I knew that the information The Pretender had sent to Andy in April had included Johnny's address in Mariah. I asked him if he had investigated it at the time and he said that he had actually done so about three or four days after the date when he had been told that "Jonathan" would be moving out in late April. Although Johnny was still there at the time, Andy said that he hadn't seen anything that would indicate he was actually there. That was unfortunate because it might have saved Andy five more months of entanglement.

In the process of untangling the web of lies that Johnny had woven, I forwarded Andy a copy of the e-mail that "Jonathan" had sent to me in which he had told me that he had been invited to "Warren and Joanne's" the weekend that, in *reality*, he had shown up at Andy's apartment at midnight wanting sex and had "scared the hell out of [him]." Because I had never had any concrete proof that Warren and Joanne were real people, I had eventually come to believe they were probably no more real than Chase was. I certainly knew that some of the e-mails "Jonathan" had sent to me in which he had claimed he was in Paladin with the Tomlinsons had actually been sent from Mariah, which made me doubt they even existed.

In response to the e-mail, however, Andy wrote back informing me that they *did* exist and that he knew who they *really* were: Warren and Joanne were *his* stepfather and biological mother.

Andy also confirmed that, far from being the best of friends, "Jonathan" had actually spoken to Joanne only once, on the phone, and had never actually met either Joanne or Warren in person. Overall, Andy was "appalled" to learn that Johnny had dragged them into his fantasies and had been using them as his mouthpieces. I told him that wasn't the first time Johnny had done that and that it was just another example of his standard practice of using the personas of real people, without their knowledge, for his own purposes.

If Chase was really Andy in some form, I wondered how much of Andy's actual life Johnny had incorporated into the character of "Chase." I asked Andy if he played the piano, but he told me he didn't. I asked him about the story that "Jonathan" had told me about how they had met, which involved the two of them getting high and ending up in bed together, but he told me that had never happened and, further, that "pot suck[ed]." Although I didn't ask him, I inferred that Andy had never attended the university in Hawthorn or, to my knowledge, post-secondary school at all. I suspected, then, that Johnny had simply gotten the idea that Chase was a student there from *me*.

I was also interested to know more about the "agreement" that "Jonathan" and Andy had been in the process of formulating. Andy had said that "Jonathan" had offered to buy him an expensive car (as he had Chuck and Jack), so I assumed that he was offering to provide for Andy in other ways. According to Andy, the agreement was supposed to protect both "Jonathan" and him financially and legally in the event that "Jonathan" died from complications related to his accident. "Jonathan's" family proposed the agreement and asked Andy to make suggestions for his compensation based on what he understood "Jonathan" wanted for him. In response, Andy suggested the continuation of his current salary of $50,000 a year, a supplement of $10,000 a month—$120,000 a year—complete medical coverage, reimbursement for travel, transportation costs, and the maintenance of an American residence for at least one year after his arrival in England.

Finally, the contract included an "infidelity clause": If Andy cheated on "Jonathan" and was caught, the contract became null and void. I didn't ask, but I assumed the same stipulation didn't apply to "Jonathan."

Altogether, Andy would have been making about $180,000 a year with generous fringe benefits. All in all, not a bad deal—*if* it had been real.

In one of his e-mails, Andy exclaimed that it would be wonderful to get back at Johnny for what he had done, although he wasn't sure how to do it. I suggested that we could taunt Johnny by taking a picture of the two of us together and sending it to him.

In response, Andy told me that although he thought my heart was in the right place, he was afraid that Johnny might use the picture, as well as other information he had about him, to create an alternate identity. Andy felt that Johnny had too much to work with the way it was. Apparently, "Jonathan" had told Andy that he wanted the two of them to go to China and had told him that he wanted Andy to send him a picture of himself that he could use in a visa application. Of course, the trip never happened, but Johnny now had both copies of the picture, which made Andy nervous. I thought his concern was valid, given how much they looked alike.

The scenario Andy outlined sounded all too familiar. I thought of all the contortions I had been put through in arranging the trip to England—a trip that Johnny knew from the beginning would never happen. Knowing now that Chase did not exist, I also began to wonder if Johnny had concocted the scenario in which he and Chase had slept together specifically with the intention of alienating me enough that I would not only conveniently relieve him of the burden of inventing a convincing explanation for why we couldn't go, but also allow him to save face, as he loved to do. The incident had allegedly occurred only a week before we were supposed to leave and the timing now seemed suspicious to me. I would never know the truth behind that lie, but I did know that our trip had been just another of Johnny's pathological games.

I was interested to learn how *Glenn* had been incorporated into Johnny's fantasies that had involved Andy. "Jonathan's" relationship with Andy was occurring at the same time that Glenn was missing, so I was certain it had come up in some fashion. I was not disappointed. Andy told me that Glenn was supposed to have been killed in an automobile accident on his way to visit his parents in the south of England. Apparently, Glenn had become so fixated on "Jonathan" while he was comatose that Glenn's health had begun to deteriorate. Concerned for his well-being, "Jonathan's" parents had sent Glenn to visit his own parents, something he was reluctant to do. On his way back, Glenn's car was hit by a truck, killing him. Andy didn't say when this was supposed to have happened, but it was during the time that Glenn was missing.

Through his story about the accident, Johnny was obviously expressing either his fear that Glenn was dead or, as Miranda had suggested, his desire to see Glenn dead. I didn't know which was true, but neither was good.

I also thought about the e-mail I had received from "Jonathan" only a few days after I had met him in which he had told me that "Alexander," a close friend of his in England whom he had known for 14 years, had died. "Jonathan" had described "Alexander" as a "dear, warm loving person who just wanted to be loved and happy" and had said that he would miss him "every day for the rest of [his] life." Given that "Alexander" was Glenn's last name and that references to the ending of a long-term relationship stretching back for many years had appeared in Johnny's ads, I had to wonder if the feelings his e-mail had expressed had somehow related to Glenn, to the sense—or the wish—that he had somehow died. I didn't know, would never know.

As far as any plans to abandon his life in the United States and move to England were concerned, Andy assured me that throughout everything that had happened between him and "Jonathan," he had never put himself in a position where he could be harmed and would never put his life in jeopardy for anyone. I was profoundly relieved to hear that, since that had been my primary concern from the moment that I had first learned about the "Andy thing" some nine months before. Even though Andy had fallen for Johnny's lies, he had actually had far more sense and solidity than I had ever realized.

■

After Andy and I had exchanged information for a couple of weeks, he, as Laura had, finally reached the point that he decided to reveal to the person whom he now knew as *Johnny* that he knew the truth. "Jonathan" had told him that he was in the process of moving back to Paladin but had been giving him vague and false information about where he was going to be living so Andy could not, of course, find him. Around the beginning of October, Andy wrote to "Jonathan" and asked him for specific information, but in response, Andy received what he described as "blather." Having had enough of the charade that had wasted more than a year of his life, Andy finally wrote the message that was long overdue.

After calling him a "boob," Andy went on to point out how casually "Jonathan" dismissed his lies, "as if they were a fundamental part of [his] life." As Laura had, Andy expressed astonishment at how he had believed "Jonathan's" lies for so long.

He then went on to detail how, in looking back, he had gotten pulled into "Jonathan's" lies through the help of invented family members and friends, who had seemed real to him. Andy said he didn't care what was true and what was not, but he did want "Jonathan" to know that he had been found out.

Andy traced the transformations of "Jonathan's" persona over time as he changed from upper-crust millionaire to struggling invalid to object of suitors to victim of repression and finally to a man who had only a commoner's means, a status that would neatly allow "Jonathan" to weasel out of making good on his promises to Andy. He expressed his thankfulness that "Jonathan" hadn't gotten any money out of *him*, which meant that he had no legal case to bring against him, but he understood that several people in the area did. He also expressed his hope that his victims took the opportunity to bring a criminal like him to justice. He said he thought that perhaps the investigation into his crimes could begin in his birthplace—not Eiseley, but his *real* one...in the *Midwestern state*. He commented on how interesting it all was, then called him not by his assumed name, "Jonathan," but by his *real* name, *Johnny*. He concluded by telling him that normally he would say "talk to you later," but that, in Johnny's "pathetic" case, he thought not.

Johnny didn't respond. That day, "Jonathan" finally died from the mortal wound that was the truth.

■

The details of his experience with Johnny that Andy had provided were enlightening and fascinating, but in some ways I was less interested in *what* had happened than in *why* it had happened. What had pulled Andy into his relationship with "Jonathan?" The overwhelming motivation, it appeared, was money. From the moment we sat down to talk, Andy admitted that he had "dollar signs in [his] eyes" and thought he stood to profit financially from the relationship. "Jonathan" had told him that the family fortune amounted to some £500 million—roughly $800 million US at the time—and that he stood to inherit a substantial portion of it. Andy also said that he was more fundamentally motivated by what he termed "self-preservation." Apparently, he saw grabbing some of "Jonathan's" millions as his greatest opportunity yet to "preserve" himself. Andy, then, was one person who had actually gotten snared in Johnny's web of deceit because he had thought he stood to profit.

In spite of the paramount financial motive for his involvement with "Jonathan," Andy did add that he had emotional reasons for becoming and remaining snared in the situation. First, he said that he genuinely liked "Jonathan" and felt sorry for him—something that I understood because that, in part, had kept *me* in *my* relationship with him. Second, he said that he was driven by what he described as "the love that gay men so desperately seem to need." I didn't know if gay men needed love any more desperately than anyone else did, but Andy certainly gave me the impression that *he* desperately needed it. He didn't perceive himself to be successful with other men and, at the end of one instant-message session, lamented that he was "off to the gay bar for a beer, and if I am lucky prince charming wil[l] show up so I can see him fall in love with someone else."

In addition, Andy seemed to be socially isolated—something to which "Jonathan" had actually alluded earlier in the spring—and had told me that he would come to Hawthorn to see me rather than the reverse because he "[didn't] get out much." He also told me, when we were instant-messaging one time, that he and his roommate had *seven* computers going and were carrying on multiple instant-message sessions at once. Although he had real friends in the real world, he seemed to spend much of his time interacting with people through the Internet rather than in person. He seemed relatively introverted and cerebral, which seemed to place something of a barrier between him and others.

On top of all of this—or perhaps because of it—Andy appeared to have a drinking problem, although I was never able to gauge the extent of it. He once concluded an e-mail by telling me that he was "a little sloshed" and another e-mail was somewhat difficult to read because many of the words had missing letters, which suggested he had been drinking. In instant-message sessions, he sometimes talked about the drinks he was drinking and, of course, went off to the bar at the end of one to have a drink. Overall, I thought that his social isolation, need for love, desire for "self-preservation," and drinking had all conspired to make him especially vulnerable to someone like Johnny.

After our initial, intensified contact in late September and early October, Andy and I continued to correspond more intermittently throughout the next few months. I thought he was an interesting person, but I also thought he was opportunistic. Apart from his bald admission to me that he had become and had remained entangled with "Jonathan" because he had had "dollar signs in [his] eyes," Andy's most revealing comment regarding what drove him came in January when I told him that I was thinking about writing a book about my experience with Johnny. To that, he instantly responded, "[m]y information is now for sale." If he couldn't get millions out of an injured and possibly dying man, it appeared, then maybe he could get a few bucks out of *me*. Although he relented on his position and continued giving me information free of charge, his spontaneous reaction said it all. In the end, I came to believe that of all of Andy's motivations for his relationship with Johnny, it was really the love of money more than anything else that had been at the root of it all.

Eventually, we stopped communicating, more because we seemed to have nothing left to say to each other than because we had some kind of difficulty. Sometime after the beginning of 2003, I didn't hear anything further from "Chase"—Andy in disguise—and for *me*, the "Andy thing," as "Jonathan" had called it, finally ended.

—43—
GOOD DAN

Richard: "He said you didn't want me...there, which is why I stayed away." Dan: "That's not true...he constantly berated you and made fun of you while he was here..."

By the beginning of October, I had spoken with Laura and had spoken with Andy and we had replaced the lies that Johnny had told us with the truth. There was, however, one person who had been a significant player in the drama of the previous year but whose *real* part in that drama was now called into question: Dan.

For me, "Jonathan" had cast Dan in the role of the villain, as an abusive alcoholic with severe intimacy issues who compulsively cruised the Internet and local parks for anonymous sex and whose erratic mood swings, which caused him to fluctuate wildly, almost psychotically, between Good Dan and Evil Dan, had driven him to make life a living hell for "Jonathan" and the "girls" until they had managed to escape. But, given that Johnny was a pathological liar, and given the excessive—implausible—drama of his experience with Dan, I now operated on the assumption that *nothing* Johnny had told me about what had happened there was true.

More specifically, my doubts about the truthfulness of "Jonathan's" version of events were raised by something Laura had said. "Jonathan" had told me that Dan didn't want me to visit his house because I was "too obviously gay" and if the neighbors saw me there, they might become suspicious of Dan. In speaking with Laura, however, she had told me that "Jonathan" didn't like me "in that way" because I was "too gay"—the precise phrase he claimed *Dan* had applied to me. If I hadn't had cause by then to suspect that what "Jonathan" had told me about Dan was untrue on basic principles alone, that "coincidence" by itself would have made me suspicious. I was also curious to learn more about Dan's lawsuit against Johnny, something to which Laura had alluded. I was determined to discover the truth.

I had what I thought was Dan's e-mail address, so on the morning of Tuesday, October 1, I decided to send Dan my own "I know I am probably the last person you expected to hear from" message. In the message, I referred to Johnny as "Jonathan" because I assumed that Dan had probably not learned Johnny's true name. I told him that I had learned that "Jonathan" had caused a great deal of trouble for him and that he had done the same for me. I told him that over the previous several months, several others and I had learned that "Jonathan" was not only a pathological liar and a deeply disturbed individual, but also a criminal personality in ways that probably went well beyond what he knew. I told him that he might be interested in what we knew and that it might prove helpful to him in some way. I also told him that "Jonathan" had told me various things about him, about what he had said and done, but that now I was believing none of it without some kind of validation. I told him that if we could talk, it might prove helpful to us all.

A couple of hours later, Dan replied. He seemed excited to have heard from me and expressed his regret that "the devil," as he called Johnny, had taken advantage of me as well. He told me in brief that he had several e-mails in which "Jonathan" had threatened him and which he had turned over to the sheriff. He told me that "Jonathan" had missed a court date—he left it unclear if it was for the bad check, the threats, or both—and that there was now a warrant for his arrest, which I knew. Dan knew that "Jonathan" had also scammed Laura and complained that legally she wouldn't do anything, although I sensed he didn't know about the kind of manipulation Johnny had used to bully her into submission. He begged me to contact him because he needed to vent to another of "Jonathan's" victims about what he had done to him.

I already knew about the harassing messages that Johnny had posted on *Gayteway* and elsewhere, but I didn't know that Johnny had actually *threatened* him. "Jonathan" had always made it seem as if the only person who had done any threatening was Dan. By now, though, I was thoroughly familiar with Johnny's inversions of reality and was certain that Johnny had done far more to Dan than I had ever suspected. I wanted to know more, to know everything. I had a right to know everything and so did Dan. I wrote him back, asking him if he could call me. After my extended conversations with Laura in the weeks before, my phone bill was astronomical and I needed to minimize my expense. Around 5:30 that afternoon, the phone rang. It was Dan.

After spending a couple of minutes exchanging small talk, we finally got down to exchanging our experiences with "the devil."

"So, he took you too?" Dan asked.

"Yes, he did," I said. "He got away with about $4,000."

"Oh, Richard," he said regretfully.

I explained what the expenses were for, which included the expenses related to the move. Dan told me that "Jonathan" had told him that his *father* had paid for the move from Paladin and for the storage of his things, but I made certain that Dan knew who had *really* gotten stuck with *that* bill. The truth was beginning to emerge.

I asked Dan what "Jonathan" had told him about who he was. "Jonathan" had apparently given Dan an autobiography similar to the ones that he had given to Andy and me, although there appeared to be differences. I told Dan that I had learned in the previous months that none of that was true. I told him that I had spoken with his brother and had learned that his real name was actually "Johnny" and that he was actually from the Midwestern state. I told him that his brother had told me that Johnny was a pathological liar and had been involved in various kinds of criminal activity, including credit card fraud, against him.

Dan then told me more about his experience with "Jonathan." I already knew from Laura about the warrant that had been issued in Dan's county for "Jonathan's" arrest and knew that Johnny had defrauded Dan out of almost $650, but I still didn't understand fully what had happened. Dan made everything perfectly clear.

Dan told me that when "Jonathan's" car had broken down on Tuesday, September 4 of the previous year, they had taken it to a garage in Rowen to have it repaired. After going without the car for a little over a week, "Jonathan" had finally gotten it back on Thursday, September 13. When "Jonathan" had gone to pay the bill, which had amounted to $642.59, the garage had refused to accept his check, since it had been written off an account from an out-of-state bank. Dan had agreed to pay the bill himself, but had told "Jonathan" that he needed the money back to make his house payment. "Jonathan" had then written Dan a check off the same account. I already knew all of that from "Jonathan," but I didn't know the rest.

On the Thursday after Laura and her sons had "rescued" "Jonathan" from Dan on Monday, September 24, Dan had received a statement from the bank informing him that the check was invalid, having been written off a closed account that Johnny had apparently shared with his father. That day, Dan had called "Jonathan" at Laura's and told him what had happened. He had asked "Jonathan" what he was going to do about it, but "Jonathan" had become evasive. Dan had then told him that he wanted him to come to Credence the next day and pay him what he owed him. "Jonathan" had said something vague about possibly coming up the next Monday, but otherwise he had avoided making specific plans. At that point, Dan, who apparently saw "Jonathan" for what he was, had said, "Oh, I get it. You're a con man—nothing but a con man." When Dan had threatened to turn the matter over to the prosecutor, all hell had broken loose.

Johnny had retaliated by threatening to out Dan in his community as well as file charges against him for sexual harassment. It was at that point that Johnny had begun posting the harassing messages on various gay message boards in which he had given Dan's full name, address, and telephone number with descriptions of his alleged behavior and warnings to avoid him. Undaunted, Dan had pursued legal action against Johnny. Dan had shown the sheriff of his town the threatening and harassing messages and the sheriff had e-mailed Johnny, warning him that he was close to violating my state's statute on harassment and to cease and desist. The prosecutor had filed charges of check deception against Johnny and had sent him a letter ordering him to pay Dan or face additional legal action. When he didn't, a court date had been set for sometime that November. Johnny had failed to appear to address the charges against him, however, and with that, the highest court in Dan's county had issued a bench warrant for Johnny's arrest.

Unfortunately, the warrant, as it stood, couldn't be served, since the police didn't have an accurate date of birth or Social Security number for Johnny. Even if the warrant had been complete, however, Johnny had moved back to Paladin, then to Mariah, during that time, so neither Dan nor the police knew where he was. I thought again of "Jonathan's" comment, in relating the bogus story about the murder of Ted Kanner's niece and fiancé, that the police had been looking for him to ask him questions about "enemies" but that they hadn't been able to find him because he had kept moving. Now I understood even more of what had probably inspired that comment. *I* had known where he was—and if *only* I had known.

More disturbingly, Dan also told me that the day Johnny was supposed to appear in court, he had received an e-mail from someone calling himself "Dulcimer" in which he said that he knew Dan's car and would get him. The next day, Dan had attended a bazaar sponsored by the art association in Rowen, and when he was going to leave, he had discovered that someone had placed two long spike nails and a large rusty screw behind the rear tires of his SUV. Dan believed that "Dulcimer" was Johnny playing yet another of his many characters. It astounded me to think of Johnny making a then-150-mile round trip specifically to pull such a juvenile prank...but I had also come to know, the hard way, that Johnny would stop at nothing to wreak vengeance on those who refused to tolerate his psychopathic behavior.

According to Dan, check deception was normally classified as misdemeanor, but since Johnny had failed to appear in court, the crime, Dan believed, might have worsened to a felony. If Johnny could finally be caught and convicted, perhaps this would stop him, at least for a while.

Most disturbing of all, perhaps, was the fact that shortly after Johnny had turned on him and had started harassing and threatening to out him, Dan's health had begun to decline. In particular, he had started having mild heart attacks and other assorted maladies. I didn't think it was coincidental. I believed the problems were stress-induced, induced by the stress that Johnny had caused him. Terry could not have been more right when he had said that Johnny left a wake of destruction wherever he went.

We spoke for about forty-five minutes and, at the end, Dan asked me if I wanted to come to Credence the next day so we could talk at greater length. I told him that because I had to work the next two days, I wouldn't be able to come until Friday. I asked him if I could record our conversation so I could have an accurate account of his version of events, but Dan was adamantly opposed. I thought I could understand his reservations, though, given his desire for anonymity and concern that the recording could fall into the wrong hands.

In anticipation of my visit later that week, I spent much of that evening assembling documents that I thought Dan might want to see, including four e-mails that "Jonathan" had sent to me the October before. In three of them, he voiced his desire to expose Dan, and in one of them, he admitted to being the one who had posted the harassing messages on the Internet. Apart from simply wanting to help Dan, I also felt guilty about how I had encouraged "Jonathan" in his efforts to expose and hurt Dan the previous fall. Although I had been manipulated as much as anyone to feel the way I had, I was still going to set right what I felt I had done wrong.

On Friday, the weather turned windy and rainy and generally nasty, so I e-mailed Dan to ask him if I could postpone my visit until sometime that weekend. In addition, I had slept badly the night before and didn't know how up I was to making a two-and-a-half-hour trip, regardless of the weather. Even so, I wanted to continue our discussion, so I asked Dan if he had the instant messenger system that I had and, if he did, if we could exchange more information that way. After I finished and sent the message, I began composing another in which I gave Dan specific directions to Johnny's apartment.

Dan said that one of his friends who lived in Mariah had seen Johnny's car at the hospital's mental health center in recent months and that the driver's side window was apparently being held up with duct tape. He didn't know if he was working there or just visiting, but I told him I suspected he was just visiting. If he *had* been working there, it certainly would have been a case of the inmates running the asylum. The revelation was interesting, in light of his claims that he and Glenn were together again and that Glenn and he (or both) were seeing a psychiatrist. If that was true, then it was difficult to know who needed to see the psychiatrist worse.

I told Dan that in the previous month, I had been inundated, or so it seemed, with people wanting more information about "Jonathan." Dan asked me if one of these people was "Jonathan's" "friend" *Tony*. I had never heard of a Tony, so I asked Dan who that was supposed to be. Dan said that "Jonathan" had told him that Tony was a college kid who lived in Paladin and whom "Jonathan" had claimed he had once dated. According to "Jonathan," Tony was the reason he had gotten fired from Intellex, where he had told Dan he worked. Apparently, Tony had followed "Jonathan" to Hong Kong, to the displeasure of his father, the CEO of Exxon. In retaliation, Tony's father had pressured "Jonathan's" boss at Intellex to fire him. Of course, none of that had ever happened and it was just another example of the grandiose, self-flattering fantasies that were an expression of his pathological narcissism.

Far more interesting, however, Dan told me that he had gone with "Jonathan" to the police station when he had been questioned about a theft at Intellex. *The* theft. I told him I had heard that he had stolen money from Intellex and Dan told me the amount was $18,000. That seemed to correspond to the amount Miranda had said had come up missing. Dan said that before he had gone into the police station, "Jonathan" had given him $18,000 from the trunk of his car to hold for him in case he needed to post bail. That also corresponded to Johnny's practice of using the trunk of his car as a kind of safe and reminded me of the time that "Jonathan" had taken $2,000 out of his trunk. Later, Dan told me that "Jonathan" had managed to satisfy the police by saying that it didn't make sense for him to steal $18,000 when he made much more than that. The logic of that explanation escaped me—perhaps that wasn't an accurate reporting of events or perhaps that explanation had had enough superficial plausibility to satisfy the investigator—but whatever the case, the fact remained that Johnny had managed to weasel out of a crime that to both Dan and me he had clearly committed.

Dan also had a perplexing story to tell me about "Jonathan's" "father"—one that mirrored my own about "Jonathan's" "mother." Dan said that while "Jonathan" was living with him, a man had called who claimed to be "Jonathan's" father. Dan had answered the phone and said the man, who had a British accent, had asked for "Jonathan." Dan claimed he had also spoken with the same man on the phone when he had once visited "Jonathan" when he was still living on Millstone Drive. I assured Dan that was *not* his father, that *Johnny's* parents were *American*, and speculated that perhaps these were people he had met while in England who had somehow gotten drawn into Johnny's insanity. It certainly didn't square with Laura's story about talking to his father on the phone, someone who had apparently had an *American* accent and who had called his son *Johnny*. Of course, he was telling Laura that he was from the United States, while he was telling Dan, Andy, and me that he was from England, so it all appeared to be just another part of his attempts to maintain his disparate façades.

In trying to figure out who was who, Dan checked his phone bills from the time that Johnny had lived with him. I later learned that Johnny had made somewhere between 60 and 70 long-distance calls from Dan's phone in the two and a half weeks he had lived there. Dan said that Glenn, who "Jonathan" had claimed was vacationing in the Caribbean Islands, was making so many collect calls, all of which "Jonathan" was accepting, that Dan had finally had to have a block put on the phone. *That* part was true—but twisted to make Dan look like a monster rather than someone who had taken reasonable measures to stop out-of-control behavior that was harming him. Undeterred, however, "Jonathan" had then resorted to sneaking down to the den and placing long-distance calls behind Dan's back. The final total for all the calls that "Jonathan" had made was somewhere around $250. That meant that with the $650 he still owed him for the repairs on the car, Johnny had taken Dan for at least $900 in the 18 days he had lived with him.

I was very interested to know whom Johnny had been calling. He had left behind some unpaid phone bills at Laura's, and although she had given me the names of some of the places he had called—for example, Glenn's town in the Great Lakes states—she had thrown them away before I could ask her to send me copies of them. In looking at his phone bills, Dan found calls that Johnny had placed to Paladin, Mariah, Hawthorn, St. Alban, Rowen, two small towns near Credence, and Viridian, all in my state, as well as Johnny's former city of residence in the South, a town in the Northeast, and two towns in the Caribbean Islands. The bills also included numerous directory assistance calls at $1.50 apiece.

I asked him about the calls to Hawthorn. I remembered that he had called me at least once from Dan's—the night he had called after midnight panicked that Dan was going to throw him out and had wanted to know if I could come and "rescue" him if he did—but I also wondered if he might have made *other* calls to Hawthorn...namely to *Chase*. By that point, I was convinced that the Chase "Jonathan" had presented to me was not a real person, was in fact Andy in disguise, but I had to ask. Dan checked and confirmed that the only calls Johnny had placed to Hawthorn had been to me.

I also asked him about the call to Viridian, since the only place of significance there was my workplace. Dan confirmed that Johnny had called the main office at my workplace in Viridian on Tuesday, September 4 of the previous year at 8:54 P.M. I then recalled that was the Tuesday night during the move that I'd had to teach class in Viridian and "Jonathan's" car had broken down at Dan's, forcing him and Laura to drive back to Paladin in Dan's SUV. I hadn't gotten the call because I had left work early so I could hurry back to Paladin.

I forgot to ask Dan if he had actually called Greg Carroll, which "Jonathan" had claimed he had. The number in the Northeast appeared to belong to him. "Jonathan" had told me that when Dan had called, Greg had told him never to call him again and had hung up on him. "Jonathan" had made it seem to me that Dan was harassing his friends—something he had made it seem to others that I was doing as well—but if "Jonathan's" story *was* true, then I wondered if Dan had simply been trying to find "Jonathan," who had defrauded, harassed, and bullied *him* and Greg had been brainwashed into thinking that "Jonathan" was the victim. I knew how easy it was to be conned and how difficult it was to see the truth once your perceptions had been shaped to see something else.

I wondered, too, about the *real* relationship between Johnny and Greg. "Jonathan" had told me that Greg worked for a particular IT company and I had learned that the company had an operation in Eiseley, where "Jonathan" had claimed that he had grown up. Since he obviously hadn't, I suspected that part of his story had been inspired by his connection to Greg.

In trying to determine the people to whom some of the calls had been placed, Dan offhandedly mentioned something that, by that point, should not have shocked me as much as it did, but did so perhaps because it abruptly replaced free-floating suspicion with well-defined fact. Dan told me that while "Jonathan" was living with him, he had "met a guy named Jim at the park one night and they [had] spent a lot of time together," and Dan thought that some of the calls might be to him. My suspicion had come less from the ads that

Johnny had posted while living with Dan than from his practice of attributing his own unflattering behavior to others: When he had accused Dan of compulsively cruising the parks for sex, it was actually *Johnny* who had been doing the cruising. Dan confirmed that, indeed, there was "definitely a lot of that going on." I felt as if I had been slapped in the face. So much for "Jonathan's" assertion to me that he had behaved "honourably."

Jim. "Jonathan" had mentioned that name before. *Jim* was supposed to be the gay police officer who had moved out of the apartment below "Jonathan's" when "Jonathan" had moved to Mariah. Apparently, that was just another example of Johnny's practice of taking real people and recasting them into whatever role for which he saw fit to use them. It was also consistent with his practice of shifting details, sometimes ever so slightly, to one side or another to throw people off the trail that would lead to the truth. I was certain that Johnny had taken great delight in his cleverness at putting one over on me. That lie, though, like many others, was now exposed.

I told Dan that I had come to suspect that it was actually *Johnny* who didn't want me there and told him that Johnny had told me that *he* didn't want me there, which is why I stayed away. Dan told me that wasn't true and that "Jonathan" "constantly berated [me] and made fun of [me] while he was [there]." I asked him what he was saying about me and Dan said that it was "mostly about the 'lazy' eye." "Jonathan" had said that he "never knew where to look so [he] would look at [my] mouth." I had always been sensitive about my strabismus and to have it ridiculed in such a juvenile way by someone for whom I had turned my life upside down upset me badly.

I asked Dan who "Jonathan" had told him I was. Although he had, despite occasional wavering, led me to believe that he viewed himself as my boyfriend, I knew he had been telling others that he was not, so I expected to hear a similar story from Dan. What I heard was somewhat less neutral. Dan told me that, according to "Jonathan," I was a "needy queen who needed his dick." I didn't ask Dan when the insults had begun, but knowing from Laura how enraged he had become when he had learned I was "Chaz," I suspected that he had reacted in similar fashion when I had confronted him about the ads he had posted while living with Dan. I understood now why "Jonathan" had been reluctant to hug me the day I had left him at Dan's: He didn't want Dan to know I was his boyfriend.

I was finally beginning to realize that *all* of the reasons that "Jonathan" had given to me for not visiting him at Dan's, at Laura's, in Mariah—especially the ones that had demonstrated his "concern" for me—had all been ruses to keep me away so he could do God-knew-what to God-knew-whom behind my back while perpetuating the illusion that he genuinely cared about me and, with that illusion, continue to manipulate me.

In spite of "Jonathan's" claims that Dan had sexually harassed him, Dan said that nothing sexual had ever happened between them…and nothing ever would. He said that when he had first laid eyes on "Jonathan," he was "repulsed" and had thought he was a "wimp." He had already commented on his body odor and general lack of hygiene, two things that, even in small measure, Dan would have found repellent. His reaction was interesting because it reminded me of my own the day I had first met "Jonathan." I didn't think of him as a wimp, but I did feel vaguely repelled. I had to wonder if part of Johnny's problem with Dan wasn't that Dan was sexually attracted to him, but that *Johnny* was sexually attracted to *Dan*. After all, upon seeing a picture of Dan in full uniform during his days in the military, "Jonathan" had referred to Dan as a "cutie." "Jonathan" had also insisted that when he had left Dan's, Dan's vindictiveness indicated that he was acting like a "high school girl who got dumped," but it seemed more likely that *Johnny* was the one behaving like an overgrown child.

My telephone and Internet conversations with Dan had done an incalculable amount to restore the truth, but there were two things that I needed to do, for myself, directly. First, I needed to revisit the place where Johnny's "nomadic" phase had begun, perhaps because I had been kept away only because of his lies, only so he could keep on lying by hiding the truth. I needed to be readmitted to a place from which I had been told I had been barred and I needed to revisit the scene of the crime. And, second, I needed to show Dan for myself where Johnny now lived. Simply *telling* him wasn't good enough. I—*I*—wanted the privilege of leading Dan to the criminal's hideaway myself.

■

Later that afternoon, the weather cleared, making the prospect of traveling to Dan's more appealing. After verifying that it was still all right to come that night, I packed a change of clothes and gathered the documents I thought Dan should see. Around 6:30, I set out for Credence.

Around 9:00, I arrived at Dan's. The last time I had been there was more than a year before, the day in early September that I had left "Jonathan" with Dan after the move and the day before the drama of Johnny's nomadic phase had begun. "Jonathan" had claimed that Dan hadn't wanted me to visit, but when I arrived, Dan greeted me with open arms, both figuratively and literally, hugging me once I stepped inside. I could not have received a warmer welcome.

After getting settled, Dan led me downstairs to the den. He showed me the damage that Johnny's dogs had done to the utility room, where Johnny had allowed them to defecate. I could understand why Dan had gotten so upset and had told "Jonathan" the dogs would have to go—something that Dan confirmed was, for once, true—because if Johnny had been allowed to continue, unrestrained, he would have turned the utility room, and perhaps the whole downstairs as well, into another shitpile, as he had his residences in Paladin and Mariah. After a brief tour of the utility room, Dan and I went back out into the den, where we continued to untangle the web of lies that Johnny had so carefully woven.

I already knew that "Jonathan" had told Dan the same basic "facts" about himself that he had told me, but I learned that Dan and I had each received a different version of that "truth." Apparently Dan had never heard of Colin, who was supposed to be "Jonathan's" best friend in England. He had also never heard of Marcus, who was supposed to have been the great love of his life and whose tragic story surely would not have gone untold—had it been true. Dan had, however, heard about *David*, the *lawyer*, who had died from a heart attack and had left "Jonathan" his house in London. That was a new one to me. The only David whom "Jonathan" had ever mentioned to me was David Garrett, the *dancer*, who actually did exist and with whom Johnny had actually had some type of relationship, although the nature of that relationship was unclear. In addition, whether the house was supposed to be the property that the private investigator had discovered or the "small mews house"—which were located in different sections of London—was equally unstated.

Dan confirmed that the story "Jonathan" had told me about how the two of them had met was just as invented as everything else that Johnny tried to pass off as the truth. "Jonathan" had told me that when he and Glenn were planning to move to my state, he had posted several messages on various gay message boards in which he had asked about what gay life in my state was like. "Jonathan" had said that Dan had responded and, after that, they had become good friends. According to Dan, that was not how it happened. Apparently Dan, as I, had responded to one of "Jonathan's" numerous—and fraudulent—ads. I had already discovered an ad that Johnny had placed on *Gayteway* in May 2000 that Dan had publicly answered. I showed it to Dan, but he couldn't recall if that was actually the one through which they had met. Indeed, I wondered just how well

Johnny had actually gotten to know Dan before I met him. In at least two different e-mails that "Jonathan" had sent to me in July 2001, around the time that he had first started mentioning Dan, he had described Dan as living in *Rowen*, not Credence. For someone with whom he was supposed to be such good friends, "Jonathan" hadn't seemed to know even basic facts about Dan.

As far as his interaction with Glenn was concerned, Dan said that he had never actually met Glenn. Indeed, Dan was so unfamiliar with Glenn that Dan referred to him as the "CI (Caribbean Islands) guy." As far as I could tell, Johnny had placed his first ad on *Gayteway* in April 2000, after he and Glenn had gone their separate ways, and since it was apparently through one of these ads that Dan and "Jonathan" had met, Dan would not have entered the picture until after Glenn had exited.

Dan told me that he had also never met Cliff, at least in the way that "Jonathan" had said. "Jonathan" had told me that Dan and Cliff *had* met and that Cliff hadn't liked Dan because of his drinking; according to "Jonathan," Cliff had told him to avoid Dan, which, given the sway that Cliff had allegedly held over him, he had for two months. In addition, "Jonathan" had told me that initially Dan hadn't had a favorable impression of me because I wasn't "forceful" like Cliff. What "Jonathan" had told *Dan* about Cliff differed considerably from what "Jonathan" had told *me*. While "Jonathan" had told me that he and Cliff had been involved in an almost preternaturally intense love affair, "Jonathan" had told Dan that he and Cliff had simply been roommates. Apparently, "Jonathan" had said that although Cliff was after him to be his lover, he wasn't interested—obviously the *complete* opposite of the feelings he'd told *me* he harbored toward Cliff.

Dan verified that Cliff had called while Johnny was staying with him, which was the first time he'd spoken to him, and said that he'd been "cool" toward him because of what "Jonathan" had told him about how he felt about him. I thought of the letter that Johnny had written to Cliff the evening he had posted the ad I had answered, the letter that had ended, "I love you madly and I always will." It was hard to tell if that was the truth or more manipulation. Even if Johnny were capable of loving, I had come to realize that like most of what he said, his "I love you" meant nothing, *was* just another form of manipulation.

"Jonathan" had also told Dan that Cliff was involved with a lawyer—a story that sounded suspiciously similar to "Jonathan's" story about his alleged involvement with David. He had also told Dan that Cliff and the lawyer were building a mansion in Paladin—again, a story that sounded suspiciously similar to "Jonathan's" story about the expansion of *Mike Harmon's* mansion...or to a story that Miranda had told me in which "Jonathan" had told Cassandra and his coworkers that he was building his *own* mansion. Needless to say, "Jonathan" had said nothing to Dan about his and Cliff's relationship having been torn asunder by the demands of Cliff's career.

Dan also had another interesting tidbit to tell that tangentially involved Cliff. "Jonathan" had told me that when Cliff had reestablished contact with him in July, revealing that he was not 2,000 miles away, as "Jonathan" had believed, but only 100 miles away, he had been devastated. He had claimed that Dan had come from Credence to see how he was doing and had found him in such bad shape that he had decided to spend the night. Dan affirmed that he had indeed driven to Paladin to see "Jonathan" because "something had happened," but in the version of events that Johnny had crafted for Dan, what had happened was that *his brother Michael had committed suicide.*

In the version of reality that Johnny had crafted for me, his brother *Malcolm* was the one who had committed suicide, years before I met him. Indeed, in January, "Jonathan" had slipped up and had started saying that it was actually *Michael*, not Malcolm, who had killed himself. At the time, I attributed the slip-up to "Jonathan's" mental state, but now I realized that it was just another, inaccurately remembered lie. This was just another example of how Johnny "recycled the same stories," as I had once described Johnny's modus operandi to Andy or, in "Jonathan's" own words in reference to Dan—but more applicable to himself—how he "shuffle[d] facts around like a deck of cards."

I asked Dan if Johnny had ever said anything to him about Chase. In at least two e-mails that "Jonathan" had sent to me in the summer of 2001, he had made references to having told Dan about him. Not surprisingly, however, Dan had never heard of Chase.

Indeed, Dan later said that he had never even met any of "Jonathan's" friends until he had met Laura, "fat" Greg, and me around the time he had moved in with him. Apparently, Johnny had done the same thing to Dan that he had done to me, either failing to produce "friends" who didn't exist or keeping us apart from people to whom he had given different versions of the "truth," or perhaps a little of both.

Dan told me that of *his* friends whom "Jonathan" had met, his friend Patty had thought that "Jonathan" was a "phony" and didn't trust him. I remembered "Jonathan's" mentioning to me, in an e-mail that he had sent to me on 9/11, that he had met Patty and had gotten the impression that she didn't like him. Patty's intuition was obviously correct, but unfortunately, Dan hadn't paid enough attention to her perception, as I hadn't mine the day that "Jonathan" and I had gone to the zoo. If we had, we might have been spared months of suffering.

Perhaps now, however, some of that suffering would be soothed. After a year of not knowing where "Jonathan" was and, therefore, not being able to pursue legal action against him, Dan now knew exactly where he was, thanks to me. To make sure that Johnny *was* still there, since it had been three months since I had seen him for myself, Dan and I decided to visit Mariah the next day. Of the many trips that I had made to Mariah, this was the one that I would enjoy the most.

■

I slept poorly that night. I was too keyed up to relax enough to drift off until sometime around 4:00. In addition, I was sleeping in the same bedroom in which "Jonathan" and I had slept when I had stayed at Dan's before "Dan" had forbidden "Jonathan" to have overnight guests. The room hadn't changed at all in the intervening year and it provoked a flood of odd memories.

Saturday morning, I was up around 8:00, although Dan, early riser that he was, had already been up for some time. I wasn't operating on rested energy, only nervous energy, but I had the latter in abundance. I was ready, *eager*, to guide Dan to Mariah, to the exact spot where Johnny, as far as I knew, was still living...or, more properly, *hiding*.

After having a breakfast burrito, Dan showed me the e-mails that Johnny had sent to him after the confrontation on the phone the September before. I had seen the harassing postings that Johnny had placed on the gay message boards, but I had not seen the e-mails. They embodied the same psychopathic rage that he had aimed at Laura, and me, once his cons had been exposed.

In the first one, which Dan had received on the morning of Friday, September 28, "Jonathan" had begun his assault by calling Dan "nasty, bitter, lonely and a drunk," and adding that it wasn't just his opinion, since Dan's son seemed to feel the same way. In response to Dan's accusation that he was a "con man," "Jonathan" accused Dan of giving false information about himself in his personals ads in order to "lure" men to visit him and told him that people didn't know what Dan was really like. "Jonathan" wondered what the people in Dan's church would think if they knew the truth about Dan's personal life.

"Jonathan" told Dan that the bad check was a "mistake" and the matter would be corrected, but he also claimed that he had spoken to an attorney in Paladin and knew where he stood legally and what he needed to do to protect himself. He told Dan that Dan's "scare tactics" wouldn't work and that now, he would "go after [Dan]…any way that [he could]," which included telling everyone what Dan was really like. "Jonathan" reminded Dan that he still had the painting he'd given to him, which he said was assuredly worth more than everything in Dan's "ugly" house put together. Ironically, "Jonathan" accused Dan of not acting like a "gentleman" and said that if only he had, the matter could have been easily resolved and they could have remained friends. In the end, he expressed his opinion that Dan deserved to be "who he was," which was "pitiful." Not unexpectedly, Johnny's reaction had been far out of proportion to what it would have been for a normal person.

In response, Dan threatened to refer the people in his community to Intellex so they could learn about the money he had stolen or at least about the cloud of suspicion that surrounded him. In his reply, "Jonathan" began by telling Dan to refer them anywhere he liked, since the matter had been settled months before. Accusing *Dan* of theft, he told Dan that *The Tempest*, which he had given to him, was worth $4,000 and, claiming now that it was not rightfully Dan's, informed him that theft in that amount was a felony.

Then, he returned to his previous threat of exposing Dan for who and what he really was, saying of Dan that even though he didn't like con men, Dan's entire life was "a lie and a con and a facade" and it was time to tear it down. He told Dan that if he wanted to "sling mud," he could sling back and informed Dan that he had "enough names and phone numbers of people who [knew] who and what [Dan was] and [would] spread all the muck that [he could]." Calling him a "fat old ugly queen," he informed Dan that if he wanted to "do battle," he would take him down with him, and that by the time he was done, Dan wouldn't be able to show his "5 chins" anywhere. "Jonathan" ended on a threatening note, telling Dan that perhaps he would show up at the art center that Sunday, where Dan would be, and "begin to chat."

Dan then replied by challenging "Jonathan" to prove any of his accusations. In response, "Jonathan" told Dan he was "half witted" if he thought he couldn't. He claimed that his attorney would subpoena Dan's computer, which was full of incriminating information. He told Dan that he would tell people he'd had to leave because of Dan's sexual advances and would drag five of Dan's sex partners and "everyone at the park" into the fray, saying they would "make the paper." He said that he still had all the e-mails Dan had sent to him in which Dan had told him about the men he'd had sex with, which "Jonathan" threatened to forward to the people at Dan's church and "everyone else." "Jonathan" assured Dan that enough of his accusations would stick and promised to destroy Dan's façade of heterosexuality and respectability. Calling him an "old drunk," "Jonathan" told Dan that he had more on him than he realized and told him, ominously, to "wait."

The next morning around noon, "Jonathan" sent Dan his most elaborate e-mail yet in which he attempted to bully him into submission. In it, he began by claiming that he had just spent the last hour and a half meeting with an attorney in Paladin. In the convoluted fashion he preferred for giving his lies an air of reality, "Jonathan" claimed that the attorney, who was also a former prosecutor, was the cousin of a friend of his, who was a state trooper. He said that after meeting with the attorney, he finally knew where he stood legally, then launched into an equally convoluted explanation of the circumstances that had led to the check situation. I had heard this story before.

Claiming that he had two checking accounts, both with the same bank, "Jonathan" said that the two checkbooks looked identical, except for differing check numbers. He claimed that the funds from one account had recently been rolled over into the other, rendering the checks in the old book invalid, but that in the chaos of the move, he had accidentally put the old checkbook into his briefcase instead of the new one. He claimed it was "a mistake, but an unintentional and honest mistake." He claimed that after having examined the checkbooks and considered the associated circumstances, as well as "Jonathan's" illness and its "documented" side effects of "intermittent confusion and memory loss" coupled with his ability to pay, his attorney had concluded there would be "no long term repercussions."

Always one to go "over the top," "Jonathan" didn't stop there. He went on to inform Dan that he was planning to file charges against him for sexual battery. He claimed that after his attorney had reviewed Dan's e-mails, in which Dan had supposedly suggested that "Jonathan" have sex with some of his partners, and Dan's postings, which contained various types of false information, the attorney had concluded that sexual battery had "probably" taken place. Knowing that nothing physical had ever happened between them, "Jonathan" was quick to add that battery "[did] not mean or include physical contact"—which, as any knowledgeable lawyer knew, was untrue. He told Dan that if he were convicted, he would follow up with a civil suit for monetary damages. "Jonathan" claimed there would be an "open investigation and people [would] be questioned" and stated that he wasn't afraid to "let daylight" into his life, since he was neither a married man nor "someone hiding from the world"—a statement I found laughable in the extreme.

Always trying to present himself in the best possible light, "Jonathan" had told Dan that he was filing charges against him "reluctantly" but felt that it was necessary to protect himself against Dan's "threats and bullying," assuring Dan that it was a course of action made "necessary" by Dan's behavior. "Jonathan" evinced the same "compassion" to Dan that he had to me in response to the "Heorshema" message in which he had told me that although Warren had wanted to turn the message over to the police, he had resisted the idea because he didn't want to do me, someone who was obviously mentally ill, further harm. Johnny's "compassion" astonished me— especially when it was in direct contrast to his statements from the day before in which he had viciously attacked Dan and had described, in meticulous detail, how he planned to destroy him.

"Jonathan" then resumed his now-familiar refrain about how deceitful and hypocritical Dan's life was, once again mentioning that even Dan's son hated him. He ended by accusing Dan of knowing how his illness left him depleted and dazed, but even so, Dan cruelly tried to frighten and bully him. He told Dan that his behavior showed what little character he had and that as a Christian, Dan had "no charity nor true spirit." He concluded by assuring Dan, "Hypocracy is always exposed in the end."

Indeed it was. So was Johnny.

Although I knew that Johnny had never spoken with an attorney and had simply been engaging in scare tactics of his own, I checked the timing of the correspondence I had received from him that Saturday to see if the scenario was plausible. I discovered that he had sent me an e-mail timed at precisely 10:00 in the morning (one in which he stated that Dan had accused him of stealing—"absolutely not true," he insisted—and mentioned his plans to destroy him, in particular, for keeping him from speaking to Glenn). The e-mail he had sent to Dan had been sent at 11:55, one hour and fifty-five minutes later. According to "Jonathan" he had spent "an hour and a half" speaking to the attorney, which would have left him twenty-five minutes to drive to Paladin from St. Alban, drive back to St. Alban from Paladin, and write a lengthy e-mail to Dan—a totally implausible scenario.

Dan also showed me the e-mail he had received from the person who had called himself "Dulcimer"—who he believed was Johnny. The e-mail had been sent on Saturday, November 10 of the previous year, the same day that Johnny had posted the ad on *Gayteway* under the name "Banzai," in which he had once again attempted to out Dan. It had also been sent the day after someone—who he believed was Johnny—had placed the rusted nails and screws beneath the tires of his SUV. In the succinct message, "Dulcimer" told Dan that he knew who he was, calling him a "disgusting old fag," and stated that he also knew his "green car." He then informed Dan that he wanted the world to know what a "swish[y] queen" he was and promised that he would get Dan out of "that closet" and let everyone know who Dan was. "Dulcimer" ended the message by telling Dan to "eat shit."

The message was chilling for more reasons than one. The singsongy, semi-psychotic tone was strikingly similar to that of the threatening letters I had received in May as well as the "Heorshema" e-mail that "Jonathan" had forwarded to Laura. Although "Dulcimer" had used lowercase letters instead of uppercase ones, that seemed a minor point. While I was there, I showed Dan a copy of the "Heorshema" e-mail, which I had brought with me. After reading it, Dan emphatically said, "He wrote this."

After reading the message from "Dulcimer," I no longer had any doubt that my ex-brother-in-law was not, and never had been, The Pretender. Now, there was no doubt in my mind that The Pretender, "Dulcimer," and "Heorshema," were the same person as "Gayman," "GayMan," "GayDaddy," "GayBear," "Stiff," "Top," "Friendly," "Banzai," "Naughtyboy," "Tough," "DoIt," "Maine," "2Hot," "Logan," "Nigel," "Iain," "Alcuin," "Colin," "Cliff," the 33- to 52-year-old, 5'7" to 6'0", 165- to 180-pound, sandy-, brown-, dark-, salt-and-pepper-, gray-haired, blue-, green-, brown-eyed, single, coupled, married, divorced, gay, bisexual, British, American, business man, COO, factory worker, doctor, travel agent, hospice worker, biker, millionaire, object of desire, pleaser for people, father figure, world traveler, caretaker, innocent victim, stalking victim, accident victim, heart disease patient, comatose patient, shattered man, dying man, Glenn's father, Mike Harmon's contacts, "Cassandra" in the insurance fraud scheme, "Terry" in the numerous identity theft schemes—"Jonathan"—and multiple additional personas known, unknown, and unknowable... In one of his last messages to Laura, Johnny had told her that he really had wanted to "be and do everything." And he *did*. Unfortunately, everything he was, everything he did, was a lie.

I thought it ironic that I had called the person behind the chaos The *Pretender* because now that title seemed to fit more than ever. Although I would never have all the answers I wanted about who did what, how, and why, I had enough. Ultimately, The Pretender issue became little more than a footnote in a tangled story of mental illness, of a brilliant mind, a promising life, gone tragically wrong.

Before we left for Mariah, I used Dan's computer to check my e-mail. While I was online, I decided to visit the *Gayteway* site and show Dan which of the ads on our state's board were actually Johnny's. As Dan watched, I pointed out the ads. "That's him." I scrolled down a little, again pointed to the screen. "That's him." I scrolled and pointed, scrolled and pointed, scrolled and pointed. "That's him—That's him—That's him." Dan was stunned. Between the beginning of April and the beginning of October, Johnny had posted or replied to ads under no less than *twenty-five* different personas. That didn't count the ones he'd posted on *Sex Now* or other boards during the same period. All told, he had concocted a new persona on average about once a week. Although much of the information in the ads was roughly similar, virtually none of it was true. Ironically, several of them insisted that he was "real." He was anything but.

Around 11:00, Dan and I headed for Mariah. Dan was now driving a white vehicle, not the "green car" that "Dulcimer" had claimed he knew. I asked Dan if Johnny knew this vehicle and he said no, that he had gotten it after Johnny had left. That made me feel more comfortable because I wanted to remain as inconspicuous as possible.

The weather was beautiful and the drive to Mariah uneventful. During the trip, I took the opportunity to ask Dan every unanswered question that came to mind about what Johnny had done, or what had gone on in general, while Johnny was living with him. In particular, I told him that "Jonathan" had told me the pastor at Dan's church was gay and had kept making passes at him. Dan told me that was ridiculous. That was apparently yet another manifestation of his pathological narcissism in which he believed, liked to believe, or liked others to believe that everyone was sexually attracted to or in love with him. Over time, the list had grown to include not only the pastor, but also Glenn, Chase, Cliff, the man at Tolliver's, the young man at Starbuck's, the realtor's boyfriend, Kyle, Javier, Frank, Lester, James, Lucas, the conductor of the London Philharmonic Orchestra, Rudolph Nureyev, David Garrett, Laura, Dan, Art, Hope, Andy, Logan, Jack (in the Andy fantasy), Miranda, David, Tony… Pathological lying wasn't Johnny's only problem and the extremity of his disordered behavior never ceased to amaze me.

We arrived in Mariah sometime around noon. I wanted to help Dan, but I also wanted some kind of revenge. I thought of "Jonathan's" paranoid e-mails from February in which he had expressed his fear that Dan would find him and do something to him. I realized now, of course, that those expressions of fear had been just as fraudulent as everything else Johnny said and did, carefully calculated to reinforce the image of Dan as the bad guy and himself as the good guy, the innocent victim of fate who kept running afoul of all manner of evil people who wanted to do him harm when in fact it was quite the opposite.

We drove by Johnny's apartment slowly, giving Dan enough time to get a good, long look at the place to which Johnny had escaped, where he had hidden from Dan for an entire year. Now Dan knew exactly where Johnny had run, but could no longer hide.

Johnny's car was gone, but his tchotchkes were plainly visible in the kitchen window. I was astounded that he was still living there—not because I thought he had fled to evade the law, but because I thought surely he would have been evicted by now for not paying his rent. He had received the summons to appear in court for non-payment at the beginning of July and it was now the beginning of October—three months later and $2,000 more owed. I doubted he was working—he hadn't worked for almost a year now—and, unless he had sold off some of his belongings, some of his scams had succeeded, or he had snared some dumb sucker like me who was gullible enough to bankroll him, he wouldn't have had the money to pay Joan Vogel what he owed her—now at least $5,200.

Once Dan was satisfied, we returned to Credence. I hoped that now that Dan knew where Johnny was living, he would be able to see the justice done that was long overdue.

I left Dan's that day feeling a profound sense of satisfaction. I was satisfied to think that the information I had given to Dan would finally lead to Johnny's having to account, legally, in some way for his actions, to suffer, in some measure, for having made the rest of us suffer. But, I was more satisfied that I was, for yet another person, able to replace Johnny's lies with the truth and that yet another person had done the same for me, even if some of that truth was hurtful. *Not* knowing the truth had been, was, even more hurtful. In the space of a little more than a month, three of Johnny's victims, three of the bigger flies that had gotten trapped in his web of lies, had been freed. And, with each one that was freed, I became freer.

Perhaps now, the one to lose his freedom was *Johnny*.

—44—
OBSTRUCTION OF JUSTICE

[The police] didn't appear to care much.

The day after I showed Dan where Johnny lived, Dan instant-messaged me to tell me that, legally, "the ball [was] in motion." He said that a friend of his worked for the highest court in his county and he had called her about how to proceed. He said that she was typing up a new warrant and would have the judge sign it on Monday. He said he was supposed to contact the sheriff's deputy with whom he had spoken before and give him the information I had given him. After that, the sheriff of the county in which Mariah is located would be notified and Johnny would be apprehended. He said his friend would notify him when he was picked up and a court date was set. After a year of immobility and consequent frustration, I thought Dan must have found that extremely satisfying. He concluded by asking me if I cared to go to court with him.

Was he *kidding*? *Nothing* at that point would have given me more satisfaction than to see Johnny answer for at least part of what he had done. I wouldn't have missed it for the world. I envisioned myself sitting in the front row, as close to him as possible, making sure he knew that *I* was the one who had led Dan, and the law, to him.

Unfortunately, things did not proceed as quickly as we'd hoped. After two weeks, there had been no movement. In an attempt to prod the law into action, Dan had me write him an e-mail that he intended to give to the police in which I expressed my concern that Johnny might be leaving Mariah soon. Although I *did* think it was a possibility, my message exaggerated the urgency. In my message, I explained that recently Johnny had told at least two different people that he had actually found a place in Paladin and was already in the process of moving some of his things there. In addition, my informants had claimed that he was splitting his time between his apartment in Mariah and a friend's in Paladin while he completed the transition. I said I thought it made sense that Johnny would be moving now, since his current lease was probably about to expire. Instead of leaving Mariah in April, as he had told me he would, he had apparently renewed his lease for at least another six months. Although I didn't know exactly what the last day of the new lease would be, I said, it could be as soon as the end of October and probably no later than the middle of November. If everything I'd heard was correct, I warned, then he could be gone within the next two or three weeks—if not sooner. The message was really just speculation based on what was probably false information, but I hoped it would prod the police into action.

On Friday, the 25th, Dan instant-messaged me to tell me that he'd taken my e-mail to the prosecutor. He said they would issue another warrant with the corrected address. Dan said that hopefully the police would arrest Johnny soon, but added that they "didn't appear to care much." He told me they had simply said that they would turn the new address over to the court, but otherwise, they didn't seem that motivated to pursue the matter. The crime he had committed was, after all, "just" a misdemeanor, which didn't spark much interest. I was just as frustrated as Dan at the police's indifference when they, if anyone, should have been helping us.

■

Dan was becoming increasingly concerned that Johnny would leave Mariah before the police arrested him. He was being pursued legally by various parties for various crimes and, as time passed, more and more of the enemies he'd made were discovering where he lived—thanks in no small part to me. Otherwise, he had no incentive to stay and every incentive to leave. Therefore, Dan began making periodic forays to Mariah to see if Johnny was still there. On the evening of Thursday, October 24, he and a friend drove to Mariah to check on him. Dan told me they had seen his "crap"—his tchotchkes—in his kitchen windows, but the curtains had been pulled, which hadn't allowed them to see anything further. At least Johnny hadn't yet made his break, although it was just a matter of time.

On Sunday, November 3, Dan drove to Mariah again to check on Johnny and found him still there. The following Tuesday, he called the sheriff's office to talk with the deputy, but unfortunately, it was his day off. He planned to call him again on Wednesday.

On Wednesday, the 6th, something interesting happened. Dan wrote to tell me that he'd received a call for "Jonathan" Frazier from a woman whose number had appeared on his caller ID. Dan said that she hadn't been at liberty to say what she had wanted to talk to "Jonathan" about, but in case it was for employment, Dan had told her about him and his "capers" with him, Laura, and me. He had also told her there was a warrant out for his arrest. The woman had said that if she was able to contact him, she would give Dan a call. Dan had called the number that had appeared on the caller ID and we established that it was, in fact, a company that apparently wanted to talk to "Jonathan" about a position. Dan didn't hear from the woman again, but it was satisfying to think that Dan's information had probably cost Johnny a job.

On Thursday, the 7th, Dan's friend who worked for the court called him to inform him that the warrant had been returned because they needed Johnny's date of birth and Social Security number. Without them, the warrant was incomplete and could not be served. Dan had managed to get the SSN, but had been unable to get the date of birth. The latter had always been something of a mystery. Even Terry didn't seem to know exactly when his brother had been born. Although "Jonathan" had given me a birth day in mid-November and Terry's ages for his brother suggested a birth year somewhere between 1948 and 1950, that wasn't precise enough. I didn't know how to find out, which was going to be an obstacle.

On Friday, the 8th, Dan instant-messaged me to tell me that in checking the SSN, he had discovered that it had been issued in the Mid-Atlantic state in which Terry had told me his family had relatives. Dan was confused, but I explained the connection. Even so, I wondered whose SSN it actually was.

Later, Dan instant-messaged me to give me additional information about the SSNs. He had discovered that Johnny had been using not one but two SSNs. One had been issued in the Mid-Atlantic state and the other in the Midwestern state. Until that point, I had forgotten that Miranda had said the private investigator working for Intellex had also discovered that Johnny had two SSNs. I wasn't surprised. This was a typical con artist tactic and explained, in part, how he was able to pass credit and employment checks—he simply used the "good" SSN. Dan had also learned that Johnny was known not only by the name "Jonathan," but also by a third name that started with the letter J that neither of us had ever heard. The aliases were piling up and I was no longer surprised by anything I learned.

Dan thought that if he had Johnny's license plate number, a friend of his who worked in law enforcement could run the number and learn his date of birth. At first, I thought Dan would have to make another trip to Mariah to obtain it, but then I remembered that when I had left Johnny's apartment the day I'd confronted him, I had driven past his car and had jotted down his license plate number before heading to St. Alban. At the time, I didn't know how I might use it, but I was trying to collect as much information about him as possible and thought it might come in handy. I gave it to Dan, hoping it would help.

On Monday, the 11th, Dan instant-messaged me to tell me that "we [were] on the move again." He explained that the deputy, with whom he had finally spoken, had offered to help him and was tracing the license number.

Dan and I had been thinking of ways to keep tabs on Johnny. Dan was making regular trips to Mariah to see if Johnny was still there, but I figured out a way to determine, from home, if he was at the apartment at particular times. My method capitalized on the fact that whenever someone who subscribed to *Sex Now* visited the site, it announced that he was online. Since Johnny was compulsively placing ads on the site and had nothing better to do with his time, I knew that he would be checking it frequently. We hoped we could catch him while he was at home so Dan could call the police in Mariah and let them know, with certainty, that he was definitely there at that time. We hoped this would make the police more persistent in apprehending him. Ultimately, though, this tactic didn't prove to be of much help, since we caught him online only infrequently and the police remained as uninterested as ever.

On Thursday, the 14th, I e-mailed Mike Harmon explaining the situation with Johnny and asked him if he would give us the date of birth that Johnny had supplied on his application. Unfortunately, I didn't receive a response. I didn't know if he didn't want to be further involved or simply didn't care to help, but it seemed like just another stumbling block along the path to seeing Johnny brought to justice.

For several weeks after I first contacted Dan, he continued to express a strong distrust of Laura. First of all, she was the one who had "rescued" "Jonathan" from him, and because he had led her to believe that Dan had mistreated him, she and Dan had ended up on unfriendly terms. Second, Dan believed that Laura was somehow protecting Johnny by refusing to give him information about him, especially his whereabouts. Third, Dan couldn't understand why Laura hadn't filed charges against Johnny for check fraud and wondered what had *really* happened between them. And, fourth, Dan couldn't understand why she and Johnny had remained in contact, on friendly terms, when Johnny was supposed to have committed a crime against her. I tried to explain precisely how Laura had been just as manipulated, deceived, and bullied as the rest of us had been, but it still took some time for Dan to overcome his year-long feeling of distrust.

One outgrowth of this distrust was that Dan forbade me to tell Laura that the warrant had been renewed and that the police now knew where Johnny lived out of fear she would tell him and he would flee. After learning what I had learned from Laura about what Johnny had done to her and her family, I knew that she had *no* incentive to do something like that and wanted to see him punished just as much as we did. Although I continued to correspond with Laura sporadically, I kept my promise not to tell her what was going on, even though I thought Dan was overreacting and I felt guilty for doing it.

By the middle of November, Dan had finally overcome his distrust enough to give me permission to tell Laura what had been happening. On Sunday, the 17th, Dan instant-messaged me to tell me that the deputy had just called and said that he was calling Mariah to have them serve the warrant. He also told me he had given the deputy Laura's and my phone numbers so we could tell him our stories. I decided to call Laura to tell her what had been happening, but I didn't explain why I hadn't told her before now when I felt she deserved to know.

In talking to her, I did explain that Dan and I hoped that by hearing our collective stories, the authorities would finally feel motivated enough to take action against Johnny. Laura was skeptical that throwing Johnny in jail would change him in any way—so was I—but as I told her, whether it would change him or not, he would still be in jail, unable to menace the rest of us.

In talking to Laura, we continued to untangle some of the smaller threads in the web of lies that Johnny had woven for us. First, Laura told me that in Mariah, "Jonathan" was supposed to have had a maid whose name was Luella. That was a name I had heard before. *Luella*, in the version of reality that "Jonathan" had crafted for *me*, was supposed to have been the aunt of the black executive at whose soul-food restaurant he was supposed to have eaten when he was supposed to have traveled to the Midwestern state on business in August the previous year. I recalled the lengthy list of foods that "Jonathan" had claimed she had served him—including the chitterlings with which he had become obsessed—and how, in appreciation of her hospitality, he had given her flowers and a music box instead of a bottle of liquor since, as a "church-goin' woman," she didn't touch the "devil's brew." Laura and I couldn't help laughing, which seemed to be the best response. In the early days of our "relationship," "Jonathan" had mentioned having had three different housekeepers, all of whom were inadequate, since he had lived in Paladin. It was clear, however, that "Jonathan's" claims about domestic help were just as fraudulent as everything else he'd claimed, designed to make him appear more impressive than he actually was, and that their alleged incompetence was just an excuse for his own inadequacy in performing even the simplest household chores.

Less humorously, Laura confirmed Dan's statements about Jim, saying that "Jonathan" had mentioned him to her and had spent time with him while he was living with her. I wondered if Jim's life had been affected adversely through his encounter with "Jonathan."

Most significant, Laura asked me about what Johnny had done for Christmas the previous year. I told her that he had been in Mariah at Christmas and that I had stayed with him, in Mariah, for two weeks beginning the day after Christmas. Not surprisingly, "Jonathan" had told her an entirely different story about what he had done for Christmas, one that, again not surprisingly, involved Cliff. "Jonathan" had told her that he and Cliff had spent Christmas in the Midwestern state. I understood now why "Jonathan" hadn't wanted to go to St. Alban to retrieve his things from Laura's the Friday after Christmas: If he had gone to St. Alban with me, then that would have destroyed his story about being in another state with Cliff. It would have destroyed a lot of other lies as well. At least *now* they *had* been destroyed, although it was a year too late.

At the conclusion of our conversation, Laura told me to tell Dan hello. If there had ever been hard feelings between the two of them because of Johnny's lies, those were gone now. The truth had finally healed that wound as well.

Even so, I didn't know if the police would contact her, do anything more than they already had, which was little. I was disappointed and discouraged that the people who were supposed to protect *us* against people like Johnny were, through their indifference, actually protecting *him*. Like Dan, I had a growing concern that before the police intervened, Johnny would escape.

—45—
LIKE A THIEF IN THE NIGHT

When I was at his [apartment], all the crap was out of the windows, [there was] no car in the garage and [there was] trash in the garage...

Around the end of November—almost a year to the day that "Jonathan" had lost his job at the hospital and the Mariah act of the drama had, in earnest, begun—Dan e-mailed me to tell me that he was "fed up" with the lack of action in bringing Johnny to justice. Earlier that day, he had once again spoken to the police in Mariah about picking up Johnny. The police had told him that they had been to Johnny's apartment "three or four" times that month to arrest him, but he was never there. Dan said he'd made sure they knew what kind of car he drove and plates it had so they would know for sure that he was home. Dan said they'd told him they would put the warrant on the "clipboard," which all the officers looked at each shift, so they would continue to pursue him. Despite the fact that the crime was "just" a misdemeanor, despite the problems with the warrant, despite the fact that Johnny often seemed to be gone, I felt the police had been dragging their heels. By the end of November, it had been almost two months, and since Mariah didn't appear to be ridden with crime, the police seemed to have adequate time to accomplish this one simple but important thing. They just didn't care. "My luck," Dan had added, discouraged.

Frustrated, Dan decided to take another tack. He decided to write his father a letter, detailing what Johnny had done to him as well as some of what he had done to Laura and me. His purpose was to "advise [them] of the problems [Johnny was] cau[s]ing people, using them with no regard to their welfare" with the hope they would do something in response. He sent the letter to the address given on the bad check, hoping it was still current.

Throughout the second half of the fall, Johnny continued to post his infamous sex ads on *Gayteway* and *Sex Now*. On Saturday, November 2, he posted the same ad, under the name "Toofer," on both sites in which he and his unnamed partner were looking for men for group sex. The location he gave was vaguely correct, but his age was at least ten years younger than he actually was. It was similar to other ads he had been posting since mid-April in which he claimed to be part of a couple. On Friday, November 15, he posted a reply, under the variant "2Fer," to an ad on *Gayteway* from someone who was advertising for "bears"—big-built, hairy men—in which he gave similar information.

Since I had pointed out all of Johnny's *Gayteway* ads to Dan when I had visited him in early October, I had been making sure he knew which new ads were his as well. I informed him that the author of the two sets of postings was Johnny. Venting his frustration toward the appropriate target, Dan posted his own "reply" to the "2Fer" reply under the provocative name "Cautchu" as well as an independent ad under the same name on Wednesday, November 27, letting Johnny know he was on to him.

On the same day, Johnny posted a lengthy ad under the name "The Two Bears." In the ad, he stated that he and his partner were looking for a "baby bear" to join them for the winter or possibly longer. After describing himself as ten years younger than he was as well as giving other skewed "facts," Johnny stated that he and his partner had been together for 16 years and were "stable and secure financially and emotionally." He said that although they lived in the Midwest, they had a home in the Southern state where they preferred to spend the winter. As far as the perfect "3rd" was concerned, he stated that "[a]ge and looks [were] less important then personality and attitude," and that they would be willing to relocate the right person.

The similarities between his original ad that I had answered as well as some of his earliest e-mails to me and "The Two Bears" ad were striking. In his ad that I had answered, "Jonathan" had described himself as "emotionally and financially secure"—a total lie—and said he would "relo[cate the] right guy." In his first e-mail to me, he had stated that "[p]ersonality and intelligence [were] more important to [him] then looks" and had said that he had a home in the Southern state. I couldn't help wondering if "The Two Bears" ad somehow related to me.

A week later, on Tuesday, December 3, Johnny informed the world of the outcome of "their" ad. The rambling message began by announcing the "arrival" of their new "cub," Nathan, who had been delivered "by stork" that day. "Nate" was described as being 24, standing 6'1", having dark brown hair and blue eyes, being a "fab kisser," and being in graduate school "studying for his Master's in Psych." According to Johnny, "they" and Nate had actually known each other for almost a year but they hadn't known that he was interested in them and "this arrangement" until he had unwittingly answered their ad. Johnny described the outcome as a "huge relief and coincidence." After joking that they would be accepting sexual accessories from a fictional sex shop as gifts, Johnny said that they had hoped they would find someone like Nate when they had posted their ad. He said they loved Nate and Nate loved them and, after thanking everyone who had apparently (or allegedly) responded, Johnny expressed his hope that everyone could find "some[one](s)" to make them happy.

This message was, in some ways, the most bizarre that I had yet seen. That was saying something. The fact that "Nate" largely resembled me except for his age and eye color and was studying for his "Master's in Psych" certainly didn't escape me. Johnny had incorporated me into his fantasy life and lies in a variety of ways, but this was somehow the most unnerving.

On Thursday, the 12th, Dan instant-messaged me to tell me that he'd driven to Mariah that day to check on Johnny. He said that his tchotchkes were still sitting in the kitchen window, indicating he was still there. Afterwards, Dan had gone to the police station and asked them to try to serve the warrant that evening if they drove past and saw lights on as well as to make sure to park where Johnny couldn't see the police car. Dan was really trying.

Throughout December, little happened. I had become focused on finishing the semester and preparing for Christmas. *This* Christmas wasn't going to be anything like the previous one had been and I was looking forward to it.

On Christmas Day, Johnny posted a response to a message on *Gayteway* in which the author was looking for a "gangbang." The response stated that the "3 of us live together as an extended family and like to party with other hotties." I wondered if Number Three was supposed to be Nate, the young man who was studying for his master's in psych. In any event, when the author replied, Johnny posted an interesting response. After instructing the author to leave "them" a way to e-mail him, he stated "they" would send him "their" phone number so that all of them could talk on the phone before hooking up. "They" apologized for being so indirect and explained that they had just had "a bad experience with someone [they had] met on the net." That person, presumably, was *me*.

This time, I couldn't help being amused. I had obviously made a big impression on him if he was still obsessing about me after so many months.

Two days after Christmas, Dan instant-messaged me to tell me that the letter he'd sent to Johnny's father had been returned unclaimed. In frustration, Dan exclaimed, "They're all con men!" I didn't believe they were, but I understood Dan's feelings. Whether by accident or design, Johnny's parents were well insulated from what their older son was doing to the rest of us, even as they seemingly continued to be supportive of him. I didn't believe they were aiding and abetting him in any way, but I did believe they were in deep, deep denial about their older son.

The next day, Dan instant-messaged me to tell me he had just gotten back from Mariah. He had checked to see if Johnny was still there and had seen lights in the apartment and Johnny's car in the garage. Next, he had gone to the police station, only to discover why nothing had happened in the previous two weeks. Apparently, the Mariah police had lost the warrant and, in contacting the authorities in Dan's county to obtain another one, they had been misinformed that the warrant didn't contain Johnny's date of birth or Social Security number, making it invalid. As it turned out, they had looked at the original version of the warrant, not the amended one. "Ready to blow," as he described it, Dan had driven to the nearby police station where they had found the amended warrant and faxed a copy of it to the police in Mariah. Dan described the Mariah police as "more than helpful," but I felt they could have done more in the three months since Dan had first gone to them.

Following Dan's lead, I decided to write my own letter to Johnny's parents, detailing what their older son had been doing over the past year and a half. The address to which Dan had sent his seemed invalid, but I thought I would send mine to Terry and have him forward it to them. I didn't know how much Terry had told them of what I had told him, but I wondered if they hadn't done anything because they didn't appreciate just how bad the situation was. Perhaps they didn't and if they did, they would finally stop providing for their older son while he thieved from the rest of us. I also knew how Johnny had reacted to finding out that I had spoken to Laura, and I assumed that, as he had done with Laura, Johnny had convinced his parents that I was insane and shouldn't be believed.

To deal with both issues, I wrote a lengthy letter that detailed everything I knew about Johnny's pathological behavior and its damaging effects on others. To counter the possibility that Johnny had convinced his parents that I shouldn't be believed, I included copies of the storage unit rental contract; the receipt for the $900 cash advance; the canceled check for the February rent; credit card statements showing the charges for the storage unit, the moving van, and the cash advance; selected e-mails he had sent to me, Dan, Laura, and Andy that highlighted his psychopathic behavior; and contact information for the people involved so Johnny's parents could corroborate the information themselves. Since I didn't have Terry's home address, I decided to send the information to Terry's workplace, where I assumed he would receive it. I sent the package around the beginning of January.

A week passed, but I heard nothing from Terry. Curious, Dan e-mailed his assistant and asked her if Terry had received the package I'd sent. She didn't respond. A week later, Dan offered his opinion that Terry had probably told her not to respond to us anymore. I would not have been surprised if he had.

On Friday, January 24, Dan instant-messaged me to tell me that he thought Johnny had been "too quiet" and expressed his concern that he might have moved. By that point, Johnny hadn't posted an ad for almost a month, which was odd, considering how compulsively he had been doing it. Dan wanted to know if I wanted to drive to Credence so we could drive to Mariah, which I declined to do. I wasn't going to make a two-and-a-half-hour drive to Dan's home on a freezing winter night just so we could drive to Mariah together when it was simpler for Dan to do it himself.

On the afternoon of Saturday, the 25th, I went to one of the local parks that I hadn't visited since October to enjoy nature on a sunny, if chilly day. It was the park where I had prayed that Andy would know the truth and close to which we had met less than two weeks later to untangle some of the threads in the web of Johnny's lies. When I returned home that afternoon, I checked my instant messages and found that I had received one from Dan. The news, as he described it, was "bad."

Dan told me that he had driven to Mariah to see if Johnny was still there. He said that when he had arrived, however, he had found that the tchotchkes that had been sitting in the kitchen windows and the furniture that had been stored in the garage were gone. Johnny's car was missing as well, and although there were tire tracks in the snow in the driveway, they appeared to be old. By all appearances, Johnny was gone—not just from home, but from Mariah.

I didn't know what to think. I thought about going to Mariah myself to confirm what Dan had said, but I refused to drive to Mariah again.

I was stunned and discouraged. I was frustrated, too, that the Mariah police had had *four months* to arrest Johnny, but had failed to do so. They had proven to be no help. Mariah might as well have been Mayberry. And now, Johnny was gone.

By the end of January, more than three weeks had passed since I'd sent the packet of information to Terry, but I still hadn't heard from him. Prompted by Johnny's disappearance, I sent Terry an e-mail on Tuesday, the 28th telling him about the package and asking him if he'd received it. I also informed him that Johnny had disappeared and explained that I was concerned for my safety, which in some ways I was.

That evening, Terry sent me a very reactive response. In it, he told me that he hadn't received the package because he visited that particular workplace only a few times a year and hadn't been there to get it. In response to my concerns about my safety, he said that he had never known his brother to be physically dangerous, only a pathological liar, and gave me the impression he thought I was overreacting. Quoting Cain, he said that he was "not [his] brother's keeper" and that when he had told me in July that he was "out of it," he'd meant it. He told me that he didn't want me to contact him further and concluded by telling me that if any of the information I had sent to his workplace hurt him in any way, he would "have to look into [his] legal options."

I was shocked by the vehemence of his response. Terry may not have been psychopathic, but in some ways, dealing with him was almost as bad as dealing with his brother. I was also beginning to see certain similarities between him and his brother, especially their way of reacting with threats of legal action when they felt their "images" were threatened. Terry had described his brother as a bully, but now, *Terry* was trying to bully *me*. Terry seemed far more concerned about maintaining his public image, with saving his own ass, than he did with helping anyone. In some ways, he was just as self-obsessed and lacking in social conscience as his brother was. He wasn't responsible for his brother's actions, no, but he also didn't seem to give a damn about anyone his brother had hurt. Terry may have given me the basic truth about Johnny, but he had also taken as much as he'd given.

Frustrated but unnerved, I wrote a placative message in which I assured him I was "not [his] enemy," but reminded him that if someone used the information I had sent to him to hurt him, then it was *their* legal problem, not mine. After all, the package was addressed to *him*, which meant that no one else could legitimately, legally open it. I couldn't imagine what someone would, or could, do with that information, though, since none of it contained anything damaging about Terry. I told him that if something did happen, I would do whatever I could to help him prosecute the person(s) responsible. To try to reduce the possibility of having the information fall into the wrong hands in the first place, I asked Terry to try to retrieve the package and return it to me. I concluded by thanking him for telling me the truth about Johnny.

I did what I could to cool the situation and hoped my efforts pacified him. Even so, I still didn't know what he might do. I certainly didn't think he would do anything that even remotely approached the psychopathic reactions that I'd suffered from his brother, but I did think he might do something within the "normal" range to make things difficult for me for the "wrong" he perceived I had done him. When it came to preserving his public image, Terry was hypersensitive and overreactive and threats to it, whether real or imagined, brought out a distinctly irrational side. I regretted having broken my vow not to contact him again.

As it happened, my fears were unfounded. After that day, I didn't hear anything out of Terry again. That was fine with me because he had made it clear he wasn't going to help and I didn't want to deal with him further. For the next several weeks, every day the mail came, I went to the mailbox hoping to find the package I had sent to him. It never came. I don't know if he ever retrieved the package or not, but I do know that *I* never received it. To this day, I don't know what became of it.

A few days after I'd e-mailed Terry, I *did* receive a package—from Laura. In September, she had told me that she had found some pictures in Johnny's things and, after I had expressed interest in seeing them, she had told me that she would send them to me. By the time we spoke in November, she still hadn't done so and I restated my interest in seeing them. I had totally forgotten about them, since it had been two and a half months since we'd discussed them and since more significant things had been happening. The note she enclosed indicated that she and her family were doing well, which I was glad to hear.

Among other things, the package included about twenty-five 4" × 6" prints and about fifty negatives. I had seen some of the pictures before. The prints were the ones that "Jonathan" had found in the kitchen drawer and had shown to me the week he was packing to move from Paladin. Although the pictures weren't dated, they appeared to have been taken in the late fall and early winter of 1999, around the time that Johnny and Glenn had moved to Paladin. All of them were shots of either the interior or the exterior of the house or shots of either Johnny or Glenn. Some of the pictures showed paintings that were sitting on the floor along the wall, waiting to be hung. Others revealed the time of year by showing a fireplace flanked by stockings or scenes of the lawn and its ornaments covered with snow. Two others showed Johnny's and Glenn's birthday cakes, respectively, that year. Interestingly, Johnny's birthday cake did not say "Happy Birthday *Johnny*," but "Happy Birthday *Jonathan*." I assumed that Glenn was the one who had bought the cake, and apparently even Glenn didn't know Johnny's real name.

In looking at the pictures of Glenn, I saw him in an entirely different light than I had when I had seen them a year and a half before. Now, I saw him not as the privileged member of the British upper crust that "Jonathan" had depicted him to me to be, nor as a pathologically symbiosed co-conspirator in Johnny's psychopathic schemes, nor as an underintelligent, intermittently psychotic and violent inmate of a mental institution. Now, I saw Glenn as just another victim of Johnny's insanity.

The pictures of Johnny revolted me. One showed him holding a present and regarding it with mock surprise. At least *this* deception was obvious, unlike his others. I also noticed that his eyes bore the same dark rings they had when I had first met him, long before he was supposed to have been worn down by the demands of his stressful position and the effects of life-threatening sickness. He had never shown me *that* picture and I had to wonder if he hadn't not because it was unflattering—which it was—but because it would have betrayed his claim that he didn't develop the rings until much later, something he had explicitly told me the day I had met him.

I found another picture especially repulsive. Apparently taken on Christmas Day, it showed Johnny dressed in a gaudy robe lounging on the living room sofa. He wore an expression of ennui, and with the darkened rings encircling his eyes, he almost looked as if he were wearing makeup, like some kind of bored, time-ravaged drag queen. One of the "girls," one of his pretentious poodles, was seated next to him. He looked bloated and overindulged, like a pampered prince expecting to be waited on hand and foot. Miranda had once speculated that Johnny had been some type of royalty in a previous life, which had left its imprint, but whether or not that was true, it was undeniable that Johnny viewed himself as something akin to royalty in *this* life. I had never seen him look so ugly and I was utterly disgusted.

At first, I decided to throw the pictures away. Then, I decided that wasn't good enough: I decided to burn them.

Not all of them—just the ones of Johnny. I also decided to burn the rest of the flammable things he had given to me. The day I received the pictures, I e-mailed Laura to tell her I'd gotten them as well as my intentions to burn them. I also told her some of what had happened over the past couple of weeks—Johnny's disappearance and Terry's overreaction—and its effects on me.

In response, she wrote an especially thoughtful, encouraging message, telling me she was sorry to hear that I wasn't doing well, but assuring me that by trying to put the experience behind me, I was on the right track to feeling better. She said she knew exactly how I felt. She said that she still thought about what Johnny had done to her at least once a day every day but was able to say, "What an asshole!" and go on with her day. She told me to take care of myself and let her know from time to time how I was doing. She concluded by telling me to roast some hot dogs and marshmallows over my fire.

She *did* know exactly how I felt, having suffered in her own way at Johnny's psychopathic hands. I hoped that one day *I* would feel different. That day, however, was not *that* day.

I didn't ignite the bonfire that day. I waited until a sunny, somewhat warmer day sometime around the end of February or the beginning of March to carry out the immolation. That afternoon, I took everything that I intended to burn, along with a box of matches, to the garage. We had an ordinance that prohibited burning within the city limits and, although it would have been a small offense, I still felt the need to be surreptitious. I took a metal trashcan and, sitting it in the middle of the floor, I began setting the papers ablaze.

I have an especially clear memory of watching the Valentine's Day card he'd given to me a year before go up in flames. The sentiment it expressed was just as fraudulent as everything else he did and was—perhaps more so—and so its destruction was especially important.

When the ashes had cooled, I dumped them out onto the ground and ground them into dust with my feet. Nothing remained except the atoms of which they had been composed.

Although Johnny had apparently left Mariah, I knew that his ads usually said that he was living near, if not actually in, the place that he was really living. Throughout the next several weeks, I checked *Gayteway* periodically to see if he had posted anything new, anything revealing. I also began checking boards other than the one for my state. Perhaps he had gotten a job in another state, and if so, he might be posting messages on other boards. I concentrated on the United States and checked about ten different boards a day, which took me only about five minutes.

Finally, I found an ad he had posted the previous October on the board for one of the Great Plains states. He described himself as part of a "masculine, gay male couple" [who would] be moving to ——— in about a month due to work transfer." He—*they*—wanted information about "the city, good places to live, gay bar etc." He—*they*—also "like[d] to hook up with [a] hot 3rd or 4th for regular sessions." Cutting through the subterfuge, a job opportunity had apparently arisen in the state in question but had obviously fallen through, since he was still in Mariah more than three months later. The discovery was interesting, but irrelevant.

For six weeks following the fateful day that Dan had discovered Johnny's flight from Mariah, I found no new ads. Then, on Friday, March 7, I found a message, titled "Suck It," that had been posted on my state's board by someone who called himself "Hard." The author claimed that he had just moved to Rowen and was looking to "hook up." He described himself as being in his late 30s and having brown hair and blue eyes as well as having a voracious sexual appetite. The message said that it was posted by "Hard," but between the lines, it had "Johnny" written all over it.

I wrote to Dan, telling him that "Hard" was Johnny. Dan was mortified because he had actually replied to the ad. In his reply, Dan had just said that he was "available," so when "Hard" replied the next day, he wanted Dan's "stats" and told him that he also "want[ed] to know something about [him] before [he gave] out [his] e address." Johnny's paranoia was at full strength, and although Dan had used an alias that Johnny must have recognized as Dan's, I couldn't help wondering if he thought it was actually *me*.

If "Hard" was really Johnny, I wondered, then why hadn't he posted anything on the board for over two months? I wondered if Dan and I had scared him off for a while and after two months he'd built up his nerve again. The person in the posting sounded cautious. I also wondered where he was now. I doubted he was in Rowen, however. I asked Dan if he was sure everything had really been gone from the apartment when he'd checked in late January.

In response, Dan assured me that it had been. He was afraid that Johnny had actually moved to Rowen, but I told Dan that I doubted it. The thought provoked an unpleasant reaction. Dan said that "it [was] starting all over, [his] hatred!" I was sorry that the wound that Johnny had inflicted on him was still so raw.

He said that he had written to the attorney general for my state, but their office had said they couldn't help. I wondered what the point was in having a legal system if it protected criminals through its inefficiency and indifference.

On Wednesday, March 19, Johnny posted another ad as "Hard." In this one, he said that he had just moved to Rowen and was using the board because he thought "the park [was] full of trolls and old men"—an ad obviously aimed at Dan. Then, a week later, he posted an ad as "Tallulah." When I told Dan that "Tallulah" was Johnny, he decided to post a response. Under the name "Cautchu," which he had used before to taunt Johnny, Dan posted a reply to the second "Hard" ad, which said simply, "watch for the sheriff." "Hard" didn't respond.

The posting as "Tallulah" was significant because it appeared to be the last time that Johnny posted an ad on the *Gayteway* board for my state. Indeed, it appeared that he stopped using the site altogether. After the end of March, I found no more new ads that Johnny, under one of his many guises, had posted.

Later, after I had located and analyzed all of the ads that I could find that Johnny had posted, beginning with the first one he had posted, under the name "Jonathan," on April 15, 2000 and ending with the one he had posted under the name "Tallulah" on March 26, 2003, I discovered that he had used no fewer than *sixty* aliases in those three years. His posting behavior accelerated markedly after our breakup, and during the last nine months of 2002, he posted ads under some 35 aliases. During the second and third quarters of 2002, he was posting a new one, on average, once a week. During the fourth, he had dropped to "only" one every 12 days. The nine-month average was one every eight days. By comparison, his "normal" rate outside this time frame was about one every six weeks. After our breakup, most of his ads began to claim that he was part of a couple (although in some he still claimed to be single); he became younger (usually mid- to late 30s when previously he had been early to mid-40s); and the list of acts that he, or he and his "partner," enjoyed tended to be lengthier and "kinkier."

This, though, included only his *Gayteway* ads. It did not include his *Sex Now* ads or the ads he had posted on other boards about which I didn't know. The actual number of ads he had posted was undoubtedly much higher. Almost none of the information in the ads was true. Ironically, though, many of the ads—about one in six—insisted that he was "real." He was anything but.

I thought of all the disruption, the damage, his fraudulent ads had caused. Most of the disruption had taken the form of Johnny giving people the runaround, stringing them along with the promise of sex when he never had any intention of meeting them, but some of it had taken a much worse form, turning people's lives upside down and inside out emotionally, financially, socially, mentally, spiritually.

I wondered if the fact that Johnny stopped using the board had anything to do with me. I liked to think so. Perhaps I flattered myself, but I liked to think that I had frightened him off the board, given that I had learned to see through his personas to the fraud who had created them, then had exposed him time after time. Whatever the case, Johnny stopped using the board through which I had met him that fateful day in May two years before, and because he had, no other unsuspecting person using the board would be snared by the web of lies Johnny wove.

Johnny was gone.

But, what he had done remained.

—46—
GETTING UNSTUCK

Seeking revenge is like drinking poison and expecting it to hurt your enemy.
—Unknown

For the next several months, my hatred toward Johnny burned stronger than ever. No one had ever hurt me as badly as he had hurt me and plenty of people had hurt me badly. I was also shocked and angered that someone like him could do what he had done to me, and so many others, and just get away with it. The law had done nothing, his family had done nothing, and most of his victims had decided to "go on with their lives" and do nothing. People's passivity in stopping him only encouraged him to continue victimizing others with impunity.

I hated him so badly that oftentimes I would lie awake in bed at night and fantasize about killing him. *Literally* killing him. My feeling were fueled not only by my hatred, but also by a perception that the only way to stop him—finally, fully stop him—would be to kill him. He was a menace to society and needed to be stopped. Since he was never going to change and was never going to be restrained, the only way to keep him from hurting anyone else would be to kill him.

I would never have seriously done anything like that, but I did think about lesser things that I could, and would, do to him if I ever saw him again. God could deal with him in the next life, but *I* would deal with him in *this* one. Vengeance was *mine* and *I* would repay.

For a long time, I carried a heavy emotional load.

Around the end of June, I happened to be at home one day flipping channels when I ran across a program on a Christian station.

Normally, I didn't watch Christian programming, not only because I didn't see things from the Fundamentalist perspective that appeared to dominate the airwaves, but also because I was repelled by the constant, obsessive fixation that so many of them seemed to have on the issue of homosexuality. I had been deeply damaged by the unrelenting condemnation and contempt that many so-called "Christians" mercilessly visited upon gay people in our society, and although I had largely overcome the damage I had suffered, I still felt a strong aversion to much of the "Christian" programming I encountered. Normally I would have flipped past the program as quickly as possible, but today was different.

The guest on the program was a woman who was talking about how sometimes in life we become emotionally "stuck" because of our inability to let go of the effects of the wrongs that others have inflicted on us. As expected, she emphasized the need to forgive others for what they have done, but gave a deeper, more psychological interpretation of forgiveness than had traditionally been expressed. Her interpretation of forgiveness emphasized the need to detach oneself from the emotional effects of the offender's actions, to do it for one's own sake if not for the other's.

I was already familiar with that more modern, psychological interpretation of forgiveness, but it wasn't until that day that I realized just how ensnared, emotionally, I still was in what Johnny had done to me. On that day, I realized that I had spent far too much time, far too much energy, far too much emotion hating Johnny for what he had done, how he had violated my life. Hating people was hard work and damaged the hater far more than the hated, only revictimized the victim. It was with that realization that finally I began to let go.

There were other realizations that helped me to begin to let go. First of all, I had begun to appreciate the fact that I was not the only one of Johnny's victims. I had understood that intellectually for some time, but only now was this understanding beginning to affect me emotionally. Johnny hadn't singled me out exclusively for victimization, as if I were uniquely flawed or deserving in some way the others weren't. Johnny had damaged the lives of *everyone* he had encountered, without discrimination and without exception, and some of them had been injured far worse than I had. Although it was cold comfort, it was *some* comfort to realize that there was nothing special about me, that I was just one of many.

Second, like many people, I drew comfort from my spiritual beliefs. I no longer accepted the Fundamentalist Christianity of my childhood, but throughout my 20s, I had developed a set of well-defined beliefs based largely on the scientific studies of near-death experiences and reincarnation. From these experiences, I had come to believe that no one gets away with anything. One of the recurring features of near-death experiences was the "life review" in which experiencers do not simply see their lives replayed, as if on a movie screen, but actually relive their lives, not from their perspective, but from the perspectives of everyone with whom they have interacted. In some sense, they *become* those people. Experiencers are made to feel how their actions affected others without the ability to shield themselves from the full impact of those actions. I believed that someday, Johnny was going to have to go through the life review and *feel* how his victims had felt when he had hurt them, *feel* how his behavior had affected their lives for the worse. In addition, I believed that in a future life, Johnny would have to be on the receiving end of the behavior he had meted out to so many in this life—not as a punishment, but as a learning experience. I hoped that in that life he *would* learn, although I knew he would have to learn the hard way.

Finally, I have long believed that to understand all is to forgive all. I have always found it easier to forgive someone for what they have done to me if I understand, or at least feel that I understand, why they did it. I have long believed that people do harmful things not because they are inherently evil, as my Christian upbringing had emphasized, but because they are flawed. I had understood, since I had found the e-mails to Andy a year and a half before, that Johnny was mentally ill, and what I had learned in the year that had followed had only emphasized just how ill he was. Whatever it was that allowed most of us to relate to others as people and not as things to be used was missing from him. I didn't know why, but it was and that was the fact. Consequently, he had no more of an ability to understand how his actions made others suffer than a mentally challenged person had to understand calculus. Intellectually, he had the maturity of a 50-year-old, but emotionally, empathetically, he had the maturity of a 5-year-old, and he seemed inherently incapable of growing beyond that level. That fact did not *excuse* his behavior— he *was* an adult and was *fully* accountable for his actions—but it did *explain* it. At least it did to me.

Eventually, I began to feel a limited sympathy toward him. Later, I became able, on occasion, to pray for him.

For the first time in two years, I truly began to feel free.

—47—
LOOSE THREADS, II

The time is long overdue that you learned the truth.

By August, Dan was still trying to figure out ways to find Johnny. I suggested that if we could somehow get Johnny to e-mail one of us, we might be able to use the IP address included in the reply to determine at least the general area where he was. I suggested that Dan send some kind of provocative message like, "Just wanted to let you know we're still after you!" and see if Johnny would respond. I gave Dan two "official" e-mail addresses that I knew Johnny had used within the previous year (though under the name "Jonathan") and he agreed to send a message.

The one he sent was definitely provocative. Addressing him as "mother fucker," Dan told him the warrant was still active. He said that he wanted to "see [him] and discuss old times," but to be warned that his 20 years in the military had taught him a lot and that he would "love to smash [his] face in." He told him that he wasn't alone, though, that there were three of us who were now looking for him, and told him that intimidation wouldn't work with us anymore. He said that he had friends who worked in law enforcement who were pursuing him. He ended by telling him that unlike the ones Johnny had invented, *his* were real.

Dan sent it to the two "legitimate" addresses. Although it wasn't delivered to one, it was delivered to the other. When he told me this, I sent him a list of five alternate addresses, primarily ones that Johnny had used in perpetrating his fantasies and ads. Dan never received a response, although we were hardly expecting one.

On Friday, the 8th, I suggested to Dan that, in trying to locate Johnny, it might be useful to contact Cliff. At the least, I felt that

Cliff needed to know what Johnny had done to him, something of which he probably didn't have an inkling. The September before, I had encouraged Laura to tell him what was going on, since most of it had been directed at her, but she had refused. I had gotten the feeling that she was transferring her feelings toward the fake "Cliff" onto the real Cliff and that dealing with him made her uncomfortable. Whatever the reason, the fact was that since she hadn't, Cliff had never been informed. However, if Cliff learned the truth and got as outraged as he should, then he might be willing to help. In addition, if it *was* true that Cliff had a high position in business and, therefore, had access to people who could help—private investigators, lawyers—then it might be worth our while. I suggested that Dan do it because first, it was more his desire than mine to find Johnny, and second, Dan knew him slightly better than I did, since he and Cliff had at least talked on the phone, while Cliff didn't even know I existed. I gave Dan Cliff's legitimate e-mail address, the one that I'd found in the "Iain" account, and hoped he would contact him.

On Sunday, the 10th, the second anniversary of the day that "GayDaddy" had posted his fraudulent ad and the night before I had seen "Jonathan" the weekend after he had said that he'd slept with Chase, Dan wrote to tell me that he had decided not to contact Cliff. He said that he wasn't going to try anymore and that "we both need[ed] to get on with our lives"—which we did and which I had tried to do.

Later that evening, however, Dan sent me a second e-mail saying that he should "never drink wine and get on the PC" because, while tipsy, he had impulsively written to Cliff. Dan said he would keep me posted and I wondered what would happen.

To my surprise, Cliff actually responded. He said simply, "What did he do, or what has happened to him this time?" Apparently, Cliff already had some hint that Johnny was trouble, although he didn't know the half of it.

In response, Dan told him, in two separate e-mails, what Johnny had done to him, Laura, and me. Dan forwarded the e-mails to me, and although they seemed thorough, Dan didn't mention the fraudulent e-mail account that Johnny had created in Cliff's name, the fact that "Jonathan" had not been on his deathbed in a hospice in November 2001, or the fact that "Iain Winslett" was Johnny in disguise. For the next couple of days, I waited for Cliff to respond to Dan's e-mails, but he didn't.

Feeling that Dan's e-mails were incomplete and wanting to tell Cliff what I knew from my point of view, I wrote to him myself. In my e-mail, I told him, in condensed form, about my "relationship" with "Jonathan" and how he had damaged me. Then, I told him about discovering, during the last couple of months of our relationship, how he had not only been deceiving and manipulating him, but also created the fraudulent e-mail account through which he had been pretending to be him. As proof that "Jonathan" was not in a hospice on his deathbed in November 2001, but was, in fact, alive and well (physically if not mentally) in Mariah, I referred Cliff to the hospital web site, which still contained the story about "Jonathan's" hiring. I also told him that he could contact both the hospital and his landlady to verify that he was, in fact, in Mariah working for the hospital at that time.

I emphasized in particular how "Jonathan" had used "Cliff" to bully Laura into shutting up about the bad checks and how Laura had lived in fear that if she antagonized "Cliff" in any way, he would use "his" powerful lawyers to prosecute and destroy her. I told him that "Jonathan" had used his persona to do all of his dirty work for him so he could assume the role of innocent victim and thereby stay in good with Laura and her family in order to avoid prosecution and continue exploiting them. I told him that, although Laura had finally learned the truth, unfortunately she could do nothing legally against Johnny because in filing for bankruptcy, she had forfeited her right to collect the money he owed her.

I also mentioned how Johnny had used the fraudulent e-mail address in his name in various sex ads he had posted on the Internet, including the "Naughtyboy" ad through which I had ultimately learned about the lies that he had been telling to Laura and her family about the two of them.

I told him that Johnny had also claimed that "Cliff" wanted to kill me—"literally"—and was, therefore, making death threats in his name as well.

I told him, in condensed form, all the garbage "Jonathan" had told me about their "perfect," but star-crossed relationship and told him that I would be interested to know how much of it was actually true, although I didn't know if he would be willing to enlighten me. All in all, I told him, "Jonathan" had painted a picture of someone who was self-centered, thoughtless, self-indulgent, and deceitful, while he painted a picture of himself as someone who tolerated his insensitive, almost sadistic behavior only because he had once loved him so much.

I concluded by apologizing for dumping everything that I had onto him because I knew it might be difficult to assimilate—I knew the feeling—but I also told him that, although he already seemed to know that Johnny was nothing but trouble, he needed to gain a fuller appreciation of the fact that Johnny was a "very dangerous man" and that it was important to know just how dangerous so he could protect himself.

Neither Dan nor I ever heard back from Cliff. In some way, it didn't matter because at least someone had finally told him the truth.

In addition, I came to believe that Cliff had no real power to do anything because, as I later learned, he didn't appear to be the person "Jonathan" had claimed him to be. Three and a half years later, I discovered Cliff's profile on one of the social networking sites. On it, he listed his profession as something totally unrelated to what "Jonathan" had told me, and mentioned that he was working on an associate's degree, which seemed like an unlikely thing for a high-powered, presumably well-educated businessman to be doing. In addition, he listed his age as 31 (almost 32) when by that point he should have been around 40. Therefore, Cliff would have been only 25, not 35, when he was supposed to have been romantically involved with Johnny. Cliff seemed to have no more power than the rest of us to stop Johnny and possibly less.

I wondered, though, about the real nature of Johnny and Cliff's relationship—if they had even had one. First, none of the pictures of Cliff that "Jonathan" had shown to me had included Johnny, the house on Millstone Drive, or anything else that would have connected the two of them romantically. Second, "Jonathan" had told Dan that Cliff and he had just been roommates and that even though Cliff was after him to be his boyfriend, "Jonathan" wasn't interested, presenting a far more blasé attitude to Dan than he had to me. And, third, in researching the sex ads that Johnny had posted on *Gayteway*, I found two, posted around the end of 2000, that mentioned recent breakups, but that offered wildly different details. The first, posted on Friday, November 24, advertised for a "pussyboi" to service his every need and said that his last "boi" had been with him for six years but had just left because his job was transferred. (This ad ended with the lines, "We sure had fun. Now it's your turn," the lines that, in modified form, had ended the ad that I had answered six months later.) The second, posted on Saturday, December 30, said that he had just broken up with his boyfriend of 13 years—something I believed was an allusion to Glenn. Neither ad seemed to refer to Cliff in any straightforward way.

In the end, I came to believe that Cliff was just another innocent young man who had gotten snared in the sticky web of Johnny's mental illness and lies like the rest of us. I never knew the extent of the damage that Johnny had done in Cliff's life, but I hoped that he was able to disentangle himself from Johnny in whatever ways necessary and move on with his life.

■

For quite some time, I also thought about contacting Art to see what had *really* happened when Johnny had lived with him. Since "Jonathan" had rarely discussed Art, his involvement had always seemed tangential. I did wonder, though, if Johnny had damaged him financially. I remembered "Jonathan's" story about Art expecting him to pay rent for December even though he wasn't going to be living there in December and his asking me if that was expected behavior in America. Knowing how Johnny projected his own misdeeds onto others, and knowing how he made a point of discussing what he was doing to others as if they were doing it to him, I wondered if Johnny had actually owed Art legitimate rent and had failed to pay it. I wondered if he had simply not bothered to make the gesture to pay him at all or if he had "paid" him with one of the bad checks he'd tried to foist onto countless others. "Jonathan" had seemed to want to avoid Art for some reason and I suspected that reason was that he had done something to Art as well. "Jonathan" had claimed that after he'd lost his job in Mariah he couldn't go back to Art's because by then Art had gotten another renter, but now, I suspected that Johnny had invented the story to make not returning seem palatable when in fact he had *done* something to make returning impossible.

I also wondered if Johnny had led Art on while he had lived with him. "Jonathan" had mentioned that he was concerned about giving him the impression that he was interested in him when he was not, but knowing how Johnny characteristically disowned responsibility for his less-than-flattering qualities, I wondered if leading Art on was precisely what he had done. In any event, I could at least see Johnny manipulating Art with the suggestion of sleeping with him.

Although I still had Art's home address and phone number, I decided in the end not to contact him. First, I suspected that "Jonathan" had told Art things about me that I didn't want to hear and had done things behind my back that I didn't want to know. Although I was becoming inured to the effects of finding out new information about Johnny, I still feared it would hurt more than it would help.

Second, I didn't know how Art would benefit from knowing what I knew. On a practical level, I didn't know where Johnny was, so if Johnny had done something criminal to Art but Art had been unable to proceed against him because he couldn't find him, I couldn't help him. On a personal level, I realized that Johnny had lived in Art's house for a month and, from my own moral point of view, I thought that entitled Art to know the truth about the psychopath he'd unwittingly harbored, but I wondered what good it would do. My great-grandmother was of the opinion that "the more you stir a turd, the worse it stinks," so I thought perhaps it was best to let this one lie.

In the end, Cliff at least learned the truth about the person who had claimed to me that he had experienced one of the most intense relationships he had ever had with him but had claimed to Cliff that he was lying in a hospice on his deathbed when he was alive and physically well in Mariah. What he did with that truth was his choice. Art didn't learn the truth, at least from me, but I hoped that if he had suffered because of Johnny, he had at least found peace, which was to me almost as important as the truth.

—48—
DÉJÀ VU ALL OVER AGAIN

I noticed a message you had posted for Jonathan Frazier. He was just evicted from my property in Paladin. Do you know him?

For the next year, I lived in peace.

Relative peace. During the fall of 2003, I became embroiled in teaching several classes at school, including another basic math class that I found uncomfortable because of my weaknesses in math, and a college skills class that I found difficult because of the disparity in motivation and maturity between the younger and older students. In addition, I had decided to try to pursue a Ph.D. in psychology and began an earnest attempt to study for two important tests on which I would need to do well in order to be considered for doctoral work. Given my weaknesses in math, I found myself spending most of my free time focused on algebra and geometry, wondering how my ability to determine when two trains that had left from different cities and were heading toward each other would meet related to the study of mental processes and behavior.

Throughout that fall, I heard from Dan a few times wondering if this or that person he'd encountered on the Internet was actually Johnny. One of them had the same (real) name as Johnny and it even turned out that he was gay, but it wasn't him. He didn't understand why he wasn't continuing to post his infamous sex ads and neither did I. Perhaps he'd grown tired of that game…or afraid to play it. Even so, in late September, Dan posted a message on *Gayteway*, as the infamous "Cautchu," with Johnny's last name as the title, just in case he was still visiting the board. Dan didn't get a reaction, though it wasn't clear why. In December, Dan said that he was planning to go to Mariah to look at Christmas lights and thought he might drive by the apartment to see what he could see. In the end, he came down with the flu and didn't go, but I was convinced that Johnny was in fact long gone and it wouldn't have mattered anyway.

The spring of 2004 was much more subdued than the fall had been. I was teaching only three classes instead of four, having decided not to teach the math class again, and work seemed much more manageable, much less stressful. When I wasn't working, I spent much of the first half of the semester renovating my bedroom. Progress was rather slow and the project, which commenced around the last week of February, wasn't completed until the first week of April. I also decided to create an insect garden in my back yard so I wouldn't have to run to the local parks every time I wanted to photograph the indigenous insects; now, I would have them come to me. I concentrated on determining as many plants that would attract insects as I could and began collecting seeds as soon as they became available.

Around the middle of February, I visited a local psychic whom I'd visited intermittently for the previous seven years. I had last visited her in May 2002, only weeks after my "relationship" with "Jonathan" had ended and only a week after I had first spoken to Miranda. The reading I received that February was one of the most extraordinary experiences I'd had in a long time. After having an intellectually stimulating conversation that we both enjoyed, we went to the room where she performed her readings. Without knowing anything about my interest in entomology, she told me that I was going through a "metamorphosis" and that she saw "butterflies in my aura." She later asked me if I was also into botany, saying that she saw "wildflowers popping up around [me]." I was astonished. She had been accurate before, but this was uncanny. She told me that my interest was "cool" and that she had once dated an entomologist. She encouraged me to "keep going with it" and to try to sell my photographs. Whatever the cause, the experience was exhilarating and I left feeling that I was on the right track.

By the end of March, I had received the last of several rejection letters from the schools to which I had applied for doctoral work. In spite of having strong credentials, except perhaps for my math score, I hadn't made the cut. I knew how competitive doctoral programs in psychology were—only a handful of students were admitted out of hundreds—so I was prepared to be rejected. At first I was disappointed, but then, I began to feel relieved. That feeling told me that perhaps being accepted would have been the wrong move for me, that perhaps I had applied only because I had felt that I should, not because I had sincerely felt that I wanted to make this my life's work. Although I didn't have a university position, I was still able to teach and do research in the position I had, which was fulfilling. I had always seen myself as someone who should have a Ph.D. in something, but I realized that in psychology, the master's level was as far as I wanted to go.

That summer, I ended up teaching three classes, the most I'd ever taught during the summer. Although I was busy, the classes were scheduled during the middle of the week, which meant that I still had several days on either side to do other things, like my photography, and generally enjoy my summer. The year 2004 was proving to be the smoothest, most fulfilling year I'd had in quite some time.

I hadn't gone anywhere on vacation in years, so that summer, I decided to go somewhere, even if for the day. Around my birthday, I took an overnight trip to visit a historical site of personal significance. Although I had never been to the site, I had no difficulty finding my way there because the site lay only 30 miles from Mariah and the path I took to reach it was the one I had already taken many times as I had gone to be with "Jonathan."

The next day, I returned. On the way back home, I decided to make a detour to Mariah. To the apartment. I had vowed that I would never visit Mariah again unless I did so for myself and now I was definitely visiting for myself. In addition, the detour would be only ten miles out of the way and take only twenty minutes to make, so I was able to remain true to my vow.

I wanted to drive past Johnny's apartment because I wanted to see for myself whether or not he was there. Dan had assured me that he had moved out a year and a half before, despite fleeting doubts, but I had to see for myself. No one I knew had been to Mariah, to the apartment, since Dan had driven past in January 2003 and it was marginally possible that Dan had been wrong. Rationally, I realized it was unlikely that Johnny was still living there, given his problems with landlords, but my motivations for checking were not rational. They were purely emotional because I felt that if I could see for myself that he was no longer there, there would no longer be a part of me that psychologically was connected to that place, to that time, to him. I felt that if I could see for myself that he was gone, I would finally be free.

Initially, I had some difficulty finding the apartment, not because the layout of Mariah had changed but, I think, because *I* had changed. Despite the fact that I had spent so many long days at the apartment during the four months of the Mariah phase of our "relationship" and had driven to and through the neighborhood more times than I cared to count, my memory of the area was beginning to fade. That was probably a good sign, since it meant that the imprint of my experience with Johnny had grown weaker, retreated farther into the past. Eventually, though, I found the apartment.

This was the first time I had seen the apartment since Dan and I had gone there almost two years before. Outwardly it hadn't changed much in the intervening time. Otherwise, I looked for telltale signs that Johnny was actually still there—his car, his tchotchkes, anything that might indicate he had in fact not left. I found nothing. Johnny was gone and it was no longer an abstract concept but a concrete reality. Now, I felt that in some way I, too, could leave.

Finally, I felt that I could put the past in the past. I left with a sense of freedom, of peace.

That feeling lasted for all of six weeks.

∎

On the evening of Tuesday, August 10, I was giving my evening psychology class their final exam and having those who wanted to do it give me data for a psychological study I was doing. While they worked on those tasks, I slipped off to check my e-mail.

I was surprised to find an e-mail from Dan. Except for an e-mail in July in which he had simply told me that he was closing down one of his e-mail accounts, I hadn't heard from Dan since the previous December. In this e-mail, he had forwarded to me what proved to be an unexpected but interesting message that he had received two days before.

The sender, whose name was "Crystal," said that she had found a message that Dan had posted for "Jonathan Frazier" on the Internet. Interestingly, she told Dan that he had recently been evicted from her property in Paladin. Crystal ended the brief message by asking Dan, "Do you know him?"

Did he know him? I thought that question should have won the Innocent Question of the Year Award. Did he *know* him...

At first, Dan wasn't convinced that "Crystal" was a real person. He thought it might actually be Johnny playing games with him, just trying to accumulate enough incriminating e-mails from him to send to people in Credence in order to out him. Given that Johnny had threatened to do that before, it was a valid concern. I, however, wasn't convinced that Dan was right. "Crystal" didn't write like Johnny—a writing style with which I had become intimately familiar—and he didn't know that we knew about his pattern of being evicted for not paying his rent. Knowing how Johnny liked to portray himself as the aggrieved party, the innocent victim, I thought it would be uncharacteristic of him to portray himself in a negative, certainly criminal light. Even so, Dan wasn't convinced that I was right, since he couldn't understand how "Crystal" had certain pieces of information about him that he claimed he'd never published in connection to Johnny. Consequently, Dan sent an insulting e-mail to "Crystal" in which he told her that he thought she was really Johnny and that the warrant was still active (although by that time it wasn't). When he didn't receive an immediate response, he was more convinced than ever.

Dan was obviously upset by the thought that something painful he'd tried to push aside was being dredged up again. "Damn, Richard, I was almost over this mess and ready to put it behind me," he told me. I told him, as he had once told me, that it would get to him only if he let it get to him—something, though, that I knew was easier said than done.

Finally, on Friday, the 13th, "Crystal" replied. Seemingly confused by Dan's message, she said that she didn't think it was intended for her and explained that she'd just replied to one of his messages. Later, I determined that the message to which Crystal referred was the taunting message that Dan, as "Cautchu," had posted on *Gayteway* in September 2003 that had contained Johnny's last name and that was still there. Presumably, Crystal had done an Internet search on the name "Jonathan Frazier" and had found the posting, which had contained not only Johnny's last name, but also indications of his criminal activities as well as Dan's e-mail address, which Dan had forgotten he'd included.

In another e-mail to Dan, which she sent the same day, Crystal explained in more detail what she had suffered at the hands of "Jonathan." Reiterating the fact that he had just been evicted from her property in Paladin, where he had apparently lived from May to the beginning of August of that year, she stated that he had never paid his rent and had written her and her husband two bad checks in the amount of $1,900. She said that they'd contacted the local prosecutor's office about a month before he was evicted, but the police had never gone to arrest him—a pattern that reminded me of what had happened in Mariah. She said that he had left her property two weeks before, but since she didn't know where he'd gone, she couldn't pursue him. She said she had a file "about 2 inches thick" from an attorney who had been pursuing him for check fraud. She said that she had learned that "Jonathan" had been moving every three to six months without paying rent and writing bad checks—continuing the pattern he had established—or had continued—in Paladin. She said that in the three months that "Jonathan" had lived at her property, he had ruined it. I had seen the condition of the house in Paladin and the apartment in Mariah, so I could only imagine. She said that she hated him and was glad that she lived in another state because she would have killed him. She concluded by stating, "He is a true sociopath"—something that I, and many others, had come to learn the hard way.

It was clear that Crystal was a real person and was only the latest victim of Johnny's psychopathic behavior. She was the newest member of a club that was becoming less and less exclusive.

Crystal was different, though, because she seemed to be the most capable of any of Johnny's victims of whom I knew of seeing him brought to justice. In one of the e-mails she'd sent to Dan, she'd told him that a friend of hers, who we later learned worked for my state's *Most Wanted*, had created a web site through which to try to expose Johnny. Crystal sent Dan the link, which he then sent to me. When I visited the site, I was delighted to see a picture of Johnny with a headline that read, "DO YOU KNOW THIS SCUMBAG?" The site then gave a brief account of what Johnny had done, insofar as Crystal knew it. Two years before, I had thought about creating a similar site myself when I had thought about pursuing legal action of my own against Johnny and wasn't sure where he was. In the end I hadn't, since I wasn't certain of the legality of doing so, but now I was thrilled that someone had actually taken that initiative.

I had already decided to write to Crystal myself, to tell her some of my experience with Johnny. Now that I was on between-semester break, I had some time to compose a concise but detailed account. I sent my message on Tuesday, the 17th, a week to the day after Dan had forwarded me his first message from her.

In looking at the web site, I'd noticed that the picture of Johnny that Crystal had posted was the one from the hospital's web site, which was still there after almost three years. It was a small black-and-white photo that didn't do him justice, so I sent Crystal the three large color pictures of him that Johnny had sent to me the day before he had left Dan's. I also sent her a detailed physical description of him to complete the "picture." There was no misidentifying him now.

I had given Crystal a list of all of Johnny's e-mail addresses of which I was aware, which now amounted to at least 12. Those were, of course, just the ones I knew about and surely were not all of the ones he used. Apparently, the "legitimate" one that he'd created when he'd first moved to Dan's three years before was still active and Crystal, to taunt him, sent Johnny the link to the web site. We were never sure if he got it because he never reacted, but the damage was done. I wondered, however, if such a site would enflame his narcissism or, perversely, reinforce it.

I also made sure that she knew his real name wasn't *Jonathan*, but *Johnny*.

In response, Crystal said that it was "scary" what Johnny was capable of doing—an opinion with which I fully, and unfortunately, agreed. She said that she had already heard from at least seven other victims who wanted to see justice done and that the more she investigated, the more victims emerged. Although she didn't know where he was at the moment, she hoped that if enough people came forward and he was adequately exposed, he could be found and stopped.

In one fell swoop, I learned, at least in broad outline, what Johnny had been doing in the year and a half that we had lost track of him. Apparently, after leaving the apartment in Mariah at the end of January the year before, he had eventually made his way back to Paladin. Sometime after returning, he had rented from a man named Harry, whose property lay near the storage unit. That left me to wonder if Johnny had managed to keep his belongings at the unit some one year after I had transferred the financial responsibility for them back to him or if it was just a coincidence. Crystal didn't say if Johnny had lived elsewhere in Paladin either before renting from Harry or between renting from him and from her. I surmised, however, that he had been living in Paladin for at least the past year and probably longer. He had always wanted to move back to Paladin and apparently his wish had come true. Before, I had half-thought that he had probably slipped off to another state, but now, I was unnerved to discover that he had been living next door the entire time, where the drama had begun.

It was from Harry's lawyer that Crystal had received the "about 2 inches thick" file regarding Johnny's recent criminal behavior. It revealed that Johnny had perpetrated the same scam with the last several people from whom he had rented. Apparently, he told potential landlords that he worked for TekNetium and that he and his son were moving from the Southern state to Paladin. He said that he wanted to sign a two-year lease and have his rent direct-deposited. The landlords fell for his lies, then never saw anything more than the deposit and first month's rent. Crystal said that she had had no idea Johnny would cause so much trouble for her and her family—a type of naïveté with which I was all too familiar. She said that she had never met him in person, having only spoken to him on the phone, and that a friend of hers had shown him her property. I doubted she would have been less fooled than I had been if she had met him in person.

She also stated that there was an open warrant for his arrest for indecent exposure that involved an address in Paladin. I was surprised—but not shocked—to learn that Johnny had been exposing himself—I realized that sexually he was disturbed—but it wasn't clear if he was living where the incident had occurred. Unfortunately, the warrant was under a pseudonym and, like the warrant in Dan's county, couldn't be legally served until it was amended with his real name, which apparently no one had known.

Describing him as a "filthy pig," Crystal said that once she received some additional information from Dan regarding the bad check that Johnny had written to him, she was going to forward everything she had to *America's Most Wanted*, hoping for national exposure. She said she had already contacted a news station in Paladin, but hadn't yet gotten a response. She said that in the meantime, she was going to update her web site with the new information she had, putting his activities into chronological order. She ended by saying that "now [was] the time" to stop him. The time was actually long overdue.

I e-mailed Dan to tell him that I'd contacted Crystal. In response he said that he'd spoken with Crystal the day before for at least forty-five minutes. He was very impressed with her, describing her as "my kind of people." His only problem was that the web site wasn't "readily available to many people," although I knew it would be only a matter of time before the site became indexed, allowing anyone who did a search under Johnny's name to find it, and word of its existence became more widespread. Dan also told me that he'd sent Crystal a copy of his bad check, Laura's damning e-mail to Johnny outlining what he had done to her, and his phone bills so she could try to trace the phone numbers in the cities in the Northeastern and Southern states, the latter of which Dan thought belonged to Johnny's parents.

From Dan, Crystal learned about Terry and, as I had two years before, she contacted him. Predictably, he responded with what appeared to be his standard-issue threat of legal action if he were publicly or professionally connected to his brother. Apparently he was still as reactive and self-obsessed as ever. Interestingly, Crystal asked Dan if he thought that "Terry" was actually Johnny playing games, something I had wondered myself when I'd received the threatening e-mail from Terry when my niece had innocently contacted him, thinking he was someone else. Dan told her no, that I'd gotten the same response.

I'd had it. I was tired of his family turning a blind eye to what Johnny was doing to the rest of us, tired of their seeming lack of social conscience. Frankly, I didn't care how much they had been traumatized by their psychopathic relation; the rest of us had been traumatized, too, and we needed their help in finding him. I believed that even if Terry didn't know where he was, his parents did. When Johnny had been living in Mariah, he had received mail from his father. Obviously, his parents had known his previous address, so if they were staying in touch with him, then they might know his current one. We had no way of contacting his parents directly—but Terry did. Terry had refused to get his parents further involved, which meant that he was actively preventing interested parties from talking to them. My understanding was that if someone deliberately withheld information, or prevented someone else from getting information, that could lead to the apprehension of a criminal, then wasn't that obstruction of justice…which was a crime? I told Crystal this and she, in turn, told Terry.

That seemed to make him back off. In response, Terry said that we were *all* his victims and implored Crystal to not let Johnny's behavior reflect on him or his family. He said he would love to help Crystal stop "this person," as he referred to his brother, from hurting others, since that would be the best thing not only for others but also for Johnny. Trying to dissociate his family from Johnny and his behavior, he described his parents as "old, sweet, HONEST" people and said they didn't understand why Johnny was the way he was. Crystal had apparently mentioned the fact that their father's name was on the checks that Johnny had used and Terry made it clear that "the scumbag," as he described his brother, had stolen them from their father. He also told her that his brother had done worse to him and had both his Social Security number and other personal information. The latter comment finally clarified what should have been obvious to me for two years, which was that Johnny's second SSN was actually *Terry's*.

In spite of his advice to me to "heal and move on," it was clearer than ever that Terry had not. I sympathized with his situation, since in some ways his situation was my situation, but I couldn't tolerate the neurotic ways in which he was dealing, or not dealing, with his brother's behavior. At some point, sympathy had to end in the name of self-preservation and I decided then and there not to have anything further to do with someone whose own behavior hindered as much as it helped, harmed as much as it healed.

■

On Saturday, the 21st, my mother and I took a trip to the Paladin zoo. I hadn't visited the zoo since that fateful day in June three years before when I had met "Jonathan" face to face and had received the intuition that something was profoundly wrong, an intuition that I had, unfortunately, ignored. In spite of the recent revival of the Johnny issue, I found that I had finally healed enough from my experience with him that the zoo held no negative associations for me. Indeed, I had a wonderful time. I was also delighted to discover a sun-filled conservatory, brimming with exotic plants, that housed a variety of tropical butterfly species that, until then, I had seen only in photographs and films. After spending an hour absorbing the beauty of the longwings, owl butterflies, and morphos, I left feeling rejuvenated, emotionally metamorphosed. Even though I believed that Johnny was still somewhere in Paladin, only miles away if not closer, I thought about him only vaguely.

When I got back home around 6:00, I found that Crystal had called. Later that evening, I called her back. I was even more impressed by her on the phone than I had been through e-mail, although in that way I had already been impressed enough. Her intelligence, her straightforwardness, her moral sense, her sense of outrage at having been taken by Johnny and not helped by the law—a feeling I knew all too well—came through even more forcefully in direct conversation.

I elaborated on my experience with Johnny as well as the experiences of others. I gave her as much information as I possibly could to use however she could in her pursuit of Johnny. I hoped that perhaps now, we would see some action and maybe some justice.

In talking to Crystal, I learned that she had finally gotten the copy of the bad check that Johnny had written to Dan. The check number was 209. The checks he'd written to Crystal, off the same closed account, were in the 800s. Although it wasn't clear how many checks between those numbers Johnny had written, the thought that he'd written *six hundred* bad checks in three years was mind-boggling, if not surprising.

In some ways the most interesting thing I learned from Crystal was that Glenn was with Johnny again. "Jonathan" had told me in April two years before that Glenn had been found and returned to my state, but I had always questioned it. In addition, "Jonathan" had told Laura that Glenn was with him, but again, I had questioned it, thinking that Johnny was once again wanting to portray himself as the self-sacrificing, caretaking father figure. Apparently, though, Glenn had in fact returned at some point, although it wasn't clear when. Although Crystal had never spoken with Johnny, or Glenn, in person, the friend of hers in Paladin who was taking care of her property there had. Crystal told me that her friend had described Glenn as sounding "retarded," which dovetailed with Miranda's description of his intelligence. In addition, I thought of Miranda's belief that their pathological relationship wove in and out and apparently, Johnny had snared Glenn in his web once again. I also thought it ironic that Johnny had been so worried about my becoming physically violent toward him when Glenn, who had actually beaten him up at least twice and probably more, was now with him every moment of the day.

We spoke for two hours. After we got off, I was left feeling, for the first time in a year and a half, that finally, we might be able to do something to stop Johnny.

■

The fall semester, which started the following Monday, proved even more difficult than it had been the previous year. Although I wasn't studying for challenging exams, I was teaching five, three-hour classes, three of which met back to back on Thursdays. I would arrive at work at 9:00 in the morning and not leave until 9:00 in the evening, only to return the next afternoon to teach yet another. It was draining and somewhat debilitating and I usually needed much of the weekend to recover. On top of that, things were going badly in other ways at work and the number of major tasks that needed to be done at home had built up to the point that I began to feel paralyzed and depressed.

Yet, despite the problems with work and home, I felt optimistic about other areas of my life—one area in particular. On the Tuesday of the first week of the fall semester, Dan sent me an e-mail in which he mentioned that he'd received an e-mail from Crystal in which she'd told him that her neighbor in Paladin had just seen Johnny lurking around her property. By that point, he'd been gone for at least three weeks, although to where we still didn't know. The neighbor, however, had gotten a description of the car and the license number, which could, of course, be traced. It wasn't his Cadillac, though, and I wondered if it was even still working. Either he'd somehow gotten a new one or it belonged to someone else who had assumed his position in the long line of Johnny's victims. Unfortunately, when Crystal had the number run, it matched the wrong car. Whether her neighbor had made a mistake in recording the number or the plates were stolen, the fact remained that ultimately the number proved to be of no help.

Even so, Crystal continued to try. She had contacted the detective in Paladin who was working the case who said he would pull up some numbers close to the one she'd gotten to see if any of them matched. In addition, the bad check from Dan, which the authorities in Paladin had finally received, had made them more interested in the case.

Crystal had also learned the name of the movers who had moved Johnny from her property. Apparently, the same movers had moved him the last three times—in the previous year alone—but had refused to give her further information because she could be a "stalker." She couldn't believe it. She wondered if he had a friend working for the company because, as she commented, "What must a normal person think when they see these properties?" I had to agree. I thought of the times that I had helped him to move and of his later attempts to discredit me by claiming that I was stalking him.

Crystal also mentioned that she had spoken to Miranda, who had promised to send her a copy of her own bad check. She also said that she had e-mailed all of the major news stations and two newspapers in Paladin with an expanded version of her story about Johnny. It contained more information about Johnny's schemes and crimes and included accounts from Terry, Dan, and me about what Johnny had done to us. She also posted the information on the web site through which she hoped to flush him out.

In reading the information that Crystal had compiled, I learned even more about the rental scam that Johnny had been perpetrating in some form since he'd moved to Mariah and probably longer. His modus operandi was always the same. First, he would find property owners with nice homes for rent in the $800 to $1,200 per month range. After contacting the owner, he would play the now-familiar father/son charade involving Glenn, explaining that he worked for TekNetium as a contract employee and was moving up from the Southern state. He would then give the owner a false Social Security number to pass the credit check and begin the scam in earnest. Johnny would pay the first month's rent and deposit in order to move in, but when the second month's rent came due, he would begin a series of threats and demands against the property owner. He would always claim that the property was unlivable and that repairs had to be effected before he would pay further rent. Unfortunately, he never had any intention of making further payments of any kind because he knew that, by law, he couldn't be forced to leave until he was officially evicted. That could take months. Apparently, he had managed to stay at places for as long as six months without ever paying any more than the first month's rent.

Interestingly, I also learned something about Johnny's behavior that cast the problems with his house on Millstone Drive in an entirely different light. During the summer of 2001, "Jonathan" had experienced persistent problems with his water heater. When I had first begun visiting him in June, it wasn't working, then after having it fixed later that month, it had malfunctioned again only days later. Consequently, he'd gone without hot water throughout most of that summer. Now, I understood that the malfunctions were no accident, no stroke of misfortune. According to Crystal, Johnny had been deliberately damaging the properties at which he had lived as part of his scheme to avoid being evicted for not paying rent. After moving in, he would do things such as damage the water heater, the plumbing, the walls, then refuse to pay rent until the problems were fixed. Once they were, he would repeat the ploy. I realized now that he had been damaging the water heater at the house on Millstone Drive in an attempt to avoid having Ted Kanner evict him, a tactic that ultimately had failed. I also remembered how the toilet had come perilously close to overflowing the Tuesday before "Jonathan" had vacated the house the next day and I began to suspect that Johnny had deliberately clogged the toilet to take one last stab at his landlord, who'd had the gall to expect Johnny to pay for living in his house. Once again, I couldn't believe how much deception had gone on under my nose, how far things had been from how they had seemed.

In addition, I learned that in the roughly year and a half that he'd been in Paladin during what I came to call "Act III" of the Paladin drama, he had lived at four different places: Harry's, Crystal's, and two others. Johnny had been a busy little bee—or scorpion—stinging everyone in the process.

Finally, I learned that one of the investigations had turned up two files that indicated that Johnny had been institutionalized in the Southern state in 1993 and that apparently that was where he and Glenn had met. That confirmed what Miranda had told me when I had first spoken to her in May 2002. I recalled my nonplused reaction when she had told me about the institutionalization, how it was official confirmation that I had been having a relationship with a crazy person.

Over the next few days, I compiled an even more extensive account of my experience with Johnny, which included the experiences of his victims to whom I had spoken. That was only a fraction of the total, which counted many times greater. Around the middle of September, I sent it to Crystal.

By the end of September, I hadn't heard from Crystal for a month. I sent her an e-mail asking her for an update, and eventually she responded. The news, unfortunately, was discouraging.

She said she had received the expanded account of my experience with Johnny and had forwarded it to a reporter who worked for a news station in Paladin, but the reporter hadn't responded. She said she had tried to contact Miranda at least three times since she'd spoken to her about the check, but she hadn't responded, either. She said she had left two messages each on the voicemails of both the prosecutor and the detective who were working the case, but neither of them had responded. She said she hadn't heard from Terry lately, who ultimately decided that we just needed to hire a private investigator to track down his brother, but who otherwise made it clear that he was not going to help. Crystal was becoming discouraged, especially with the police, who didn't seem to care that much about what Johnny had done. I knew all too well how she felt.

She said that Johnny was probably going to be evicted again soon, so she thought she might call the small claims court in Paladin to see if any papers had been filed, papers that might give us an address. She also said that she was planning to be in the Paladin area around Christmas and that if we found out where he was living then, maybe we could go find him. It seemed a slim hope.

I forwarded Crystal's reply to Dan. In response, he said he thought that Johnny led a charmed life, managing to get out of all the trouble he had gotten into. Defeated, he said he gave up trying, since it wasn't worth the headaches anymore. He said that he wished Crystal the best, however, and that I was right: Now she knew how we felt.

In the e-mail, Dan also reported that he'd had a sixth heart attack. I was very concerned about him, both physically and emotionally. The reactivated stress was destroying him.

By the middle of November, there had still been no progress. We still didn't know where Johnny was and the web site hadn't brought us any leads, although it was profoundly satisfying to see his ugly face and even uglier crimes displayed on the Web that he had used so adeptly to snare, poison, and suck dry the rest of us. In addition, none of the prosecutors, detectives, or journalists, who should have been helping, was doing anything, which was deeply frustrating, but equally familiar.

Thinking he might still be in Paladin, I decided to contact Andy. We hadn't been in contact for almost two years, and even though he was no longer entangled with Johnny, I wondered if he, or one of his friends in the gay community, insofar as he seemed to have them, knew where Johnny might be. His response was brief and to the point. He said simply that if Dan and I wanted to pursue the matter, then that was our business, but he himself wanted nothing further to do with it. His response only reinforced my perception of Andy as an opportunist who refused to help anyone but himself unless he could somehow profit from it. I was disgusted by his behavior, by him, and decided to have nothing further to do with him.

Out of frustration, I decided to do an online search for pages containing the name "Jonathan" Frazier, the name he seemed to prefer. In the process, I discovered that Crystal's web site had finally been indexed, which meant that anyone who tried to find more information about Johnny through the Internet, as Crystal had, would find the site.

In addition, I discovered something else. I found a recent posting for a position at an IT company in the city where Johnny had lived before coming to Paladin. When I read the ad, I found that the person who had posted it was none other than "Jonathan" Frazier. It couldn't have been anyone else.

In checking the company's web site, I didn't find additional information about him, but the posting had given me his e-mail address and the web site provided telephone numbers. I forwarded the information to Crystal.

Taking a more active approach in verifying the information, Crystal called the company and actually spoke to Johnny. She told him that she was going to forward all the information she had about his criminal activities to his company and asked him how long he thought he'd have a job. In response, he called her a "fat, ugly, nigger bitch," thinking she was black. She told me that he was "really freaked out," and was amused. She then gave me his work number in case I wanted to contact him—to taunt him. She told me not only that he was he working in that office, but also that the receptionist had told her that he lived nearby. We now knew where he was.

Apparently, sometime between mid-August and mid-November, Johnny had managed to finagle a position at the company as a human resources manager, a position similar to the ones he'd held before. Presumably, they knew nothing about his history of criminal or antisocial behavior, which he had once again managed to keep secret. Johnny had returned from whence he had come five years before to weave his web and wreak his havoc in my state.

Crystal quickly compiled an abbreviated account of Johnny's activities in my state and e-mailed it to his employer, hoping they would investigate further and take appropriate measures. At my suggestion, she included contact information for several legal officials who had been involved in his case so his employer didn't have to take her word for it. I myself had been in the position of trying to convince indoctrinated, or at least unsuspecting, people that "Jonathan's" stories were lies and I knew how important concrete proof was in persuading them. His employer had no idea how much trouble potentially they were in.

In the account, I finally learned just how much he owed the owners of the properties from whom he had rented but to whom he had paid no rent: $50,000. I figured that, taken together, what Johnny had stolen from, cheated out of, or otherwise cost the people of my state—at least six landlords, at least two and possibly three employers, one hospital, Laura, Dan, Miranda, my mother, me— amounted to at least $170,000. That didn't include what he owed to the IRS, what he owed to those to whom he'd written other bad checks, and to everyone else whom he'd taken and of whom we were unaware. The true figure was certainly in the hundreds of thousands and possibly more, when totaled throughout his lifetime.

■

On Friday, December 3, Dan e-mailed me to tell me that while he had been looking through the closet in his guest bedroom that afternoon, he had found a briefcase belonging to Johnny. He said that he'd looked in the closet a few times since "Jonathan" had lived with him, but always for something specific, so he hadn't noticed it before then. He said the briefcase contained, among other things, a few paid parking tickets, some pay stubs, some names and phone numbers, and a few addresses of gay web sites, all of which dated back to when he had lived in the Southern state before coming to our state. He said he would go through it more thoroughly to see if there was anything Crystal might be able to use. I told him I would be interested to know exactly what he found. It amazed me that for such an intelligent con man, Johnny was so stupid when it came to leaving potentially incriminating evidence lying around.

The matter dropped for the next two months, then around the end of January, Dan e-mailed to tell me that he'd finally gone through the briefcase more carefully and would send me the contents so I could see them for myself. I received them on Tuesday, February 1. The contents were unremarkable, but interesting. Among them were several pay stubs and other work-related materials indicating that throughout 1998, the year before he had come to my state, "Jonathan" had worked at two different human resources firms and had business cards to the effect that he had been the vice president of one of them, whatever that meant in real terms. They did not confirm, however, whether or not he had worked at TekNetium, but they did suggest that he had not worked there throughout the entire time frame (mid-1996 to mid-1999) that he had given to me. The pay stubs also indicated that throughout 1998, Johnny had been making base salaries ranging from $55,000 to $62,000 a year. Those figures accorded with the salaries that he had been making in 1999 and

2000, which the W-2 forms that Laura had found had revealed. I had received my credit card statement that morning as well and seeing the balance—which still included some of his debt—combined with seeing how much he made, did not sit well with me.

It also contained a page that indicated that he, along with Horatio and another friend, had planned to form their own business, apparently an HR concern, with "Jonathan" as head, of course. It also verified that Horatio was in fact a real person instead of an invention of Johnny's pathological mind but functioned not as an executive, as "Jonathan" had suggested, but as an office worker.

The page was interesting not so much because of the fact that they were planning to form a business as because of the hyperbolic, even manic, way in which their venture was described. It portrayed "Jonathan" as having "amazing contacts and networks," the people involved as having an "amazing desire for success," and the opportunity as having the potential for making everyone "extremely wealthy." It also said it would give them the satisfaction of "owning, operating, and running a business with a tremendous sense of pride." I couldn't help thinking that if Johnny was involved, it wasn't the healthy kind of pride but, rather, the kind of pride that had gotten Lucifer kicked out of Heaven.

It concluded by listing the group's major long-term goal: "January 2000 all three of us buy matching Porsche 911 turbos with customized plates." Obviously he hadn't achieved that goal, since he was still driving the ratty Cadillac with what I had learned were expired plates when I'd met him a year and a half after the target date. *What an asshole*, I thought. It reminded me of his grandiose story to Miranda about how his father was going to buy him a white Jaguar. It only reinforced the fact that with Johnny, it was *all* about money and power and presenting an impressive façade.

It also contained the information for gay sites that Dan had mentioned. Actually, the information consisted only of a few web site and e-mail addresses scribbled down on notepaper. One of them, I could not help noticing, was the one for *Gayteway*, the site through which we had met and through which he had posted so many of his fraudulent ads. This must have been the original record of the web site he would use for future reference, the point at which everything, as far as I was concerned, had started. The note had an almost primal quality to it, as if I were seeing the spot at which the main strand in the web that would, in time, link many tangled threads had begun to be extruded. After more than six years, things had come full circle.

The contents of the briefcase helped to fill in more pieces about the person who had deceived me in such an extravagant fashion for an entire year. Although I had long gotten over the emotional damage that my encounter with Johnny had wreaked, finding out exactly who Johnny was remained an intellectual puzzle that provided me with satisfaction when additional pieces fell into place.

■

By the middle of January, I hadn't heard from Crystal since we'd discovered that Johnny had slithered back to the state from which he had come. On Tuesday, the 18th, I e-mailed her to see how things were going. In response, she said that she had just started school and had a job interview the next day, so things were going well for her. As far as Johnny was concerned, she said that she was trying to get her judgment against him turned over to an attorney in his state so she could get his wages garnished if he was still working. I held out hope that at least she would succeed where the rest of us had failed, but I didn't hold out much hope.

That spring, I taught five classes again, and although I was making more money than I ever had, the spring semester proved to be just as wearing as the fall semester had. The summer proved to be much more subdued and, in addition to teaching only two classes, I spent much of the summer making renovations and repairs to my house, doing photography and research, and cultivating plants, although severe storms that passed through my area in the middle of August destroyed much of my garden. That fall, I went back to my typical fall schedule, although now I had decided to become a student again myself—not in psychology, but in biology. I had always been interested in biology and might have had a career in it if circumstances hadn't directed me elsewhere. During the fall, I made the necessary preparations for beginning in the spring.

I continued to check the Internet for indications of Johnny's activities. I was especially interested in knowing whether or not he was still working at the IT company. In late January, Dan had told me that he'd called Johnny's work number and had gotten his voicemail, indicating that he was still there two months after we had found him. Over time, I discovered ads for positions at the company that Johnny had posted as late as the end of June. Apparently, the company hadn't acted on the damning information that Crystal had sent to them. I couldn't help wondering if he had gotten to them with some kind of carefully crafted story to discredit her, as he had tried to do with me. Even so, I thought they still should have taken some of the information seriously, just in case. I didn't know what it would take. Johnny did appear to live a charmed life.

By the end of September, I hadn't heard from Dan since the beginning of May. I e-mailed him to find out how he was doing. In response, he said that he was continuing to have health problems, including another heart attack and gastrointestinal bleeding from the medications he'd been given, which had caused him to need four units of blood. In spite of his health, he said that he had been traveling extensively throughout the United States and was thinking about visiting Europe in the spring, having decided that if he was going to have a "short life span," he would see some of the things he wanted to see. I didn't know what to think of his fatalism but I was glad that he was enjoying his life when "the bastard," as he called Johnny, had done so much to undermine it.

Finally around the middle of October, when I'd found no new postings for three months, I called Johnny's office one weekend when I knew he wouldn't be there to answer. He wasn't and he didn't, but strangely, I also didn't get his voicemail, which I should have. He'd kept the jobs he'd had in Paladin for only about six to eight months—a pattern that the documents in the briefcase suggested had also prevailed when he'd worked in the Southern state before—which made me wonder if he had finally been fired. Or, hopefully, worse.

By the end of October, I hadn't heard from Crystal since January, so I contacted her to see how things were going. I was curious to know if she'd made any further progress in her dealings with Johnny and I wanted to tell her about my failed attempt to find out if he was still working at the IT company, which made me wonder if he was. I was also curious about the file that Crystal had described as "about 2 inches thick" that she had gotten from Harry's lawyer and I thought I would ask her to send me a copy.

I didn't hear from her for a month. After apologizing for taking so long to respond, she told me that she'd gotten a job working for a big law firm. The attorney for whom she was now working was drafting a demand letter to Johnny for the judgment she had against him. I also learned that, contrary to my concerns, Johnny was still working at the IT company. She said that she had called the day before to make sure because she was sending the demand letter to him at work. To me, she sarcastically "congratulated" him on having kept his job at the company for over a year—which amazed me, given his track record, and dismayed me, given that his employer had apparently done nothing to verify the information she had sent to them a year before and take appropriate measures. She said that she was fortunate because she would have his wages garnished if he didn't send her payment in full. "Will keep you posted," she concluded.

That was the last I heard from her. I never learned if she reclaimed any of her lost money. I, however, had given up long before trying to reclaim any of my own lost money, having placed far more importance on reclaiming my half-lost self.

Around that time, I also heard from Dan. He told me again that he had been traveling and had recently gone to Las Vegas, where he had lost $350 gambling. At least *that* loss had resulted from a known risk, willingly taken, unlike the loss he had suffered from the unsuspected, unselected risk he had endured at the hands of Johnny. Dan ended his message by stating, "He still roams free!! Hard to believe! Life!" That seemed to me to be the best assessment of the outcome of the Johnny situation.

It *was* hard to believe that Johnny was still roaming free. Numerous people in numerous ways had ensured that freedom. In the end, I learned, however, that those of us who have suffered the damage that psychopathic personalities can inflict on us can have an even greater freedom: the freedom that comes from the knowledge, the self-knowledge, that permits us to untangle ourselves from their web of manipulation, exploitation, and lies, that prevents us from becoming entangled in it in the first place.

—49—
TIED THREADS

Stories like these never seem to end, although hopefully, as time passes, the drama and damage inherent in them diminishes in presence and impact.

■

Needless to say, my experience with Johnny left me profoundly damaged, especially when it came to being involved with gay men. I was afraid to become involved with them because of a fear that I would encounter someone like Johnny again. For at least two years after the experience, I suffered from a form of post-traumatic stress disorder and was occasionally assailed by flashbacks to certain aspects of my experience with him that would overwhelm and paralyze me. I was also afraid of being injured further by gay men in general, since I had already had enough bad experiences with them and didn't want to repeat them. I had been injured not only romantically, but also in every other way by them. Gay men had always made me feel that I was second best, that I was not Mr. Right but Mr. Right Now, that I was "good enough to fuck but not good enough to love," as I once described it. I felt that I was supposed to look, behave, and be a way that was not natural, possible, or desirable for me in order to be accepted by them. Gay men only brought pain and I wasn't going to suffer any more because of the damaging behavior they seemed to be so skilled at inflicting on me. It was better to live my life without them.

For the four years between November 2002 and November 2006, I had very little deliberate contact with other gay men. The only gay men with whom I maintained even marginal contact were Dan and another friend whom I had met in late April 2002, between the time I had ended my relationship with "Jonathan" and had started finding out the truth about "Johnny." Even here, the contact was confined exclusively to e-mail and I would sometimes go for long periods—in one case, for two years—not communicating with them at all. At work, gay students would pass through my classes, but I never made any attempts to open up to them about who I was, to try to connect with them on that level. I used the excuse that they were students and that it wouldn't be appropriate, but it was just an excuse. I wasn't really out at work, although I was less concerned about repercussions from straight people than I was from gay ones. I retreated into a self-protective shell and the world, for the most part, saw only bits and pieces of my true self—not just my sexual self, but my entire self. Except for a few, close, trusted friends, no one knew who I really was.

In the spring of 2005, I went through a period of about a month when I regained some interest in having at least casual sexual contact with other men and even placed a couple of ads online, which drew considerable interest. Even so, when it actually came to meeting one of the men in person whom I'd met online, I couldn't go through with it. As the time to meet him grew near, I grew increasingly anxious, since this would be the first time that I'd been sexually involved with a man, even casually, in two and a half years. The prospect of doing so only reactivated my fears about gay men, about what they could and would do to me. In the end, I explained some of what I was going through to him and he seemed to understand, but there was no further contact. Shortly thereafter, I removed my ads and retreated back into my self-protective shell.

I stayed there for another year and a half.

In the meantime, I returned to school in the spring of 2006 to study biology. In the process, I began to have some interesting experiences that slowly began to break down the self-protective wall with which I had surrounded myself.

In one of my classes, I met a young man named Rod. At first, I wasn't certain if Rod was male or female, appearing to be androgynous. Eventually, when I began to work with him, I discovered that he not only was male, but also had once lived as a woman and performed drag. At first, I was somewhat judgmental of him because I felt that he reinforced destructive stereotypes about gay men, but as I got to know him, I realized what a remarkable person he was. Knowing that I had a background in psychology, he took me aside one day and told me much of his life story because he thought I would understand. I realized he had endured far more as a gay person than I ever had, but constantly tried to respond to hate with love. After that, I never viewed him the same way again and was reminded of the wrongness of judging someone without even knowing him. Even someone who had suffered because of irrational prejudice could still be prejudiced himself in some ways. I was left feeling ashamed of myself for how I had reacted, but I was also left enlightened. He told me he thought I would understand about him because of my background in psychology, but I didn't tell him the *real* reason I understood. I was still in my shell, but because he seemed different, less victimizing than most of the gay men whom I had encountered, he left a chink in my armor.

Later that fall, I had a series of experiences in rapid succession that finally brought the wall I had built around myself crashing down. A former student of mine with whom I had become friends sent me an e-mail containing a Thanksgiving joke involving a gay man that I found somewhat offensive. I wrote her back, telling her briefly that I didn't know how I felt about the joke before moving on to other things. In response, she apologized for any offense it had caused and told me that she thought I would appreciate it because she had always assumed I was gay. I wasn't sure why she thought that, but it was obvious that I wasn't hiding myself as much as I'd thought, that my solid shell was something of an illusion.

Only days later, a young woman in one of my classes in which we were discussing prejudice opened up in class and spoke about the prejudice she had suffered because she was a lesbian. I was stunned by her unexpected display of candor, of seeming comfort at revealing something about herself that could have made her the victim of further prejudice. No one around her seemed to have much of a reaction, however, which astonished me. I began to wonder why I was going to such lengths to maintain my wall, to keep people away. Perhaps I was really healing.

That semester, I was taking a class through which I met a young man named Austin. Austin was very mild-mannered and one of the most non-threatening people I have ever met. Slowly, I began to suspect that Austin was gay. Then, around mid-November, I found out for certain that he was. I found myself attracted to Austin and decided to do something that I had not done in many years: ask a gay man for a date. Austin wasn't interested, but we did go on to have an interesting friendship that, despite some complications, wove in and out for the next several months. Eventually, I realized that Austin reminded me of two other heterosexual men with whom I had been infatuated and that I was projecting my unrequited feelings for them onto him; a relationship with him, then, would have been built on an illusion, which wouldn't have been good for either of us. Even so, my encounter with him proved to be the *coup de grâce* that completely shattered my self-protective wall and opened the gay world to me again.

I decided that at 40, it was finally time to finish tearing down the wall that still separated me from the rest of humanity. Although my sexuality wasn't the most important aspect of my personality, I still felt it was important to take my place in the world as a totally out gay man. I was also going to try to reconnect with other gay men, though from what I had learned from my previous experiences with them, I planned, or at least hoped, to do it the *right* way this time. With the hard-won wisdom of age and experience, I vowed that I was not going to make some of the mistakes that I had made before and would not allow myself to be hurt any more than I had been or had to be. The shell was gone and in its place I now wore a flexible membrane that, like the membrane of a cell, selectively filtered in what was good for it while rejecting what was bad for it and interacted with its environment instead of retreating from it.

By this point, the social networking sites had become the rage and I decided to create one that fall through which I would "blog" about my experiences in trying to reestablish a life as a gay man and through which I would try to connect with other gay men. In the process, I went through a second adolescence and with something of the emotional turmoil and upheaval of the first one, I slowly established an emotional and social equilibrium regarding gay men that I wished I had gained the first time. Ultimately, the results were mixed, but although I encountered certain problems from various sources, I also encountered a number of gay men who, for the first time in my life, made me feel accepted. Part of why I had become and remained entangled with Johnny was that I had never gotten the kind of "acceptance" from someone that I felt I had gotten from him, except that now, it was *real* acceptance, not the fraudulent acceptance of a psychopath who was using the façade of love to manipulate me. Because of their reinforcement, their validation, I was strengthened in a way that made me increasingly resistant to the kind of mistreatment that comes from wanting acceptance at almost any cost.

That proved useful when I finally went on my first date in five years the next spring. After meeting someone through the main social networking site through which I was operating, we arranged to go on a date. Unfortunately, he proved to be one of the most self-absorbed people I have ever met. A performer, he was always "on stage" even when he wasn't and wanted constant attention and reinforcement. I felt that he didn't want a boyfriend as much as he wanted an adoring fan. In addition, he was still living with his ex-boyfriend, whom he had failed to mention until well into our exchange of information about each other and which made me wonder just how "ex" he really was. After ten hours of being subjected to his narcissism, I left, vowing never to see him again. In many ways, he reminded me of Johnny, except that he was just narcissistic, not psychopathic. That, however, was bad enough. I felt that I was being tested, and this time, I passed the test by doing what I should have done to "Jonathan" at the zoo six years before: I walked away and never looked back, taking my self-respect and well-being with me.

In the end, I realized that I enjoy being single and don't have a strong need to be involved in a relationship the way many people do. Now, it is a preferred state, not a neurotic one born of fear. I do know that if I do become involved with someone, it will take someone very special to make me abandon my singledom. Despite Johnny's accusations that I didn't know how relationships worked, the fact is that I *do* know how both normal *and* abnormal relationships work and, having had my share of abnormal ones, I will now settle only for the normal type. That involves someone who treats me with equality, dignity, and respect. Anything less is lessening and unacceptable. My experience with Johnny taught me the ultimate, and I believe, final lesson about *real* relationships and how "this was not one of them." Someone like Johnny, or the countless lesser versions of him, people whose self-centeredness comes before everyone and everything else, will never be allowed to injure me badly again.

■

On the evening of May 30, 2011, I was staying up late, as I preferred to do. The night was clear and warm and the Scorpion sparkled in the south. Mars was far away, clustered with the Moon, Mercury, Venus, and Jupiter in Aries, and Pluto, drifting slowly eastward, had finally reached Sagittarius. Ten years to the day that I met "Jonathan," the arachnid had lost its power to do anything but intrigue with its mysteries, inspire with its beauty, as it previously had.

■

By May 30, 2011 the following developments had taken place in the lives of some of the "flies" who had, for a time, fallen into the web that Johnny had woven:

"Dan"

Over the years, I stayed in closer contact with Dan than I did with any of Johnny's other victims. By the fall of 2005, Dan, who was now in his late 60s, had begun experiencing recurring heart problems that, perhaps not surprisingly, had started around the time that

Johnny had turned on him and he had suffered several heart attacks. In addition, he had started having kidney problems as well as some lesser maladies. In spite of—or, more accurately, because of—his declining health, he had decided to make the most of his life if he was going to have a "short life span," as he had described it. He had been traveling extensively throughout the United States and was thinking about visiting Europe the following spring. Although I thought he was being fatalistic, I was glad that he was taking the opportunity to enjoy his life, regardless of how much time he had left.

After not having heard from him for a year and a half, I e-mailed Dan in April 2007 to find out how he was doing. In response, he reported that nothing much had changed, although he had been hospitalized for additional heart and kidney problems. Even so, he said he was "on the mend again." He concluded his reply by saying that he was glad "the pig," as he described Johnny, was out of our lives and that we had moved on. I couldn't have agreed more.

At least that was how it seemed. In February 2011, after not having heard from him for almost four years, I decided to contact Dan. Still alive and well, he replied the next morning. I was stunned, however, by his message. After stating that in getting my e-mail his "prayers [were] answered," he went on to explain that he had lost my e-mail address but had wanted to write to me to tell me about something upsetting that had happened only days before.

He told me that he had gotten a response to one of his personals ads from someone who lived in the city to which Johnny had fled six and a half years before. The two-sentence message asked him if he was "still in the closet" and if he had "finish[ed] the painting." He was convinced it was Johnny, who was still trying to harass him after nine and a half years.

Disturbed by the possibility, I took a look at the sender's profile, but was able to determine, thankfully, that it wasn't him. Unfortunately, the incident reenflamed Dan's hatred for Johnny, which was once again as strong as it had ever been. I wrote Dan a long message in which I explained what I had learned about why Johnny had been able to deceive me and made certain he understood that he had deceived *everyone* he had encountered until it was too late. It was *not* just him. In response, he told me that my message had made him feel better. I hope it did. Unfortunately, for some of Johnny's victims, "the pig" still wasn't fully out of their lives.

"Laura"

By the fall of 2005, I hadn't heard from Laura for more than two years, not since June 2003. That June, I had written to let her know how I was doing and to ask her how she was doing. She told me that she was doing "great," having moved to a better home and gotten a better job. So, in September 2005, I sent her a message in which I again let her know how I was doing and asked her how she was doing. I did make one, tangential reference to Johnny, but otherwise, I did not mention the person who had initially brought us together and had caused us so much pain. She had also encouraged me to let her know how I was doing once in a while, so I didn't feel I was intruding. Unfortunately, she never replied.

In the spring of 2007, I found one of Laura's social networking pages, which offered little information about her. When I checked another one at the end of 2010, I found that she was now the owner of a small business and seemed to be doing well. In mid-2011, that still appeared to be true.

Laura's social networking pages also contained links to her sons' pages. In mid-2011, Chuck, who had joined the military in 2002 but was now a civilian, was living in another state with his wife and four children. All in all, he and his family seemed to be doing well.

Jack, who had in some ways been one of Johnny's most hapless victims, also seemed to be doing well. Like his big brother, he had apparently joined the military. The first of his social networking pages that I checked also answered one lingering question that Johnny had "answered" more than five years before: whether or not Jack was gay. He was not. Apparently, Johnny's insistence that he was had simply been a reflection of his own sexual fantasies. I could understand, though, why Johnny had developed sexual feelings for him because the pictures on his page, the best ones of him that I had seen, revealed a young man who was extremely good-looking. Unfortunately, when I saw the pictures for the first time, it was hard for me not to think of how he must have looked when he was lying in a hospital bed after having attempted to take his life because of Johnny.

"Cliff"

Through the social networking sites, I learned more about Cliff—the *real* Cliff. His profile information, though limited, made it clear that he was not the high-powered executive that "Jonathan" had made him out to be. In addition, he stated that he had only a high school diploma, not the college degree one might have expected. Finally, his age was listed as 31, which would have made him only 25 when he had run afoul of Johnny.

Interestingly, his profile confirmed some of the facts that "Jonathan" had given to me about him, including his hometown, his current location, and his "five-year" relationship with "Loren," which would have begun at the time that "Jonathan" had said it had. Based on the pictures that Cliff had posted on his page, my impression was that Loren was a sugar daddy and that Cliff had been looking for a sugar daddy when he had encountered Johnny, who doubtlessly had presented himself as such.

Interestingly as well, the profile also listed the names of his two Great Danes, one of which was named "Sadie." *Sadie* was, of course, the name of the Great Dane that "Jonathan" had claimed he was keeping for Horatio while he worked overseas and had later given away when keeping her had become too burdensome. I had seen Johnny hand over Sadie to her new owner myself, so unless there was a connection between the new owner and Cliff, then Cliff's Sadie was a different dog from "Jonathan's" Sadie. I wondered if Johnny had gotten a Great Dane in imitation of Cliff, but I never really knew.

I also never knew how he had reacted to or acted on the information that Dan and I had sent to him in the summer of 2003. I hope that it somehow made his life better, although I also wonder if Johnny, true to form, got to him with one of his elaborate lies to discredit Dan and me and Cliff has remained snared in Johnny's web of deceit.

"Art"

Around the end of 2009, an equally intriguing piece of information came to light regarding the identity of the mysterious "Dulcimer," who had sent Dan the threatening e-mail in November 2001. In doing an Internet search on that username, I was stunned to learn that it was the username of an e-mail address that belonged to Art. His connection to the threatening message, however, was unclear. Given Art's mild-mannered personality, it seemed unlikely that he had authored the message. More plausible, given his habit of appropriating other people's identities without their knowledge and pretending to be them through the Internet, is that Johnny simply accessed Art's e-mail account while he was living with him in November 2001 and sent the message from it. If that was true, then given the similarities among the "Dulcimer" message, the "Heorshema" message, and The Pretender letters, that only strengthened the case that Johnny was the author of all of them. Assuming this to be true, I e-mailed Art in February 2011 to tell him what I believed Johnny had done, but the "Dulcimer" address now proved invalid. Although I knew Art's phone and house numbers, I decided not to make further attempts to contact him. I resumed my previous position that I would leave him in peace.

"Miranda"

In mid-2011, Miranda was still alive and well and doing a healthy business in Paladin. From late 2008 to early 2009, I made three attempts to contact her either by e-mail or by letter to ask her additional questions, but she never replied. Even so, Miranda will always have the honor of being the first person to help me begin the long, messy process of untangling my mind and life from Johnny, of replacing his lies with the truth.

After learning the birth dates of most of the major players involved, at least from my standpoint, I discovered something interesting that Miranda would appreciate. Fully half of the people involved were Scorpios—Johnny, Miranda, Andy, Crystal, Art, Cassandra—and at least one-quarter were Cancers—Dan, both of Johnny's parents, me—a proportion that statistically appeared unlikely to have occurred by chance. Miranda had commented to me about the receptivity between Scorpios and Cancers, since they were both water signs, and her belief that the situation was karmic. Whether it was or not, there was no question that some kind of "receptivity" had drawn all of us together.

"Crystal"

In the fall of 2008, I e-mailed Crystal at the last e-mail address I had for her to ask her if she had been successful at reclaiming any of her lost money from Johnny. Unfortunately, I didn't receive a response. I eventually found her profile on one of the social networking sites and not only had the chance to see what she looked like for the first time, but also learned that in the three years or so since I'd been in contact with her, she had gotten divorced and had moved back to my state, where she had grown up. She owned her own business and seemed to be both successful and happy. When I checked again in mid-2011, the business had closed and she had moved to one of the Western states. She had a different last name, appearing to have reclaimed her maiden name, but still seemed to be doing well. Crystal hadn't had the emotional entanglement that some of the rest of us had had with Johnny, but even if she had, she always seemed like the kind of person who wouldn't let something like an encounter with a psychopath stop her in her tracks and keep her from living and enjoying her life.

"Andy"

The most interesting development, in my opinion, involved Andy. Around the beginning of 2006, I found an abbreviated profile he had posted online. In it, he stated that he was in a period of reevaluating his life, had gone back to church, and—to quote the remainder of the sentence exactly as given—had "removed myself fr—." The sentence not only broke off in midstream, reminding me of the fragmented e-mails I had occasionally received from him, but also left wide open the question of what he had removed himself from. I had my suspicions, however. Given his statement that he had returned to church, and given my perception that he viewed himself as some sort of failure as a gay man, I suspected he had planned to say "removed myself from *the gay community*," but had been unwilling to complete the sentence. It made me wonder about the circumstances under which he had written it and I wondered if, as he had been on occasion when he had written to me, he had been drunk. I didn't know what to think and since I had no intention of corresponding with him further, no further clarification was forthcoming.

Then, in the spring of 2007, I found one of his social networking pages. Interestingly, he had left blank the section of the profile that asked for one's sexual orientation. Even so, his blog made it clear that he was in fact gay, since one of them discussed at length his latest failed gay relationship. Then, when I checked the page again in the fall of 2007, only six months later, things had changed in an utterly unexpected direction. Now, he was claiming that he was *straight* and the blog in which he had discussed his *gay* relationship had been removed.

I was surprised...yet I was not. I had already suspected that he was trying to move away from a life as a gay man and toward a life as a straight one, possibly under the influence of his church. I actually felt sorry for him, having seen this pattern among certain gay men and lesbians who, finding unhappiness and unfulfillment in the gay world, fled into an illusion of social and spiritual acceptance in the straight world at the expense of their true selves.

Alternately intrigued and disturbed by what I considered to be an unfolding disaster, I couldn't help following the development of Andy's "straight" life. By 2008, a new person had entered the picture: his *fiancée*. Apparently, he had met and become engaged to a woman. Her own social networking page featured a picture of the engagement ring that Andy had apparently given to her. Then, sometime in 2009, they married. I couldn't help wondering what she knew, if anything, about Andy's "former" life. If she didn't, then what Andy was doing to her was in some ways just as bad, the same, as what Johnny had done to him. By the middle of 2011, they were still married, their pictures on their social networking pages depicting them as nothing but the happy couple.

It was clear to me that Andy was disturbed more deeply or differently than I'd believed and I hoped that his fiancée, whom I believed he was using to convince either others or himself that he was straight, would learn the truth and, like me, remove herself from someone whose pathology would only bring her pain and loss.

"Edward Frazier"

In January 2009, I decided to do an Internet search in an attempt to find more up-to-date information about Johnny, if there was any to be had. Knowing that his real parents were already old and in poor health more than six years before, I wondered if either of them had died in the intervening time. In searching an Internet site that collects obituaries from papers throughout the country, I found that, indeed, Johnny's father had recently died.

The obituary, which was quite lengthy, was a revelation, clarifying many points that until then had remained unclear. The obituary revealed someone who was extremely intelligent, well educated, and cultured and had made significant contributions to his field. It stated that he had been born and educated not in England, but in the Mid-Atlantic state, and had later moved to the Midwestern state to pursue a lengthy, productive career in teaching and research. "Jonathan" had occasionally alluded to having connections to the Mid-Atlantic state and "Iain" had actually told "Chaz" that he was from there. Later, Terry had confirmed that they had relatives in that state and one of the two Social Security numbers Johnny had been using had been issued there. Although Johnny's father had a Ph.D. and not an M.D., which "Jonathan" had claimed about the British version of his father, his Ph.D. was in a biology-related field in which "Jonathan" had said that the British version of his father was involved. The obituary also confirmed that "Jonathan" had actually used his real mother's real name, although it also revealed that, far from having seven (or eight) siblings, he had only one. Terry had stated that financially his parents were "comfortable," but not rich, and his parents' background did indeed seem more American middle-class than British upper-crust. Overall, Johnny's father seemed like a very impressive person who had led a full and accomplished life. I knew, though, that he had suffered more than I, or anyone else, had because of his older son and I wondered how much this had undermined his life. I hoped he was finally at peace.

"Terry"

By mid-2011, Terry was still involved in the same field that he had been when I had first discovered the seemingly discrepant, but ultimately accurate, web page in June 2001 that had discussed "Jonathan's" younger brother. He didn't appear to be hobnobbing with the level of celebrity that he formerly had, but he seemed to be content doing what he was doing. Under other circumstances, Terry and I might have been friends or at least friendly, but the damage that his brother had inflicted on him and that Terry, in turn, had inflicted on me precluded that. I don't wish him ill and will always be thankful to him for having snapped the biggest strands in the web of Johnny's lies, but I will also always wish that things between us could have been different.

"Glenn"

In 2009, I discovered one of Glenn's social networking pages, which indicated that he, too, was living in the Southern state, although it didn't specify where. In 2011, however, I discovered a police report online in which Glenn had been arrested for a minor, but unspecified crime that placed him in the same city with Johnny in the spring of 2010. Presumably they were together. If that was true, then Glenn had never gotten away from Johnny, as he had tried to do. I wondered if their strange, symbiotic relationship was continuing, would ever end, and what kind of damage it was causing, had caused, would cause. I wondered, too, if he would ever break free of Johnny's snare.

In addition, while performing a police record search on Johnny for crimes he committed in Paladin, I decided to perform one on Glenn. In the process, I uncovered information that shed light on Glenn's whereabouts during at least part of the time he was supposed to have been missing while I was involved with "Jonathan." Far from being in the Caribbean Islands or the southern United States, he was in Paladin. According to a police report filed around the end of December 2001, Glenn had stayed with a man in Paladin for about three weeks before becoming "stressed" and leaving the man's house on Christmas Eve—a pattern that sounded familiar. The report also suggested that Glenn had been staying at a homeless shelter in Paladin before he had gone to live with the man. When he had left the man's house, Glenn had stolen the man's credit card and had gone to a nearby hotel, where he had checked in under the man's name and had used his credit card to pay for his room. On the day after Christmas—Boxing Day—the man's credit card company had contacted him to alert him of excessive activity on his card, at which time the man, who didn't know his card was missing and being used, had informed the company that no one had permission to use it. The company had then placed a stop-use flag on the card. When the hotel had run the card again the next day, the flag had appeared. When Glenn was questioned about it, he had become uncooperative, and the police were called.

When they arrived, they had gone to Glenn's room, where he had given them his real name and a Social Security number that was issued in a Northeastern state—a place to which I had not previously been able to connect him. After claiming that he had permission to use the card but otherwise being unable to prove the truth of what he was telling them, he was arrested. The charges against him included forgery, theft, and fraud. The outcome of the case was unclear.

At the time, I had wondered where Glenn was, how he was spending Christmas. Now I knew.

I am convinced that when Glenn was in Paladin in late 2001-early 2002, Johnny knew he was there even if he didn't always know exactly where. Johnny had mentioned the idea that Glenn had been staying at a homeless shelter, and I suspect that he knew he had been staying at the one alluded to in the report. I also suspect that through either Glenn's mother, his own investigations, or both, Johnny learned, in early December 2001, that Glenn had disappeared from the shelter but couldn't determine where he'd gone, provoking the frantic reaction expressed in his e-mails to me from December 10. The message directed at Glenn that Johnny posted on the *Gayteway* board for my state in mid-January suggests that Johnny still didn't know where he was more than a month later but assumed that he was in my state, since he didn't post similar messages on the message boards for the Caribbean island or the Southern state.

I do suspect, however, that after coming to Paladin in the fall of 1999, Glenn continued to be in or near the Paladin area far longer than Johnny had led me to believe. Mike Harmon's acknowledgement that Glenn worked for him during the second half of 2000, "Jonathan's" comment to me in mid-June 2001 that "the ex," after learning about his health problems, wanted to "come over" to comfort him, and the police report stating that Glenn was in Paladin in December 2001 together suggest that Glenn was still there more than a year and a half after he was supposed to have left. He may have gone to what appears to be his home town in the Great Lakes state and visited the Caribbean island at different points, but how those places figure into his life during 2000 and 2001 is unclear. I suspect, too, that precisely where Glenn's wanderings took him will always remain a mystery to me.

"Johnny"

As of mid-2011, Johnny was still living in the city in the Southern state to which he had escaped seven years before. In doing a background check on Johnny in early February 2011, I learned that he had continued to have "problems with landlords," as Mike Harmon had described it. In early 2007, Johnny was sued for "forcible entry and detainer"—which, translated from the legalese, meant that his landlord had sued to evict him from her property and repossess it after Johnny had refused to leave. In addition, it appeared that he had lived at several residences in those seven years, although it wasn't clear if he kept getting evicted or simply kept moving. Given the 2007 case, as well as his unreformed personality, the first possibility seems more likely.

In addition, I received confirmation of something I already knew: Johnny had been evicted from the house on Millstone Drive in Paladin. Ted Kanner had started eviction proceedings against him on August 29, 2001, the day after Johnny had e-mailed me to tell me that he and Ted had made the "deal" in which Ted would reclaim the house and "Jonathan" would move out, something that "Jonathan" had presented to me as a mutual idea. By the end of that August, Johnny owed Ted over $5,200 in unpaid rent. I came to believe that "Jonathan's" original story about how he would still have to pay rent on the house for four months after he left actually referred to four months' *back* rent that he owed. Although I finally tracked down and contacted Ted Kanner twice in 2011 and he verified that he was in fact the correct Ted Kanner, unfortunately he ignored my attempts to gain further information from him about what had happened between him and Johnny.

By mid-2011, Johnny was no longer working for the IT company in the Southern state, although it wasn't clear when he had stopped working for them or why. As far as his employment history is concerned, I was finally able to piece together that in the five-year period between 1996 and early 2001, Johnny had held at least six different middle-management positions, all of which he had held for only a few months before something had happened. It wasn't clear if he had worked during his tenure in Paladin between 2003 and mid-2004, although it seems unlikely, given that he was telling landlords an obviously false story about his employment situation. Otherwise, it appears that apart from the job at the hospital in Mariah, which he'd held for a month, and the job at the IT company in the Southern state, which he'd held for at least a year, though possibly not much longer, Johnny had barely worked in ten years. By 2011, he was in his early 60s, which meant that he was now old enough to draw various retirement benefits, but it was unclear how he had gotten by before then. Presumably he had been continuing to live the parasitic lifestyle of the typical psychopath, conning the unsuspecting out of their honestly-earned money and failing to pay money he had promised to them to fund his life of exploitation, manipulation, and deceit.

I also discovered that in the late 1980s, Johnny and his father had gotten into legal trouble after violating certain financial laws at a company of which Johnny's father was president and Johnny was, unfortunately, chief financial officer. My suspicion was that his father wasn't involved at all in the financial misdealings, that it was all Johnny's doing, but I also saw another example, if later behavior was an indicator, of Johnny's father overlooking his older son's pathological behavior, presumably out of some misguided "fatherly" desire to protect his son, even when it hurt him. That pattern, unfortunately, had disastrous consequences for the rest of us.

Around the same time that he and his father had gotten into legal trouble at their company, Johnny had been charged with seven counts of "uttering a forged instrument"—which, translated from the legalese, meant signing another person's name to a document then presenting that document to a third person. Although unclear, I suspected that in Johnny's case, that meant passing bad checks, possibly under his father's name. In addition, he had been charged with one count of grand theft, although it was unclear what he had stolen.

Otherwise, I learned that Johnny had not been keeping up the payments on the car he'd had when I was involved with him. In June 2001, the creditor who had loaned Johnny the money for the car had filed a case in small claims court in the county in which Paladin is located to try to reclaim almost $1,100 in unmade car payments. Somehow, though, Johnny had managed to hold on to the car for at least a year and a half longer, until he left Mariah, and possibly longer still. I doubt that he settled up with his creditor, however, and believe that he kept his car through some type of evasion. The day the case was filed was the day that he wrote me the first of his fraudulent e-mails concerning his father's health and only two days before we physically met. Interestingly, I had told him that I was renting a car to come to Paladin because mine wasn't reliable and in response he had said that "[m]aintaining and servicing a car [was] another one of those daily chores that [he did] reluctantly." Apparently, *paying* for one was another chore he didn't do at all.

In performing the police record search on Johnny for crimes he had committed in Paladin, I discovered that in the fall of 2003, Johnny had been arrested at an adult bookstore during a vice investigation. Because certain details of the incident were labeled confidential, I wasn't able to obtain more than the basic fact, but I suspect that this was none other than the "indecent exposure" incident to which Crystal had alluded. Although the bookstore was located at a different address from the one she had mentioned—an address at which Johnny had apparently lived sometime during his 2003-2004 tenure in Paladin—I suspect the address she had mentioned was simply the one at which he had lived when the incident had occurred. I viewed the incident as yet another example of Johnny's sexual disturbance.

In doing an online search using the formal form of his real first name—the one that had appeared on warrants before—I discovered that in the fall of 2010, Johnny had been arrested for operating a motor vehicle without a valid license. The site that offered the information also contained a mug shot of Johnny. This was the first time since the day in July 2002 that I confronted him in Mariah that I had seen what he looked like. The picture was shocking. In addition to having aged well beyond the eight years that had passed between 2002 and 2010, Johnny looked like someone who had been picked up out of the gutter and photographed. He looked haggard, drained, heavy-lidded, as if he were exhausted or drugged. Within the mixture of negative emotions that I felt upon seeing him for the first time after so many years and after expecting never to see him again, I felt that what I was seeing was a reflection of the truth about who Johnny really was. The mug shot put the lie to the façade of superiority that he always liked to project and his deteriorated condition was, I believe, an inevitable product less of age than of the life he had lived, continued to live.

Using a combination of records, I was finally able to determine the precise date that Johnny was born—something that, like so many other things, he had never wanted me to know. Surprisingly the day he had given to me appeared to be correct, while the year corresponded to the true age that Terry had estimated Johnny to be. I was able to determine as well, based on his father's whereabouts around the time Johnny was born, that Johnny had actually been born not in the Midwestern state, but in the Mid-Atlantic state. When Terry had told me that Johnny was from the Midwestern state, he had apparently meant that he had grown up there, not that he had been born there. His alter ego "Iain" had told my alter ego "Chaz" that he was from the Mid-Atlantic state, one of the few statements Johnny had made that was true. The Social Security number that Johnny had been using that had been issued in the Mid-Atlantic state, then, was apparently his own. This, however, was simply reconfirmation of one of the most important facts that I had learned about Johnny: He was as American as I was.

Finally, by mid-2011, I found no further sex ads on the sites that Johnny had used while living in my state. That did not mean, however, that there couldn't be others, undiscovered, on one or more of the numerous other gay sites on the Internet. All I could do was to hope that there *were* none, that Johnny's attempts to snare unsuspecting people through fraudulent personas on the Internet had finally stopped.

—V—
—Unmasking the Mimic—

We are all fascinated by illusions, by things that differ from how they seem. The syndrome of psychopathy is inherently fascinating for this reason: It represents a severe form of psychopathology that is concealed by an outer façade of normality—what Hervey Cleckley described as a "convincing mask of sanity." Like Amyciaea lineatipes, *a species of arachnid that mimics the physical appearance of ants on which it preys, psychopathic individuals readily gain the trust of others because they come across on initial contact as likeable, adjusted, and well meaning. It is only through continued interaction and observation that the psychopath's true, "darker" nature is revealed.*

—Christopher J. Patrick,
Handbook of Psychopathy

UNMASKING THE MIMIC

*...even the most severely and obviously disabled psychopath
presents a technical appearance of sanity...*
—Hervey Cleckley, *The Mask of Sanity*

Introduction

In this section, I will explore four aspects of my experience with Johnny: First, I will try to understand Johnny's seemingly incomprehensible behavior and place it into some kind of comprehensible psychological framework. Second, I will detail at least some of the ways in which people like Johnny operate. Third, I will discuss several things that I believe you need to do to become disentangled from the emotional damage that an encounter with a psychopath can inflict on you. And, finally, I will discuss ways in which you can, hopefully, recognize and avoid becoming entangled with the psychopathic personality in the first place.

A—Unmasking the Insanity

Before exploring the different ways in which Johnny was able to deceive, manipulate, and use those of us who were snared in his web of lies and discussing how to avoid the webs that such people weave, it is important to understand the underlying problem that caused Johnny to behave the way he did. Throughout this book, I have used terms such as "psychopathic" and "narcissistic" to describe Johnny's behavior, although I have used those terms somewhat loosely. These terms technically refer to different *personality disorders*, a group of psychological disorders that involve some type of disturbance in an individual's personality that causes him or her to behave in ways that are destructive to himself or herself, others, or usually both. Personality disorders are different from the majority of psychological disorders in that they do not "come and go" as do many other psychological problems and represent a more fundamental way of relating to oneself, others, and the world. Psychopathic and narcissistic personality disorders represent two specific patterns.

To describe these disorders briefly, people with *narcissistic* personalities are fundamentally self-centered, believing themselves to be superior to the rest of us. They tend to believe they are special or unique and, viewing most of humanity as inferior to them, they strongly prefer to associate or align themselves with others whom they perceive to be equally special or unique. They typically come across as arrogant and self-important, displaying little humility or ability to recognize their failures, faults, and flaws. Although they may actually be highly accomplished, they tend to exaggerate their abilities and achievements to make themselves appear to be even more than what they really are or simply expect to be recognized and admired as accomplished without an equivalent degree of ability or achievement. They are often preoccupied by grandiose, self-flattering fantasies that usually revolve around the themes of success, power, wealth, brilliance, beauty, or perfect love. Like the psychopathic personality, they lack empathy for others and have little concern for our rights, feelings, and dignity. They have a profound sense of entitlement and expect us to comply with their requests or demands regardless of the personal cost to us. Unlike the psychopathic personality, however, the narcissistic personality tends not to cross the line into criminal behavior. When their grandiose, self-flattering sense of self is challenged, they will react with either shame or rage, although the rage usually takes the form of verbal, not physical, attack. Overall, the behavior of the narcissistic personality, though troublesome, usually doesn't present the same potential for damage as that of the psychopathic personality.

People with *psychopathic* (also known as *antisocial* or *sociopathic*) personalities function with little or no conscience, which gives them the freedom from the emotional restraints that feelings of guilt, shame, or remorse impose on the rest of us. The disastrous result of this dysfunction is that they view the rest of us not as beings with rights, feelings, and selves that matter, but as tools to be used for their purposes, then callously discarded when our usefulness to them has ended. To them, we are things, not people. On the surface, the psychopath often comes across as charming, intelligent, concerned about our welfare. They may even appear to be the best thing that has ever happened to us, some kind of dream come true. Nothing could be further from the truth, however, and on closer inspection, the dream proves to be a nightmare. Beneath the surface, behind their façade of charm, intelligence, concern, of seeming normality, they are deceitful, manipulative, and irresponsible to an extent that far surpasses anything that the "normal" person displays. Their façade of normality, their "mask of sanity," is simply another tool in the arsenal of weapons they use in the self-serving war they wage against us, another thread in the web of exploitation they weave and in which they ensnare us. Psychopathic personalities are much more likely to react with physical violence than narcissistic ones are when threatened, although they usually resort to non-physical methods of reestablishing their sense of self, gaining reinforcement, or seeking revenge. They are human predators, wolves in sheep's clothing, and we are their prey.

There are different systems for conceptualizing and diagnosing personality disorders, although some are more well known and used than others. Even so, similar concepts seem to appear from system to system, regardless of the specific name that is given to a particular disorder within a particular system. Many of these systems contain personality disorders that roughly correspond to one another and that are usually labeled narcissistic personality (disorder) and psychopathic (or antisocial/sociopathic) personality (disorder). One commonly used system is that presented in the *Diagnostic and Statistical Manual of Mental Disorders (DSM)*, which, as of 2012, was in its fourth (revised) edition (*DSM-IV-TR*). There, the two disorders are labeled Narcissistic Personality Disorder and Antisocial Personality Disorder. Of the nine features that an individual with Narcissistic Personality Disorder may exhibit, Johnny displayed all nine, while of the seven core features that an individual with Antisocial Personality Disorder may exhibit, Johnny displayed four (criminality, deceitfulness, irresponsibility, and lack of remorse). Exhibiting only five of the nine features for Narcissistic Personality Disorder and only three of the seven core features for Antisocial Personality Disorder, respectively, is required to diagnose someone with those disorders. In other words, Johnny personality structure, according to the *DSM*, was predominately narcissistic with antisocial (psychopathic) traits.

Robert Hare, who has done extensive work in trying to understand the psychopathic personality in particular, has derived a set of symptoms that in many ways overlaps with those for the *DSM-IV-TR* Antisocial Personality Disorder, but expands on them by including more internal (psychological), as opposed to purely external (observable), traits, something that the *DSM-IV-TR* version emphasizes in order to increase the reliability of diagnosis.

Consequently, Hare (and I) prefer the term *psychopathic* because of its inclusiveness. Hare developed the *Psychopathy Checklist-Revised (PCL-R)*, which includes 20 features that those with psychopathic personalities are likely to possess. A subject being evaluated using the *PCL-R* is given a rating for each item, reflecting the degree to which that symptom is present, that can range from 0 to 2, where 0 = not present, 1 = moderately present, and 2 = markedly present; total scores, then, can range from 0 to 40 (Hare, 1999; Hare, Harpur, Hakstian, Forth, Hart, & Newman, 1990).

In evaluating Johnny's level of psychopathy using the *PCL-R*, Johnny received a total score of 30 out of a possible 40. The cutoff score for considering someone to be psychopathic, at least among North American samples, is 30. In other words, various scales for measuring psychopathic behavior, in spite of some overlap in proposed symptoms, lead to the conclusion that Johnny's personality, in addition to having a strong component of narcissism, had a significant component of psychopathy.

Narcissistic and psychopathic traits appear to be related and, although they can occur independently in different people, they can and do frequently coexist. Theodore Millon, who has done extensive work in trying to conceptualize personality disorders, suggests that both narcissistic and psychopathic personalities are fundamentally related in that both of these personality types employ an "independent" style of gaining reinforcement, or encouragement, to continue thinking and behaving as they do. Instead of relying on others to give them the reinforcement they need, they receive reinforcement from themselves, largely through how they view themselves in relation to others. Narcissists gain reinforcement through a "passive" independent style, which means that they do so by continually convincing themselves that they are superior to others and deflecting implications that they are not by devaluing the negative evaluations of others, whom they see as inferior. Psychopaths gain reinforcement through an "active" independent style, which means that they take a more aggressive approach in gaining reinforcement by maintaining an attitude of contempt for others and feeling superior through their ability to intimidate, deceive, manipulate, and damage the remainder of society (Millon, 1981, 1996; Millon & Davis, 2000).

Otto Kernberg, who has done extensive work on understanding narcissism, similarly suggests that narcissistic and psychopathic traits are related, existing along a continuum that ranges from "normal" narcissism to pathological narcissism to psychopathy. (Kernberg also includes *malignant* narcissism in his system, lying between pathological narcissism and psychopathy, but for the sake of simplicity, I am excluding this point in the continuum from the current discussion.) Some of the main traits of interest include 1) one's self-perception relative to others, 2) one's ability to empathize with the feelings of others, and 3) one's level of concern for the welfare of others. As one moves from "normal" narcissism to psychopathy, the traits in question gradually deviate farther and farther from what is considered normal and become more destructive, especially to others (Kernberg, 1998, p. 47).

"Normal" narcissism includes healthy self-esteem in which one sees oneself as being just as good as others without seeing oneself as being superior to them, an adequate ability to empathize with the feelings of others and to respond to them accordingly, and concern for the welfare of others in which one operates from the basic premise of "do unto others as you would have them do unto you." This type of "narcissism" is essential for healthy psychological functioning and basic social stability, since one sees oneself as fundamentally equal to everyone else.

Pathological narcissism, which occupies the midpoint of the continuum, involves inflated self-esteem in which one sees oneself as superior to others, a diminished ability to empathize with the feelings of others, and lessened concern for the welfare of others in which one increasingly believes that one is "above the law" that governs ethical social interaction. People at this point in the continuum would generally be regarded as having narcissistic personality disorder.

Psychopathy, which occupies the far end of the continuum from "normal" narcissism, involves grossly inflated self-esteem in which one's feelings of superiority to others assume an increasingly hostile, aggressive tone, an absent or nearly absent ability to empathize with the feelings of others in which one's emotional life is shallow or narrow, and no concern for the welfare of others in which the only law that one obeys is one's *own* law and the moral, ethical, and legal standards that society has established are seen as irrelevant at best, ridiculous and contemptible at worst. People at this point in the continuum would generally be regarded as having psychopathic personalities or antisocial personality disorder.

Visually, the continuum can be illustrated as follows:

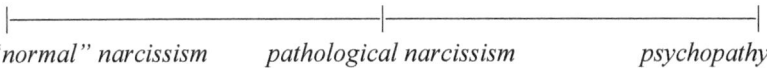

"normal" narcissism   pathological narcissism   psychopathy

Given that he met all of the criteria for Narcissistic Personality Disorder and at least half of those for Antisocial Personality Disorder, Johnny appeared to occupy a point roughly midway between the pathological narcissism and psychopathy regions of the continuum:

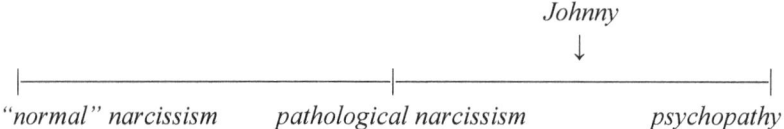

In short, Johnny's high intelligence, combined with his unshakable belief in his superiority to others as well as little or no conscience to inhibit his behavior, made him a dangerous predator capable of doing unparalleled damage in the lives of those whom he encountered.

B—The Threads in the Web

How in the hell could two intelligent people be so gullible? We are both aware of a psychopathic personality and behavior...
—Dan

Johnny used various techniques for manipulating the people he encountered, techniques that capitalized on blind spots in human psychology. Johnny was fully aware of some of these blind spots and deliberately, skillfully used them to maneuver his victims, but he was probably less aware of others whose exploitation was more second nature to him. Regardless, they all proved useful in manipulating us and bear closer examination.

There are two sets of behaviors that I will examine, which I have broken into two groups: 1) pathological lying, which was Johnny's most effective and widely used technique, as well as related factors that enhanced its effectiveness, and 2) other manipulative techniques that did not involve pathological lying.

1. Pathological Lying and Related Factors

The most striking aspect of Johnny's behavior, at least to me, was his pathological lying. Almost everything Johnny told me was a lie and almost everything he told others was a lie. This feature of his behavior also stood out prominently in the minds of many of the people who had encountered him. In at least three cases, people independently made references to his pathological lying. It was also his pathological lying that wreaked the most havoc in the lives of the people who ran afoul of him.

How does "pathological" lying differ from "normal" lying? Unfortunately, the psychological community has done very little research on the nature of pathological lying, despite its presence in several psychological disorders (e.g., psychopathy). Currently, the debate about pathological lying in psychiatric (and, to some degree, legal) circles appears to revolve around two issues: 1) how "pathological" lying differs from "normal" lying and 2) whether or not pathological lying should be considered a disorder in and of itself and not simply a symptom of a broader disorder. As far as the first issue is concerned, I have come to the conclusion that pathological lying differs from normal lying in the following ways:

1. Pathological liars obviously lie considerably more often than "normal" liars do.

2. Pathological liars lie more often to reinforce their perceived sense of self (e.g., to appear more impressive than they actually are) than to gain practical advantage (e.g., to avoid punishment).

3. Pathological liars are often less consciously aware that they are lying than "normal" liars are or lie more automatically than "normal" liars do.

4. Pathological liars often seem to believe, or half-believe, their lies, while "normal" liars do not.

5. If exposed, pathological liars are more likely than "normal" liars to show indifference toward the importance and impact of their lies (though not necessarily to having their lies exposed). They may react with intense anger (e.g., Johnny's reactions to my uncovering the lies he was telling me and others and my revealing those lies to them), rationalization (e.g., "If I lie sometimes on the Internet, I don't think that I am the first or only person to do it"), minimization (e.g., "In the end, where is the harm?"), or projection (e.g., "Remember, despite your motives, you have lied and concocted a whole person to someone else."). To them, lies are morally and ethically equivalent to truths and ultimately they take no responsibility for the effects of their lies.

Overall, Johnny seemed to lie much more for psychological reasons than for practical ones. Certainly, he did the latter (e.g., to avoid honoring financial obligations, to avoid being prosecuted, to conceal his devious behavior), but the psychological motives seemed paramount. He informed me that by uncovering and intruding into the fantasy world he had created between him and Andy, I had "destroyed" him more thoroughly than "anything" ever could. Although I believe this statement was mainly offered as some kind of manipulative lie, I also believe it reflected the truth. Johnny's propensity to lie—and to believe his lies—was far more central, far more crucial to his sense of self than it is in the "normal" person. In his final message to Johnny, Andy perceptively remarked that Johnny behaved as if his lies were a "fundamental part" of his life. They were.

In retrospect, it is difficult for me to believe that I could have believed Johnny's lies for so long. I certainly didn't believe everything he told me, even before I discovered the extensive lies he was feeding Andy, Cliff, Joan, Laura, Jack, and others, but I *did* believed *most* of what he said. I, apparently, was not alone, and other people whom Johnny had deceived had almost identical reactions of amazement at their "gullibility." Andy told him that he was "completely amazed" that he had believed Johnny's lies for as long as he had. Laura told him that she was "kicking herself" for not figuring out that Johnny had been deceiving her sooner than she had. Dan asked me how two intelligent people who had formal backgrounds in psychology could have been "so gullible." Why did we, and so many others, believe his lies?

I believe there are a variety of reasons why we believed that "Jonathan" was telling us the truth. Below, I have outlined the primary reasons that, at least to me, seem to be the most influential ones in allowing Johnny to deceive us and others as well and as long as he did.

Assumption of Honesty

Whether we realize it or not, we tend to operate on the assumption that most people are truthful about most things most of the time. This is sometimes referred to as the *truth bias*. Consequently, we are not prepared to encounter someone like Johnny, where that fundamental assumption is completely overturned. In Johnny's case, he was *un*truthful about most things most of the time or, to quote Mike Harmon, "You can believe only about ten percent of what he says...[a]nd you can't be sure about that ten percent." In this regard, Johnny was like a creature from science fiction that came from a parallel universe in which the laws that govern that universe are the opposite of what they are here. Unfortunately, assuming that he was like everyone else and that our assumption that people are basically honest held true for him as well, we made what was probably our most fundamental, and fatal, error in dealing with him.

Assurance of Honesty

At least in the beginning, Johnny constantly assured me that he was being honest with me. He told me, "I always tell the truth because the truth is easier." He also told me, "The more info[rmation] that you take in [about me], the better you can understand who and what I am… There are really no, or very, very few secrets (and they must be unconscious ones as I don't know what they would be at this point) here. What you see is what there is." He also "joked" that "[m]aybe I'm giving you just enough truth to make you think I'm being truthful about everything when I'm not," and told me, again "jokingly," that he was not "Iain." Although his assurances of honesty probably didn't sway me as much as other things he did, in the absence of firm evidence that he was lying, his assurances probably did have some kind of impact that helped to shift my thinking about him in what was for him a favorable direction.

Detail

An important reason that Johnny's lies were so convincing was that they were so detailed. In this book, I have attempted to illustrate the level of detail that he incorporated into his lies. The events of life are specific, not general, so to be believable, lies must also be specific. In his lies, Johnny gave specific names, dates, times, and acts, all of which combined to give his lies the specificity of truth. If his lies had been more general or vague, lacking in detail, I might have called them into question earlier than I did, all other things being equal. Although mentally it is very demanding to create stories with the level of detail that Johnny incorporated into his, his high intelligence and vast knowledge base allowed him to do it to a degree that probably most liars cannot. In addition, he had a well-stocked mental larder of lies that he had concocted in the past, ones that he had "tested out" and confirmed that they could pass the believability test. To me, the sheer amount of detail that Johnny included in his lies made them believable above and beyond almost any other characteristic.

Consistency

Johnny was a shrewd observer of human nature and behavior and knew what sets of behaviors were psychologically plausible for a particular person or persona. He functioned quite effectively as an amateur psychologist or fiction writer and was able to create characters or characterizations that convinced others of their reality. Even though I never had any direct proof of the truth of anything he was telling me about his family, friends, associates, or associations, I believed he was telling me the truth about them, in part, because his information was so consistent and plausible. Although some inconsistencies did creep into his stories from time to time—for example, the name of the Frazier child who died—the inconsistencies were kept to a minimum and the ones that did occur were not usually seen for what they represented: loose threads that if pulled hard enough, would have unraveled the lie into which they had been woven.

Fluency

Like a spider that can effortlessly extrude and weave its sticky silk into complex patterns, Johnny was able to deliver his elaborate lies with an ease that is usually reserved for the truth. To quote the Cubist painter Georges Braque, "Truth exists; falsehood is only invented," and because the truth doesn't need to be invented, because it is already *there*, fully formed and ready to be related, the truth is transmitted with ease. Falsehood, however, must be invented, and because its invention is a complicated process, it is difficult for most of us to create then convey falsehood with the same effortlessness that we can relate the truth. Certainly, Johnny had the advantage of perpetrating much of his fiction through the Internet, which gave him the luxury of leisurely concocting carefully crafted scenarios as well as obviating the complications that can arise from having to create convincing lies on the spot and convey them in an equally convincing manner. However, many of his lies were delivered in person, where the advantages of the Internet were absent.

In Johnny's case, several factors combined (or conspired) to gift him with the fluency necessary to make his lies seem like the truth. First, by the time I met Johnny, he had already had at least 40 years (if not longer) of practice at inventing and delivering truthful-sounding lies, so he was an "old pro." He had had many years to learn, through trial and error, what worked and what didn't and had honed his ability to create and present convincing lies to laser-like precision. Second, Johnny had accumulated an extensive knowledge base from which to draw facts or pseudo-facts that he incorporated into his lies. Finally, Johnny's high intelligence gave him the cognitive ability to collect, connect, and generally coordinate vast amounts of information in a cohesive and convincing manner, something that is not true of all pathological liars and something that Johnny, by chance, had working to his advantage. In both quality and quantity, I have not personally encountered, either before or since, a liar who lied with the level of fluency that Johnny did.

Superficially Plausible Explanations for Suspicious Behavior

When psychopaths are questioned about their suspicious behavior, they habitually offer positive explanations that *sound* plausible. When examined more deeply, however, these explanations are often found to be illogical, irrelevant, even blatantly nonsensical. For example, when Johnny was summoned to the police station and questioned about the money he was suspected of stealing from his place of employment, he told the authorities that it would have made no sense for him to steal "only" $18,000 because he made much more than that. His explanation seemed to satisfy them, which caused them to let him go. That probably wasn't the only factor, but it was certainly a contributing one. Unfortunately, the authorities didn't take the time to look beneath the superficial plausibility of his explanation to discover that it was, in reality, illogical.

When I asked Johnny how he had obtained "Iain's" account information, he told me that when the question of "Iain's" identity had arisen several months before, he had searched the Internet for information that might prove to me that he was not "Iain" and, in the process, had discovered a file directory containing "Iain's" *Sex Now* account information. Although superficially this sounded plausible, especially to someone with limited knowledge of what is possible to do through the Internet, the explanation, on closer examination, is implausible. Account information is stored in secure files that to be retrieved would have required that Johnny hack into the server on which they were stored. To someone who is unknowledgeable about how this process works it might seem plausible that Johnny *could* have found "Iain's" account information by searching the Internet, where you can, as the perception goes, find anything. Psychopaths are masters at covering up their suspicious behavior by effortlessly offering positive and plausible-sounding explanations for it that, like a high-powered tranquilizer, lull their victims into a false sense of security about who they are and what they're really doing.

Information Overload

Johnny was an extremely prolific liar. Because he was neither working (except for the month at the hospital) nor doing anything else productive throughout the entire time that I, and others, knew and were dealing with him, he had plenty of time to invent and distribute information-packed stories. He barraged me, and others, with so much information that mentally it was overwhelming. Johnny said to me early on that "the more info[rmation] that you take in [about me], the better you can understand who and what I am" and he supplied it, even though it was all largely false. Whether he consciously intended or understood it, his barrage of information gave us so much information that it was virtually impossible to sort through it and to separate the wheat from the chaff, even if we had been inclined to do so. In some ways, if he had provided less information, it might have been easier for us to see the incorrectness or inconsistencies in it, but overloaded as we were with the products of his pathological imagination, it became virtually impossible.

Exploiting Areas of Limited Knowledge

Johnny was highly educated and highly knowledgeable about a variety of fields, including business, art, and British culture, to name several. He was able to use this knowledge not only to maintain the façade of intelligence and impressiveness that many narcissists like to project, but also to manipulate those who didn't have the same level of knowledge about particular subjects that he did. For example, in one of my first e-mails to him, I expressed my ignorance of business when I told "Jonathan" that I thought his degree in strategic planning indicated that he was in the military. With my limited knowledge about business, he was able to weave complex stories about his business dealings that sounded completely convincing to me, but that might have sounded implausible to someone more knowledgeable. Andy made the same comment regarding the business dealings in which *his* version of "Jonathan" claimed to be engaged.

In addition, I had a certain level of knowledge about art, but my ignorance of some aspects of it—for example, the details of the process of auctioning expensive works—kept me from seeing how Johnny was actually just coming up with one excuse after another for not selling his paintings. And, finally, my ignorance about some aspects of British culture played a significant role in his ability to perpetrate his charade that he was British for as long as he did without my being able to see through it. Although some of what he told me sounded suspect—for example, claiming that the word *boyfriend* meant something different in England than it did in the United States (which it does not) or that British law maintained the position that someone was "guilty until proven innocent" (which it does not)—I accepted most of what he told me without question. Taking advantage of people's ignorance is perhaps one of the most effective techniques that a psychopath can use to deceive and manipulate.

Telling People What They Want To Hear

One of the most powerful techniques Johnny used to trap and keep his victims was telling them what he thought they wanted to hear. In his final message to Johnny in which he informed him that his lies had been exposed, Andy told him that he saw how Johnny, using his various guises, had collected information about who he was and what he wanted in life and had manipulated him by constructing his deceits around them. Johnny did the same to me. He took my loves and hates, my wants and needs, my fears and hopes and used them to snare and increase his stranglehold on me.

In the beginning, "Jonathan" made it seem, made me feel, that somehow our meeting was "destined." For example, when I told him only a few days after we met that I was in a process of reevaluating and redirecting my life, he said that it was "funny how we are both at a crossroads at about the same time" and that "[m]aybe there is fate after all." He also made other statements to the effect that our meeting was more than accidental, that something deeper than the obvious lay behind it. Although he used this technique more frequently toward the beginning of our relationship than later, he used it in some form throughout the duration of our entanglement.

More compellingly, however, Johnny made me feel special. He told me that, aside from Marcus, I was "the most compassionate person [he had] ever known." He told me that while everyone else had turned their backs on him or only wanted to use him, I was the only one on whom he could depend and to whom he could turn for help. He told me that he had decided not to have anything further to do with Chase because he finally realized what was important, *who* was important. He told me that I was one of only two American men with whom he had considered spending the rest of his life, the other being Cliff, a man with whom he had experienced "the most intense relationship [he had] ever had." He told me that he wanted us to live together, and when it seemed that no one else was going to come to help him pack, that it was "just the two of us—not just today, but from now on." He told me that I was so important to him that he refused to return to England, where he could resume a cushy, upper-crust life, and was remaining in Mariah, in reduced circumstances, until his situation improved and we could finally be together in Paladin. And, of course, he told me that he loved me, which is the simplest and strongest way to manipulate someone.

Psychopaths are experts at making you feel special above and beyond everyone else until you realize, too late, that to them, you are nothing except just another tool to be used to gratify their pathological need.

Plausible Explanations for Errors of "Fact"

Pathological liars, even ones as intelligent and consistent as Johnny, do occasionally slip up and say or do something inconsistent with the lies they have led you to believe. The good ones, like Johnny, always have ready-made excuses for their mistakes, though. In general, Johnny used the idea that he was having memory problems that resulted from the effects of his endocarditis. Once he had established this idea, I found myself failing to question his memory lapses, excusing them myself as products of his illness.

For example, in August, he told me that his brother who had committed suicide was named *Malcolm*, but in January, he told me that it was *Michael*, who he had previously told me was the professor of economics at Cambridge who was quite alive. In addition, he gave various "alternative" spellings of his siblings names, names he should have been able to spell. For example, he spelled the name "Terrence" variously as "Terrence," "Terrance," and "Terence" and gave similar "alternative" spellings of the names of people who either didn't exist or at least didn't exist in their given form.

Finally, I recall an incident that happened in the fall that I was involved with him when we were sitting in a restaurant in Paladin and were discussing Cliff. He mentioned that Cliff's birthday was in a month other than he had said it was and when I corrected him, he became teary-eyed at his "inability" to remember and ran to the restroom, where he remained for several minutes before returning, pretending to compose himself. I simply excused the mistake as an effect of his illness. (In addition, the incident served to increase my sympathy for him, which further blinded me.) The skilled psychopath will always have plausible-sounding excuses when his carelessness threatens to undermine his façade of truth.

Minimal Outward Indications of Lying

Most "normal" people experience some level of anxiety when they lie, out of fear that their lie will be exposed and they will somehow be punished. In more obvious forms, this anxiety can manifest itself in such ways as avoiding eye contact (having "shifty" eyes), stammering, throat clearing, having an unsteady voice or unusual pitch, rapid blinking, fidgeting, and sweating. It may also cause the person to become defensive, displaying anger, sarcasm, or forced humor, want to change the subject, or even accuse *you* of lying. Because the truth is fundamental to our ability to understand and interact with people meaningfully, the ability to detect lies is of the utmost importance.

Unfortunately, people are lousy lie detectors. According to research summarized by Don Grubin (2005), participants in experimental studies are, on average, able to detect lies no more than 50% of the time (i.e., no better than chance) and people who are trained in the art of lie detection (e.g., experienced detectives, Secret Service personnel, CIA agents) are, on average, able to detect them only about 70% of the time. Therefore, relying on someone's outward behavior to determine whether or not that person is lying is often useless.

Grubin suggests that apart from the truth bias that leads people to label statements as true when they are actually false, people are misled because they usually pay more attention to body language than to statement content in determining whether or not someone is telling the truth. Body language isn't always a helpful indicator of someone's truthfulness because liars who don't experience anxiety (or are skilled at concealing it) when they lie won't appear nervous, while people who are telling the truth may be visibly anxious for reasons that have nothing to do with lying. For example, there have been occasions when I have been telling the truth but my honesty was questioned because I appeared nervous from being under stress or from being afraid that I wouldn't be believed. In addition, I often don't look people in the eye when I speak to them, especially when I have something complex to tell them, because I find it distracting; in my case, that behavior is more strongly associated with being introverted or having social anxiety than with being a liar. Appearing to be lying is no more an indication of deception than appearing to be telling the truth is an indication of honesty.

Even if outward behavior were an accurate indication of one's truthfulness (or lack of it), the fact remains that in the hundreds of hours that I interacted with him, Johnny gave no outward indication that he was lying. The *only* reaction he ever had was a brief pause before answering when asked to explain something he had said or done that seemed suspicious. This, of course, was simply the time it took him to invent a satisfying lie or to retrieve one that was ready-made and seemed suitable. Otherwise, he rarely displayed any obvious reactions that indicated he was lying. Almost always, he *looked* as if he were telling the truth.

I also believe that part of the reason that Johnny came across as so convincing is that he half-believed his lies. Although on one level he knew they were lies, on another level he wanted many of them to be true to the point that for him, they had the force of reality. Much of his lying appeared to represent a defense mechanism that reinforced his sense of who he was, so it was crucial for him to deceive *himself*, first and foremost, into believing his lies were somehow true before he could do such an excellent job of deceiving others into believing they were true. Johnny reminded me of an actor who becomes so absorbed into a character that he is playing that he begins to half-believe he *is* that character. Lying, apparently, is the most convincing and the most effective in deceiving others when you yourself believe your own lies.

The Use of the "Web"

I titled this book *The Tangled Web* in part because one of Johnny's favorite methods for perpetrating his lies was, of course, the Internet. This tool has become notorious for allowing people to pretend to be whoever and whatever they want to be, sometimes to the detriment of others. In recent years, we have all become aware of the more flagrant forms of Internet deception, such as those involving pedophiles who pretend to be pre-adults in order to lure unsuspecting or vulnerable children or teenagers into compromising situations in which the latter are molested or even murdered, as well as the less flagrant and more frequent ones, such as those involving the telling of "white" lies or half-truths about oneself in order to obtain the social, psychological, or sexual attention, acceptance, or approval that one's real self might otherwise not. The Internet is a liar's paradise and the full effects of this tool of easy deceit are, I fear, only beginning to be felt.

In my own experience interacting with people on the Internet, I have discovered a disturbing level of naïveté among otherwise sophisticated users regarding their uncritical acceptance of what strangers tell them to be true about themselves. Even people who know full well that the Internet is filled with liars of one variety or another routinely ignore this knowledge and behave as if the virtual world is filled only with truth. It is fascinating to me how easily and quickly our critical faculties, our common sense, break down when we go online. Perhaps this comes from the truth bias, our naïve willingness to believe that people are basically honest, or perhaps it comes from our belief that at some safe remove, the person at the other end of the thread in the Web can't hurt us the way someone in a dark alley can. Unfortunately, some of them can hurt us just as badly, if not worse. The Internet is not only a liar's paradise but a fool's one as well, one in which many of us are far too willing to believe the "truths" that strangers, people whom we have no *real* reason to trust, lead us to believe about themselves.

Although con artists were around long before the Internet was even a thought in the mind of its inventor and were able to deceive people in person (as Johnny did me), their ability to deceive by using the Internet has increased their effectiveness, and their menace, immeasurably. The Internet has become the psychopath's playground. Nowadays, the Internet gives the psychopath (or other disturbed person) a previously unimagined opportunity to masquerade as whoever they wish to be without question, to act out whatever maladjusted impulses they have without repercussion. Because of its anonymity and absence of ways to enforce normal social behavior, the Internet has the effect of turning many otherwise "normal" people into miniature psychopaths, acting without conscience because of an awareness of a lack of consequences. For the constitutional psychopath, however, the ability to masquerade as whoever he wishes, to weave webs of deceit and manipulation as complex and sticky as he desires with far less chance of detection than he would risk in the "real" world, is taken to an entirely new, and frightening, level.

Through the Internet, Johnny was able not only to spin elaborate, detailed lies at his leisure, but also to reinforce his charades by using a variety of alternate e-mail accounts in the names of both fictional and real people—family, friends, acquaintances, associates—that presented the illusion that information was coming from a variety of sources, something he could not possibly have accomplished in person. And, it was only through the Internet that he could have woven his webs of deceit that involved so many supporting, and seemingly real, characters. Johnny created dramas, comedies, tragedies as complicated as, and only slightly less well acted than, any that Shakespeare created, and we, like the viewers of a play, suspended our disbelief, our critical faculties, that otherwise might have alerted us to the fact that it was all just fiction. Unfortunately, unlike the viewer of a play, who *knows* that it *is* just a play, those of us whom Johnny deceived didn't have the privilege of knowing that it *was* all fiction.

The Confirmation Bias

The *confirmation bias* is the tendency to accept only that information that confirms our pre-established beliefs about what is true. Once we begin to believe that something is true, that things are a certain way, we begin to selectively filter information in such a way that we accept only what fits with our already-held belief and reject whatever contradicts it. As time passes, the process snowballs and our belief in the truthfulness of what we have come to believe as true only grows stronger and we accept more confirmatory evidence and continue to ignore discrediting evidence. In the process, it becomes increasingly difficult to accept disconfirming evidence and admit the possibility that we could be wrong. Emotionally and cognitively it's taxing, even threatening, to have to reinterpret old facts through a new framework that's different from the old one, and the more different, the more discrepant, the new framework is, the more taxing, or threatening, it will be to employ it.

The confirmation bias operated with frightening efficiency in my, and others', experience with Johnny. When Miranda first told me what she knew or believed to be true about Johnny, I found it difficult to accept. It wasn't that I thought she was lying; it was more that I thought she was misinformed. Although I tried to remain open-minded, mainly because I already had my own suspicions about Johnny, her information, her perspective, was so different from what I had come to accept as true that I had difficulty assimilating it. In the days that followed my first face-to-face conversation with Miranda, I found myself listening to my recording of our conversation repeatedly, almost obsessively, in an attempt to absorb what she had said. Once the doorway to another interpretation of Johnny's behavior was open, however, I was able to allow in, with increasing momentum, the information that I later learned from his other victims. Even so, it still took some time before I fully reinterpreted Johnny's behavior in terms of his being a *psychopath* and finally saw him for what he really was.

The confirmation bias also operated with Laura and Andy, to their detriment. When I went to Laura after confronting Johnny and told her the truth about him, she was skeptical or at least unsure, but willing to admit that Johnny was mentally ill. Although I had opened the door to the truth a crack, Johnny then slammed it shut with a thunderous thud when Laura went to him wanting the truth. In response, he wove an incredibly elaborate, detailed web of lies through which he convinced her that I was insane and, therefore, should not be believed. Although Laura said that in the end she wasn't sure which of us to believe and had remained open to the possibility that I *could* be telling her the truth, she was far more inclined to believe Johnny. In the process, she was afraid to talk to me, tried to warn me away from "Jonathan's" "powerful friends," threw away Johnny's address in Mariah that I had given to her, and remained in contact with "Jonathan" for the next two months until finally he pulled the thread of credulity to the point that it snapped.

Part of the reason that Laura believed him over me—perhaps the largest part—was simply that Laura had become so indoctrinated to accept one version of reality that it was difficult, virtually impossible, in fact, to accept another, until her doubts and his behavior built up sufficient power to overcome her resistance to an alternative interpretation of the facts. By that point, Laura had been indoctrinated for an entire year to believe that Johnny's version of reality was the truth, so the amount of evidence and doubt needed to counteract her beliefs about what was true was considerable. Even if Johnny hadn't been such a skilled liar, Laura probably would have still believed him once he had established his "credibility" and begun manipulating her to see things the way *he* wanted her to see them purely because of the increasingly compelling power of the confirmation bias.

From what I gathered, Andy initially refused to believe what The Pretender had revealed to him, referring to it as a "smear campaign." Even though he had no concrete proof that anything that "Jonathan" was telling him was true, Andy had, by April, been indoctrinated to believe "Jonathan's" (as well as "Jonathan's" "co-conspirators'") version of reality for at least nine months. Although Andy had doubts, as did Laura, he ignored them until "Jonathan's" excuses, Andy's inability to find verifying evidence, and most compelling of all, Andy's fateful encounter with "Jonathan" in Mariah finally forced Andy to reinterpret the previous fourteen months in an entirely different light. Unfortunately, it took months for Andy to reach the point that he was prepared to accept the truth that I had to tell him, which is yet another testament to the overwhelming power of the confirmation bias.

Explaining Away Behavior

Johnny's victims played their part in "helping" him maintain an air of plausibility. One thing they, certainly *I*, did was to explain away his incongruous or suspicious behavior for him. This wasn't the result of being stupid, just unsuspecting. Indeed, an intelligent, well-educated person's intellect can actually work against him. In retrospect, I realize that my extensive background in psychology, which included a more detailed than normal knowledge of cognitive and abnormal psychology, gave me a variety of psychologically plausible explanations for the inconsistencies in "Jonathan's" behavior in addition to the ones he gave to me.

For example, I explained away the fact that he didn't dress up for work because he either changed when he got there or could get away with it because he was COO rather than because he wasn't really working. I explained away the temporary loss of his British accent as an effect of fatigue rather than as an indication that it wasn't his real accent. I explained away the fact that he couldn't fill out the storage unit rental agreement because he was too upset and confused from the effects of his illness and the stress of losing his home rather than because he was manipulating me into assuming financial responsibility for the storage. I explained away the "Iain" messages as "inconclusive" rather than seeing them as the clear proof they were that "Jonathan" was deceiving me. I explained away his superior attitude as the result of his upper-class upbringing rather than as an indication of a narcissistic personality. I explained away the lies he was telling others, especially the elaborate scenarios he was presenting to such people as Andy, Laura, and Cliff, as a need to retreat from the reality that he couldn't bear rather than as the psychopathic manipulation it actually was. And, I explained away much, much more. Apart from what Johnny so masterfully did to me, I did plenty to myself to further my undoing.

2. Other Forms of Manipulation

Subtle Control

For the most part, psychopaths, especially the more intelligent and cunning ones, prefer to exert subtle as opposed to blatant forms of control. The more subtle the control, the less likely it is that the other person will recognize that he or she is being controlled and thwart the psychopath's attempts to manipulate. This, of course, permits psychopaths not only to maintain whatever control they have already managed to gain, but also to gain progressively more control as time passes. One is, of course, much more likely to notice the sharp pain of a heart attack than the dull ache of a slowly-spreading cancer and much less likely to take measures to stop it before it is too late.

From the very day that I met Johnny, he began trying to exert control over me in subtle ways. Immediately, he decided that he didn't like my underwear and began "encouraging" me to change it to the bikini briefs that he preferred (and that he himself wore). He would persuade me to do so in low-key, but nonetheless manipulative ways, such as by saying that *Kyle* had taken his advice to change *his* style of underwear. At the same time, Johnny began "encouraging" me to have my hair buzz-cut (again, a style that he himself came to wear) and constantly pointed out other men on television or in real life who had buzz cuts and who Johnny thought looked attractive. As with the underwear issue, he tried to "encourage" change by inciting whatever feelings of romantic rivalry I might have by telling me that *Chase* had gotten *his* hair cut and that it looked "fetching." Sometimes, especially as the relationship continued, he would try to manipulate me into doing what he wanted by saying, "If you really love someone, then sometimes you do things to make them happy even though you don't want to do them." *He*, of course, was *never* willing to make changes for *me*, either ignoring me or even becoming actively hostile when I would ask for something in return. It was all about what *he* wanted and, usually, trying to obtain it in the most devious way possible.

The subtler forms of control that Johnny used with his other victims are less clear to me and I didn't ask them in detail to tell me how he manipulated them using such techniques—which they may not have even recognized anyway because of their subtlety—but the psychopath, especially the con artist type, will generally prefer the subtle approach over the blatant one so that his victims won't realize what's happening and try to resist, thereby making his job of manipulation that much easier.

Blatant Control

If subtle forms of control fail, as they sometimes do, then psychopaths feel no hesitation about exercising more blatant forms of control. Although Johnny had a temper and flew into a rage when his deceptions were exposed, he was never physically threatening, though many psychopaths are. The more obvious forms of control that Johnny utilized included intimidation, harassment, and character assassination. When Dan called Johnny a "con man" and threatened to sue him for the money he owed him, Johnny immediately retaliated by threatening to expose the details of Dan's sexual life to the people in Credence and actually posted messages on the Internet that included Dan's full name, address, telephone number, and other identifying information. Johnny's intentions were much more obvious in such statements as, "You want to battle, I'll take you down with me," and "I promise to tear down that facade of yours," and "I can't wait to begin to let people [in Credence] know who and what you really are." The effect was to leave Dan deeply fearful that Johnny would actually expose and destroy him, and although Dan didn't entirely back down, he was more passive in trying to seek justice, at least at first, than he might otherwise have been and developed what appeared to be stress-related health problems that persisted for years afterwards.

Similarly, when Laura began pressuring Johnny to address the issue of the bounced checks, he created a fraudulent e-mail account in Cliff's name and began threatening her, as Cliff, that if she pressed the issue, he, with the help of his "Big Six" lawyer, would file charges against her for having "undue influence" over a sick person, which is a felony. The effect was to make Laura so afraid that financially and personally she and her family would be destroyed that she totally backed off from pursuing legal action against Johnny, which left her bankrupt and suicidally depressed.

Finally, when I told Laura how Johnny had deceived her, he immediately retaliated with not one, but several, lengthy, extravagant messages that outlined, in great detail, that I was suffering from a dissociative disorder and was obsessed with and stalking him, thereby attempting to demolish my credibility. He apparently did something similar with Andy, although Andy didn't give me the level of detail about it that Laura provided me. I suspect that as soon as he learned that I had found out how he was deceiving Laura and Andy, Johnny began putting a plan into place to discredit me should I decide to reveal the truth to them, but even if he didn't, he, like the typical psychopath, did not hesitate to take the aggressive approach when the subtle approach failed.

Separation

A common tactic that psychopaths use to maintain control is to isolate their victims from sources of support or information that could help them break loose from that control. As mentioned above, psychopaths are "control freaks" and will do almost anything to maintain control over those whom they use or those who would try to take away their control. In extreme cases, psychopaths will go to the length of physically imprisoning their victims, depriving them of any contact with the rest of the human world. In most cases, however, they seek to separate and isolate their victims in more subtle ways.

In my case, Johnny worked to keep me isolated from the other people who were involved in the situation. He didn't and couldn't do this physically, since I could have contacted most of the people involved at any time and Johnny could have done little to stop me, but he *did* succeed in doing it *psychologically* by turning me against many of the people involved. For example, although he told me that

Dan didn't want me to visit him while he was living with him, which kept me away, "Jonathan" also painted Dan as a disturbed drunk who would (and allegedly did) lie about him out of spitefulness. In addition, although he led me to believe that visiting him at Laura's would cause trouble, he mainly led me to distrust Laura, causing me to discount anything she said that contradicted what "Jonathan" told me as some kind of manipulative ploy. It was clear that in various ways Johnny did the same thing with me, depicting me to Dan, Laura, and others in ways that led them to discount my claims that I was his boyfriend or that I played any kind of significant role in his life.

Almost all of the interaction I had with Johnny in the ten months I was involved with him took place in the absence of other people. That, of course, made it easier for him to separate people to whom he had given differing and conflicting versions of reality. When he lost his ability to control the flow of information, however, he naturally became extremely nervous. When Laura and I continued our conversation outside the Saturday we were helping Johnny pack when he was leaving the house on Millstone Drive, Johnny eventually discovered us and nervously asked if something was wrong. Nonchalantly, we told him no, but he either intuited or outright learned from Laura that we'd exchanged conflicting sets of information about him. Immediately afterwards, he embarked on his program to discredit Laura to me and, presumably, to discredit me to her.

Miranda made the same observation about Johnny's behavior and offered the more dramatic example of the time that Johnny brought Glenn to see her. Afraid that Glenn would undermine his lies with the truth, Johnny told Miranda—in private—that Glenn probably wouldn't be willing to speak to her by himself and suggested that he be present at the reading. Since Glenn didn't want Johnny in the room, however, Miranda sent Johnny away. Being away from Glenn, being unable to control the information that flowed from him, made Johnny extremely nervous. As Miranda said, "...it freaked [Jonathan] out. I could feel it from the other room. I could just feel him, like, run the gamut of, like, fear, jealousy...the whole thing." Above everything else, psychopaths fear the truth.

I find it interesting that the *only* time that Johnny, who almost always came across as cool and self-controlled, became enraged was when his lies were exposed and there was no way left for him to restore them, nowhere left to "run." Then, he became like a cornered animal that turned aggressive. He did react with anger when I called into question his attempts to change and control me that ignited our first fight in July, but that didn't seem to provoke the same level of unmitigated rage that my exposure of his lies unleashed. He also became enraged when Dan confronted him about the bounced check and accused him, accurately, of being a con man. His rage was confined exclusively to the revelation of the truth about him, which is a direct indication of what he felt was more important to him than anything else.

C—Escaping the Spider's Web

I had several reasons for writing this book. The first was simply to untangle the web of lies in which I, and others, had become ensnared and the format and length of a book seemed to be the ideal, possibly the only, way to do it. The second, and more personal, was to try to understand how I could have allowed something like this to happen to me and, by understanding it, hopefully to avoid a similar situation in the future. A third reason was simply that I, and many others, had never encountered someone like Johnny, encountered someone with his unique combination of pathology, in particular the pathological lying, and that by itself was fascinating. More generally, because the psychological community appears to have devoted only limited attention to understanding the nature of pathological lying, I hoped this book would be a helpful addition to the literature, albeit one written in a popular style, on pathological lying in particular and the narcissistic and psychopathic personalities in general.

But, I had a fourth reason for writing this book. I wanted something good to come out of an experience that caused me so much pain and hoped that by telling my story and sharing what I had learned from what I went through, I could help others avoid people like Johnny and the havoc they wreak in our lives. By going through this experience, I learned far more than I had ever learned from any psychology course or book about psychopathic personalities and how they operate and, more importantly, I learned how I participated in my own undoing.

If you have had the misfortune of running afoul of a psychopath, there are several things that you need to do, or at least consider, in order to begin to overcome the effects of your experience. Below, I have outlined what I believe to be seven of the most important. This list is by no means exhaustive nor should it be viewed the "final word" on a specific aspect. There are undoubtedly elements of recovery from an encounter with a psychopath that I have failed to consider, but the seven I have given can be seen as starting points in your attempts to heal from the harm you have suffered at the hands of a psychopath.

Don't Minimize the Impact of Your Experience

An encounter with a psychopath will inevitably leave you with some kind of damage—physical, psychological, financial, social, spiritual. Damage is what they do best. Except for damaging me physically, Johnny damaged me in every other way. In response, I felt betrayed, violated, belittled, exploited, abused—*wronged*. Your encounter with a psychopath is going to leave *you* feeling wronged. Among other feelings, you will undoubtedly feel anger, even rage, over what the psychopath has done to you. Those feelings can occur at varying levels of intensity and persist for varying lengths of time. In my case, I spent an entire year hating Johnny to the point that I wanted to see him dead. My hatred was so intense that I remember many nights lying awake in bed plotting his murder in such a way that I wouldn't get caught. I never would have actually done something like that, but it *is* an indication of just how intense my animosity toward him was.

I certainly wasn't the only one who felt enraged over what Johnny did to me. For example, in her letter to Johnny in which she revealed that she finally knew the truth about him and vented her feelings toward him, Laura made several references to her and her family members' desire to physically injure him. Although she made these statements only a few days after she discovered how she and her family had been deceived and damaged by Johnny and her anger gradually diminished over the next few months, they are an indication of the kind of intense hostility her experience with Johnny provoked in her.

Crystal's reaction was similar, though more subdued, perhaps because of her differing personality or because of the fact that she wasn't as deeply entangled and damaged financially, personally, or emotionally as Laura was. Even so, Crystal did state in her e-mail to me that she was glad that she lived in another state because she might have "killed" Johnny if she'd encountered him directly.

Dan's hatred toward Johnny burned perhaps the strongest of all. In October 2002, when I first contacted him and one year after Johnny had defrauded and threatened to expose him, Dan expressed the desire to "kill" him or do some kind of bodily harm to him. The next March, a year and a half after Johnny had victimized him, Dan told me, in response to the possibility that Johnny had moved to nearby Rowen, "it's starting again, my hatred!" toward Johnny. The following August, some two years later, Dan's taunting e-mail to Johnny read, in part, that he wanted to "smash [his] face in." The August after that, when Crystal contacted him and some three years after Johnny had swindled him, Dan's anger, which he thought he'd put behind him, returned as strong as ever. When I contacted him in early 2011, nine and a half years after the incident with Johnny, Dan's anger was still present and potent. An encounter with a psychopath can leave you feeling all kinds of unpleasant, intense, and even disapproved emotions, ones that you and others may not be willing to accept or deal with directly.

Consequently, something that you might be tempted to do is to minimize the impact that your experience had on you. Perhaps you try to convince yourself that you don't feel the way you do or that what happened didn't really matter *that* much, thinking that you can spare yourself the discomfort, the inconvenience, the pain of feeling the emotions your experience provoked. Unfortunately, *anything* that interferes with your ability to feel what you feel will prevent you from recovering. It can seem doubly unfair not only that someone has done something so damaging to you, but also that *you* are the one who is stuck with the job of cleaning up that damage. It is. But, the unfortunate fact is that you *are* the one who has been stuck with cleaning up the mess that someone else made. And, the first step in cleaning up that mess, I believe, is feeling the anger, the outrage, the pain that it's caused you. Do *not* try to pretend that you don't feel what you feel because if you do, you will only prolong the recovery process and cause *yourself* more pain in the end.

Avoid "Revictimizing" People

Unfortunately, other people who haven't gone through what you have may not understand why you feel the way you do or may be uncomfortable with your feelings, especially if those feelings are intense or socially unacceptable. For example, I spent many nights lying awake in bed plotting Johnny's death in such a way that I wouldn't get caught. I hated Johnny badly enough that I literally wanted to see him die, preferably at my hands. This type of thinking is very disturbing to many people, but the fact that it's so disturbing to them is just an indication of their inability to understand what you've been through and how it's provoked such feelings of hostility in you. Even less "antisocial" feelings may not be understood by people who haven't experienced what you have and may be subject to the same kind of disapproval that more intense feelings are.

Because of their lack of understanding, you cannot always rely on others to help you recover from your encounter with a psychopath or other damaging personality. If these people haven't gone through what you've gone through, had it affect them the way it's affected you, then they will have at best a two-dimensional understanding of why you're thinking, feeling, and generally experiencing what you are. That will obviously limit their ability to empathize with you and possibly lead them to have various reactions that are designed to lessen the impact of your reactions, less on you than on *them*. Your preoccupation, your emotions, may make them aggravated, uncomfortable, or even afraid, so they may try various maneuvers—usually unintentional and sometimes well intentioned, but still problematic—to buffer themselves against whatever negative feelings your expression of your experience has on *them*.

For example, they may try to minimize what you've been through, telling you that it wasn't *that* bad or that it *couldn't* have been that bad and making you feel that you're overreacting or being unreasonable, if not irrational. They may criticize you for having the feelings you have, telling you that it's wrong, morally, for you to feel the way you do and that you need to stop feeling the way you do. They may insist that you need to forgive the perpetrator, that you need to put it behind you, that you need to "heal and move on." They may stop wanting to listen to you and become actively disgusted or hostile when you raise the issue. They may have other reactions that are just as dismissive and invalidating of what you've been through. They may genuinely believe that they're behaving the way they are toward you "for your own good," that they're only trying to make things better for you, but the fact is that their behavior is only serving to shut down your normal emotional reactions and actively thwart the recovery process, which is based, in large measure, on feeling what you do and having those feelings validated. If you feel that others are invalidating your feelings about what has happened to you, then it is time to turn away from them and toward others who *will* support you.

Family and friends or people who have an unsophisticated understanding of psychology aren't the only ones who may be uncomprehending and dismissive of the impact of what you've experienced. Mental health professionals to whom you might turn for help can have reactions that are just as ignorant and detrimental. In some cases, they can actually do more harm than good. I didn't seek professional help in dealing with my feelings toward Johnny, but I did have some bad experiences with therapists when I was younger that taught me that "professionals" can be just as bad as lay people.

When I was a teenager, I was emotionally abused by other teenagers to the point that I developed what is now known as social anxiety disorder and, later, agoraphobia that made it difficult, if not impossible, to engage in many normal activities, such as work or live on my own. In telling the clinical psychologist whom I was seeing at the time how I felt, someone who had clearly not been through what I had been through, he actually told me that "it can't be *that* bad." He then went on to tell my mother that she should throw me out of the house in order to "make me stand on my own two feet." His reaction and "treatment" was not only irresponsible, but also indicative of the fact that he had *no* idea what I was going through.

Yes, what I went through *was* that bad, and the effect of his statement, and his subsequent behavior, was to alienate me from the mental health system, make me feel that I could no longer turn to the people who presented themselves as professionals and who I had been led to believe by a psychology-worshipping culture were the people to whom I should turn for "salvation." In the end, I had to study psychology on my own and help myself, since no one else seemed willing or able to do it.

Therapists have their blind spots, their areas of insufficient knowledge, experience, and empathy. These blind spots sometimes come from their training in which future therapists are indoctrinated to view and relate to the world and their clients in particular and sometimes narrow ways and they sometimes come simply from being human and, therefore, limited. Some therapists simply don't know what they're doing and some do more harm than good, despite their motives. That is unfortunate but true and you cannot allow a therapist, no matter how well-meaning, to harm you further.

If you discuss your experience with a therapist and that therapist begins to indicate to you that he or she doesn't really understand what you have been or are going through, expects you to recover more rapidly than is realistic or comfortable for you, or minimizes or criticizes you for feeling the way you do, it's time to leave. It is *very* important to remember that in spite of the "intimacy" that a therapeutic situation fosters, which may make it difficult for you emotionally to leave, the therapist is, fundamentally, a professional whom you have hired to perform a specific job for you: the job of helping you to become healthy or at least healthier. If the therapist isn't doing that job, it's time to fire him or her and take your business elsewhere. Whether he or she intends to do so, he or she is only doing you further damage and you have been damaged enough. It's not your responsibility to spare his or her feelings because it's *your* feelings that are important and his or her negating behavior isn't sparing *yours*. Don't allow yourself to be revictimized by people who are supposed to be doing the opposite.

In addition, you cannot always rely on the legal system to help you if you have been the victim of a crime. The legal system proved largely useless in helping his victims in my state bring Johnny to justice. Despite Dan's repeated attempts to have the police in Mariah arrest Johnny, the police's behavior seemed uninterested and half-hearted, despite the fact that Mariah was a relatively small city with little crime to overwhelm their resources. The same was true of

Crystal's experience of trying to have Johnny arrested after he had defrauded her in Paladin. The same was true of his other victims—employers, landlords, private citizens, others—who attempted to bring Johnny to justice for the crimes he had committed against them. Having the law not help you when it should be helping you can only add insult to injury and further complicate the process of recovery. In my opinion, your well-being, ultimately, should not be based, even in part, on what the law may or may not do for you, but you will have to decide for yourself if seeking justice is worth the stress and possible disappointment of trying to do so.

Refuse the "Victim" Role

Having said what I have about refusing to minimize the impact that your experience with a psychopath has had on you, I believe that it is *extremely* important not to assume the role of *victim*. If you are an American, you are currently living in a society that glorifies The Victim in a way that is excessive and ultimately damaging. The reasons that our society venerates the victim mentality are complex, but the ultimate effect is that oftentimes we encourage people who have experienced some type of emotional injury to wallow in that injury without really taking steps to recover from it. Although emotionally it can be quite satisfying to acquire sympathy, attention, a sense of importance, and even a sense of rightness from playing the victim, assuming that role will, in the end, do you far more harm than good and actively prevent you from recovering.

I believe that in suffering any kind of psychological injury, there are at least three stages that one can pass through. The first is what I will call the *wounding* stage, in which the injury occurs. The second is what I will call the *victim* (or *martyr*) stage, in which one is wallowing, to one degree or another, in one's pain, feels at the mercy of the pain one is suffering, and ultimately looks to someone other than oneself to take responsibility for making things better (usually the victimizer). The third is what I will call the *healing* stage, in which one realizes that ultimately the *only* person who is ever going to make things better is *oneself* and takes *full* responsibility for doing what one needs to do to achieve that goal. It is natural, in fact necessary, I believe, to spend some time in the victim stage because it is only by allowing the pain to be felt and expressed that you can then really begin the process of releasing that pain and recovering. It is important, however, to realize that the victim stage *is* not and *should* not be the final stage in the process of recovering. If you don't realize that, then you will never be free.

To be perfectly blunt, the fundamental reason why psychopaths take advantage of us is that, on some level, we *allow* them to take advantage of us. This may sound harsh, but it's true. No one can hurt you psychologically unless you *allow* him to hurt you. We allow others to do this by being unaware of our weaknesses. Psychopaths find our weaknesses then use them against us. But, in order to do that, there must first be weaknesses they can use. This is a cold truth, but also a liberating truth. If the "problem" ultimately lies within *you*, then ultimately so does the solution. It means that far from being powerless over the effects of what has happened to you, *you* ultimately are the one who has the power to recover from your experience and change your life for the better.

Don't Feel "Stupid"

Your experience may also leave you feeling "stupid," wondering how you could have possibly fallen for what the psychopath led you to believe. As mentioned above, several of Johnny's victims were dismayed by their gullibility and berated themselves for it. In addition, Miranda advised, "You shouldn't feel stupid" because she knew that questioning my intelligence for not recognizing Johnny for what he was sooner than I did might be an issue for me. Fortunately, I *didn't* feel "stupid" because I realized how cunning psychopaths are, but many people *do*, not realizing why they were deceived.

The fact that you were taken in has *nothing* to do with your intellectual capacity. As discussed at length above, psychopaths capitalize on blind spots in human psychology as well as weaknesses in human personality, and because there are quite a few of them, it's practically impossible to be aware of all of them at once and to keep from being undermined by at least some of them. This is true even if you know what you should be aware of, but most people have *no* idea that they should be on guard until it's too late.

The main reason we let down our guard in the first place is simply that, as poetically and accurately described by Hervey Cleckley, psychopaths wear a "mask of sanity" that makes them appear not only normal, but also more captivating than the average person. That allows them to slip in underneath our intellectual radar and do their damage. Unfortunately, there appears to be an inverse relationship between intellect and emotion, the former growing weaker as the latter grows stronger. As long as you're human, your emotions will always exert an interfering influence on your intellect, which is why otherwise smart people sometimes end up making stupid mistakes...and psychopaths know very well how to intensify your emotions precisely so you *will* make "stupid" mistakes, in their favor. You shouldn't feel any more "stupid" than anyone else for falling victim to a "weakness" that we *all* share.

Focus on Improving Yourself

Because psychopaths are by definition self-centered in the extreme, expecting you (or allowing you) to focus exclusively on *them*, it is easy to lose yourself to one extent or another through your contact with them. I know I did. What I wanted to accomplish, who I was, became subverted, at least while I was entangled with Johnny. It wasn't until afterwards, in assessing the damage he did, that I realized just how much I had lost myself. An important part of repairing the damage your psychopath caused, then, is to concentrate on yourself and your self-improvement (in a healthy as opposed to selfish way). You can do this by finding or resuming activities, interests, and goals that are meaningful and fulfilling to you and that further what you want to accomplish in life.

After my experience with Johnny, I felt an especially strong need to put my life back on track by immersing myself in pursuits that reflected who I was or wanted to be. By focusing on *me* instead of *him*, I was counteracting the self-centeredness of another that had undermined my life. First, I rediscovered my childhood interest in entomology and embarked on a "mission" to photograph and collect as much information as possible about the local insect fauna. That activity, for one, satisfied both my artistic and my scientific sides and ultimately proved to be one of the most fulfilling things I have ever done. Second, I resumed my writing, another pursuit that my encounter with Johnny had derailed, but something that I had been doing in one form or another since I was a child and that also gave me a strong sense of fulfillment and accomplishment. Third, I eventually returned to school and studied subjects that I had always been interested in but that I had incomplete knowledge about and whether or not the activity led to a better or different job, it proved to be intellectually and socially satisfying and led to further "adventures" that also promoted my understanding of life and my growth.

And, finally, I eventually realized that my self-protective isolation, though necessary and therapeutic at first, had become self-destructive, which prompted me to reconnect to other gay men in a constructive way and to take my place in the world as a totally "out" gay man, in spite of the risks (more from gay people than from straight ones). In short, my life became immeasurably richer in many ways after my encounter with Johnny, not simply because his disruptive influence had finally been removed from my life, but mainly because the experience so forcefully focused my attention and motivation on doing what I needed to do to improve myself and my life.

Not knowing you, I don't know what does or would give you a sense of accomplishment, satisfaction, and fulfillment; only you can determine that for yourself. If you don't know, I believe that one effective way of answering that question for yourself, of putting things into perspective, is to ask yourself the "deathbed" question: *When I am lying on my deathbed, thinking over the life I have lived, what will I regret not having done with my life?* That is actually *the* question that *all* of us should be asking ourselves on a regular basis, regardless of what's happened to us, regardless of the state of our lives, because the goal of not regretting the life you have lived is, I believe, the ultimate goal that should inform our lives.

Before I conclude, I want to make something perfectly clear that I also believe is of utmost importance in reclaiming your life. In saying that you need to focus on yourself and your own fulfillment, I do *not* mean to say that it is acceptable to do this *at the expense of others*. If your attempts at "self-actualization," to use the psychological term, are injuring others, then what you are doing is no better than what your psychopath did to you. Indeed, true fulfillment comes, in part, from finding a mutually satisfying give and take in your relationships with others. You are no less deserving than others, but you are no *more* deserving, either. You have been victimized by another's selfishness and know what that has done to you; in this case, do *not* do unto others as this one other has done unto you.

Learn to Trust Again

One of the deepest forms of damage that the psychopath can wreak is damage to your ability to trust. Psychopaths are, by definition, liars, leading you to believe things are one way when in fact they're very different. When you discover how you've been deceived, it can shake or even shatter your ability to trust people who are in similar positions as the deceiver was or even people in general. Once damaged, your ability to trust can be difficult to reclaim.

Trust is fundamental to our ability to interact with other people. In fact, developmental psychologist and psychoanalyst Erik Erikson believed that the issue of whether or not we can trust other people is the first major issue that we deal with in life. Even as infants, we somehow sense that trust, our assurance that other people will be there for us and won't hurt us, is *the* foundation for our ability to coexist and interact with others. If we don't feel that we can trust others, that feeling will undermine, perhaps destroy, our ability to interact with others in a healthy way. Of course, we deal with issues of trust not just in infancy, but throughout our lives, and every relationship we attempt to forge and maintain with others is in some way a constant test of our ability to trust. Trust, that first crucial issue that confronts us at birth and follows us until death, is the human bond that can be the easiest to destroy and the hardest to restore.

For several years, I refused to deal with other gay men, especially in a romantic or even casual sexual context, because it was in that context that my ability to trust was the most directly and severely damaged. Although my experience with Johnny wasn't the only experience I'd had in which my ability to trust gay men had been shaken, it was, by far, the worst and proved to be the *coup de grâce* that damaged my ability to trust gay men far more deeply than any of the others did. For years, I didn't feel that I would ever be able to trust another gay man on *any* level again enough to really open myself up to one in any meaningful way. Although I have come a long way in the years since I realized that my relationship with "Jonathan" was nothing but a lie, I still have a certain amount of difficulty being able to trust gay men, especially in a romantic context, and it is still easy to have that wound to my ability to trust them reopened. I am still working on it. But, I *am* working on it now instead of allowing my experience with Johnny to continue to color my perceptions and control my behavior, something I did for far too long and something that eventually did me more harm than good.

It is important for me to remind myself, though, that the chances of encountering someone like Johnny again, someone who displays his level of deceit, are small. It is important for me to remind *you* that the chances of encountering another psychopath, becoming enmeshed in a similar situation again, are small. These people, though more common than the serial-killer type psychopath, still constitute a fraction of the population. With most people you encounter, you will have to deal only with "normal" trust issues (although that can be complicated enough). Don't take your experience with a psychopath and apply it to all of humanity. It isn't warranted and even if you think you're doing it out of self-protection, you will ultimately be doing yourself more harm than good. Most people can be trusted in most ways most of the time. Trust is crucial to healthy human relationships and to take the attitude that you can't or won't trust anyone again will only deprive you of relationships in which having trust in the other person is justified, relationships that are necessary to your well-being. Don't become mistrustful of humanity because of the atypical experience, the excessive damage to your ability to trust, that you suffered at the hands of one abnormal individual.

Find Meaning in Your Experience

The most profound thing that you can do, I believe, is to find meaning in your experience with a psychopath. Not knowing you, I cannot tell you how you can best find that meaning, but I *can* tell you that doing so will do more to free you from the psychopath's emotional snare than perhaps anything else you can do. It is fascinating to me that we can bear the most unimaginable pain when we believe there is some kind of meaning behind it, but find it difficult to endure even the slightest ache when we believe it is meaningless. The need for meaning underpins our existence whether or not we are always aware of or acknowledge it.

Viktor Frankl, a Jewish doctor and psychiatrist who was living in Vienna during World War II, was captured by the Nazis in September 1942 and imprisoned in various concentration camps, including the infamous Auschwitz, until he was finally liberated in April 1945. By the time his ordeal was over, he had lost his parents, his wife, and two and a half years of his life. Yet, instead of allowing his horrific experience to destroy him, Frankl rose above it by using his experience, and the lessons he learned from it, to help and inspire others. Frankl developed a powerful type of psychotherapy called *logotherapy*, which loosely translates as "meaning therapy." Frankl believed that it was possible to find meaning even in the most seemingly meaningless experiences. Largely because of his ability to find meaning in his experience, Frankl went on to live a highly productive life in which he became one of the outstanding figures in his field, garnered almost 30 awards, wrote several influential books, including *Man's Search for Meaning*, his most important, and actively, even zestfully, pursued life until his death at the age of 92.

My experience with Johnny drove home the importance of finding meaning in my life in a way that few other experiences have. I found meaning in my experience in a variety of ways. I found meaning by replacing Johnny's lies with the truth, both for myself and for others whom he had snared. I made certain that as many people knew the truth about him as possible and was somewhat successful in supplying Johnny's victims with information they needed to help themselves intellectually, emotionally, or legally to untangle themselves from the web of Johnny's psychopathy. My role as an information collector and disseminator was probably the way in which I found the greatest meaning in my experience.

I found meaning by realizing, after my experience with Johnny was over, just how far my life had gotten off track, how much of myself I had lost, or misplaced, through my experience with him. The experience forced me to reevaluate myself, my life and either to rediscover, or to discover for the first time, the activities, goals, and values that gave me the strongest sense of who I was and wanted to be. Although it was a disorienting, damaging experience, it ultimately helped me to redefine, or strengthen the definition of, who I was and spur me on to additional experiences that helped to give meaning to my life.

I found meaning, as many people do, in my spiritual beliefs, which inform me not only that my encounter with Johnny was prearranged to further my personal growth, but also that after his life has ended, he will have to go through a "life review" in which he will have to feel the feelings of those with whom he interacted, those whom he harmed, and will have to compensate his victims *karmically*, a type of law he *cannot* evade. In the end, Johnny did far more harm to himself, spiritually, than he did to any of his victims—something, incidentally, that is a source not of satisfaction, but of sorrow.

And, finally, I found meaning by writing this book, not only by untangling the complex set of threads in the web of psychopathology that Johnny wove in order to help myself both intellectually and emotionally, but also by using what I learned from my experience to (hopefully) help others.

A Final Thought

Something that you *must* understand, if you don't already, is that the recovery process is *not* straightforward. It is not an unswerving ascent ever upward, but is instead filled with peaks and valleys, the latter of which can sometimes be very deep. Although the recovery process, if it is proceeding as it should, will be marked by gradual improvement over time, less preoccupation with the thoughts and feelings your encounter provoked in you and more focus on the present and the positive, you will have periods—moments, hours, days, weeks—when you will feel that you have slid backwards, that you are losing ground, and become preoccupied with what happened in ways that seem more typical of earlier points. That is *normal*. That does *not* mean that you are not making progress. Your recovery from your experience with a psychopath is in some ways no different from your adjustment to the loss of a loved one, a divorce, the loss of a job, or any other emotionally important loss that we experience in life. If you have periods when you feel that you've somehow regressed, gone backwards, know that *it is only temporary* even if it doesn't feel that way. You *are* making progress and as long as you continue to further the process of recovery, you will eventually reach the point that Johnny's victims and I finally reached, where we can now go about our daily lives and have our encounter with our psychopath be the *last* thing on our minds. It happened for us and it *will* happen for *you*.

D—Avoiding the Spider's Web

The best way to avoid the damage the psychopath can do to you is, of course, not to become entangled with him in the first place. Below, I have outlined what I believe are some of the more important factors that will allow you to do this. The advice I give below is certainly not complete or foolproof, as there are undoubtedly aspects that I, in my limitations, have failed to consider and that you, in your limitations, may fail to implement. Hopefully, though, they can help to reduce the possibility of being snared by a psychopath and allow you to avoid the damage one can wreak in your life.

Trust Your Intuition

The first mistake that I made was not listening to my intuition, my gut instinct that told me that something was wrong with "Jonathan." I knew literally from the day I met Johnny in person and interacted with him in the flesh that *something* was wrong with him, although I didn't know rationally what. Because I didn't have any facts to support my intuition, I ignored it, writing it off as nervousness about being on a first date or some other source. In looking back, I realize now that my feeling that something was wrong probably stemmed from the conversation that Johnny and I had had before we went to the zoo in which he grilled me about my previous relationships and his eventual conclusion that I had "never really been in a long-term relationship." That was odd behavior for a first date and I felt as if I were less on a date than on a job interview in which I was being asked to justify my qualifications to be his next boyfriend. In retrospect, I realize now that his attitude and approach were those of someone who was looking for weaknesses that he could use to manipulate me, and the fact that he later used my history of "semi-relationships," as he called them, to manipulate me (unsuccessfully) into believing that his pathological behavior was normal only confirms that intention. What he revealed, and what apparently had an adverse effect on me that day, was only a small sliver of a much larger, if unseen, problem.

My pattern of ignoring my intuition continued throughout much of our relationship. At many points I would sense that something was wrong, that he was lying to me or somehow manipulating me, but often I had no concrete evidence to back up my suspicions. I have generally always been a scientist, a rationalist, in my approach and, like all good scientists, I was unwilling to accept an idea as true without evidence. That was especially true in the "Iain/Chaz" situation in which I had, in the end, accumulated enough evidence that "Iain" was actually Johnny to have been persuasive in a court of law, but since I didn't have ultimate, incontrovertible proof until I found that Johnny had used "Iain's" e-mail address in the *Sex Now* ad, I was unwilling to be persuaded in the court of my own mind. I realize now that I should have listened to my intuition that day in June that told me something was wrong and saved myself ten months—and, in some ways, years—of suffering.

Since that time, I have become very attuned to my intuition and I have to say that the only time I've regretted heeding it is when I *haven't* heeded it. My intuitions about situations, about people, are pretty much infallible. For example, as a teacher, I can go into a classroom of new students at the beginning of the semester and tell not only which are going to be good groups, but also which are going to harbor problem areas. My instincts always prove to be right and not because I create a self-fulfilling prophecy in which I treat the classes and students I perceive to be good differently than the ones I perceive to be trouble. The students themselves often second my perceptions as they attend and interact with the other members of the class. The same thing has happened in my interactions with other people and my involvements in various situations and whether my intuition has told me that this is a good person or situation or a bad one, it has rarely if ever been wrong. Again, the only time I have made mistakes in listening to my intuition has been when I haven't listened to it.

Therefore, if a situation, a person, feels wrong to you, then that situation, that person, probably is. Even if you can't define the problem rationally, there is still probably a legitimate, if unseen, reason for your feeling. Listen to that feeling and behave accordingly. Remove yourself from the situation, the person, as delicately or as assertively, but as quickly, as possible and don't look back.

Counteract Psychological Biases

As discussed as length above, psychopaths are able to deceive and manipulate us because they capitalize, whether intentionally or incidentally, on a number of blind spots or biases in human psychology. The way not to fall prey to them, then, is not only to be aware of them but also to counteract them using various techniques. Below I have offered ways of minimizing the damaging effect that these biases can have on you.

- *Assumption of honesty*: Although you can assume that people *in general* are being honest about most things most of the time, do not assume that *specific* people are being honest about most things most of the time. I am not advocating a paranoid or constantly doubtful attitude, but always be aware of the fundamental fact that trust should always be *earned*, *not* unreservedly bestowed. You should always reel out trust a little at a time and the person in whom you are placing that trust always needs to prove that he will honor that trust before you reel out more. In addition, different areas of your life demand different levels of trust. The greater the impact that a violation of trust could have on you, the more evidence the person needs to provide that he can in fact be trusted before you should. Obviously, trusting a person to pick up milk at the grocery store involves far less risk to you than trusting him with your life savings...or with your life. Ideally, the evidence that you can trust him should come not from his words but from his *deeds* as well as from the experiences of *others* in addition to your own, if the latter is an option. You should place your trust in another person's hands *only* to the extent that he has *proven* that he deserves that trust and is unlikely to violate it.

- *Assurance of honesty*: If someone tells you that you can trust him, especially repeatedly, you probably can't. Honest people will convince you of their honesty through their *deeds*, *not* their words, letting their deeds speak for themselves. If their deeds don't speak as loudly as their words, if their deeds and words are saying two different things, then they probably cannot be trusted.

- *Detail, consistency, and fluency*: Do *not* assume that even if what someone is telling you is highly detailed, self-consistent, and fluently presented it's the truth. How many political speeches and sales pitches have you heard that were full of lies? Completeness, cohesiveness, and eloquence are *no* indication that something you're being told is true. The *only* thing that makes something true is, of course, whether or not it reflects reality.

- *Superficially plausible explanations for suspicious behavior*: If someone gives you what appears to be a plausible explanation for some kind of suspicious behavior, especially if it doesn't seem to ring true, then look beneath or beyond it to determine if it actually is. For example, Johnny told the authorities that he couldn't possibly have stolen the $18,000 from Intellex because he made much more than that. Why should that have stopped him? Eighteen thousand dollars is eighteen thousand dollars and it's a lot, even for someone who presumably is making a high salary. In addition, when I asked "Jonathan" how he had obtained "Iain's" account information, he said that he had performed an Internet search and had found it online. Although that *sounds* good, on closer examination, that explanation is implausible, since account information is stored on secure computers, making it inaccessible to the average person.

My experience has been that the explanations the person gives you are often delivered with a casualness, an offhandedness, that makes it seem as if the person is innocent or the person may even turn the tables on you and make *you* out to be the one who is in the wrong. As far as the latter is concerned, Johnny did that to me, for example, when I asked him if he was the author of the "GayMan" posts, asking me in return what *I* was doing on the *Gayteway* board and accusing *me* of looking for sex myself. But, even though you will occasionally receive a defensive response, more likely than not, you will receive a nonchalant one. The psychopath who prefers subtle as opposed to blatant control believes that "playing Mr. Innocent" is more effective in pacifying you and keeping you from questioning further than faking indignity when his "honesty" is called into question, something he understands may spur you on to try to look even deeper to justify your suspicions to him. With the subtle type, it's not uncommon to experience a pattern of having him raise your suspicions then receiving casually delivered, seemingly plausible explanations when questioned. Normally, someone who is *genuinely* innocent will display less neutral reactions because for someone who has a conscience and isn't guilty of what you believe he may be, he will be *genuinely* disturbed that his honesty is being questioned and probably not be able to conceal it. It is definitely suspicious for someone to be too unruffled too often.

If you have doubts about someone's behavior, especially when it comes to important matters that have a major impact on you, and he offers what seems to be explanations that are too easy and too casual, look beyond what the person wants you to believe by trying to determine if what he's telling you is genuinely logical and factual, not just superficially appealing.

- *Superficially plausible explanations for "factual" errors*: None of us is perfect and sometimes we give others a fact that is inconsistent with what we have already told them. That doesn't mean that we're lying, just that we've made some kind of mistake. Sometimes, however, a "fact" that someone gives us that isn't consistent with everything else is a lie. When you are presented with a fact that doesn't fit with what the person has already led you to believe is true, place it into the "questionable" category. This doesn't mean you should actively seek out inconsistencies like a lawyer who is trying to collect damning information to use against an opponent, but don't *habitually* dismiss such inconsistencies as innocent mistakes. They *could* be an indication of something larger, another reality behind a façade.

- *Explaining away behavior*: Do not explain away someone's suspicious or inconsistent behavior. If something he says or does doesn't fit logically into everything else he's said or done, it could be an indication that he hasn't been truthful with you. If the information strikes the wrong chord, accept it for what it is and don't attempt to twist the information to make it easier to accept. Your first reaction is probably an accurate one and should be heeded. If it strikes you the wrong way, then there probably *is* something wrong and probably not with you. My perception is that the people who seem to be the most susceptible to the tendency to reinterpret incongruent information in a favorable direction are those who are insecure about the stability of the relationship and need to reassure (or deceive) themselves as well as those who have (or feel they have) a number of ready-made explanations for particular behaviors (like someone with a background in psychology) or both. Regardless of the underlying motivation, however, resist the temptation to impose a positive interpretation on the person's words or deeds when they provoke a feeling of wrongness in you; that feeling of wrongness is probably an indication that you are right.

- *Information overload*: If someone barrages you with information-packed stories about himself and his life, it can be very difficult to sort through all of the information and determine what is true or plausible and false or unlikely. Therefore, my advice is to concentrate on those areas that have the greatest importance to and impact on you and focus on trying to verify the truthfulness of what you're being told. For example, whether or not "Jonathan" had really had a relationship with Rudolph

Nureyev was irrelevant, but whether or not he was really from England was of fundamental importance. Only a few days after I met him, I discovered the story about his brother Terry, which stated that he was from the United States. I should have gotten more information about this discrepancy (from a source other than Johnny), but I was already succumbing to the power of the truth and confirmation biases, which caused me to discount the accuracy not of "Jonathan," but of the story. (I did, of course, try to get answers to my questions about his sexual behavior, but I had other reasons for not acting as I should have.) I should have tried to verify the truth of many other significant "facts" that "Jonathan" led me to believe when I had doubts, such as why he didn't dress up for work when he was the COO of a company, why he couldn't afford to hire a nurse and have the house on Millstone Drive cleaned and repaired, why I couldn't visit him if not spend the night at Dan's when others could visit him, why he was still doing as well as he was months after he had been diagnosed with a rapidly spreading, potentially fatal heart infection and was receiving no treatment…why…why…why… Those should have been obvious questions, but much of the reason I didn't ask them and try to answer them as I should have was simply that the signal was lost amidst all the noise that surrounded it and was not adequately perceived.

- *Areas of limited knowledge*: Try to find more information about important areas about which you have questions or, if possible, locate people who are more knowledgeable than you and ask them if what you've been told is accurate or plausible. In retrospect, I should have asked people who were more knowledgeable than I was about many things, including a medical professional about endocarditis, a lawyer about landlord-tenant agreements, a businessperson about business matters, and someone knowledgeable about specific aspects of British culture. Living as we do in the so-called Information Age, when knowledge is as available as air and especially via the Internet, it is harder than ever for someone who is trying to capitalize on your ignorance and control the flow of information to you to keep you from learning what you need to know. Take full advantage of that unparalleled opportunity and get the answers to crucial questions that you need to know.

- *Telling you what you want to hear*: This is perhaps one of the most difficult forms of manipulation to detect and resist because it provokes such a feeling of *rightness* within us, a feeling of fulfillment, of inevitability, of destiny. It makes us feel as if the other person understands us, connects to us, completes us, in a way that no one else has or can. We *want* to believe what we're being told. Unfortunately, if it sounds too good to be true, it probably is. The feeling of rightness that such statements provoke is precisely the feeling that should tell you that what you're being told is *wrong*.

As mentioned above, "Jonathan" expressed his belief that our meeting was "destined"—the result of "fate" or "kismet." He told me that, apart from Marcus, I was "the most compassionate person [he had] ever known." He told me that I was the only one on whom he could depend and to whom he could turn. He told me that, apart from Cliff, I was the only American man with whom he had considered spending the rest of his life. He told me that I was so important to him that he refused to return to a comfortable, upper-crust life England, choosing instead to remain in Mariah, in great hardship, to be with me. He told me that he loved me. He told me many other things that he knew that I, and most of us, wanted to hear, all of which made me more amenable to what he wanted. Once again, the feeling of rightness, of specialness, that such statements provoke is usually a sign of wrongness and should raise red flags.

- *Use of the Web*: Although people can deceive you in person, they can do it much more effectively online. Take *everything* that someone tells you online with a grain of salt, especially if you don't know him. You have *no* reason to believe that what he's telling you is true until further evidence of his truthfulness—preferably from an independent source—is forthcoming. Even if you feel you know the other person and have had direct interaction with him, as I did Johnny, that still doesn't mean that what he's telling you online (or in some other indirect way) is correct. Although it can be difficult to do and easy to forget to do, it is very important in your online dealings to remain skeptical, rational, and critical about what someone says about himself (or others) and resist, as strongly as possible, the urge to be unjustifiably trusting.

- *Confirmation bias*: One of the most difficult obstacles that confronted me was trying to overcome the confirmation bias, the resistance that some of Johnny's victims, who had been indoctrinated to view things from his perspective for months, displayed in accepting the new facts, and the new interpretation of those facts, that were presented to them. It is *extremely* important not to be seduced by the power of this insidious bias. If someone comes to you with new information about the person you've come to view in a particular way that doesn't fit with what you already believe to be true about him, do *not* reject it no matter how inconsistent or unpleasant it may seem. It may be false...but it may be true. Give the person giving you the differing information the benefit of the doubt and try, if possible, to gather more information—preferably from independent sources—to determine if it fits with the differing information you've been told. Do *not* allow yourself to be deceived and damaged merely because you have trouble accepting what may be the crucial truth about someone you thought you knew and could trust.

- *Outward signs of lying*: Rely not on *outward behavior*, but on *message content*, especially the inaccuracies and inconsistencies, to determine if someone is lying. As noted above, outward behavior allows the average person to detect lies only about 50% of the time—no better than chance—so relying on it as an indication of lying is often useless. In fact, if you are dealing with a psychopath, someone who doesn't have normal anxiety reactions or is good at hiding them, then your chances of detecting his lies from his outward behavior drop even further.

- *Talk to other people he knows about what he is telling them*: One of my biggest mistakes was failing to find out as much as possible from Johnny's other victims about what he was saying and doing to them *at that time*. While the events were transpiring, I should have spoken in greater detail with Laura, Dan, Art, Joan, "fat" Greg, all of whom I already knew, and contacted Miranda, Ted Kanner, and Mike Harmon, whom I didn't know then, but who had been mentioned. After the conversations I had with Laura and Greg when we were helping Johnny move, and especially after I had already found the "GayDaddy" ad that even then I believed Johnny had posted, my suspicions about him were raised and should have been pursued. Unfortunately, I allowed Johnny to manipulate me into distrusting Laura and others who could have provided me with the truth.

    Confronted with the same situation today, I would have allowed *nothing* to dissuade me from finding out whatever I could and forming my own opinion about what should be believed. One of the psychopath's greatest weapons against you is your ignorance, so the best way to undermine him is with knowledge. If you believe that the person with whom you have become involved isn't what he seems to be and you have the opportunity to talk to others who know him (or think they know him), then please go to them and find out as much as you possibly can from them. If you're lucky enough to have several people to talk to, then eventually a consistent pattern will emerge in which their stories will either agree with what the person you doubt is saying as well as each other's or betray clear discrepancies between those that the person you doubt is telling as well as each other's. In any event, find out as much as you possibly can from whoever is involved about what the person in question is saying and doing to others.

- *Form your own opinions about people*: A related mistake that I made was allowing "Jonathan" to form my opinions of other people for me instead of doing it myself. That, more than anything else, was what kept me from finding out more than I did at the time about what he was doing and saying to others who were entangled. Don't allow another person to poison your mind against someone, especially someone who might have crucial information. As you should *always* do, *think for yourself.*

Know Your Weaknesses

The most powerful way to avoid becoming entangled in the psychopath's web, apart from using your intuition and counteracting the psychological biases noted above, is to know your weaknesses. Psychopaths prey on our weaknesses, so it is important to become and remain aware of those weaknesses. All of us have blind spots, things we either can't or won't see within ourselves, and that fact played a huge part in why I became and remained snared in Johnny's web of deceit and manipulation for as long as I did. Despite being an intelligent person, despite having studied psychology for almost 15 years, despite having a bachelor's and a master's degree in psychology, despite having taught psychology for several years, despite having engaged in a certain amount of self-analysis, I still had weaknesses that either I couldn't or I didn't want to admit to myself. In retrospect, I see them more clearly and now understand more about why I became snared. These are just a few:

First of all, in the year and a half before I met Johnny, I had suffered a major setback in which I had come to doubt my ability to take care of myself. When things had gone so disastrously wrong in Paladin, when I had lost my job, lost my ability to pay my bills, lost my ability to maintain my home, lost my emotional and physical well-being through one of the worst depressions I had ever suffered and one health problem after another that assailed me in rapid succession, and limited social support, I somehow felt reduced almost to the level of a child, to the level of someone who needed his mother to take care of him. I had already suffered that feeling in the past because during my mid-20s, I developed agoraphobia shortly after graduating from college and lost the ability not only to work, live on my own, and generally be self-sufficient, but also, at my worst, even to leave the house or to control the anxiety reactions of my own body. I endured that situation for four long years before I was finally able to gain control over it.

My failure in Paladin only reinforced my feelings from what had happened before, made me feel that I was incapable of surviving on my own, without help. Indeed, that feeling stretched all the way back to adolescence when I was psychologically abused by other teenagers to the point that I developed social anxiety disorder and recurring depression and was left with so little self-confidence and self-esteem that I started doubting my ability to function in life on any level, to do even the minimum amount required to survive. I developed a deep fear that my weaknesses would eventually cause me to become homeless, a fear that persists even to this day in some form. Therefore, I was left with the unresolved need to attach myself to a more powerful, or at least available, person who could take care of me when I could not.

Consequently, when I stumbled upon "Gayman's" ad in which he presented himself as a powerful, successful figure who would take care of all of his new boyfriend's material needs, I was irresistibly reeled in. I was interested not in leeching off a sugar daddy, but in merely surviving. Andy had said that was in some form the major motivation for his involvement with "Jonathan"—that he was concerned about what he called "self-preservation." I didn't learn enough about Andy's past, present, or personality to know what might have happened to make "self-preservation" a concern beyond the ordinary, but apparently, in spite of having a good-paying job, he somehow felt that wasn't enough and was lured in by the prospect of having a seemingly powerful, affluent person (or persona) provide for his material needs. Although Laura's motivation for having "Jonathan" move in with her seemed to revolve more around a genuine desire to help someone she cared about who was in need, the fact that (in spite of Johnny's attempts to paint her as a money-grubber to me) she perceived "Jonathan" as someone who could help her and her family financially was, undoubtedly, a motive, at least on an unconscious level. Many people are motivated to attach themselves to a (seemingly) more powerful figure who can provide them with the stability and security, however that is defined, that they need, and because of my perceived inability to provide these things for myself, I was pulled into a situation in which, ironically, *I* became the powerful one.

Second, I had been raised to believe that one of the most important things that you do in life, one of the most important things that defines you as a person, is that you help others who are in need, regardless of the extent to which you have to go to do it, regardless of the effects your generosity has on you. This attitude and the resulting behavior came directly from my mother. My mother, who firmly believes in and practices the Christian virtue of charity, not only explicitly taught me to be "generous to a fault," but also demonstrated this belief through example in her behavior.

Unfortunately, this guiding belief, though laudable when kept in balance, became pathological. There are many instances of my mother's feeling that after helping people, she had been taken advantage of, although her perception ultimately did nothing to alter her behavior. I realize now that beyond whatever was motivating her behavior from a purely philosophical perspective, she was also driven less constructively by a strong need to "buy" other people's love (especially her mother's) through the money or things she could give to them. Mindlessly, I imitated the extremity of this behavior and also rationalized it as doing the "right" thing. I even derived a sense not simply of satisfaction, but of superiority from what I was doing. Because I perceived myself as more generous than other people, I thought I was *better* than other people—which is, ironically, the opposite of what generosity, properly felt and displayed, is supposed to do.

My experience with Johnny changed all that. After losing thousands of dollars that I didn't have, after putting thousands of miles on my new car to be with and help someone for whom nothing I did was ever enough, after losing my emotional and to some degree physical health, after neglecting my own life to the point that it almost fell apart as completely as it had two years before, after doing everything that I could for someone who always wanted *more*, I felt slapped across the face hard enough to make me see the madness of how I was behaving, how out of control my need to give had gotten. Once I realized what I was doing, I stopped.

Now, in dealing with people, I operate by the "golden rule" in which I treat others the way that I myself want to be treated: I give only as much as I receive. This rule doesn't apply to people who are genuinely needy, genuinely down-and-out and unable to give back, but to people who have the ability to reciprocate or to provide for themselves. Although the truth was different, the *character* of

"Jonathan" was someone who presented himself as having options, as having alternate methods of aid, some of which most of us don't. He could have returned to England, where his wealthy family could have erased his debts and he could have resumed the cushy, upper-crust life from which he had come. He could have taken a more active role in selling his paintings, which were allegedly worth hundreds of thousands of dollars. He could have gone to live with Greg in California. The character of "Jonathan" had many options and even though none of them really *were* options, I believed they were…yet behaved as if *I* was the *only* one who could help him. In retrospect, I realize fully that my behavior in this regard was irrational and out of control. It no longer is. I now have a much healthier, much saner attitude toward doing for others what they can do for themselves, toward giving and receiving in general, an attitude that prevents me from being taken advantage of the way that I allowed myself to be taken advantage of by Johnny.

Third, my behavior was driven by a certain amount of competitiveness. Although I am not strongly competitive in every aspect of my life, I do become *very* competitive when I am confronted with a challenge that is important to me. In these cases, I become so driven to be the best that I usually outperform everyone else, through sheer determination if not always talent. In my relationship with "Jonathan," I was presented with certain challenges that I was determined to overcome. When "Jonathan" complained that somehow I wasn't doing enough for him or for our relationship, this drove me to do even more. When Jonathan revealed his "perfect" relationship with Cliff and that Cliff wanted to resume his relationship with "Jonathan," my insecurities and competitiveness made me want to strive even harder to be the "perfect" boyfriend. These tendencies came through even more strongly when "Jonathan" presented his growing relationship with Chase and sometimes made comparisons between him and me that were not always flattering to me. Normally, someone who is subjected to this kind of insulting behavior would balk against it and probably end the relationship, but to me, it simply spurred me on to be a better boyfriend because I wasn't going to allow someone I considered to be an obnoxious, overgrown child to win. The relationship was filled with such challenges, real and invented, and oftentimes my behavior was driven to overcome these challenges in order to prove something either to someone else, usually "Jonathan," or to myself.

This kind of irrational behavior will never happen again. As mentioned above, I refuse to do more for someone than he is willing to do for me. "Jonathan" once rationalized his self-centered behavior by saying that "[s]ometimes relationships [were] not all 50-50 due to events." That's true, but I've also come to believe that how far the balance should deviate from 50-50 depends on the strength and longevity of the relationship. Having things become unbalanced after ten years of a strong, reciprocal relationship is, in my opinion, very different from having them be unbalanced from the beginning of a relationship with someone with whom you have only a developing bond, especially when the relationship chronically displays no real indication of becoming equal. Nowadays, I am willing to give people a certain amount of leeway, a certain amount of time to "prove" themselves, but my patience is no longer infinite and if the person appears to indicate that he will persistently take more than he gives, then I have no hesitation about cutting off the relationship before too much damage is done.

In addition, I have developed a healthier perspective on the issue of jealousy, something "Jonathan" was able to use throughout the relationship to manipulate me. Jealousy is, of course, based on insecurity, and at the time, I had my share of insecurities about myself that caused me to develop some fairly strong rivalrous feelings, primarily toward the nonexistent Chase. At the time, it created an equally strong feeling of competitiveness in which I attempted to "prove" myself to "Jonathan," but now, I react to attempts to make me feel jealous with a sense of contempt for the person who is making them. Anyone who tries to provoke feelings of jealousy in another person is, at heart, someone who is deeply insecure about himself and his relationship and doesn't feel he can get what he wants in honest, straightforward ways. Someone like that obviously has a weak personality and that weakness is usually associated with other forms of weakness—in general, the need to control—which should indicate to you that you will experience further trouble if you continue to be involved with that person and that you need to leave.

Fourth, I believe that I wanted the social validation that goes along with being involved with someone. In our society, being coupled is seen as the norm and those who are in relationships are viewed more favorably than those who are single. Indeed, people who are single are often seen by others, and themselves, as "failures." When I became involved with "Jonathan," I hadn't been involved with anyone for a long time, and now that I was, I wanted, on an unconscious level, to maintain whatever emotional or social benefits I felt went along with my coupled status.

The antidote to that type of thinking involves realizing that singlehood is only as inferior, neutral, or superior as you make it. Being single can give you opportunities for self-development and accomplishment that the demands of a relationship can oftentimes thwart. For me, I find that I am the most productive—and, in those areas, the happiest—when I am single. Indeed, it is better to be single than to be in a relationship because you are mainly deriving some kind of social benefit from it; that is *not* what a relationship is supposed to be about. It is *certainly* better to be single if you're involved with someone who is turning your life upside down because of some type of pathological behavior.

And, finally—and most compellingly—I became and remained involved with Johnny simply because I wanted to be loved. Andy said that one reason he had become entangled with "Jonathan" was that he was driven to obtain "the love that gay men so desperately seem to need." I don't know if gay men need love any more desperately than anyone else does, although I do know that I myself had never had a relationship with another man in which I felt that he truly loved me. At 35, I was still looking, still longing to experience this. In the end, Johnny contemptuously labeled me a "needy queen who needed his dick" and, far worse, stopped me from trying to find real love for years. In the end, I received the precise opposite of what I was looking for. Fortunately, the experience was so painful, so powerful, that it forced me to confront myself in such a raw way that I could no longer deny that I was willing to have love, or the façade of love, at almost any cost to myself.

Our unconscious motivations can sometimes be far more powerful than our conscious ones, and because we are not aware of them, they can control our behavior in ways that are far more devious, far more destructive than our conscious ones can. It's almost as if we have some kind of internal psychopath, trying to fulfill its needs by manipulating us into behavior that is ultimately self-destructive. However, in the same way that an actual psychopath can be stopped by the power of truth, our metaphorical one can be stopped by the power of self-truth, self-understanding. When we replace their lies to us—and *our* lies to *ourselves*—with the truth, we replace our weakness with strength.

■

I hope you never encounter and become entangled with a psychopath. It can be one of the most destructive experiences you will ever have. But, if you do, it can also be one of the most enlightening, if you learn the lessons that it can teach you, not only about people, but mainly about yourself. It can become a tool of self-understanding and self-improvement. I hope that whatever has happened or will happen to you, my story will in some way give you a greater insight into humanity and into yourself.

REFERENCES

The literature on the psychopathic and narcissistic personalities is vast. Much of the scientific variety is highly technical and largely incomprehensible to the average person, and much of the popular variety is unequal in quality. Below, I have given a brief list of the sources that I have mentioned in this book as well as a handful of others that might prove useful or of interest to you. (Works mentioned in the text are indicated with an asterisk.) Most of these sources contain numerous additional references that may also be of help to you.

∎

American Psychiatric Association. (2000). *Diagnostic and Statistical Manual of Mental Disorders* (Revised 4th ed.). Washington, DC: Author. The latest edition (as of 2012) of the *DSM*, the so-called "bible" of psychological disorders published by the American Psychiatric Association. 943 pp.*

Cleckley, H. M. (1976). *The Mask of Sanity: An Attempt to Clarify Some Issues about the So-Called Psychopathic Personality* (5th ed.). St. Louis, MO: Mosby. Originally published in 1941, this is the most recent printed version of Cleckley's seminal and highly influential work on the psychopathic personality. As of 2012, a PDF version prepared by Emily Cleckley for non-profit educational use could be found online at http://www.cassiopaea.org/cass/sanity_1.PdF. Contains 301 references. 471 pp.*

Dike, C. C., Baranoski, M., and Griffith, E. E. H. (2005). Pathological lying revisited. *Journal of the American Academy of Psychiatry and the Law, 33(3)*, 342–349. Excellent overview of the psychological and legal issues involved in the phenomenon. Contains 31 references spanning roughly 100 years illustrating a shift from a more psychological emphasis to a more legal one throughout time regarding pathological lying. Available online at http://www.jaapl.org/content/33/3/342.full.

Erikson, E. H. (1993). *Childhood and Society.* New York: W. W. Norton & Company. Originally published in 1950. Erikson's seminal work outlining his eight-stage theory of personality development throughout the lifespan. Does not deal with narcissistic or psychopathic personalities. 448 pp.*

Frankl, V. E. (2006). *Man's Search for Meaning: An Introduction to Logotherapy.* Boston, MA: Beacon Press. Originally published in German in 1946 under the title *...trotzdem Ja zum Leben sagen: Ein Psychologe erlebt das Konzentrationslager.* Frankl's classic work on his experience as a Nazi concentration camp prisoner and the psychological therapy he developed from it. Does not deal with narcissistic or psychopathic personalities per se in spite of the relevance of the latter to the subject of the book. 168 pp.*

Grubin, D. (2005). Getting at the truth about pathological lying. *Journal of the American Academy of Psychiatry and the Law, 33*, 350–353. Attempts to distinguish between "normal" lying and pathological lying and comments on the average person's inability to detect lying at better than chance level as well as the need to focus on statement content rather than body language in detecting lies. Contains 15 references. Available online at http://www.jaapl.org/content/33/3/350.full.*

Hare, R. D. (1999). *Without Conscience: The Disturbing World of the Psychopaths Among Us.* New York: Guilford Press. A popular presentation of Hare's research on the psychopathic personality with vivid real-life examples illustrating different facets of psychopathic behavior. An excellent starting point for the average reader in understanding the psychopathic personality. Does not contain a bibliographic section per se, but does contain extensive notes with references to various popular and scientific works on the psychopathic personality scattered throughout. 236 pp.*

Hare, R. D. *"Without Conscience": Robert Hare's Web Site Devoted to the Study of Psychopathy.* http://www.hare.org. An extraordinary resource for information about the psychopathic personality by one of the leading researchers in the field.

Hare, R. D., Harpur, T. J., Hakstian, A. R., Forth, A. E., Hart, S. D., and Newman, J. P. (1990). The revised Psychopathy Checklist: Reliability and factor structure. *Psychological Assessment, 2(3)*, 338-341. A scientific paper assessing the usefulness of the PCL-R emphasizing its reliability and two-factor structure. Contains 13 references.*

Kernberg, O. F. (1998). Pathological narcissism and narcissistic personality disorder: Theoretical background and diagnostic classification. In E. F. Ronningstam (Ed.), *Disorders of Narcissism: Diagnostic, Clinical, and Empirical Implications* (pp. 29-52). Washington, DC: American Psychiatric Press. Discusses in part Kernberg's concept of the narcissistic continuum. Numerous references are listed at the end of each paper. 512 pp.*

Millon, T. (1981). *Disorders of Personality: DSM-III, Axis II*. New York: John Wiley & Sons. A technical work outlining Millon's theory and system of personality disorders emphasizing their correspondence to the personality disorders listed in the third edition of the *Diagnostic and Statistical Manual of Mental Disorders* (1980). Narcissistic and antisocial personalities, as well as their relationship to each other, are discussed in chapters 6 and 7, respectively. Contains 323 references, although most refer to other personality disorders or issues. 458 pp.*

Millon, T. (1996). *Disorders of Personality: DSM-IV and Beyond* (2nd ed.). New York: John Wiley & Sons. A revised and updated version of Millon's 1981 work emphasizing their correspondence to the personality disorders listed in the fourth edition of the *DSM* (1994). Narcissistic and antisocial personalities are discussed in chapters 11 and 12, respectively. Contains 800+ references, although most refer to other personality disorders or issues. 832 pp.*

Millon, T. and Davis, R. D. (2000). *Personality Disorders in Modern Life*. New York: John Wiley & Sons. A technical, but somewhat more accessible, version of Millon's 1996 work designed for students at the advanced undergraduate or beginning graduate level. Antisocial and narcissistic personalities are discussed in chapters 4 and 9, respectively. Contains 553 references, although most refer to other personality disorders or issues. 581 pp.*

Patrick, C. J. (Ed.) (2006). *Handbook of Psychopathy*. New York: Guilford Press. A collection of 31 papers from leading researchers in the field of psychopathy that deal with a wide range of issues related to the psychopathic personality. 651 pp. Numerous references are listed at the end of each paper.*

Ronningstam, E. F. (2005). *Identifying and Understanding the Narcissistic Personality.* Oxford: Oxford University Press. A somewhat technical, but generally accessible, book about different facets of narcissism. Contains 414 references. 239 pp.

INDEX

Absolutely Fabulous, 254
A.I. (film), 68, 101
Aidan (*Sex and The City*), 81
Alcuin (alleged nephew), 12, 13, 15, 309, 322, 550, 603
   as Johnny alias, 488
   "Jonathan's" "shared" e-mail account with, 488
Alexander
   as possible reference to Glenn, 582
   e-mail from "Jonathan" to Richard about death of, 14, 22, 582
   See also Glenn, "Jonathan's" belief in, being dead
Alicia, 59
America's Most Wanted, 639
Americans With Disabilities Act (ADA), 344
Amounts loaned to "Jonathan", 147, 151, 229, 254, 261, 308, 324, 366, 379-380, 430, 440-441, 489-490, 498, 503, 515, 520, 535, 539, 545, 588, 616
Andrea, 59
Andy
   as narcissistic reflection of Johnny, 572-573
   assumption of heterosexual life, 661-662
   concerns about Johnny's using photographs of, to create false documents, 581
   "contract" with "Jonathan", 578-579, 580-581
   differences between "Chase", 580
   engagement and marriage to woman, 66-662
   events surrounding January 2002 "breakup" with "Jonathan", 577
   final e-mail to "Iain", 350-351
   final e-mail to "Jonathan", 582-583
   first conversation with Richard, 571
   first e-mail to Richard, 569-570
   first meeting with "Jonathan", 573
   "Gayboi" as Internet alias of, 315, 322, 483
   investigation of "Jonathan's" apartment in Mariah, 579
   Johnny's lies to, 322-323, 574-576
   "Jonathan's" allusions to Richard to, 68, 310
   "Jonathan's" story about Easter weekend to, 577-578
   "Jonathan's" story about returning to the United States to, 579
   "Jonathan's" visits to, 576-577
   mid-2011 update, 661-662
   motives for becoming involved with "Jonathan", 583-585
   passkey to apartment, 576
   physical appearance, 572
   plans to move to England, 322-323

Andy (cont.)
  reality questioned, 462, 463, 483, 542, 543, 568, 569
  refusal to help find Johnny, 645
  Richard's letter about "Jonathan" to, 357
  Richard's meeting, 572, 573
  self-identification as "Chase", 577, 580
  sighting of "Jonathan" in Mariah, 571
  similarities between "Chase", 573, 576-577
  suspicions about "Jonathan", 571
  trip to China proposed by "Jonathan" to, 581
"Andy thing", 352, 353, 356, 451, 567, 568, 572, 576, 582, 585
Antisocial Personality Disorder, 672-673, 675-676
  See also Psychopathic personality
Apartment in Mariah
  condition of, 274, 304
  description of, 244, 246, 247
  showing of, 246, 247
Are You Being Served?, 305
Art, 163, 248, 250, 251, 257, 466, 521
  description of, 245
  house of, 245
  "Jonathan's" inability to return to live with, 286, 418
  "Jonathan's" reservations about living with, 214-215
  mid-2011 update, 659-660
  offer to have "Jonathan" move in with, 131-132
  reclaiming belongings from, 304-305
  rent expected from "Jonathan" for December by, 252
  Richard's decision not to contact, 447, 630-631, 660
  Richard's meeting, 246
  Richard's pattern of visiting "Jonathan" while living with, 249
  sexual interest in "Jonathan" by, 252-253, 604
  shopping trip with "Jonathan", 255
Ash (*Alien*), 26, 515
Austin, 654
Avoiding entanglement with psychopath, 706-719

  counteracting one's psychological biases, 707-714
  knowing one's weaknesses, 714-719
  trusting one's intuition, 706-707

"Banzai" (Johnny alias), 255, 602, 603
  See also Gayteway (web site), Johnny's harassing messages about Dan posted on
Beaches (film), 51
Ben (alleged employee at OutSource), 60, 121, 511
  identification of Johnny as, 502
Bettina (alleged sister), 425
  "Jonathan's" biography of, 11
Big (*Sex and The City*), 81
"black mammy" objects, 82-83
Blanche Devereaux (*The Golden Girls*), 68
"Boi", 217-218, 234, 378, 380
"Boystown", 42
Braque, George, xxi, 392, 680
Brian (*Queer As Folk*), 43, 105
British accent
  Americans' reactions to, 15, 33, 41-42, 68, 87, 508
  "Jonathan's" faking of, 464, 508, 518
  "Jonathan's" loss of, 136
  "Jonathan's" use of, 15, 492, 521
British Museum. *See* Johnny ("Jonathan"), employment as assistant curator at British Museum.
"Business drag", 40, 55, 60, 80, 153, 419

Cadillac, 56, 571, 642, 648
  license plate number of, 609, 642
  See also Crimes committed by Johnny, non-payment of car loan
Cancer (astrology), 3, 476
  personality of person born under, 3-4
Caribbean island
  as home of Glenn's mother and stepfather, 200
  envelope postmarked on, 286, 557
  Jeanne's report of Glenn's absence from, 283
  "Jonathan's" claim to Dan about Glenn's vacationing on, 592

Caribbean island (cont.)
  "Jonathan's" plan to search for Glenn on, 238
  telephone calls from Johnny to, 592
Carlson, Mike, 578
Carrie (*Sex and The City*), 81
Carroll, Greg (alleged best friend in United States), 124, 145, 195, 446
  as employee of information technology company, 124, 450, 593
  as narcissistic reflection of Johnny, 572
  Dan's attempt to contact, 207, 593
  finding of Glenn, 437-438
  invitation to have "Jonathan" live with, 418, 419, 428
  possible connection between Eiseley and, 593
  Richard's attempt to contact, 447, 542
Cassandra, 497, 498, 499, 598, 603
  as employee at Intellex, 501
  as name on fraudulent insurance claim, 499
  introduction of "Jonathan" to Miranda by, 460
  See also Crimes committed by Johnny, insurance fraud scheme at OutSource, theft of money at Intellex
"Cautchu" (Dan alias), 613, 621, 632, 636
Charmaine (alleged sister), 28, 86, 97, 309, 370, 425, 509
  "Jonathan's" biography of, 12
Chase (alleged boyfriend), 382
  instant-message session between "Jonathan" and Richard about, 112-113
  insults toward Richard, 106-107, 108
  intensification of pursuit of "Jonathan", 105, 106, 107, 108
  invitation to performance of music in "Jonathan's" honor, 108-109
  "Jonathan's" admission of sleeping with, 109-110
  "Jonathan's" attempts to discourage pursuit, 105-106, 108
  "Jonathan's" biography of, 103

  "Jonathan's" decision to disassociate from, 140
  "Jonathan's" decision to go to auction house with, 396, 400, 401, 402, 412
  "Jonathan's" description of circumstances leading to sleeping with, 111
  "Jonathan's" final meeting in mid-August 2001 with, 114
  "Jonathan's" first "date" with, 104-105
  "Jonathan's" initial attitude toward, 104
  "Jonathan's" later attitude toward, 108
  "Jonathan's" renewed interest at Thanksgiving in, 268
  "Jonathan's" stated reasons for sleeping with, 112-113
  "Jonathan's" visit on January 20, 2002 with, 346
  Justin on *Queer as Folk*, self-compared to, 105
  music inspired by "Jonathan" by, 108
  passkey to apartment, 408
  reemergence of, into "Jonathan's"' life, 250
  Richard's attempts to learn more about, 180, 415
  Richard's reactions to "Jonathan's" admission of sleeping with, 110-111
  Richard's reasons for remaining with "Jonathan" after admission of sleeping with "Chase", 114-115, 120-121
  Richard's visiting "Jonathan" after sleeping with, 114
  sighting of Richard, 106
  view of "Jonathan" as symbol of ideal life by, 103-104, 105, 106, 108
  See also Andy
"Chaz" (Richard alias), 228, 229, 232, 235, 322, 331, 487, 488, 493, 503, 508, 510, 515, 522, 554, 556, 572, 594, 662
  autobiography of, to "Iain", 221-222
  plans to meet "Iain" of, 222, 223, 224, 225-226, 233-234

"Chaz" (Richard alias) (cont.)
  Richard's conclusion of exchange with "Iain" as, 234
  Richard's discovery of e-mails in "Iain" account between "Iain" and, 321
Cheryl, 145
Chester (alleged friend), 113, 577-578, 579
Chris (Richard's friend), 224, 249-250
Christmas
  exchange between "Jonathan" and Richard about, 288-293
  hospitalization of Richard's aunt at, 297, 528
  "Jonathan's" family's activities at, 292-293, 297
  "Jonathan's" feelings about, 288, 294, 295, 296, 297, 298, 299
  Laura's desire to see "Jonathan" at, 293, 294
  Richard's inability to invite "Jonathan" for, 288, 407, 411
  See also Tomlinsons, invitation to "Jonathan" to spend Christmas with
Chuck (Laura's son), 141, 566
  expectation to have "Jonathan" pay for dental work, 211
  expectation to have "Jonathan" pay for truck, 279, 544
  feelings about "Jonathan", 559
  mid-2011 update, 658
  repossession of truck, 545
  request for money from "Jonathan", 279
  Richard's meeting, 244
Clarian
  car shopping in, 196, 201
  Richard's teaching in, 129, 198
Cleckley, Hervey, xi, 669, 700
Cliff (alleged boyfriend), 98, 239, 332, 347
  "Big" on *Sex and The City*, compared to, 81
  Dan, feelings about, 124, 597
  "Jonathan's" reservations about living with, 163
  "Jonathan's" "shared" e-mail account with, 381, 390, 520
  letter from May 2001 from "Jonathan" to, 414, 597
  lie to "Jonathan" about whereabouts, 75-76
  masochism in "Jonathan's" relationship with, 167, 179, 180, 181, 196-197, 215, 283, 284, 358
  mid-2011 update, 658-659
  offer to have "Jonathan" move in with, 163, 179, 181
  physical appearance, 80-81
  reemergence into "Jonathan's" life, 73-75, 81
  relationship with "Jonathan", 72-73, 237, 238
  telephone calls to "Jonathan", 167, 181, 196, 215
  See also "Cliff" (as Johnny alias)
"Cliff" (as Johnny alias)
  confrontation between "Jonathan" and Richard over deception of Laura's family as, 387, 389
  e-mails from "Jonathan" to Jack as, 383, 384, 386
  e-mails from "Jonathan" to Laura as, 385, 386
  "Jonathan's" giving Richard password to e-mail account of, 381
  promise to have Jack live with "Jonathan" and, 384, 385, 386, 389, 543
  Richard's reasons for doubting Cliff's knowledge of *xxcliff* e-mail account, 383, 390-391
  Richard's theories about "Jonathan's" pretending to be, 386
  threat to file charges against Laura for undue influence by, 545, 558, 563, 565
Cole, xix, 95, 232
Colin (alleged best friend), 15, 76, 100, 124, 289, 306, 318, 347, 359-360, 551, 603
  as character in Andy fantasy, 322, 331, 575
  as doctor in "Kev" exchange, 490-491, 492-493
  Dan's ignorance of, 596
  "Jonathan's" biography of, 13
  "Jonathan's" "shared" e-mail account with, 330-331, 390, 399, 450, 488
Compazine, 277-278, 302
Confirmation bias, 688-689, 711, 712-713

"Control freaks", 6, 92, 514, 533
Credence, 124, 155
  as Dan's town of residence, 77, description of, 159, 161
  distance between Paladin and, 77
  "Jonathan's" confusion with Rowen as Dan's home town, 597
  "Jonathan's" description as "Hooterville", 168
  Richard's first visit to, 155
Crimes committed by Johnny
  acquisition of credit card in Terry's name, 510, 588
  check fraud, 636, 640, 641, 642, 647
  check fraud against Crystal, 636, 641, 643
  check fraud against Dan, 520, 544, 587, 588, 589, 590, 599, 601, 613, 639, 641, 642
  check fraud against Laura, 544-545, 558, 565, 609, 628
  check fraud against Miranda, 478, 496, 520, 544, 643, 644-645
  checks stolen from father, 559, 640
  forcible entry and detainer, 665
  grand theft, 666
  indecent exposure, 639, 666-667
  insurance fraud at OutSource, 499
  non-payment of car loan, 666
  non-payment of rent to Crystal, 636
  non-payment of rent to Harry, 638
  non-payment of rent to Joan Vogel, 517, 605
  non-payment of rent to Ted Kanner, 665
  operating motor vehicle without valid license, 667
  theft of money at Intellex, 460, 481, 497, 499, 501, 591, 600
  theft of money from bank in northern Europe, 510-511
  uttering forged instrument, 666
  violating financial laws, 666
Crystal, 641, 642, 643, 646
  attempts to contact Terry, 639
  attempts to locate Johnny, 639, 644
  conversation with Johnny, 646
  experience with "Jonathan", 636-637
  first e-mail from Richard, 637-638
  first e-mail to Dan, 635
  first e-mail to Richard, 638-639
  identity questioned by Dan, 635-636
  information about Johnny's criminal activities sent to Johnny's employer by, 646
  mid-2011 update, 660
  web site for exposing Johnny, 637, 646
  See also Crimes committed by Johnny, check fraud against Crystal, non-payment of rent to Crystal
Cuomo, 218

Dahmer, Jeffrey, 555
Daisy (*Keeping Up Appearances*), 210
Dame Edna Everage. *See* Humphries, Barry.
Dan
  amount owed by Johnny to, 592
  attempts to have Johnny arrested by, 606-610, 614, 615
  attempts to locate Johnny by, 626
  biography of, 124
  checkbook mixup, "Jonathan's" story about, 601
  cleanliness/neatness, attitudes about, 160, 183
  Cliff, "Jonathan's" story about, 597
  control over "Jonathan", attempts to exert, 161-162, 164, 169, 170-171, 172-173, 174, 183, 184, 186, 188, 193, 203
  conversation with Crystal, 639
  conversation with job recruiter about "Jonathan", 608
  conversation with "Jonathan's" "father", 592
  Crystal's first message, reaction to, 636
  denial of having met "Jonathan's" friends before August 2001, 598
  distrust of Laura, 609-610
  drinking behavior, 124, 170, 172, 173, 174, 175, 176, 177, 178, 185, 188, 192, 194, 196
  e-mails to Cliff, 627
  erratic behavior, 171, 183, 186-187, 190, 191

Dan (cont.)
  events surrounding "Jonathan's" leaving, 200
  "Evil", 187, 188, 190, 192, 586
  experience with "Jonathan", 587-590
  façade of heterosexuality, 175, 177, 178, 182-183, 189, 601
  father's paying for move from Paladin, "Jonathan's" story about, 588
  friend of, seeing Johnny in Mariah, 591
  "Good", 187, 190, 191, 192, 586
  Greg Carroll, attempt to contact, 207, 593
  health problems, 590, 645, 650, 656-657
  homophobia, 183, 184
  hypocritical behavior, 178
  ignorance of "Chase", 598
  impression of Richard, 125, 126
  inconsideration toward "Jonathan", 162, 164, 168, 169, 171, 172, 173, 182, 194
  Johnny's departure from Mariah, discovery of, 616
  Johnny's leaving Mariah, concerns about 607
  Johnny's parents, attempts to contact, 612-613, 615
  Johnny's second Social Security number, discovery of, 608
  "Jonathan's" autobiography to, 588
  "Jonathan's" denigration of Richard to, 594
  "Jonathan's" development of hatred toward, 188, 189, 204
  "Jonathan's" dogs, feelings about, 135, 160, 162, 163, 166, 168, 170, 172, 173, 175, 177, 182, 183, 184, 188, 189, 190, 194, 196, 200
  "Jonathan's" perceptions of behavior of, 173, 182
  "Jonathan's" plans for escaping from, 163, 164, 165, 166, 167, 168, 169, 173, 175, 185, 186, 187, 188, 189, 190, 191, 193, 195
  "Jonathan's" reservations about living with, 135
  meeting "Jonathan", story about, 596-597
  meeting, "Jonathan's" story about, 124
  "Michael's" suicide, "Jonathan's" story about, 598
  mid-2011 update, 656-657
  motives for taking in "Jonathan", 166, 176
  offer to stay with "Jonathan" after father's surgery, 100
  perception of Richard as "too obviously gay", 182, 374, 586-587
  physical appearance, 125
  Richard's first impression of, 125
  Richard's meeting, 123-125
  Richard's visit to Mariah with, 604-605
  sexual behavior, 124, 125, 174, 175, 176, 177, 178, 184, 185, 186, 192, 197
  sexual interest in Johnny, denial of, 595
  sexual interest in "Jonathan", 204
  stalking by, "Jonathan's" claim of, 371-372, 374, 520
  stealing, accusation against "Jonathan" of, 202, 203, 204, 256
  telephone calls from Glenn, refusal to accept, 172, 200, 203, 204, 592
  theft at Intellex, going to police station with "Jonathan" about, 591
  visit to "Jonathan's" after Cliff's revelation of whereabouts, 77-78, 598
  visitors, feelings about, 163, 168, 171, 174-175, 182
  See also "Cautchu" (Dan alias); Crimes committed by Johnny, check fraud against Dan; *Gayteway* (web site), Johnny's harassing messages about Dan posted on; Johnny ("Jonathan"), harassment of Dan
Daniel Jackson (*Stargate*), 80-81
"Darin" (Richard alias), 488, 524, 548
Devon (alleged friend), 113
Diagnostic and Statistical Manual of Mental Disorders (DSM-IV-TR), 673

Dogs
  damage done to properties by, 130, 304, 596
  described as "classy", 18, 27
  Frizzie, 27, 130, 196, 244, 334, 360, 433
  "Jonathan's" plans to give up, 334, 335, 336, 337
  Prissy, 27, 130, 334
  referred to as "the girls", 28, 32, 40, 153, 155, 156, 159, 160, 174, 181, 185, 186, 190, 193, 196, 244, 263, 273, 294, 295, 307, 334, 337, 341, 362, 518, 586, 619
  Sadie, 28, 36, 40, 146, 659
  Sweetie, 27, 130, 160, 162, 244, 321, 328, 334, 360
  See also Dan, "Jonathan's" dogs, feelings about
"Drifting", 305, 442
"Dulcimer", 604
  similarity of e-mail from "Heorshema" to that from, 603
  threatening e-mail to Dan from, 589, 602-603
  See also "Heorshema", The Pretender
Dwayne, 494-496
  Richard's trip to Mariah with, 494-495

Ealing Broadway IRA bombing, 120
Easter
  Richard's inability to invite "Jonathan" for, 407, 411
  See also Andy, "Jonathan's" story about Easter weekend to; Richard's mother, letter about Easter to "Jonathan"; Tomlinsons, invitation to "Jonathan" to spend Easter with
Egyptian faience scarab, 152, 345, 442, 496
  authenticity questioned, 479
  birthday gift from "Jonathan" to Richard, 36-37
  gift from "Jonathan" to Miranda West, 479-480
Egyptian Museum (Berlin), 37, 479, 480
Eiseley, 116, 485, 571, 577
  as "Jonathan's" birthplace, 11, 583
  "Jonathan's" story about Malcolm hanging himself in home in, 126
  meeting of "Jonathan's" parents and sisters at home in, regarding "Jonathan", 310
  possible connection between Greg Carroll and, 593
Elfriede (alleged aunt)
  "Jonathan's" biography of, 12-13
England, trip proposed to Richard by "Jonathan" to, 116
  cancellation, 121-122, 123, 378
  preparations for, 118-121
  Richard's acquiring passport for, 116, 117, 118
  Richard's feelings about meeting "Jonathan's" family and friends during, 119
Erikson, Erik, 702

Family and Medical Leave Act, 500
Fights between "Jonathan" and Richard
  breakup, 418-427
  July 2001, 93-101
  March 2002, 402-406
  October 2001, 234-239
  provoked by Andy's final e-mail to "Iain", 351-356
  provoked by "Naughtyboy" ad, 378-383
  reasons for Richard's remaining with "Jonathan" after July 2001 fight, 89-93
  reasons for Richard's remaining with "Jonathan" after October 2001 fight, 241-242
  reconciliation after July 2001 fight, 101-102
  reconciliation after October 2001 fight, 240
Frankl, Viktor, 704
Frazier, Edward (father), 45, 117, 121, 175, 195
  attempts to have "Jonathan" declared "diminished", 309, 310
  attitude toward "Jonathan's" predicament at Dan's, 164, 183-184, 191
  colon cancer, 50, 99-100, 104, 116, 306
  gift of £10,000 from, 184-185, 307

Frazier, Edward (father) (cont.)
"Jonathan's" biography of, 10
"Jonathan's" leaving house on Millstone Drive, reaction to, 133
mid-2011 update, 662
Richard's attempts to locate, 485-486
ultimatum to "Jonathan" to return home, 325, 337, 341, 345, 347
See also Crimes committed by Johnny, checks stolen from father, violating financial laws

Frazier, Helena (mother)
"Jonathan's" biography of, 10
"Jonathan's" comparison to "Lovey Howell" on *Gilligan's Island*, 10, 119
"Jonathan's" leaving house on Millstone Drive, reaction to, 133
portrait of, and children, 28, 196, 244, 286, 361, 510

Freud, Sigmund, 69, 88, 573

Garrett, David, "Jonathan's" e-mail to, 398
See also Lovers/sex partners claimed by "Jonathan", David Garrett

Gayteway (web site), 6, 219, 370, 529, 603-604
"Chaz" ads posted on, 221, 321
exchange between Richard and "Jonathan" on, 409
first ad by "Jonathan" answered by Dan on, 596
first ad by "Jonathan" on, 597
Johnny's harassing messages about Dan posted on, 205, 219-220, 236-237, 239, 255, 587, 589, 599
"Jonathan's" visiting travel page on, 315-316, 323
notepaper found in Johnny's briefcase with address of, 648
Richard's April 1, 2002 ad on, 416
See also Johnny ("Jonathan"), harassment of Dan; Sex ads posted by Johnny

Glenn (boyfriend), 13
Andy's story about, 581-582
as American, 502, 556
as employee at OutSource, 502
as narcissistic reflection of Johnny, 572
as "son" of "Jonathan", 367, 460, 465, 474, 483, 502, 512, 532, 533, 638, 643
birthday, 276
"CI (Caribbean Islands) guy", referred to by Dan as, 597
Dan's denial of having met, 597
delusions about Hitler, 470
differences in Johnny's stories to Laura and Richard about, 556, 557
disappearance in September 2001, 200, 212-213, 261, 474, 663-664
disappearances before September 2001, 200, 201, 262, 461, 474-475
dissociative (identity) disorder, 470-471, 473, 477, 532
dreams of "Jonathan" about, 293, 368-369, 438
dying hair red, 473, 532
escapes from "Jonathan" attempted by, 465, 473, 475, 530, 533
family relationships, 261-262
fugue states, 461, 470
hallucinations and delusions, 461, 470, 473-474, 475-476, 531
homophobia, 470, 474, 529, 532
"Jonathan's" belief in, being dead, 202, 213, 284, 469, 582
"Jonathan's" reservations about living with, 163
life in England, alleged, 71
mid-2011 update, 663-664
photographs of, 141-142, 618-619
physical abuse against Johnny, 461, 464, 556
physical abuse by, admitted by "Jonathan"', 149-150, 262
physical appearance, 142
physical violence committed by, concerns about, 477, 532
prejudice, 474, 532
private investigator hired by "Jonathan" to find, 240, 284, 367, 465, 502
relationship between "Jonathan" and British version of, 70-72
residence in Paladin after breakup with Johnny, 557, 664

Glenn (boyfriend) (cont.)
   schizophrenia, 470, 477
   schizophrenia of, denied to
      Richard by "Jonathan", 149
   telephone call to Laura's in
      October 2001, 212
   "trust fund" (psychiatric
      disability), 284, 557
   white supremacist/Nazi ideas
      expressed by, 470, 529, 531-532
Gobi, 316, 318, 320
"God Gave Me Everything"
   (Jagger), 297
Golden Dragon, 247, 263
"Great Lakes" state
   as Glenn's home state, 556, 592
   as "Iain's" former state of
      residence to "Chaz", 223, 556
Greg, "Fat/Big", 167, 177, 178, 195, 197, 282, 503, 598
   asking Dan personal questions
      about "Jonathan", 166
   conversation with Richard on
      September 1, 2001, 148
   involvement in move from house
      on Millstone Drive, 145, 151
   visits to Dan's, 168, 174-175, 193, 194
Grubin, Don, 685

Half-Time, 68
   "Jonathan's" and Andy's meeting
      at, 573
Hamish (alleged nephew), 12
   involvement in IRA bombing at
      Ealing Broadway, 120
Harald (alleged friend), 63, 124,
   "Jonathan's" acquisition of
      scarabs from, 37, 479
   "Jonathan's" biography of, 13
Hare, Robert, 673-674
Harmon, Mike (CEO of OutSource), 128, 135, 138, 192, 207, 257, 344, 498, 578. 609
   citizenship of "Jonathan",
      speculation about, 501
   conversation with Richard, 499-503
   feelings toward "Jonathan" for
      taking leave of absence, 184
   financial damage done by
      "Jonathan" to, 503
   firing of "Jonathan" from
      OutSource, reason for, 500
   Glenn's employment at
      OutSource discussed by, 502, 557
   "Jonathan's" biography of, 59
   "Jonathan's" late-night meeting in
      July 2001 with, 59, 504
   "Jonathan's" pathological lying
      mentioned by, 500
   "Jonathan's" posing as different
      people through e-mail to, 502, 603
   "Jonathan's" "problems with
      landlords" mentioned by, 501
   "Jonathan's" psychological
      problems mentioned by, 502, 503
   "Jonathan's" requesting leave of
      absence from, 136, 137
   refusal to let "Jonathan" go to
      England, 121-122, 123, 128
   remodeling of mansion, 59, 597, 598
   suspension of "Jonathan's"
      executive privileges by, 155
   See also OutSource
Harry (landlord), 638, 644
   "2 inches thick" file on Johnny's
      criminal behavior from, 636, 638, 650
   See also Crimes committed by
      Johnny, check fraud against
      Harry
Hawthorn
   as business destination of
      "GayMan", 217
   as location of "Boi", 217
   as Richard's home town, xv
   distance between Art's house and, 249
   distance between Credence and, 171
   distance between Mariah and, 249, 264
   distance between Paladin and, 25
   distance between St. Alban and, 244
   "Jonathan's" not visiting, 97, 98
   Richard's experience of being gay
      in, 122
   Richard's teaching in, xvii, xviii, 129, 206, 273, 278, 315, 336, 337, 347, 360, 395, 396, 399, 444, 536, 537
   university in, xv, 5, 66, 103, 180, 255, 392, 580

Health problems of "Jonathan",
  alleged, 47-48, 52, 162, 164, 166,
    171, 173, 174, 175, 178-179, 184,
    192, 197, 208, 211, 243, 275, 276,
    277-278, 292, 294, 364, 405, 424,
    428, 576
  angina/chest pain, 46, 47, 48-49,
    76, 246
  effects on relationship, 53-54, 69,
    193, 504
  endocarditis, 51, 53, 211, 243,
    298, 405, 500, 501, 564, 566
  heart abnormalities, 46
  heart institute losing tests results,
    47-48, 575
  "Jonathan's" feelings about, 49-
    50
  lack of appetite, 184, 193, 275,
    277-278,
  mental confusion, 144, 209, 241,
    244, 254, 275, 291, 329, 336,
    338, 481, 545, 561, 563, 565,
    598, 601
  nausea/vomiting, 45-46, 50, 52,
    165, 181, 182, 231, 278, 293,
    424
  problems staying warm, 277, 301
  stress as possible cause, 45, 46, 48
  tests, 46, 47-48, 50, 51, 52, 99,
    100, 101, 117, 211, 281, 283,
    285
  travel restrictions because of, 50,
    52
  treatments for, 47, 51, 52, 53, 192,
    211, 243, 278, 301-302, 468
Heaven (nightclub), 31, 37, 360
heilhitler (password), 448, 470, 481.
  See also The Pretender
Henri, xix, 95-96, 232
"Heorshema", 455, 551, 552, 565
  e-mail to "Jonathan" from, 453,
    481, 482, 548-549, 602, 603
  feelings about Kathryn expressed
    by, 549
  feelings about Richard's mother
    expressed by, 549
  threat against Richard by, 549
  See also "Dulcimer", The
    Pretender
Hershey, Barbara, 51
Hope, 604
  invitation of "Jonathan" to
    Thanksgiving dinner by, 265,
    453
Horatio, 90, 95, 146, 184, 185, 186

"Jonathan's" biography of, 28
"Jonathan's" story about falling
  down escalator while helping,
  150
proposed business venture with
  "Jonathan" and friend, 648
Hospital in Mariah, 193, 206, 210
  description of job at, 152, 193,
    194, 247
  distance between apartment and,
    246
  emotional reactions of "Jonathan"
    to firing from, 270, 271, 272,
    273, 274, 276, 277, 278, 279,
    280, 281, 282
  firing of "Jonathan" from, 270,
    273, 274
  hiring of "Jonathan" at, 202
  interviews for job at, 169, 175,
    184, 187, 188, 191, 193, 194
  "Jonathan's" fear of parents'
    reaction to firing from hospital,
    271, 274, 279, 280
  refusal of "Jonathan" to return to
    hospital, 277
  Richard's visit to, 247
  story about "Jonathan's" hiring on
    web site of, 243, 522
Humphries, Barry, 306

"Iain Winslett" (Johnny alias)
  as hospice worker to Cliff, 321,
    350, 378, 390, 576
  as travel agent to Andy, 323, 575
  autobiography to "Chaz" by, 222,
    223
  e-mails from "Jonathan" to Andy
    as, 322, 323
  e-mails from "Jonathan" to
    "Chaz" as, *See* "Chaz"
    (Richard alias)
  e-mails from "Jonathan" to Cliff
    as, 321, 324
  "Jonathan's" denial to Richard of
    being, 232, 233, 256, 319, 320
  "Jonathan's" description of, as
    Richard's "phantom lover",
    256, 575
  "Jonathan's" suggesting of
    password to e-mail account of,
    to Richard, 320-321
  questioning of "Chaz's" identity
    by, 224, 225
  self-identification as "GayMan"
    by, 221

"Iain Winslett" (Johnny alias) (cont.)
  similarities between "Jonathan"
    and, 223, 224, 228
  similarities between writing style
    of "Jonathan" and that of, 226-
    228
Immigration and Naturalization
  Service (INS), 275, 280, 292, 303,
  340, 342, 346, 370, 485
Intellex, 591, 600, 608
  allusions by "Jonathan" to
    working at, 79, 501
  employment of "Jonathan" at,
    500-501
  See also Crimes committed by
    Johnny, theft of money at
    Intellex

Jack (Laura's son), 141, 244
  as "suitor" of "Jonathan", 574
  e-mails from "Jonathan" as
    "Cliff" to, 566
  homosexuality, 251, 252
  Johnny's acquisition of Social
    Security number, 544
  mid-2011 update, 658
  request to live with "Jonathan",
    251, 293
  suicide attempt, 545
Jagger, Mick, 297
Jeanne (Glenn's mother), 262
  "Jonathan's" biography of, 261,
    262
  letter to "Jonathan" about Glenn
    from, 283, 285, 286
Jeopardy, 305, 335, 337, 481
Jerry Springer Show, 80, 305, 316,
  351, 567
Jim, 264, 594
  Dan's confirmation of Johnny's
    relationship with, 593
  Laura's confirmation of Johnny's
    relationship with, 611
Johnny ("Jonathan")
  activities from January 2003 to
    August 2004, 638, 644
  age, 509, 608
  American driver's license,
    concerns about not having, 42,
    151, 510
  amounts owed to people in
    Richard's state by, 647
  apathy of authorities in pursuing,
    606, 607, 609, 611, 612, 615,
    616-617, 621, 636, 645

arrogance, 87, 389
Art Deco bed, purchase of, 255-
  256, 263
attempts to find job, 335, 337,
  339, 342, 344, 355, 359, 368,
  372, 375, 401, 403, 407, 410,
  413-414, 418, 424
autobiography to Richard, 7-8, 9,
  13-14
birth date, 667
breakdown at storage facility,
  143, 144
breakdown/repair of car, 154, 161,
  162, 168, 169, 171, 172, 173,
  174, 520, 588
breakup, stated reasons for, 428
Brian on *Queer as Folk*, Chase's
  comparison to, 105
briefcase left at Dan's by, 647-
  649
building of mansion, 598
business dealings with company
  in California, 58, 100, 121,
  128, 132, 133, 134, 135, 184
Carrie on *Sex and The City*, self-
  compared to, 81
cash, possession of large amounts
  of, 56, 254-255, 261, 467-468,
  591
celebration of "45th" birthday,
  257-258
childlike behavior, 274, 311, 329,
  534
Cliff's lie about whereabouts,
  reaction to, 76-77, 78-79
conversation with "mother", 263-
  264, 509
damage to properties to avoid
  paying rent, 643-644
denial of encouraging Richard to
  access e-mail accounts, 329,
  336, 453
denial to Richard of Glenn's
  schizophrenia, 262, 461
disability, long-term, 275-276,
  278, 285, 344, 355, 424, 437,
  438
disability, short-term, 152, 208,
  275, 307
dishonesty suggested by, 127, 236
dislike of "gay yuppie scum" in
  Paladin, 86-87, 245
dislike of women, 86, 97, 145,
  471, 474
drug/alcohol use, 468

Johnny ("Jonathan") (cont.)
   effects of separation from Richard on, 178, 181, 182, 188, 196-197, 205, 206, 265, 267, 268
   employment as assistant curator at British Museum, 8, 9, 37, 55
   employment at bank in northern Europe, 55, 510
   employment history from 1996 to 2011, 665-666
   façade of heterosexuality, 460, 465
   fainting in lobby of hotel, 136
   family's attitude toward helping, 280, 307, 370
   family's attitude toward homosexuality, 13
   family's description as "unusual", 311
   favorite television shows, 43, 305
   feelings of being "unsafe", 77, 112, 129, 132, 167, 192, 207, 271, 419, 453, 454, 481, 482, 523, 551, 560
   financial behavior, 307
   finding Glenn, story about, 437-438
   gay men, feelings about, 86-87, 471
   "Good For You" e-mail to Richard from, 506-507
   harassment of Dan, 203, 204, 205, 206, 207, 220, 255, 371, 372, 378, 589, 599-602
   health, plans for regaining, 131, 132, 136, 137
   height, feelings about, 16
   homosexuality, feelings about, 69, 572-573
   income, plans for generating, 307, 342, 374
   Independence Day, feelings about, 36, 507
   information on company web site about, 17-18, 93
   Internet/e-mail, problems with, 334, 335, 367, 368, 369, 370, 408, 409, 411
   Internet, "Jonathan's" claim of staying off, 363, 370, 404, 408
   investigation of, 467
   IP (Internet Protocol) addresses used to locate, 487, 490, 626
   "J", referred to as, 558
   leaving Paladin, feelings about, 132, 134, 137
   living together suggested to Richard by, 134, 206, 247, 272, 348, 354, 355, 374
   "Lord Jonathan" in Andy fantasy, referred to as, 322
   mail, problems with, 376-377, 430
   manipulating others through use of "illness", 54, 207-208, 230, 231, 232, 233, 251, 257, 321, 382, 422-423, 424, 560, 561, 562
   marriages of, 512
   meeting at Mike Harmon's in July 2001, 59, 504
   meeting of Glenn in institution, 471, 474, 530, 561, 644
   mid-2011 update, 665-668
   mug shot of, 667
   nervous breakdown story to Laura, 540, 545-547
   nervousness over conversation between Laura and Richard, 148
   obsession with Glenn, 200-201, 204, 206, 212-213, 230, 238, 240, 261, 283-285, 293, 294, 297, 358, 359, 368-369, 371, 403, 426, 432, 437, 464, 529
   obsession with soul food, 84-85
   photographs of, 196, 513, 618-619, 637
   physical appearance, 17-18, 26, 518
   prejudice, 474
   prejudice against Americans, 82
   prejudice against Arabs/Muslims, 85-86, 169-170, 173
   prejudice against blacks, 82-84
   prejudice against Hispanics, 85
   prejudice against Indians, 85-86, 257, 258
   prejudice against "mud people", 86
   prejudice against Pakistanis, 85-86, 257
   previous relationships, questioning Richard about, 29, 30

Index   737

Johnny ("Jonathan") (cont.)
   profession of love to Richard by, 144
   promises to repay Richard, 144, 228-229, 231, 254-255, 303, 308, 324, 325, 348, 400, 403, 428, 433, 438
   "proposal" to Laura, 544
   "proposal" to Richard, 142-143
   psychiatrist, claim of seeing, 413, 453, 481, 511, 548, 551, 552, 591
   refusal to reclaim belongings from Laura's, 305, 611
   relationship with Richard denied to others by, 125, 146-147, 148, 150, 212, 233, 386-387, 388, 404, 426, 522, 550, 555, 594
   reluctance to hug when leaving Dan's, 161, 594
   remaining in United States to be with Richard, 307, 338, 341, 353, 354, 355, 381, 397, 400
   rental scam, 638, 643
   repaying Richard, tactics to avoid, 229, 230, 231, 232, 324, 325, 326-327, 400, 430, 481-482, 486
   repayment to Richard of $360 in November 2001, 254-255, 259, 261, 308, 324, 428, 489
   retirement plans, 6, 9, 10, 56, 152
   retirement trust, 307, 342
   return to Paladin, intention to, 303, 355, 382, 389, 403, 405, 407-408, 410
   returning to England suggested by, 163, 287, 325, 327, 341, 347, 353, 354, 355, 400
   Richard's appearance, reaction to, 17
   Richard's attempts to learn about family, reaction to, 92-93, 505-506
   Richard's learning about "Andy" fantasies, reaction to, 328-329
   Richard's status as boyfriend, questioning of, 252-254
   salaries, actual, 541, 647-648
   salaries, alleged, 56, 500
   self-centeredness, rationalizations for, 405, 421, 426
   self-description to Richard, 7, 8-9
   Sex Now site used to locate, 609
   sex, stated attitudes toward, 7, 9, 44
   sexual attention, ability to attract, 67-68, 167
   sexual behavior as young adult, alleged, 61-62
   sexual behavior toward Laura, 148
   sexual behavior toward Richard, 69, 127
   sexual development, 512
   sexual interest in Dan, 595
   sexual involvement with Catholic priests, 64, 306
   "shit" e-mail, 138-139
   suicidal thinking, 276-277, 338
   telephone calls made from Dan's by, 592-593
   telephone service, relinquishing of, 368, 369, 409, 411
   threats to file charges against Dan for sexual harassment, 256, 589, 601-602
   trunk of car used as "safe", 56, 468, 591
   truthfulness, assurances of, 75, 236
   Valentine's Day card to Richard, 361, 620
   weekend activities during summer 2001, 40-44
   work activities described, 56-59
   work behavior, 59-60, 503-504
   See also Crimes committed by Johnny; Health problems of "Jonathan", alleged; Sex ads posted by Johnny
"Jonathan" (Johnny alias). *See* Johnny ("Jonathan")
"jonathan iain" (Johnny alias), e-mail to Richard from, 523, 529
Justin (*Queer As Folk*), 43, 105

Kanner, Ted (landlord), 130, 252, 644
   "deal" with "Jonathan" to vacate house on Millstone Drive, 131, 132, 134
   eviction proceedings against Johnny by, 665
   murder of niece and fiancé, 248-249, 502, 589
   repossession of house on Millstone Drive, 156

Kanner, Ted (landlord) (cont.)
  See also Crimes committed by Johnny, non-payment of rent to Ted Kanner
Kathryn (Richard's sister), 39, 47, 52, 53, 117, 196, 240, 271, 290, 361, 362, 424, 425, 434, 448, 456, 475, 481, 513, 514
  biography, 34
  "Jonathan's" feelings about, 35, 95, 97, 98, 363, 381, 422, 471, 483, 523
  "Jonathan's" meeting, 35
  See also "Heorshema," Kathryn, feelings expressed by; The Pretender, Kathryn, feelings expressed by
Keeping Up Appearances, 210, 305
Kernberg, Otto, 674-675
"Kevin (Kev)" (Richard alias), 553
  exchange between "Colin" and, 490-493
King, Carole, 197
King, Stephen, 172, 199, 203

Lauper, Cyndi, 327
Laura
  bankruptcy, 545
  biography, 141
  breakup with "Cliff," "Jonathan's" story about, 543
  checkbook mixup, "Jonathan's" story about, 565
  Christmas, "Jonathan's" story about, 611
  conversation with Richard on July 6, 2002, 519-522
  conversation with Richard on July 7, 2002, 525
  conversation with Richard on November 17, 2002, 610-611
  conversation with Richard on September 1, 2001, 146-148
  conversation with Richard on September 1, 2002, 540, 545
  e-mail confronting Johnny with truth from, 558-560
  e-mail to Richard on September 1, 2002, 538-539
  e-mails from "Jonathan" as "Cliff" to, 566
  financial motive for involvement with "Jonathan", 150, 151, 163, 208, 209, 210, 214, 215, 251
  Glenn's abuse of "Jonathan" revealed to Richard, 147
  Glenn's "medication" mentioned by, 142
  Glenn's schizophrenia revealed to Richard, 147, 262, 461
  incriminating documents discovered in "Jonathan's" belongings by, 541
  jealousy toward Richard, 180, 209, 244
  job at hospital, "Jonathan's" story about, 521
  "Jonathan's" belongings left behind with, 245, 301, 305, 541
  "Jonathan's" plans for escaping from, 203, 207, 208, 210, 214, 215, 243, 244, 245
  "Jonathan's" promises to, 539, 540, 543, 544, 562
  "Jonathan's" psychological problems discovered by, 539, 540
  "Jonathan's" reaction to learning about "Chaz" deception to, 522
  "Jonathan's" reservations about living with, 163, 175, 190
  medical leave, "Jonathan's" story about, 521
  mid-2011 update, 658
  offer to have "Jonathan" move in with, 163, 175, 189
  possessiveness toward "Jonathan", 180, 203, 210, 243
  "powerful friends," "Jonathan's" claim of having, 525, 542, 565
  "proposal" to "Jonathan", 210, 211
  Richard's first impression of, 141
  romantic interest in "Jonathan", 142, 148, 149, 150, 163, 175, 178, 190, 208
  suicidal thinking of, 545
  theft of "Jonathan's" money by sons, 209, 210, 229
  threatening messages from "Cliff" to, 545, 563, 564, 565
  See also Crimes committed by Johnny, check fraud against Laura; "Trevor" (Laura alias)
Leandra (alleged sister), 28, 100, 120, 370, 425, 509
  "Jonathan's" biography of, 11
Lithographs, 38, 347, 367, 412, 495
  attempts to sell, 359, 393-396

Lithographs (cont.)
  insurance on, Joanne's offer to pay, 400
  insurance on, "Jonathan's" inability to pay, 364, 393
  plan to sell, 302-303, 325, 355
  smaller of, as collateral against money owed to Richard, 324, 326
  value, actual, 393
  value, alleged, 302, 393, 394
Logan (alleged friend), 574, 603
  as suitor of "Jonathan", 574, 604
  beliefs about Dan's behavior, 176, 177, 184, 189, 194
  "Jonathan's" biography of, 176
Logotherapy (Frankl), 704
London, 31, 36, 37, 62, 63, 306, 402, 427, 486, 571, 575
  as Bettina's current home, 11
  as birthplace of "Trevor", 554
  as business destination to David Garrett, 398
  as Charmaine's current home, 12
  as Glenn's current home, 71
  as "Jonathan" and Marcus's home, 71
  as Leandra's current home, 11
  as location of family's Christmas celebration, 292
  as parents' current home, 10, 306
  as Sarah's current home, 10
  house left to "Jonathan" by "David" in, 596
  "Jonathan's" home in, 7, 70
  property in "Jonathan's" name in, 501
  "small mews house" in, 556
London School of Economics, 71
Loren, 74, 77, 179, 215, 659
Lovers/sex partners claimed by "Jonathan"
  conductor of London Philharmonic Orchestra, 62, 604
  David, 596, 597, 604
  David Garrett, 64, 398, 519, 556, 596, 604
  Frank, 67, 604
  James, 63, 604
  Javier, 66, 67, 604
  Kyle, 65-66, 67, 89-90, 604
  Lester, 67, 604
  Lucas, 63, 604
  realtor's boyfriend, 66, 604

Rudolph Nureyev, 62-63, 64, 604
Tony, 591, 604
young man at apartment in Mariah, 432, 433, 434
See also Chase, Cliff, Glenn, Marcus
Luella
  as "Jonathan's" maid in Mariah, 610
  as aunt of black executive, 84-85, 258, 610-611

Make Way for Lucia (Benson), 38, 427, 495
Malcolm (alleged brother), 126, 133, 195, 338, 425, 598
  death by falling out of window, 126
  death by suicide, 126
  reaction of "Jonathan's" parents to death of, 126-127
Malcolm in the Middle, 43
Man's Search for Meaning (Frankl), 704
Marcus (alleged boyfriend), 78, 79, 179, 276, 291, 294, 298, 332, 382, 405
  Boxing Day accident, 72, 297
  Dan's ignorance of, 596
  relationship with "Jonathan", 71-72
Marcus (alleged brother-in-law), 12
Margarita, 117
Mariah
  as location of "Colin", 491
  as location of "Naughtyboy", 376, 377
  distance between Paladin and, 191
  indications of "Jonathan's" remaining in, 435, 436, 469, 486, 487, 490
  "Jonathan's" description as "Hooterville", 343
  "Jonathan's" negotiations on housing in, 203, 204, 207, 213, 214, 231, 240
  move to, 207, 208, 210, 231, 257, 259, 261
  Richard's impression of, 246
  See also Hospital in Mariah
"Mary", 222, 223
Mata Hari, 476
Michael (alleged brother), 126, 578
  death by suicide to Dan, 598
  "Jonathan's" biography of, 11

Michael (alleged brother) (cont.)
  "Jonathan's" confusion of Malcolm with, 338, 598
"Mid-Atlantic" state
  as birthplace of Johnny, 667
  as "Iain's" birthplace to "Chaz", 222, 510, 662
  relatives of Frazier family in, 510, 662
  Social Security number issued in, 608, 662
"Midwestern" state, 223, 499, 508
  as "Iain's" former state of residence, 222, 508
  as Johnny's home state, 508, 518, 520, 583, 588
  as "Terry's" home state, 18, 166, 505
  fraudulent insurance account in, 499
  "Jonathan's" business trip to, 84-85, 123, 508, 610-611
  "Jonathan's" claim to Laura of spending Christmas in, 611
  "Jonathan's" friends in, 84, 508
  Social Security number issued in, 608, 640
Millon, Theodore, 674
Millstone Drive, house on, 25, 132, 137, 146, 154, 244, 245, 258, 259, 260, 261, 263, 282, 305, 385, 427, 462, 463, 468, 494, 501, 541, 574, 592, 629, 643-644,
  appearance of, 25-29
  condition of, 130-131, 304
  "Jonathan's" reasons for wanting to leave, 42, 79, 129
  last day at, 155-156
  Richard's arranging for move from, 132, 133, 134, 135, 136
  Richard's drive-by visit in November 2001, 255
Misery (King), 172
"Money Changes Everything" (The Brains/Lauper), 327
Morrison, Jim, 137
Morte d'Arthur (Malory), 24
Moving van, 151, 153
  arrangements to rent, 132, 133, 134, 135, 136
  breakdown, 154
  cost, 147, 151, 228-229, 259, 489, 616

Narcissism
  "normal", 674-675, 676
  pathological, 591, 674-676
  See also Narcissistic personality
Narcissistic personality, 498, 522, 671, 672, 673, 674, 675, 676, 690, 694
Narcissistic Personality Disorder, 673, 675, 676
  See also Narcissistic personality
Nathan (Nate), 614
  similarities between Richard and, 614
  See also Sex ads posted by Johnny, "The Two Bears"
Nigel (alleged friend), 574, 603

Other forms of manipulation, 690-694
  blatant, 691-692
  separation, 692-694
  subtle, 690-691
OutSource, 55
  insurance fraud scheme at, 518
  "Jonathan" as COO of, 9, 17, 18, 22, 55, 70, 207
  "Jonathan" as general manager at, 499, 500
  "Jonathan's" firing from, 500
  "Jonathan's" leave of absence from, 136, 137, 152, 164, 184, 192, 207
  "Jonathan's" length of employment at, 500
  "Jonathan's" salary at, 56, 307
  nature of, 498, 500
  Richard and "Jonathan's" drive-by visit to, 245-246
  See also Crimes committed by Johnny, insurance fraud at OutSource; Harmon, Mike (COO of OutSource)

Paladin
  art museum in, 37, 168
  as "Jonathan's" city of residence in 2001, 7
  distance from St. Alban and Credence, respectively, to, 202
  "gay elite" in, 73, 113
  "Jonathan's" move from Southern state to, 9, 42, 70
  letters from The Pretender postmarked in, 444, 448

Paladin (cont.)
    trip to zoo on August 21, 2004, 640-641
    trip to zoo on June 16, 2001, 30-31
"Paladin Incident", xvi-xvii, 8, 22, 140-141
Pastor at Dan's church, 170, 604
    "Jonathan's" plan to expose Dan to, 189-190
    sexual advances toward "Jonathan" by, 167, 179
Pathological lying and related factors, 676-678
Patty, 168
    as Dan's girlfriend, 183
    "Jonathan's" plan to expose Dan to, 189-190
    perception of "Jonathan" by, 598-599
Paxil, 468
Personality disorders, 460, 671-672, 673, 674
Phantom of the Opera, 250
Phenergan, 52, 468
Projection (defense mechanism), 88
Prozac, xviii, 166, 368, 371, 387, 442
    Richard's acquiring, from doctor for "Jonathan", 338-339, 404, 486
    sexual side effects of, xviii-xlx, 19, 380
Psychopathic personality, 522, 671, 672-674, 675, 676
Psychopathy, 526, 669, 674-676, 677
    See also Psychopathic personality
Psychopathy Checklist-Revised (PCL-R) (Hare), 674
Purple chair, 29, 36, 41, 261, 535
    "Jonathan's" beliefs about, 461-462

Queer As Folk, 43-44, 305
    Chase's comparison of himself and "Jonathan" to characters on, 105

Reaction formation (defense mechanism), 534
Reasons for believing lies, 678-690
    assumption of honesty, 678-679
    assurance of honesty, 679
    confirmation bias, 688-689
    consistency, 680
    detail, 679
    explaining away behavior, 689-690
    exploiting areas of limited knowledge, 682-683
    fluency, 680-681
    information overload, 682
    minimal outward indications of lying, 685-686
    plausible explanations for errors of "fact", 684
    superficially plausible explanations for suspicious behavior, 681
    telling people what they want to hear, 683-684
    use of Internet, 686-687
Recovering from entanglement with psychopath, 694-706
    avoiding "revictimizing" people, 696-699
    finding meaning in experience, 704-705
    focusing on self-improvement, 701-702
    learning to trust again, 702-703
    not feeling "stupid", 700-701
    not minimizing impact of experience, 695-696
    refusing "victim" role, 699-700
Reginald (alleged brother), 424-425, 509
    attempt to take control of "Jonathan's" affairs by, 578, 579
    "Jonathan's" biography of, 11
Reginald (alleged brother-in-law), 11
    "Jonathan's" biography of, 10
Reptilian, 475
Richard
    "Aidan" on *Sex and The City*, compared to, 81
    anxiety problems, 3, 21-22, 25
    attraction to "Jonathan", reasons for, 18-22
    bathhouse in Paladin, meeting "Jonathan" at, 177, 204, 205, 208, 245, 251
    breaking into garage by, "Jonathan's" claim of, 523, 551, 554
    burning Johnny's items, 619, 620
    contacting Johnny's parents, 615, 616, 617

Richard (cont.)
  contacting "Jonathan's" friends, 447
  confrontation with Johnny about money, 516, 518
  confrontation with Johnny about money, reactions to 526
  conversation with "Jonathan" about trust, 399, 400
  conversations with "Jonathan" about Andy situation, 329, 330, 331, 332, 336, 337
  death of cousin, 310
  depression, 3, 21-22, 358, 368, 369, 371, 373, 380, 387
  difficulties in having "Jonathan" stay with, 44, 164, 266, 288, 407, 411, 427
  dissociative identity disorder of, "Jonathan's" claim of, 453, 454, 455, 459, 470, 481, 482, 548, 549, 553
  distance driven by Richard to be with "Jonathan", 290, 379, 431, 432
  doubts about Dan's "too obviously gay" comment, 586, 587
  e-mail accounts compromised, 440, 441, 443, 444, 446, 448
  e-mail to Cliff, 627-629
  emotional breakdown on Valentine's Day, 361, 362, 381, 382, 456
  events from fall 2002 to spring 2007, 652-656
  events from mid- to late April 2002, 442
  events from mid-August 2003 to mid-August 2004, 632, 633, 634, 635
  events of July-August 2002, 527, 529
  exchange with "Jonathan" about repayment of money on January 13, 2002, 324, 325, 326, 327
  family relationships, 21, 39
  feelings toward "Jonathan", 39, 145, 241, 336, 367
  first conversation with "Jonathan", 15-16
  hacking into e-mail by, "Jonathan's" claim of, 453, 450, 488, 523, 542, 548, 550, 552, 554,
  harassment by, "Jonathan's" claim of, 488, 523, 542, 548, 550, 552, 553, 554, 593
  "Iain" e-mail account, reaction to discovering contents, 326, 327, 328
  ignorance about business, 7, 10, 135
  inability to trust "Jonathan", 147, 219, 232, 236, 324, 352, 380, 397, 398, 399, 403, 413, 434, 455
  interests, 3, 4, 5, 8, 9-10, 15, 20, 30, 31, 37, 38, 527, 528, 569, 633, 634, 649
  Johnny's whereabouts in November 2004 discovered by, 646
  "Jonathan's" non-repayment of money, concerns about, 324
  "Jonathan's" posing as Cliff discovered by, 378
  legal action against "Jonathan" pursued, 486, 489, 493, 538, 637
  letter to "Jonathan" in mid-March 2002, 402
  loan of $900 to "Jonathan", 307, 308
  "message" web site, 409, 449, 523, 569
  misgivings about "Jonathan", 30, 31, 139, 219, 228, 242, 273, 308, 309, 318
  monitoring of "Jonathan's" Internet activities, 315, 316, 350, 351, 370, 371, 377, 398, 414, 487
  obsession by, "Jonathan's" claim of, 523, 542, 550
  payment of "Jonathan's" rent in February by, 366
  personality, 3-4
  physical appearance, 16-17
  plan to help "Jonathan" reestablish life, 300-303
  problems at work in February 2002, 361, 364, 365, 372, 373, 374

Richard (cont.)
  purchase of new car, 196, 201, 204, 206
  relationship between "Jonathan" and Cliff, feeling about, 73, 74, 79, 80, 81, 98, 179, 180, 181, 215, 283
  relationships, feelings about, 44
  remaining with "Jonathan", reasons for, 114-115, 274, 356, 417
  reservations about moving to be with "Jonathan", 236, 348, 349, 414
  revisiting former workplace in Paladin, 140, 141
  stalking by, "Jonathan's" claim of, 488, 538, 539, 542, 643
  teaching, feelings about, 167
  telephone call to "Jonathan" on June 21, 2002, 492, 553
  theories about Glenn's behavior, 262, 263, 461
  theories about "Jonathan's" behavior regarding e-mail accounts, 332, 333
  use of Internet to meet gay men, 5-6
  visit to apartment in Mariah in summer 2004, 634-635
  visit to Mariah to give "Jonathan" spreadsheets, 432, 433, 434, 435
  visit to penthouse in Paladin, 79-80
Richard's mother
  automobile accident, 528
  gift of $100 to "Jonathan", 281
  hospitalization for possible blood clot, 239, 240, 241
  "Jonathan's" feelings about, 95, 97, 98, 191, 240, 282, 288, 289, 327, 421, 422, 423, 424, 425, 428, 433, 434, 450, 451, 471, 483
  "Jonathan's" thank-you note to, 282
  letter about Easter to "Jonathan", 411, 421
  reaction to photographs of "Jonathan", 196
  second letter to "Jonathan", 422, 423, 424
  sisters' deaths, 528, 529
  subdural hematoma, 528

Rod, 653-654
Rowen, 164, 173, 175, 187, 189, 192, 195
  art center in, 162, 172
  as location of "Dulcimer" incident, 589-590
  as location of "Hard", 621
  Dan's concerns about Johnny's having moved to, 621
  Dan's driving home drunk from, 194
  garage in, 171, 588
  location, 162
  park used as "cruising" area in, 175, 176
Ryan (Andy's friend), 336, 573, 575

Sarah (alleged sister), 509
  attempt to take control of "Jonathan's" affairs by, 579
  children of, in Andy fantasy, 578
  "Jonathan's" biography of, 10-11
Schafer, Natalie, 10
Scorpio, 476, 535
  constellation of, 4, 489, 558
  personality of person born under sign of, 67
"Separation thing", 202, 205, 208
September 11, 2001 ("9/11"), 86, 168, 169, 170, 216, 598
  Dan's reaction to celebrants in Baghdad on, 86, 173
Sex ads posted by Johnny
  "2Fer", 613
  analysis of, 622
  Christmas Day 2002, 614-615
  December 30, 2000, 629
  "DoIt", 451-452, 493, 603
  "Friendly", 220, 223, 603
  "GayBear", 217-218, 220, 603
  "GayDaddy", 138, 139, 147, 217, 218, 220, 603, 627
  "Gayman", 6-7, 8, 138, 216, 220, 483, 603
  "GayMan", 216-217, 218, 219, 220, 221, 232, 241, 317, 321, 324, 331, 376, 378, 416, 483, 603
  "Great Plains" state, 620
  "Hard", 621
  "Maine", 427, 603
  March 2003, 621-622
  "Naughtyboy", 376, 377-378, 603, 628
  November 24, 2000, 629

Sex ads posted by Johnny (cont.)
  September 5, 2002, 562
  "Stiff", 217, 218, 220, 603
  "Sucker" reply, 316, 398
  "Tallulah", 621, 622
  "The Two Bears", 613-614. *See also* Nathan (Nate)
  "Toofer", 613
  "Top", 218, 219-220, 603
  "Tough", 415, 603
Sex and The City, 43, 305
  "Jonathan's" comparison of himself, Cliff, and Richard to characters on, 81
Sex Now (web site), 316, 317, 319, 331, 577, 604, 609, 613, 622
  Richard's discovery of "Jonathan's" profile as "Iain" on, 316-317
"Southern" state, 55, 280, 471, 500, 639
  as Glenn's location in 2011, 663
  as "Iain's" former state of residence, 222
  as Johnny's location in 2011, 665
  as Johnny's parents' state of residence, 506, 509
  as "Jonathan's" former state of residence, 7, 23, 223, 283, 307, 342, 346, 398, 462, 592, 638, 643, 647
  as location of winter home in "The Two Bears" ad, 613
  coconut patties from, 278, 509
  fraudulent insurance account in, 499
  "Jonathan's" employment with information technology company in, 646, 649, 650
  location of Glenn in December 2001, alleged, 283, 285, 663
  produce from father from, 337, 462, 509
  psychiatric institution in, 471, 474, 561, 644
  trip proposed to Laura and family by "Jonathan" to, 544, 563
  trip proposed to Richard by "Jonathan" to, 117
St. Alban, 384, 478, 540, 592
  as Laura's current city of residence, 141, 200, 466
  Dan's "stalking" of "Jonathan" in, 371, 520
  distance between Paladin and, 231, 602
  relative distances to Paladin from Credence and 202, 231
  retrieving "Jonathan's" belongings from, 301, 611
  Richard's trip to, in order to expose "Jonathan" to Laura, 518-519, 609
  Richard's trip to "rescue" "Jonathan" in, 243, 244-245,
"Stiffyitis", 19, 51
Still Life, 37-38, 244, 303, 304, 345, 346, 347, 355, 356
  attempts to authenticate, 359, 392, 393, 394
  attempts to sell, 393, 394, 395, 396
  "Jonathan's" father's reaction to selling, 345
  plan to sell, 38, 302, 341, 342
  plan to syndicate, 412, 414, 422, 433, 438, 482
  sale postponed until June, 325
  value, alleged 38, 302, 392
Storage unit, 153, 159, 260, 281-282, 283, 301, 305 361, 433, 453, 461, 638
  contract for, 144, 535, 572, 616
  cost for, 134, 144, 147, 228-229, 254, 259, 261, 379, 489, 535, 588
  investigation of, 143-144
  "Jonathan's" story to Laura about Richard's showing up at, with forged letter, 540
  Richard's attempt to meet "Jonathan" at, 439, 442-443, 446
  Richard's letter to "Jonathan" left at, 409, 412
  Tomlinsons' offer to remove and store items from, 381, 403, 408, 423
Stonehenge, 119, 293
Stress Center, 48, 113, 140, 147, 323, 461, 502, 503, 561
  homicidal client at, 552, 604
  "Jonathan's" interaction with Chase at, 103, 104, 105, 106, 107, 108, 114
  "Jonathan's" interaction with "fat" Greg at, 145
  "Jonathan's" interaction with Laura at, 141, 148, 545

Stress Center (cont.)
  non-payment of fees, Johnny's dismissal for, 559
  Richard's drive-by visit to, 197
Surrealist vase, 38
  "Jonathan's" desire to bequeath, to Richard, 146, 159, 432
Survivor, 475

TekNetium, 280
  as employer in rental scam, 638, 643
  as "Jonathan's" former employer, 55, 70, 191
  client position in Winford at, 342, 344
  confirmation of "Jonathan's" employment at, 500
  Johnny's length of employment at, 647
Terrence (British version of brother), 28, 93, 124, 547, 551
  discrepant information about, 18, 166, 505
  "Jonathan's" biography of, 12
  "Jonathan's" claim of, filing harassment charges against Richard, 523, 550
  offer to have "Jonathan" move in with, 195, 237
  plans visit "Jonathan" at Dan's, 163, 165, 166, 172, 185
  report of fraudulent credit card in father's name by, 308, 510
  Richard's contacting, 447, 505-506
Terry (actual brother), 529, 590, 603, 643, 645
  accent, 507
  birth date of Johnny, uncertainty about, 509, 608
  bullying behavior of Johnny, 511, 516
  conversation with Richard on July 4, 2002, 507-512, 542
  conversation with Richard on July 5, 2002, 514
  conversation with Richard on July 7, 2002, 524
  mid-2011 update, 663
  modus operandi of Johnny described, 511
  parenting of Johnny criticized, 511
  parents described, 508-509, 547
  pathological lying of Johnny, 508
  psychiatric history of Johnny, 511
  refusal to help victims, 524, 529, 617, 639, 645
  Richard's letter about Johnny sent to, 615-616, 617, 618
  Richard's younger niece's contacting, 514
  sexuality of Johnny not acknowledged to parents, 512
  siblings of "Jonathan" denied as actual siblings by, 509, 530
  threats of legal action against victims, 513, 617, 639
  See also Crimes committed by Johnny, acquisition of credit card in Terry's name; Terrence (British version of brother)
Thanksgiving, 344, 379, 402
  "Jonathan's" desire to see others raised at, 265, 267, 268, 269, 272
  plans for, 266, 267, 268
  Richard's inability to invite "Jonathan" for, 266, 288, 407, 411
  See also Tomlinsons, invitation to "Jonathan" to spend Thanksgiving with
The Antiques Road Show, 305
The Brains, 327
The Fly (film), 1, 35
The Mummy Returns (film), 120
The Pretender, 440, 488, 529, 549, 550, 568-569, 571, 579, 603
  e-mails to Andy as Richard, 449-450
  e-mails to Andy as Richard's mother, 448-449
  feelings about Kathryn expressed by, 444
  feelings about Richard's mother expressed by, 444
  first letter from, 444
  identification as Johnny, 549, 565, 603
  "Jonathan's" reaction to e-mails to Andy from, as Richard, 450-451
  origin of name of, 456
  possible motives for "Jonathan" assuming role of, 481-483
  probable sources of material for e-mails from, 456

The Pretender (cont.)
  Richard's attempt to identify, 444-446
  Richard's belief in ex-brother-in-law as, 444-446, 448, 455
  second letter from, 448
  "suicide notes" as Richard, 451
  See also "Dulcimer", "Heorshema"
The Tempest (painting), 159, 203, 600
Tiffany chandelier, 244, 286, 304
Tolliver's, 8, 9, 31-32, 68, 78, 224, 233, 249, 604
Tomlinson, Joanne
  as Andy's biological mother, 580
  as "Chase's" mother, 266
  "Jonathan's" biography of, 266
  reaction to Richard's mother's letter to "Jonathan", 421, 422, 424
Tomlinson, Warren
  as Andy's stepfather, 580
  as "Chase's" father, 266
  feelings about Richard, 425
  INS deception, 303, 340, 342, 344, 346
  "Jonathan's" biography of, 266
Tomlinsons
  attempts to verify existence of, 480, 481, 579, 580
  invitation to "Jonathan" to spend Christmas with, 289
  invitation to "Jonathan" to spend Easter with, 408
  invitation to "Jonathan" to spend Thanksgiving with, 266, 267
  Johnny's true relationship with, 580
  "Jonathan's" alleged visits to, 342, 343, 344, 345, 346, 347, 396, 401, 402, 408, 409, 410, 412, 414, 415, 418, 421-422, 423, 424, 487
  Richard's letter to, 410, 411
  See also Tomlinson, Joanne; Tomlinson, Warren
"Trevor" (Laura alias), 539, 540, 541, 553
  exchange between "Jonathan" and, 553-556
  "Jonathan's" mention of Richard to, 554, 555
Truth bias, 678, 685, 687, 711
Turkey, 223

"currency" incident involving "Jonathan" in, 510-511

VeraMed, 348-349, 460, 467
Victor/Victoria (film), 197, 205
Viridian, 347, 395, 592
  location of, 3
  Richard's teaching in, 3, 40, 44, 114, 129, 133, 153, 271, 278, 315, 340, 360, 361, 374, 397, 419, 432, 492, 536, 537, 593
Visa, 280, 303, 348
  hospital's decision about "Jonathan's", 279-280, 306
  requirements for remaining in United States, 275-276
Visits of Richard with "Jonathan"
  August 18-26, 2001, 123-128, 219, 378
  December 11-16, 2001, 286
  December 26, 2001-January 10, 2002, 300-310, 611
  June 29-July 4, 2001, 35-39, 72-73, 90
Vogel, Joan (landlord), 247, 295, 368, 397, 414, 460, 512, 519, 572
  conversation with Richard about "Jonathan's" rent, 366-367
  "Jonathan's" concerns about being evicted by, 348, 359, 363, 365, 375, 377
  Richard's attempt to contact, in May 2002, 486
  Richard's meeting, 246
  See also Crimes committed by Johnny, non-payment of rent to Joan Vogel

Warrants for Johnny's arrest, 498, 520, 587, 588, 589, 606, 607, 608, 610, 612, 614, 615, 626, 636, 639
West, Miranda
  "alien" stories recounted by, 475
  Cliff mentioned by "Jonathan" to, 534, 535
  conversation with Richard on August 3, 2002, 529-536
  conversation with Richard on May 14, 2002, 459-462
  conversation with Richard on May 16, 2002, 463-484
  danger posed by "Jonathan", concerns about, 462
  firing from hospital, beliefs about "Jonathan's", 466, 467

West, Miranda (cont.)
   first letter from The Pretender, beliefs about, 529
   Glenn, description of, 464, 473, 530
   Glenn, perceptions of, 473
   invitation to have "Jonathan" stay, 369
   jealousy to manipulate, "Jonathan's" attempts to use, 478
   Johnny and Glenn's assuming identities of others, beliefs about, 531
   "Jonathan", perceptions of, 469, 472, 473, 531, 532, 533, 534
   "Jonathan's" ability to evade responsibility remarked on by, 476
   "Jonathan's" biography of, 14-15
   "Jonathan's" claim of being British dismissed by, 462, 464
   "Jonathan's" discomfort at leaving Glenn alone with, 473, 474, 530
   "Jonathan's" paranormal experiences recounted to, 461, 462, 475, 476
   "Jonathan's" story about Laura to, 478
   location of home of, 463
   metaphysical interpretation of involvement with "Jonathan", 472, 476, 477, 535, 536
   mid-2011 update, 660
   murders committed by Johnny and/or Glenn, concerns about, 530, 531
   physical appearance, 463
   reading for "Jonathan" on October 2, 2001, 201, 207
   relationship between "Jonathan" and Glenn, perceptions of, 469, 470, 477, 478, 529, 530, 533
   Richard's visit in late June 2002, 496
   Richard's visit on July 6, 2002, 519
   romantic relationship claimed by "Jonathan" with, 460
   "rug" story recounted by, 461, 475
   sexual abuse suffered by Johnny, belief in, 534
   storage unit discussed with Richard, 535
   The Pretender, belief in "Jonathan" as, 470
   "white Jaguar" story recounted by, 467, 648
   See also Crimes committed by Johnny, check fraud against Miranda

Will & Grace, 199
   "Iain's" comparison of living situation at "Mary's" to that on, 221, 223
   "Jonathan's" comparison of living situation at Laura's to that on, 190, 203, 223, 478

Wind in the Willows (Grahame), 24

Winford, 285, 301, 306
   airport in, 575
   as location in "Maine" ad, 427
   "Kev's" and "Colin's" plans to meet in, 490
   TekNetium client position in, 324

"Wynken, Blynken, and Nod" (Field), 23-24

www.ingramcontent.com/pod-product-compliance
Lightning Source LLC
Chambersburg PA
CBHW070934180426
43192CB00039B/2169